Books by John Toland

JOHN TOLAND
INFAMY
PEARL HARBOR AND ITS AFTERMATH

BERKLEY BOOKS, NEW YORK

This Berkley book contains the complete text of the original hardcover
edition. It has been completely reset in a typeface designed for easy reading,
and was printed from new film.

INFAMY

A Berkley Book / published by arrangement with
Doubleday & Company, Inc.

PRINTING HISTORY
Doubleday edition published 1982
Berkley edition / February 1983
Sixth printing / December 1984

ISBN: 0-245-07664-4

A BERKLEY BOOK ® TM 757,375
Berkley Books are published by The Berkley Publishing Group,
200 Madison Avenue, New York, New York 10016.
The name "BERKLEY" and the stylized "B" with design
are trademarks belonging to Berkley Publishing Corporation.
PRINTED IN THE UNITED STATES OF AMERICA

To the Victims of Pearl Harbor

Contents

Cast of Principal Characters

BEFORE PEARL HARBOR

Washington
Franklin Delano Roosevelt, President of the United States
Cordell Hull, Secretary of State
Henry L. Stimson, Secretary of War
Frank Knox, Secretary of the Navy
Harry Hopkins, the President's adviser and confidant
Harold L. Ickes, Secretary of the Interior
Frances Perkins, Secretary of Labor
Admiral Kichisaburo Nomura, Japanese ambassador
Saburo Kurusu, Japanese special envoy
Captain Johan E. M. Ranneft, Netherlands naval attaché
Colonel F. G. L. Weijerman, Netherlands military attaché
Dr. Alexander Loudon, Netherlands minister

U. S. Navy Department
Admiral Harold R. Stark, Chief of Naval Operations
Rear Admiral Royal E. Ingersoll, Assistant Chief, Naval Operations
Rear Admiral Richmond Kelly Turner, Chief, War Plans Division
Rear Admiral Leigh Noyes, Chief, Communications Division
Commander Laurance Safford, Chief, Security Intelligence Communications (Op-20-G)
Rear Admiral Theodore Stark Wilkinson, Chief, Intelligence Division, Office of Naval Intelligence (O.N.I.)

Lieutenant Commander Alwin Kramer, Chief, Translation Section, O.N.I. (attached to Op-20-G)

Commander Arthur H. McCollum, Chief, Far Eastern Section, O.N.I.

Captain John Beardall, White House naval aide

Lieutenant Lester Robert Schulz, assistant to Beardall as White House communications duty officer

War Department
General George Catlett Marshall, Chief of Staff

Major General H. H. Arnold, Deputy Chief of Staff for Air

Colonel Walter Bedell Smith, Secretary, General Staff

Brigadier General Leonard T. Gerow, Chief, War Plans Division

Brigadier General Sherman Miles, Chief of Intelligence (G-2)

Colonel Rufus S. Bratton, head, Far Eastern Section (G-2)

Colonel Otis K. Sadtler, Signal Corps, operations officer

William F. Friedman, chief cryptographer, Signal Intelligence Service (S.I.S.)

Honolulu
Robert L. Shivers, agent in charge, F.B.I.

Lieutenant John A. Burns, head, Honolulu Police Espionage Bureau

Nagao Kita, Japanese consul general

Ensign Takeo Yoshikawa, Japanese naval spy

Hawaiian Department
Lieutenant General Walter C. Short, Commanding General

United States Pacific Fleet
Admiral Husband E. Kimmel, Commander in Chief

Lieutenant Commander Edwin T. Layton, fleet intelligence officer

Fourteenth Naval District (Pearl Harbor)
Rear Admiral Claude C. Bloch, Commandant

Lieutenant Commander Joseph J. Rochefort, Communications Security Unit

San Francisco

Captain Richard T. McCollough, Chief, Intelligence, Twelfth Naval District

Lieutenant Ellsworth A. Hosner, an assistant

Seaman First Class Z, Hosner's assistant

Station M:
The U.S. Navy's East Coast Intercept Installation

Ralph T. Briggs, one of the qualified operators assigned to monitor Japanese intercepts

Chief Radioman DW, his superior

Java

General Hein Ter Poorten, Commander in Chief, Netherlands East Indies Army

Dr. Walter Foote, U.S. consul general

Brigadier General Elliott Thorpe, U.S. military observer

Others

Admiral James O. Richardson, Kimmel's predecessor

Dusko Popov, British double agent, code-named "Tricycle"

Kilsoo Haan, agent for the Sino-Korean People's League

Major Warren J. Clear, U. S. Army intelligence agent in the Far East

Captain and Mrs. Harold D. Krick, close friends of Admiral Stark

Tyler Gatewood Kent, code clerk at the U. S. Embassy, London

Dr. Henry Field, special assistant to President Roosevelt

C. A. Berndtson, Commodore of the Matson Fleet and commander of the S.S. *Lurline*

Rudy Asplund, chief radio operator, *Lurline*

Leslie E. Grogan, first assistant radio operator, *Lurline*

AFTER PEARL HARBOR

Admiral Ernest J. King, Stark's successor and Commander in Chief of the U. S. Fleets

Admiral Chester W. Nimitz, Kimmel's successor

James V. Forrestal, Knox's successor

Harry S. Truman, Roosevelt's successor

Thomas K. Kimmel, Kimmel's son

Edward Kimmel, Kimmel's son

Manning Kimmel, Kimmel's son

Charles B. Rugg, Kimmel's chief counsel

Lieutenant Edward B. Hanify, USNR, Kimmel's assistant counsel

Captain Robert A. Lavender, U. S. Navy, Retired, Kimmel's assistant counsel

Admiral Thomas Hart, U. S. Navy, Retired, Stark's counsel

Lieutenant David W. Richmond, USNR, Stark's assistant counsel

Captain Robert Diggs, Marshall's counsel

Percy L. Greaves, Jr., chief of minority staff during Joint Committee hearings

The Nine Investigations

1. Knox personal inquiry   December 11–12, 1941
2. Roberts Commission   December 18, 1941,
                                                    to January 23, 1942
    Associate Justice Owen J. Roberts, U. S. Supreme Court, Chairman
    Admiral William H. Standley, U. S. Navy, Retired, member
    Rear Admiral Joseph M. Reeves, U. S. Navy, Retired, member
    Major General Frank R. McCoy, U. S. Army, Retired, member
    Brigadier General Joseph T. McNarney, U. S. Army, member
3. Hart Inquiry   February 22 to June 15, 1944
    Conducted by Admiral Thomas C. Hart, U. S. Navy, Retired
4. Navy Court of Inquiry   July 24 to
                                                    September 27, 1944
    Admiral Orin G. Murfin, U. S. Navy, Retired, President
    Admiral Edward C. Kalbfus, U. S. Navy, Retired, member

Vice Admiral Adolphus Andrews, U. S. Navy, Retired, member

Commander Harold Biesemeier, judge advocate

5. Army Pearl Harbor Board   August 7 to October 6, 1944

    Lieutenant General George Grunert, President

    Major General Henry D. Russell, member

    Major General Walter H. Frank, member

6. Clarke Investigation   September 20, 1944
                                     to August 4, 1945

    Conducted by Colonel Carter W. Clarke, U. S. Army

7. Clausen Investigation   January 24
                                     to September 12, 1945

    Conducted by Major (later Lieutenant Colonel) Henry C. Clausen, JAGD

8. Hewitt Inquiry   May 14 to July 11, 1945

    Conducted by Admiral H. Kent Hewitt, U. S. Navy

    Counsel: John F. Sonnett

    Assistant Counsel: Lieutenant John Ford Baecher, USNR

9. Joint Congressional Committee on the Investigation of the Pearl Harbor Attack   November 15, 1945
                                     to May 31, 1946

    Alben Barkley, senator from Kentucky, Chairman (D)

    Jere Cooper, representative from Tennessee, Vice Chairman (D)

    Walter F. George, senator from Georgia (D)

    Scott W. Lucas, senator from Illinois (D)

    Owen Brewster, senator from Maine (R)

    Homer Ferguson, senator from Michigan (R)

    J. Bayard Clark, representative from North Carolina (D)

    John W. Murphy, representative from Pennsylvania (D)

    Bertrand W. Gearhart, representative from California (R)

    Frank B. Keefe, representative from Wisconsin (R)

    William D. Mitchell, general counsel (through January 14, 1946)

Gerhard A. Gesell, chief assistant counsel (through January 14, 1946)

Seth W. Richardson, general counsel (after January 14, 1946)

Samuel H. Kaufman, associate general counsel (after January 14, 1946)

Foreword

In *But Not in Shame* I concluded that every American would have to accept a share of the blame for the disastrous attack on Pearl Harbor, and that it had been a largely unprovoked act of Japanese aggression. Nine years later, after considerable research in Japan, I came to the startling conclusion in *The Rising Sun* that Pearl Harbor had been the result of American as well as Japanese miscalculations and mistakes. "A war that need not have been fought was about to be fought because of mutual misunderstanding, language difficulties, and mistranslations as well as Japanese opportunism, *gekokujo,* irrationality, honor, pride and fear—and American racial prejudice, distrust, ignorance of the Orient, rigidity, self-righteousness, honor, national pride and fear." At that time I saw no villains or heroes on either side and could not, above all, believe that President Roosevelt knew ahead of time that a Japanese striking force was approaching Pearl Harbor.

Even so, many aspects of Pearl Harbor had troubled me. The various investigations left too many crucial questions in doubt and in limbo. Was it possible that Roosevelt had engineered a conspiracy to get America into the war with Hitler by the back door? Had some of our military and civilian leaders lied under oath? Had some good men been persuaded or threatened into perjuring themselves? Had there truly been a "winds" execute message in early December 1941? Had the nine investigations, in short, been an elaborate cover-up to place the blame primarily on Admiral Kimmel and General Short while whitewashing those in Washington?

Forty years after the "date which will live in infamy," I have attempted to answer these and other questions that have been nagging Americans and Japanese all these years. Upon embarking on this quest I was warned that the recent wholesale release of controversial Pearl Harbor material under the Freedom of Information Act was a smoke screen and that the cover-up of Pearl Harbor was still in force. On the contrary I found the U. S. Navy and the National Security Agency not only open but helpful; they made only a few deletions of the highly controversial material submitted to them, and these only for security purposes.

And now into the murky depths of Pearl Harbor.

Part 1

TANGLED WEB

"Oh, what a tangled web we weave,
When first we practise to deceive!"

Sir Walter Scott

Chapter One

"HOW DID THEY CATCH US WITH OUR PANTS DOWN, MR. PRESIDENT?" DECEMBER 6–7, 1941

1.

On Saturday morning, December 6, 1941, one of the translators at Op-20-G, the Security Intelligence Section of U.S. Naval Communications, in Washington, D.C., began skimming through a pile of intercepted Japanese messages in the consular code. She came across one sent three days earlier from Consul General Kita in Honolulu to Tokyo, transmitting a scheme of signals regarding the movement and exact position of warships and carriers in Pearl Harbor. The translator, Mrs. Dorothy Edgers, had been on the job only a month but at first glance she thought it was important enough to be completed immediately. She asked the senior translator, Fred Woodrough—her brother—if she should remain after the noon closing time to finish the message. He thought it was "a crank deal" but of sufficient import to stay over. As she translated the details she became excited, for the message told about giving signals from the window of a certain house on Oahu to Japanese

3

ships hiding offshore. Fascinated, she showed what she had written to the yeoman presiding over the six translators. It was "interesting," he said, but didn't warrant attention on a weekend.

Even so, Mrs. Edgers stayed at her desk and by 3 P.M. was finishing the message just as Lieutenant Commander Alwin Kramer, chief of the Translation Section, walked in. He had studied Japanese assiduously but Mrs. Edgers, like her brother, had been brought up near Tokyo and her command of the language was far superior. She waited expectantly while he read the entire telegram standing up. He seemed more annoyed than electrified even though the last paragraph read:

> If the above signals and wireless messages cannot be made from Oahu, then on Maui Island, 6 miles north to the northward of Kula Sanatorium . . . at a point halfway between Lower Kula Road and Haleskala Road (latitude 20°40′ N., longitude 156°19′ W., visible from seaward to the southeast and southwest of Maui Island) the following bonfires will be made daily until your EXEX signal is received; from 7 to 8, Signal 3 or 6; from 8 to 9, Signal 4 or 7; from 9 to 10, Signal 5 or 8.

Nicknamed "The Shadow," after the radio character, Kramer was tall and slender with a pencil mustache. He combined the traits of a dreamer with extreme punctiliousness. Every message that passed through his hands had to be meticulously, painstakingly corrected and recorrected. He told Mrs. Edgers the intercept needed a lot of work and she should run along home. They could finish editing it sometime next week. She protested but he politely insisted she leave.

Kramer himself was busy supervising the decryption of a long message in the Japanese code known as Purple. This was the most secret system used to transmit information between Tokyo and foreign embassies. First had arrived a pilot message from Tokyo alerting Ambassador Nomura to make ready to receive a crucial message—the answer to America's reply to Japan's final offer in the long negotiations between the two countries in an attempt to end their difficulties in peace, not war. Thirteen parts of a fourteen-part message that was in English were decrypted by dark and these made it obvious the Japanese were completely dissatisfied with the American reply, which was a repudiation of their offer.

As soon as President Franklin D. Roosevelt read these thirteen parts that evening, he turned to Harry Hopkins, his chief adviser, and said, "This means war."

Even so no warning was sent to Hawaii where the Pacific Fleet was based at Pearl Harbor. In fact, no Purple intercepts had been sent to the fleet's commander, Admiral Husband Kimmel, for months. Nor did he have a Purple machine which would have enabled his intelligence officers to read the series of disturbing messages being exchanged between Tokyo and Washington.

The message in the consular code that attracted Mrs. Edgers' interest had been intercepted in Hawaii by MS-5, a special Army monitoring station at Fort Shafter. But General Walter Short, the Army commander in Hawaii, had not been cleared for any of the decrypted Japanese messages known as Magic. Short did not even know of MS-5's existence. Nor had the Army major in charge of the station been given decrypting facilities. His orders were merely to ship the intercepts air mail to Washington in their original form.

The consul's message was by no means the only one that morning which indicated the Japanese might be planning a surprise attack on Pearl Harbor. Two months earlier S.I.S., the U.S. Army Signal Intelligence Service, had decrypted a message from Tokyo to Consul Kita dividing the waters of Pearl Harbor into five areas and asking for the exact locations of Kimmel's warships and carriers. Both Army and Navy intelligence officers in Washington guessed this could be a grid system for a bombing attack. Several of these men urged that Kimmel and Short be warned but for some reason their superiors would not allow this. Three other messages between Tokyo and Kita also indicated unusual Japanese interest in Pearl Harbor.

One instructed Ensign Takeo Yoshikawa, a naval spy posing as one of Kita's assistants, to report all ship movements in Pearl Harbor "twice a week"; another ordered Yoshikawa to subject the fleet air bases on Oahu to special scrutiny; and a third, on November 8, requested information about strategic points around Honolulu. None of these messages was sent to Kimmel or Short. And there were eight other revealing telegrams which the overworked Americans had not yet had time to decrypt, including two sent December 6 by Yoshikawa. One listed ships presently anchored in Pearl Harbor, noting that it appeared no air reconnaissance was being conducted by the fleet air arm. The other reported that the battleships probably did not have torpedo nets, and also stated, "At the present time there are no signs of barrage balloon equipment. In addition, it is difficult to imagine that they have actually any. However, even though they have actually made preparations, because they must control the air over the water and lava runways of the airports in the vicinity of Pearl Harbor, Hickam, Ford, and Ewa, there are limits to the balloon defense of Pearl Harbor. I imagine that in all probability there is considerable opportunity left to take advantage for a surprise attack against these places."

These two messages were immediately monitored by MS-5 at Fort Shafter and started off on the erratic air route to Washington. Twice a subordinate naval intelligence officer in Washington had urged his superiors to allow Kimmel's intelligence officer to decrypt these consular messages upon reception at MS-5. Both times permission had been refused on the grounds that such information was no business of Kimmel's.

What did Kimmel and Short know on December 6? For months they had been aware that war with Japan was not only a probability but undoubtedly a certainty, and both had been preparing their forces for battle. On November 27, the day after Secretary of State Cordell Hull sent his reply to Tokyo refusing to bow to Japan's unacceptable conditions, warnings from the two heads of the Army and Navy, General George Marshall and Admiral Harold R.

"Betty" Stark, were sent to their commanders in the Philippines, the Panama Canal and Hawaii.[1]

General Douglas MacArthur in Manila got this message: NEGOTIATIONS WITH THE JAPANESE APPEAR TO BE TERMINATED TO ALL PRACTICAL PURPOSES WITH ONLY THE BAREST POSSIBILITIES THAT THE JAPANESE GOVERNMENT MIGHT COME BACK AND OFFER TO CONTINUE PERIOD JAPANESE FUTURE ACTION UNPREDICTABLE BUT HOSTILE ACTION POSSIBLE AT ANY MOMENT PERIOD IF HOSTILITIES CANNOT, REPEAT CANNOT, BE AVOIDED THE UNITED STATES DESIRES THAT JAPAN COMMIT THE FIRST OVERT ACT PERIOD THIS POLICY SHOULD NOT, REPEAT NOT, BE CONSTRUED AS RESTRICTING YOU TO A COURSE OF ACTION THAT MIGHT JEOPARDIZE YOUR DEFENSE. . . .

A similar message was sent to General Short but it also ordered him to do nothing "to alarm civil population or disclose intent." Short took all this to mean he should institute only a sabotage alert. He informed Washington of this but apparently nobody there read his reply carefully. He was never told he had missed the import of the instructions.

Stark dispatched to Kimmel and Admiral Thomas C. Hart, commander of the Asiatic Fleet in the Philippines, the same message: THIS DISPATCH IS TO BE CONSIDERED A WAR WARNING X NEGOTIATIONS WITH JAPAN LOOKING TOWARD STABILIZATION OF CONDITIONS IN THE PACIFIC HAVE CEASED AND AN AGGRESSIVE MOVE BY JAPAN IS EXPECTED IN THE NEXT FEW DAYS X THE NUMBER AND EQUIPMENT OF JAPANESE TROOPS AND THE ORGANIZATION OF NAVAL TASK FORCES INDICATES AN AMPHIBIOUS EXPEDITION AGAINST EITHER THE PHILIPPINES THAI OR KRA PENINSULA OR POSSIBLY BORNEO X EXECUTE AN APPROPRIATE DEFENSIVE DEPLOYMENT PREPARATORY TO CARRYING OUT THE TASKS ASSIGNED IN WPL [WAR PLAN] 46 X. . . .

No other warning had been sent either Kimmel or Short and, on December 6, both assumed the negotiations were continuing.

[1] Although the Army message bore Marshall's name, he was out of town and it was dispatched by Secretary of War Henry L. Stimson.

Short, like Marshall, a graduate of V.M.I., was noted for his efficiency, and he had brought his troops to a high point of effectiveness. In his supervision of the Civilian Defense Force, he had shown his diplomatic ability to deal equally with local leaders while getting results.

Roosevelt had selected Kimmel over the heads of men who outranked him. Promoted to the temporary rank of full admiral, he was now one of the few four-star admirals in the Navy. Kimmel was known for his ability to get the best out of his subordinates. Brilliant, energetic and hard-boiled, he was a work horse who drove himself as hard as he did others. Curt, authoritative and crusty, he had never strived to be loved by his men. But they respected him, for he was easy to get along with as long as they produced; and they knew he never demanded more of them than he did of himself. He had left his wife in California upon taking over command of the fleet in early 1941 so that he could dedicate all his time and energy to whipping his forces into war readiness. Kimmel had accomplished this by December 6. His fleet was primed and eager to fight.

It was Short's responsibility to protect Oahu against enemy air and sea attack and to provide short-range air reconnaissance while Kimmel took care of long-range reconnaissance. By December 6 men and machines of both air arms were in poor shape after so many missions. Both Kimmel and Short had been complaining for months of shortages of personnel, planes and radar but Washington's main attention had gone to the Atlantic where American war materials were being convoyed to England in the desperate fight against Hitler. To make matters worse, most of the Flying Fortresses which were to assist Kimmel in long-range reconnaissance had been sent on to the Philippines.

Kimmel and Short knew that the main Japanese carrier force had left home waters only to disappear in late November. It was assumed it was probably with the invasion force heading south toward the Philippines, Thailand or the Kra Peninsula. On December 2 Kimmel was informed by his intelligence officer that the carriers were still missing. If this disturbed Kimmel he didn't show it; in fact, he facetiously asked, "Do you mean to say that they could be rounding Diamond Head this minute and you wouldn't know?''

"I hope they would be sighted by now, sir."

But no one in Hawaii seriously considered an attack on Pearl Harbor; the Japs weren't that stupid. Marshall and Stark agreed. So did their staffs.

Six carriers, along with fast battleships, two heavy cruisers, a light cruiser, eight destroyers, and a train of three oilers and a supply ship were bound for Hawaii. This formidable striking force, *Kido Butai,* was scheduled to hit Army and Navy airfields and Pearl Harbor at dawn, December 8, Tokyo time. On December 3 *Kido Butai* received a message in a new code: "Climb Mount Niitaka 1208." This meant: "Attack as planned on December 8." In Hawaii it would be Sunday, December 7.

Kido Butai was cruising eastward at a modest 14 knots to conserve fuel, advancing in ring formation with three submarines ahead scouting for neutral merchant ships which, if found, were to be boarded and seized. A chance encounter with the U.S. Pacific Fleet, however, could not be handled so easily. Admiral Chuichi Nagumo ordered all ship captains to start traveling with no lights and to inform their entire crews of the Pearl Harbor attack. That night a spirit of intense, subdued excitement swept from ship to ship. By late morning of the next day the final major reservicing point was reached—42 degrees north and 170 degrees east—and all ships were refueled.

On December 6 *Kido Butai* was still undiscovered, so it seemed, as it sped southeast at 20 knots through gales and high seas. Several of the exhausted lookouts had already been swept overboard and the fog was so thick it was often impossible to see the ship ahead.

That night the thirteen parts of the vital Japanese message were delivered not only to Roosevelt but to Admiral Theodore Wilkinson, Chief of Naval Intelligence, who happened to have as a dinner guest General Sherman Miles, Chief of Army Intelligence. Marshall and Stark could not be located.

In Hawaii, Short spent the evening at the Officers Club in Schofield Barracks; Kimmel left a party at Honolulu's

House Without a Key, at 9:30 P.M. He wanted to get to bed. He had a date to play golf with Short in the morning.

Kido Butai was racing full steam at 24 knots toward the launching point, two hundred miles north of Pearl Harbor. The pilots and crew were routed from their bunks at 3:30 A.M., December 7, Hawaiian time. They put on clean *mawashi* (loincloths) and "thousand-stitch" belts, then ate a breakfast of red rice and tai, a red snapper eaten at times of celebration.

In Washington it was 9 A.M.. The fourteenth part of the Japanese message had come in and was already decrypted. It stated that it was "impossible to reach an agreement through further negotiations." Admiral Wilkinson took the entire message to Admiral Stark. While they were discussing what actions should be taken another intercept was brought in instructing Nomura to submit the fourteen-point message to Hull "at 1 P.M. on the 7th, your time."

"Why don't you pick up the telephone and call Admiral Kimmel?" asked Wilkinson.

Stark did pick up the phone at about ten forty-five. It was an ungodly hour to call Kimmel in his sleep, especially since the November 27 "war warning" to him was enough to keep the Pacific Fleet on its toes. Besides, an attack on Pearl Harbor was unthinkable. Stark decided instead to call the President but his line was busy.

In the meantime Colonel Rufus Bratton, an Army intelligence officer, had been frantically trying to find Marshall, who had dropped out of sight since early Saturday evening. The 1 P.M. note had sent Bratton into "frenzied" action. Convinced that "the Japanese were going to attack an American installation," he literally ran to the office of his chief, General Miles. But he was at home. Bratton phoned Marshall's quarters at nearby Fort Myer. An orderly said the general had just left for his Sunday morning horseback ride.

By the time Marshall is said to have finally reached his office it was 11:25 A.M. At that moment *Kido Butai* was at the launching point. The first faint light of dawn glimmered in the east. Forty-three fighter planes began leaving the six carriers. Then would come forty-nine high-level and fifty-one dive bombers; and finally forty torpedo planes.

After reading the long message and the 1 P.M. note, Marshall hastily jotted down a dispatch to his Pacific commanders: "The Japanese are presenting at 1 P.M. Eastern Standard Time today what amounts to an ultimatum. Also they are under orders to destroy their code machine immediately. Just what significance the hour set may have we do not know, but be on the alert accordingly." He telephoned Stark, who offered to send the warning through the Navy's rapid transmission facilities.

"No, thanks, Betty, I feel I can get it through quickly enough," said Marshall, and marked the message "First Priority—Secret." It was sent by Western Union.

At 1:23 P.M. Zeros were approaching Pearl Harbor where it was 7:53 A.M. At that moment the flight commander radioed Admiral Nagumo TORA, TORA, TORA! The repeated code word, meaning, "tiger," stood for "We have succeeded in surprise attack." Two minutes later torpedo bombers began diving on Battleship Row.

2.

Admiral Kimmel was putting on his white uniform, for he had been informed that the destroyer *Ward* had sighted and sunk an unidentified submarine. Hearing the sound of distant explosions, he rushed outside.

Planes were darting overhead, the Rising Sun on their wings visible. They circled and began diving on the ships in the harbor. "There goes the *Arizona!*" exclaimed Kimmel's next-door neighbor, Mrs. Grace Earle. He said not a word but she would never forget that "he looked stricken, and was as white as his uniform."

A car pulled up. Kimmel jumped in and shortly reached his temporary shore headquarters at the submarine base. Even as he rushed inside he noticed a sailor on a tied-up tug pumping away at a 50-caliber machine gun "as fast as he could get the thing going."

Inside Kimmel joined several of his officers at an open

window. As he watched the attacks on Battleship Row, Kimmel could not help but admire the planning that must have preceded the Japanese attack. All at once a spent 50-caliber bullet struck the left breast of his white uniform. It smacked into his glasses case and fell to the floor. He picked it up, put it in his pocket and said, "I wish it had killed me." His career was over; he should somehow have prevented what was happening. Still looking cool, the austere Kimmel strode into an inner room. When he emerged a few minutes later, Chief Yeoman Ken Murray, his writer, noticed his four-star shoulder boards had been replaced with two-star boards. He had demoted himself from his temporary rank of full admiral to his permanent rank of rear admiral.

"Oh no, Admiral," a young aide said.

"Hell, yes, son."

It had been a warm December in Washington but today was brisk. At 1:50 P.M. the following message arrived from Kimmel's headquarters:

AIR RAID ON PEARL HARBOR THIS IS NOT A DRILL.

Soon the message was relayed to Admiral Stark. Secretary of the Navy Frank Knox was about to order lunch when Stark burst into his office. "My God," said Knox, "this can't be true! This must mean the Philippines!" He telephoned the President, who was in his study lunching from a tray with Harry Hopkins.

"No!" said Roosevelt incredulously. Hopkins said there must be some mistake. Surely the Japanese would not attack Honolulu. "The President discussed at some length," recalled Hopkins, "his efforts to keep the country out of the war and his earnest desire to complete his administration without war, but that if this action of Japan's were true it would take the matter entirely out of his own hands, because the Japanese had made the decision for him."

At 2:05 P.M. Roosevelt called Hull, who was about to receive the two Japanese diplomats, Saburo Kurusu and Nomura. They were obviously bringing a declaration of war but Hull was not to let on that he knew the attack had already been launched "but to receive their reply formally and coolly and bow them out."

But Hull had a temper and gave the two Japanese strong Tennessee mountain language. "In all my fifty years of public service," he told them, in the official expurgated version, "I have never seen a document that was more crowded with infamous falsehoods and distortions—infamous falsehoods and distortions on a scale so huge that I never imagined until today that any Government on this planet was capable of uttering them."

Secretary of War Henry L. Stimson was lunching at his nearby estate, Woodley, when Roosevelt called to ask excitedly, "Have you heard the news?" Stimson said he knew about the Japanese advances in the Gulf of Siam. "Oh, no, I don't mean that. They have attacked Hawaii. They are now bombing Hawaii!"

Throughout America radio programs were interrupted with brief announcements of the Hawaii and somewhat later Manila bombings. In Chicago the New York Philharmonic concert was broken up by an announcer so excited he twice pronounced the program as "Philharminic." Most people were stunned but there were no scenes of panic. Strangers in the street began to look at each other with a new awareness. Personal problems were overshadowed by national catastrophe; and the bitter wrangles between the interventionists and America Firsters suddenly had no meaning. With few exceptions 130,000,000 Americans accepted total war with determination and unity.

The Washington correspondent of the Domei News Agency, Clark Kawakami, felt not only shock but shame. An American citizen, he wrote his newspaper colleagues at the Department of State, "I cannot tell you how deeply I was shocked by Japan's action. . . . That shameful double-dealing coupled with the equally shameful manner in which she launched her attacks on Sunday, without warning, indicates how completely the militarists in Tokyo have gone over to the methods of Hitler and the Nazis. Not only I but my father, too, feel that these acts constitute the blackest and most shameful page in Japanese history."

Another Japanese newsman named Hatanaka was apologizing to C.L. Sulzberger at the Grand Hotel in Moscow. Bowing and smiling, he said, "So sorry, we sank your fleet this morning. Supposing we are at war."

At 8:20 P.M. that evening members of the Cabinet began arriving at the White House. As they were assembling in a semicircle around the President's desk in the Oval Office, Knox, his face white, whispered to Stimson that they had lost seven battleships.[2]

"The President was deeply shaken," recalled Attorney General Francis Biddle, "graver than I had ever seen him." Roosevelt told what he knew and answered a few questions; then a group of congressional leaders arrived and he repeated his story. There was silence for a tense moment. Finally Senator Tom Connally, his face purple, sprang to his feet, banged the desk and shouted, "How did they catch us with our pants down, Mr. President?"

With head bowed, the President muttered, "I don't know, Tom. I just don't know." But everyone in the room including Roosevelt knew they had to find out who was at fault—and fast. Once the shock of the attack wore off, the public would begin demanding to know who was to blame: Washington, Hawaii, or both?

Secretary Morgenthau returned to the Treasury Department and told his intimates, "It is just unexplainable. And they caught us as unprepared as the others—just the same." The battleships were a perfect target: and all the Army planes were crowded together to prevent sabotage. "That's what Stimson kept saying," said Morgenthau. "He kept mumbling that all the planes were in one place. They have the whole Fleet in one place—the whole Fleet was in this little Pearl Harbor. The whole Fleet was there. . . ." He was stunned, puzzled. "They can never explain this. They never will be able to explain it."

All over America people were wondering who was to

---

[2] Eighteen ships had been sunk or seriously damaged, including eight battleships. All but two of the battleships—*Arizona* and *Oklahoma*—were later salvaged. At the airfields 188 planes were destroyed—96 Army and 92 Navy. Of the 2,403 killed, 2,008 were Navy, 109 Marines, 218 Army, and 68 civilian. Nearly one half died on the *Arizona*.

blame. To the hard-core isolationists the answer was simple: Roosevelt. But to most people it was: Kimmel and Short.

Army cryptanalyst William F. Friedman, whose team had solved the Purple code, found it difficult to believe what had happened. All he could do was pace back and forth, so his wife recalled, and mutter to himself repeatedly, "But they knew, they knew, they knew."

Aboard a tramp steamer three days' sailing from New York, Dusko Popov, a British double agent, code-named "Tricycle," heard the captain announce in a funereal voice the attack on Pearl Harbor. Popov was triumphant. That fall he had personally passed on to the F.B.I. a detailed plan of the Japanese air raid which he had obtained from the Germans. "It was the news I had been awaiting. I couldn't say anything to relieve the tension of my fellow passengers, but I was sure the American Fleet had scored a great victory over the Japanese. I was very, very proud that I had been able to give the warning to the Americans four months in advance. What a reception the Japanese must have had! I paced the deck, no, not paced it, I floated about it exultantly."

Chapter Two

MR. KNOX GOES WEST
DECEMBER 8–16, 1941

1.

The next morning two adjacent buildings on Constitution Avenue were the center of activity. These were the outmoded barracks-like Munitions and Navy Buildings, which had housed military and naval headquarters during World War I. Stimson walked from his office on the second floor of the Munitions Building along the corridor to the connecting bridge to the Navy Building and on to Knox's office. He did so "just to show that I was not going to be one of those who attack the Navy when it is down. I took as an excuse a paper that I wanted him to sign but he appreciated my call very much." Secretly Stimson was seething at the unconscionable neglect and inefficiency of Admiral Kimmel, whom he blamed primarily for the disaster.

Yesterday scarcely a uniform was in sight but today any serviceman who possessed one wore it with pride. Tailors all over the city were busy making uniforms for officers who had been borrowing a friend's for special occasions.

Tin Pan Alley was also in operation and patriotic songs such as "You're a Sap, Mister Jap," were being prepared for popular consumption. By dawn Max Lerner had composed a more thoughtful one, "The Sun Will Soon Be Setting on the Land of the Rising Sun."

Behind the nation's bravado was a nagging question: How could tiny, backward Japan with pilots who wore glasses and flew inferior planes bring such a crushing defeat? Why were the Army and Navy caught napping? Who were to blame? Public officials as well as private citizens were asking the same questions. That morning it was reported in the New York *Times* that Senator Tom Connally, a Democrat, apparently had already given Knox "uncharted hell" for Pearl Harbor. Connally made no comment, except to wonder where American planes and patrols had been during the attack.

The White House had a new look that morning, with military police and sentry boxes set up at intervals inside and outside the picket fence. The White House police were already being reinforced by the metropolitan police, and the Secret Service was rushing extra men from field stations. On both the office and house blackout curtains were being put up.

By late morning the last changes had been made on the President's speech to Congress. He delivered it to a joint session of Congress in the chamber of the House of Representatives at 12:30 P.M., beginning with words that would be long remembered: "Yesterday, December 7, 1941, a date which will live in infamy, the United States of America was suddenly and deliberately attacked. . . ." Then he called for a declaration of war for this "unprovoked and dastardly attack." Ordinarily plaudits for the President at such appearances came only from the Democrats but not today. "The applause, the spirit of cooperation," recalled Samuel Rosenman, who helped write Roosevelt's speeches, "came equally from both sides of the chamber."

Thirty-three minutes later Congress passed a resolution declaring that a state of war existed between the United States and Japan.

Roosevelt cabled the news to Churchill:

. . . TODAY ALL OF US ARE IN THE SAME BOAT WITH YOU AND THE PEOPLE OF THE EMPIRE AND IT IS A SHIP WHICH WILL NOT AND CANNOT BE SUNK.

The night before Churchill had gone to bed "and slept the sleep of the saved and thankful." Today when someone at the War Cabinet meeting suggested continuing the same gentle approach to America used before Pearl Harbor, he replied, "Oh! that is the way we talked to her while we were wooing her; now that she is in the harem, we talk to her quite differently." After all, the Americans were amateurs of war and had to be shown how to wage it.

Rumors were multiplying in Hawaii. Paratroopers had landed and twenty-one Japanese transports were offshore, waiting to sneak in. Many Navy officers were still in shock. When Admiral Raymond Spruance, commander of a division of five cruisers, entered Pearl Harbor that Monday morning to see the shattered wrecks of beloved battleships he was stunned. Years of study had not prepared him for such a sight. He found Kimmel's staff unshaven, still wearing their mud-splattered white Sunday uniforms. He was heartbroken to see Kimmel, a man he had always admired, dazed and disheveled. Others sat numbed and stunned.

Noted for his own coolness, Spruance's self-control collapsed by the time he reached home. Choked with emotion, tears running down his cheeks, he tried to tell his shocked wife and daughter what he had seen and felt. It was the most shattering experience of his life.

In his office Kimmel was telling two of his staff, "If I were in charge in Washington I would relieve Kimmel at once. It doesn't make any difference why a man fails in the Navy, he has failed." The two captains protested; nothing like that would happen. But Kimmel knew he was right.

2.

On the West Coast there was understandable panic because of the large Japanese-American population. False rumors of enemy air attacks were followed by widespread fear of a Japanese landing although it would have taken a force many times the size and strength of the Imperial Navy to land a single division on the American mainland.

In Washington, Knox had already asked the President for permission to leave Washington. Where was he going? "Pearl Harbor," said Knox, "with your permission." Somewhat reluctant to let him go, Roosevelt wondered what he thought he would accomplish. "I can find out a great deal more than here." Knox was deeply concerned by the rumors of dereliction of duty at Pearl Harbor and feared the thought of "a nasty congressional investigation."

By Tuesday evening the Knox party was in El Paso in time to hear the President's fireside chat. "The sudden criminal attacks perpetrated by the Japanese in the Pacific," Roosevelt began, "provide the climax of a decade of international immorality. Powerful and resourceful gangsters have banded together to make war on the whole human race." Every single man, woman and child in America was now a partner in the most tremendous undertaking of its history. "We must share together the bad news and the good news, the defeats and the victories— the changing fortunes of war. So far, the news has been bad. We have suffered a serious setback in Hawaii." The Philippines were being attacked and it seemed likely that Guam, Wake and Midway islands would be seized. He urged the people to ignore rumors, and the newspapers and radio stations to cease dealing out "unconfirmed reports in such a way as to make people believe they are gospel truth."

The road ahead, he said, was going to be difficult. "We must be set to face a long war against crafty and powerful bandits." But America "can accept no result save victory final and complete. Not only must the shame of Japanese treachery be wiped out, but the sources of international brutality, wherever they exist, must be absolutely and finally broken."

Despite the favorable public reception to Roosevelt's speech, there were stirrings of discontent in Congress. The next day a Republican representative complained that the

President gave no details of the losses at Pearl Harbor and
then quoted a damning dispatch from news correspondent
Leland Stowe in Chungking:

> . . . It seems incomprehensible here how the Japs
> were able to get the Army's big airfields in Oahu,
> losing a few planes, and without large numbers of
> American fighters getting in the air promptly. . . . On
> Sunday evening [Chungking time], at least one hour
> before the Jap blitz on Hawaii, an official of the
> United States gunboat *Tulitz [Tutuila]* warned your
> correspondent: "It is going to happen tonight."

Before dawn of December 11, battle stations were
sounded aboard the Knox plane, a Navy flying boat, as it
neared the Hawaiian Islands. The passengers donned life
preservers and parachutes. Machine guns were manned.
They were prepared for the worst. They broke radio silence, got a fix and soon were landing at Kaneohe Bay.
Knox was appalled. The air station hangars were hulks and
wreckage of seaplanes could be seen on the ramps and in
the water. The party was driven to the Royal Hawaiian, a
grim contrast to the holiday hotel of peacetime. Kimmel
met them there and escorted them to his headquarters.

From the submarine base Knox got his first view of what
was once Battleship Row. It was a shambles. Smoke was
still pouring from the wreckage of the *Arizona*. "Did you
receive our dispatch the night before the attack?" Knox
asked. Kimmel had not. "Well, we sent you one. . . ."

That day Adolf Hitler solved another of Roosevelt's
problems by declaring war on America. If the President
had been forced to act first, he would have risked opposition from a substantial segment of the country.

On Capitol Hill, the debate in Congress over responsibility for Pearl Harbor resumed. Republican Senator
Charles Tobey of New Hampshire expressed disappointment at the President's failure in his speech to make "a
definite statement as to the losses suffered in the debacle at
Pearl Harbor."

A Democrat instantly came to the Administration's defense. The Japanese undoubtedly still didn't know how much damage they had done. The public should be told the truth "but I think as this struggle proceeds we must all realize that sometimes it is better Americanism not to withhold the truth when it can be told, but to withhold it when it aids our enemies more than it serves our own people." There was a burst of applause from the galleries.

Unabashed, Tobey then began attacking Knox and quoted an article in the *Christian Science Monitor* entitled, "Why, Mr. Secretary—why?" criticizing Knox for not taking proper precautions. Where were the patrols that were supposed to protect the fleet?

It was obvious that the unity brought by Pearl Harbor had abruptly ended in Congress and the battle between interventionists and isolationists, however subterranean, would be resumed.

"Now, all that I feared would happen has happened," wrote isolationist leader Charles Lindbergh in his diary. "We are at war all over the world, and we are unprepared for it from either a spiritual or a material standpoint." It probably would be the bloodiest and most devastating war of all history. "And then what? We haven't even a clear idea of what we are fighting to attain."

During the day Stimson held his first press conference since the disaster. With Marshall's help he jotted down brief notes and then talked effectively to the newsmen. "Altogether," Stimson wrote in his diary, "much is brewing. We are doing our best to keep from having a row with the Navy. There is bitterness on both sides over the failure at Hawaii and the younger and less responsible—and some of the irresponsible older men—are all trying to throw the burden off on the other Department."

On his own initiative, Stimson had already sent two of his own people to Hawaii to investigate the Army side of the attack, a major general and a colonel, the former to relieve General Short. On the afternoon of the twelfth their B-18 took off from Phoenix, Arizona, destination Hamilton Field, California. It crashed into the snow and ice of the high Sierras.[1]

[1] The wreckage was not found until early May 1942, two miles northwest of Burch Mountain at an altitude of 11,000 feet.

Unaware that Army investigators had been sent to join Knox in Hawaii, the President was dodging questions about the attack at his own press conference. There was no need to be uneasy about being scooped, he assured the White House press corps. He told them that Knox had arrived in Hawaii the night before and warned those who planned to "tell all, and publish all" they had better wait until the Secretary of the Navy made his report.

3.

On Sunday, December 14, Stimson finally had time for his first relaxation in a week. But after a good horseback ride with his military aide he found a new crisis: two urgent telegrams from MacArthur in the Philippines asking for help. "He was instigated to do so by a conference he had had with Admiral Hart who took the usual Navy defeatist position and had virtually told MacArthur that the Philippines were doomed, instead of doing his best to keep MacArthur's lifeline open."

That afternoon he showed the President the two telegrams. "He read them most carefully with tremendous interest, if not excitement. To my great joy he took the position which Marshall and I took and against the Navy." Stimson had brought along a memorandum of his plans for reinforcing MacArthur. "I read this to the President and it all fitted into the same plan so that by the end he had fully made up his mind to side with us against the Navy." Stimson was delighted at his success in "upsetting the Navy's defeatist plan." That evening he exulted on having apparently gotten the President firmly on his side: ". . . and so tonight I went to bed with a feeling we had probably gotten over the hump, so to speak, and were going to embark on an aggressive constructive policy which will bring the end of the war just that much nearer."

He did not know that Knox was already at the White House. He had returned from Hawaii and at ten o'clock personally delivered a typed report to Roosevelt. The Japanese attack, he said, came as a complete surprise to both Kimmel and Short. "Its initial success, which included almost all the damage done, was due to a lack of a state of readiness against such an air attack, by both branches of the service.''

Knox did not accuse either Kimmel or Short of dereliction of duty and pointed out that neither had been privy to the Magic intercepts. He also reported that Kimmel and his staff had been convinced that the principal danger to the fleet was a submarine attack for which they had taken the necessary precautions. As for Short, he feared sabotage and bunched his planes so they could be more easily protected; but this, of course, made them easy air targets for the Japanese. Knox also pointed out that several factors were beyond the responsibility of the two commanders: Japanese fifth columnists and inadequate fighter planes and anti-aircraft guns.

Clearly displeased with a report practically exonerating Kimmel and Short, Roosevelt next morning summoned Knox, Stimson, Hull and other high officials. He instructed the War and Navy secretaries to hold separate press conferences and cover *only* the parts listed on a piece of paper he handed Knox. Nothing else, Roosevelt said, repeat, nothing else in the Knox report was to be made public at this time. It was to be admitted that neither military nor naval forces had been prepared for the air attack but that, once engaged, the defense was heroic. The burden of blame, by inference, was to fall on Kimmel and Short.

At the press conference later that day, Knox held his audience spellbound as he graphically revealed the story of the gallant actions after the sneak attack. ''You could have heard a tiny pin drop on the carpet of the room,'' recalled a Navy public relations officer. ''Hardened veteran war correspondents present were visibly moved.''

Knox's formal statement was almost a verbatim version of the President's notes. ''The United States services were not on the alert against the surprise air attack on Hawaii. This fact calls for a formal investigation which will be initiated immediately by the President. Further action is, of course, dependent on the facts and recommendations made by this investigating board. We are entitled to know if (a) there was any error of judgment which contributed to the surprise, (b) if there was any dereliction of duty prior to the attack.'' He then read off Roosevelt's list of those ships lost: the battleship *Arizona;* the target ship *Utah;* an old minelayer; and three destroyers.

The reaction to the drastically revised Knox report was enthusiastic. The *Nation* called it "as fairly extensive and unvarnished" as was possible until after the war. The New York *Times,* satisfied that some information about the attack had been disclosed, noted that "it was almost possible to hear the immense sigh of relief that arose yesterday when news of [Knox's] statement reached the American public." The sigh of relief would not have been so immense if Knox had revealed that the actual losses were far greater than those on Roosevelt's list.

The most important difference between the original Knox report and the one released was the omission of the fact that Kimmel and Short had not been privy to the decoded Japanese message indicating a surprise move was imminent. If it had been made public, the Japanese would have known the United States was decrypting their top secret diplomatic code. This necessary suppression, however, misled the American people into placing the burden of blame on the two local commanders; nor was the public informed that there were insufficient fighter planes, antiaircraft artillery and radar on Oahu. And so the truth about Pearl Harbor was kept from the public. The question was how long could the cover-up last.

Late in the afternoon Knox called Stimson. He had just seen the President, who wanted to appoint a commission of two Army and two Navy officers and one civilian to investigate the responsibility for the losses at Pearl Harbor and to make recommendations. The Secretary of the Navy was going to recommend two former commanders of the fleet, Admirals Joseph Reeves and William Standley—and a federal judge in Chicago named Sullivan. What did Stimson think of these choices?

"I'll get right on it and let you know later," he said, and took the problem home to Woodley. That evening he queried friends about Judge Sullivan but no one knew him well. The Assistant Secretary of War, John J. McCloy, suggested Supreme Court Justice Owen Roberts. McCloy had been active in the Black Tom explosion case which had been tried before Justice Roberts. Stimson also had been impressed by Roberts' investigation of the Teapot Dome scandal and he was inclined to recommend him.

That evening Mrs. Charles Hamlin dined with the Roosevelts. "Our pièce de résistance were two pheasants from Hyde Park," she recalled, and the President, looking well and in fine spirits, carved them. He said he was going to appoint Owen Roberts to head the Pearl Harbor inquiry. The justice, he remarked, "seemed very friendly lately." As Roosevelt was being wheeled off to his study he said with a twinkle, his cigarette tipped at its usual angle, "Hungary, Roumania and Czecho-Slovakia have all declared war against us. I told Cordell to take no notice of them and I will not inform Congress."

Later Knox arrived. At the press conference he had assured the reporters that there would be no reassignments until after the investigation. But now he felt Kimmel should be relieved immediately since his name was inescapably associated with disaster. Roosevelt concurred, and they both agreed that Admiral Ernest J. King should be appointed to a new, independent post as head of the Navy. They would sleep on who should replace Kimmel.

4.

By early morning Stimson had made up his mind on the military members of the commission. Before 8 A.M. he telephoned Marshall to say he had definitely decided on Frank McCoy, a trusted friend for thirty years,[2] and they should pick an airman for the second. Marshall agreed and returned his call a little later. Joseph McNarney, he thought, was the best man. Recently promoted to brigadier general, he was Marshall's trustworthy right hand.

---

[2] As Secretary of State in Hoover's administration, Stimson had been unable to bring the President around to his anti-Japanese views. So he persuaded the League of Nations to appoint General McCoy to the committee investigating Japanese actions in Manchuria. McCoy was so successful in pressing Stimson's ideas that Japan withdrew from the League.

Stimson now telephoned Knox at his apartment just as he was getting up. How about Justice Roberts for the civilian? he asked. Knox agreed and said he would back Roberts.

Stimson immediately wrote the President his suggestions, adding a paragraph which was the first disclosure outside the War Department that the Hawaiian top commanders were to be fired *before* the investigation. "Most confidentially we are sending to Hawaii two men to relieve Short and [F. L.] Martin, the present Army Commander and Air Commander and I think nothing should be said about it until they arrive to take command."

In a rather informal postscript Stimson wrote, "My opinion is that the housecleaning which I describe in the last paragraph should be synchronised with a similar housecleaning in the Naval Command, and all announced at the same time."

Knox was already at the White House discussing Kimmel's replacement. It took little time for them to agree on Rear Admiral Chester W. Nimitz, Chief of the Bureau of Navigation. "Tell Nimitz to get the hell out to Pearl and stay there till the war is won," said Roosevelt.

Nimitz was startled to be selected. Upon learning that he was going to be the new commander in the Pacific, his wife said, "You always wanted the Pacific Fleet. You always thought that would be the height of glory."

"Darling, the fleet's at the bottom of the sea. Nobody must know that here, but I've got to tell you."

That afternoon the President summoned Knox and Stimson. After a long wait, they were informed that their recommendations for Army and Navy members of the investigating commission had been accepted. Then Supreme Court Justice Roberts was brought in. He agreed to head the commission and promised to turn up at Stimson's office next morning for instructions.

The two secretaries were pleased. All their selections had been accepted and the crucial investigation was now in hand. With the wrong members the unity of the nation might have been jeopardized. Both Knox and Stimson were Republicans, appointed for their agreement with

Roosevelt's interventionist policy. Both were men of positive views, confident that theirs was the right way.

But of the two Stimson was the stronger. He was now convinced that both Short and Kimmel had been derelict in their duties and he resented any suggestion that they had not. The fault was in Hawaii, not in Washington. He was particularly unsympathetic to Kimmel, who he felt was most to blame. In fact, Stimson was suspicious of admirals in general. Most of them were defeatists like Hart.

A graduate of Yale University, Henry L. Stimson still took seriously its motto, "For God, for country, and for Yale." He carried this messianic message through life, staunchly convinced that the principles of his class and country were best for all the world. An ardent believer in exercise, he rode horseback, chopped wood and participated in active games, particularly deck tennis, played by tossing a quoit over the net. Only close friends knew he was blind in one eye; and his aide was careful to pick opponents. Vice-President Henry Wallace, for instance, was never invited after an aggressive first match. His idol was Theodore Roosevelt, whose motto he also took seriously: "Speak softly and carry a big stick." Stimson had carried his big stick in service to Taft as Secretary of War, to Coolidge as governor of the Philippines, and to Hoover as Secretary of State. Despite all these titles, the one he chose for personal use was "Colonel." He had earned this in the Great War and still sentimentalized over his Army service. To him the greatest virtues were soldierly. He had never looked upon war as evil but as a necessary fact of international life.

His firm lips and set jaw were indicative of a one-track mind, and once he had made it up would stick tenaciously to his decision. This was proven in his persistent hatred and fear of Japan. It had begun, while he was Hoover's Secretary of State, with the Japanese conquest of Manchuria in 1932. Stimson took this as a personal affront, and the bombings of Shanghai further ignited his hot temper. His solution was to apply against the Japanese drastic economic pressure and, if necessary, military and naval force. Hoover was equally offended by Japan's aggression but with him it was a moral and legal protest. He would not tolerate force.

In 1940 Stimson found a President more to his taste, albeit a Democratic one. He agreed to serve as Roosevelt's Secretary of War, and in the next months consistently pressed him to get tougher with both Nazi Germany and Japan. It was Stimson, above all, who convinced the President to freeze Japanese assets in July 1941. Since America had been Japan's major source of oil imports, this left Japan in an untenable position. To the New York *Times* it was "the most drastic blow short of war." To Japan's leaders it was even more. This freezing was the last step in the encirclement of their empire by the ABCD (American, British, Chinese, Dutch) powers, a challenge to their nation's very existence.

Throughout the fall of 1941 Stimson kept pressure on Roosevelt to take a stronger stand against the Japanese. The President was reluctant to provoke a war in the East when the real danger was in Europe. But Stimson, seething with moral indignation at Japanese depredations, persisted. For a while Roosevelt was tempted to make a compromise reply to the final Japanese offer of settlement in late November since Stark and Marshall had urged conciliation, both arguing that America would not be ready for war until the following spring. But Stimson and his adherents won out, and on November 26 Hull sent the strong reply to Tokyo that had resulted in Pearl Harbor.

Now Stimson's task was to beat both the Nazis and Japanese and save the world. To do this the Pearl Harbor controversy had to be quelled. If the Administration and George Marshall could not be completely exonerated of all culpability, the war effort would be seriously impeded. And, in his opinion, this was unthinkable to any true patriot. Therefore, Kimmel and Short had to take the blame.

Chapter Three

"SOME ADMIRAL OR SOME GENERAL IN THE PACIFIC MAY BE MADE A GOAT"

Herbert Hoover

DECEMBER 17, 1941– JANUARY 29, 1942

1.

The Roberts Commission, with the exception of Admiral Standley, met next morning before ten o'clock in Stimson's office. The Secretary said that the Army and Navy wanted to cooperate fully with the commission, adding that he felt it was not a question of Army versus Navy or Navy versus the Army. Then he turned to Knox. "How about that, Frank?"

"That is absolutely right."

Praise was already coming to Roosevelt for securing such a prestigious commission. The selection of Justice Roberts was particularly applauded, for it guaranteed, as one eminent judge wrote, "that the whole truth concerning the unhappy eventualities of December 7th will be revealed in an irrefutable and satisfactory manner." Unmentioned was that Justice Roberts had been an active member of William Allen White's aid-to-Britain organization.

Herbert Hoover sent his congratulations to his old friend, General Frank McCoy, on his appointment. Then, with apologies, added a warning:

> When Hull's ultimatum was delivered to the Japanese on the 26th of November [1941] I and many others of some experience knew that sooner or later it meant war, and said so. . . . My point is: Did the State Department apprise the Army and Navy of the ultimatum and its serious import? If so, did the Washington heads of these departments transmit it to the forces in the field? Now the only reason why I write this is the feeling that some Admiral or some General in the Pacific may be made a goat for action or lack of action higher up, and thus a great injustice done.

At about 10 A.M. the membership, still without Standley, convened down the hallway at the Board Room, 2309. After preliminaries, General Marshall, assisted by the Chief of the War Plans Division, General Leonard T. Gerow, outlined a number of warning messages sent to General Short.

Standley was just landing at the Washington airport. Retired in 1938 after four years as Chief of Naval Operations he had been ordered to proceed immediately from San Diego and report to the Secretary of the Navy. He was blunt, outspoken and inclined to be crusty to those he regarded as fools. "Well, Admiral," greeted Knox, "we're in a mess and, as always, we need your help." Standley had no idea what he meant until the Secretary explained about the commission. "That's your first job, Admiral."

Standley found Justice Roberts sitting at the head of a table flanked by three men, obviously his three colleagues. But what was General McNarney doing there? What right had a member of the Army General Staff to be a member? How could he possibly have an objective view of Washington's responsibilities in the case? In fact, he himself was somewhat prejudiced. "I knew from first-hand experi-

ence the shortcomings of our base at Pearl Harbor, for
which Short and Kimmel were in no way responsible.''

"Hello, Betty," said Standley to Stark, present as a
witness, and they shook hands. He was presented to Justice Roberts and spoke to the other members.

Once the questioning of Stark was finished Standley was
determined to discover what he had gotten into. Was this,
he asked, an Army or Navy board or a joint commission or
what? Would they go by Army, Navy or civil procedure?
Could they summon witnesses, administer oaths and take
testimony? "The answers I got were not at all reassuring." It was a mixed commission with no precedent. The
recorder had little or no court-martial experience; and a
Marine Corps colonel was provost marshal. Most astounding was that none of the witnesses had been sworn in.[1]
Shocked at such irregularity, Standley protested so vigorously that his colleagues agreed to have Congress pass a
joint resolution giving them the authority to subpoena witnesses and administer oaths. Why this hadn't been done
earlier, particularly by a body headed by a Supreme Court
justice, puzzled Standley. Had this strangely constituted
body been purposely set up informally so as to whitewash
the Washington authorities for their failures and place the
blame primarily on Short and Kimmel? Standley feared
that if it came to a vote he could only count on McCoy.

In the House that day the commission was discussed and
praised by a Democratic representative from Michigan.
"There is no question but that under the chairmanship of
Mr. Justice Roberts the testimony will be fair and fearless
and that the findings of the Board will be equally fair and
fearless. Such facts as cannot, because of military necessity, be revealed, can be passed over by the people without
uneasiness when they are assured by this Board that concealment of such facts is necessary."

Next day the commission again met at 10 A.M. in Room
2309. They listened to the Army and Navy intelligence
chiefs and to the officer in charge of communications for

---

[1] A transcript of the witnesses' testimony was not taken. The only known
minutes of this and the next day's testimony are brief and unrevealing
summaries by the recorder.

the War Department. And so by the time of adjournment soon after noon, the commission had been provided by the Army and Navy with "every document that could have bearing on the situation at Pearl Harbor."

So Justice Roberts thought. But except for the fourteen-point message of December 6–7 none of the other numerous Magic intercepts was produced and, without these messages, it would be impossible for the commission to determine how much Washington knew in advance of the attack and how much had been sent on to Kimmel and Short.

Based on these two days of unsworn and unrecorded testimony, the commission formulated its plans and by the time the members left the Washington airport at 4:17 P.M. bound for Hawaii the general feeling was that they had been thoroughly prepared to proceed with the investigation.

After a long, tedious trip they arrived in Honolulu at 7:20 A.M. on the twenty-second. The day was spent in preparations at Fort Shafter and it was not until nine the next morning that the first Army witness, General Short, was interrogated. He said he regarded Marshall's warning of November 27 as an order to prevent sabotage uprisings and subversive action among the many Japanese living on the islands. While he had been warned "hostile action possible at any moment," he was cautioned to let "Japan commit the first overt act . . ." and that reconnaissance and any other measures he deemed necessary "should be carried out so as not to alarm civil population or disclose intent." He had replied the same day, "Department alerted to prevent sabotage. Liaison with Navy." Two days later he sent another wire giving details of the full precautions he was taking against subversive activities and was never told he had misunderstood instructions.

No meeting of the commission was scheduled for Christmas. Early that morning Nimitz arrived from Washington by flying boat. It came to a halt on the choppy waters of Pearl Harbor. As the door was thrown open he was met by an appalling stink of black oil, charred wood and burned and rotting bodies. On the launch trip to shore through steady rain, an escorting officer explained that the boats moving in the harbor were fishing out bodies. They were grotesquely bloated, still rising to the surface.

"This is a terrible sight," murmured Nimitz, "seeing all these ships down." After breakfast he was joined by Kimmel. Ordinarily of imperious presence, Kimmel seemed stooped and deflated. "You have my sympathy," said the shocked Nimitz. "The same thing could have happened to anybody."

There was still a grim spirit in Washington. Churchill, arrived three days earlier for conferences, went with the President to a service at the Foundry Methodist Church. General Marshall and his wife were eating Christmas dinner at home alone. But the Starks were entertaining friends, including four children, in the festive aura of a brightly decorated Christmas tree in the hall surrounded by presents. Stimson had risen early for a horseback ride before driving to his office.

The next day Churchill told Congress how thankful Great Britain was for all the help America had sent. These were indeed dismal days but there were some good tidings from across the Atlantic. Hitler was suffering in Libya and the lifeline of supplies from America was flowing steadily and freely. "If the United States has been found at a disadvantage at various points in the Pacific Ocean, we know well that it is to no small extent because of the aid which you have been giving to us in munitions for the defense of the British Isles and for the Libyan campaign, and, above all, because of your help in the battle of the Atlantic, upon which all depends, and which has in consequence been successfully and prosperously maintained."

On the twenty-seventh the Roberts Commission moved to Pearl Harbor where the day was spent in the wardroom lounge of the submarine base interrogating Kimmel. The admiral brought with him an old friend, Rear Admiral Robert Theobald, to help locate papers pertinent to his testimony. Roberts told Theobald with a smile, "Of course, you are not here in the capacity of a defense counsel because you and Admiral Kimmel both understand that no charges have been preferred against him; he is not in the status of a defendant." Theobald bowed silently but thought Roberts' statement was incomprehensible. How could any investigation of the Commander in Chief of the United States Fleet be conducted without regarding him as a defendant—and without counsel?

Late that afternoon Roberts began questioning Kimmel "in a loud tone of voice; in fact, in a manner more to be expected of a trial lawyer in a lower court." Kimmel felt he was being treated not as a witness but as a guilty defendant, and that Roberts was not a judge but a prosecutor. Admiral Standley also was unhappy. It seemed as if Roberts was angry at Kimmel because his statement to the commission was not as orderly as Short's. The justice should have realized that most of the admiral's staff had gone to sea after the attack and he had been unable to draft a comprehensive report by himself. Moreover Kimmel, not having been allowed to be present at the inquiry previously held at Fort Shafter, had no idea what testimony or documentary material had been presented.

After adjournment Roberts, Reeves and Standley visited the basement headquarters of Commander Joseph Rochefort, chief of the Communications Security Unit. While the two admirals were in close conference with Rochefort, Roberts asked Commander Jasper Holmes, an intelligence officer, to see the charts and logs kept during the attack. Holmes also mentioned some of the relevant information they had discovered since the attack by decrypting Japanese consular messages. If only they had had access to consular messages before the attack, they might have stopped the Japanese, lamented Holmes, who did not know that many of those messages had been decrypted in Washington before the attack.

The following day Roberts must have had some feeling of dissatisfaction with his own harsh conduct and half apologized to Kimmel. Although inwardly seething Kimmel replied "that he desired to offer no objection to the treatment he had received from the Commission up to that time."

As the inquiry continued it became evident to Standley that the sixty-nine-year-old Admiral Reeves, a veteran of naval aviation's most formative years, shared Roberts' conviction that the two Hawaiian commanders, and particularly Kimmel, were entirely at fault. Standley could not subscribe to this view. "I felt that, with all the information available to them in Washington, Admiral Stark and General Marshall were equally culpable."

Kimmel was frustrated that he had no opportunity to confront the other witnesses or to submit evidence on subjects they discussed. He had no idea what the others had testified or what material had been placed in evidence since each witness had been ordered to keep his testimony secret.

When the commission resumed its inquiries after the New Year holiday Standley asked Lieutenant Commander Edwin Layton, Kimmel's intelligence officer: "Has the Naval Intelligence in Washington all the information for making the estimates of the situation and drawing conclusions?" Yes. "If that is true, wouldn't they be in a better position to estimate the whole situation than you are here?"

."That is the way the system is laid."

This line of questioning would inevitably lead to criticism of Washington and Roberts took over. "If you are an intelligence officer for the Commander of the Fleet of the United States, you do not expect that anything of value to you as to any important situation would be withheld from you by the authorities in Washington, do you?"

"No, sir," said Layton.

On January 5 the commission convened at Suite 300 of the Royal Hawaiian Hotel. Yeoman Ken Murray accompanied Kimmel to the hotel that morning with a large box of correspondence relating to the admiral's efforts throughout ten months to improve the defenses of Pearl Harbor. Murray was not permitted inside the hearing room and sat outside for two days without being summoned. Finally he was instructed to take the papers back to headquarters and file them.

Adding to the problems of both Kimmel and Short was the inefficient recording by the two stenographers brought from Washington by Roberts. One, an adult, had little or no experience in court reporting, and the other was a teenage young man who at times could not even read his own notes and omitted considerable material. Kimmel found the transcript of his first days of testimony so muddled that it took him a day and a half to correct it. Omitted was his entire main statement. Theobald protested to the recorder, who reported that Roberts was opposed to any extensive correction. Theobald tried to explain that Kimmel had no desire to modify his testimony in any respect, only to bring it in accord with what he had originally said before the commission. The answer was that Roberts was "opposed to any correction of the testimony other than by numbering the errors and placing the correct statements in an addendum to the Commission's report." But what reader would bother to turn to an addendum every few words?

Although Theobald appealed to Standley, he confirmed that Roberts would not permit the original transcript to be altered. "But Mr. Roberts is only one member of the Commission," protested Theobald, "and there are four military men on that Commission who must know how this matter is handled in case of testimony before a military court." Did Roberts' wishes control the actions of the entire commission?

"Theobald," said Standley, "you and Kimmel fully understand what Kimmel is up against in this inquiry, don't you?"

"Of course we do."

Next morning Kimmel renewed his request to Roberts himself in the presence of Standley. "Admiral," said Roberts, "you are not on trial."

"Words don't alter facts," replied Kimmel. "In the eyes of the American people I am on trial and nothing you can say will alter that."

On January 10 the commission left Honolulu, arriving in San Francisco the next day. En route to Washington by train the group began to draft their findings. On the evening they arrived Standley reported to Knox. "Mr. Secretary," he said, "under the circumstances, Admiral Kimmel and General Short had to be relieved of their commands. Yet, I can't help regretting that Admiral Kimmel had to go. I have never seen the Fleet in a higher state of efficiency than was evidenced during the course of our investigations at Pearl Harbor.''

2.

It took three days for the commission to finish the draft of their findings. Then on the nineteenth, they spent much of the day in Room 2905 of the Navy Building, interrogating General Marshall. Unlike Short and Kimmel, he was treated with extreme consideration. He was asked few penetrating questions and no embarrassing ones concerning the alert sent to Stark on November 7 and the warning of December which did not reach the recipient until long after the Japanese attack. His explanation of why this second message was sent by commercial cable and not by radio or telephone was accepted at face value. Nor was he asked why it had taken the Chief of Staff until 11:25 A.M. to get to his office that fateful day.

The next morning, the twentieth, the commission went into executive session to draw up its report. That evening the chairman dined at the home of a fellow justice of the Supreme Court, Felix Frankfurter. Present also was Stimson, who as a district attorney in 1906 in southern New York State had launched Frankfurter, just out of Harvard Law School, on his career as his assistant in several trust-busting cases. ''We sat up until twelve o'clock,'' Stimson wrote in his diary, ''talking over with Roberts the view he had formed on the general situation in Hawaii as distinguished from his decision which is not yet ready for announcement. He has been impressed in the same way that I have with the defensive spirit of the Navy and he has been impressed as I have with the fact that Hawaii is no longer a safe advance base for the Navy under the conditions of modern sea and air warfare.'' Stimson was pleased that Roberts thoroughly approved of sending more troops to Hawaii. ''We sat until midnight and it was a fruitful evening.''

The board room in the Navy Building became an arena

of battle during the next few days, Reeves insisting that
Kimmel was completely at fault, while Standley maintained that the burden of blame belonged in Washington.
The conflict between the two men was open, their enmity
dating back to when Standley, as Chief of Naval Operations, refused to recommend Reeves's reappointment as
commander of the Pacific Fleet. As a result, deduced
Standley, Reeves's animosity "apparently persisted long
after we both had retired and seemed to motivate his actions during our service on the Roberts Commission."

Standley was so shocked by the prejudicial attitude of
his colleagues that he warned Knox that if Kimmel was
ever court-martialed he would take his case and see that he
was acquitted. But Knox was so successful in persuading
him to work with the group that Standley agreed not to
submit a minority report lest it divide the country and
harm the war effort. On the twenty-third he reluctantly
signed Roberts' report, though he later wrote that "it did
not present the whole, true picture. The findings as to sins
of commission presented true enough statements, but the
many sins of omission in the picture were omitted from
our findings because the President in his executive order
setting up the Commission had specifically limited its
jurisdiction."

Roberts wanted to release his report directly to the
newspapers but Roosevelt insisted on seeing it first. It took
two hours for the President to study the document in full
and ask Roberts a few questions. Then, pleased by what
he had read, he said, "Is there any reason why this report
should not be given to the public in its entirety?" There
was not. Roosevelt tossed the document across his desk to
one of his secretaries. "Give that in full to the papers for
their Sunday editions."

Stimson spent the next morning poring over newspaper
accounts of the report. He was as pleased as Roosevelt.
"It is an admirable report, candid and fair, and thorough
in its study of the facts. It points out with merciless thoroughness the faults in the defense of Hawaii on December
7." The commission, thought Stimson, had done its work
well. In the conclusions it found that Hull and Knox had
fulfilled all their obligations by keeping the Army and

Navy Departments informed of the course and significance of negotiations with Japan. And Marshall and Stark had fulfilled theirs by consulting with each other and their superiors. Moreover, both had fulfilled their command responsibilities by warning Short and Kimmel of probable hostilities and ordering them to take appropriate measures.

The lack of readiness in Hawaii, concluded the report, was laid to the failure of Kimmel and Short "to consult and cooperate as to the necessary action based upon the warnings and to adopt measures enjoined by the orders given them by the chiefs of the Army and Navy commands in Washington."

Although unnamed officers in the War Department were scolded for leading Short to believe that sabotage was the only danger, the great burden of blame fell on Short and Kimmel. "The Japanese attack was a complete surprise to the commanders, and they failed to make suitable dispositions to meet such an attack. Each failed properly to evaluate the seriousness of the situation. These errors of judgment were the effective causes for the success of the attack."

Asked for a comment, Senate Majority Leader Alben Barkley declared that the report was a "comprehensive and admirable view of the facts and the people are justified in believing that nothing will be kept from them." This should end all suspicion, he added, "now that everybody knows what happened."

The majority of Americans agreed with this verdict. Letters poured into the White House calling for prompt disciplinary action. "I am hopeful," wrote Mrs. Herman Groth of Oak Park, Illinois, "that Kimmel and Short will put an end to their lives even before you make your decision as to their punishment. In this way they would at least apply the same lack of consideration for their own lives as they did for the lives of those fine American boys who perished as the result of their negligence."

This apparently ended the Pearl Harbor dispute for most Americans. But there remained many who regarded the report as prejudicial and one-sided. Vice Admiral Joseph Taussig wrote Kimmel that he knew he was "not guilty of anything either in the way of dereliction of duty or in your judgment'' despite the findings of the Roberts board. ''I, probably as much, if not more, than any high ranking officer have studied the Hawaiian Defense—and the Pacific situation in general, having spent 8 years at our War College—been Chief of Staff of the Fleet, and Assistant Chief of operations. . . . I have always felt that the entire blame for this whole affair lies right in Washington—but, of course there is no way that I can see to get at the culprits. So they have to find a goat and the mantle falls on you, who through circumstances happen to be the CinC.''

Support for Kimmel and Short also came from the Congress. Senator David Walsh, a Democrat, pointed out that there were important facts which the Roberts report had omitted and that ''the public will demand to be informed.''

Senator Robert La Follette, Jr., charged that some of the blame lay in Washington. Even Felix Frankfurter, who had suggested the private meeting between Roberts and the President, was concerned. That day he told Roberts, ''Naturally it stirs many reflections from what I think I can fairly read between the lines. . . .'' There was, he said, ''an inert and unimaginative mentality in command at Pearl Harbor'' which still remained in the Army General Staff and the Office of Naval Operations.

Upon reading the report that morning in Oklahoma City Short was completely dumbfounded. ''To be accused of dereliction of duty after almost forty years of loyal and competent service was beyond my comprehension.'' He immediately telephoned Marshall, an old and trusted friend for thirty-nine years. The Chief of Staff said he had not yet seen the report. He'd been in New York.

''What should I do?'' asked Short. Having the country and the war in mind, should he retire?

''Stand pat,'' said his old friend, ''but if it becomes necessary I will use this conversation as authority.''

Short replied that he was placing himself entirely in Marshall's hands, having faith in his judgment and loyalty. ''After I hung up I decided it wasn't fair to him to have to use the conversation as authority, so I wrote out a formal application which I enclosed in a personal letter to him.''

Dear General Marshall:

I appreciate very much your advice not to submit my request for retirement at the present time. Naturally, under existing conditions I very much prefer to remain on the active list and take whatever assignment you think it necessary to give me. However, I am enclosing application so that you may use it should you consider it desirable to submit it at any time in the future.

Short then pointed out that the Roberts report did not mention that twelve B-17s had arrived from the mainland in the midst of the attack with skeleton crews, without ammunition, and with guns packed in heavy grease for preservation.

From my point of view this is a strong argument that the War Department agreed with me that sabotage was the most dangerous thing to the Hawaiian Department and for that reason did not direct me to take action against an air attack although it had known since November 28th of the precautions taken by me. . . . I shall appreciate very greatly anything you may be able to do in my case.

On Monday morning Stimson talked over with Marshall what they should do in respect to Short since the President had left it in their hands. Marshall pointed out that Short had already telephoned him making an application for retirement, and that Stark was hoping Kimmel would do likewise. Stimson warned of the danger of acting too hastily ''as I feared it might give the impression that we were trying to let off these people without punishment because we felt guilty ourselves. Of course this would be a wholly false inference on both sides, for the retirement would not legally affect a court martial which could still be had, and on the other side I pointed out to Marshall that the Roberts Report seemed to me to be such an accurate analysis of the facts that our consciences could rest clear on its statements. Congress and the press are showing signs of going through a ghost hunt for victims and the isolationists are beginning to take up that cry in Congress, but it seems to me that the report virtually met all such trials.''

To Stimson's dismay a ground swell of protest came from the press and Congress for further investigation. ''The Roberts Report has left the FBI, Naval Intelligence and Military Intelligence under a cloud,'' commented a columnist in that day's Washington *Times-Herald*. ''Congress should penetrate that cloud and fix due guilt for negligence where it belongs.'' In New York City both the major papers agreed. The *Times* objected that the Roberts conclusions ''seemed too sweeping in exculpating their superiors in Washington from blame and in too easily finding that each of these 'fulfilled his obligations.''' And the *Tribune* charged, ''The want of foresight at Pearl Harbor was paralleled higher up.''

In Congress Democratic stalwarts, led by Barkley, were predictably supportive and the Administration critics predictably skeptical. Senator Dewey Short felt the guilt extended to Washington. ''It's high time we were getting rid of these incompetents. We've got a lot of gold-braiders around here who haven't had an idea in twenty years. They should be court-martialed.'' Another isolationist senator went further, demanding an investigation of Stimson and Knox.

On Tuesday the attack on the Administration spread. In the House Naval Affairs Committee momentum was growing for a ''thorough study'' of Pearl Harbor. A similar uprising in the Senate so concerned Harry Hopkins that the President's chief adviser, in a confidential memorandum, accused Senator Walsh, chairman of the Naval Affairs Committee, of hating ''the British more than he cares for our country.'' He also charged that another senator was ''a Nazi-minded person.''

Despite these rumblings, Stimson still expressed faith in the commission's findings. ''This is just a hasty line,'' he wrote to Roberts, ''to tell you what an admirable job I think that you and your colleagues have done in your difficult task of drawing the report on the disaster at Pearl Harbor. I think it is a masterpiece of candid and accurate statement based upon most careful study and analysis of a difficult factual situation.''

Two days later, on Thursday the twenty-ninth, the Democrats in Congress counterattacked. In the House Naval Affairs Committee meeting the motion for an investigation was defeated 14 to 6. "I think it is regrettable that the committee voted as it did," countered a Republican congressman from Minnesota. "The Roberts report settled nothing fundamental. It fixed the local blame, but not the real cause of Pearl Harbor. . . ."

Roosevelt had been kept informed of the course of this debate by House Majority Leader John W. McCormack, who warned that the second-ranking minority member of the Naval Affairs Committee, James W. Mott, was now requesting that the stenographic report and documents of the Roberts Commission be brought before the committee. Roosevelt reacted aggressively. "If you think it would be a good thing to have me send for Mott and give him a fatherly talk about how a war has to be run, I will do so," he wrote McCormack. But the scolding was not necessary. The House majority leader stifled the attempt by having Mott's request tabled. In the Senate a similar move for an investigation was choked off.

All seemed under control and Stimson wrote that evening that the Pearl Harbor business which came up at his press conference "went off very well." But the criticism had by no means ended. In a week the magazine comments began coming in. David Lawrence of *U.S. News* flatly charged that Roosevelt was responsible for the failure to coordinate defense operations and his Chief of Staff and Chief of Naval Operations should have made sure Kimmel and Short had taken the necessary precautions. Lawrence hoped that the two local commanders would not be made scapegoats for "the negligence in Washington"; and in the next issue openly accused the Administration of suppressing a congressional inquiry.

By now it was obvious that the Roberts report had only opened the door to a wider investigation. It could not come in the foreseeable future but it was bound to take place, for too much discontent, suspicion and bitterness had been raised in both civilian and military circles. "I cannot conceive of any honorable man being able to recall his service as a member of that commission without great regret and the deepest shame.'' These words came from the man who had turned over command of the Pacific Fleet to Kimmel, Admiral J. O. Richardson. ''A more disgraceful spectacle has never been presented to this country during my lifetime than the failure of the civilian officials of the Government to show any willingness to take their share of responsibility for the Japanese success at Pearl Harbor. . . .

''It is my firm belief that, when the President realized the extent of the damage done by the attack at Pearl Harbor, he lost his nerve and lost his head, and ordered the convening of the Roberts Commission, believing that he could best protect his own position by focusing public attention on Pearl Harbor.''

Richardson's indignation was shared by leading admirals on active duty. The new head of the Navy, Admiral King, later wrote, ''It seems to me that this committee did not get into the real meat of the matter but merely selected a 'scapegoat' to satisfy the popular demand for fixing the responsibility for the Pearl Harbor debacle. For instance, Admiral Kimmel was not asked the important questions nor was he given the proper chance to speak for himself. In fact, he and General Short were 'sold down the river' as a political expedient.'' The continuation of the Pearl Harbor cover-up had been done with the approval of the President on the grounds that revelation of the whole truth would impede the war effort. But there was another possible motive: did Roosevelt have something to hide?

"SETTLE YOURSELF IN A QUIET NOOK SOMEWHERE AND LET OLD FATHER TIME HELP THIS ENTIRE SITUATION"

Stark to Kimmel

JANUARY 25, 1942–FEBRUARY 1944

1.

Kimmel had already joined his wife in Long Beach, California, when he was informed on January 25 that General Short had submitted a request for retirement. Until then the admiral had not even thought of submitting a similar request. But he "took this as a suggestion" that he do likewise and submitted his own resignation the next day as a patriotic act, declaring himself in readiness "to perform any duty to which I may be assigned."

Several days later he received a personal letter from Stark. "I showed the Secretary and the President your splendid letter stating that you were not to be considered and that only the country should be considered." The general feeling in Washington, Stark added, was that, until definite action was taken regarding Kimmel's future orders, it was "better for you not to return to any temporary duty."

Kimmel was puzzled. Nor was he reassured by Stark's next words:

> I do want you to know that we will try and solve the problem on the basis of your letter—whatever is best for the country; that is about all I can say.
>
> That you are sitting on a question mark hoping for something definite at the earliest possible moment, we realize and I can assure you you are very much in our thoughts.

Even so, Kimmel promptly informed Secretary Knox on the twenty-eighth, "I desire my request for retirement to stand, subject only to determination by the Department as to what course of action will best serve the interests of the country and the good of the service."

That afternoon, at a private conference with Stimson, the President was personally directing the method of handling the Kimmel and Short requests for retirement. He ordered the Army and Navy to act in concert. "Wait about a week," he instructed, "and then announce that both officers have applied for this immediate retirement and that this is under consideration." Then, about a week later, it should be announced that the applications had been accepted with the condition that acceptance did not bar subsequent court-martial proceedings.

Courts-martial of Kimmel and Short, of course, would have revealed the inequities of the Roberts report and had to be avoided at all costs; and so such proceedings were to be described as impossible "without the disclosure of military secrets."

Stimson agreed so completely with the Roosevelt plan of action that he regarded it as his own; and it was he who put it into operation. He brought Knox into the picture. "I told him the way in which I had arranged with the President we should treat the problem of Kimmel and Short and he agreed to it."

While everyone concurred that courts-martial were out

of the question, the Administration wanted to avoid public criticism for barring them. On the other hand, it did not wish to stimulate the public or Kimmel and Short to expect or demand such proceedings. The wording of the condition in the acceptance of the requests for retirement was the most troublesome matter. All concerned labored over the language, finally agreeing that the phrase to be used in acceptance was "without condonation of any offense or prejudice to future disciplinary action."

Kimmel and Short were each retired by letter. The latter's was handed to him personally at Oklahoma City on February 18. Kimmel got his the next morning at eleven-five. He was stunned, and birthday greetings from Stark three days later did not help: "I wish for you, amid the clouds of uncertainty, COURAGE—courage that will enable you to think bravely, act wisely, and endure. . . . Make over your own world. Let your courage be its architect. May God give you strength, wisdom, balance, courage, and hope." This advice was followed by more later in the day: "Pending something definite, there is no reason why you should not settle yourself in a quiet nook somewhere and let Old Father Time help this entire situation, which I feel he will—if for no other reason than that he always has."

Kimmel replied in words indicating he was not yet ready to settle in his quiet nook. He protested the wording of his retirement:

> I stand ready at any time to accept the consequences of my acts. I do not wish to embarrass the government in the conduct of the war. I do feel, however, that my crucifixion before the public has about reached the limit. I am in daily receipt of letters from irresponsible people all over the country taking me to task and even threatening to kill me. . . . I have kept my mouth shut and propose to do so so long as it is humanly possible. . . . But I do think that in all justice the department should do nothing further to inflame the public against me. I am entitled to some consideration even though you may consider I erred grievously.

Before this letter was received Stark wrote another, this one addressed to "Dear Mustapha," Kimmel's nickname. They all had a tough year ahead and would need courage to think bravely and act wisely. "I do not have to tell you that my faith in one Husband Kimmel and in the fine fiber in his innermost makeup is such that I know it will carry him through, regardless of how rough the going."

Ignoring Kimmel's request, the disclosure of the retirement applications was about to be made public when the President, who had been kept in bed several days with bronchitis, summoned Stimson and Knox to the White House on February 25. The President said that, after sizing up the situation, he had concluded that "the temper of the people" required courts-martial for Kimmel and Short, and he preferred they request them. Then they could be delayed until a time "commensurate with the public interest." Why punish the two Hawaiian commanders severely? They should merely be reprimanded enough to placate the public.

Stimson was astonished that the President had completely changed his position but could do nothing but follow orders. He summoned Marshall, who was also shocked. The Chief of Staff sought advice from his Judge Advocate General, who advised against issuing a statement that Kimmel and Short were going to be tried by courts-martial. There was no law that authorized those two officers to request courts-martial; such trials had to originate from sworn charges and specifications. Armed with this information, Stimson pried a compromise from the President: the retirement disclosure would also announce that charges were being prepared against Kimmel and Short for trials by courts-martial, alleging dereliction of duty. These trials would not be held "until such time as the public interest and safety would permit."

Announcements were made by the Army and Navy on the last day of February. But the compromise between Roosevelt and Stimson, designed to defuse the Pearl Harbor controversy, loosed a flood of indignation and hatred upon Kimmel and Short from all over the country. "Why," a New Jerseyite asked the President, "do you protect or shield for one solitary minute your Messrs.

Kimmel and Short from the punishment of death and ignominy which in my candid judgment and that of countless but probably inarticulate fellow-citizens, these two individuals have so completely and indubitably earned?" Thousands protested the granting of pensions of six thousand dollars a year to commanders guilty of dereliction of duty. Hadn't Representative Andrew May, chairman of the House Military Affairs Committee, urged in a speech at Pikesville, Kentucky, that these two men should be shot? One man named Mix, a Yale graduate and a former circuit judge, advised Kimmel to show that he was a real man "by using a pistol and ending your existence, as you are certainly of no use to yourself nor the American people."

The families of the two officers were subjected to hate mail. How dare the three Kimmel sons serve in the Navy when their father was an infamous traitor! As the months went on there were increased demands to punish the guilty men. At the same time a growing minority was looking upon the two men as scapegoats created by the Administration to cover up its own dereliction.

Even so the Pearl Harbor controversy was far overshadowed throughout the nation by events in the Pacific. Late that February the Japanese Navy inflicted a crushing defeat on a combined Anglo-American-Dutch fleet in the Java Sea. This resulted, a few days later, in the fall of Java itself. The Southwest Pacific area was now in Japanese hands except for two bastions in the Philippines, Bataan and Corregidor.

By the beginning of April the Japanese had driven the American-Filipino defenders of Bataan to the end of that peninsula, forcing the surrender of over 76,000 defenders, including 12,000 Americans. It was the greatest capitulation in U.S. military history. This humiliation had been preceded by the forced flight of MacArthur from Corregidor to Australia. Then came the long, tragic Bataan Death March of prisoners of war to internment camps, and the fall, on May 6, of Corregidor itself.

From despair came a sudden, shocking victory less than a month later. Thanks to a group of cryptanalysts at Pearl Harbor, Admiral Nimitz was able to learn that the target of Japan's next major naval assault would be Midway Island.

On June 4 gallant Navy and Marine pilots sank four Japanese carriers in one of the greatest sea battles of history. It signaled the turn of the tide in the Pacific.

2.

That June General Short journeyed to West Point for the graduation of his son. At a garden party given by the superintendent of the Academy, General Marshall came across the lawn to speak to the Shorts. They talked for five minutes about their early service together but not a word was said of Pearl Harbor or Short's retirement.

Kimmel was now living in Bronxville, New York, working in New York City for the shipbuilding firm of an old friend, Admiral Frederic R. Harris. Kimmel was involved in drawing up drydock blueprints for areas in the Pacific where docks were unheard of. In his spare time he began planning for an eventual court-martial. He asked the Secretary of the Navy for access to the files on the attack. Knox gave him permission to study the files and get copies of whatever he needed.

Two of his sons, Manning and Tom, were submarine officers on duty in the Pacific. The latter, now a lieutenant, was in Australia. His submarine, the *S-40*, had escaped, after harrowing adventures, to Perth. While his boat was maneuvering in the harbor, a Dutch liner, one of the few ships that survived the exodus from Java, approached. Aboard was Nancy Cookson, who had met young Kimmel on a ship bound for China, the *President Adams*, several years earlier. The daughter of a consultant on a Malayan rubber plantation, she was escorting four children out of the battle zone. "I know that man on that submarine," she told a friend. "That's Tom Kimmel."

That afternoon she went to the Perth Post Office to send word to her parents that she was safe. By chance Kimmel was also there sending a three-word message to his family: "Well and thinner." Three months later they were married and in late August 1942 they left for America on a Danish ship. When the young couple arrived in Bronxville Tom was amazed by the strange welcome he received. His parents thought he was not supporting his father since he had written nothing about the Pearl Harbor controversy. Knowing only that his father had been relieved of command, he was astounded to learn about the Roberts report, the hate campaign launched against the family and how Stark had let down his father.

Later in the year Kimmel's third son, Ned, also a Navy officer, chanced to meet Stark, now commander of naval forces in Europe, on the *Ranger,* which was anchored at Scapa Flow. Having no idea there was bad feeling between his father and Stark, Ned expected Stark, who had known him since he was a boy, to embrace him warmly. But the admiral was very cool. "Oh, how are you?" he said, and ended the conversation.

3.

Allied joy over the Midway triumph had been followed a few weeks later by dismay at the fall of Tobruk to Rommel. Then came news on the second of July that Sevastopol in the Crimea had fallen to Hitler's troops. On the same day the British Eighth Army was compelled to retreat to the gates of Alexandria. What if the German forces in Russia broke through to the Caucasus and linked up with Rommel? Then it would be only a question of time before an even more ominous link-up with the Japanese.

On the other side of the world, however, an American assault on the island of Guadalcanal in the Solomons, Japan's southernmost outpost, was already under way. In the first week of August, 11,000 Marines landed on Guadalcanal. Despite vigorous attempts to dislodge the invaders by ground assaults and sea bombardments, the Americans enlarged their gains.

That fall the raging ground and sea battles in the Solomons along with the German assault on Stalingrad so occupied the minds of politicians and public alike that the Pearl Harbor controversy did not become a major issue in the congressional elections. There were attempts by the Administration to purge the most outspoken prewar isolationists but these efforts failed and the Republicans

emerged with forty-four additional seats in the House and
nine in the Senate, giving them a total of thirty-seven,
enough to block a two-thirds vote. And in the House the
Democratic majority had dwindled to two. These gains, at
the expense of liberals and New Deal supporters, furthered
the coalition between Republicans and Southern Democrats which had begun some four years earlier.

The period of November 1942 to the summer of 1943
was one of significant victories for the Allies. In the Pacific, the bloody Battle of Guadalcanal had ended in a
desperate escape of the surviving Japanese troops; and
MacArthur was driving across New Guinea toward Lae.

Hitler's successes in North Africa and Stalingrad had
turned into catastrophic defeats; and Field Marshal von
Manstein's mass tank assault near Kursk was stopped so
decisively that the initiative on the Eastern Front now belonged to the Soviets. A fourth blow came fifteen days
after an Anglo-American force landed in Sicily on July 10,
1943: Mussolini, forced to resign, was placed under arrest.

4.

By the fall of 1943 Admiral Kimmel was convinced that
he would have to spend full time defending himself. He
submitted his resignation to Admiral Harris and prepared
to leave for Washington. Harris strongly urged him to reconsider. The people in Washington would destroy him.

"That is the chance I will have to take. But I have to
live with myself and my mind is made up." Knox had
agreed to let him examine all records in the Navy Department bearing on Pearl Harbor.

The problem now was to get a good lawyer. Already
several had offered their services. "I had a feeling they
were planted by the administration in an effort to sabotage
any effort I might make."

At "my wit's end," Kimmel finally sought out a retired
Navy captain, Robert A. Lavender, a patent lawyer familiar with court proceedings. He refused to act as Kimmel's
chief counsel since he didn't have enough experience. But

he knew a man who had: Charles B. Rugg, of the Boston law firm of Ropes, Gray, Best, Coolidge and Rugg.

Ropes, Gray was one of the most prestigious firms in New England and Charles Rugg one of the most respected counselors in the country. Son of a chief justice of the Supreme Judicial Court of Massachusetts, he was a graduate of Amherst and Harvard Law School. In 1930 Herbert Hoover appointed him Assistant Attorney General of the United States. His individual participation in litigation was characteristic of his prodigious energy and capacity. In three years on this assignment he personally argued more than seventy-five cases before the Court of Claims, and thirty-five cases involving separate and distinct issues before the Supreme Court. Nor did he argue from a brief written by others but took an active part in the draftsmanship of each brief, its arrangement, its selection of cases and its style. He earned the respect of the justices of the Supreme Court and one, Justice Butler, commented that he had "the soul of an advocate."

Since 1933 Rugg had returned to private practice where his skill in presenting evidence and his powers of persuasion won scores of cases. His speech was picturesque, his laughter contagious, and he dominated a courtroom with his wit and carefully laid plan of attack. He was, in short, just the kind of fighter that Kimmel needed. He carried his brief case into the courtroom as if it were a weapon, and his "I object" crackled like a rifle shot.

Early in 1944 Kimmel was invited to Boston and, upon entering Rugg's office, was disconcerted to see a signed photograph of Roberts hanging on the wall. For two hours Kimmel gave a history of what had happened to him since Pearl Harbor. "I did not spare the Roberts Commission nor Mr. Roberts himself but castigated the Commission and Mr. Roberts in particular with every invective at my command." These invectives brought a frown to Rugg's face.

Kimmel was not intimidated. "If you believe what I have told you," he said, "I would like to have you act as my counsel. If you don't believe me, I don't want you." Rugg did not hesitate. "I will take your case," he said, then added, "I shall have to ask some embarrassing questions." "Go ahead," said Kimmel. "I hold nothing back. No question can embarrass me."

"We are going to get along fine together." A moment later Kimmel described Roberts as "that son of a bitch."

"Admiral," protested Rugg, "please don't call him such names. He is an old friend of mine."

"I won't call him any names," Kimmel promised, "until I hear you doing it."

On the train ride back to New York, both Kimmel and Lavender read most of the way. As the admiral was getting off at 125th Street he said, "Lavender, this will be the first night since Pearl Harbor that I can go home and sleep."

By the time the three men had met, Rugg had read the transcript of the Roberts Commission proceedings. "You were right about Roberts," the lawyer said.

A few days later the chance Kimmel had long been awaiting suddenly came. On February 12 Knox wrote Admiral Hart ordering him to examine witnesses and take testimony under oath pertinent to the Japanese attack on Pearl Harbor. In view of the fact that Admiral Kimmel had an interest in the matter, Hart was instructed to "notify him of the times and places of the meetings to be had and that he has the right to be present, to have counsel, to introduce, examine, and cross-examine witnesses, to introduce matter pertinent to the examination and to testify or declare in his own behalf at his own request." Although not a court-martial, this was the first step in allowing Kimmel to tell his story—and with the aid of counsel.

Kimmel's good fortune continued nine days later with the appearance in his New York office of Captain Laurance Safford, head of Op-20-G, the Navy's cryptologic organization. Years earlier Safford had served briefly as a gunnery officer on a ship commanded by Kimmel. The admiral had observed, "He couldn't shoot a gun worth a damn," and told him, "Safford, you're not cut out for this, so I'm going to see that you're transferred." Since then Safford had not only founded the Navy's communications-intelligence organization but constructed a new cipher machine which greatly surpassed any known at the time. Brilliant and innovative, he was recognized as the Navy's foremost cryptanalyst.

Safford revealed that, when Congress was demanding the admiral's court-martial, he had expected to be called as a witness. To prepare his testimony and to refresh his memory he examined the secret files of the intercepted Japanese messages which had come through his office. To his amazement, he said, he discovered for the first time that none of these messages had been transmitted to Kimmel. Until then Safford had condemned Kimmel for dereliction of duty. Now he was outraged that all this vital information had been denied the admiral.

Kimmel's excitement can be imagined. He scribbled on a pad as Safford told of the messages from Tokyo indicating that war was inevitable and imminent. But his elation was mixed with a surge of resentment, particularly when he learned about the fourteen-point message received on December 6 and 7. Why had Washington deprived him of this knowledge? How had they dared to accuse him of dereliction![1] For three hours Safford talked but finally had to excuse himself. He was in the city, he explained, to attend an exhibition of his wife's paintings and had to get back to the gallery. His wife, a talented artist, was a domineering woman with a temper. Safford himself was a professional, a quiet man fanatically dedicated to his work. He was slightly stooped, an unforgettable sight as he hurried down the corridors of the Navy Building in short, rapid steps, his diminutive secretary, Miss Feathers, scurrying at his heels, pad in hand, jotting down his latest inspiration. He was now willing to jeopardize his career by revealing the truth.

Kimmel took his penciled notes to Rugg, who agreed that the Safford testimony would be of the greatest importance. The lawyer was faced with an unusual responsibility. His first duty was to preserve and record this new material in the best interest of his client. Yet he had to protect Safford's career from destruction, and the captain

---

[1] Ned Kimmel recalled that these revelations by Safford "got father's dander up" and, "by God, he turned into a tiger."

himself from possible punishment or liability. Further, there was the transcendent consideration of the national interest. Nothing could be done in defense of his client to disclose to the Japanese that their codes were still being read.

Since the Hart Inquiry would be conducted in secrecy, Rugg advised Safford "to make a complete disclosure of the existence and substance of the intercepted messages. Then, in any future proceedings, counsel for Kimmel could request access to this record and have it available for further legitimate inquiry."

At last Kimmel would have his day in court, his fate dependent on a canny lawyer from New England and a quixotic Navy captain.

Part 2

PANDORA'S BOX

Chapter Five

MUTINY ON THE SECOND DECK

1.

Among the many ironies surrounding Pearl Harbor was the fact, unknown to the public, that the Roosevelt Administration had freely given to the British throughout 1941 much secret information denied Kimmel and Short. The most secure Japanese code, the one used by Tokyo to communicate with their embassies abroad, had been solved by a team of code breakers led by William F. Friedman, chief cryptanalyst of the Army Signal Corps. Eight machines were constructed to duplicate the original Japanese machine. There were four in Washington, two for the Army and two for the Navy; one in the Philippines at Cavite; and three in London. But none went to Hawaii. It was in this code, known to Americans as Purple, that the controversial fourteen-part message to Admiral Nomura in Washington was sent on December 6. If Kimmel or Short had been informed of its contents even a few hours before the Japanese attack, the American losses could have been reduced and perhaps the attack been seriously blunted.

When Kimmel's intelligence officer had learned that Cavite had the Purple machine, he asked Washington for another. On April 22, 1941, Commander Arthur H. Mc-

Collum, head of the Far Eastern Section of O.N.I. (the Office of Naval Intelligence), refused. "I thoroughly appreciate that you would probably be much helped in your daily estimates if you had at your disposal the DIP [the diplomatic code]. This, however, brings up matters of security, et cetera, which would be very difficult to solve. . . . The material you mentioned can necessarily have but passing and transient interest as action in the political sphere is determined by the Government as a whole and not by the forces afloat. . . . In other words, while you and the Fleet may be highly interested in politics, there is nothing that you can do about it."

Once the British learned the Purple code had been solved they requested the Joint Army-Navy Board in Washington for a machine. In return the British Chiefs of Staff agreed to reciprocate with a German Enigma cipher machine. After much haggling, two Purple machines had been sent to London in January 1941; whereupon the British refused to turn over the Enigma on the grounds that British intelligence was under the Foreign Office and any agreement made by the British Chiefs of Staff was null and void.

Once this was reported to Rear Admiral Leigh Noyes, director of Naval Communications, he exploded, accusing Rear Admiral Richmond Kelly Turner, chief of War Plans, of involvement in the double cross. Although slender, Turner was a forbidding sight with lantern jaw and heavy, black eyebrows. He was a feisty Irishman known as "Terrible Turner" because of his sulphuric temper. He retorted with vitriol. Thus began a feud on the second floor of the Navy Building that reached a climax early that fall. While Noyes was a gentle soul, a fine tennis player, and a favorite of ladies in Navy society, he surprised observers by opposing the abrasive Turner. Well known as a "fusser" in his Academy days, Noyes also had a habit of hoarding dispatches and then permitting the recipients only a glance at them. Even as recipients were initialing such messages, Noyes would snatch them away in his overzealous protection of secret material. Such behavior further infuriated Turner. "That Noyes!" he would rage in open contempt. "He and his goddamn secrets!"

His conflict with Noyes was aggravated by an even more critical one with Captain Alan Kirk, the new chief of O.N.I. Kirk, once naval attaché in London, was one of the few men junior to Turner who dared stand up to him. Turner resented this and was extremely irritated to learn that Kirk felt it was his responsibility to keep Kimmel informed concerning Japanese diplomatic moves and had actually sent him an occasional Purple intercept. Regarding this as intolerable interference, Turner complained to Stark that he was being impeded by O.N.I. His own mission was to prepare the estimate of enemy intentions, interpret, evaluate and disseminate all information on possible enemy nations. O.N.I. was simply a collection agency. "Betty" Stark greatly esteemed Turner and, some whispered, was dominated by him. In this case, at any rate, the chief of Naval Operations, an affable and accommodating man, sided with Turner.

Despite Turner's coup, Kirk felt obliged to keep Kimmel informed and during July 1941 sent him information from ten more important Purple intercepts. General Marshall, fearing this might tip off the Japanese that their top code had been solved, pressured Stark into cutting off any more such information.

To make matters worse, Kimmel was given no explanation and thenceforth labored under the delusion that the cessation of messages was only because there was nothing of importance to report. Even more important, he was also denied a look at the steady flow of messages to and from Honolulu and Tokyo via the Japanese consular code.

On September 24 a Mackay cable was delivered to the Japanese Consulate at Nuuanu Avenue in Honolulu. It was addressed to Nagao Kita, the consul general. Although the radiogram was signed Toyoda, for Foreign Minister Teijiro Toyoda, Kita knew it was from Captain Ogawa of Naval Intelligence. It was marked "very urgent" and when decoded read:

HENCEFORTH PLEASE MAKE YOUR REPORTS CONCERNING VESSELS ALONG THE FOLLOWING LINES INSOFAR AS POSSIBLE:

1. THE WATERS (OF PEARL HARBOR) ARE TO BE DIVIDED ROUGHLY INTO FIVE SUB-AREAS. (WE HAVE NO OBJEC-

TIONS TO YOUR ABBREVIATING AS MUCH AS YOU LIKE.)

AREA A. WATERS BETWEEN FORD ISLAND AND THE ARSENAL.

AREA B. WATERS ADJACENT TO THE ISLAND SOUTH AND WEST OF FORD ISLAND. (THIS AREA IS ON THE OPPOSITE SIDE OF THE ISLAND FROM AREA A.)

AREA C. EAST LOCH.

AREA D. MIDDLE LOCH.

AREA E. WEST LOCH AND THE COMMUNICATING WATER ROUTES.

2. WITH REGARD TO WARSHIPS AND AIRCRAFT CAR-RIERS, WE WOULD LIKE TO HAVE YOU REPORT ON THOSE AT ANCHOR, (THESE ARE NOT SO IMPORTANT) TIED UP AT WHARVES, BUOYS AND IN THE DOCKS. (DESIGNATE TYPES AND CLASSES BRIEFLY. IF POSSIBLE WE WOULD LIKE TO HAVE YOU MAKE MENTION OF THE FACT WHEN THERE ARE TWO OR MORE VESSELS ALONG THE SAME SIDE OF SAME WHARF.)

Kita summoned Ensign Takeo Yoshikawa, who was posing as a consular official but was in reality the sole Japanese Navy spy in Hawaii. The ensign explained that Ogawa was setting up a grid system for Pearl Harbor and wanted the exact locations of ships pinpointed for the benefit of bombardiers and torpedo pilots.

This message was intercepted that day by MS-5, the monitoring station the U. S. Army had set up recently at Fort Shafter, but General Short had not been cleared for any of the Magic messages and did not even know of MS-5's existence. Nor had the major in charge of the station been given decrypting facilities. His orders were merely to ship the intercepts air mail to Washington in their original form. The next Pan American Clipper flight, scheduled to leave in two days, was canceled by bad weather and so the important message was sent by ship. It arrived in Washington on October 6 and was decrypted by S.I.S. (the Army's Signal Intelligence Service) three days later.

That same day the message was transmitted to the Navy. Realizing it could be a bomb plot for an air attack on Pearl Harbor, Kirk urged it be sent to Kimmel. As had happened so often in the past months, Turner objected.

Nor did he relent when Captain H. D. Bode, head of Foreign Intelligence, sided with Kirk. Turner appealed to Stark and once again the chief of Naval Operations backed him. The intercept, which would become known as the Bomb Plot message, was never sent to Kimmel; and a few days later both Kirk and Bode were "detached" from intelligence and reassigned.

Captain Kirk was replaced by Theodore "Ping" Wilkinson, the fourth chief of O.N.I. that year. Top of his class at Annapolis in 1909, he was a tall, handsome man who had won the Medal of Honor in 1914 at Vera Cruz during the Mexican campaign for "leading his men with skill and courage." Scholarly, bright and intelligent, he was completely inexperienced in intelligence. Any hope that he and Turner could work harmoniously was dispelled immediately. The chief of War Plans was openly antagonistic. Perhaps Turner, still bitter that he had been fifth in the class of '08, could not abide the fact that Wilkinson had been first the following year. He bullied the newcomer relentlessly in an overt effort to dominate O.N.I. Taking advantage of Wilkinson's lack of experience, Turner began assuming some of his responsibilities. All decryptions from O.N.I. and Communications directed to Stark's office now had to be cleared through Turner, which made him, in effect, the ultimate censor. At the same time this gave him the option to release to Wilkinson and Noyes only that information he chose.[1]

---

[1] The feud on the Second Deck (the second floor of the Navy Building) was continued during the Battle of Savo Island off Guadalcanal in 1942. It was perhaps America's most humiliating naval defeat and is still bitterly debated and recollected with rancor and shame by men of the U. S. Navy. At the beginning of the battle, Admiral Turner, in command of the amphibious force, sent out a desperate call for help. His old adversary, Admiral Noyes, now in charge of the air support group, refused three times to send his carrier and destroyers to Turner's aid. "Both officers were good haters," Safford later commented. "Turner had his little victories in Washington: and now Noyes had his revenge." The latter was relieved of command for incompetence after losing his carrier, *Wasp*, several weeks later.

Captain Bode also was ruined by the Savo Island battle. In temporary command of *Chicago*, he inadvertently steamed away from the main battle. He committed suicide.

The problems of those on a lower level at O.N.I. were compounded by their own differences with the Communications chief, Noyes. Commander Safford was as concerned as Kirk and Bode about the Bomb Plot message. It was obvious to him that Lieutenant Commander Joseph J. Rochefort, head of the Communications Security Unit of the Fourteenth Naval District located at Pearl Harbor, should have the message as well as the keys to the consular code so future intercepts could be solved on the spot. He drafted a message of instructions to Rochefort but this was disapproved summarily by Admiral Noyes, who remarked irately, "I'm not going to tell any district commandant how to run his job!"

A few weeks later Rochefort's monthly report for October arrived with its last paragraph requesting instructions. Safford made a second attempt to comply but again Noyes dissented.

Despite the confusion on the Second Deck caused by rivalries and cross-purposes remarkable progress was being made because of a talented group of junior officers. "It was a strange madhouse," one of them recalled, "with sane inmates ruled over by madmen." This dedicated group included Safford, Lieutenant Francis Raven, Ensign Prescott Currier, Lieutenant George Linn and Commander Arthur McCollum. The last was chief of the Far Eastern Intelligence Section. Born in Nagasaki, he understood the Japanese and their language. He was not embroiled in the Bomb Plot message argument only because he was in England at the time and on his way home was one of two survivors in an air crash. But he, like Safford and others, agreed that the commanders in the Pacific were not getting sufficient information. On December 1 he warned both Turner and Stark that in his opinion "war or rupture of diplomatic relations is imminent." Had Admiral Hart in the Philippines, he asked, been "adequately alerted"? Given categorical assurance that this had been done, he still worried. What with Turner's bullish antagonism and Noyes's secretive nature, there was no telling what had actually been sent out to the Pacific. On December 4, McCollum was so convinced war with Japan was imminent that he drafted a brief, condensed dispatch warning all commanders from the Caribbean to the Philippines. He took it to Wilkinson, well knowing that he would only be shunted on to Turner, and once the War Plans chief saw the dispatch he began revising it. With a scowl Turner showed McCollum the war warning message sent to Kimmel on November 27.

"Good gosh," said McCollum. "You put in the words 'war warning.' I do not know what could be plainer than that, but nevertheless I would like to see mine go too."

"Well, if you want to send it, you either send it the way I corrected it, or take it back to Wilkinson, and we will argue about it."

McCollum scanned the diluted dispatch and, deflated, took it back to Wilkinson, who said, "Leave it here with me for a while."

The emasculated warning was never sent. Noyes chanced to see it and remarked characteristically, "I think it is an insult to the intelligence of the Commander in Chief." He was referring to Kimmel who, having received no warnings since November 27, had the feeling the alert was over.

2.

On the first of January, 1942, Safford was promoted to the rank of captain. But two weeks later, on the day the Roberts Commission arrived in Washington, he was called to Noyes's office to be informed that his professional career was virtually ended. Noyes explained that Admiral King felt his job was too big for a single officer to handle and that it would be split into its component parts. Safford would retain the smallest part, cryptographic research. He had performed this duty eighteen years ago with the rank of lieutenant. "No other reason was given by Noyes," Safford wrote in an unpublished memorandum, "and there was no criticism of Safford's performance of duty." What Noyes said was at variance with a written directive of the previous day ordering Commander John R. Redman to set up and head a Radio Intelligence and Deception Section. This directive blandly ignored the fact that such an organization had been set up under Safford, seventeen years previously, and that it numbered about a thousand people on January 15, 1942.

Safford was appalled "but there was nothing to do but bow to fate. There was a war on and the United States was taking a terrible beating from the nation which our Top Brass had badly underestimated and had refused to take seriously." Wilkinson's assistant commiserated with Safford. "You have been capsized," he said, "just as we have been capsized."

Perhaps Safford was unaware that his downfall had been plotted by Captain Joseph Reasor Redman, Noyes's assistant, who became chief of Communications that February. A shrewd bureaucrat, he had always disliked Safford's informal, disorganized working style, regardless of his accomplishments. Safford's erratic management had gone unnoticed by high quarters before Pearl Harbor but, with America now flung into a two-ocean war, Redman reasoned that it was essential Op-20-G have a tighter organization to intercept and break the German U-boat codes and thus protect the vast convoys that would soon be crossing the Atlantic. And so Captain Redman, an efficiency expert, maneuvered his younger brother into taking over the major part of Safford's job.

The entire operation expanded under the efficient Captain Redman and Op-20-G, with allied agencies, moved from the old building on Constitution Avenue into the red brick structures of a former girls' school near the intersection of Nebraska and Massachusetts avenues.[2] Here, Safford was shoved aside into an office where he was supposed to be primarily "tinkering with gadgets."

"Although in the official doghouse, Safford managed to contribute essentially to the War in the Atlantic," he later wrote, "and to mitigate in some degree one of Admiral King's worst blunders." Safford was far too modest. His contribution would rank high among the unsung feats of the war. He not only uncovered a blunder that was costing America numerous ships and lives but ended that unnecessary destruction. Since early 1941 he had suspected the security of the code being used for high-level com-

[2]Today the Naval Security Command Headquarters at the same address faces the new Japanese Embassy.

munications between the British and the United States, Naval Cipher No. 3. It was exactly like the Japanese Fleet code, JN 25, "except that it was lacking in the protection afforded by the complexity and ambiguity of written Japanese." While "tinkering" at his little office in the former girls' school, Safford confirmed his suspicions that the Germans had broken Naval Cipher No. 3, which was still in use. He was positive that the appalling toll of Allied shipping in the Atlantic by German submarines was because the enemy was now "reading solid" all the U.S.-British communications pertaining to convoy-and-routing as well as anti-submarine warfare.

He warned his superiors but they did not take him seriously. Neither did a British technical expert whom he alerted that summer. In desperation Safford took action. In all haste he succeeded in designing a system that would thwart the Germans by "'marrying' the British-Type-X cipher machine with the American ECM [the Electronic Countermeasure device created by the S.I.S. cryptographer Friedman]. . . . By working from each machine towards a common meeting-point, Safford succeeded in developing a third type of cryptographic principle which would enable the two radically different machines to intercommunicate." Within eight months he had designed and built working models of the necessary adapter units for both machines. Simple and comparatively inexpensive, they could be installed and removed without tools in seconds. "Most important, when removed the two machines operated in their original, unique cryptographic principles."

Before placing a production contract for his Combined Cipher Machine, that November Safford urged temporary use of the ECM devised by Friedman. The suggestion was forwarded to the U. S. Joint Chiefs of Staff, who rejected it.

Even so the stubborn Safford, spurred on by the appalling losses in the Atlantic, began building his own machine from scrounged material. In the next four months almost two million gross tons of shipping were sunk at the cost of but fifty U-boats. It was evident that if Doenitz's wolf packs were not rendered harmless Germany would win the

Battle of the Atlantic. Still Safford's new system, although now completed, was not put into use. In mid-October of 1943 one of the leading cipher experts on the British Military Mission in Washington visited Safford privately. "You were right about Naval Cipher No. 3," he said. "It is no good and the Germans have been reading it all along as you predicted. Our faces are very red and your stock is very high in London."

Several days later Friedman also made a private visit. "General Marshall has just learned that a British troop ship was sunk and 900 U.S. soldiers drowned because the Germans had broken the Naval codes. He is boiling mad and ready to raise hell over it. He has instructed me to make a personal investigation as to the circumstances, find out who is to blame, and what emergency measures should be taken to prevent recurrence of such losses."

Safford unraveled the whole story: How Admiral Robert Ghormley had accepted the British proposal to use Naval Cipher No. 3 for "possible" combined U.S.-British naval communications as one of his first official acts in November 1940 after assuming office as special naval observer in London. How Stark had approved of this decision before conferring with Noyes. How Noyes would not ask Stark to reconsider the matter or even permit Safford to talk to Stark about it. How Safford's efforts to alert his superiors had failed. "I further informed Friedman that the three men to blame [Admirals Ghormley, Noyes and Stark] had subsequently been relieved of command for incompetence, and that nothing would be gained by raising hell."

The conversation with Friedman ended Safford's frustration. In December 1943 his Combined Cipher Machine at last came into use in the North Atlantic, and the effectiveness of Doenitz's wolf packs was terminated.

3.

Several months earlier Safford also had had time to gather materials on Pearl Harbor for what he believed would be the impending court-martial of Kimmel. "I realized I would be one of the important witnesses, that my memory was vague, and I began looking around to get everything that I could to prepare a written statement which I could follow as testimony. That was the time when I studied the Roberts Report carefully for the first time and noted no reference to the 'winds' message or to the message which McCollum had written and which I had seen and I thought had been sent.''

Up to this time he had been convinced that Kimmel, derelict in his duty, deserved his harsh fate. But now he began to suspect that perhaps the admiral had *not* been given all the information about Japanese intentions that Safford had been led to believe. The ''winds'' message referred to one of the most important Japanese intercepts. On November 19, 1941, the Japanese Foreign Office advised its representatives abroad in the consular code that, in case diplomatic relations were about to be severed with the United States, Great Britain or Russia, a signal in the form of a false weather report sent in the clear would be broadcast and all code papers were then to be destroyed. If the signal was *''Higashi no kaze ame* [East wind, rain]'' that meant a break with America; *''Kitano kaze kumori* [North wind, cloudy]'' a break with Russia; and *''Nishi no kaze hare* [West wind, clear]''' a break with Britain.

After this message was decoded and translated in Safford's office on November 28, everyone on the Second Deck was alerted to watch for the crucial execute of the ''winds'' code. All interception stations were instructed to forward all such weather reports. Safford distinctly remembered seeing a message reading ''East wind, rain'' about the third or fourth of December. He had assumed the warning had been transmitted to Kimmel but failure to find the so-called ''winds'' execute in the files aroused his suspicions. Moreover, further study of the Roberts report convinced him Kimmel had been made a scapegoat. Realizing he himself had done the admiral an injustice, Safford threw himself into further investigation with the same intensity and fervor he had exerted on ridding the Navy of Cipher No. 3. He went through files and queried many colleagues. By mid-November 1943 he began to suspect that Kimmel had been deliberately deprived of this information; that he was not only a scapegoat but the victim of a complex frame-up. In December he uncovered more material which practically confirmed his suspicions and on the twenty-second he wrote for additional information to Lieutenant Commander Alwin Kramer. Before Pearl Harbor, O.N.I. had loaned Kramer to Op-20-G as head of the Translation Section. Since Safford could not understand Japanese, he had relied heavily on Kramer, who had studied the language.

Kramer was currently stationed at Pearl Harbor and Safford's greeting, "My dear Kramer-san," was followed by the announcement that he was "preparing a secret paper" covering events taking place in early December 1941.

I realize that your reply will have to be censored and therefore you must be guarded as to what you state. Also, I am phrasing my questions very carefully, in the event that my letter might fall into unauthorized hands. I am saving a copy of my letter so it will be merely necessary to give the *question number* and a brief answer, which should not disclose anything to an outsider.

He then asked what time on December 6 Kramer had brought the Japanese intercept to the President, whom he referred to as "Mr. R." Was Hull ("Mr. H.") with him? When were Admirals S. (Stark) and W. (Wilkinson) informed of the message? He also asked what time Kramer reached the Navy Building on the morning of the seventh. And were Mr. K. and Mr. S. (Kimmel and Short) telephoned or notified in any way? He also asked what happened to "the original Weather Report." It had disappeared from the files. He was referring, of course, to the "winds" execute, "East wind, rain."

Safford continued his assiduous research. Clearing Kimmel had become a crusade. The days passed but there was still no answer from Kramer. Finally on January 17, 1944, he received a memorandum from Hawaii. Kramer revealed he had taken the fourteenth part of the Japanese message to Stark at about nine o'clock on the morning of December 7. This indicated to Safford that there had been plenty of time, about three and a half hours, to send Kimmel the warning he never received until after the attack. Convinced that he had "absolute proof" that Kimmel had been framed, Safford sent Kramer an excerpt from a *Saturday Evening Post* article on Admiral William F. Halsey, commander of the Third Fleet, in the December 25, 1943, issue by J. Bryan III. "Halsey's devotion to Kimmel, an Annapolis classmate, is almost religious," wrote Bryan. "He was shocked to see him cast as a scapegoat. When the Roberts Committee of Investigation asked Halsey how he, almost alone, happened to be ready for the Japanese attack, his answer was, 'Because of one man—Admiral Kimmel.' It would surprise none of Halsey's friends if, on retirement, he applied himself to Kimmel's exoneration." The clipping was pertinent since Kramer had just been ordered to Halsey's staff. On a blank space in the article, Safford had typed:

My dear Kramer:
    When the proper time comes, show the above to Admiral Halsey as a sort of letter-of-introduction. Assure him that his ambition will come true. And it will not be necessary for him to wait until his retirement to see Admiral Kimmel completely exonerated. But we will need Admiral Halsey's help. Do not hesitate to tell him *everything*.

Three days later, on January 22, 1944, Safford wrote Kramer at length. "What a break for you, as well as the cause, to be ordered to Admiral Halsey's staff. I can see the hand of Providence in it. . . . With regard to taking Admiral Halsey into confidence, wait patiently for the proper moment, and then shoot the works. Tell him everything he will listen to and show him whatever documentary proof you may have. Use your own judgment and don't force the issue." Kramer was to be prudent and patient. "I am just beginning to get things lined up on this end. No one in Opnav [Navy Operations] can be trusted. Premature action would only tip off the people who framed Adm. Kimmel and Gen. Short, and will also get Kramer and Safford in very serious trouble. Yet we must have backing, the rank, and the prestige afforded by Adm.

Halsey.'' Kramer was to tell Halsey that Safford "has overwhelming proof of the guilt of Opnav and Gen. Staff, plus a list of about fifteen reliable witnesses.''

Fearing their correspondence might be "tapped" by those trying to hide the truth, Safford also sent a condensation code for future correspondence. It was like something out of a spy novel. No. 1 meant Roosevelt. 2 was Hull, 3 was Stark. He himself was 8 and Kramer was 10. The Son of Heaven (The Emperor) was 109. There were numbers for every department, for codes, for messages, for cities (Pearl Harbor was 92) and even for dates (December 6, 1941, was 136, December 7 was 137, and 1325 Eastern Standard Time, December 7, was 138).

Prepared to go the limit to reveal the truth, Safford journeyed to Kimmel's office on February 21, 1944. First he was screened by Admiral Harris, who asked "Were you ever on his staff?" He wasn't. "Are you a close personal friend?"

"No, sir, just a casual acquaintance."

"Then why do you wish to see Admiral Kimmel?"

"Because Admiral Kimmel is the victim of the dirtiest frame-up in the history of the Navy. And I have the proof of it."

"In that case," said Harris, "you can see him."

*On February 1, 1944, Nimitz island-hopped from Tarawa
all the way to Kwajalein in the center of the Marshalls.
His next goal was another bold leap all the way to the
Marianas from whence the new B-29 Superfortresses could
bomb Japan.*

Chapter Six

THE HART INQUIRY
FEBRUARY–JUNE 1944

1.

Soon after sending Rugg the notes on Safford's revelations, Admiral Kimmel had second thoughts about the Hart Inquiry. Was this really the best way to bring his case before the public? After all it would hardly be a free and open trial, merely a taking of testimony, and it might prevent him from getting a proper hearing later. Lavender and Rugg agreed and it was concluded that the admiral should not participate. Safford's testimony alone should provide grounds for a genuine trial. "I feel that I am entitled to a speedy and public trial and to be informed of the nature and cause of any accusation against me," he wrote Knox. "To date I have been offered neither." The Hart Inquiry, he added, will be restricted in scope, "will not be free and open and will not be of the character to which I am entitled."

Knox replied, "It must be well known to you that the public interests make a speedy and public trial impossible at this time. Similarly Admiral Hart's examination cannot be 'free and open' since matters of a very secret nature will be dealt with and their disclosures would be inimical to the war effort." In any case the Hart Inquiry would proceed and he hoped Kimmel would participate.

With the help of Rugg, Kimmel replied at length why this was impossible. The simple recording of testimony was "entirely inadequate." Also the absence of formal charges made it impossible for him "to prepare and intelligently to cross-examine witnesses who may testify before Admiral Hart and to enable me to present evidence in my own behalf. . . ." Limiting witnesses to members of the naval forces was also unfair. "In the nature of the case, it is apparent that personnel of the Army as well as civilians are intimately concerned in the events pertinent to the Pearl Harbor attack." He and Rugg of course were thinking of such key witnesses as Knox himself, Stimson and Marshall.

On February 22 the Hart Inquiry began. During the next four months he recorded the testimony of forty naval officers, most of them admirals, in Washington, San Francisco and the Pacific area. One whose testimony turned out to be particularly unfavorable to Kimmel was Admiral Turner. He met with Hart at Pearl Harbor on April 7. Since coming to the Pacific as commander of amphibious forces of the Pacific Fleet he had lived up to his reputation as a man difficult to deal with and shared the title of Most Hated Man in the Navy with King. But he was a brilliant tactician and had been promoted to vice admiral. What many did not realize was that his drinking problem was getting out of hand, although so far he had been able to bound back from hangovers and operate at his usual high efficiency.

He stated that he was "not in the least" surprised by the attack on Pearl Harbor. He and Stark and other senior assistants all considered a surprise air attack "a strong possibility." Moreover, he had sufficiently warned Kimmel. "The letters and dispatches on that subject initiated by my office are not many because we felt, and it was the Chief of Naval Operations policy, not to nag on matters of that sort. The problem was put where it belonged, in the hands of the Commander-in-Chief." That is, Kimmel. The "war warning" message of November 27 was all that Kimmel needed to be on the alert for any surprise attack. Turner's testimony, an indictment of Kimmel, went in the face of sworn statements to Hart made by Kimmel's staff.

Back home there was increasing pressure for a public trial of Kimmel and Short. During his April 11 press conference, Secretary Knox was questioned in connection with Congress' extension of the time for Kimmel's trial. As a former newspaperman, Knox was accustomed to speaking freely and replied spontaneously that he was going to seek the Judge Advocate General's legal opinion since he was "confused." That officer must have shuddered; fearing the Navy might lose the initiative in the case, he quickly drafted a press release in Knox's name stating that he had received a memorandum from Admiral King officially declaring that "certain officers in the Navy now serving on battle fronts in various parts of the world, could not be withdrawn from their military duties in order to participate in court-martial proceedings in connection with Pearl Harbor." The release pointed out that Kimmel had long since signed a waiver "and there is now no necessity to construe any acts of Congress on this subject."

Kimmel regarded this latest announcement as another trick to deny him a trial. "I presume you have noted the recent maneuvers in Washington by Mr. Knox," he wrote his oldest son, Manning, "and his contradictory statements issued in regard to the court-martial. From this mass of confusion I think it is becoming quite clear that the Administration has absolutely no intention of bringing General Short and me to trial."

2.

Kimmel now had additional counsel. Edward Hanify, formerly of Rugg's law office but now a Navy lieutenant j.g., was permitted by the chief of the Bureau of Naval Personnel to assist Rugg. Hanify had come to Ropes, Gray in 1936 after Holy Cross and Harvard Law School, and greatly admired Rugg, with whom he had often worked. On his way to see Kimmel in Bronxville, he read the Roberts report. It was so damning, he felt there would be difficulty defending Kimmel but a few minutes with the admiral changed Hanify's mind. He was impressed by the decisiveness of the admiral's actions and the profound look of deep sadness in his eyes. "I said to myself, 'There's something the matter with the Roberts Report because this is not the type of man who could be guilty of any carelessness.'"

While digging up background on the case, Hanify interviewed Admiral Richardson. The admiral said he was going to tell a story that the lieutenant could regard as a parable. "Assume," Richardson said, "you were the leader of the greatest nation in the world, and assume that you saw, in another hemisphere, the development of a power which you regarded, with reasonable support, as a total threat to Western civilization as you knew it. Supposing, however, that for various reasons, your conception of the danger was not shared by your constituents, your own people. And you saw the total destruction of Western civilization in the hands of this adversary, and you detected in your own people, at the time, on the basis of everything they knew, a lack of appreciation of the problem. Assume that you saw that the only salvation of Western civilization was to repel this particular power but that that required you to enter a foreign war for which your people were not psychologically or militarily prepared. Assume that what was needed to galvanize your own people for a unified approach towards this basic danger to civilization was an incident in which your posture was clearly of passive nonaggression, and apparent unpreparedness; and the incident in question was a direct act of aggression which had no excuse or justification. Assume that you saw this potentiality developing on the horizon and it was the solution to the dilemma, as you saw it, of saving civilization and galvanizing your own people. It is conceivable, is it not, that you might be less disposed to create a situation in which there might be doubt as to who struck the first blow. You'd want to be sure that whatever the incident, it happened under circumstances where it was perfectly clear that you were not the aggressor, and the resulting incident galvanized your own people to a realization of the terrible threat which they faced from this totalitarian force. Now just think about that. I don't say it's an hypothesis even. It's a fable. You just think about that fable as you study some of this material. And it's conceivable that it might have some enlightening factors.''

In the meantime Hart's investigation continued. Admiral Halsey staunchly defended his friend Kimmel. ''I did not feel that we were well informed on what the Japs were doing and I felt we were operating in the dark. I had the personal feeling, entirely personal, that they knew a lot more in Washington than we knew out there and that we should have been informed.'' Had he discussed this with Kimmel? ''I recall, vaguely, discussions along that line and damning them for not letting us in on the information.''

On April 17 Hart finished his examinations in Hawaii and started back to Washington. On the twenty-ninth the most important witness, Captain Safford, reported to Admiral Hart at the Navy Building. First they talked off the record. When Safford told of the ''winds'' execute and how all copies had been destroyed, the admiral sternly observed that such remarks should not be entered as evidence. ''I have just come from the front office, and I have seen your 'winds' message. Now don't make statements that you can't verify.''

Heartened by confirmation that someone else had seen the ''winds'' execute, Safford agreed to withdraw from his testimony any mention of destroyed messages. But he insisted on testifying under oath how, on December 3, he had prepared a dispatch warning Kimmel of imminent danger. ''Before drafting my message, I called Commander McCollum on the telephone and asked him, 'Are you people in Naval Intelligence doing *anything* to get a warning out to the Pacific Fleet?' And McCollum replied, '*We* are doing everything *we* can to get the news out to the Fleet.'

McCollum emphasized both 'we's.' In sending this information I was overstepping the bounds as established by approved war plans and joint agreement between Naval Communications and Naval Intelligence, but I did it because I thought McCollum had been unable to get his message released.''

Hart asked if the units at Pearl Harbor had any material from which they could have gained this information through their own efforts. ''No, sir, they did not have the material and they could not possibly have gained this information.''

Hart had no wish to continue this line of questioning but Safford insisted on telling in detail about ''winds.'' He revealed how, on December 4, McCollum drafted a long message quoting the ''winds'' execute, ending with the positive warning that war was imminent. Captain Wilkinson approved this message and then discussed it with Admiral Noyes in Safford's presence. Wilkinson had then asked, ''What do you think of the message?'' ''I think it is an insult to the intelligence of the Commander-in-Chief,'' observed Noyes.

''I do not agree with you,'' Wilkinson had replied. ''Admiral Kimmel is a very busy man, with a lot of things on his mind, and he may not see the picture as clearly as you and I do. I think it only fair to the Commander-in-Chief that he be given this warning and intend to send it if I can get it released by the front office.''

Safford explained that at the time of Pearl Harbor he had assumed the warning was sent. He hadn't realized until two years later, after studying the Roberts report carefully, that it had never gone out. As he recalled it, the ''winds'' execute was received during the evening of December 3 but Safford did not see it until the next day. ''Lieutenant A. A. Murray, U.S.N.R., came into my office with a big smile on his face and a piece of paper in his hand and said, 'Here it is!' as he handed me the 'Winds Message.' As I remember, it was the original yellow teletype sheet with the significant '*Winds*' underscored and the meaning in Kramer's handwriting at the bottom.'' He gave a list of those who must have read the ''winds'' execute, those who had heard about it by hearsay; and those who should have some recollection of it.

"The 'Winds Message' was last seen by myself about December 14, 1941, when the papers which had been distributed in early December were assembled by Kramer, checked by myself, and then turned over to the Director of Naval Communications for use as evidence before the Roberts Commission, according to my understanding at the time."

Although there was no way all this information could be made public, it had at last been put on the record, despite Hart's reluctance; and it would greatly assist Kimmel once he got his day in court.

The findings of the Hart Inquiry were not to be revealed to the public until after the war and its significance could only be guessed at by those outside of top naval and Administration circles. Hart filed no report but he did write Admiral Stark in London that what he had learned threw some suspicion on the Navy Department's role in the Pearl Harbor debacle.

Something the President told him would also concern Hart for the rest of his life. "I happened to remark to him," he later revealed in a taped interview, "that perhaps it was unfortunate that the Japanese heard too much about the date of 1 April [1942] being given as the date on which General MacArthur and his forces would be ready for war. The President replied that he had been assured by General Marshall in November [1941] that the Army's forces in the Philippines were ready then! Now I understand that at that date Secretary Knox was assuring the world that our fleets were entirely ready for the Japanese, but I still wonder if General Marshall really did say that. Anyhow, the President said, and I'm quoting his words, 'If I had known the true situation, I could have babied the Japanese along quite a while longer.'"

By the beginning of June 1944 Italy had surrendered and the Allies ruled the Mediterranean. On the Eastern Front it was only a question of how long the Wehrmacht could hold back the resurgent Red Army. Attacks by American daylight bombers on fuel plants in central and eastern Germany had already seriously endangered Hitler's entire armament program. And the Allies were making final preparations for a massive landing in France.

In the Pacific an armada of 535 ships was approaching Saipan. It carried 127,571 troops, most of them Marines.

Chapter Seven

THE ARMY AND NAVY CLUB
JUNE–OCTOBER 1944

1.

Even before the Hart Inquiry closed, Rugg realized that it was time to attack "to prevent the whole story from being shelved and buried." The statute of limitations for prosecuting Kimmel and Short was nearing its deadline. If it were not extended the two men might never get the open hearing they both wanted. It was, thought Rugg, an anomalous situation. His client, the accused, was anxious to confront his accusers while the powers that be were obviously hoping that the matter would die. There were legal reasons to wonder whether a congressional extension of the statute would withstand attack. "Kimmel's waiver of its provisions might be treated as incapable of curing a jurisdictional defect," commented Hanify later. "No others but Kimmel and Short had waived the statute." Hence, Rugg decided it was essential that Congress not only extend the statute further "but combine the extension with a mandate to the Secretaries of the Army and Navy severally to investigate the Pearl Harbor disaster."

"Admiral, this is the crossroads," Rugg told Kimmel. "If I go down to Washington and have this statute passed, we're going to be in for a tempestuous time. The other course may be that they will drop this business and you will be free from any more public discussion."

Kimmel was a fighter. "I am determined that the American people know this story, and you are authorized to go all out and see that it is done. I am prepared to face the consequences, embarrassment, misunderstanding, time, anything. Go to it."

And so in mid-April Rugg and Hanify went to the capital. Rugg himself drew up the substance of the statute; the next day Hanify dressed up the preamble and put on the formal, finishing touches. Hanify took the draft to the Supreme Court Library where he studied it before rewriting the final draft by hand. Having no typewriter, he took the draft to the office of Senator Walsh of Massachusetts. Walsh was chairman of the Naval Affairs Committee. "To my great consternation," recalled Hanify, "when the thing was finished and was to be delivered to Congressman [Dewey] Short's office, Walsh called in a Navy yeoman assigned to his committee to make the delivery. And I thought to myself, 'If this youngster ever happens to divert the document and the Secretary of the Navy and the Secretary of the Army discover that a lieutenant j.g. is getting laws prepared on this delicate subject, you will end up on some atoll very soon.'" But the messenger reported straight to Congressman Short, who publicly demanded a further extension of the statute of limitations and courts-martial for the two commanders.

On May 24 a senator telegraphed Kimmel asking what his position was regarding extension of the statute. He replied that he wanted a trial by court-martial as soon as possible. "I have wanted it since Pearl Harbor and have said so in letters to the Secretary of the Navy. I want a free, open and public hearing. I am ready now." For two and a half years he had waited for the Navy Department to bring him to trial. "In the critical years following Pearl Harbor I understood why I had to bear, in silence, the burden of shame heaped upon me by the report of the Roberts Commission and by published interpretations of that report. Now, with our armed forces on the offensive on all fronts, I owe it to my family, to my friends and to the public to make it clear that I want a trial by Court-Martial at the earliest practicable date." He had been accused of dereliction of duty by Roberts. "I want to answer that accusation in a formal and public way. . . . To be held under a shadow of blame for an additional prolonged and indefinite period is intolerable. The public has a right to know what happened. I have an American's right to my day in court."

The following day he got a telegram from Senator Homer Ferguson, a Republican from Michigan, asking the same question. Kimmel gave a similar reply. The senator's response was to introduce a bill to extend the statute beyond its June deadline. This, he hoped, would force an immediate trial before the fall. Debate over the proposed extension might give the Republicans, and anti-New Deal Democrats, the opportunity to link the White House with the Pearl Harbor debacle. And it would come at the best possible time—the months preceding the presidential election.

The debate on Congressman Short's resolution in the House on June 5 turned out to be promising. When a Democrat from North Carolina opposed any wartime inquiry he was greeted with a loud chorus of boos and shouts of "Shame! Shame!" "Mr. Chairman," proclaimed a Republican from Illinois, "why is it necessary, after two and a half years, to continue to insist upon keeping the truth about Pearl Harbor a secret? Can it be that the court-martial of Admiral Kimmel and General Short will reveal that our military and naval commands were not negligent but rather the negligence was on the part of the civil heads of the Government? . . . The administration fears an adverse public reaction to what the court-martial would reveal on the manner in which the 'affairs of state' were handled prior to the war and, with an election approaching, the administration is determined to keep the true facts about Pearl Harbor hidden.''

The debate spilled over to the next day, the sixth, and some Democrats tried to whip up a patriotic counteroffensive by exploiting the D-Day invasion which was thrilling the nation. ''It would be a splendid contribution on the part of the Members of the House,'' said Emanuel Celler of New York, ''. . . if we would no longer continue deliberations on this bill and discard it. That would be a fitting tribute to the brave and intrepid commanders of our armed forces and the boys under them.'' But the Republicans and their anti-New Deal colleagues would have none of such rhetoric. Even supporters of the Administration realized it was a losing battle and Dewey Short's provision for immediate courts-martial and a three-month extension was passed overwhelmingly, 305 to 35.

A week later both houses passed a joint resolution directing the Secretaries of War and the Navy to proceed forthwith with an investigation into the facts surrounding the catastrophe of December 7. At last Kimmel and Short would have their day in court; that is, if the President did not veto the bill. Franklin Roosevelt, reading the temper of Congress, again proved what a master politician he was. He was confident, he said in a formal statement, that Congress ''did not intend that the investigation should be conducted in a manner which would interfere with the war effort. On the strength of this confidence I have approved the resolution.'' This implied that it was Stimson and James V. Forrestal (successor to Knox as Secretary of the Navy after the latter's death by heart attack five weeks earlier) who were attempting to impede trials for Kimmel and Short and not he. He undoubtedly had in mind the coming presidential campaign during which the Republicans would be likely to make Pearl Harbor a major issue.

2.

On July 8 the Army Pearl Harbor Board was appointed with Lieutenant General George Grunert as president. But the Navy had not selected their members by the thirteenth when Kimmel wrote Rugg that he still felt such an inquiry was inadequate to investigate the case fully. ''Nothing short of an impartial investigation of the Executive and the War and Navy Departments will ever set forth the facts clearly. . . . Just how far a Naval Court of Inquiry can go in an investigation of the War and Navy Departments will depend upon the character of the members and the pressure that will be brought to bear on them by these and other agencies. It is conceivable that a Naval Court of Inquiry might be stopped if they pursue certain phases too tenaciously.''

That same day the Navy Court of Inquiry was finally selected. Admiral Orin G. Murfin, formerly judge advocate general and commander of the Asiatic Fleet, was the chairman. The two other members were also well-known retired admirals. Adolphus Andrews, a former aide to three Presidents, had commanded the Eastern Sea Frontier, responsible for protecting the East Coast in the early years of the war. Edward C. Kalbfus, president of the Naval War College for all but one year from 1934 to 1942, was the most sympathetic to Kimmel, being already convinced that he should not be held solely responsible for Pearl Harbor.

The three members of the Army Board were still on active duty. Grunert, once a private, was a close friend of Marshall and very well thought of by the War Department. Convinced that Short had been derelict, he desired to vindicate the War Department. The Army Air Force representative, Major General Walter H. Frank, was the only West Pointer on the board. He too was convinced that Short must suffer the consequences since he surely had enough information before the attack. The third member, Major General Henry D. Russell, was an odd choice. He had commanded a National Guard division until his relief in May 1942. He disliked Marshall intensely, blaming him for the anti-National Guard policy held during the war. He admired Short but had been reluctant to serve on the board. Wincing at the thought of getting involved in a controversy over the Army's role in the disaster, he accepted for the sake of giving Short a fairer hearing.

On July 17 the Navy members began preparations for the inquiry. A week later they were sworn in. They would be ready to start procedures on the last day of July.

Admiral Kimmel was already in Washington making last-minute preparations with Rugg, Lavender and Hanify. So far he only had Safford's unsupported word that there were incriminating intercepted Japanese messages in the secret Navy files. Now was the time to produce such messages, if they did exist. He went to Secretary of the Navy Forrestal's office. By lucky chance Admiral King happened to be Acting Secretary that day, and after Kimmel asked permission to have an aide search the files, King readily complied. "Mr. Knox promised you access to all the files so I can see no reason to refuse."

That same afternoon Kimmel sent Lavender to unearth the missing messages. "I knew pretty well the general subject of them," Lavender recalled, "but I was astounded when I was shown into a room and there was a stack of papers two and a half feet high of intercepted messages." He had a limited time for search but Safford had given him the numbers of the most important intercepts. Also very helpful was the man in charge, a former junior member of Kimmel's staff. Lavender extracted some forty-three messages typical of what he thought should have gone to Kimmel. "As I sat back in my chair and looked over the selected messages and then at the piles of other messages I became nauseated when I realized what the information in my hands would have meant to Kimmel and the men of the Fleet who died."

That evening Rugg and Hanify dined with Lavender at the Willard Hotel. "I found the messages and many more," he told them but was still so sickened by what he had uncovered that he could not eat.

The messages had the same effect on Hanify. "I cannot now describe the revulsion I felt as the war and its carnage continued and I pondered why the highest leaders of the government of the United States reading the most secret designs of their potential enemy would keep this material from trusting and loyal commanders at the distant, lonely, and inadequately protected bastions of defense with the lives of my fellow citizens in the armed forces at risk. Was this an incredible, fantastic, gargantuan series of mistakes or was there operating some sinister design?''

The following day Marshall's deputy telephoned the director of Naval Communications to vigorously protest Lavender's visit to the secret files. Orders, he said, forbade such an inspection. When the director said he had received no such orders, the deputy hastily explained he merely meant that orders *should* forbid such inspection.

Even though the messages had been segregated and authenticated, the copies were not delivered to Lavender but kept in the custody of Naval Communications. There was nothing for Rugg to do but wait until the court of inquiry began. Then his demand for the intercepts would be a matter of record.

Admiral Stark was also preparing his defense. After his dismissal as chief of Naval Operations, he had been sent to England as commander of the United States naval forces in Europe. "It appeared that this assignment had been made originally because the President wished, for political reasons, to have Stark out of Washington." [1] So wrote Admiral King in his biography. But Stark was convinced King himself was involved in his being "kicked upstairs." Ordinarily a man of remarkably even temper, Stark was not one to hold a grudge. But in this case he could not forgive King, whom he had personally selected as commander of the Atlantic Fleet. Although his new position in Europe was an important one, Stark felt he was being rushed out of the country in semi-disgrace. As he said good-by to his former aide, Commander Harold Krick, he was downcast. The Kricks were close personal friends of the admiral and he treated their children as his own grandchildren. "He was hurt and disappointed and crushed," recalled Mrs. Krick, who had often played golf with him.

[1] "I have never been able to understand," wrote King after the war, "how or why FDR could fire Admiral Stark without doing the same to General Marshall. In my opinion one could not possibly be more suspect than the other."

In England, Stark was in charge of the logistical planning for the Normandy invasion and its success was due in part to him. News of the Navy inquiry came as a surprise to him and he had made no preparations for his defense by the time he arrived in Washington with Lieutenant David Richmond, a law school graduate who had little court experience. Richmond was to assist Admiral Hart, who had offered to act as Stark's counsel. The Judge Advocate General sent several lawyers to assist but they did not appear very enthusiastic and Stark dismissed them. "I'm not really very excited about having a lawyer," he told Hart and Richmond. "That looks as though I have something to hide. I haven't. I may not remember all this but I've nothing to hide."

Both inquiries began on the morning of August 7 within a few hundred yards of each other in the elongated connected headquarters of the Army and the Navy. Someone observed it was like an annex of the Army and Navy Club. The Army Pearl Harbor Board convened an hour later than their Navy colleagues, and their first witness was George Catlett Marshall, the most revered and admired military leader in the country.

Marshall admitted his recollection was "very hazy" about the controversial "war warning" message to Short on November 27, 1941, since he was in North Carolina at maneuvers that day and didn't return until that night. He was also hazy about Short's reply that he was only preparing for sabotage. When General Frank asked if the Hawaiian reply was satisfactory, he said, "In the first place, as I told you, I have no very distinct recollection of the matter. The first definite reaction I have on it would be confused with the 'backsight' state of mind."

A few minutes later General Russell, his old antagonist, began putting pressure on him. Was he rather well acquainted with the foreign policy of the United States as related to Japan? "Yes, sir." Did he regard that policy as a rather definite and firm policy? "I don't believe I could comment on that. In the first place, I don't quite understand the question, and in the next place I would rather not be involved, as a military official, in expressing myself on the foreign policy of the United States." After a few more questions he abruptly announced, "I have got to go. I have got something that just won't wait."

It was incredible that the Chief of Staff should have been called away from his office in the Pentagon while more than a million Allied troops were attempting to smash their way across France.[2] It was also a pity that other military and naval officers found themselves involved in two lengthy inquiries at such a critical moment. The blame for this expenditure of time and energy was being placed upon the Republicans by the Democrats whereas it was the latter's Administration that had caused it. There need have been no wasteful investigations of Pearl Harbor if Roosevelt had called upon the people in 1941 to await all judgments in the national interest until victory was won. But the Administration had felt it necessary to fix blame and made scapegoats of two good men. This had aroused such indignation, not only among private citizens but within the Army and Navy, that further investigations could not be avoided.

Four days later Short took the stand. His answer to Marshall's warning, he said, had simply been that his command had been alerted by Washington to prevent sabotage. During the long session Short repeated himself and spoke without eloquence. But his feeling of frustration and indignation was so eloquent that Russell was swayed if not his two colleagues.

The Navy inquiry was far more charged with emotion. Kimmel, outwardly cool to Stark, had broken off their personal correspondence since he felt Betty had walked away unscathed to let him shoulder all the blame. Although hurt, Stark was careful to say nothing in his testimony that would reflect on his old friend. He still admired Kimmel and on his last fitness report for the period ending 17 December 1941 had written: "I have always considered Ad-

[2] Construction on the Pentagon began August 11, 1941. Immediately after its completion on January 15, 1943, Army personnel moved in but it was not until seven years later that Navy top-level officials left the Munitions Building for the Pentagon.

miral Kimmel an outstanding officer in ability, integrity and character. I still do.''

At every session Rugg had requested to no avail that the authenticated copies of the intercepts be introduced into evidence. On August 11 Rugg added a new twist. He had Kimmel read a statement that he had been informed that the judge advocate had received a letter from the Acting Secretary of the Navy denying to the court certain data on file at the Navy Department. If this material was of such a highly secret nature that it could not be presented to this court, Kimmel suggested, why not request that the members of the court alone inspect it?

Kimmel conferred with Rugg. ''I don't wish to be insistent in this matter,'' said Kimmel, ''and I don't want to be in any sense disrespectful, but I think I must emphasize the fact that this data which I have requested is essential for proper examination of the witness now on the stand, Admiral Stark, that what I have requested is to show affirmatively in the record that I have exhausted every means at my command to accomplish the introduction of this data at this time.''

Admiral Murfin called for a resumption of testimony but Kimmel interrupted. ''Just a suggestion—that the decision made by the Secretary is now an accomplished fact. It has been decided that this data is denied the court.''

''Denied *you*, sir,'' cut in Commander Harold Biesemeier, the judge advocate.

Kimmel insisted on his wording. ''Denial to me and the judge advocate is not nearly as important in my mind as denial to this court, in order to arrive at a proper verdict; and that is the burden of every statement I have made on this subject. I would respectfully like to be informed of the decision of the court as to how they will proceed in this matter.''

Biesemeier was just as persistent. ''The judge advocate would like to advise the court, in his capacity as legal adviser to them, that, in response to Admiral Kimmel's request that they view this evidence themselves in the files of the Navy Department, it would be highly irregular and illegal for the reason that it does not permit of usual cross-examination by other interested parties or the judge advocate, and the court would be receiving the information from a source not set forth in the record.''

''I admit that extraordinary conditions require extraordinary procedures,'' said Kimmel.

Admiral Murfin had had enough of this and ordered the inquiry to proceed with Stark's testimony. He couldn't remember anything about December 6. ''Do you recall what time you left the office after the routine day, the time in the afternoon or evening?''

''No, I do not.''

''Do you recall what you were doing Saturday evening, 6 December?''

''No, I couldn't say what I was doing that evening. My remembrance is—I think I was home but I couldn't say. I don't recall clearly.''

''Do you recall receiving at your home, or wherever you were, between 9 and 10 P.M., Washington time, important intelligence information brought by an officer messenger?'' This was in reference to the fourteen-point message from Tokyo, of which thirteen points were delivered to a number of officers' that night.

''No, I haven't the slightest recollection of anything of that sort on that evening.''

Admiral Adolphus Andrews was not a sympathetic listener. There was a rumor that Andrews blamed Stark for his not being promoted.

The drama continued with the next witness, Rear Admiral R. E. Schuirmann, formerly Stark's liaison officer with the State Department. Upon being asked if November 25, 1941, was regarded as the deadline for all negotiations between the Japanese and the United States, he refused to answer on the grounds that it would disclose information detrimental to the public interest. He claimed his privilege against revealing state secrets.

After the court honored Schuirmann's claim, Rugg tried another line. ''Do you recall whether you had information from Naval Intelligence that the deadline originally determined or fixed, was extended at some later date?''

''This is the same line of questioning and the same objection to it,'' said Schuirmann, and the court said he need not answer the question. But Rugg pressed the attack. Now was the time to get the Japanese intercepts. "I feel that Admiral Kimmel is entitled to have indicated on this record the fact that he seeks information from this witness, not once but as to the several items of information; that the cross-examination of this witness is being precluded to Admiral Kimmel on that ground and I see no way of accomplishing that other than asking several questions on different lines of information more or less on the line that I asked Admiral Stark yesterday afternoon."

The court repeated that this line of questioning could not be continued on the ground of security.

Rugg asked the same question in slightly different words. Again Schuirmann claimed his privilege against revealing state secrets. And again the court told him he need not answer. Now Rugg made a veiled reference to the "winds" message. "Do you recall whether on or about November 26 you received information from the Office of Naval Intelligence that it had specific evidence of Japan's intention to wage an offensive war against both Britain and the United States?"

Once more Schuirmann protested. If this line of questioning continued, he threatened to leave the courtroom. Murfin again upheld him.

As Rugg calmly, doggedly proceeded with the cross-examination, it was becoming apparent that the Boston lawyer was trying to get so much on the record that the intercepts would have to be released. "During the early part of December, December 3rd or December 4th, do you recall receiving information from the Office of Naval Intelligence that Japan would wage an offensive war against both the United States and Britain?"

This was a direct reference to the "winds" message, and now Judge Advocate Biesemeier himself realized what Rugg was doing. "I must object to the question," he said, "on the ground that counsel is getting into the record the specific sort of information that he is trying to get, although he knows that it is objectionable on two grounds, one of them being national security, and the other being that it is beyond the scope of the direct examination." The harried Biesemeier requested that the court be cleared.

Young Richmond, unaware of Magic, asked Hart what the fuss was about. "You'd better stay and see what goes on," said Hart, and left the room.

A few minutes later the court was reopened with the announcement that the judge advocate's objection was not sustained but Schuirmann need not answer the last question.

Rugg insisted on continuing his line of questioning on the ground that this was essential to the interests of his client. "On December 4th or 5th," he asked Schuirmann, "do you recall receiving information from the Office of Naval Intelligence that the Japanese consul in Hawaii was furnishing Tokyo with intelligence as to the number of United States warships in Pearl Harbor, and their location in the harbor?"

The judge advocate again objected on the same ground as before. Objection not sustained. Again Schuirmann claimed his privilege. And again the court told him he need not answer. It seemed like a standoff but Rugg had cleverly managed to get a good deal of information on the record. His persistent line of questioning had also given Admirals Murfin, Kalbfus and Andrews much pause for thought.

When the Navy Department still refused to release the vital forty-three intercepts that had not been forwarded to Kimmel, Rugg suggested that the admiral write a letter to Secretary Forrestal requesting that, since the intercepts could not be submitted in evidence, they should be sealed in the presence of Captain Lavender until the time they could be divulged. Kimmel personally delivered the letter to the assistant chief of Naval Operations.

In the meantime the inquiry continued. After Vice Admiral William Pye, Kimmel's chief of staff, had completed his testimony on August 19 he came to Kimmel's temporary office where he was handed a copy of Captain Safford's testimony at the Hart investigation.

The usually calm Pye became excited as he read. "Here it is! Here it is!" he exclaimed.

"What do you mean?" asked Kimmel.

"Why, here is what you told me last April. I thought you were crazy. I believed this thing had preyed on your mind so much that you had gone nuts." That all this information had been withheld from the commanders in Hawaii was so incredible to Pye that he could not believe it. "Here was a man," wrote Kimmel, "whom I had known all my adult life who concluded I was crazy when I told him of the evidence I had discovered. What chance had I to convince the public of these incredible facts except by indisputable evidence." Both he and Rugg concluded that they must break loose the intercepts at all cost.

At this time word came to the Navy Department that the U.S. submarine *Robalo* had hit a mine off Palawan Island in the Philippines. Its commander, Captain Manning Kimmel, had gone down with his boat. King instructed Rear Admiral Walter DeLany, a close friend of Kimmel's, to inform the admiral. He arrived at Kimmel's office while he was discussing a statement with Hanify. DeLany said he had some bad news. "Manning?" asked Kimmel, and, after DeLany nodded, simply said with little show of emotion, "Those things happen." But later he told his son Ned, "That son of a bitch"—he meant Roosevelt—"has now killed my son!"

He hastened to Bronxville to console his wife but after a few days returned to Washington to testify before the Army Board.

3.

Little of import had happened at the Munitions Building since Short's testimony. There was talk of the "war warning" of November 27 that was not clearly understood; and of the radar report on the morning of the seventh which was not heeded. But nothing new had been revealed.

There was a stir of excitement when Kimmel appeared on August 25. He told the Army Board how well, despite false reports, he and Short had cooperated. At the end of his testimony, General Grunert asked if there was anything else he wanted to say. Lieutenant Hanify, who had accompanied Kimmel, suspected that the Army Board knew nothing of the intercepts and was operating in the dark. And so he and Kimmel had prepared a statement which Kimmel now read. Vital information in the hands of the

War and Navy Departments, he said, had not been sup-
plied to Short and himself. In Washington they knew the
Japanese had set a deadline of November 25; that a day
later an ultimatum had been sent to Japan. As Kimmel
read of other secret messages he noticed that one could
have heard a pin drop. "All this information was denied to
General Short and me." On December 7 the precise time
of the attack was known. "Had we been furnished this
information as little as two or three hours before the attack, which was easily feasible and possible, much could
have been done."

Grunert thanked the admiral. The Board had had some
intimation that this kind of material existed, he said, but
thus far had not gotten it. Russell had paid little attention
to Kimmel's previous testimony but the statement brought
him to sharp attention. He put his head in his hand, then
looked up and asked, Could the admiral supply the Board
with the source of this information?

"I will cooperate to the best of my ability, in con-
formity with the restrictions which have been imposed
upon me." Kimmel was thinking: "They all know where
to get it . . . every Goddamn one of them."

Since there had been no answer to his last letter to Forrestal, Kimmel inquired when he would receive an answer.
He was told his letter had been misplaced. Would the admiral kindly submit another? He wrote again repeating his
request for the forty-three messages, delivering it in person, as he had the first letter, to King's assistant, Vice
Admiral Richard Edwards. "Dicky," he said this time,
"it won't do you a Goddamn bit of good, and you can tell
those SOB's in the Secretary's office it won't do any good
to lose my letters, because from this day forth I am going
to send a letter here every day until I get my answer." His
voice carried well, and Kimmel was sure everyone within
fifty yards heard it. Very soon a clerk came running.
"Here, Admiral, here's your letter." The original, by a
remarkable coincidence, had just been located.

A day later Kimmel was informed that the forty-three
messages would be sealed in the presence of Captain Lavender as requested. Since this satisfied neither Kimmel nor

Rugg, the latter suggested they resort to dramatics. After the session at the Navy Inquiry on August 27, Kimmel began speaking to Lavender as they walked into the corridor. In a booming voice that could be heard by everyone in the room, he remarked that since it was apparent the messages would not be released he would have to hold a press conference and reveal that vital information essential to the case was being withheld.

The ruse succeeded. The next morning the judge advocate announced that he had certain documents he would like to introduce into evidence. Lavender would never forget the reactions of Admirals Murfin, Kalbfus and Andrews as the intercepts were read into the record. "Well, I never saw three officers, who were able officers, just simply blanch as they did when they heard these things read out. . . . Admiral Murfin threw his pencil down on his desk so hard that it bounced about ten feet. Admiral Kalbfus simply shrunk and Admiral Andrews—I never saw anybody look so terrible. From then on we got our stuff in." Hanify recalled that Murfin, a slight, wiry man, said, "Jesus Christ, we'll adjourn!" and flung his pencil down. "He couldn't believe it."

Kimmel had never told Short about the intercepts because he suspected his counsel, Brigadier General Thomas Green, was a Marshall man. But as soon as he left the courtroom the admiral telephoned Green, only to learn that Short was in Texas. "Why in the hell isn't he up here looking after his interests? Send him a telegram and tell him I have something for him."

Upon Short's return to Washington, Kimmel told him about the intercepts. "Short," he then said, "Marshall is your enemy. Haven't you found that out yet? He is doing everything he can to doublecross you and has been right from the very beginning. I know from what I have heard and from what I have seen that this is so and if you stick with him you will be in a hell of a fix. I can tell you that."

On the twenty-ninth the drama at the Navy Building reached its crisis. Captain Laurance Safford, looking professorial and inoffensive as he peered through horn-rim glasses, took the stand. After appearing before Hart, Safford had scoured the files for the intercepts but could not even locate the fourteen-part message. He asked a reserve officer on duty in the Code Section where the Pearl Harbor intercepts were now kept. The answer was that Kramer had turned over the packet with a request that they be placed in the safe. Safford promptly searched Kramer's files and found all but one, the "winds" execute. After making copies for his own convenience, Safford returned the originals to their proper file.

Safford told the Navy Board in detail about the "winds" execute. He was extremely tense, and as he spoke in a rather high-pitched voice his eyes searched from side to side. "It was an alert apprehensiveness which I think was a mannerism," recalled Hanify, who guessed such wariness had come from years of dealing with codes and ciphers.

The following day Stark was asked why he had not telephoned Kimmel on the morning of December 7 as a subordinate had suggested. "The telephone is purely hindsight with me as to wherein I was wrong that I didn't do more to alert them." A remarkable admission, he then underlined it. ". . . and I regret that I did not pick up the telephone, regardless of secrecy, as things have turned out, and notified them." This regret was all post-Pearl Harbor? "Yes, it is all hindsight, and it is in search of my own conscience as to what I might have done."

He weakened his position even more a minute later when asked if he had considered it advisable to keep Kimmel informed in detail of the progress of events in relation to Japan. "I didn't consider it. I endeavored to keep him informed of what I thought would be useful to him in the main trend."

Then Stark admitted he knew nothing about the original "winds" message which had caused such a stir in Naval Intelligence and Communications; and that he couldn't even recall the important note Hull sent to the Japanese on November 26.

After the session, Stark confided to Hart that he wished he had just gone in and expressed his thoughts. "Perhaps I was tired," he added. "Perhaps part of the trouble was my fondness and loyalty to Kimmel, my actual desire to share the burden and protect him so far as I could, and trying too hard to be so one-hundred-percent-plus honest, so that in spots I may have made more or less a mess of it."

Three days later George Marshall walked down the long corridor from the Munitions Building to the Navy court-room. There was subdued excitement as he entered. David Richmond for one was apprehensive. "I don't know how Marshall's going to take questions by a lieutenant," he told Hart.

"Well, I've got four stars here. Just go ahead and ask him any questions you want. If there's any trouble, I'll stand up. But you go ahead." After an early clash with the judge advocate, Hart had no wish to interrogate and instructed Richmond to take over.

Rugg realized he would have to be very cautious in his handling of Marshall since this was not in a civil court. If he too aggressively pressed a man surrounded by the aura of the Army's highest rank before a body composed of officers, he would run the risk of endangering Kimmel's case. At the same time, to dig out the truth he had to be incisive and exhaustive.

With patience he kept probing Marshall about the events of December 6 and 7 but he would only say he didn't recall where he was on the night of the sixth and was hazy about the seventh. And to Rugg's penetrating questions about the Hull note of November 26 and the November 27 warnings to Hawaii, the Chief of Staff three times could not recollect. He also replied once with "No, I don't know about that," thrice with "I don't recall," and five times with "I don't recall that."

What a cool and calculating witness! thought Hanify. There was no animus in the long exchange. Marshall and Rugg were obviously sparring and there was no apparent victor. But in so deftly evading the questions the general had not enhanced his credibility.

4.

The Army Board had been taking testimony at the Presidio in San Francisco since August 29 about the possible connection of Colonel Theodore Wyman, Jr., with a suspected German spy, Hans Wilhelm Rohl. Wyman, district engineer in Honolulu in 1940–41, had been in charge of many activities including construction of hangars, landing strips and the aircraft warning system. The testimony had been conflicting, inconclusive and boring. The Army Board postponed this tedious line of questioning on September 5 and made plans to transfer their activities to Fort Shafter on Oahu.

The Navy Inquiry, after concluding the Marshall testimony, also was making plans to go to Hawaii. Rugg would stay in Washington while Lavender and Hanify would accompany Admiral Kimmel. On the flight to Hawaii in a Navy flying boat, there was camaraderie among the group. After most of the members had gone to sleep, Hanify chatted at length with Admiral Andrews, who finally asked what the lieutenant thought of Roosevelt's unconditional surrender formula. "To give you an honest answer, Admiral, I think it's a tragic mistake." To his surprise, Andrews said, "I couldn't agree with you more. I think it is a disastrous policy." Here, obviously, was a man of independent mind, thought Hanify. It boded well for Kimmel's case.

The Navy interrogators began work at the Navy Yard in Pearl Harbor the following day. Rugg had instructed Hanify to interview Kramer informally before he had been confused or intimidated by the court, the advocate general or the counsel for Stark. Rugg wanted fresh testimony and Hanify was entitled to interrogate him informally since there were no property rights in witnesses. On the morning Kramer was scheduled to testify Hanify and Lavender waited in the corridor. As the commander got off the elevator, the two lawyers introduced themselves. "We don't know what else you'll be asked at this inquiry," said Hanify. "We have these questions for you."

Kramer was willing to talk.

"Did you ever see, or do you recall, an execute of the Winds Code?"

"Yes," he said decisively without hesitation.

"What is your best memory of the words used in the Execute?"

Without pause he said, *"Higashi no kaze ame.* East wind, rain." Both Hanify and Lavender were convinced Kramer was telling the truth. He had just arrived from the war zone, no one had prompted or harried him, and he had spoken freely.

A few minutes later, on the stand, Kramer testified how he had seen the "winds" execute about the third or fourth of December. He had taken it to his superior "and from that point Captain Safford took the ball. I believe Captain Safford went directly to Admiral Noyes' office at that time."

Could he recall what the Japanese-language words were? *"Higashi no kaze ame,* I am quite certain. The literal meaning of *Higashi no kaze ame* is East wind, rain. That is plain Japanese language. The sense of that, however, meant strained relations or a break in relations, possibly even implying war with a nation to the eastward, the United States." Lavender and Hanify were delighted. His testimony here was as straight as in the corridor.

Kramer believed the message was typewritten on teletype paper. This would indicate it came from a U.S. intercept station. He added that he had received the execute from the watch officer who received information coming from the teletype.

Was Kramer the one who went to the communications officer and said, "Here it is"?

This time Kramer gave Safford his former rank. "I believe I used that expression when I accompanied the watch officer to Commander Safford's office. . . . I left Commander Safford's office as soon as I knew he had the picture and knew what the message was, and I believe he at once went to Admiral Noyes' office. I knew that Admiral Noyes was highly interested in that particular plain language code [the "winds" code] because of his previous instructions to me to make out these cards so that he could leave it with certain high officers and the Secretary [Knox], all with the view of getting the word to those people promptly, whether it was any time of the day or night."

"When the original Winds message was received, was that to your knowledge sent to the Office of the Chief of Naval Operations?"

"I'm sure it was, yes, sir." This was the message Stark claimed to have no knowledge of. It was, explained Kramer, "a message which we had been looking for many days and that we had made special provisions to handle for many days."

By September 13 the Navy Board had finished its work in Hawaii and was on its way to San Francisco. Here, two days later, it met at the Federal Building for interrogation of Admiral "Terrible" Turner. At first he stated he knew nothing about an execute of the "winds" message but later corrected himself. "Admiral Noyes called me up on the telephone. What day or time of day I don't recall. I think it was December 6. He said something like this: 'The Winds message came in,' or something of that sort." Was Stark told of the message? "Not from me. I believe Admiral Noyes informed him."

Did Turner consider that the message was of such high significance that action should be taken immediately to transmit that information to Kimmel?

"No, I assumed that he had it."

Then came a rather startling piece of information. Lavender asked if Turner knew that Kimmel was not receiving the decrypted, intercepted Japanese diplomatic messages. "I have never received such information." He had assumed that Kimmel was reading *all* the intercepts.

There was much more to come. Turner reiterated that he had thought a Japanese air attack on Hawaii was a possibility, wasn't "in the least" surprised when it came. "I knew our carriers were out, and with the warnings which had been given, I felt we would give them a pretty bad beating before they got home by our shore-based aircraft and by our carriers."

It was apparent that Turner had let his mouth run away with him. And those who knew him intimately wondered if he had been drinking again.

The judge advocate was puzzled by Turner's remarks since no warnings had been sent to Kimmel since November 27. "Well, if you felt this strongly, Admiral," he asked, "did you discuss this probability with the Chief of Naval Operations?"

Turner did not answer this direct question but rambled

on, first admitting that the Navy Department knew Kimmel didn't have enough patrol planes, and then acknowledging that the Japanese attack on Pearl Harbor could not have been averted. "I think the destructive effect could have been considerably lessened, but I don't believe that the attack could have been stopped from coming in, except by luck."

The three admirals must have been stunned by such talk from the former head of Navy War Plans. Turner not only thought an air attack on Pearl Harbor was a lively possibility but recognized that Kimmel had neither sufficient planes for a proper search nor a strong enough force to avert an air attack when it came. Lavender and Hanify found it unnecessary to cross-examine Turner. His testimony couldn't have been better for their client.

The following morning Admiral Noyes was interviewed at the Federal Building. He confused matters by denying he had received any "winds" execute and had not even talked to anyone about it; and then by charging that Admiral Turner must have known Kimmel was not getting the intercepts. "It is my remembrance that Admiral Turner asked what was our set-up in regard to intercepted messages and it was fully explained to him." The session was adjourned at 12:30 P.M. and plans were made to leave for Washington.

5.

On September 19 Stimson was preparing his testimony before the Army Board, which would probably come the following Monday. "General Marshall came in in the last part of the morning and he with McCloy, who happened to be present, and I talked over the same matter, Marshall telling me what had developed in his two hearings before the Army Board and the Navy Board respectively, and I telling him what I had dug up in regard to my own testimony." In the afternoon he attended a meeting with American and British scientists. "The meeting lasted for three hours and was a pretty long strain. Part of the time we called in General Groves to give us information." The conversation with Groves, overseer of the Manhattan Project, obviously was about the atom bomb.

On Monday the twenty-fifth the Navy Inquiry was winding up its investigation where it had begun, on Constitution Avenue, but the Army Board was by no means finished. The following day Stimson was interrogated at the Pentagon. "I am somewhat in the position, roughly speaking, of a district attorney in his relations with the grand jury," he told them. "And, by becoming a witness, I have to 'watch my step' very carefully that I do not get into a position of advocacy or bias towards any person who may afterwards be proceeded against or concerned with the action which your report may recommend."

General Grunert said the Board thoroughly understood his position, adding, "And the Board is not a bit timid!"

General Russell demonstrated this by aggressive questions on the warning to Short, which Russell termed ambiguous. Then he asked if Stimson had envisaged an air attack from Japanese carriers at the time the warning message went out.

"Well, I envisaged it as one of the possibilities. . . ."

"Then you were not surprised at the air attack on the 7th of December?" prodded Russell.

"Well, I was not surprised, in one sense, in any attack that would be made; but I was watching with considerably more care, because I knew more about it, the attack that was framing up in the southwestern Pacific."

Stimson could not have been altogether happy with the treatment he got from the three generals, but he wrote Roosevelt, later that day, a reassuring letter. "I was sorry to learn . . . that you had been worried by rumors as to what the Army Pearl Harbor Board might find in its report." That morning he had spent two and a half hours before the Board "and I think satisfied them on the subject matter of some of these speculations. One can never tell but I felt at the end of the hearing that they were satisfied with my account of the sequence of the events. I had the advantage which, so far as I know, none of the other witnesses have had of having kept a daily account of my meetings and work during that critical period so that my testimony was all based upon records and thus lifted above the danger of faulty memory. For myself, I can hardly imagine a picture of more close cooperation and anxious desire to warn our outposts of impending attack than was shown by this documented record. According to my memory, you were yourself so painstakingly on the job throughout that period that I should be greatly distressed if you were victimized now by ignorant or malicious rumors.''

The Board returned to the Munitions Building on Friday, September 29. At ten-thirty that morning Marshall returned to admit that he had not considered telephoning Short on December 7. And if he *had*, he would certainly have called MacArthur first and then the Panama Canal. Besides, from his own experience it took too long to get a telephone call through. ''You put the other thing through in a hurry.'' And, if Short, who was waiting outside to testify, had been present, he would have found it difficult not to interject that the ''hurry'' message had not arrived until hours after the attack.

In the afternoon Short appeared and it was obvious that he had taken Kimmel's warning to heart, for he was now looking upon Marshall not as a friend and protector but as an enemy. He brought up the final part of Admiral Kimmel's testimony before the Army Board. ''He makes a statement that I would like to have read to the Board, and then I would like to comment on it.''

Short's counsel read the Kimmel testimony revealing that there had been considerable information regarding the imminence of war that had not been transmitted to either Kimmel or Short.

''I feel that Admiral Kimmel would not have made that statement,'' Short said, ''unless he had factual data to corroborate it. I haven't had access to that data, and, from reading Admiral Kimmel's testimony, it does not appear that the Board has been furnished with it.'' He had written a letter that day to the Secretary of War asking that a search be made of War Department files; and if not found there the Navy should be required to furnish it.

''General,'' said Frank, ''are you putting the Board in the position of working for you?''

''I am putting the Board in the position, I hope, where I

feel that they should want to consider everything, that this should not be a one-sided investigation; but that here is something that is tremendously important from my point of view.''

Frank took offense. ''Have you found anything in the proceedings of this Board that has indicated that this Board has not tried to conduct an impartial proceeding?''

''No, I have not; but I have found nothing in this Board's proceedings—now, they may have done it; the Board may have had access to everything that Admiral Kimmel has in mind, but I feel that he definitely would not have made that statement without he had data to support it.'' He was so upset, his tongue had got twisted. If the Board had such information and it was off the record, then he hoped the letter to Stimson would cause it to be made available to him. ''I do not know what the Board has had, off the record. They may have had everything I am asking for.'' He turned indignantly to Frank. ''I do not think your statement is a fair one that I am trying to have the Board work for me. I am really just hopeful that they will get everything before the Board that is necessary for a complete understanding of the case.''

''That is just what we are endeavoring to do,'' said Frank.

The Board responded by sending Marshall a list of questions to be answered either in person or by a signed statement by the following Monday. Was there information in the War and Navy Departments on December 6, 1941, ''that the order of attack was momentarily imminent''? Had the Chief of Staff known that between November 27 and December 7 the alert in effect in Hawaii for the Army forces provided security for sabotage only? Why wasn't the telephone used on December 7 to warn Short? What warnings were sent to Short from October 21, 1941, until November 27? There were many other questions but none directly asking that the Japanese intercepts be released and put on record by the Board.

6.

On Saturday, the last day of September, Colonel Rufus "Togo" Bratton was called before the Board. Serious, competent and meticulous—if not brilliant—the industrious Bratton was well qualified for his position in 1941 as chief of the Far Eastern Section of Army Intelligence. He was responsible for Japanese matters. His interest in all things Japanese had come from three long terms in Japan. Being a scholar as well as a soldier, he had delved into the history and customs of the Japanese and could write as well as speak the language. He and Colonel Otis Sadtler, a senior intelligence officer of S.I.S., had also been involved in a minor uprising as a result of the Bomb Plot message from Tokyo to the Japanese consul in the fall of 1941. Like their Navy colleagues involved in the mutiny on the Second Deck, they too felt this important message should be transmitted to the Pacific commanders. After the Navy failed to get permission to send off their warning, these two West Point colonels managed secretly to transmit theirs through a special channel to Spencer Akin, MacArthur's chief signal officer. This information alerted General Charles Willoughby, MacArthur's G-2, who later wrote, ". . . this was no longer a case of diplomatic curiosity; coordinate grid is the classical method for pinpoint target designation; our battleships had suddenly become 'targets.'" Spencer Akin was uneasy from the start. "We drew our own conclusions and the Filipino-American troops took up beach positions long before the Japanese landings." This was the information denied both Kimmel and Short.

The involvement of Sadtler and Bratton in this and succeeding incidents had made them outcasts. Bratton, a heavy-set bear of a man, had confided his concern to Colonel Ivan D. Yeaton in early 1942. Yeaton, a Far East expert, had just been assigned to the War Department General Staff. Bratton felt, Yeaton wrote in his unpublished memoirs, "that he had given both G-2 [General Miles] and the chief of staff sufficient warning that they should have been sleeping in their offices instead of comfortable at home. He was well aware that this testimony would be considered disloyal by Marshall and probably mean the end of all chance of promotion.''

Later in 1943, Army Intelligence had been ordered by the White House to produce a study on Japanese preparations for war from 1935 to Pearl Harbor. Bratton wrote it. "The morning after it had been sent up to the chief of staff," recalled Yeaton, "I found Bratton at his desk with his head in his hand, looking down at the Far Eastern manuscript. Looking over his shoulder, I could see the margin notes and lined out words and phrases. 'Who dun it'? I asked. 'The Old Man himself,' he answered. Marshall had edited out all the parts most damaging to him, leaving the remainder too vague to be interpreted as cause for immediate concern over Japanese intentions. I urged Bratton for his own protection to have the entire volume photostated at once and to keep the evidence in a safe place.'' This he did.

Bratton, a sophisticate who talked like a college professor, had a ruddy complexion with a face that reminded one colleague of a "friendly bulldog." He had already been interrogated by Marshall's special investigator, Colonel Carter Clarke, and must have been apprehensive by the time he faced the Army Board that Saturday. He told how he had received the translations of the two Japanese intercepts between eight-thirty and nine on the morning of December 7. These were immediately apparent as of such importance that he had telephoned Marshall's quarters only to be informed he was riding horseback. "I requested his orderly to go out and find him at once and ask him to call me on the telephone as soon as practicable, as I had an important message to deliver to him." He finally got the call from Marshall sometime between ten and eleven. "He said to report to him in his office, as he was on his way there. I reported to him at about 11:25, immediately upon his arrival.''

Over the weekend there was discussion at the War Department on how to handle General Short's request to release secret material to the Board and his own counsel. If the request were denied for reasons of national security, one staff officer warned Marshall, "politicians may question our motives and thus embarrass the President.'' This advice may have influenced Marshall to recommend that Stimson send Short a letter permitting his counsel to examine the records ''in the presence of a member of the Board.'' Stimson did so on Monday, the day Marshall was to appear a third time before the Board.

The witness preceding him was Captain Safford. He told how Kimmel had managed to get permission to inspect files for some sixty or so Japanese intercepts—he was referring to the forty-three messages Lavender had discovered—and how these documents had finally, after many efforts, been introduced as evidence in the Navy Inquiry.

''Who has the official custody of these sixty messages at the moment?'' asked Frank. The recorder of the Navy Court of Inquiry, answered Safford. ''If it was the desire of these Boards to get a copy of those sixty messages, to whom should the request be made?'' The Secretary of the Navy. Safford was then asked if the ''winds'' execute was among these messages. ''That is still missing.'' He told how he had discovered its absence from the files. He also told how Kramer had told him all about delivery of the Japanese fourteen-part message on December 6 and 7.

''When did he make these statements upon which you base your evidence now?'' asked Russell.

''Kramer made his statements the 8th or 9th of December immediately after the event, when I discussed it fully with him. I called for statements. I talked to everybody concerned, to see if my people had been negligent in any way, that this thing had in any way been our fault. I made a very careful investigation.'' Russell credited Safford's testimony, as well as his claim that the ''winds'' execute had been purposely done away with. ''It is my personal belief that it was destroyed for a reason,'' wrote Russell later. ''Neither Marshall nor Stark wanted it to be made public. Marshall knew about it.''

In the afternoon Marshall returned with answers to the questions submitted by the Board. He told of regulations regarding the extreme secrecy to be used regarding ultra-secret information. That was why they had to be so cautious in sending messages to Short and Kimmel in 1941.

Then General Frank asked why the thirteen-point message of December 6 had not been delivered to Marshall that night.

Russell was amused that today Marshall's attitude was different. "No longer was he the talkative salesman. Now he was the somewhat irritated executive, very brusque and direct in his answers, employing just as few words as possible. Apparently my criticism of General Marshall about his treatment of the Board had reached him."

Russell took over the interrogation. The Board had learned, he said, that there had been a G-2 investigation of Pearl Harbor shortly after the attack. It appeared that a lot of things discovered at that time were not transmitted to the Army Board and had just come to the Board's knowledge the past week. He was referring, of course, to the intercepts.

Marshall's close friend, Grunert, now joined in. The G-2 witnesses, he said, had all had the opportunity of giving this information to the Board but had not. "Now, evidently they either forgot or didn't recall, or else they didn't tell us this information which we have gotten of late."

Marshall hedged. "Well, I don't know." He hadn't seen or talked to General Miles, the G-2.

Grunert told how the Navy Board had managed to pry their information out of the Navy. "Of course, naturally, the Board thought that, well, if they held out from the Board information which is now coming up, what do we know but that something else is being held out?"

"And information that is rather vital, too," added Frank.

"Well, I don't know," said Marshall.

"I cannot imagine that it is intentional," said Grunert.

"The only thing that I can think of in connection with that," said Marshall, "is that everybody that is concerned with this top secret thing is very cagey about saying anything about it."

"That is what I attribute it to," said Grunert.

"And naturally he feels no freedom whatever to speak about it unless he is specifically authorized," said Marshall; and then ended the session with a curt "I have nothing else I can think of."

He was followed by Bratton, who was asked about a message sent out to Hawaii on December 5. He admitted he had seen it that very morning but was unable to get it.

"And it is over there in the files, but they won't let you have it?"

"Well, they wouldn't let me bring it over here, if that is what you mean, sir."

"Now, do you know who has issued the instructions that we are not to be given those messages, Colonel?"

"No, sir. I mean by that, I don't know the ultimate authority."

After sidestepping that question, Bratton admitted he had received the first thirteen parts of the long message on the night of December 6 and had delivered it to Marshall's office as well as to the watch officer in the State Department. He remembered when he turned it over at the State Department—about half past ten; but had no recollection of exactly when he placed the message on Marshall's desk.

Bratton was obviously under stress and, after further probing about delivery of the message, finally said, "I am trying to remember, sir, what I did with the copies that went to General Miles and General Marshall and General Gerow. I can't verify it or prove it, at this time, but my recollection is that those three officers got their copies the evening of the 6th."

"By 'the three officers,' you mean whom?"

"General Marshall, General Miles and General Gerow," he said fearfully, as if, one witness recalled, expecting to be struck by lightning. All at once he seemed to remember everything. "Now, it was my practise to deliver to them their copies before I went to the State Department." That would make it before 10:30 P.M.

Did he deliver a copy to Marshall personally that evening?

"No. I very seldom delivered it to him in person. I gave it to his secretary, in a locked bag."

"And what is the name of the secretary to the Chief of Staff?"

If Togo Bratton had been concerned for his future before, he must have blanched that day. "Colonel Smith, Bedell Smith, now Lieutenant General," he said. Yes, he was the one who got Marshall's copy on the night of December 6.

7.

The following day the three members of the Board increased pressure for release of the secret material. Russell could see only one reason for not doing so: "Marshall and his close associates on the General Staff did not want the Army Pearl Harbor Board to know that they were in possession of so much important information, none of which had been sent to Short on the Islands."

During the day Grunert did something definite about it. "May I call on War Department agencies to produce files and personnel having knowledge thereof, without in each case getting some higher-up's O.K.?" he asked Marshall's deputy. The answer was, "Yes," and Grunert promptly wrote back a top secret letter stating that the Board had verified that the Army had a file of these intercepts. "It is requested that the file referred to be made available for the Board's examination. . . ." If permission was denied, Grunert requested "that that decision be communicated to the Board in writing."

The next day Grunert's request was approved. At last the Army Board had Magic. It came in time to be recorded at the last interrogation of witnesses on October 6, which featured the testimony of Colonel O. K. Sadtler who, like Bratton, still held the same rank he had in 1941.[3]

Sadtler told the Army Board that he was telephoned by Admiral Noyes on the morning of December 5 and told, "Sadtler, the message is in!" It was a "winds" execute and Noyes wasn't sure which enemy was indicated. He

---

[3] "We knew nothing of the reasons for continuing them in their grades of colonel," commented Russell; "but we do recall that in one of our informal conversations, some officers said that the pattern was perfectly clear. If an officer wanted to be condemned forever, it was only necessary for him to have guessed Pearl Harbor correctly."

thought it meant the Japanese were going to war with Great Britain. "I asked him for the Japanese word, and he didn't know it, but to please tell G-2."

Sadtler reported all this to General Miles "and then I went down to see General Gerow, who was head of the War Plans, told him to the effect of what Admiral Noyes had said, and didn't he think we should send a message to Hawaii. I don't mean Hawaii—to Panama, the Philippines, and Hawaii. He says, 'I think they have had plenty of notification,' and the matter dropped. I then went in to the Secretary of the General Staff and talked to Colonel [Bedell] Smith about the same thing, and he asked me what I had done, and I told him I had talked to G-2 and War Plans; and he didn't want to discuss it further."

Why, asked Russell, was Sadtler so concerned that he went the "second mile" to discuss the matter with both Gerow and Smith? "I was sure war was coming, and coming very quickly." The previous day, December 4, at a meeting of the Defense Communications board he had been asked by the Assistant Secretary of the Treasury what he thought about the imminence of war "and I said that I thought they would have war within 48 hours. He turned to Captain Redman, who represented Admiral Noyes at the meeting, and asked him what he thought, and he said he agreed with Colonel Sadtler."

So ended the Army Pearl Harbor Board hearings. Now there was the task of writing a report. The Navy was well along with theirs and it was submitted to the Secretary of the Navy on October 19. It completely reversed the findings of the Roberts Commission. Kimmel had not received all available information from Washington and could not be blamed for something he could not expect. Admiral Stark, however, had "failed to display the sound judgment expected of him in that he did not transmit to Admiral Kimmel . . . important information which he had regarding the Japanese situation."

The following day came the Army report. To Russell's delight, his two colleagues had supported his own conclusions. He was gratified that they had not flinched from the truth even if it might "undermine such faith as the great masses of the people still had in the Army." Russell himself did not care what Marshall might think. ''There was nothing that he could do to or for me which concerned me in the least.''

Although the Army report stated that Short had made an ''earnest and honest'' effort to implement plans for defense, he was criticized for adopting only a sabotage alert. He was also charged with failing to reach an agreement with Kimmel to implement joint Army-Navy plans. But these were mild scoldings compared to the counts against Marshall:

1. Failure to keep Short fully informed as to the international situation and the probable outbreak of war.
2. Failure to note Short's message that he was only preparing for sabotage without taking any action.
3. Failure to alert Short on the evening of December 6 and the early morning of December 7 that an almost immediate break with Japan was coming.
4. Failure to investigate and determine the state of readiness of Short's command after the November 27 warning despite the impending threat of war.

But the most scorching criticism came in a supplemental top secret report. Marshall and the War Department were censured for sending Hawaii so little of the mass of information it had of impending war. ''The messages actually sent to Hawaii by either the Army or Navy gave only a small fraction of this information. No direction was given the Hawaiian Department based on this information except the 'Do-Don't' message of November 27, 1941. It would have been possible to have sent safely information, ample for the purpose of orienting the commanders in Hawaii. . . .''

Much vital information, which had been distributed to the War, Navy and State Departments, ''did not go out to the field, with the possible exception of the general statements in occasional messages which are shown in this Board's report. Only the higher-ups in Washington secured this information.''

The report went on for several more pages about the ''winds'' execute and the poor handling of the fourteen-point message, ending with a devastating list of Marshall's delinquencies.

There, therefore, can be no question that between the dates of December 4 and December 6, the imminence of war on the following Saturday and Sunday, December 6 and 7, was clear-cut and definite.

Up to the morning of December 7, 1941, everything that the Japanese were planning to do was known to the United States except the final message instructing the Japanese Embassy to present the 14th part together with the preceding 13 parts of the long message at one o'clock on December 7, or the very hour and minute when bombs were falling on Pearl Harbor.

At the Pentagon that October 20 there was anger, indignation and consternation. The repercussions were felt even more at the White House. With the Roberts report so dramatically turned about by both the Army and Navy inquiries, the new findings would have to be suppressed until they could be refuted. And in little more than two weeks the nation would go to the polls to elect a President.

That evening James Forrestal did publicly reveal that the Navy Court of Inquiry report had been presented to him. For the present, at least, he told the press, it would be kept confidential. He had asked Admiral King to ascertain how much of this material sufficiently affected present military operations as to merit a security classification.

Rugg sent Forrestal this telegram:

I REQUEST IMMEDIATE RELEASE OF FINDINGS OF NAVY COURT OF INQUIRY AS TO INNOCENCE OR GUILT OF ADMIRAL KIMMEL. FOR NEARLY THREE YEARS HE HAS BORNE PUBLIC BLAME FOR PEARL HARBOR DISASTER. HE HAS REQUESTED AND BEEN DENIED COURT MARTIAL. HIS TREATMENT HAS BEEN UN-AMERICAN. IN YOUR LETTER TO ADMIRAL MURFIN RELEASED TO PRESS ON OCTOBER 20 YOU INTIMATE THAT FACTS, NOW THREE YEARS OLD, FOUND BY NAVY COURT MAY BE WITHHELD AS "SECRET" OR "TOP SECRET" ON GROUND DISCLOSURE WOULD INTERFERE WITH WAR EFFORT. CERTAINLY RELEASE OF FIND-

INGS OF COURT AS TO KIMMELS INNOCENCE OR GUILT
CANNOT AFFECT WAR. PAST INJUSTICES CANNOT NOW BE
REMEDIED. SIMPLE JUSTICE AND COMMON DECENCY RE-
QUIRE IMMEDIATE PUBLIC ANNOUNCEMENT OF COURTS
FINDING AS TO KIMMELS INNOCENCE OR GUILT.

But there was little doubt in knowledgeable Washington
circles that the Navy would find it all top secret, and the
Pearl Harbor cover-up would continue.

"YOU DO NOT HAVE TO CARRY THE TORCH FOR ADMIRAL KIMMEL" JUNE 1944–SEPTEMBER 1945

1.

A month before the Army and Navy inquiries opened, it appeared as though an event only distantly related to Pearl Harbor would endanger Roosevelt's attempt to win his fourth presidential election. It was a curious case in camera, unique in the American experience. A young U.S. code officer in the London Embassy had been seized on May 20, 1940, by British police; and, with the connivance of Ambassador Joseph Kennedy, arrested. The officer, Tyler Gatewood Kent, was then secretly tried in Old Bailey under the Official Secrets Act of 1911 for stealing official documents and sentenced to serve seven years in a British prison.

Kent was a clean-cut, good-looking young man from a well-known Virginia family. A descendant of Davy Crockett, he was born in Newchwang, Manchuria, where his father was the American consul. He had been educated at the Kent School, Princeton, the Sorbonne, the University of Madrid and George Washington University. Six years earlier he had entered the consular service. He was sent to Moscow as a code and cipher clerk and became alarmed by the dispatches of his ambassador, William C. Bullitt, as well as the cables sent on from Warsaw by Ambassador Anthony Drexel Biddle urging the Poles to resist Hitler. To Kent this was all evidence that American diplomats were ''actively taking part in the formation of hostile coalitions in Europe . . . which they had no mandate to do.''

Being an isolationist as well as an anti-Communist, he began to think of ways he could reveal such information to the U.S. Senate or the press. This resolve was strengthened, soon after being transferred to London in October 1939, upon reading the secret correspondence between Churchill and Roosevelt which, contrary to protocol, bypassed the British Foreign Office. These messages were far more alarming than anything he had yet seen. Here was the President of the United States and the First Lord of the Admiralty conniving to oust Chamberlain as Prime Minister so that they could put an end to the ''Phony War'' carried on by Chamberlain. They were both dedicated to a genuine all-out war against Nazism. The messages also indicated that Roosevelt was in touch with Eden, Duff Cooper and other members of the ''War party'' who were vigorously opposing Chamberlain's attempts to make a compromise peace with Hitler.

This secret correspondence continued even after Churchill became Prime Minister in the spring of 1940. Convinced that Roosevelt would draw America into the war unless he were exposed, Kent felt it was his duty to do so no matter the cost to himself. Recently he had met a Russian émigrée, Anna Wolkoff, whose father had been naval attaché in London at the time of the 1917 revolution. She shared Kent's detestation of Communism and introduced him to Captain A. H. M. Ramsey, a hero of the First World War and a Tory member of Parliament who was equally anti-Communist. He was also convinced that a vast Jewish conspiracy had taken over England from within.

Kent showed copies of some of the Roosevelt-Churchill

correspondence to Ramsey, who thought they might be made the subject of a question in Parliament. This would not only expose Churchill's plot against Chamberlain but reveal to a peace-minded American public that their President was secretly working to that end. At this point Kent made the mistake of letting Anna Wolkoff borrow some of the messages. At his trial Kent testified that he thought she was going to take them to Ramsey.

Two days before Kent's arrest, a Scotland Yard officer informed Ambassador Kennedy that one of his code clerks "had become the object of attention by Scotland Yard through his association with a group of persons suspected of conducting pro-German activities." One was Anna Wolkoff, who was believed to be in communication with the Germans. This raised the question of whether Kent had been giving the Germans, through Wolkoff, secret cables involving the President. Since Kent was an American citizen, entitled to diplomatic immunity, and the documents were American property, the Scotland Yard man wondered what should be done.

Without consulting Washington, Kennedy waived Kent's immunity and then asked permission from Hull to do so. The approval came in a "very secret cable" two days later. In the meantime Kent, despite the serious charges against him, had been allowed to carry on his duties.

On the morning of May 20 he was arrested at his flat at 47 Gloucester Place. Two Scotland Yard detectives and an officer of British Military Intelligence searched the room and found some fifteen hundred copies of confidential documents in an unlocked cupboard and a brown leather bag. Kent was arrested and soon was facing Kennedy. How on earth, asked the ambassador, could Kent break trust with his country? Confident that he had only acted to prevent his country from being driven into a catastrophic war, Kent "never batted an eye." Then Kennedy asked why he had taken all this material. The reserved Kent said he did so because they were "important historical documents."

Now, by the choice of his own government, Kent was a British political prisoner with no American rights. It was not until two months later that he was finally formally charged in a closed session of Bow Street Police Court. "I don't think there was any intention originally of pressing any charges against me,'' Kent later said. ''I believe it was done as a result of pressure from officials of the United States.'' This was likely since, three days after his arrest, the Home Office had issued a deportation order indicating the British were willing to expel him from the country.

But this would have meant a trial in the United States at a time when Roosevelt was preparing his 1940 campaign for re-election. Since a secret trial in America at this time would have been impossible, the revelations in open court could have meant Roosevelt's defeat. But in England all trials under the Official Secrets Act were held in camera. That October Kent was taken to the Old Bailey. He told how disillusioned he had become with American foreign policy, and that Roosevelt had not been straight with the people. They ''were not being adequately informed, they were . . . being told half-truths, instead of the strict truth.'' Alarmed by the cables he read, he had decided to reveal Roosevelt's chicanery to the U. S. Senate or the press; and had finally decided the only way he could do so was through Captain Ramsey.

Didn't he feel he owed allegiance to his employer, Ambassador Kennedy? Yes, he replied, but this was not his only duty. ''To whom did you consider you had another duty?''

''Well, putting it in a dramatic way, to the American people.''

''Which duty did you consider the higher of the two?''

''Naturally, the one to the people of America.''

Despite Kent's admission that he had let both Ramsey and Wolkoff borrow some of the documents, it would be difficult to convict him under the Official Secrets Act unless it could be proven to the jury that Wolkoff was a foreign agent. The only evidence to show this was an intercepted letter addressed to ''Lord Haw-Haw,'' who broadcast anti-British propaganda over the German radio; the letter contained advice to launch stronger attacks on the Jews. Even flimsier was evidence that Wolkoff had been friendly with a military attaché at the Italian Embassy in London *before* Italy declared war. The Solicitor General, the Earl Jowitt, later admitted "there was no evidence that she had passed any secret information to such attaché." Even so Wolkoff was named a "foreign agent" by the court under the special definition contained in the Official Secrets Act that such an agent was anyone reasonably suspected of having committed an act prejudicial to the safety or interests of the state. Jowitt admitted that "Anna Wolkoff was not employed by any foreign power, nor did she ever receive any payment from any foreign power."

Still, by definition, she was a foreign agent; and Kent, found guilty, was sentenced to seven years in prison. He was still convinced he was a loyal citizen of the United States. He admitted he had committed an offense "but the motive or purpose of an act that is committed is of prime importance." While the British claimed it was for a purpose prejudicial to the interest and safety of the state, Kent never believed it was at all prejudicial to the interest and safety of his own country. Quite the contrary. The majority of Americans wanted to stay out of war in Europe.

From the beginning Kent's mother, Mrs. Anne H. P. Kent, waged a battle to return her son to America where he could be tried under U.S. law but her letters to Roosevelt and the State Department brought no satisfaction. It was not until June of 1944 that the news of Kent's imprisonment was released by chance. It came after a member of Parliament asked a question about Captain Ramsey, who had been imprisoned the past four years without charge. It was then revealed that Kent had given him some of the secret Roosevelt-Churchill messages. An American reporter filed this story, which surprisingly passed the British censor. The result was a tempest in Washington on June 19. "I cannot understand how an American citizen could be tried in a British secret court," Burton Wheeler stated in the Senate. What would happen, "if we should arrest a member of the British Embassy here and endeavor to try him in an American secret court? Of course, the British Government would immediately protest, and we would not try him in a secret or a public court."

The chairman of the Senate Foreign Relations Committee, Democratic Senator Tom Connally of Texas, replied,

"The State Department says that the British government before prosecuting submitted the documents to the United States Government, and before the prosecution was begun our Government examined the documents and concluded that Kent ought to be prosecuted and waived his diplomatic immunity." Connally said he had no pity for Kent. "It is all very well to beat your breasts and say, 'We will try Americans in American courts,' but here we find a man who is conspiring, and under the British law he is concluded to be guilty. I have no tears to shed for him." He also claimed the stories of the so-called Churchill-Roosevelt private correspondence were only gossip.

"This is not gossip," retorted a Republican senator. "I am amazed that the British censor should pass it, but since he has, I assume it has the imprimatur of the British Government. No one on the floor of Parliament denied the statements." Another Republican observed that the reported secret negotiations between Churchill and Roosevelt preceded the President's 1940 campaign pledge "again and again and again" that American boys would not be sent to fight foreign wars.

This stung. "Why can we not have unity until the war is over?" pleaded Connally. "Why cannot we stop this sniping and shooting behind the lines?"

The heated Senate debate was echoed in the House where a Republican declared that Roosevelt and Churchill, then First Lord of the Admiralty, "were carrying on a correspondence, the purport of which was to involve us in the present war." He also revealed that he had been informed of the case more than two years earlier by Kent's mother. "I was unable at the time to get accurate information as to the facts but, if the story is false, the facts should be spread upon the record. No harm could possibly be done to the military effort."

Concern among Democrats preparing for the presidential election in the fall was echoed across the Atlantic. In a memorandum to the Foreign Office, Viscount Halifax noted that the isolationists in Congress had generated a sizable issue out of the Tyler Kent case. "If any fact about the Kent-Ramsey case could be made public without prejudice to security it would do much to clear the air. Otherwise there is considerable danger that issue re: alleged collusion between President and Mr. Churchill behind backs of United States Congress and people to make American entrance into war inescapable will be injected into election issues to our detriment and continue to cloud pages of journalists and historians long after.''

The State Department received so many letters inquiring whether Tyler Kent had been fairly treated that it was felt necessary to release a statement early in September, most of which was accurate, but it read more like a spy thriller than a sober State Department report with its injudicious mixture of suspicions and proven facts. For example, at one point it intimated that Kent was a spy by stating that the police had ''established that some of the papers found had been transmitted to an agent of a foreign power.''

Mrs. Kent protested to Secretary Hull. ''Very few persons besides his mother are interested in Tyler Kent *per se*,'' she wrote, ''but 130 odd million Americans are vitally concerned to learn whether or not it is true that in time of peace, one year before the Lend-Lease bill and other measures were put before the Senate, they had been planned 'between the American President and the British Navy head.'''

The incident was inflamed the next day by former Ambassador Kennedy, who had just visited Franklin D. Roosevelt, whom he had endorsed in a surprise, last-minute radio speech in 1940. In an exclusive interview with Scripps-Howard reporter Henry J. Taylor, Kennedy mentioned matters that were never touched upon in the Kent trial and made unfounded allegations that far exceeded those in the State Department statement.

When asked how and why Kent transmitted the secret information to Germany, Kennedy said, ''Kent's reported friendliness with the Russian girl, Anna Wolkoff, had its place in his attitude but apparently she didn't have safe and regular channels into Germany. . . . But Kent used the Italian Embassy to reach Berlin. For the most part he passed our secrets out of England in the Italian diplomatic pouch. Italy, you recall, didn't enter the war until after Kent was arrested. If we had been at war I wouldn't have favored turning Kent over to Scotland Yard or have sanctioned his imprisonment in England. I would have recommended that he be brought back to the United States and been shot.''

He gave a dramatic twist also to his version in the discovery in Kent's flat of ''a locked box'' containing fifteen hundred copies of cables in an unbreakable code.

That night America's diplomatic blackout started all over the world. I telephoned the President in Washington saying our most secret code was no good any place, and I told Mr. Roosevelt that the Germans and Italians, and presumably the Japanese, had possessed the full picture of the problems and decisions and everything else sent in and out of the White House and the State Department for the past eight months, as critical a period as any in the history of the war. . . .

The result was that for weeks, right at the time of the fall of France, the United States Government closed its confidential communicating system and was blacked out from private contact with American embassies and legations everywhere. At this critical time, with decisions of the highest importance needing to be made and communicated hourly, no messages could be sent or received by the President, Mr. Hull or anyone else. This lasted from two weeks to a month and a half—until a new unbreakable code could be devised in Washington and carried by special couriers throughout the world. . . .

Nobody ''railroaded'' Kent. The British sentence that put him on the Isle of Wight for seven years was mild beyond measure. The only thing that saved Kent's life was that he was an American citizen and we were not yet at war.

This concoction of fact and fiction, labeled by Taylor as ''the most important spy case yet revealed in this war,'' successfully ended Republican efforts to make Kent an election issue. It also ended whatever public sympathy there had been for Kent. The man was an out-and-out spy who had betrayed his country, probably for the love of a glamorous Mata Hari. (She was, in truth, middle-aged and described by one observer as "the ugliest woman" he had ever seen.)

Kent managed to cable his mother that the Kennedy statement was a tissue of lies. It was. The story that Kent had smuggled American secrets in the Italian diplomatic pouch was sheer conjecture based on the fact that Wolkoff knew an Italian Embassy employee. In his trial Kent was not even accused of conspiring with her. In a letter, produced at Old Bailey, the Public Prosecutor declared that he had no intention of charging that Kent "participated in, or had any knowledge of, her attempt to communicate with Germany."

The diplomatic blackout caused by Kent was another fabrication. Kennedy himself, during the days following Kent's arrest, sent very confidential cables which would eventually be published by the State Department. Moreover, to describe the code used to transmit the Churchill-Roosevelt messages as "unbreakable" and "our most secret code" was ludicrous. This was the notoriously unconfidential Gray code which had been read with ease by the Germans and other foreign powers since 1918. It became so familiar to American Foreign Service officers that in the late twenties a senior consul in Shanghai made his retirement speech in Gray.

2.

Although the Kent case had been successfully submerged, Pearl Harbor remained the most volatile issue of the election. It came to a climax in late August through a mistake in judgment by the Democrats' candidate for Vice-President. In the August 26 issue of *Collier's*, Senator Harry Truman called for a consolidation of the Army and Navy, opening his argument with the statement that the Pearl Harbor attack revealed "the danger that lies in a division of responsibilities." He went on to imply that Short and Kimmel were not on speaking terms prior to the attack, and stated that at no time "did Admiral Kimmel ask or receive information as to the manner in which the Army was discharging its highly important duty." He also charged that Kimmel had never conducted any distant air reconnaissance except during drills and maneuvers. Nor had General Short ever ascertained how the Navy was handling this task.

Kimmel wrote Truman that his allegations were false since they were based on the Roberts report, which did not contain the basic truths of the Pearl Harbor catastrophe. ''I suggest that until such time as complete disclosure is made of the facts about Pearl Harbor, you refrain from repeating charges based on evidence that has never met the test of public scrutiny. I ask for nothing more than an end to untruths and half truths about this matter, until the whole story is given to our people, who, I am convinced, will be amazed by the truth.''

Publication of Kimmel's letter, which was never answered, set off a storm of controversy, with Republicans and anti-Administration forces rushing to his defense. The author, Rupert Hughes, made a speech over radio calling the plight of Kimmel and Short an American Dreyfus case. ''Dreyfus was on Devil's Island for four years. Kimmel and Short will have been in purgatory for three years in December.'' The Administration was covering up the entire affair. ''Of course, if Thomas E. Dewey is elected,'' he promised, ''the fur will begin to fly. . . . It took a new President of France to get Dreyfus out of his cruel inferno.''

Republicans in the House took the ball from there, one charging that Truman, the possible ''assistant Commander in Chief,'' had himself reopened the question of Pearl Harbor responsibility and, moreover, ''had prejudged it, in allocating the blame, before all the facts have been made known.'' Full disclosure of the controversial incidents surrounding the catastrophe was demanded.

A few days later another Republican charged that Short had only acted according to information transmitted from Washington. ''There appears to be an abundance of evidence that 72 hours before the attack, the Australian Government advised the American Government in Washington that an aircraft carrier task force of the Japanese Navy had been sighted by Australian reconnaissance headed toward Pearl Harbor.''

House Majority Leader McCormack responded. "A dangerous rumor of this kind cannot be treated lightly or brushed aside, as most political statements are, with a smile," he said, and produced an official denial that Washington had received the alleged Australian warning. "There would appear to be a bottomless cavern wherein cheap politics begets unforgivable war rumors."

To counter this accusation a Republican two days later read into the record a statement by Colonel Sidney Graves, son of the commanding general of American forces in Russia in 1918–20. He claimed he had heard Sir Owen Dixon, then Australian ambassador to the United States, discuss the warning at a Washington dinner on December 7, 1943. Dixon said, in substance, "About 72 hours before Pearl Harbor, I received a flash warning from my Naval Intelligence that a Japanese Task Force was at sea and Australia should prepare for an attack; 24 hours later this was further confirmed with a later opinion of Intelligence that the Task Force was apparently not aimed at Australian waters and perhaps was directed against some American possessions."

Dixon denied he had made any such remarks and in his press conference on September 22 Roosevelt made a joke of the matter. "There will be lots of things like that, flocks of them—morning, noon and night—until the seventh of November." Although his airy dismissal of the Dixon case was successful, Roosevelt remained concerned about other rumors or charges that might be revealed before Election Day. Stephen Early, the presidential press secretary, had already informed him that Charles Rugg was supplying information on Pearl Harbor to Senator Robert Taft and the Republican National Committee. The White House was also getting large numbers of letters urging the Administration to stop hiding the truth about Pearl Harbor and reveal Washington's part in the disaster. "The American People demand the TRUTH be told about Pearl Harbor before November 7, 1944," wrote one citizen. "Did Harry Hopkins transfer 250 Navy planes which were needed at Pearl Harbor before the attack?"

What worried Roosevelt most, according to Stimson, was "fear there would be an adverse report by the Army

Pearl Harbor Board" just before the election. "The President rather characteristically isn't worried at all about the Navy Inquiry but is worried about the Army and was anxious to have the termination of the inquiry postponed until after Election." But the Army Board still had a few weeks to go and Stimson knew it would be impossible to stop proceedings. All he could do was hope that it would not include politically damaging information.

There were also rumors that Dewey had already gathered many facts about Pearl Harbor and would use them in his next major speech. The man who took action on this was not the President but George Marshall, who feared revelation of secret material might endanger the security of the Purple code. On September 25, the day Dewey was scheduled to speak in Oklahoma City, he drafted a letter of caution to Dewey and sent it to Admiral King with this note: "A recent speech in Congress had deadly implications and I now understand much more is to be said, possibly by Governor Dewey himself. This letter, of course, puts him on the spot, and I hate to do it but see no other way of avoiding what might well be a catastrophe to us." The whole thing, he added, was "loaded with dynamite but I very much feel that something has to be done or the fat will be in the fire to our great loss in the Pacific, and possibly also in Europe." The letter was approved by King, and Marshall decided to have it hand-delivered by Colonel Carter Clarke, a trusted assistant of Marshall's.

That evening Dewey made a strong speech that put the Democrats on the defensive. He claimed that Roosevelt was accountable for "the shocking state of our defense programs" in the months preceding Pearl Harbor. America was grossly unprepared for war.

The following afternoon Carter Clarke, in civilian clothes, arrived in Tulsa where arrangements had been made to meet Dewey in a private room at the Tulsa Hotel. Clarke made sure they were alone before handing over the letter from Marshall. "Well, Top Secret," said Dewey. "That's really top, isn't it?" He began reading:

I am writing you without the knowledge of any other person except Admiral King (who concurs) because we are approaching a grave dilemma in the political reactions of Congress regarding Pearl Harbor.

What I have to tell you below is of such highly secret nature that I feel compelled to ask you either to accept it on the basis of your not communicating its contents to any other person and returning this letter or not reading any further and returning the letter to the bearer.

Dewey looked up from the letter and asked Clarke, "Are you a Regular Army officer?" He was. Would Clarke give his word that he had been sent by Marshall? Yes. At this point, so reported Clarke, the governor said he did not want his lips sealed on things he already knew about Pearl Harbor. "He then asked if I were authorized to say to him in the name of Gen. Marshall that he already had in his possession the identical information that was contained in the letter, that he would then be released from all obligations to keep silent."

After Clarke said he had no such authority, Dewey said, "I cannot conceive of General Marshall and Admiral King being the only ones who know about this letter." Nor could he conceive of Marshall approaching an "opposition candidate" and making such a proposition. "Marshall does not do things like that. I am confident that Franklin Roosevelt is behind this whole thing." The letter had been lying in his lap. He picked it up. "Let me read those first two paragraphs again." He started to read, laid down the letter. "I have not reread them because my eye caught the word cryptograph. Now if this letter merely tells me that we were reading certain Japanese codes before Pearl Harbor and that at least two of them are still in current use, there is no point in my reading the letter because I already know that." He paused. "That is the case and I know it, isn't it?"

"Governor," said Clarke, "I am merely a courier in this case."

"Well, I know it and Franklin Roosevelt knows all about it. He knew what was happening before Pearl Harbor and instead of being reelected he ought to be impeached." He handed back the letter. "I shall be in

Albany on Thursday and I shall be glad to receive you or General Marshall or anyone General Marshall cares to send to discuss at length this cryptographic business or the whole Pearl Harbor mess.''

Marshall responded by writing a second letter requesting Dewey only to agree not to disclose information of which he was not already aware. He was persisting in the matter, he wrote, only ''because the military hazards are so serious that I feel some action is necessary to protect the interests of our armed forces.''

This letter was delivered by Clarke on September 28 at the Executive Mansion in Albany. But Dewey refused to look at it unless his personal adviser could also read it. He then suggested Clarke phone Marshall. Clarke replied that he did not want to do so from the Executive Mansion but would go to a pay booth. ''Oh, hell,'' said Dewey, ''I'll phone Marshall. I've talked to him before and this will be all right.'' He conversed several minutes with Marshall before handing the phone to Clarke. Marshall authorized the colonel to give the letter to Dewey, to leave it with him and to discuss the case technically in the presence of his personal adviser. A moment later Dewey put the letter down. ''Well, I'll be damned if I believe the Japs are still using those two codes.''

Clarke assured him that they were and that one of them was America's lifeblood in intelligence. Dewey read how vital the Purple code was to the war effort, and a final appeal from Marshall to help keep it a secret. ''You will understand from the foregoing the utterly tragic consequences if the present political debates regarding Pearl Harbor disclose to the enemy, German or Jap, any suspicion of the vital sources of information we possess.'' Further speeches such as the one recently delivered in Congress by Representative Forest Harness of Indiana would clearly reveal to the Japanese that we were reading their codes. ''I am presenting this matter to you in the hope that you will see your way clear to avoid the tragic results with which we are now threatened in the present political campaign.''

Dewey still believed Roosevelt's administration was responsible for Pearl Harbor but, despite urging from some

Republicans to expose what he already knew about the codes, he promised to keep the issue out of the campaign—and did.

Another issue kept from the public was Roosevelt's failing health. A photo taken at the Democratic Convention had revealed a haggard President with mouth hanging listlessly open. *Time* and *Life* kept hinting about his fragile health since Henry Luce was now unabashedly supporting Dewey. Yet early that month he made a decision that might have won Roosevelt the presidency. *Life's* managing editor showed Luce some two hundred Roosevelt pictures for upcoming issues. "In about half of them he was a dead man," recalled Luce. "We decided to print the ones that were the least bad. And thereby—by trying to lean over backward being fair or something, or kind—we infringed our contract with readers to tell them the truth. Actually the truth *was* in the pictures." The big irresponsibility of the American press, confessed Luce, "came when we did not indicate, especially in *Life's* pictures, that Roosevelt was a dying man."

Lies about his health had been coming from the White House since early in the year. That March a checkup on Roosevelt at Bethesda Naval Hospital had confirmed indications of "hypertension, hypertensive heart disease, failure of the left ventricle of the heart, and fluid in both lungs. FDR had a persistent cough, a grayish pallor on his face, a noticeable agitation of the hands, a blue cast to lips and fingernails." And yet a month later Admiral Ross McIntire, his personal physician, assured a reporter from *Time* that Roosevelt was in good health. "Considering the difference in age, his recent physical examination is equally as good as the one made on him twelve years ago."

And so, on November 7, the American public went to the polls unaware that the Army Pearl Harbor Board and the Navy Inquiry had just placed the burden of blame for Pearl Harbor, not on Kimmel and Short, but on Washington. Nor did the voters know that one of the candidates was a dying man. As a result the President won thirty-six states with 432 electoral votes. Dewey took only twelve states with 99 electoral votes. The Democrats won seven more senatorial seats than their opponents, with two races still in doubt. In the House the score was 242 to 185 in favor of the Democrats. It must have particularly pleased Roosevelt that two of his favorite enemies, isolationists Hamilton Fish and Gerald Nye, were defeated. Upon his return to the capital from Hyde Park the President was greeted by a crowd of several hundred thousand despite a downpour. He was in a jovial mood, remarking that he hoped news writers "won't intimate in the papers that I expect to make Washington my permanent residence for the rest of my life."

3.

By Election Day MacArthur had landed a substantial force on Leyte with more than 100,000 tons of cargo. In the great naval battle that followed in Leyte Gulf, the Americans sank some 300,000 tons of combat shipping. It was the virtual end of the Imperial Navy.

In Europe the Allies, confident of imminent victory, were preparing to storm the Siegfried Line, unaware that Hitler was preparing a surprise counterattack in the Ardennes designed to reach Antwerp and destroy thirty U.S. and British divisions.

The morning before the election Forrestal and Stimson had conferred about Pearl Harbor for an hour and a half. "We each told the other the substance of the reports of our respective investigating boards," Stimson wrote in his diary. "I was relieved to find that the Navy were apparently not going to try to whitewash their people and Forrestal seems to look at the matter in a very cooperative spirit." By afternoon Stimson had "finally gathered myself together and decided practically what my decision will be in the Pearl Harbor case." Having reached the decision, Stimson "took the bit in my mouth" and told the Judge Advocate General and the assistant recorder of the Pearl Harbor Board that he was going to reverse the Board's findings. "To my relief I found that they agreed with me and were very helpful in working out the general outlines of it. In fact I think we were all finally agreed on it by the time the long talk of the afternoon was over. It was a great relief to my mind to have gotten that far.''

At Navy Headquarters, Admiral King was presented with a proposed endorsement to the Navy Inquiry report for his signature. In it Stark was criticized for not keeping Kimmel properly informed and the latter for not being sufficiently alive to the dangers of the situation. ''Since trial by general court-martial is not warranted by the evidence adduced, appropriate administrative action would appear to be the relegation of both of these officers to positions in which lack of superior judgment may not result in future errors.'' Although he had not yet read the proceedings of the Navy Inquiry, and although he felt that Kimmel had been made a scapegoat, King signed the endorsement.

The Secretary of War, with the help of two assistants, worked diligently to finish his endorsement to the Army Board report and by the following Monday he could write that ''by the grace of God by the end of the day we had done so practically.'' What concerned him most were the ''pinpricks'' in the Army Board's conclusions about Marshall. ''That's what makes all the trouble.'' Although Marshall was held in the highest of esteem throughout the Army and the Administration, the charges against him would damage his position. They also would reflect on Stimson and Roosevelt. Marshall himself had only recently read the report and was despondent. On November 14 he told Stimson that the shocking conclusions of the Board had destroyed his usefulness in the Army. ''I told him that was nonsense, to forget it.''

Later in the day Stimson had lunch with Forrestal at the Navy Department. Afterward Stimson brought out the draft of his statement. Forrestal read it, then handed over the endorsement signed by King. The two Secretaries concluded they were ''not very far apart and that there was to be no clash between the standards and views of the two Departments in regard to the situation.''

On the twentieth Stimson sought advice from General Alexander Surles, who handled Army Public Relations. First Surles read Stimson's latest draft, then the Secretary read him the conclusions of the Army Board. Surles had not seen these before and was so staggered that "his first reaction was to try to keep back the findings. He was afraid that the Navy will somehow or other ride in behind our publicity and escape it themselves and leave us to bear the whole brunt of it." Although Surles approved of Stimson's statement he was not sure they could "afford to take the big publicity" that would surely result from the criticisms of Marshall. "This was natural and not unexpected but of course it was a heavy blow to me to have to carry the whole load alone myself. Surles has usually been such a support and his judgment has always been so good that this was another staggering swipe to me."

Throughout the night he was also troubled because he hadn't yet heard from the Navy. He had shown Forrestal his own report but still had no idea what his fellow Secretary was going to say. "So this morning I called him up and said that I wanted to have their report before I saw the President or at least to know what they were going to do." Stimson knew Forrestal had seen Roosevelt the previous week and he suspected the two had come together "more or less."

Forrestal revealed that he had not finished his report but would send it over before Stimson saw Roosevelt. When it arrived late that morning Stimson was appalled. "After all the preliminaries, the preambles, and recitals, it consisted of just one sentence in which he said that, owing to the situation and the circumstances which existed, it was not in the public interest or something like that to take any proceedings against any naval officers. Well, my group who at once got together again, as well as myself, decided that in the face of that, if the Navy put that out, why our report with our frankness and our frank criticism of our own people would get all the publicity and unfavorable publicity in the sense that the people would do all the speculating about the big names that have been mentioned."

By then it was time to go to the White House. Stimson had lunch with the President in his penthouse with Roosevelt's daughter, Anna Boettiger, present. "That of course cramped a little bit our style . . . so during the luncheon I sat quiet and listened to the chitchat that went on." Finally Roosevelt brought up the Pearl Harbor report. "I think," he remarked, "the less said the better."

Stimson guessed the President must have seen and approved Forrestal's draft. "I told him that I had been completely cut off from my proposal by that plan because we could not afford to go ahead and be frank when the Navy was not being frank." Stimson explained his own plan and argued that frankness was the best policy. Then he handed the President the conclusions of the Army Board.

Roosevelt read them very carefully. "Why, this is wicked!" he said. "This is wicked." He studied Stimson's report carefully and at length. Very good, he said, but still thought it would be safer to follow Forrestal's line.

After Stimson expressed fear that Congress would get at the papers and the facts, Roosevelt said they should take every step against that, and also must refuse to make the reports public. "He said that they should be sealed up and our opinions put in with them and then a notice made that they should only be opened on a Joint Resolution of both Houses of Congress approved by the President after the war, this resolution to say that it was in the public interest to do so."

Stimson left the White House disgruntled. His influence there was apparently waning. He knew that Harry Hopkins was conniving against him on the grounds that he was ill and too old. What stung most was that Forrestal's method had been chosen, not his. Stimson reluctantly complied with the President's order to prepare a shorter news release, but was stubborn enough to include that the Army Board had found that "certain officers in the field and in the War Department did not perform their duties with the necessary skill or exercise the judgment which was required. . . ." He also criticized Short by name.

In a covering letter to the President, he wrote, "The enclosed draft goes as far in condensation as I believe I can properly go. To say merely that I believe that the facts do not warrant the institution of any proceedings against any officer of the Army would, I believe, inevitably give the impression that I was trying entirely to absolve all

Army officers from any criticism including General Short. . . . This is an impression I am unwilling to father."

The proposed news release and the letter were sent to Hyde Park by a courier who had been instructed by Stimson to wait for an answer. But the President said he couldn't reply that day and would like to compare it with the Navy proposition since he wanted both departments to coordinate. "His wish for coordination . . . is reasonable," Stimson wrote in his diary, "but I have gone a long long step towards giving up what I think is the wisest plan and I think it is time for the Navy to come and meet me. In any event I do not feel like yielding to him at all. In fact it is a matter of conscience—any yielding to the Navy form. I can't help feeling that if I did that I would lose the respect of the people whom I most value because they would say that I was doing a complete whitewash of the entire Army in a situation where such a position was untenable. That criticism will come to Forrestal if he doesn't change his form of statement."

Although the next day was Thanksgiving, Stimson went to his office as usual. He talked on the telephone to Forrestal, whom he found "not as stiff as the draft statement which he sent me the other day." The Navy Secretary was also in favor of admitting there was something wrong in the Navy but Stimson had his doubts and these were strengthened upon hearing rumors that the Navy was going to whitewash everyone including Kimmel. And so Stimson called back on the twenty-fourth. Forrestal assured him he was going to admit the guilt of some of his officers. But there was still nagging doubt in Stimson's mind. He would have "an uneasy feeling" till the thing was done.

On the way home he read the new critique of the Judge Advocate General on the Army Board's report. It was, thought Stimson, "really a humdinger," since he "handled the Pearl Harbor Board without gloves and had analyzed very carefully and yet fairly all their mistakes."

The Judge Advocate's memorandum largely reconfirmed the findings of the Roberts Commission. It also stoutly defended Marshall, stating baldly that none of the Board's criticisms of the Chief of Staff was "justified."

Forrestal was far more sensitive to the Army's problem than Stimson realized. If the Navy criticized Stark that would reflect unfavorably on Marshall. Yet it would not be fair only to place blame on Kimmel. "The exercise of hindsight is probably the easiest intellectual function available to man," he wrote in his diary on the twenty-seventh but he was still forced to conclude that neither those officials in the Navy Department nor those in Hawaii had taken adequate precautions for the Japanese attack. At the same time he had to protect the reputation of the Navy.

His dilemma apparently weighed so heavily on him that when he talked on the phone to Stimson the latter got the impression that Forrestal was backsliding, for he bitterly noted in his diary that the Secretary of the Navy was "turning back to his old form of impossible statement or rather a statement the form of which is impossible for me. It was another body blow to me."

Still another came that day with the announcement that Hull was being replaced by a much younger man, Edward Stettinius. "The departure of Mr. Hull means a tremendous loss to me personally and officially. Hull, Knox and I have kept so close together all through these four years that it has saved many a bad slip, and now both Hull and Knox have gone. So tonight I felt pretty solemn and alone." It must have made him aware of his age—and of Harry Hopkins' continuing efforts to get rid of him.

His differences with Forrestal were solved in the next few days; Stimson found Forrestal's latest draft to be "a very good job." On the last day of November they met to make their two statements "as parallel as they could be under the circumstances." After final tinkering the two men called up the President at Warm Springs, Georgia, and read aloud their reports. Roosevelt approved and authorized release to the press. "Now I feel as if I had a burden off my back for the present," wrote Stimson, yet still felt it was a grave mistake not to have made a frank and full statement—"but it is as much as Forrestal and I could accomplish under the President's direction that we should not go too far."

This was one time Stimson's political instinct was superior to his chief's. The general editorial response to the two statements on December 1 was negative. Newspapers and magazines attacked the Administration for continuing to suppress the Pearl Harbor story. Great numbers of letters and telegrams flooded into the White House. "What do you think Americans are?" a man from Edgewood, Rhode Island, asked the President. "Just ignorant and dumb cattle? Freedom of Speech: Freedom of Press? . . . Can't tell us now about the responsibility for the Pearl Harbor catastrophe because it will undermine the morale? The Government's cover-up of the responsibility for that catastrophe has done more to undermine morale than any other single event of the past three years. The thinkers of America, and there are millions of them, won't stand for such guff. I am but one of the millions of Americans today who are shocked, humiliated and indignant because of this announcement."

In his column in the New York *Daily News,* John O'-Donnell wrote that a police court aroma hovered over the case. Partisan debate in Congress broke out anew. The Democrats defended the two press releases. What more should be disclosed during a war? The Republicans repeated their charge of suppression of vital information. In any case, it was obvious that full revelation of facts and an open investigation of Pearl Harbor could not come about until the war was over.

Neither Rugg nor Kimmel had been surprised by the news releases since the latter had been kept informed of the rumors floating around the corridors of the Navy Building and the former had collated this information into an accurate prediction. The Roosevelt-Stimson-Forrestal tactic aroused the admiral's fighting spirit and he immediately demanded an audience with the chief of Naval Operations. It was fitting that the interview was granted on the third anniversary of the Japanese attack. Kimmel found the crusty King in a friendly and sympathetic mood, treating an admiral-in-disgrace as if he were still in the inner circle. With disarming frankness Ki, as he was known to a few intimates, stated that it was he who had recommended to Forrestal that Betty Stark be relieved of his command and placed on the retired list. "He strongly implied, without definitely stating it as a fact," Kimmel wrote in his memorandum of the interview, "that the Court of Inquiry had completely cleared me of all blame in connection."

King's frankness even extended to revelation that the Army Board had vigorously censured Marshall "for his action or lack of action" in the days preceding the catastrophe, and that Stimson himself had "sweat blood" over his news release. "The publication of any part finding any fault of Marshall's was voted down," confessed King. The President, he said, had not only turned down King's proposal to relieve Stark on the ground that he was performing valuable services, but made it clear that Marshall was irreplaceable. "He would not consent to the publication of any remarks in the slightest degree derogatory to Mr. Marshall." Roosevelt, in fact, had been "fit to be tied" when he read the Army Board report.

After King asserted he had also recommended against publication of the Army and Navy findings, Kimmel bluntly asked what assurances King could give that the record and findings of the Navy Inquiry would not be tampered with or destroyed. The Navy commander in chief indignantly replied that he was amazed at such a question. Under no circumstances could the findings be tampered with! "You need not be amazed," retorted Kimmel, "as such things have happened and might happen again." He told how he had heard Stark commit perjury at the Navy Inquiry. "And after hearing that, I think anything might happen."

King showed such shock that Kimmel asked him point-blank, "Have you read the record of the Court of Inquiry? Stark's lies are spread there for anyone to read, and the fact that he was lying is unmistakable."

King admitted he had not read the testimony. Kimmel assured him that at least half a dozen other witnesses had heard Stark's testimony. "I am convinced that Stark lied before the court under oath," said Kimmel. "After listening to Stark I was ashamed of the Navy."

4.

The criticism that followed the news releases impelled
Stimson to seek new information that would refute the
Army Board charges. He turned over the job to Major
Henry Christian Clausen, who had served as assistant recorder for the Board. An attorney before he entered the
Army, he had served as assistant U.S. attorney for the
Northern District of California and then become chief
counsel for the chief engineer during the construction of
the Golden Gate Bridge. At the outbreak of war, Clausen
volunteered direct from practice in law in San Francisco.
He had prosecuted a court-martial involving an air scandal
in Ohio, bringing about ultimate convictions. This, together with a letter of recommendation to the War Department from Senator Truman, had resulted in his assignment
to the Army Pearl Harbor Board. Currently he was on the
staff of the Judge Advocate General, a strong dissident of
the Army Board findings, who submitted to Clausen a list
of unexplored leads to be followed up. Among the most
important witnesses to be "subjected to further questioning" were the controversial Colonels Bratton and Sadtler.

To be selected by Stimson for the new mission was an
honor. The Secretary of War was the great man of the war
to Clausen, and he himself had not been in total agreement
with the Army Board report, finding the condemnation of
Marshall too severe. Clausen was, in short, a very appropriate choice from Stimson's point of view for a difficult
and sensitive task.

After preparing himself, he began interrogations in
Washington in February 1945, concentrating on the
"winds" execute. Colonel Moses Pettigrew, Bratton's assistant in the intelligence branch before Pearl Harbor, testified that someone he did not now recall showed him "on
or about 5 December 1941" the "winds" execute "which
indicated that Japanese-U.S. relations were in danger."
He had taken this message "to mean that anything could
happen" and, consequently, at the request of someone he
did not recall, he had prepared a message to Hawaii.

Colonel Carlisle Dusenbury then signed an affidavit that
he was the one who had instructed Pettigrew to draw up

the message, which read: "Contact Commander Rochefort immediately through Commandant Fourteenth Naval District regarding broadcasts from Tokyo reference weather."

"The reason which I recollect for sending the secret cable," testified Dusenbury, "was that the trend of translated intercepts which had been received by G-2, especially the 'Winds Code,' indicated danger to the United States."

Clausen was keeping Stimson periodically informed of his progress. In early March he reported that he was uncovering important evidence that Short had more information about imminent war with Japan than he had admitted. He knew about the "winds" code and had advance notice that the Japanese were going to destroy their secret codes and papers at embassies just before the attack.

Convinced that Clausen, now a lieutenant colonel, was on the trail of discrediting the Army Board findings, his superiors sent him on to Pearl Harbor for more proof.

At Yalta the Big Three had agreed on the perimeters of the postwar world. Victory was in sight. The Russians had crossed the Oder River and the Americans, after recovering from a setback in the Battle of the Bulge, crossed the Rhine. In Berlin Hitler was living like a mole in his bunker, nurturing an impossible dream—that the British and Americans would come to their senses at the last moment and join his crusade against Godless Red Russia.

The efforts to bury the facts about Pearl Harbor were being turned over to loyal Democrats in the Senate. Both Stimson and Forrestal sent identical bills to the chairmen of the Senate and House Armed Services Committees prohibiting disclosure of any coded matter. On March 30 Senator Elbert Thomas introduced his bill in the Senate.

The next day Kimmel happened to read an obscure item in the New York *Herald Tribune* about the bill. He immediately telephoned Rugg in Boston and then hurriedly packed and left his apartment in Bronxville for Washington. While he was attempting to find out what was going on, he received a call from Rugg. The bill, he said, had been passed in the Senate while Senator Ferguson was in the Caribbean; it had been sent to the House.

In desperation Kimmel began telephoning congressmen and senators only to learn that if the House followed the Senate's example that was the end to all disclosures about Pearl Harbor. As a last resort he telephoned the publisher of the Washington *Post*, Eugene Meyer, to whom he had been introduced by Admiral Harris in New York. By the time he reached Meyer's office the publisher had two of his top writers on hand. The four discussed the matter and the next morning headlines in the *Post* attacked the Thomas bill. A stinging indictment of the Democratic attempt to hide the facts of Pearl Harbor followed in the April 12 issue. "It is regrettable to note that we can no longer depend upon the Senate to protect the Nation against executive deprivation of our liberties." Only one hearing had been held prior to the bill's passage and that in camera. "Either from inertia or somnolence, either from lack of interest or just plain complacence, the Senators approved the say-so of Chairman Thomas of the Military Affairs Committee. Yet this bill would gag anybody who would publish any information which originally took the form of a coded message. The effect would be to put the history of this storied period under wraps, for all of that history could be traced back to a coded message. And you may be sure, if this bill is enacted, almost everything that it sought to keep from the prying eyes of the public will first be put in code."

Later in the day came news that Franklin Delano Roosevelt was dead in Georgia. It was shocking to all, friends and foes, for it was the end of an era.[1]

Rugg came down from Boston and, with the help of Hanify and Lavender, wrote speeches for their friends in Congress. These were so effective that the Senate approved Ferguson's move to reconsider the Thomas bill; and by the time the bill to gag the facts was brought to the floor of the House, the matter had been aired so thoroughly that it was defeated by that body. "I have wondered always," Kimmel later wrote, "if we would have

[1] That day MacArthur talked to his military secretary, Brigadier General Bonner Fellers, as they drove to their quarters. "Well, the old man has gone," said MacArthur, "a man who never told the truth if a lie would suffice."

been successful if Franklin Roosevelt had not died on April 12, 1945."

On the eighteenth of April Forrestal met with the new President. He informed Truman that Admiral H. Kent Hewitt had been selected to pursue the Pearl Harbor investigation. "I told him that I felt I had an obligation to Congress to continue the investigation because I was not completely satisfied with the report my own Court had made. . . ."

The Hewitt Inquiry began amidst national rejoicing over the unconditional surrender of Germany six days earlier. Although Admiral Hewitt was the nominal head of the inquiry and would do much of the interrogation, the real work was carried on by John F. Sonnett, a special assistant to Forrestal, and his own assistant, Lieutenant John Ford Baecher.

His most important witness was Captain Safford, who was first informally quizzed in Room 1083A of the Navy Building. Sonnett, a New York lawyer of some distinction, asked many questions pertaining to Safford's testimony before previous investigations and they discussed the discrepancies between his testimony and that of other witnesses.

"It was apparent to me on my very first meeting with Lieutenant Commander Sonnett," Safford wrote in a Confidential Memorandum for the record, "that he was acting as a 'counsel for the defense' for the late Secretary Knox and Admiral Stark rather than as a legal assistant to the investigating officer. His purpose seemed to be to refute testimony (before earlier investigations) that was unfavorable to anyone in Washington, to beguile 'hostile' witnesses into changing their stories, and to introduce an element of doubt where he could not effect a reversal of testimony. Above all, he attempted to make me reverse my testimony regarding the 'Winds Execute' message and to make me believe I was suffering from hallucinations."

Safford again talked informally to Sonnett on May 18 and a day or so later. "On these latter occasions, like the first, Sonnett tried to persuade me that there had been no 'Winds Execute' message, that my memory had been playing me tricks, that I had confused the 'False Winds message' with what I had been expecting, and that I ought to change my testimony to permit reconciling all previous discrepancies and thereby wind up the affair. In some cases the idea was stated outright, in some cases it was implied, and in other cases it was unexpressed but obviously the end in view.''

During the course of the three conferences Safford distinctly recalled Sonnett using these statements:

''You are the only one who seems to have ever seen the Winds Execute message.''

''How could the Winds Execute be heard on the East Coast of the U.S. and not at any of the places nearer Japan?''

''It is very doubtful that there ever was a Winds Execute.''

''It is no reflection on your veracity to change your testimony.''

''It is no reflection on your mentality to have your memory play you tricks—after such a long period.''

''Numerous witnesses that you have named have denied all knowledge of a Winds Execute message.''

''You do not have to carry the torch for Admiral Kimmel.''

But the clever barrage of assorted suggestions, insinuations, veiled threats and wheedlings had no effect on Safford when he appeared officially before Admiral Hewitt on May 21. He repeated the testimony he had previously given with only a few minor changes.

As he was leaving the room Safford asked Hewitt if there were still any doubts in the admiral's mind that there had been a ''winds'' execute. Hewitt, according to Safford's memorandum, looked startled but before he could reply Sonnett said, ''Of course, I am not conducting the case and I do not know what Admiral Hewitt has decided, but to me it is very doubtful that the so-called Winds Execute message was ever sent.''

Hewitt thought a moment or so before replying to Safford: ''You are not entitled to my opinion, but I will an-

swer your question. There is no evidence of a Winds
Execute Message beyond your unsupported testimony. I
do not doubt your sincerity, but I believe you have confused one of the other messages containing the name of a
wind with the message you were expecting to receive.''

For his part, Safford did not doubt Admiral Hewitt's
integrity, ''but I do believe that Sonnett has succeeded in
pulling the wool over his eyes.''

Safford was also convinced that Sonnett used similar
tactics on Alwin Kramer, now a captain. That same afternoon he summoned Kramer to a private conference and
showed him a number of intercepts. But what had failed
with Safford succeeded with Kramer, who was recovering
from illness and mental fatigue. The following day he
drastically altered the positive testimony he had given before the Navy Court that he had seen the ''winds'' execute
in early December and it read, ''East wind, rain.''

Although he admitted he had seen the ''winds'' message, he now could not recall the wording. ''It may have
been, *'Higashi no kaze ame,'* specifically referring to the
United States, as I have previously testified at Pearl Harbor, but I am less positive of that now than I believe I was
at that time.'' He explained that he had revised his original
statement after thinking it over.

''For that reason, I am at least under the impression that
the message referred to England and possibly the Dutch
rather than the United States, although it may have referred to the United States, too.''

A little later he admitted that his memory had been refreshed the previous afternoon by Sonnett, who had shown
him a number of messages. If Kimmel and his counsel had
been allowed to be present their cross-examination could
have brought out full details of the informal meeting with
Sonnett, and whether pressure had been applied on Kramer
to change his testimony.

Rugg would also have vigorously protested Hewitt's announcement at the next session that, in view of the testimony of Kramer, it was decided not to call Admiral Noyes
as a witness; the admiral's previous evidence was good
enough. Moreover, it appeared from Safford's own testimony that he only *''thought* that a 'Winds' message relat-

ing to the United States was received about 4 December 1941, and was shown to him by Captain Kramer and a watch officer and then delivered to Admiral Noyes. . . . There is yet no other evidence to the effect that a 'Winds' code message relating to the United States was received.''

In late June Safford was recalled by Hewitt but was asked no questions about the ''winds'' execute. That, apparently, was a dead issue in the eyes of Hewitt and his assistants. Safford left Washington for a vacation in Marblehead and on July 3 called on Charles Rugg. He told about his ordeal with Sonnett and his belief that the same measures were being used on other witnesses favorable to Kimmel, particularly Rochefort and Kramer.

Rugg asked what would be the probable results of the investigation. Safford thought Hewitt would file a report absolving Washington of all responsibility and divide the blame between Short and ''an act of God.'' He had no opinion as to whether they would try to pin any errors of judgment on Kimmel.

As he was leaving Safford asked if Rugg would act as his counsel if he got into any trouble in connection with anything that he might have done. ''One of the reasons why he suggested this,'' noted Rugg in a memorandum, ''was that that relationship with me would make it possible and legal for him to talk freely to me about matters of interest.''

In his official report Hewitt concluded that ''no message was intercepted prior to the attack which used the code words relating to the United States [East wind, rain].'' Stark was criticized for not warning Kimmel of other intercepted Japanese messages, particularly during the week prior to the attack, but Hewitt still found that Kimmel had ''sufficient information in his possession'' to indicate that the outbreak of war was imminent.

Even before he learned of the conclusions Kimmel was bitter. He had specifically asked Hewitt if he could appear but had been refused. ''I studied carefully every word of testimony in each of the earlier investigations, including, of course, all the statements of Admiral Kimmel himself,'' Hewitt later wrote to Kimmel's biographer, Donald Brownlow. ''As to his appearance before me, I would have been glad to hear him, although, frankly, I did not see how anything of import could be added to what had already been said. However, Secretary Forrestal himself disapproved of the Admiral's further appearance. It was an unfortunate decision, for the result was misunderstanding and bitterness and the loss of some old friendships.'' By laying the blame on Forrestal, Hewitt had raised a point that was never resolved. Although the Secretary of the Navy had refused to allow Kimmel to cross-examine witnesses and have counsel, he had authorized the admiral's appearance before Hewitt as a witness, ''whether it be at his request or on your own initiative.'' Had Forrestal previously instructed Hewitt to ignore this written permission or had the admiral acted on his own initiative?

Hewitt had never felt that Kimmel was in any way guilty of dereliction of duty and in his conclusions praised him as ''energetic, indefatigable, resourceful and positive in his efforts to prepare the Fleet for war.'' He had neither intended to whitewash the Navy Department nor make Kimmel a scapegoat. But as Forrestal read the Hewitt report he took it as corroboration of his own misgivings about the conclusions of the Navy Inquiry.

5.

By this time another one-man investigation was under way at the instigation of Marshall. During his interrogation by Hewitt, Safford had mentioned a third-hand story that the ''winds'' execute message had been destroyed by a Colonel Bissell ''on the direct orders of General Marshall.'' This account had come, he reluctantly revealed, from William Friedman, the man credited with the solution of the Purple code. Hewitt subsequently interviewed Friedman, who testified that he had heard this story from Colonel Sadtler.

Colonel Carter Clarke, who had brought Marshall's letters to Dewey, was again utilized by the Chief of Staff, this time to find evidence refuting this and other charges. On July 14 Sadtler confirmed that he had been told about the destruction of messages. ''Some time during 1943

General Isaac Spalding at Ft. Bragg, North Carolina, told me something to the effect that J. T. B. Bissell had told him that everything pertaining to Pearl Harbor was being destroyed or had been destroyed.''

Three days later, on July 17, General Spalding admitted to Clarke that he had discussed the matter with Sadtler but first wanted it to appear on record that it was his ''full belief that the Secretary of War, Mr. Stimson, and the Chief of Staff, General Marshall, are not involved in any way whatsoever with the testimony which I am about to give, and it is my belief that neither one knew anything of it.''

After this cautious disclaimer, which anyone who has served in the armed forces would understand, Spalding related that in 1943 he had talked to Colonel John T. B. Bissell at Fort Bragg about the Pearl Harbor incident. Spalding had expressed amazement that General Miles and the Navy had not been able to track the Japanese task force. ''I was astounded at their ignorance or inability to detect that! I remember shooting off my mouth about Sherman Miles for whom I didn't have a very high regard professionally, and I think I remember telling him . . . that I thought Sherman Miles was a 'stuffed shirt.' . . .'' Spalding also revealed that Bissell had told him ''certain messages had been received and were in the files of G-2 and he deemed it most necessary to destroy them. I got the impression that these messages were derogatory to the War Department and that he [Bissell] on his own responsibility destroyed them. I had the impression that they were secret information which it was most desireable that the President, Congress, the public, Mr. Stimson and Gen. Marshall not know about. I had the feeling that Bissell destroyed them without even Gen. Raymond Lee, the G-2 at that time, knowing they were in existence.''

Next it was the turn of Bissell, now a brigadier general, to testify. He admitted discussing Pearl Harbor with Spalding and confirmed he had heard Miles called a stuffed shirt. But he denied saying that any messages had been destroyed. Nor had he ever heard of any messages being destroyed except in 1940 when the World War I files were cleared out.

"Did you tell Gen. Spalding at any time, in substance, that you had destroyed what you would call vital records, records which if known to exist would be very unpleasant to the War Department?"

"I did not."

As far as the War Department was concerned this categorical denial closed the incident. But it seems reasonable to assume that, if Bissell had done anything improper or illegal, he would have denied the allegation under any circumstances. It is just as likely to believe that he was probably telling the truth to Spalding, an old friend, never dreaming that the story would be investigated officially.

6.

Colonel Clausen had been traveling to the Pacific and Europe. In Frankfurt am Main he had interviewed Bedell Smith, now a lieutenant general and Eisenhower's chief of staff, early in June.[2] At first Smith objected to being interrogated. He "pulled rank" on Clausen, a mere lieutenant colonel, insisting the matter go up to Ike. But Clausen was not one to be intimidated, having a directive from someone of higher rank, Stimson. During the interview Smith flatly denied Colonel Sadtler's claim that he had asked Smith and Gerow on December 5 to authorize him to send Hawaii a warning, and both had refused. He also denied Colonel Bratton's claim that he had delivered the thirteen-part message to him on the eve of Pearl Harbor. He had left his office, he said, about 7 P.M. on December 6 and therefore could not have been in his office when Bratton delivered it.

---

[2]Earlier that year Lieutenant Richmond, Stark's counsel, chanced to ride in the same car with Smith and General Marshall in Malta. "I don't know if you remember me, General," Richmond said, "but I had a little set-to with you down in Washington." Marshall thought he had seen Richmond someplace before. "I was Admiral Stark's counsel at the Court of Inquiry, and I assisted Admiral Hart and asked you some questions."

"Oh yes," said Marshall. "By the way, they got me all tangled up in that thing." He couldn't remember anything about the weekend of December 6 and 7. *(Continued on page 148)*

Several weeks later Clausen saw Gerow in Cannes. He too denied the Sadtler testimony. Moreover, he had never seen any "winds" execute. "If I had received such a message or notice thereof, I believe I would now recall the fact, in view of its importance." He also denied that Bratton had ever delivered to him the thirteen-part message on the night of December 6.

Bratton was now chief of Intelligence of the staff of Berlin District. The chief of staff of Berlin District, Brigadier General Paul Ransom, regarded him as "an exceptionally good officer and especially well qualified in the field of intelligence. He did excellent work in Berlin under circumstances made difficult by Russian intransigence."

That July Bratton was on the Autobahn encircling Berlin, on his way to the British Sector headquarters, when a British car overtook and flagged him down. Colonel Clausen stepped out, told what his mission was and that he had authority to interrogate Bratton. Once they had settled in Bratton's billet, Clausen discovered he had left papers necessary for the interrogation in Paris. He radioed Army Intelligence requesting the papers be flown to Berlin by courier but was informed this material was top secret and the interrogation would have to take place in Paris.

In a state of trepidation, Bratton went to a friend, Lieutenant Colonel William F. Heimlich, head of Combat Intelligence, Fifteenth Army. Bratton related how he had to go to Paris with a Colonel Clausen and he feared he might not return. He then described in detail the events preceding the Japanese attack as he saw them unravel at the Munitions Building; and of his problems with Marshall later. Removing a carefully wrapped brown envelope from his office safe, he explained that the contents were copies of intelligence summaries submitted to Marshall in the months preceding Pearl Harbor. They had been prepared for the President, and Bratton called Heimlich's attention

Smith interrupted. "General, there's a book that has all that in it. You had everybody write a memorandum the day after Pearl Harbor about everything they could remember about that pre-Pearl Harbor period and the day itself, and it was all put away in a single volume. I did it."

Marshall wanted to know what in the devil happened to the book and Smith said it was still in the safe at the Chief of Staff's office.

to numerous paragraphs which had been crossed out and initialed on the side "G.C.M."

"In the event he did not return," recalled Heimlich, "I was to hand-deliver them to his family. He did not give a reason why he might not return and I assumed he might continue on directly to Washington from Paris."

The interrogation took place at the Hotel Prince of Wales on July 27. Clausen showed Bratton a number of affidavits he had collected in his travels. After seeing those of Generals Bedell Smith and Gerow, Bratton promptly changed his previous testimony that he had delivered the thirteen-part message on Pearl Harbor to one of these two officers. In the affidavit refuting himself, he said, "Any prior statements or testimony of mine which may be contrary to my statements here . . . should be modified and considered changed in accordance with my statement herein. This affidavit now represents my best recollection of the matters and events set forth, and a better recollection than when I previously testified before the Army Pearl Harbor Board, and is made after having my memory refreshed in several ways and respects."

Chastened, Bratton returned to Berlin where he reclaimed his photostats from Heimlich without comment.

Clausen's next witness was Sadtler. On August 13 they met in Washington and he, like Bratton, repudiated his previous testimony. No, he had never conferred with Generals Gerow and Smith on December 5 concerning a warning to Hawaii. Nor had he ever seen any "winds" execute message.

Three days later the indefatigable Clausen, who had already journeyed some fifty thousand miles in his quest for information, went to Boston to see Miles. The general denied that he had ever met with Colonels Sadtler and Bratton on December 5 concerning information supposedly received by Sadtler from Admiral Noyes of a possible "winds" execute.

Clausen's findings pleased Stimson. Although the peripatetic colonel had uncovered some evidence which raised serious doubts as to the extent of information Washington had sent Short, the War Secretary's mind was eased by the refutation of Bratton's and Sadtler's damaging testimony concerning Marshall's assistants. And no new information had come up that would further implicate the Chief of Staff himself. Indeed, the net result of both the Clausen and Clarke reports was to acquit the War Department of the charges made by the Army Pearl Harbor Board.

7.

In another part of the Pentagon, Forrestal was similarly relieved by the conclusions of Hewitt. In his endorsement to the admiral's report, Forrestal found no negligence on the part of Washington officials with respect to withholding from Kimmel vital information clearly indicating an attack on Hawaii. And he particularly denied the existence of any intercepted "winds" execute. But he did censure Kimmel and Stark for failing to demonstrate "the superior judgment necessary for exercising command commensurate with their rank and their assigned duties."[3]

Forrestal was so satisfied with the Hewitt report that he felt there was no reason to withhold any longer from the public the report of the Navy Inquiry. He discussed this three days after V-J Day, August 17, with President Truman, who had gotten himself mixed up in the Pearl Harbor controversy with his attack on Kimmel and Short in the *Collier's* article. He regretted that act and was now determined to detach himself and his Administration from the issue. After all, he had not been involved in prewar policy and wouldn't have to defend his own action. The problem, as a loyal party man, was to protect the Democratic Administration from new attacks without causing further acrimony. He agreed with Forrestal that the best solution was to terminate the entire issue as soon as possible: and the first step should be disclosure of the Army and Navy reports. No longer could the excuse be made that Pearl Har-

[3] In a taped interview in the Oral History Collection, Columbia University, Hewitt later stated, "Secretary Forrestal had some very set ideas about the thing. And he wanted me to find certain things which I couldn't find and didn't find. I think he was disappointed that I didn't make a report in accordance with some of his ideas." It is unfortunate Hewitt didn't say what Forrestal's "ideas" were.

bor secret data must be concealed for the sake of national security now that the war was over. The denial of such material, said the astute Truman, "only added to and accentuated the atmosphere of mystery surrounding such an event of broad national interest as Pearl Harbor."

Stimson may not have liked the idea but he made no protest, and on the morning of August 29 Truman, his advisers, and officials from the War and Navy Departments began working out the final details of releasing the two reports. But Forrestal, apprehensive that Truman was being "stampeded" into action, had second thoughts. The two endorsements of the Navy Court's report by himself and King were so critical of Kimmel that Forrestal feared their release might prevent the Hawaiian commander from receiving the unbiased court-martial promised by Knox in 1942. At the same time the Secretary of the Navy realized that withholding release of the Navy Court findings could result in charges of a cover-up.

The solution of this dilemma, Forrestal told Truman, would be either courts-martial for Kimmel and Short or formation of another commission to study the case. While announcing a new trial for the commanders, he suggested, why didn't the Army publish its report and the Navy publish nothing?

Stimson's two representatives at the meeting both objected strenuously. Why should they accept a proposal that placed the burden of culpability on the Army? At this point the President ended the controversy. Kimmel, he promised, would receive a fair trial despite all the publicity.

At his press conference that morning Truman announced that the two reports would be released with the endorsements. He noted that there were criticisms of General Marshall in the Army Board report to which Stimson, in his statement, took sharp issue and characterized as entirely unjustified, and that the Chief of Staff had "acted throughout with his usual 'great skill, energy and efficiency.' I associate myself wholeheartedly with this expression by the Secretary of War." Then he added, "Indeed, I have the fullest confidence in the skill, energy and efficiency of all of our war leaders, both Army and Navy."

The release to the public of the Army and Navy reports was done in such a manner that they were overshadowed by the endorsements from Stimson and Forrestal condemning them. In fact, some readers got the impression that the Army and Navy had confirmed the guilt of Kimmel and Short.[4] The majority of newsmen and radio commentators found fault with the disclosures. The Navy Department's own Office of Public Information found unfavorable reaction from 64 per cent of the editorials, 54 per cent of the columnists, and 68 per cent of the radio commentators. The *Kiplinger Washington Letter* called it a cover-up. "These high-ups are now sitting in judgment on their own acts. They are ducking all blame, and applying the whitewash to each other, and tell partial truths. This may be natural but it is not honest. . . ."

Political commentator Gabriel Heatter's instant reaction over the Mutual Broadcasting System was typical of those defending both the Roosevelt and Truman administrations. "If anybody were to ask tonight who stands with complete confidence behind General George C. Marshall, I would reply: Put me down . . . with tens of millions of other Americans."

Truman did nothing to stem the tide of dissatisfaction at his press conference the next day. From the opening he was bombarded with pointed questions: Why had the reports been put out on the day American troops entered Japan? Were they a whitewash as some charged? Was he ordering courts-martial for Kimmel or Short? Why had communications broken down between Washington and

[4] When one of the members of the Army Board, General Russell, read the first dispatches from Washington he was disgusted. "As the stories were 'rigged' in Washington little was said in the press about the Board's findings. The criticisms of those findings were featured. In a small way the President and the Secretary of War defended Mr. Hull, who was criticised very mildly in our report, but Marshall was the one to whose rescue they went in a big way. Poor old Stark, whose derelictions were almost identical with Marshall's, was completely forgotten. In fact, the findings of the Navy Board, which resulted in driving him from all responsible official duties, were actually approved. How strange it is that conduct which virtually eliminated Stark from the Navy—was described by the President and Secretary of War as the exemplification of great skill, energy, and efficiency on the part of Marshall."

Hawaii? To this last question he gave an answer that would only generate more suspicion. "I came to the conclusion that the whole thing is the result of the policy which the country itself pursued. The country was not ready for preparedness. . . . I think the country is as much to blame as any individual in this final situation that developed in Pearl Harbor."

This statement was received with widespread indignation, typified by that expressed by the Nashville *Banner:* "The attempt to place the blame on the American people is a national insult." But what promised to be the most devastating result of the reports was the demeaning of George Marshall. "There is no getting away from the fact that the public reputation of General Marshall has been smirched," reported an Office of War Information press summary; ". . . his name has been bracketed with Kimmel and Short, the two men whom *[sic]* the American public has long been led to believe were primarily responsible for the Pearl Harbor tragedy." There were rumors throughout Washington that Marshall planned to retire and demand a court-martial to clear his name. This story was branded as "poppycock" by officials but the Washington rumor mill took this as only confirmation.

In any case the demand was growing from many sources for a final and thorough investigation of Pearl Harbor. By the beginning of September it seemed likely that Congress would approve a full and impartial inquiry. On the fifth two investigation bills were introduced in the House and one in the Senate was expected the next day from Senator Ferguson. Speaker Sam Rayburn made a feeble effort to halt any congressional investigation. "I wish Congress could forget about it," he remarked wistfully, then added, with a sigh, "But I guess it can't."

It couldn't. And Majority Leader Barkley asserted that the President not only approved a full investigation but urged it. At his press conference Truman confirmed this. His only purpose, he said, was to get the truth, the whole truth and nothing but the truth.

"While the name of the late President Roosevelt was not mentioned in the debate," declared the Chicago *Tribune,* "the remarks of Barkley, Ferguson and several other senators indicated clearly an awareness that only a Congressional inquiry could be expected to fix responsibility upon Mr. Roosevelt, if the evidence brings it out.''

The Senate measure was sent to the House where prompt consideration was promised by Rayburn. Overwhelming passage was assured and the public was at last to be admitted to an open hearing of a controversy that had threatened the unity of the United States since December 7, 1941.

Part 3

CONGRESS DANCES

"IF I HAD KNOWN WHAT WAS TO HAPPEN . . . I WOULD NEVER HAVE ALLOWED MYSELF TO BE 'TAGGED'"

William D. Mitchell

NOVEMBER–DECEMBER 1945

1.

By the beginning of September a Joint Congressional Committee to investigate Pearl Harbor had been appointed, composed of five senators and five representatives, three of each being Democrats and two Republicans, thus giving the Administration about to be investigated a majority of six to four.

It also gave the majority members the choice to pick the committee counsel. They chose a nominal Democrat, William D. Mitchell, who had also served with Stimson in the Hoover Cabinet and shared many of his beliefs. A lawyer from New York, he was seventy-one and held the conviction that Army and Navy officers did not lie. He was serving without fee, as was his chief assistant, a young retired

New Dealer, Gerhard A. Gesell, at that time a $35,000-a-year partner in the law firm of the Under Secretary of State, Dean Acheson.

John Sonnett, who had so effectively assisted Admiral Hewitt's investigation, no longer headed the influential Navy Pearl Harbor Liaison Group. He had been promoted to Assistant Attorney General of the United States and replaced by his able assistant. The Army Liaison Group included several bright young lawyers with New Deal leanings.

Such a line-up would give the Democrats a decided edge in the hearings and among some Republicans there was fear that Mitchell, a man with a prestigious record, would lean decidedly toward the majority views. From the first preliminary meeting of the committee there were sharp arguments, particularly over the release of classified material to individual members. The argument was carried to the Senate on the second of November with the senior minority member, Senator Owen Brewster of Maine, complaining that under a ruling of the majority of the committee that morning no member was to be permitted to look at records.

Brewster, an aggressive anti-New Dealer, whose voice could be heard in the farthest seat, angrily charged during the heated two-hour debate that the Democrats were blocking the probe of Pearl Harbor by this measure. "I simply ask the right to go to the chairman of the committee, tell him there are certain records and files which I should like to examine, ask him to designate a member of the counsel's staff to accompany me—I would not desire to go there alone, and be allowed to examine the records and see whether any rumors or reports I had received were correct."

The second Republican senator, Homer Ferguson, was equally irate. "It is absolutely impossible for the committee to function properly to cross-examine witnesses, if we don't have the records. The fact that files are missing and that records are missing is material to this investigation." The composition of the committee, charged Ferguson, was unfair. Every controversial issue at executive session that morning had been decided by a strict vote along party lines and therefore favored the Democrats. In addition, he said, Chief Counsel Mitchell had "taken it upon himself to say what is competent and what is not competent."

The Republican imputations continued a few days later with Brewster's revelation that he had been advised by Mitchell that files of four government monitoring stations covering the critical period before Pearl Harbor were missing, and the records of one had been destroyed for lack of storage space. The following day, November 6, the two Republican representatives on the committee brought other charges to the floor of the House. Representative Bertrand Gearhart of California, an anti-New Dealer and isolationist whose chief claim to fame was advocacy of Iceland as the forty-ninth state, charged that a key message, known as the "winds" execute, was also missing; and Frank Keefe of Wisconsin declared that he was not allowed to see an important witness, a Captain Kramer, who was in the psychopathic ward at Bethesda Naval Hospital and that "whole legions of stories have arisen about the manner in which he was broken down in mind and in health." Another Republican congressman, not on the committee, added dark hints. "I'm surprised they've only locked him up. I'm surprised he hasn't been liquidated."

In the Senate the Republicans were also demanding freedom to examine the personal files of Roosevelt. This brought fire from Scott Lucas, one of the Democratic senators on the committee. A reliable New Dealer; except for one lapse in 1937 when he denounced Roosevelt's court-packing scheme, he had since consistently supported the Administration's internationalist foreign policy. "I shall never grant permission to any single member to examine these files. I cannot understand why any member of the Senate would wish to go down and look over by himself, the personal files of a former President of the United States. I simply cannot understand it—any more than I would want to look at the personal files of the Senator from Michigan."

In an effort to placate the Republicans, President Truman signed a directive on November 9 authorizing disclosure of additional information to individual members of the committee. Sam Rosenman and the Attorney General protested that this went too far, but the Republicans were not at all satisfied. Brewster said that Truman's modification "seemed to have been designed by the President's advisors with devilish ingenuity to leave the heads of executive departments in doubt as to what they are to do."

Brewster's protest was joined by one from Senator Burton Wheeler, a long-time foe of Roosevelt's interventionist policies. The gag being imposed on the Pearl Harbor investigation, he said, was unprecedented in his twenty-two years' experience in the Senate. "The Teapot Dome investigation in which I played a part, would have been a complete failure if such tactics had been permitted."

Senate Majority Leader Alben Barkley retorted next day, "Neither I as chairman nor the committee as a whole will countenance any effort to keep from the public any fact material to the inquiry. Our task, as I see it, is to lay all the facts before the public, no matter whom they hurt in high or low places, and we propose to conduct the inquiry accordingly."

William Mitchell was so upset by the rancor aroused that he wrote a close Republican friend, "It is very distressing to me to have these charges and countercharges publicly made. When I took this job I told the Committee that I wanted it understood there was to be no hush-hush stuff, and there was to be no restraint on me in getting the truth out, and they were unanimous in saying they would back me in that to the limit. I have seen no trace among the Democrats of the slightest inclination to suppress anything or to place any restraints on me. . . . It is a tough situation, and if I had known what was to happen, and that political feelings and charges of suppression were to be bandied about, before anyone had a look at what my staff can produce, I would never have allowed myself to be 'tagged.'"

A shadow of doubt was cast on the hearings and the Republican minority still had hopes that the whole truth might be extracted if they were aggressive enough. At least they would finally have the chance of cross-examining Stimson, Hull, Forrestal and other Administration leaders. The proceedings began on November 15 in a Hollywood atmosphere at the Senate Office Building's stately, bechandeliered caucus room where national scandals like Teapot Dome had seen light of day, and where the classic picture of a midget on J. P. Morgan's lap was taken. Large maps and charts hung about for the benefit of the members, their counsel and the witnesses who sat at long tables placed in T formation. In front of each man was a microphone. A hundred reporters sat at tables paralleling each side of the T. Behind crowded some four hundred onlookers, straining to see the principals, while five newsreel cameras, aided by glaring klieg lights, filmed the scene.

The proceedings began on an inauspicious note. Just as Chairman Barkley rapped for order the room went black. A fuse had blown. After a considerable wait the lights came on and Chief Counsel Mitchell began his opening remarks. Few could hear what he said since the poor loudspeaker system could not compete with the grinding of cameras and bursting of flash bulbs.

The first session featured a narrative by an admiral and a colonel of the conditions that prevailed at Pearl Harbor on December 7 and the events of that momentous day. Perhaps the most intent listeners were Admiral Kimmel and General Short, both wearing civilian clothes. They sat at a small table with their lawyers.

It was not until the second day that the spectators were treated to the first lively exchanges. To questions as to whether Washington ordered Kimmel, Short and MacArthur in the fall of 1941 "not to fire unless the Japs fired first," the Navy narrator could only reply that he did not know. Gearhart was so exasperated, he shouted, "Is the reason that they have you people up here to read hearsay testimony so you can always reply you were only sent up to say that is 'not in my province to answer'?"

Barkley, ordinarily affable, became so annoyed at Gearhart's effort to get the Navy narrator to admit there was "something strangely significant" in some orders from Washington in November 1941 that he couldn't help blurting out that Gearhart was using the hearing for a political sounding board. This remark was not recorded.

There were half a dozen other flurries and by the end of the day the Republicans were in a rebellious mood. Ferguson had requested that the committee be furnished copies of all exhibits at least ten days earlier. Yet more than a thousand pages without any index had been dumped on them in the first day. Was this deluging tactic part of a plot to prevent intelligent questioning by the minority?

At a press conference that day the Republicans charged that the investigation of the Democrats' plan was merely an attempt to whitewash the Roosevelt Administration. The Democrats retorted this was just "a sneak attack upon the grave of Franklin D. Roosevelt." Robert Hannegan, the Democratic National Committee chairman, called it a "tactic of desperation by a party without a program."

To newsmen it was apparent that the hearings were going to degenerate into a battle royal between the two parties. From their conduct thus far, wrote W. H. Lawrence in the New York *Times,* "it seems almost certain that they will remain split into Democratic and Republican blocs throughout the investigation and the result will be a majority report by the six Democrats and a minority report from the four Republicans."

The early days had proved a disappointment to the press, for it seemed as if the inquiry were degenerating into inconsequential bickering. But this changed on the nineteenth with the appearance of the first genuine witness, Admiral Richardson, Kimmel's predecessor, who had previously denounced Pearl Harbor as a "damned mousetrap" and expressed his conviction that President Roosevelt, not Kimmel and Short, was responsible for the debacle. He created a stir when he told the committee of a luncheon with Roosevelt on October 8, 1940—less than a month before the presidential election—during which the admiral had urged that the Pacific Fleet should be returned to California. The President, he said, insisted that it be retained in Hawaii "to exercise a restraining influence on the actions of Japan." Richardson argued that Japan had a military government which knew that the American fleet was undermanned and unprepared for war. So how could it exercise any restraint?

"Despite what you believe," Roosevelt had replied, "I know that the presence of the fleet in the Hawaiian area has had, and is now having a restraining influence on the actions of Japan."

"Mr. President, I still do not believe it, and I know that our fleet is disadvantageously disposed for preparing for or initiating war operations." Richardson then asked the President if they were going to war. He had replied that if the Japanese attacked Thailand, or the Kra Peninsula, or the Dutch East Indies America would not get into the war, but sooner or later the Japanese would make a mistake as the area of operations expanded "and we would enter the war."

The next morning readers of the Washington *Post* were greeted with this headline:

. . . ROOSEVELT PREDICTED JAP WAR, KEPT FLEET AROUND HAWAII AS "RESTRAINT," RICHARDSON SAYS. . . .

"I have been greatly disturbed and still am about the Pearl Harbor investigation," Eleanor Roosevelt wrote Harry Hopkins that day, "because I have a feeling that none of those people are looking after the President's interests." She was referring to her husband, not Truman. "I am sure, in the long run, it will all come out all right but you have got to remember that all of the witnesses are going to look after themselves."

2.

By this time the Republicans had gathered themselves for the attack. Although Brewster was a shrewder interrogator, Ferguson had taken over the leadership because of a keener interest in the case. He had put aside his personal and social obligations and all but the most important of his other congressional duties. His chief assistant was Percy L. Greaves, Jr. (pronounced Graves). A graduate of Syracuse in 1929 *magna cum laude,* he had been head of public relations research for the Metropolitan Life Insurance Company before becoming associate research director of the Republican National Committee in 1943. Greaves and six helpers had been retained to assist all the minority members in their efforts to ferret out the essential facts which had been withheld. The money for the operation had been raised by John T. Flynn, author and columnist. A staunch foe of Roosevelt, he had devoted his energies to the fight to keep America out of the war. Now he was equally dedicated to proving that Roosevelt and his advisers had deliberately plunged the country into war by the back door, Japan.

"Since Senator Ferguson devoted more time and effort to this investigation than any other minority member," Greaves recalled, "my work simmered down to working constantly with him while reporting to Senator Brewster and maintaining liaison with Republican Representatives Keefe and Gearhart."

Most of the members of the committee had been inundated with so much material that they relied on the testimony and what little they could read in spare moments between other congressional duties. But Ferguson had instructed his staff and secretary not to interrupt him except in cases of supreme emergency. He settled down to a routine, devoting most of his waking hours to Pearl Harbor.

He and Greaves would work together about an hour before each day's hearing opened. For every witness it was necessary to know the phases with which he was familiar, what he had previously testified and what others had testified about him or the facts with which he was familiar. The previous night Greaves would have gone over his voluminous files for such information and made special note of any conflicting testimony. Just before ten every weekday morning they walked down the corridor to the caucus room with several assistants helping Greaves lug the many documents needed for the session. Once they arrived at the committee table they were usually greeted with a new stack of documents. While Ferguson was doing the questioning, Greaves sat at his side to supply the needed documents and make suggestions, should the answers take an unexpected turn.

After morning recess they would return to Ferguson's private office where a secretary would bring them soup, sandwiches and ice cream. And as they ate they would discuss procedure for the afternoon session. Often Ferguson would telephone his wife, who was ill, and she would give the senator encouragement. Following the afternoon session the two men would return to Ferguson's office, discuss the events of the day and plan the next day's program. Greaves would then hand the senator a pile of material to be read that night and they would leave at six or seven.

On November 22 the aged and ailing Cordell Hull appeared as a witness. He brought with him a 22,000-word statement to be offered in evidence to support his contention that he had striven ceaselessly to avoid war with Japan. He did not read it since the committee had been advised by Hull's physicians that it would constitute an undue strain.

Senator Walter George of Georgia, like the other two Democratic senators on the committee, had been a reluctant convert to Roosevelt's interventionist policy but once war broke out he supported the President loyally; and it was unlikely that he would now join in the Republican criticism of a foreign policy he had grown to accept. There was no reason to read the statement, said George, since all the members had been given copies. All the Democrats concurred but Brewster said Hull's remarks were so important they should be read aloud. He also suggested that Hull return at 2 P.M. for questioning. Predictably the other Republicans voted with Brewster. At that point came the first break in party uniformity. Chairman Barkley voted with the minority.

Hull, pale and shaking from long illness, was back at 2 P.M., topcoat draped over his shoulder, and underwent forty-five minutes of considerate questioning from Gesell, Mitchell's chief assistant. In a tired voice the former Secretary revealed that he had failed to foresee any attack on Pearl Harbor and denied he had known of any U.S. pledge to defend British possessions in the Pacific until early November 1941.

The Republicans had to content themselves with having a joint memorandum from Marshall and Stark read into the record. Dated November 27, 1941, it stated that, should current negotiations with Japan end unsuccessfully, "Japan may attack the Burma Rd., Thailand, Malaya, the Philippines, the Russian maritime provinces." They saw blows at five possible spots—but not at Hawaii.

The following Monday Hull appeared for another questioning by Gesell and friendly Democrats. His answers were those of an exhausted old man until someone read an excerpt from the Army Board report describing his November 26 reply to the Japanese as an ultimatum, and concluding, "It was the document that touched the button that started the war as Ambassador [Joseph] Grew so aptly expressed it." These words infuriated Hull and he erupted. Although his voice scarcely rose, the words crackled. "If I could express myself as I would like I would want all of you religious minded people to retire!" Restraining himself from using the sulphuric language at his command, he continued, his voice tired but ominous, "I stood under that infamous charge for months, when every reasonable minded person knew that the Japs were on the same march of invasion in the Pacific area to get supreme control over it in every way so that we could not even land a boatload of goods on the other side of the Pacific except under extortionate terms—" He paused for breath, almost overcome with angry indignation. Everyone, he went on, knew the Japs were on the move of conquest. ". . . and yet, somebody who knows little and cares less, now says, 'Why didn't the United States make concessions and save us from the war,' when any person knows, and if you look back on the situation as it existed during those last 10, 12, 14 days, any rational person knows just what the Japs were doing. They were off on this final attack and no one was going to stop them unless we yielded and laid down like cowards, and we would have been cowards to have lain down." His hour was up and he walked out of the room to the accompaniment of resounding applause.

It was an exit worthy of a Barrymore and effectively prevented the frustrated minority from cross-examining a witness they still felt was officially responsible for the disastrous negotiations that led to Pearl Harbor.

Despite the absence of new revelations or dramatics, interest in the investigation remained high. A hundred reporters from newspapers throughout the country, jammed shoulder to shoulder, poured out reams of copy over the four crowded wires in the Senate Office Building. "The quality of this extravagant coverage," reported *Time*, "was something else. The painful Pearl Harbor story was confused at best. It was complicated by contradiction, by varying recollections and by bitter bouts of political swordplay." The testimony was tailored to fit old prejudices. FDR PEARL HARBOR SMEAR PLOT BLOWN SKY HIGH BY EVIDENCE was the headline in New York's *P.M.* But the Washington *Times-Herald* and many other papers regarded the first week as a war-criminal trial with Roosevelt convicted daily. "One becomes appalled and frightened at the one-man, all-out ignorance and mental arrogance of the late Franklin D. Roosevelt," wrote John O'Donnell in the New York *Daily News*. "The evidence builds up to the simple brutal fact that F.D.R., the Big Brain, through blind stupidity . . . was directly and personally responsible for the blood and disaster."

SAY HULL EDICT DECIDED JAPS TO OPEN WAR, proclaimed the New York *Journal-American*. Yet the same afternoon the New York *Post* saw it differently: JAP WAR PLANS SE1 BEFORE TALKS. And so it was throughout the nation.

Little of importance was disclosed in the next few days and Representative Gearhart charged that the Democrats on the committee were "deliberately" unfolding testimony in driblets to "hamstring a real investigation." They had already accomplished their purpose, he told reporters on December 1. "They have turned this into a judicial body without any investigative duty."

A modicum of interest was added to the proceedings three days later with the arrival in Hoboken of Tyler Kent. He had come by the British freighter *Silver Oak* after serving more than five years in prison. He brought with him a copy of his secret trial which he had placed in his suitcase. The suitcase had been carried out of the prison by an unwitting Scotland Yard agent who neglected to search its contents.

As soon as Kent left ship, he was escorted by two policemen to his mother, waiting at Pier 3. They kissed and she said, "It is so nice to see you." Then he was taken to a room crowded with more than forty reporters who began firing questions at him. Why had he taken the Roosevelt-Churchill documents? "I considered that these documents contained information which the Senate and the people of the United States should know about.'' Someone else asked if he were going to testify at the Pearl Harbor investigation. He said he would be willing but hadn't been asked. ''Not as to the Pearl Harbor phase but as regards America's entry into the war.''

He admitted he should not have taken the documents to his London flat. ''But under the special circumstances I considered I had a moral right.'' Finally he broke free from the reporters and went off, guarded by two private detectives hired by his mother. ''Where are you going?'' was the last question flung at him. ''We're just disappearing,'' said Kent.[1]

3.

There was renewed interest in the proceedings once it was announced that Marshall, recently retired as Chief of Staff, would appear before the committee in early December. On November 28 Truman bestowed on him the Oak Leaf Cluster to the Distinguished Service Medal as the man who exercised ''greater influence than any other man on the strategy of victory.'' The following day, after Patrick J. Hurley resigned as ambassador to China, the President selected Marshall as his special envoy to China with ambassadorial rank.

The Marshalls were at their home in Leesburg, Virginia. At about 2 P.M. as Mrs. Marshall was starting up the stairs for a rest the telephone rang. Marshall answered it. When she came down at three the radio was broadcasting the news that her husband would leave immediately for China. She stood rooted to the floor.

Marshall got up from a chaise longue. ''That phone call as we came in was from the President,'' he said. ''I could not bear to tell you until you had had your rest.''

---

[1] Years later this author asked Kent if he would do it all over again. Yes, he said, but this time he wouldn't be caught. ''If I had more experience, I wouldn't have gotten into that situation. I would be more circumspect and careful.'' But he would still do it because Roosevelt had to be prevented from getting America into the wrong war.

Marshall left immediately for Washington and summoned Captain Robert Diggs, a lawyer in private life, who had been assigned the responsibility of preparing the general for his testimony before the Joint Congressional Committee. For the past two months Diggs, a graduate of Hamilton and the Yale Law School, had been preparing a summary of all the evidence from previous investigations which related to matters that would have been within Marshall's knowledge. Diggs was under no time pressure, since the general was scheduled to be the last witness, and was plodding through the tedious task of documenting the summaries with copies of all the relevant orders, memoranda and correspondence.

Diggs had not heard the news about China and was astounded to learn that Marshall would have to testify in a week. This meant Diggs would not only have to rush through his preparations for Marshall but also hurriedly prepare Mitchell and Gesell, who would question the general.

Marshall told Diggs that his testimony before the committee was his "number one priority until it was completed and that I was to feel free to barge into his office anytime I wished to consult with him even though someone else might be there." They immediately began a series of sessions of several hours a day. "I would sit across his desk from him and he would read through the material I had prepared. He seldom made any comments or asked any questions, and so I had very little idea of how much he was absorbing or to what extent he agreed or disagreed with the statements in the material. I was heartened by occasional remarks that he thought I didn't have the entire story or didn't have it in proper perspective and he would give suggestions of further avenues of research."

Theirs was an unusual friendship. Diggs was treated not as a lowly captain but as the former Chief of Staff's lawyer, his equal. One day they were interrupted by a group planning the trip to China. "Instead of asking me to step out he simply joined the group at a table at the far side of his office and then rejoined me at his desk as soon as he was able to oust them."

Another morning Diggs arrived at the Pentagon a few minutes early to be told by the general's secretary that he was with the Chinese ambassador. Diggs waited in the anteroom until the ambassador left. Marshall was annoyed. "Diggs," he said tartly, "at the very beginning I told you that you were to walk in at any time, no matter who was here." It was the first time Marshall had been critical or cross with the young lawyer. "I've been trying to get rid of that boring ambassador for ten minutes or more but knew you were to come at eight-thirty and give me an excuse to get rid of him. But instead of coming in you sit across the hall waiting for him to leave."

On the day before Marshall was scheduled to appear, Gerow, now promoted to lieutenant general, was brought in to testify out of order, and he caused a mild sensation by taking all the blame for the confusing war warning sent to Short on November 27.

Was he sure, asked Mitchell, that it wasn't the responsibility of Marshall and Stimson? "It wasn't their function to follow up things like that?"

"No, sir," said the bemedaled Gerow, a hero in the Normandy landing. "I was a staff adviser to the Chief of Staff, and I had a group of 48 officers to assist me. It was my responsibility to see that these messages were checked, and if an inquiry was necessary, the War Plans Division should have drafted such an inquiry and presented it to the Chief of Staff for approval. As I said, I was chief of that division, and it was my responsibility." It was refreshing to hear someone at last taking responsibility but Gerow was, in fact, only responsible for War Plans, not for sending off confusing messages to Hawaii. And the minority only saw Gerow's admittance of malfeasance as a ploy to relieve Marshall from any part of the blame and prepare the way for the former Chief of Staff's own testimony.

Just before Marshall was scheduled to start his testimony on Tuesday morning, December 6, he asked Diggs about the format of the proceedings and what was expected of him. Diggs said that the top people of the Navy had sat at a table with two or three assistants at their sides whom they would consult, sometimes at considerable length, before answering questions. "I said that I felt this created an unfavorable impression and that I thought he should sit there alone and give his own answers to the questions, pointing out that he could always say that he didn't recall as to any particular question but would be glad to furnish later on whatever additional information was requested. He agreed emphatically.''

As Chairman Barkley called the committee to order, Marshall was sitting alone, in the brilliance of klieg lights, an impressive and reassuring figure. Diggs was a mere spectator in the back of the room. ''Naturally I had a great deal of trepidation concerning his performance, having very little idea as to how he might fare.'' Marshall began his testimony, unperturbed and at ease. He answered all of Chief Counsel Mitchell's questions briskly and with authority.

''It was thrilling to me,'' recalled Diggs, ''to hear his complete command of every question put to him—reflecting not only total absorption of all the materials prepared for him but also his own perspective and grasp of the bigger underlying factors. I felt that his performance was masterful and my reaction was being proud of him not of myself.''

Although Marshall had confided to Diggs that he felt Short and Kimmel ''had let Washington down terribly,'' he was careful not to criticize either of them openly. When Mitchell asked a question about which he was uncertain he would reply, as he had before the Army Board, ''I do not recall.'' Did he know that a week prior to Pearl Harbor the Navy had lost complete track of the Japanese carriers? ''I have a faint recollection that I did not know all the time where all the Japanese ships were. I do not recall being aware of the fact that it was the carrier divisions that were the missing ones. It may be I knew it, but I do not recall.'' Nor could he recall at Friday's session where he was on the night of December 6. ''The only definite thing I have is that I had no dinner engagement.'' His wife's engagement book showed there was nothing for that night. ''Also they checked on the post movie. It was about our only recourse for relaxation, and I had never seen the picture. So I was not there. We were not calling. We were leading a rather monastic life.''

''You are sure you were not at the White House that evening?'' asked Mitchell.

"No, sir; not at all," he said, which could mean he might have been or he might not have been.

After Mitchell finished, the Democrats took over with friendly, respectful questioning. In midafternoon Barkley wondered if they could conclude the testimony the next day. What were the general's plans to leave for China? "All I can do, sir, is have a plane in readiness as soon as you release me."

"So your plans are to go forward at once as soon as we are completed?" said Barkley.

"Yes, sir."

The minority members were unhappy with what appeared to be an attempt to rush Marshall through the committee before they had time to interrogate him fully but they did get their chance the next morning. Their first interrogator, Senator Brewster, had been called out of town because of the sudden death of his father and Ferguson took over. Fortunately he had devised, with the help of Greaves, what he called a "blue plan" for questioning the general. He had it typed into a loose-leaf binder with a full set of questions on each phase of Marshall's involvement in the case. He did not mean to let him go until every single question was answered.

By the end of what must have been a most trying time for Marshall, Ferguson had succeeded in getting him to admit these damaging facts:

1. That Gerow was in charge of war plans and had no authority over Short; and therefore could not take the blame for the confusing messages to Hawaii. Moreover, Gerow had no responsibility for sending or not sending a proper alert to Short.

2. That Marshall, as Chief of Staff, was the only Army officer with authority over Short; and was therefore the only one responsible for not properly alerting Short.

3. That there was no responsible Army officer on duty on the night of December 6, or Sunday morning, who could take action before Marshall's arrival after his long horseback ride. Therefore the Army was not on full alert even though it was known the situation was critical.

4. That Marshall had appointed General Miles as head

of Army Intelligence, although aware he did not have proper qualifications.

5. That Marshall knew the British were privy to the Purple code before Pearl Harbor, and that "we have been trying to keep that quiet as much as we could."

6. That Marshall did not know why Kimmel had not been getting the information from the Purple and other codes.

7. That before the Roberts report "was made public there were certain things withdrawn and the complete Roberts Report went to the President before portions were withdrawn."

8. That the United States initiated the Anglo-Dutch-American agreements which called for unified action against the Japanese; that Marshall, Stimson and Knox had approved them; and that the agreements had gone into effect before the attack.

9. That officers of the United States, the Flying Tigers, were furnished to China for combat duty against Japan before Pearl Harbor.

At last Ferguson's relentless grilling, which visibly annoyed the Democrats, was ended for the day. The Vice Chairman, Representative Jere Cooper, a strong party man used as a Democratic trouble-shooter in the House, had said so little thus far that he was nicknamed "The Sphinx" by reporters. Now he asked if he could inquire something of General Marshall. "I understand he stated yesterday his plane was waiting to take him to his duties in China."

"It will have to continue to wait," said Marshall equably. "I am to be at your disposal until you have finished."

"Under these circumstances," said Barkley, "the committee will recess until ten o'clock Monday morning."

Ferguson resumed his bulldog tactics on the tenth, unperturbed by majority attempts to deride and discredit his interrogation. He was also back on Tuesday, "blue plan" in hand. Finally, late in the day, Marshall was excused to see the President but not before Ferguson gave warning that the Republicans were by no means through with him.

In the remaining time, General Miles was recalled. Described in *Time* as "balding, bumbling," he admitted he had read the thirteen points on the night of December 6 and later said he did not believe "it was necessary to arouse the Chief of Staff at that time of night for that message."

Ferguson ordinarily was at the extreme right end of the long table, but in Brewster's absence he moved one chair to the left. Greaves, who hitherto had sat at the head of the table, had moved over into Ferguson's original seat. During the Miles interrogation, Greaves smiled at something Senator Lucas said.

Lucas, aware that Greaves had been prompting the Republican senators, flared up, protesting that the gentleman sitting to the right of Ferguson was ridiculing him. "I would like to know who the gentleman is and what right he has to sit alongside of the committee table and chuckle at a member of the United States Senate. . . . I do not propose to sit around this table and permit some individual that I do not know anything about, who is constantly in this case and constantly reminding Senators of the type and kind of questions they should ask, to give a hearty chuckle to something I might suggest in connection with this hearing. I think it is about time that the committee find out just who he is and what his business is."

Ferguson said Greaves was in charge of Senator Brewster's Pearl Harbor files. Lucas wanted to know where Greaves had worked before that. "Was he the Republican National Committee research man in the campaign of 1944? Let him answer that."

Greaves replied that he was; and Barkley wondered who was compensating him for the services being rendered to Brewster and Ferguson.

"He is not rendering any services to me," said Ferguson.

"Not much!" said Lucas sarcastically.

Ferguson insisted he could not say who was paying Greaves but Senator Brewster surely could as soon as he returned from his father's funeral.

But Lucas had the last word: "Mr. Chairman, I do not

appreciate the gratuitous insults that have been made a couple of times by this gentleman, and I do not propose to take it much longer.''

After adjournment Greaves was surrounded by reporters and photographers. He said that anyone who wanted to know the whys and wherefores of his salary would have to ask Brewster, who would not be back until Friday. Lucas also had the last word with the press. ''It seems strange to me that a man so recently and so closely identified with the Republican National Committee should be sitting here, doing all the research work for two Republican Senators— especially when they so loudly claim that they want politics kept out of it.'' He promised the reporters that he was going to find out ''who's paying for Mr. Greaves, how much, and who's responsible for moving a prominent Republican into a non-partisan hearing.''

The next morning Greaves was back at the caucus room, this time sitting in his usual place at the head of but not behind the committee table. It was Keefe's turn to question Marshall. The Wisconsin representative was a big, imposing man. At the University of Michigan he had been president of the Glee Club and his clear, baritone voice dominated the room. Famed as a trial lawyer, it was said he could hypnotize juries with his logic and eloquence.

At first he was smiling and affable but soon he assumed the role of district attorney, which he had once been. Somewhat flustered, Marshall excused his lapses of memory. Things were being brought up ''that have been, to a large extent, rubbed out by 4 years of global war. I have not investigated these things to refresh my memory until the past few days. . . .''

At the afternoon session Keefe, with punctilious courtesy, quizzed Marshall on the ambiguous warning to Short on November 27. Should not he, as Chief of Staff, have investigated further and given further orders to General Short once it appeared that he was only alerted against sabotage?

''As I stated earlier, that was my opportunity to intervene and I did not do it.''

"Well, now, you say that was your *opportunity*," said Keefe pointedly. "That was your *responsibility*, was it not?"

"You can put it that way, sir."

"Well, *I* don't want to put it that way. I am asking *you*. You used the words, 'that was your opportunity.'"

Hiding any resentment he might have felt, Marshall again made an excuse. "Mr. Keefe," he said, "I had an immense number of papers going over my desk every day informing me what was happening anywhere in the world. . . . I noted them and initialed them; those that I thought the Secretary of War ought specifically to see I put them out for him to see, to be sure that he would see it in case he by any chance did not see the same message." He quickly added, "I was not passing the responsibility on to the Secretary of War. I merely wanted him to know. Now the same thing related to these orders of the War Department. I was responsible." He repeated that he had full responsibility in the matter, but General Gerow had "a *direct* responsibility."

"Well, now, then," said Keefe, "the fact remains that on this most important matter . . . when you and everybody else in the exercise of ordinary care must have known that war with Japan was imminent and that they might strike any time or any place, as you have said, and yet this important message comes back from Short and through some misadventure or dereliction some place no further message went to General Short or no further investigation was made." Short, sitting only a few feet away, must have been as impressed by Keefe's line of questioning as were Kimmel's attorneys, Rugg, Lavender and Hanify.

Keefe was not finished and minutes later abruptly asked Marshall if it was fair to conclude from his testimony that he fixed the responsibility for the Pearl Harbor tragedy on General Short so far as the Army was concerned.

"I have never made that statement, sir. I feel that General Short was given a command instruction to put his command on the alert against a possible attack by the Japanese. The command was not so alerted."

"Well, I will ask the same question, from a full and

INFAMY

Roosevelt addresses Congress: "Yesterday, December 7, 1941–a date which will live in infamy–the United States of America was suddenly and deliberately attacked..." *(National Archives)*

THE CONTROVERSY: A PHOTOGRAPHIC RECORD

The Roosevelts' Christmas card to friends. *(Rear Admiral Lester Robert Schulz*

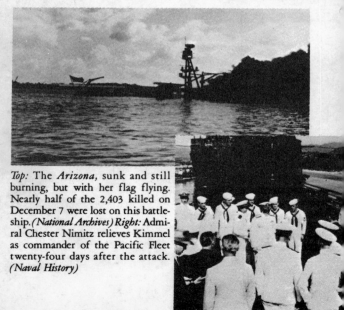

Top: The *Arizona,* sunk and still burning, but with her flag flying. Nearly half of the 2,403 killed on December 7 were lost on this battleship. *(National Archives) Right:* Admiral Chester Nimitz relieves Kimmel as commander of the Pacific Fleet twenty-four days after the attack. *(Naval History)*

eft: Knox visits the new com-
mander at Pearl Harbor. *(Naval
History) Right:* Rear Admiral Rich-
mond Kelly Turner, brilliant Chief of
War Plans, nicknamed "Terrible
Turner," for his temper. He refused

the request of Captain Alan Kirk
to send warning of possible attack
on Pearl Harbor to Kimmel. Kirk
was "detached" from his position as
head of Navy Intelligence. *(National
Archives)*

The Navy Building on Constitution Avenue, Washington, D.C. Here, on the
second floor, took place the "mutiny" of October 1941.

Top left: Rear Admiral Theodore "Ping" Wilkinson, Kirk's replacement, was also bullied by Turner. This picture was taken in Japanese waters on September 21, 1945. He met a tragic death soon after testifying at the congressional investigation of Pearl Harbor when his car plunged off a ferry. *(National Archives) Top right:* Commander (later Captain) Laurance Safford, one of the subordinates on the second deck who persisted in trying to send warnings of Pearl Harbor to Kimmel. A talented cryptoanalyst, he later risked his reputation and career to prove that Kimmel was innocent of responsibility for the Pearl Harbor debacle. *(Commander Charles C. Hiles) Bottom left:* Rear Admiral Leigh Noyes, Chief of Naval Communications, also feuded with Turner. *(National Archives) Bottom right:* Commander Charles C. Hiles, one of Safford's closest postwar friends and confidants. Their voluminous correspondence, available at the Archive of Contemporary History, University of Wyoming, is an invaluable source for researchers. *(Mrs. Charles C. Hiles)*

William Friedman, a close friend of Safford's and leader of the talented team of codebreakers that solved the Japanese Purple Code. *(George C. Marshall Research Foundation)*

The machine constructed to break the Purple Code. *(National Archives)*

The Roberts Commission placed the burden of blame for Pearl Harbor on Kimmel and Short. *Left to right:* Major General Frank McCoy, Admiral William Standley, Associate Supreme Court Justice Owen J. Roberts, Rear Admiral Joseph Reeves, and Brigadier General Joseph McNarney. Standley, the highest-ranking officer on the commission, later felt he had been grossly betrayed by Roberts and called his performance as head of the commission "as crooked as a snake." *(Wide World)*

Kimmel selected retired Navy Captain Robert Lavender as assistant defense counsel in his efforts to clear himself. Lavender, second from the left, is shown as a member of the crew of one of three Navy planes involved in the historic transatlantic flight of 1919. *(Naval History)*

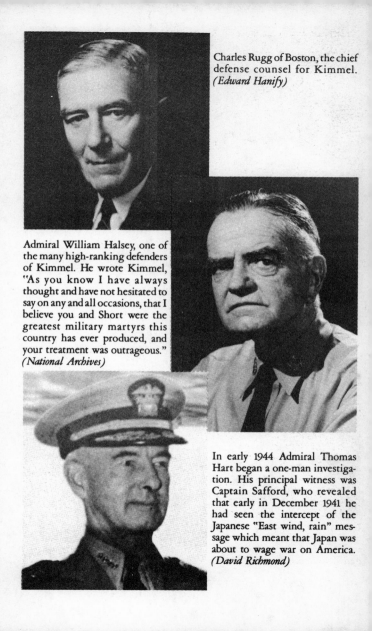

Charles Rugg of Boston, the chief defense counsel for Kimmel. (*Edward Hanify*)

Admiral William Halsey, one of the many high-ranking defenders of Kimmel. He wrote Kimmel, "As you know I have always thought and have not hesitated to say on any and all occasions, that I believe you and Short were the greatest military martyrs this country has ever produced, and your treatment was outrageous." (*National Archives*)

In early 1944 Admiral Thomas Hart began a one-man investigation. His principal witness was Captain Safford, who revealed that early in December 1941 he had seen the intercept of the Japanese "East wind, rain" message which meant that Japan was about to wage war on America. (*David Richmond*)

That July the three members of the Navy Inquiry are sworn in. *Left to right:* Vice Admiral Adolphus Andrews, Admiral Orin Murfin, and Admiral Edward Kalbfus. When they learned to their amazement and indignation that Kimmel had been deprived of vital information they reversed the Roberts findings and exonerated Kimmel. *(David Richmond)*

Members of the Navy Inquiry talk with Admiral Nimitz (back to camera) at Pearl Harbor. *(David Richmond)*

The Army Pearl Harbor Board was simultaneously convening. The members were equally appalled by similar evidence. Moreover, two of General Marshall's closest subordinates, Colonel (later General) Bedell Smith *(left)* and Brigadier General Leonard Gerow *(right)* were involved in controversial testimony. Consequently the Army Board also reversed the Roberts findings, placing much more blame on Marshall than on Short. *(National Archives)*

James Forrestal, successor to Knox as Secretary of the Navy, put an endorsement on the Navy Inquiry report repudiating its findings. Secretary of War Stimson did the same to the Army's report. *(National Archives)*

Tyler Kent, *right,* in Russia prior to transfer to London as a code officer in the American Embassy. He was imprisoned by the British in 1940 for possession of secret Roosevelt-Churchill messages. *(Tyler Kent)*

Mrs. Anne Kent worked tirelessly to free her son. The revelation that he was still in a British prison caused a stir during Roosevelt's campaign for the presidency in 1944. *(Tyler Kent)*

Vice-President Harry S. Truman entered the campaign controversy by implying that Short and Kimmel were not on speaking terms prior to the attack; he made the false statement that at no time did "Admiral Kimmel ask or receive information as to the manner in which the Army was discharging its highly important duty." Kimmel wrote Truman for a correction of the misstatements but never received a reply. *(National Archives)*

In a special investigation conducted by Vice Admiral Henry Hewitt, Captain Safford charged that he was pressed to repudiate his previous testimony about the "East wind, rain" message. Captain Alwin Kramer, who had supported Safford in the Navy Inquiry, did reverse his testimony. *(Naval History)*

Marshall testifying on December 6, 1945. The table for the congressional committee is perpendicular to Marshall. Percy Greaves *(extreme left)*, chief researcher for the Republicans, leans over to confer with Senator Homer Ferguson. Next to Ferguson, almost obscured, is the other Republican senator on the committee, Owen Brewster. *(Wide World)*

Rear view. Behind Marshall are General Short's counsel (hand to face), the general, and Counselor Rugg. *Extreme right center,* Admiral Kimmel leans back. Both Short and Kimmel show their disbelief of Marshall's testimony. *(Wide World)*

Left: Republican Congressman Frank Keefe chats amiably with Marshall, but moments later his aggressive cross-examination puts the general on the defensive. *(National Archives) Right:* Marshall insists he cannot remember where he was on the night before Pearl Harbor. Investigators failed to check the December 7, 1941, issue of the Washington *(Times-Herald).*

Percy Greaves with Senator Ferguson *(left)* and Senator Brewster *(right).* Greaves causes a tempest in a teapot on December 10 by smiling at something Democratic Senator Scott Lucas says. "I would like to know who the gentleman is," storms Lucas, "and what right he has to sit alongside of the committee table and chuckle at a member of the United States Senate." *(Wide World)*

At last, in early January 1946, General Short, weakened by illness, has his day in court. As he tells how his old friend of thirty-nine years, George Marshall, advised him "to stand pat," tears come to Short's eyes. "I told him I would place myself entirely in his hands, having faith in his judgment." Until mid-1944 Short had regarded Marshall as his friend. Then Kimmel told him about the intercepted messages. "Short, Marshall is your enemy. Haven't you found that out yet? He is doing everything he can to double-cross you and has been right from the very beginning." *(National Archives)*

Chief Warrant Officer Ralph T. Briggs with his wife and her Seeing Eye dog. He told Captain Safford he had received the controversial "East wind, rain" message a few days before the attack. Briggs offered to testify at the hearings but was forbidden to do so by his commanding officer, who told him, "Maybe someday you'll understand the reason for this."

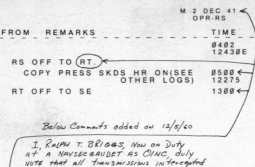

```
                                    M 2 DEC 41
                                    OPR-RS

    FROM   REMARKS                          TIME
                                            0402
                                            12430E
       RS OFF TO (RT.)
       COPY PRESS SKDS HR ON(SEE           0500
                        OTHER LOGS)         12275
       RT OFF TO SE                         1300
```

Below Comments added on 12/5/60

I, RALPH T. BRIGGS, NOW ON DUTY
AT A NAVSECGAUDET AS OINC, duly
NOTE that all transmissions intercepted
by me between 0500 thru 1300 on
the above date are missing from these files &
that these intercepts contained the
"Winds message warning code. My operation
sign was RT"

RT

In 1960 Briggs, then officer in charge of all U.S. Navy World War II communications intelligence and cryptic archives, found what he believed to be his log sheet of the "East wind, rain" message. He felt he had no right to make a copy, but did write his comments on the bottom. At the request of the author, the classified Briggs material was released by the U.S. Navy.

Safford swears that his superiors ordered him to destroy all the notes he had made of the circumstances concerning the "East wind, rain" message *(left)*. Other sensational revelations by Safford bring forth a savage, relentless cross-examination by Democratic Congressman John W. Murphy *(right)*. "We haven't touched the real meat of this," the triumphant Murphy tells reporters after the session. "There's real, genuine tenderloin in it." The next day he continues his attack until Republican Keefe protests so eloquently that the onlookers spontaneously applaud. They do so twice until rebuked by the chairman. *(Wide World)*

Safford chats with his friend Captain Kramer just before the latter testifies that there was no "East wind, rain" message. *(Wide World)*

Left: Former Lieutenant Colonel Henry C. Clausen testifies that he had been "as free as the wind" in his one-man investigation for Stimson. He also denies charges that he had brow-beaten witnesses, including Colonel Rufus Bratton, into changing their testimony. *Wide World. Right:* Colonel "Togo" Bratton admits he was not brow-beaten by Clausen–and then reveals new testimony damaging his former chief, General Marshall. *(Wide World)*

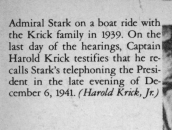

Admiral Stark on a boat ride with the Krick family in 1939. On the last day of the hearings, Captain Harold Krick testifies that he recalls Stark's telephoning the President in the late evening of December 6, 1941. *(Harold Krick, Jr.)*

Commander Lester Robert Schulz —pictured with his wife and child when he was communications assistant to Roosevelt's naval aide in 1941—causes a sensation on February 15 by revealing that on Pearl Harbor eve he had delivered an intercepted Japanese message to Roosevelt that caused him to say, "This means war." *(Rear Admiral Schulz)*

Republican Congressman Bertrand Gearhart causes consternation among the Republicans when he signs the Democratic findings. He did so, according to Washington gossip, to save his seat in Congress that November. *(Wide World)* complete knowledge of the situation and the responsibility involved, do you assume any responsibility for this disaster at Pearl Harbor?''

He would only assume responsibility in not detecting that Short's reply ''did not indicate a full alert.''

Marshall's ordeal ended the next day but not before Gearhart, taking over from Keefe, asked why Japanese intercepts, particularly those between Honolulu and Tokyo, had not been sent to Short and Kimmel. ''Don't you think the specific inquiry from Tokyo in reference to ship movements in Honolulu and Pearl Harbor was sufficiently important to convey to the commanders in Hawaii?''

He replied that ''a great many messages about a great many places'' were coming in and that if he had the final responsibility of reading all of the Magic messages, ''I would have ceased to be Chief of Staff in practically every other respect, so that that was an absolutely impractical proposition.''

By 12:45 P.M. the Republicans had finished with Marshall and he was free to leave for China. Chairman Barkley thanked him for his patient cooperation and wished him, on behalf of the committee, as high a degree of success in his new mission as he had had in other fields. An adept master of ceremonies, Barkley ended with a joke. ''The Chair would like to say personally that if after you get to China, you discover that you cannot successfully cultivate your Leesburg farm from Chungking and need a good farmhand, the Chairman of the committee feels that by spring he will be available.'' For once the caucus room was united—everyone laughed.

The majority and the legal staff all felt that Marshall's testimony had been convincing. ''Totally honest,'' was Gesell's conclusion. ''I felt that his performance was masterful,'' recalled Diggs, ''and my reaction was being proud of him not myself.'' But many Republicans, and practically all isolationists, were convinced he had lied.[2]

---

[2] According to Percy Greaves, Ferguson told Greaves and Brewster before one of the sessions that the previous night he had overheard Marshall remarking to Barkley in the men's room at a social affair that he could not say where he was on the night of December 6 because it might get ''the Chief'' in trouble. Ferguson took ''the Chief'' to mean Roosevelt.

"The General left a sorry impression on those who heard him," reported John T. Flynn in the New York *Journal-American.* "One left on me was that he revealed a surprising readiness to blame his subordinates."

Marshall himself must have been greatly relieved to leave the caucus room where, he later complained to a friend, he had to "sit and take it."

By the end of the afternoon session Chief Counsel Mitchell was in a glum mood. He called Barkley into his office to announce that he and his staff were resigning. They had been promised that the proceedings would be over in a month yet the end was far from in sight. Barkley urged Mitchell to reconsider, to at least sleep on the matter.

The next morning, December 14, Mitchell announced to the committee his decision to quit. Only eight witnesses had been examined after a month of sittings and there remained at least sixty more. Therefore he and his staff would have to be replaced since they had taken on the assignment with the understanding that the final report of the committee would be made not later than January 3, 1946. He complained that "extensive examination by some members of the committee" had gone "far beyond" what he had anticipated. And so he and his staff felt they could not see the job through to the end. "This outcome is a source of deep concern and regret to me and to the other members of my staff. I did not want the place as counsel, but under the circumstances I felt I could not refuse it." He and his staff had worked days, nights and Sundays for two and a half months, and had produced much pertinent information never before introduced by other inquiries. "We are all depressed that because of the course of the proceedings we have not been able to present it." He didn't say so but it was his quarrels with the Republicans which had forced his decision. He regarded them as obstructionists who were only playing politics, while they felt Mitchell was openly partisan to the Democrats on all important issues.

Barkley praised Mitchell and his staff and deeply regretted their decision. He himself was thinking of quitting. "I must, in my own mind, decide whether I have any further duty in regard to this investigation, and whether, if I have any duty, it outweighs my duty on the floor of the Senate in the capacity in which I have been chosen by that body, and in which I have served for more than 8 years."

Senator George added his criticism of the extended examinations by the Republicans. "Of course, I recognize the right of all members of the committee to cross-examine witnesses at any length, but I have wondered whether or not we were confusing the issue rather than arriving at any answer in which the public could have any confidence."

Mitchell did agree to stay on until early January, and business resumed with more testimony of General Gerow. Despite the tension of the morning, by afternoon both Mitchell and Barkley were in a joking mood. In discussing how safe a fortress was from attack, Mitchell noted that Fort Ticonderoga was one of the strongest British fortresses in the Revolution. "The Commander, as I remember it, was caught in bed. . . . I think he even had his trousers in his hand."

"Was he about to put them on, or take them off?" asked Barkley to the delight of the spectators.

Reaction to Mitchell's resignation depended on which newspaper was read. Pro-Administration journals denounced the minority members of the committee for unnecessarily delaying the proceedings for political gain. But opposition papers like the Cedar Rapids *Gazette* took another view. "Who in the world ever made a deal with Mitchell and his staff that the hearings wouldn't last beyond January 3? What kind of investigation did whoever made that agreement think this was going to be anyhow? An investigation of this kind is vital to America and it should be given all the time necessary to do the job right if it takes five years."

William S. White, in the New York *Times*, revealed that Mitchell's decision was not wholly unexpected by those associated with him.

What was indicated in his statement was much more evident in his manner for at least two weeks.

This was his growing impatience with committee

examinations which left counsel with little more to do than to obtain data and hand up exhibits, and his hardly repressed anger at many pointed questions from the Republican side suggested that he had perhaps not brought out all that was material on this or that point.

His exchanges, especially with Senator Ferguson, Republican of Michigan, were edged since the first week of the hearing.

4.

The following Monday Brewster explained to the committee that Greaves worked for him and had had no connection with the Republican National Committee for many months. Then he read a letter from Greaves stating that "there never was any intention on my part to insult or reflect on any members of the United States Senate by thought, word or action. . . . I am sure that the Senator from Illinois misconstrued an unconscious and which I thought was a silent smile that went unnoticed by anyone else."

Not at all appeased, Lucas said he was going to find out more about Greaves in executive session. "I think this committee is entitled to know who every individual is, what his background is, what his motives and purposes are, how much he is being paid, and by whom."[3]

Brewster retorted with a threat that if there was going to be an investigation of Greaves there could also be one "of the associations and connections of those more actively identified with the committee, but I am sure we will be embarking on something that will carry us a rather long way."

"Yes," said Lucas. The two were like fighting cocks.

"There are a good many things that have occurred which have not impressed the minority. They are matters

[3] Later Democratic Representative Clark, who had been relatively quiet during the sessions, put an arm around Greaves's shoulder. "If you ever need a counsel," he said affably, "let me know."

of record. If we are going to start on that we will make a complete job of it.''

What threatened to be a storm only turned into a tempest in a teapot. It was agreed that Greaves could stay but never again sit behind the committee table. Barkley left the caucus room shortly after the noon recess. He had a fever, he said, and his doctor had ordered him to bed. He called off the executive session that was to have been held later that afternoon. He hoped to be back next day. But instead of going home Barkley went to the White House. After a conference with Truman he told reporters he had not yet made up his mind whether he'd resign as chairman.

The following morning, the eighteenth, Admiral Wilkinson caused consternation among the majority by revealing that there had been an intercepted German message informing the Japanese that the Americans could have broken some of their codes. ''Several messages that were sent from Japan indicated that they wished their agents to be particularly careful in their reports to protect the code.'' Greaves watched to see how Mitchell would react. A month earlier Ferguson had asked the chief counsel for any information indicating that the Japanese knew the United States had broken their code. Mitchell had replied a day later in the negative.

Brewster now asked whether counsel had located these messages. Gesell, answering for Mitchell, said they had not. Whereupon Brewster turned on Mitchell like a district attorney. ''Well, I have a letter from Mr. Mitchell saying there was no evidence that the Japanese had any knowledge that we were breaking their codes or suspected it, and that the evidence was all to the contrary. Do you recall that letter, Mr. Mitchell?''

''Yes,'' said Mitchell. ''That is based on a report from the department of whom we made inquiry.'' He had forwarded the negative report to the minority.

Brewster held up a paper. It was an intercepted message from Tokyo to Mexico. He read it: ''. . . American surveillance will unquestionably be vigilant. There are also some suspicions that they read some of our codes.''

Mitchell paled and Greaves thought he was going to faint.

"Now that," continued Brewster, "of course, is squarely in conflict with the report which apparently the Navy Department gave you, is it not, indicating that at least the Japanese suspected that we were breaking their code?"

Mitchell was flustered. "I assume the Navy kept right on cracking them, so we can assume the Japs did not know that. I suppose that is why they made that statement. Obviously that one message contains a suspicion that we might be."

Brewster's voice was sharp. "Now the intercepts run from July 1 to December 7 and I asked some time ago for the earlier intercepts, after I was refused permission to examine the files, as I was reliably informed that there were five cablegrams which made very specific reference to this matter of which the admiral now speaks, that the Germans had apparently discovered something of this kind. . . . I say I am at least surprised that the Navy would give you the information that there was nothing to indicate this, if there are four or five messages of this character in their files." After Mitchell asked exactly what information Brewster was really looking for, the Republican said that was obvious: he wanted all messages indicating the Japs suspected their codes were broken. Why, he repeated, had Mitchell given him a negative report to his request for information?

The harried chief counsel replied that he had merely transmitted the report the Navy had given him. "I never asked them what their evidence was, but I assumed it was a fact because we kept on breaking the code, indicating that the Japs were not aware of it."

Brewster repeated what Admiral Wilkinson had just testified about the warning tip from Berlin to Tokyo. "I think it is unfortunate that the Navy should have given you a report of this character, if what Admiral Wilkinson says now is correct."

At last a majority member came to Mitchell's aid. "This is two or three times that the statement is in the record," protested Representative John W. Murphy of Pennsylvania. The eleventh of twelve children, he was an aggressive Irishman who relished combat.

Brewster raised his voice. "I can quite understand the concern of the gentleman over anything which seems in any way to be in conflict here, but I think it is a rather important point, on which great emphasis has been laid, and I would like to know whether or not these messages exist. . . . I have been trying for more than a month to get them. I spoke to counsel about this in executive session ten days ago, and now I am advised that they would like to know just what it is I am after."

"You are using that microphone rather loudly," chided Murphy. "This is three times that that statement is in the record now."

Vice Chairman Cooper, taking over for the ailing Barkley, tried to bring order. "I think counsel understands, Senator. I am sure they will continue to cooperate in every way possible."

Brewster was ready to resume the questioning of Wilkinson but Ferguson entered the fray. He produced the memorandum that Mitchell had written to him stating that there was "no information or indication" that Japan ever knew their code had been broken.

Mitchell looked his age but now he was angry. He could not see the significance of the matter. Why were they making such a fuss? "I am probably dumb about it, but I do not grasp it. . . ."

"I should be very happy to give you what is in my apparent simple mentality," boomed the senator from Maine. First, if Admiral Wilkinson was correct, the Navy had not been giving the chief counsel complete or accurate information. Secondly, when Marshall was examined regarding the Dewey matter, great importance was attached to the fact that Magic was a great state secret and the Japanese had no suspicion their codes were being broken. "I cannot understand why the Navy will tell you there was nothing to indicate it. If it is not of any importance, why do not they simply give us the facts and the messages, and if it is of importance, and there is any suggestion of concealment, that is something we must take into account." A third point Brewster could have added, but left unspoken, was the lively suspicion that the Navy had held back or destroyed other messages on even more important issues.

Murphy cut in to say that yesterday twenty minutes were spent "on tirades" concerning Percy Greaves, "and now we have spent 20 minutes in trying counsel, talking about the Dewey episode. I suggest we talk about Pearl Harbor. . . ."

But Keefe had complaints of his own about the delivery of requested material. He himself had made at least twenty-five requests and only two or three had been complied with. And now a month had passed on the information Ferguson asked about code breaking. "We cannot help but wonder as to what is the cause of this great delay. This has caused me great exasperation and I can only say we have been receiving spoon-fed evidence."

By the end of the day Mitchell was in such a pitiable state that his wife approached Mrs. Brewster to ask if the minority senators might be a little easier on him because of his health.

In the morning the chief counsel opened the session with an embarrassing apology. "Now, yesterday I made the mistake, without checking up on the fact, of saying or thinking that I had submitted that request to the Navy or the Army, and they had reported and it was on the basis of their report that I made that statement, and as a result of that there were some imputations made on the good faith of the Army and Navy in not producing what we asked for." His voice was weak in his humiliation. "I want to say that imputation is not justified because I now find I never did ask for that material. . . . I am quite willing to be open to criticism for not following it up, although at that time we were pretty busy getting started, and possibly I might be forgiven for that."

"I am sure we all recognize that," said Vice Chairman Cooper sympathetically. Nor were there any sharp remarks from the minority, thanks either to the good offices of Mrs. Brewster or sheer pity. Mitchell then read in the record eleven messages Admiral Wilkinson had unearthed from the files proving beyond any doubt that the Japanese indeed feared America had broken their codes.

After Wilkinson was dismissed, Admiral Turner was called, and it was remarkable that he walked into the room without a tremor. He had been a house guest of his former

aide, Captain William Mott, who had been desperately trying to sober up Turner for the hearings. After the Battle of
Savo Island his drinking problem had degenerated into al-
coholism. During the Battle of Okinawa he was drinking
straight alcohol mixed with grape juice. He would send
out for quantities to sick bay "for my foot," and would
become so drunk that Mott often could not wake him during a kamakaze raid. To Mott, Turner was the brightest
and most forceful admiral in the Navy and he had protected him for months. But the matter became so serious
he finally reported it to the fleet surgeon. Turner was relieved. On the trip back to Guam, he drank nothing but
orange juice. Arriving sober, he managed to convince
Nimitz there was nothing wrong with him and that he
should be task force commander for the invasion of Japan.

He exhibited the same recuperative powers at the hearings. Although some of his testimony was mixed up, no
one realized what his condition had been the day before.
On Thursday, December 20, he repudiated the testimony
he had given before the Navy Inquiry: that Admiral Noyes
had reported to him a "winds" execute had been received;
and that this meant a break in relations or more probably
war between Japan and the United States. Now he testified
that Noyes telephoned him on December 5 to say that the
first weather message had come in and it read "North
wind, clear."

Turner said he had been a little confused in his testimony before the Navy. But now he was clear. Under
cross-examination by Brewster the next day, the twenty-
first, he explained his changed testimony. Recently he'd
been straightened out by several officers who had studied
the matter. Listeners wondered which testimony should be
accepted: Turner's own remembrance of the "winds" incident or the repetitions of conversations he had heard in
San Francisco?

Turner also claimed that Noyes had assured him on
three occasions prior to Pearl Harbor that Kimmel and
Short were receiving the same decrypted information that
Washington had. Since Noyes had denied this at the Navy
Inquiry, Turner said, "The only conclusion that I can ar-
rive at is that I did not make my question to Admiral

Noyes clear and that he misunderstood what I was trying to do.'' It was peculiar that two high-ranking Navy officers couldn't make each other understood on three separate occasions. ''However, as a result of those three conversations at three widely separated times during 1941 I believed and so informed Admiral Stark that those officers were receiving the same information on all decrypted messages, at least concerning the Pacific, that we had here in Washington.'' By now, of course, he knew that there was no Purple machine in Hawaii.

Even so Turner harshly criticized Kimmel. If he had carried out the November 27 war warning he could have defeated the Japanese or greatly reduced the effects of their attack. Asked if Kimmel had sufficient equipment and material to have accomplished that result, Turner said, in conflict to considerable testimony to the contrary, ''Yes, sir, to have inflicted very serious damage on the Japanese Fleet.''

The session went on until 5:40 P.M., at which time Vice Chairman Cooper thanked the witness, excused him and said, ''The Committee wishes the press and all others who have worked with us a Merry Christmas and a Happy New Year, and the Committee now stands adjourned until December 31, at 10 A.M.''

Chapter Ten

THEIR DAY IN COURT
DECEMBER 31, 1945–
JANUARY 31, 1946

1.

When the committee next met on the last day of the year, a new chief counsel had finally been selected to replace Mitchell as of January 15, 1946. The unanimous choice was Seth Richardson, a staunch Republican from North Dakota, who had served the present Administration as chairman of the Subversive Activities Control Board. Long associated with the two isolationist senators from his state, Gerald P. Nye and William Langer, he himself had been a critic of Roosevelt but the majority had approved his selection to give the hearings that air of impartiality they had so far lacked. Lucas, his frequent golf partner, felt that he would not be harmful to the majority cause.

His selection created a minor mystery in Washington circles. Had it been a coincidence that his law office did business with the government and that he and Mitchell were old friends? Richardson had been selected by Herbert Hoover as Assistant Attorney General under Mitchell; and the retiring chief counsel had prepared for his successor a "Revised Order of Proof and List of Witnesses, and Ex-

planatory Memoranda.'' It revealed Mitchell's own judgment of witnesses not yet interrogated and evidence not
yet completed. In one section it was critical of Kimmel
and in another it expressed near certainty that the "winds"
execute message had never been received. Still another
dealt with the White House papers of Roosevelt which the
minority had been so anxious to get. Mitchell had requested that Grace Tully, the late President's secretary,
extract from the files for the year 1941 all papers relating
to Japan, the imminence of war in the Pacific, or general
Far Eastern developments. "Counsel has not yet had nor
requested physical access to the files," wrote Mitchell,
"but has relied upon Miss Tully's extraction of documents
coming under the broad headings noted above." Not all of
the Roosevelt files had been checked, "but, of course,
those considered likely to contain material relevant to the
inquiry have been read." Reliance upon a President's
loyal secretary to extract documents that could be embarrassing was naïve at best.

To ease himself into the task, Richardson, a bulky six-
footer, was on hand to watch Mitchell and his staff interrogate Stark on December 31. Stark, relieved of duty by
King at Forrestal's order, was again counseled by Lieutenant Richmond. He had urged the admiral to "go after"
Marshall in his opening statement. Richmond was angry
because the former Chief of Staff was "coming through
this looking like a hero, and he didn't deserve it, and I
wanted to take a good, sound whack at him." But Stark
refused. "I know you and George are good friends," said
Richmond, "but we're trying to do something here that's
of tremendous historical significance."

"Well, Dave," said Stark, "let's tell the facts about
me, and if somebody wants to point the finger at someone
else, let them do it, not me." And so he refused to make
adverse comments about Marshall, Roosevelt, Hull, Kimmel or others. He would leave evaluations to the committee. In his statement, Stark did introduce into the record a
number of letters he himself wrote in 1941. Many were
personal, and some so much so that he had suggested the
recipients burn them. In one he wrote that he had told
Roosevelt after Hitler invaded Russia, "I considered every

day of delay in our getting into the war as dangerous, and that much more delay might be fatal to Britain's survival.''

During the afternoon session Seth Richardson, who would soon replace Chief Counsel Mitchell, sat between Ferguson and Greaves, to get an idea of what was going on at the committee table. Later Greaves wrote a friend that Keefe was very enthusiastic about the new chief counsel but that Gearheart was much opposed ''and feels that if he did anything against the Administration, he would be cutting off his chief source of income as a Washington attorney. Ferguson feels that they can't do anything about it, so they might as well make the best of it.'' Richardson, noted Greaves, had conversed in a very friendly manner with Ferguson, who had neglected to introduce him. ''As yet Richardson has not decided on any assistants and I do not know that any serious effort was made to get minority help, as Lucas is branding Richardson as a Republican.''

For three more days Stark was forced to submit to harsh questioning. Unlike Marshall, he was treated by the Democrats as a defendant who was as guilty as Kimmel and Short. Then a Republican, Gearhart, queried him about his loss of memory on the night of December 6. ''In view of the fact that the Chief of Staff cannot remember where he was on that night is it possible that you and he could have been in each other's company that night?''

''I think we had no such conspiracy at that time, sir,'' replied Stark, causing some stir by the use of the word ''conspiracy.''

''Well, do you shut it out as being an utter impossibility that you and he could have been in each other's company that night?''

It was not an utter impossibility, admitted Stark, ''but I think we were not.'' The ''think'' was provocative to some observers. On January 5, Ferguson questioned him on the controversial staff conversation with the British and Canadians early in 1941 which had led to a Joint Basic War Plan directed against the Japanese. In Stark's original statement it was noted that this plan was approved by the Secretaries of War and Navy, and by the President. Stark had put a line through ''and by the President.''

"I want to know," said Ferguson, "when you put that in there, whether you were of the opinion personally that that had been approved by the President?"

"Yes," replied Stark. "He approved my sending it out, although he had not officially approved it."

This not only ended Stark's interrogation but was also the last appearance for Chief Counsel Mitchell at the hearings. In ten days the investigation would lie in the hands of Richardson, who was well meaning if ill prepared.

2.

The hearings were recessed to give Richardson a chance to study the case. His first witness on January 15 was Kimmel. Now at last the admiral would have his day in court. What had concerned the attorneys for both Kimmel and Stark was the bad feeling between the two admirals. Stark had already written Kimmel to offer anything in his files. He had also invited Kimmel to his home for lunch, but both offers had been declined. Even so, Stark told David Richmond that he was to consider himself Kimmel's lawyer just as much as his own. "I want the truth to come out. Don't spare me in any way."

At his first meeting with Kimmel's attorneys Richmond had remarked that it was an awful shame that their two principals were at such odds. "It wouldn't take much for Stark to be a good friend of Kimmel. He's not mad at him." The reply was that their fellow was pretty mad at Stark. Richmond proposed they do something and their efforts had some effect. Kimmel and Stark did shake hands and on that morning managed to greet each other publicly.

Dressed in a dark suit with a bright blue tie, the sixty-three-year-old Kimmel began to read a 25,000-word statement asserting that Washington had denied him information that might have made Pearl Harbor an ambush for the Japanese. His voice was strong and he punctuated points with aggressive finger-pointing. He had come not with bowed head but full of fight. He was angry that the committee had already released to the press his and Short's testimony given at previous investigations. "This was unquestionably done with the object of lessening the impact of my statement when it was read."

The next day Kimmel told of the abuse and threats to his life that followed the Roberts report. Asked by Richardson if there had been a close personal relationship with Stark before Pearl Harbor, Kimmel said he'd had the highest regard for him. "I trusted him, and I felt he was one of my best friends. I had that feeling, but I cannot forget the fact"—he paused as if restraining himself—"well, events that have occurred since then."

During four and a half hours of questioning by Richardson and Vice Chairman Cooper the admiral flung back quick, authoritative answers. "I could have saved the fleet if given facts," he said. "Had they given me those dispatches, dispatches that were my primary concern—the people in Washington had other things to do—I can say without reservation they would have changed my ideas considerably. My staff still feels the same way. We were there—on the ground."

Friday, January 18, was a harrowing day for Kimmel, who had trouble hearing some of the sharp questions by Lucas. Several times he protested that he was deaf. This disability was compounded by the district-attorney manner of the senator. To wind up his interrogation Lucas asked, as if it were an accusation, "From November 24 until the hour of attack did you exercise that superior judgment necessary for one of your rank and position when you knew the war was practically imminent?"

"I did."

"In other words, Admiral, you are now telling the committee under solemn oath that you did not commit any mistakes or commit any errors of judgment from November 24 to December 7?"

"I would say that is a reasonable conclusion, and it is a conclusion that the Naval Court of Inquiry, composed of three Admirals selected by the Secretary of the Navy came to when they submitted their report to the Secretary of the Navy."

On Saturday Representative Murphy of Pennsylvania continued the aggressive Democratic interrogation of Kimmel. But pressure on the admiral was relieved by an argument between Murphy and Keefe. Since the beginning of the hearings the two Irishmen had crossed swords good-naturedly but lately bitterness had crept into their colloquies.

"Now, Mr. Chairman," said Murphy, "the gentleman on the left has made a statement before I started a question and he was going to try to cut me off." Though he was a head shorter than Keefe, he was sharp of tongue and as feisty as Jimmy Cagney. He had tried forty-five murder cases as Assistant District Attorney without losing one. "We are all men. Now let us not have this needling going on. I want to conduct a fair examination and I do not propose to be cut off."

Murphy continued his acute and contentious interrogation of Kimmel for another hour before Brewster finally took over for the Republicans. At last Kimmel had an ally. "I appreciate as you do that perhaps necessarily over the past few days, this entire week now, there has been much that is repetitious in the very extended examination. I do not want to single out any of my colleagues by undue mention, but I do want to say Mr. Cooper, who is perhaps of the most belligerent variety, has questioned you in his customary style." He smiled. "When I went before him as a witness one time in the House he offered to throw me out of the room." There was laughter.

"I can appreciate the belligerency," said Kimmel. "I may have indulged in that sometimes myself. I do not object to it." What he objected to privately was the deletion of some of his own remarks from the record.

Brewster continued with questions that Kimmel was pleased to answer. Until then the committee had only been told of the defensive duties of Kimmel's Pacific Fleet. Now he was asked to enumerate the fleet's considerable offensive responsibilities. These included support of Allies in the Far East by diverting enemy strength away from the Malay Barrier; protection of sea communications of the Allies within the Pacific area; support of British naval forces in the area south of the equator; and protection of Allied territory within the Pacific area "by destroying hostile expeditions and by supporting land and air forces in denying the enemy the use of land positions in the Hemisphere.''

"Now those are rather large orders, are they not?" said Brewster.

"Yes, sir," said Kimmel, and charged that Rugg had twice pointed out to Mitchell and Gesell that the true picture of Kimmel's offensive responsibilities had not been presented to the committee.

Brewster asked what reply Gesell had made to Rugg regarding that request.

"I do not know as he made any reply, but he did not do anything about it."

A volume containing the war plans of the Pacific *had* been delivered to the committee, but only one copy made available. It was so bulky that no one had time to read it and Mitchell had kept it out of the record. Now, thanks to Brewster, Seth Richardson finally let it be entered. "It contained the first inkling of what Admiral Kimmel had been ordered to do in the so-called 'war-warning' message, first mentioned in the Roberts Report," recalled Greaves. "Unfortunately, no copies were given or shown to the press until the entire proceedings were printed many months later." [1]

"Murphy took up most of today but got nowhere in particular," Greaves reported to columnist John T. Flynn, who was spending much of his working day on Pearl Harbor. Greaves told of Brewster's success in bringing out Kimmel's offensive responsibilities. "Both Mitchell and Gesell tried to keep it out, but it is now in evidence. . . . Brewster brought out that no one would be able to judge whether Kimmel carried out his assignment without knowing what it was and there had been attempts to suppress what his full duties were. Rugg seemed very enthusiastic about the results so far."

On the following Monday Kimmel's testimony ended, this session highlighted by Gearhart's lengthy criticism of the war warning message on November 27. How could Kimmel be condemned for being caught by surprise, said Gearhart, "when everybody above him, the Commander

[1] This important document was buried among exhibits on pages 2882-883 of Vol. 18, Joint Committee Hearings. See Notes.

in Chief of the armed forces of the United States, the Chief of Naval Operations, the Chief of Staff of the Army, all insisted that they were surprised.''

To Kimmel it was a satisfactory ending. He wrote his brother, Colonel Manning Kimmel, that although only a very small part of the evidence had so far been presented, he had finally had the chance to tell completely his story about Pearl Harbor; and had it not been for this investigation he was ''confident that the Navy Department would never have permitted me to disclose this story. They would have kept it under wraps on the plea that any disclosure would jeopardize our code breaking activities and that would have left me hanging in the night. So I suppose I should be thankful for small favors and certainly telling my story in public has relieved my mind and reduced my blood pressure considerably.''

3.

The next day it was Short's turn. He was now represented by a young Army captain; his former counsel, General Green—whom both Kimmel and Rugg had suspected of connivance with Marshall—was now the Army Judge Advocate General. Short declared that he had been treated unjustly by the War Department. ''I was singled out as an example, as the scapegoat for the disaster. I am sure that an honest confession by the War Department General Staff of their failure to anticipate the surprise raid would have been understood by the public, in the long run, and even at the time. Instead, they 'passed the buck' to me, and I have kept my silence until the opportunity of this public forum was presented to me.''

The burden of examination was handed over to Samuel Kaufman, the associate general counsel. It was obvious to Greaves that Kaufman was already convinced of Short's guilt and was doing his best to shift the blame for the wrong alert from Marshall to Short by skipping over that part of the war warning message that placed full responsibility on the Chief of Staff. ''He even tried to ignore Washington's instructions to look out for sabotage. He omitted entirely the shabby way the General's retirement had been handled. From his questioning you would have thought the Hawaiian commander was a dunce while those in Washington were wise men."

Short's fourth day on the stand was the most dramatic and moving. In the presence of his son, Major Walter Dean Short, he described the Roberts Commission hearings as "star chamber" proceedings at which he had no opportunity to hear the testimony of other witnesses or cross-examine them in his own defense. In a voice still weakened by recent illness, he said, "When I read the findings of the Roberts Commission in the newspapers on the morning of January 25, 1942, I was completely dumbfounded." It was beyond his comprehension to be accused of dereliction of duty after almost forty years of loyal and competent service. "I immediately called General Marshall on the telephone."

Tears came to Short's eyes as he told how his old and trusted friend of thirty-nine years' standing said he had not seen the Roberts report until that minute. "I asked him what I should do, having the country and the war in mind, should I retire? He replied, 'Stand pat but if it becomes necessary I will use this conversation as authority.' I told him I would place myself entirely in his hands, having faith in his judgment and loyalty." But the next day Marshall had sent a memorandum to Stimson stating, "I am now of the opinion that we should accept General Short's application for retirement today. . . ." Short dabbed quickly at his eyes with his handkerchief; sitting behind him, his son did likewise. ". . . and to do this quietly," continued Short, "without any publicity at the moment."

Brewster asked if the Marshall memorandum to Stimson indicated a radically different position than the Chief of Staff had taken the day before. "Yes, sir," said Short. He seemed more hurt than angry. "And the day before he had told me to stand pat."

Later he did show anger and indignation when asked to comment on a list of possible charges to be brought against him in a memorandum compiled by the Adjutant General's office in 1942. To every charge, Short answered with spirit, "Not guilty!" and then gave his reasons. He concluded by stating that he had "never at any time tried to pass the buck to a single subordinate." He may have been tempted to add "like the War Department," but didn't.

It was fitting that the next witness be Justice Roberts. He had come reluctantly and became testy under badgering by the minority, apparently resenting the fact that a justice of the Supreme Court should be forced to endure such indignity. To Brewster's question whether there had been any mention in the commission's hearings of the "winds" message, Roberts replied curtly, "I have no recollection of any such thing. And I think you will search the testimony in vain for any reference to it."

Ferguson picked up a transcript of the testimony before the Roberts Commission. "You were the chairman, and this is your language," said the senator, and began quoting: "'It has been reported to me that about ten days before the attack a code was intercepted which could not be broken, but it was forwarded to Washington to the War Department to be broken, and the War Department found out it could be broken and did break it, and found it contained three important signal words which would direct the attack on Pearl Harbor, and that the War Department subsequently intercepted over the radio those three signal words and forwarded them to the military authorities here as an indication that the code had been followed and that the attack was planned.'" Ferguson extended the document to Roberts. "I wish you would look at that."

"You don't need to show it to me," the justice replied testily. Ferguson asked what he was talking about in that quote. "I was talking about some information that had been given me somewhere around Pearl Harbor. People were coming to me all the time telling me there was such and such a rumor. You see I say 'It has been reported to me.'"

"Wouldn't this describe the 'winds' code message?"

"Very likely it would," admitted the justice. "Very likely so."

Did Roberts follow up on the matter? asked Ferguson. "Yes, sir. We asked for all the messages there were about any broken codes and we were told we had all they had except this Magic thing.''

"Do I understand that you did not get the Magic?''

"No, we were never shown one of the Magic messages,'' said Roberts, then admitted he knew the Army or Navy had been cracking a super code of the Japanese. "They did not show us the messages, any of them, and I didn't ask them to.''

"That being true,'' said Ferguson, "how was this finding possible . . .''

Roberts angrily interrupted. "Now, Senator, is this an investigation of the Roberts Commission or an investigation of what happened at Pearl Harbor?''

Ferguson was somewhat intimidated. "I am trying to get the facts.''

"When you ask 'How is this finding possible?' I don't find you criticizing me a bit,'' retorted Roberts sarcastically.

"I am not criticizing,'' said Ferguson. "I want to know on the facts you had before you . . .''

"How we could make a certain finding,'' interrupted Roberts.

"Yes.''

"I think that is criticism.''

Though cowed, Ferguson returned to the attack. He read from another document that the Secretary of State had fulfilled his obligations by keeping the War and Navy Departments in close touch with the international situation and fully advising them respecting the course and probable termination of negotiations with Japan. He turned to Roberts and asked how the commission could make a finding if it didn't have the facts.

Roberts replied that he had spent an entire day in Hull's office. ". . . Secretary Hull showed me his personal memorandum where he had noted that on a certain day he had told the Secretary of War and the Secretary of the Navy this, that and the other thing, and where he got that information. I didn't ask him, but I was perfectly convinced and our commission was convinced from my repoi them of the testimony he brought to me, that Secret

Hull had been warning the War and Navy Departments day by day and day by day that something might happen this day or that day, that the situation was degenerating, and so on."

"All right," said Ferguson. "Now, Justice, that part of the testimony is not in the testimony furnished to us, is it?"

"Certainly not. They had a stack of memoranda of the State Department that high, or Hull's personal memoranda and in order to recap it I asked him to write the letter which is in our record." He explained that his commission had not gone into any question of Hull's or the President's policy and was limited solely to the Army and Navy.

"All right," said Ferguson. "Then we come to the next finding in your conclusions." He read:

"'The Secretary of War and the Secretary of the Navy fulfilled their obligations by conferring frequently with the Secretary of State and with each other and by keeping the Chief of Staff and the Chief of Naval Operations informed of the course of negotiations with Japan and the significant implications thereof.'

"Now," continued Ferguson, "without having the intercepted Magic messages, did you make this finding? I will put it that way."

"Why, certainly. The Chief of Staff and Admiral Stark told us and the Secretary of War and the Secretary of the Navy told us that every time Hull gave them a warning they would go and repeat it to the Chief of Staff and to the Admiral. I did not need to look at any messages to find out whether Marshall and Stark had been sufficiently warned. That is all I was interested in."

But, asked Ferguson, did he not know that Knox, Stimson, Hull, Stark and Marshall were all being furnished the Magic?

"I did not know it and I would not have been interested in it," said Roberts.

Ferguson was taken aback, as were some of the spectators.

Roberts reverted again to sarcasm. "Let's investigate the Roberts Commission. I would not have been interested in it, Senator. I wanted to know whether the military men were put on full warning and put on their toes by the men who had the information. I got a unanimous statement that they were.''

''Well, then, Justice, if your commission was not furnished all the data that we had here in Washington, how could you make a finding on whether or not they were on their toes out in Hawaii and knew all the facts?''

The justice was becoming openly belligerent. He repeated he had not seen the Magic. ''I would not have bothered to read it if it had been shown to us. All I wanted to know was whether the commanders [Kimmel and Short] had been advised of the criticalness of the situation.'' He had found from the messages sent them that they had ample warning and that they had orders from headquarters. ''Now, they could have been sent more, of course,'' he said, adding derisively, ''They could have been sent a message every two hours.''

Ferguson took him literally. ''Well, now, wait. If there was a message coming in every two hours and that information would have given them more warning wouldn't there then have been neglect on those here who did not send it?''

''Now, do you want me to make your report?'' Roberts was losing his temper.

''No.''

''Well, I have made my conclusions. My commissioners joined me in making the conclusions. If you reach a different conclusion, certainly that is your privilege but don't ask me to check your conclusions.''

He may have been intimidated, but the senator pointed out that the oral evidence of the commission amounted to 1,887 typewritten pages while the photostatic copy only had 1,862. There were twenty-five less. He asked the justice to look at the page with this information.

''I do not need to, sir.''

''Can you answer it if you do not look at it?''

''Yes; I can answer it. I do not know why the discrepancy.''

Obviously ill at ease, Ferguson pressed on. ''On the day you spent some two hours with the President, the day you made your report, did you have a discussion of the facts?''

No, said Roberts.

"Well, will you try and give us what took place there and that will answer the question."

"Well, I think it a highly improper thing but if you ask it I suppose I am bound to answer it." Reluctantly Roberts told of the conversation, which revealed nothing startling.

"Well, now, Justice, what was wrong with the question I asked you, to tell me what the President had said?"

"Well, now, Senator," mimicked Roberts, "I am not going to indicate whether Senator Ferguson is wrong. We have been inquiring about how wrong Roberts is. Don't let us get clear off that line."

"I was wondering why we shouldn't have the facts as a committee."

"Well, I'm not going to argue it with you, Senator. I said I was going to try to answer your questions."

Ferguson appeared disheartened to Greaves. "My personal reaction," recalled the latter, "was that the Senator was deeply shocked by such conduct. The Senator's own judicial background had led him to revere all Supreme Court Justices." Ferguson laid down Greaves's question list and left the battleground to Brewster. Definitely not one to be intimidated, he approached the task with relish. "I would like to take up one further matter, Justice, and I think you will understand that it is very rare for us to have an opportunity to examine a former Justice of the Supreme Court."

"Well, I hope they are having as much fun as I am."

"It is rarely we can suggest that a witness may be unduly sensitive, although without positive—"

"Oh, no," interrupted Roberts, "I am just plain Mr. John Citizen now; you know that. I haven't the high exalted position that you hold now."

Brewster hoped the justice would appreciate the difficulty of the commission's situation; and then asked why General Marshall had testified that portions of the Roberts report had been suppressed for reasons of military security.

Roberts' momentary show of good nature dissolved. He snapped, "Well, I have testified to the facts. Now if you want me to say, which I think is a very improper thing, that General Marshall was wrong, I will say General Marshall was teetotally wrong. I have given you facts. The facts are all typed, they are not my word against General Marshall's word.''

Brewster would not submit to Roberts' testiness. Raising his voice, he sharply counterattacked. ''I do not think it is questioning the integrity of General Marshall or criticizing you when your attention is called to the testimony of General Marshall before this committee, and it was called to your attention for any comment you desired to make, and I do feel very confident, in examining your distinguished record both as investigator and justice of the highest court in this country for many years, that you have found that this [situation] could be duplicated many times.''

Bowing sardonically, Roberts retorted, ''Thank you for those kind words.'' A few minutes later Barkley attempted to make a joke out of an embarrassing afternoon. ''Mr. Justice, the committee thanks you for your cooperation. It regrets the necessity of bringing you from what Horace in his 'Odes' said is a Sabine farm.''

Roberts smiled. ''I cannot get back in time to milk, Mr. Chairman.''

''I would like to have a photograph of you in that operation,'' said Barkley.

''I think that is the most irrelevant of anything that the committee has asked me for.'' There was a burst of laughter and Justice Roberts was excused.

Monday the twenty-eighth of January had provided an entertaining if sorry spectacle to the reporters and spectators in the crowded, smoke-filled room. To some it was an outrage that a justice of the Supreme Court should be treated so roughly. To others Roberts' behavior was a blow at the vaunted objectivity of that court. But an even higher drama seemed in sight with the announced appearance in a few days of Captain Laurance Safford. It was expected that he and Kramer would consume more than a week of high-tension testimony which would settle the crucial issue of the ''winds'' execute one way or the other.

Chapter Eleven

SAFFORD AT BAY
FEBRUARY 1–11, 1946

1.

The public interest in Safford, Kramer and the "winds" execute had been whetted since the previous November when Representative Keefe had charged he had proof that a Navy intelligence officer was being "badgered" to change his testimony about the "winds" message. The officer was Captain Kramer and he was being held in the neuropsychiatric ward of the Bethesda Naval Hospital. "He entered the Naval Hospital under orders," Keefe told the Associated Press. "They took away his uniform and gave him pajamas, bathrobe and slippers." He was convinced that Kramer, with whom he had had three conversations, was chafing under this restraint.

But Kramer had denied that he was being held incommunicado. "I have been a patient at the hospital for some weeks and as for being beset and beleaguered as the newspapers said, I'm feeling very well. My treatment by the Navy has been as fair and considerate as it could possibly be." He said he could leave the hospital at his discretion and was ready to testify at the congressional hearings whenever he was called.

Richardson had been well briefed by his predecessor on the "winds" execute. In a memorandum Mitchell had stated that, although previous testimony and available information left the issue in doubt, he felt it was an unimportant issue. "Our whole reaction to the whole 'winds' code episode was, and still is, that it is all much ado about nothing, because even if such a signal was sent out in a broadcast by the Japs and [had] been received by the War and Navy Departments, it would have added nothing to what our people already knew." While hoping the whole matter would be dropped, Mitchell wrote that he was aware that the sensational publicity already surrounding the issue made it necessary to continue the search for evidence.

This remained the attitude of the Democrats, who not only ridiculed the significance of the "winds" execute but were convinced it had never existed. The Republicans, as well as some neutral observers, contended that Safford's evidence could not be treated so cavalierly and that the existence of the message proved that Washington had sufficient warning of the Pearl Harbor attack to have repulsed it.

Perhaps the person most interested in the matter, except for Safford himself, was Chief Warrant Officer Ralph T. Briggs, for he clearly recalled receiving the "winds" execute in early December 1941. At that time he was one of the qualified operators assigned to monitor all Japanese intercepts at the Navy's East Coast intercept installation, Station M. A *katakana* (the Roman style of the Japanese alphabet) instructor, he was the only one on duty at Station M that night who understood the significance of *"Higashi no kaze ame,"* which meant "East wind, rain."

Briggs had come to Washington just as the congressional hearings were about to begin. He was assigned to Safford's former command, the Security Intelligence Section of Naval Communications, presently located at the ex-girls' school out on Nebraska Avenue. Concerned as he was by the innuendoes in the press that Safford was lying or confused about the "winds" execute, Briggs felt there was nothing he could do. Like others in intelligence, he was extremely security minded, having signed an oath never to reveal what he knew without official approval and release. He had no idea Safford was in a little office only a few minutes away until early in December 1945 when he got a telephone call from the captain, who asked if he'd be kind enough to come to his office in Building 18. "I want to go over some things with you that you may be able to confirm, and help me out in reference to some intercepted messages, some Orange [Japanese] traffic I'm looking for."

It was only a short walk to the south side of the grounds. Briggs found a mild-mannered, soft-spoken man who showed him some notes, then abruptly asked, "Was your sign RT?"

"Yes, sir," admitted Briggs. "I was RT." Receivers had to put their sign on every incoming message.

"I've pinned that down from the record," said Safford. "I believe you were the one who copied this particular message, this 'winds' execute message."

Briggs was edgy. "Well, it could be." He had no idea how much had already been revealed in previous investigations and was under the impression that everything was still classified Secret or higher.

"Well, do you recall getting that message?"

"I guess I did."

Safford said he didn't have the execute. Somehow it had become lost but he recalled seeing it for the last time when he had assembled it with a batch of related material for submission to the Roberts Commission hearings. "That is why I wanted to confirm this with you."

For many months Safford had searched in vain for the "winds" execute message. And at last he was sure he'd found the operator who had received it.

But the issue had already raised a storm of controversy. Could he now convince Briggs to reveal his involvement?

To his great relief Briggs admitted his role as one of the Orange intercept operators who had been alerted by Safford's own office to the three possible "winds" execute messages. He noted that the captain had a list of the names and signs of the other operators involved. Safford also brought out testimony taken at previous hearings. "It's in here," he said. "Some of it but not all of it."

It was obvious to Briggs that the captain knew what he was talking about; he had everything right. Then Safford identified Briggs as the one who had received the "winds" execute. "Of course," recalled Briggs, "I admitted I did." Late on a night in early December 1941, he had found himself copying down *"Higashi no kaze ame."* He quickly checked his watch supervisor's classified instructions and felt sure this was one of the three anticipated executes. In addition to the original message, he made two carbon copies. He entered the message in the log and then telephoned his superior, Chief Radioman DW,[1] who had quarters at the station. DW said, "Get it on the circuit right away to downtown Washington's 20G terminal." This was Safford's office, Op-20-G.

After explaining his dilemma, Safford asked if Briggs would be willing to testify as a witness at the present hearings. Briggs reasoned that Safford must have some authority to see him as well as to ask for his testimony. Therefore he agreed to appear.

A day or so after their meeting, Briggs was ordered to report to Captain John S. Harper, commanding officer of the Naval Security station. He was austere and dignified, the epitome of military bearing and firmness. A stickler for discipline and the chain of command, he felt that only one man on that post was entitled to the title of captain—himself. "Briggs," he said, "I can understand you have been holding meetings with Captain Safford in reference to the hearings." Why hadn't he, the commanding officer, been informed? "Who authorized you to do this?"

"Well, no one, sir—other than Captain Safford."

Harper's stern expression indicated this was no excuse. Didn't Briggs know that *he* was the commanding officer of the station, not Safford?

"Yes, indeed, sir, but Captain Safford didn't allude to the fact that you weren't aware of my meeting with him."

Harper didn't pursue the point but remarked that too much had already been revealed at the hearings. "I'm not

[1] Certain names and restricted material have been deleted by the U. S. Navy from an official taped interview of Briggs on January 13, 1977. These deletions only concern security and in no way affect Briggs's narrative.

at liberty to disclose the reasons for what I am about to tell you," he said. "You are not to confer with Safford any further on this subject. You are specially prohibited from meeting with him in his office, and if there are any further inquiries or requests with reference to this matter, you are to report to me at once!" Then he added, "You are not to be called as a witness at any hearings. Is that clear, Briggs?"

Briggs was taken aback. Harper himself was uneasy. "Well, Briggs," he said, softening his tone, "perhaps someday you'll understand the reason for this." He paused as though wanting to say something further in clarification but then straightened up, ramrod erect. "You understand what I've told you? That is all!"

Briggs mulled over the situation. Had Harper called in Safford and discussed this with him? There were a number of questions to be answered but Briggs realized further contact with Safford would damage his career. He had no choice but to obey Captain Harper's order. And he had an added responsibility. Recently his wife had lost her sight and required the use of a guide dog. What if something happened to him? Even so he felt he had to talk to Safford once more. He telephoned the captain and told him what had happened. There was a long, strange silence on the other end of the line.

Safford seemed stunned, at a loss for words. He finally expressed regret that the efforts to assist him had resulted in Briggs's being called on the carpet by Harper. He promised to look into the matter and get back to Briggs later. After a few days Safford did so. This time he was in complete control of himself. The decision to reject Briggs's testimony, he explained, had possibly originated from someone on the staff of the Joint Congressional Committee. Safford concluded that "higher authority" had probably been responsible for canceling any further rebuttal witnesses. He once more thanked Briggs for his information and support. Since the captain had not identified by name who he thought the "higher authority" might be or what channel had been used to pass the order down to Harper, Briggs guessed that Safford had been intentionally bypassed. The only logical explanation was that a definite effort had been made to cover up the truth. But why? And what had happened to the missing messages?

It was about this time that Lieutenant Hanify was called from the caucus room to answer a telephone call from Safford. Would Hanify please come out to his house? There was such urgency in the captain's voice that Hanify immediately took a cab to 2821 Dumbarton Avenue. No sooner had he rung the front doorbell than he was met by both Saffords in lounging robes. They hastily pulled him inside, explaining that Drew Pearson, the columnist, lived in the neighborhood. If he saw a visitor in naval uniform he might draw conclusions.

Mrs. Safford, a distinguished and imposing woman, was in great distress and it appeared to Hanify that her husband was distraught because of her.[2] They both looked as if they had spent an anxious, sleepless night. Safford explained that they were concerned over possible repercussions or reprisals if he testified as planned.

---

[2] By now the seemingly endless Pearl Harbor controversy had frayed her nerves. During a recent party one of Safford's colleagues, Prescott Currier, started to talk to him. Mrs. Safford put both hands on Currier's chest and pushed him back so forcefully that he almost fell backward. "Leave him alone," she said. "You can't monopolize him."

Mrs. Safford suffered even more than her husband during his tribulations at the hearings. Although he never held it against Kramer and other associates who repudiated him, Ruth Safford was bitter. Once she told the wife of one of Safford's colleagues over the telephone, "Your husband is a Judas Iscariot!"

After the congressional hearings she would not permit any talk of Pearl Harbor, and several times physically ejected colleagues and reporters who called at the Safford home. One such was Helen Worden Erskine, a contributing editor of *Collier's*. In 1954 she arrived unannounced at the Saffords' to gather material for an article in the Boston *Traveler*.

She was met at the door by a man with a kindly face and gentle voice. "I am Captain Safford. What can I do for you?"

"I understand you're the real hero of Pearl Harbor."

There came a scream from the upper floor: "Not Pearl Harbor, not Pearl Harbor!" Mrs. Safford rushed down the stairs shouting, "Get out! Get out!"

"Ruth, be quiet," said Safford, and turned to the reporter. "I've said all there was to say at the Pearl Harbor inquiry."

"Stop talking!" exclaimed his wife. *(Continued on page 208)*

Hanify reassured them. All Safford had to do was tell the truth and stick to the evidence. The information about the Japanese intercepts was now in the record and he could speak openly on the subject. "I had a very good idea that Laurance Safford was not going to be the most popular character in the American Navy for a long time," recalled Hanify. "There was no doubt about that in my mind. On the other hand, I did not expect that anyone would dare bring proceedings against him, because the case was already beginning to get into the public domain."

Safford said nothing about the order preventing Briggs

Safford continued politely. "I have my own opinions, but I'm not in a position to comment any more."

Abruptly Mrs. Safford grabbed Erskine by the shoulders and pushed her toward the door. "Get out!"

Safford was extremely upset by the story that appeared in the *Traveler*, particularly since both he and his wife were Bostonians. He protested in a letter to Erskine that he was not, as described, "a lonely and tragic figure" who had sacrificed his career for the truth. This, he objected, tended "to make me appear forlorn and pathetic—which I am certainly not. . . . If I had it all to do over again, I would not change a jot of it; even to the decision to give up all hopes of being an admiral. . . . It is a matter of deepest personal regret to me that you wrote so unkindly of Mrs. Safford."

Safford continued an obsessive interest in Pearl Harbor until his death, and wrote voluminous letters for years to a group engaged in publishing a revelatory history of Pearl Harbor. Their replies to Safford had to be sent to a series of mail drops, the last the residence of his old friends, Major General and Mrs. William O. Reeder.

For this project, which was headed by revisionist historian Dr. Harry Elmer Barnes, Safford wrote articles and lengthy memoranda. These had to be composed outside the home, for if his wife found any such papers she would burn them. She would check letters addressed to him at their home, and those to which she objected "went down my wife's private memory hole."

"Like all women Mrs. Safford is curious and suspicious," he warned Commander Charles Hiles in 1962. "Unlike other women she goes into hysterics at the mention of Pearl Harbor or the idea of another book about it. Fortunately I got the mail which included your letter so no harm has been done."

By 1967 Mrs. Safford had become so disturbed that the captain warned those working on the new book that "it would take very little to send her to the snakepit." More secure measures, such as the use of code names, were taken to keep the correspondence secret. This continued until Safford's death in 1973. Mrs. Safford died seven years later.

from appearing as a witness, in fact, never mentioned his name. And Hanify drove back to the Senate Building somewhat perplexed.

2.

There was an atmosphere of expectancy in the caucus room at 2 P.M. on the first of February even before Seth Richardson began interrogating Safford. After his briefing by Mitchell the new chief counsel was convinced he was about to deal with a brilliant but confused witness who stood alone in the belief that a "winds" execute had been received. The professorial-looking Safford was visibly nervous as he began to read a 28-page statement of his involvement with the "winds" code. He told his story in halting bursts and was so obviously upset that once Richardson thoughtfully asked if he were "scared." Safford said the frequent flashes of photographers bothered him. The picture taking was halted. But as he continued his nervousness remained and he would occasionally pause to bite his lips and sip from a glass of water.

His story, heightened by his own excitement, caused a sensation. "Capt. L. F. Safford, a timid, graying code expert," reported the Washington *Times-Herald*, "tossed a bombshell into the Congressional Pearl Harbor inquiry yesterday, when he declared positively that a Tokyo 'Winds Execute' message (meaning war between Japan and the U.S.) was received in Washington on December 4, 1941." Without mentioning Briggs, Safford had stated categorically that the message came in Morse code and was intercepted by a Navy listening post on the East Coast, Station M. "Safford's dramatic revelations were contrary to everything which the Congressional Inquiry has been told about the Winds messages by the Army-Navy high command—Gen. Marshall, Adm. Stark, Vice Admiral Wilkinson, then director of Naval Intelligence, and Major Gen. Miles, former War Department G-2." Equally sensational was Safford's claim that, less than a week after Pearl Harbor, the Navy Department ordered all personal memoranda concerning the disaster destroyed.

The next day, Saturday, brought new sensations. Safford accused John Sonnett, legal assistant to Admiral Hewitt, of having attempted to get him to reverse testimony before the Navy and Army boards that a "winds" execute had been intercepted. "It was apparent to me on my first meeting with Lieutenant Commander Sonnett that he was acting as a 'counsel for the defense' for the late Secretary Knox and Admiral Stark, rather than as the legal assistant to the investigating officer. His purpose seemed to be to refute testimony [before earlier investigations] that was unfavorable to anyone in Washington, to beguile 'hostile' witnesses into changing their stories and to introduce an element of doubt where he could not effect a reversal of testimony. Above all, he attempted to make me reverse my testimony regarding the 'Winds Execute' message and to make me believe I was suffering from hallucinations."

A little later he told Richardson that all copies of the "winds" execute were missing; and the one in Kramer's safe must have been stolen.

"Well," said Richardson in a tone that made it obvious he did not believe Safford, "do you think that there was a general conspiracy running from the White House through the War Department and Navy Department and through Kramer's section to destroy these copies?"

"I have never indicated the White House at any time in my testimony."

"Well, do you think there was a conspiracy between the Navy Department and War Department to destroy these copies?"

"There is an appearance of it," said Safford nervously.

"And whom do you suspect as individuals who took part in that conspiracy?"

"I have no first-hand knowledge."

"All you have is a suspicion?"

Safford said he had more than that and told in detail of his search for a copy of the controversial message. The men in charge of the files of his section did not know it was missing; "they had no record of it being missing, they had no authority for destruction and no record of destruction." Repeated searches were made but no copies ever showed up. "They had simply evaporated from the face of the earth. They were gone, and no records of them. It was an unwritten law in that section that we retain the original intercept forever, because we could never tell when it would be useful or how many years we might want to go back to verify something." Then he tried to find the original teletype at both Station M and the Bainbridge Island station near Seattle but there was no trace. Letters in connection with the search had also disappeared without a trace. "It was not only the Winds message itself; it was everything connected with the Winds message which had disappeared."

Richardson did not take any stock in these accusations. "Now, it is a fact, isn't it, Captain, that every single witness who has testified on the Winds code, on the subject of having received or seen a Winds Execute message, testifies that they never saw one; isn't that a fact? Every single one of them."

That was not true, retorted Safford. The assistant chief of Naval Operations before Pearl Harbor, Admiral Ingersoll, for one, testified he had seen it and that it meant war with the United States. The admiral wasn't sure whether he saw it before or after Pearl Harbor, but he definitely saw it and it was in writing.

Richardson brushed aside the Ingersoll testimony. "Why," he asked, "would anyone want to press the veil of secrecy, destruction, on this Winds Execute message that you say came on the 4th of December, why would they?"

"It is human to try to cover up mistakes."

"Well, what was the mistake that was made with reference to that message?"

"The fact that no war warning was sent," said Safford. "The fact that an attempted war warning in the Navy Department was suppressed by higher authority and that the War Department didn't even attempt to get a war warning out."

"Then it is your idea that, with a message in the hands of the officers of the Navy, the officers of the Army, and the President of the United States, that everybody forgot that they were interested in the war and forgot to make use of this message?"

"I do not know why the warning did not go out."

"I suggest, Captain, that the reason the warning didn't go out was because there never was a Winds Execute message on the 4th of December. You disagree with that?"

"I disagree with that," said the harried Safford.

Richardson kept asking repetitious questions until Safford could restrain himself no longer and exclaimed that the chief counsel was trying to get him to change his testimony and wasn't the first one who had tried to do so.[3]

By the time Safford left the caucus room that afternoon, he was exhausted. Now at least he would have a day of rest before returning on Monday to what was likely to be even more severe interrogation by the majority.

In a statement to the press Sonnett denied the charge that he had attempted to get Safford to change his testimony. Now promoted to Assistant Attorney General of the United States, he said, "I was instructed by the Secretary of the Navy to secure all of the facts concerning the 'Winds messages' in order to clear up the apparent mystery as to that message about which there has been so much rumor. I discovered that Captain Safford was the source of the erroneous rumors concerning the existence of such a message. . . . It should be borne in mind that, of the many people named by Captain Safford in previous testimony as having knowledge of the 'Winds message,' not a single one recalled the existence of such a message. It is impossible to believe that all those witnesses could be wrong." It was also hard to believe that Sonnett didn't know that not only Ingersoll but two others, Colonels Moses Pettigrew and Carlisle Dusenbury, had testified that they saw it. So had Kramer until his memory was altered at the Hewitt Inquiry.

[3] This part of the interrogation cannot be found in the published record. "I was sitting right behind Safford and heard every word of what was said and it was so unusual that I remember the whole thing distinctly," Lavender wrote Kimmel. This came as no surprise to the admiral. Many of his own remarks had been deleted and misquoted in the record. Greaves also recalled that key material had been deleted from the record.

3.

On Monday morning, February 4, the Democrats converged on Safford. Lucas began by asking if he had communicated with Kramer about the "winds" message. Safford admitted he had written his friend a letter about the end of 1943 but did not have a copy. "Your memory would be better then than it is now, would it not?" asked Lucas.

"As far as that aspect was concerned."

"And if in that letter you said this whole thing was somewhat vague and uncertain—I don't know whether it did or not, I haven't seen the letter but maybe we can get it—that would be true, would it not?"

"I believe I did not go into details at all. . . . And I did not suggest anything to Kramer. I was trying to ask a question."

"I see," said Lucas, and then dramatically called out, "Is Captain Kramer in the room?"

"Yes," said a voice that Safford recognized as Kramer's.

"Do you have a copy of that letter, Captain?"

"Yes, sir, I do. I made it available to counsel, Senator." Kramer put his hands in front of his face as a photographer took his picture.

It was a moment for theater with Safford and Kramer facing each other. One can only imagine what conflicting emotions Safford endured. He had fallen into Lucas' trap—because of a trusted friend. Agitated, he admitted he had destroyed his copy of the letter and then had to listen to Lucas reading out that he was preparing a secret paper and was getting details from available records. "'My memory is bad as to details . . . ,'" quoted Lucas and stopped. Was that true of the "winds" execute? he asked.

"That is true on the details," admitted Safford. "You will see I had not been able to establish the date at that time, the exact day. I knew it within two or three days."

Lucas read on: "'My memory is bad as to details, which is the reason for preparing this memorandum, and I have forgotten or am very vague as to certain things which I clearly recalled a year ago.'"

All of the Safford-Kramer correspondence was read aloud, including the code to be used giving numbers to persons, messages and places. With obvious relish Murphy, the feisty Irishman from Pennsylvania, took over the questioning. His aggressive tactics had already brought him press commendation as the ablest majority member who "has shown himself fast and shifty on his feet." Safford had previously testified that he had left his office about four-thirty on the afternoon of December 6, had gone out with friends that night and was having late breakfast on the seventh. "You were still in your pajamas the next afternoon at 2:20 having breakfast, on December 7, is that right?"

"That is right."

"At 2:20 you were still in your pajamas having breakfast?"

"That is right."

Murphy began savaging him. "And you are home at a time when you think war is coming, because you have told this committee that war was coming on Saturday or Sunday, you knew that there is going to be a time fixed which will fix the deadline and you leave on Saturday afternoon at 4:30, and you do not inquire as to anyone under you until after the war has started; that is right?"

Safford explained that one of his subordinates had sent the thirteen parts of the Japanese message to the Army for translation. That was the day the Army was supposed to do translations of Magic. Also another of his officers had called Kramer to tell him what was in the message.

"We are talking about you, in charge of 200 men!" exclaimed Murphy. "You, the one who has been accusing everybody else! We are now talking about you." The fact was, he said, that Safford had no translator on hand on December 7—"on the day you expected the war to start, did you?"

Safford admitted he had no translator in the office at that time but was not given a chance to explain that he had a watch officer on duty at all times to decrypt promptly whatever came in. And it was Kramer's responsibility to provide translation.

"And you are still in your pajamas having breakfast at 2 o'clock?" accused Murphy.

"Yes, sir."

"Do you have any sense of responsibility for the failure of this 1 o'clock message to get to the proper people in time? Do you feel responsible?" [4]

"Not in the least. . . . Three official naval investigations have listened to all the facts and none of them found me responsible."

"Not one of them have gone into this, have they? Whoever asked you about your responsibility and failure to be there on Sunday; whoever asked you that question before?"

"That question was not specifically asked."

"You believe that the best defense is an attack, don't you?"

Safford could have replied that this was exactly what Murphy was doing. "It is the oldest trick in the book," he later wrote, "—to try to put the chief witness for the prosecution on the defensive or to try to make the victim responsible for his own murder." The reason the warning to Short and Kimmel arrived too late was by no means Safford's or Kramer's fault but that of Stark and Marshall. The one o'clock message had been translated and in the hands of Stark a little after 10 A.M., three hours before the first bombs fell on Pearl Harbor.

But all the flustered Safford could think to say was, "I believe the best defense is telling the truth."

Murphy then turned to another of the letters Safford had written Kramer. He read:

[4] Murphy's accusations were grossly unfair. It was Safford who, before December 1941, had set up a twenty-four-hour watch to decrypt Magic traffic. He told an assistant that if the Japanese started anything it would be over a weekend. And if things broke Op-20-G would be held responsible for unprocessed traffic even if it was the Army's date of responsibility. He thereupon instructed his people to decrypt Army date traffic after all Navy date had been run.

Safford's vigilance and foresight paid off on December 6. The Army decrypters closed at noon but Op-20-G stayed on duty and began decryption of the message from Tokyo. Otherwise the first thirteen parts would have remained undecrypted until Sunday.

" '. . . What a break for you, as well as to the cause, to be ordered to Halsey's staff. I can see the hand of Providence in it.'

"What was the *cause?*" asked Murphy. The cause of Admiral Kimmel, explained Safford. Murphy then called attention to another paragraph.

" '. . . Be prudent and be patient. I am just beginning to get things lined up at this end. No one in #15 [the code for Office of Naval Operations] can be trusted.'

"Will you give us who you felt was not trusted in the Navy of the United States during the course of the war on January 22, 1944?"

"That is a rash statement," admitted Safford. "I will not expand on it."

Murphy pressed him to name names. Safford refused. "You will not?" exploded Murphy. "You refuse? I ask you to tell us. You are now under oath. Please tell us, sir, who you say there cannot be trusted, because, sir, that is an important accusation. It is an accusation against one of the important departments of the United States Navy during the war. You are making assertions. This is going into the papers of the country as well as are your other statements. You say 'they cannot be trusted.' Who were you saying could not be trusted? Names, please. Who could not be trusted?"

"He says all of them," said Lucas, joining in the attack.

"I would like to have names," said Murphy. "Here is a man making an accusation in writing." He made it sound as if Safford had made a public statement, not a comment in a private letter. "This is going to the papers. You, sir, a captain in the United States Navy, say: 'No one in #15 (Opnav) can be trusted.' Who did you mean? I don't want any sweeping statement. We are going to get down to details. Who could not be trusted?"

The harried Safford had no counsel to advise him. Rugg had to be careful not to talk or write to him before he testified, and would not even exchange glances with him during his testimony. Behind his horn-rimmed glasses, Safford's brown eyes darted warily with what seemed to Hanify "a combined comprehension and apprehension born of secrets known and secrets not to be told.'' It was an alert guardedness, a mannerism that probably came from his years as a cryptologist. It was obvious to Hanify that this unassuming man had a strong will. He appeared diffident and retiring but was as malleable as steel. Under his inquisitor's relentless quest for names, Safford kept silent.

Murphy kept at it like a terrier. "Names, please. I am still waiting. Waiting. Will you please give us the names as to who could not be trusted in Opnav? Please, sir. What did you mean by saying no one in #15, Opnav, can be trusted?''

"Do you wish to answer?" asked Barkley.

"I would prefer not to answer," said Safford. Rugg, Hanify and Lavender must all have heaved a sigh of relief.

"The Chair thinks you should answer if you can answer," said Barkley. Safford had no right to conceal anything that was pertinent.

"That was a private letter to Commander Kramer," said Safford stubbornly.

Murphy tried another angle. He read the next sentence.

"'. . . Premature action would only tip off the people who framed #31 (Admiral Kimmel) and #32 (General Short) and will also get #8 (Safford) and #10 (Kramer) into very serious trouble.'

"What did you mean by that?" asked Murphy. "How would it get Safford into trouble if he was doing the right thing? Will you answer that, sir? Still waiting.''

"Go ahead," said Barkley. "Answer if you can. You must have some sort of answer to that.''

"What I meant was that nothing should be done in the way of making any statement or anything of that sort until the expected court-martial or the expected investigation at that time which had been directed by Congress had taken place, so I could come on the witness stand, or Kramer could come on the witness stand and present the facts.''

"And spring a surprise," said Murphy. "Is that right?''

"Not necessarily. . . .''

"How would you get into trouble, what trouble could you get into for telling the truth, if you were telling the truth: Who would make trouble for you?''

"I was standing almost alone at that time."

"Who would make trouble for you, sir?"

The answer obviously was: the higher-ups. Safford had no one to advise him. Today he was really alone. "Anyone who doubted the accuracy of my statements," he finally said.

Who did the framing of Kimmel and Short? pressed Murphy relentlessly. "Name names, please. That also is a serious accusation. Names. Do you know that to frame anyone is one of the meanest and lowest crimes?"

Safford had no trouble in answering this. "Yes, sir."

"Now, then, you say some people did frame these two people, Admiral Kimmel and General Short. Who framed them?"

"I do not know."

"Whom do you refer to and whom are you cautioning Kramer against? Whom were you referring to?"

"I was referring to the War and Navy Departments in general, but not to any specific individual that I can identify."

"Captain, you wouldn't accuse the whole War and Navy Departments with the stigma of the vile crime of framing anybody? Can you narrow it down?"

"Well, I will narrow it down to the people concerned, the General Staff and officers."

Murphy was triumphant. "In other words, you felt that the General Staff of the United States Army under General Marshall, and the General Staff of the Navy under Admiral Stark had framed Kimmel and Short. Is that right?"

Safford licked his lips and wiped his forehead with his handkerchief. "I felt that way."

Murphy was set for the kill. "And my question is now: Can you give to the committee the name of any single witness . . . to furnish absolute proof or overwhelming proof of the guilt of Opnav and the General Staff of the United States Army?"

Safford said he could name four people who, he believed, "will give me some support if not complete support," and listed Kramer and three colonels, Sadtler, Bratton and Pettigrew.

"Did Sadtler ever say anything to you that he felt General Marshall had violated the criminal laws of the United States?"

"Not directly."

"What did he say that would make you think that he believed General Marshall, General Gerow, and the other generals would commit crime by ordering the destruction of—withdraw that. What did he say that would lead you to believe that those men were guilty of what you were referring to in this letter to Kramer? I am speaking of Sadtler."

Harried as he was, Safford had never raised his voice or displayed temper. "I cannot estimate anything that Colonel Sadtler will say specifically," he said courteously.

"Well, what do you have to offer to the committee by way of generalization as to what he might say that will prove the guilt of the General Staff of the Army? Have you any lead? Have you any suggestion? Have you any idea, that led you to believe that they will testify and support you and corroborate you in these charges? Upon what do you base your statement here today that these men will corroborate you? This is going into the papers, the statement that you made that four men will corroborate you in these charges."

"Colonel Sadtler knew of the Winds Execute," he said.

"What else?" pressed Murphy. "What will he say about the guilt of General Marshall or anybody on the staff, if you know?"

"I believe that Colonel Sadtler knows about the destruction of documents in the War Department." He had been told this by William Friedman, the code expert.

"What evidence can he give as to the guilt of the General Staff of the Army?" hammered Murphy. "You see, there is quite a difference between the alleged or actual existence of a Winds Execute and the violation of the criminal laws of the country in destruction or pilferage, stealing from the files. What evidence can he give on that subject? You say he is a reliable witness as to the guilt of the General Staff of the Army."

At last Safford got help. Keefe motioned to Cooper, who had replaced Barkley in the chair. "Mr. Chairman, I don't want to object, but aren't Colonel Sadtler and Colonel Pettigrew and these other people going to be witnesses, and won't their testimony be the best this committee can get as to what they are going to testify, instead of speculating as to what this witness may think they will say?''

A little later the committee recessed for the day and Safford, still shell-shocked, gathered his papers. Kimmel's three lawyers did not acknowledge him but their feelings were with him. Lavender thought the afternoon's grilling was cruel and gruesome. Hanify had suffered through Safford's inept testimony about his whereabouts on December 6 and 7. Why had he mentioned he was in pajamas? The majority had had a field day with that slip. They had made him look like a fool. ''That's where he betrayed the inexperience of a person who has been in a quasi-academic atmosphere all his life, and not in a competitive atmosphere,'' recalled Hanify. ''He was not a forensic type. He was not a debater. He was not argumentative.'' He was helpless without counsel in the hands of a Murphy or Lucas. But there had been something noble, thought Hanify, in the way Safford had stood up alone against all the forces arrayed against him and refused to back down. He was a modern Don Quixote.

The reporters crowded around Murphy, who was triumphant and exultant. ''We haven't touched the real meat of this,'' he told them. ''There's real genuine tenderloin in it.'' And tomorrow he would go after it.[5]

When Briggs read the stories of Murphy's ''hard-hitting, hammering cross-examination'' of Safford and how he and the other Democrats were making a mockery of his testimony about the ''winds'' execute, ''it became increasingly evident to me that the poor man was really being taken for a ride and not given an opportunity to prove his points.'' If it had been within Briggs's power to help Safford find one of the copies of the missing message, he would have done so. But he didn't know where they were or who had them.

[5] Two months later, President Truman would nominate Murphy to be U.S. district judge for the Middle District of Pennsylvania. Murphy had been Truman's floor manager in the 1944 convention that nominated him for Vice-President.

*   *   *

The next morning, February 5, Murphy resumed the attack on Safford's inaction on December 7—the day he slept late and was in his pajamas even after bombs were dropping on Pearl Harbor. Safford tried to explain why he was not responsible for the delay in sending the warning message to Kimmel and Short on December 7. It was true he slept late that morning but he was not responsible for the translation of the fourteenth part and the 1 P.M. message.

"There was not one translator in the Navy that day, was there, outside of Kramer?" said Murphy.

"I cannot answer for the translators," said Safford.

"In other words, you weren't so concerned about getting the message translated?"

"It was not my responsibility," said Safford patiently, "and I had no responsibility to issue any orders about translators."

"Weren't you interested in protecting the American Navy? You said war was going to start that day. Do I understand you to say you were not responsible for anything at all that might help with winning the war?"

Keefe objected. "Mr. Chairman, I don't think that the answer bears any such interpretation. I think it is an unfair question." There was rustling among the spectators, mostly women, who were beginning to have sympathy for Safford. "The witness is entitled to some degree of fairness and fair play."

"I expected Mr. Keefe to be concerned, and I expect he will have more trouble all day. What is the objection?"

Keefe's voice boomed out. "I object because the witness has testified that under the set-up he had no responsibility for translators. You are trying to make it appear that he did have and had no interest in protecting the welfare of the nation." The onlookers could no longer control their emotions. A wave of spontaneous handclapping swept around the big room. Vice Chairman Cooper rapped a large ashtray on the table. "The committee will be in order," he called out. "That applies to the guests."

"Mr. Chairman," said Keefe, "I have sat here all during this hearing without hardly opening my mouth. I think it is unfair on the part of the Congressman to say he expected to be interrupted by me all the time. But there is a limit to fairness even with this witness." There was another burst of vigorous applause.

Murphy was angry at the sudden turn. "I think I understand what is happening, and I am not going to be taken off the track by either certain people in the audience, or by the objection. I will proceed. I will get the facts regardless of any hindrances, sir." He turned to Safford. "The fact is, sir, that you were head of communications, and you felt war was going to start on Sunday." And it was also a fact that the translators were Kramer's responsibility, not his.

Some steam seemed to have been taken out of the Irishman from Pennsylvania and he dropped that unproductive line of inquiry. He asked if Safford ever had any trouble with Admiral Stark.

"No, never."

"Well, when was it you first turned against him? You have turned against him, haven't you? You feel he is guilty of a crime, don't you? You said he could not be trusted, didn't you? You said he was guilty of a frame-up . . ."

"I said that in a private letter . . ."

"Well, sir, you always speak the truth privately or publicly, don't you?"

"You try to," said Safford almost to himself.

"Yes. Well, now, was it or was it not your feeling when you said that you felt that Admiral Stark was guilty of a frame-up?" Safford didn't understand the question and asked for it to be reread. "Will you answer the question, sir?"

"Yes."

"Your answer is 'Yes,' Captain?" asked Cooper.

"No. I said I would answer the question." He begged Cooper's pardon.

"Take your time," said Murphy, who might have been impressed by Safford's unfailing courtesy under stress. "I will wait."

"I want a chance to get that straight."

"I don't want to ask you these questions but my job here is to get the facts." Murphy's adversary tone was dropped. "I don't want to embarrass you at all. I would rather not be here, but being here I am obliged to get the facts."

"It was not my feeling at the time," said Safford, "and if I wronged Admiral Stark I regret it. . . ."

"At any rate, you did state as an officer of the United States Navy that the leading officers, the commanding officers of the Navy were guilty of a frame-up and that, in your judgment, a frame-up is about as vile and low a thing as can be done to a human being, isn't it, or by a human being?"

"It is."

"And do you feel now, sir, today, that Admiral Stark and the members of his staff did bring about a frame-up of Admiral Kimmel?" Safford did not answer. "I won't press you upon that point."

"All right," said Safford. "Thank you."

"You have answered a good many others," said Murphy. He continued the questioning but his hammering ceased and so had hope of the tenderloin envisaged yesterday. Then the minority took over and both Ferguson and Keefe began bringing out points that supported Safford.

Keefe said one thing puzzled him: "Captain Safford, I am unable to understand any possible interest, personal interest, that you might have in this controversy, and if you have any such personal interest, I would like to have you state it."

"I have no personal interest, except I started it and I have got to see it through."

This brought a third spirited round of applause.

"The guests of the committee will be in order," warned Cooper.

"You realize, of course," went on Keefe, "that in view of the implications that have been stated in the cross-examination of you, especially by the gentleman from Pennsylvania, that you have made some rather strong charges?"

"Yes, sir."

"That may well mitigate against your career as a naval officer. Did you realize that when you came here as a witness?"

"I realized that every time I testified."

"And despite the fact that you have nothing to gain, and everything to lose, you have persisted in this story every time you have testified."

"I have."

Yesterday had been a day of trauma for Safford, today one of satisfaction. But upon his return on December 6, the Democrats made another attempt to break him. This attack was launched by Lucas and it was in the form of a threat. Didn't Safford realize that when he sent the private code to Kramer giving numbers for the President and other notables he was doing something wrong and was violating naval regulations?

This time Safford answered promptly. "Yes, sir."

"That is what I cannot understand, Captain Safford, how a man who is as intelligent as you are, and who is such a brilliant officer as you have appeared before this committee, would take a chance on the violation of naval regulations in order to help a man that you never saw or knew intimately, in order to help Admiral Kimmel, an individual whom you never served under, that you slightly knew, but you did all of this taking a chance of ruining your own career to help a man that you hardly knew. Can you explain that to me?"

Safford said that he had first been very bitter against Kimmel, assuming he was guilty for Pearl Harbor. Then he learned that Kimmel had not been sent the "winds" execute and other vital information.

As a result of this change, Lucas asked Safford, "you then felt it your duty to go all out and do everything you could for him?"

"I did."

"And in so doing you realized that Captain Kramer was probably the most valuable man you could get on your team in the defense of Kimmel?"

"Yes. That is, if Kramer was so disposed."

And if Kramer had answered Safford's second letter,

using the personal code against Navy regulations, the two of them might have been court-martialed for it?

"Yes, sir," said Safford. "Kramer used better judgment on that occasion than I did."

If Kramer *had* answered the second letter, said Lucas, then he would have been in the same boat as Safford was now in. "Isn't that right?" Safford insisted Kramer was always a free agent. "I do not want to infer," went on Lucas, "that you haven't given us your best understanding of this whole transaction, but there is a lot of testimony here against you on this Winds message and if Captain Kramer had been with you on this completely from beginning to end—which he would have had to have done, if he had answered the second letter—this committee would have had a pretty difficult time making any determination upon that question."

Brewster protested.

"I will withdraw it, if the Senator objects to it. Please don't take it, you men, for the newspapers. I will withdraw the whole thing. I do not want to get into any arguments with the Senator from Maine."

"I quite appreciate your request to the newspapers," said Brewster, "but I am afraid it will be difficult for them to completely disregard it." Lucas had implied that Safford was involved in a plot. By using pejorative words, Lucas had accused Safford of "laying a *net* for Captain Kramer and also the fact that if Kramer had responded to his letter, then Captain Safford would have had him at his *mercy,* certainly those things imply that Captain Safford was plotting in this situation, and I understand you do not mean any such insinuation. If Kramer had innocently and not evilly answered Captain Safford, that would not imply anything at all, that Captain Safford would have blackmailed Captain Kramer, or that Captain Kramer would have yielded to Captain Safford. I think all of these implications are unwarranted and unfair."

The audience applauded briskly.

"The Chair desires to say to the guests that this is not a political convention," said Barkley, who had returned to duty, "and any further outbursts in the midst of this testimony will be dealt with accordingly, no matter in whose behalf they are or in response to whose questions.'' He added that the Chair had made no objection to demonstrations on the part of the audience when a witness had concluded his testimony. ''This was true in regard to Secretary Hull, General Marshall, and the others, but the audience has repeatedly broken into the testimony of the present witness to make demonstrations. If they want to applaud when he finishes, that is their business.''

By early afternoon the committee was through with Safford and this time the sustained applause brought no objection from Barkley. As the captain, exhausted and nervous, was getting to his feet, Richardson said, ''Mr. Chairman, I would like to present Captain Kramer.''

''Captain Kramer,'' said Barkley, ''come around, please.''

Kramer and Safford passed each other. The latter, stunned a few days earlier to learn that his friend had turned over all their private letters without informing him, did not feel that he had been betrayed. He figured that the pressure of the past year had cracked Kramer and he was a sick man. Safford felt no resentment, only sorrow that his friend had been forced to undergo such harassment. They exchanged friendly words and had their picture taken together.

As Kramer prepared to testify, his wife, standing in the rear of the room, watched nervously. The minority members and Greaves were equally tense. Kramer had previously testified both ways. Which way would he go today? He began by admitting he had seen a ''winds'' execute. But it was on the fifth of December, not the fourth.

''Now it is testified here,'' said Richardson, ''that you came into Captain Safford's office with the watch officer and that you said, 'Here it is,' and handed to Captain Safford a message on yellow teletype paper in Japanese, about 200 words, 'War with United States.'''

''If I had written anything on that piece of teletype paper I would most positively have not used the word 'war,''' he said, flatly denying not only Safford's recent testimony but his own at the Navy Inquiry. The original "winds" message setting up the code, he explained, did not specify "war," merely "strained relations" with America, England or Russia.

"What country do you recall, if you do recall, was involved, in the one you recall?"

"To the best of my belief it was England." He was quite sure it was "West wind, clear" and not "East wind, rain."

It was apparent when Kramer returned to the stand the next day that he had once more had his memory refreshed—perhaps by counsel, Richardson and Kaufman, or the Democrats. This time he retreated even further from Safford. "In the last few weeks, I have had occasion to see some interrogations conducted by General MacArthur's headquarters in Japan of high Japanese officials who were concerned with these broadcasts. In view of their statements that no such weather signal [a "winds" execute] was made, it is my present belief, in the light of my recollections on this matter, as well, that what I saw Friday morning in December before Pearl Harbor was also a false alarm on this Winds system." This statement, reversing his avowal the day before that the message *was* a genuine "winds" execute, caused a stir. Some were wondering why, if he had known about MacArthur's interrogations of the Japanese for several weeks, he hadn't mentioned them the day before. Others, who knew about the interrogations, wondered why he did not add that these same Japanese officials also denied even setting up a "winds" code. Kramer's next words added to the mystery. "It was, nevertheless, definitely my conception at the time that it was an authentic broadcast of that nature. I am still of that opinion, that it used that precise wording, keeping in mind, as I indicated this morning, that my recollections on that are that only one country was involved." What did he mean? First he said that he presently believed the message was a false alarm, and now he implied it was not.

"What country was that?" asked Cooper.

"To the best of my recollection, it was England."

He became irascible under cross-examination and turned

openly irate when asked if anyone had tried to get him to change the testimony he had given at the Navy Inquiry. "There never was any such person," Kramer exclaimed, denying the charges that Sonnett had put pressure on him.

"Have you ever been 'beset and beleaguered'?" asked Murphy, referring to Keefe's charge after an earlier visit to Kramer at Bethesda Hospital.

"At no time," said Kramer sharply, "have I been beset and beleaguered."

"Did anyone 'badger' you?"

"That statement, sir, is false," he said.

He was equally upset when Cooper asked if he felt the General Staffs of the Army and Navy were crooks or would "frame" Kimmel or anyone else. "Such phenomena are inconceivable to my mind."

That evening Kramer listened to radio commentator Fulton Lewis, Jr.'s broadcast in which he referred to Kramer's testimony as "very irate," "antagonistic" and "reluctant." The following morning he was chastened, prefacing his testimony with an apology. "It may well be that he [Lewis] is accurate in this regard, inasmuch as I left this witness chair at 5 P.M. yesterday afternoon, after testifying for approximately six hours, with a slight headache, undoubtedly due to the fact that I am somewhat out of condition physically. Mr. Chairman, my effort has been to be as objective and cooperative with this committee as I possibly could. In pursuance of this policy I have been as truthful as I could. . . . If I have created any impression of irrationalism, antagonism or reluctance, I feel I am under obligation to apologize to this committee and assure the members that my only intention in tone of voice or manner was emphasis on points I was making. I will endeavor to amend my tone and manner during further inquiry."

He proceeded to apologize to Keefe for a gruff remark during the discussion on his stay at Bethesda Hospital. Keefe good-naturedly said no apology was called for.

During the afternoon session Kramer produced what the Washington *Times-Herald* described as "new fireworks" by producing from a little black satchel a hitherto secret letter which Kimmel had written to Halsey four months before the opening of the Navy Inquiry. In this letter Kimmel asked his fellow admiral to have Kramer answer a list of enclosed questions about the "winds" execute and other matters, and sign an affidavit. "I will assure him that I will make no use of the affidavit without his permission so long as he is alive."

Kramer testified that after Halsey showed him the letter he did promise to write the affidavit, then changed his mind and, instead, wrote a memorandum for Admiral Halsey setting down what he recollected and asking for Halsey's advice. Keefe strode over to the witness chair to look at the memorandum to the accompaniment of photographers' flash bulbs. It was mighty funny, he said, that Kramer had been allowed to disclose "at the tail end of this examination, what appears to be a very important and vital instrument which has been in the possession of the Navy and no one knew anything about it. Now how are we ever going to be sure unless these things are going to be turned over to our counsel in advance, what facts there are? I haven't read it, I don't know what is in it, but it seems to me, if we are to believe what Captain Kramer says, that it represents his idea as to what the facts were when he wrote this in the spring of 1944."

Kramer then revealed that he had had no intention of introducing the Safford letters or that day's material into the hearing until they were specifically requested. Ferguson was angry. "Now, is there any doubt, from now on, Captain, that you are going to give the truth, the whole truth, and nothing but?"

Kramer related that he had taken the memorandum to Halsey, who read it and handed it back. "I thought about it in fact all through the summer of 1944, and it was only after my testimony before Admiral Murfin's court of inquiry that I felt no further necessity of even thinking about that. I simply kept those papers with me."

"And up to the time you testified before Admiral Murfin's court of inquiry you had been giving a lot of thought to this question?" asked Keefe.

Only to what disposition he could make of the papers. "Not to the subject matter of that piece of paper."

"You were satisfied that the statements which you made in this memorandum prepared out there in the South Pacific were the truth?"

"Yes, sir, as of that time." He had not read the memorandum since he prepared it for Halsey.

"You mean you have had it in your possession all this time, and you haven't read it until now?" Keefe was incredulous.

"I have not read it to this moment, sir."

The committee adjourned to the Judiciary Committee room for an executive session. They decided not to put the memorandum in the record because of security; and later declined to reveal their decision to the press. They did announce that they might hold night sessions, in view of the surprising developments, with the aim still to wind up the inquiry by February 15.

The following morning, Saturday the ninth, Keefe read Kramer's testimony at the Navy Inquiry. When questioned which Japanese words were used in the message Kramer had replied: *"Higashi no kaze ame,* I am quite certain. The literal meaning of *Higashi no kaze ame* is East wind, rain. That is plain Japanese language. The sense of that, however, meant strained relations or a break in relations, possibly implying war with a nation to the eastward, the United States."

And now, asked Keefe, the captain was testifying that the Japanese words in the message were not *Higashi no kaze ame?*

"No words referring to the United States."

"Well," asked Keefe, "were there any words at all in it that you remember?"

"Yes, sir," he said, but when asked if he remembered what the words were said, "I do not, sir."

Keefe was skeptical. "Now, you, as the man in charge of translations of these messages, with the knowledge that the whole government was set to pick up this very vital and important message, who handled that message, who saw it, who read it, who checked the interpretation of the watch officer on that message, sit here before us today, and say you can't tell us what that message said, you have no recollection of what it said at all; is that correct?"

"That is correct, sir. However, I would like to point out to you, Mr. Keefe, that I think that an entirely unwarranted emphasis and importance is being attributed to that message, not only in this hearing but in past hearings, and in the press." This had been the thesis of Mitchell, who successfully passed it on to Richardson. And now Kramer had accepted it as his own.

Later that afternoon the decision to withhold the memorandum Kramer had written to Halsey was reversed. With the exception of one question, it was introduced into the records. Its importance lay in the fact that it represented Kramer's best memory of the "winds" execute in 1944 after much thought. Kramer now testified that he later showed the memorandum to Admiral Wilkinson, Captain Rochefort and a Marine colonel in charge of the Far Eastern Section of Naval Intelligence. The three occasions had occurred from December 6, 1945, to January 9, 1946. Yet Kramer insisted he himself had never reread it.

Brewster, who had been conducting this inquiry, was equally skeptical. "Do you expect that it can be credited that during this month that elapsed from December 6 to January 9, during this period when you were showing these papers to three different men because of your very great concern, apparently, over your name being used in connection with this, asking your friend the captain about it, and asking for an interview with the colonel, that during all that period you never once examined, yourself, this memorandum which you present here now?"

"I did not, Senator."

"You realize how difficult it is for anyone to credit a statement of that sort, Captain, when you were really disturbed, that you never examined this paper which you present?"

"By 'examine,' if you mean to infer that I read this paper, I did not." He repeated, "I did not." Credulity was further stretched when the distraught Kramer said, "I have, without question, looked at certain points that I may have pointed out or that they may have pointed out. I do not believe that that occurred, though, sir, I think in each case, Senator, there was practically no conversation throughout this paper."

"You were taking this to them without a statement of the background, and your recollection and your action?" asked Brewster with utter disbelief. "We are going to recess over the weekend. I wish you would ponder that question, from the standpoint of the difficulties which we face. I can see no reason why you should not have examined it. I do not think you would be subject to any criticism if you had examined it. I have been amazed from the beginning that you insisted that you did not see it, that you base your entire present recollection on the refreshment you received with officers who examined that document; that under those circumstances it must have seemed proper for you to refresh your recollection from something you wrote more than a year and a half ago in Noumea. I think it would make it far easier for us to credit your story if we could believe you examined that paper at some time in the last month."

On Monday morning Brewster was unable to attend and the questioning was taken over by Ferguson. He said he would give Kramer the opportunity to explain what had been left up in the air over the weekend. Kramer said he had pondered Brewster's request and would like to read a statement. It went on so long and was so diffuse that Richardson was visibly impatient. And when Kramer began reading from his own diary, the chief counsel interrupted, "Is there any need of carrying this on?" The only question that had been asked by Senator Brewster "was the question of keeping this memorandum in your possession without reading it." Kramer tried to explain why he had been so long-winded. "Go ahead," said Richardson. "Get through with it."

Now Murphy protested. "Mr. Chairman, in fairness to the witness, the senator from Maine did ask him to ponder."

The vice chairman was also impatient. "Go ahead, Captain," he said.

"In November last year my wife came to Washington from Miami and remained with me until our departure on November 14 for Miami. On my return alone to Washington in early December to await the pleasure of this committee I determined to keep notes in some detail of my activities, people I met, old acquaintances seen again, and so forth, so that on my expected return to Miami for the Christmas holidays she could read them over and I would thus be able to acquaint her of the above in detail without depending on memory alone." He went on and on and finally answered Brewster's question in a long, tangled sentence swearing that he had definitely *not* read the memorandum. More than half an hour had been taken up to arrive at an explanation which by no means satisfied the minority. Even some neutral observers were finding their credulity taxed. The question to most observers now was who was more likely to be telling the truth about the "winds" execute—Kramer or the quixotic Laurance Safford? Late that afternoon it was announced that the latter, in ceremonies at the Navy Department, had been awarded the Legion of Merit for "exceptionally meritorious conduct" in cryptographic research from March 1942 to September 1945. "A dynamic leader combining strong purpose and creative imagination with a profound knowledge of mechanical and electrical science and their cryptographic applications, Captain Safford was the driving force behind the development of the perfected machines which today give the United States Navy the finest system of encipherment in the world." He had, read the citation, "contributed essentially to the successful prosecution of the war." It was a shocking rebuff to those attempting to discredit and demean Safford, and indicated there were men in high naval posts who not only regarded him highly but openly supported him.

In his broadcast that night Fulton Lewis, Jr., said, "The net significance of the whole thing is a practical demonstration that the Navy has nothing against Captain Safford for what he has said before the Pearl Harbor Committee. . . . A gorgeous gesture, on very high ground, indeed, and it calls for a bow of respect to the Navy officials who were broad-minded enough to do it."

The Democratic members of the committee were indignant at the award and suggested that Kramer be granted "some medal of higher dignity than that which was given to Captain Safford."

Chapter Twelve

"TO THROW AS SOFT A LIGHT AS POSSIBLE ON THE WASHINGTON SCENE"

1.

On Lincoln's birthday a far different breed of witness appeared. Lieutenant Colonel Henry C. Clausen was not at all daunted by the committee and its battery of counsel. A lawyer himself, he faced cross-examination with refreshing cockiness. When it was suggested that Stimson and the War Department had meant him to "slant" his one-man investigation, he bridled. "No, sir. I would not have conducted it if they had." Were there instructions that he should in any way attempt to have a witness change his evidence? "No, sir," briskly.

A query from Ferguson on the pre-war American agreement with the British, Chinese and Dutch was revelatory. Clausen said that an investigation of this nature "would lead to the White House and I was told that it was beyond the scope of my functions to investigate there."

The next day Clausen talked frankly about his relationship with Stimson, whom he admired greatly. "When you made your investigation," asked Ferguson, "did you ever look into his diary?"

"No, sir."

"Why not?"

"Well, you mean I should investigate the investigator? That would be like the grand jury investigating the grand jury. You told him to do the job. If you wanted somebody else to investigate Stimson you should have said so in the law."

On February 14 Clausen assured Gearhart that he had been "as free as the wind as to what I could do so far as uncovering evidence was concerned. I mean by that, Mr. Gearhart, and I want you to believe this, there was no compulsion, no restraint, nothing put upon me except that in which I agreed."

During the day Senator Lucas read Keefe's statement in the House the previous November that Clausen "at the instigation of the War Department and Secretary of War" had apparently "browbeat" Colonel Bratton into signing an affidavit changing his previous testimony.

Then Lucas turned to Clausen, a man of average size. "What I want to specifically know is whether or not you browbeat this 225-pound colonel here into giving evidence that was other than what he considered at that time the truth."

It was a comical concept from a physical aspect.

"No, sir."

The next witness was the burly Bratton, who had first made a statement to the Army Board that he had delivered the thirteen-part message to Bedell Smith and General Gerow. Now, under the grilling of the associate general counsel, Samuel Kaufman, Bratton was trying to explain why he had changed his testimony to Clausen. "This is the point at which my memory begins to go bad on me. I cannot state positively whether there was any delivery made that night or not at this time. . . . At the time when I made the statement to the Grunert Board I had not remembered, or I did not remember, that Colonel Dusenbury was working with me in the office that night." Since making the statement to the Army Board Clausen had shown him affidavits from Bedell Smith and Gerow denying that they had received the thirteen-part message that Saturday night.

"Now, I know all these men. I do not doubt the honesty and integrity of any one of them, and if they say that I did not deliver these pouches to them that night, then my memory must have been at fault."

It was odd that after such abasement he was preparing to challenge Marshall himself. Just before leaving Berlin to testify at the hearings, he had vowed to his friend, Colonel Heimlich, that he was going "to blow the roof off that inquiry!"

He began by testifying that it was Marshall who, sometime in August 1941, had ordered him not to send Magic to the overseas theaters. But Bratton became so convinced by subsequent Magic messages that war was coming that he decided to take a chance and send a warning to Hawaii.

Then he produced the carefully wrapped package of photostats he had brought from Berlin; it was the long memorandum requested by Roosevelt on Japanese and German preparations for war from 1937 to Pearl Harbor. This was the report Bratton had discussed in 1943 with Colonel Yeaton, who had advised him to have the entire volume photostated at once and kept in a safe place.

Now at last he had nerved himself to reveal that Marshall personally had deleted vital portions of the memorandum. One stricken part dated 1937 was read aloud by Ferguson:

" 'There is a possibility, fantastic as it may seem, that Japan contemplates military action against Great Britain in the Orient at a time when she is involved in Europe, with the idea of seizing Hong Kong and Singapore, and ultimately acquiring the Dutch oil fields and control of trade routes to the Orient . . . it is not improbable that this country will be compelled to apply the Neutrality Act and ultimately become involved.'

"Now who struck that out of the report?" asked Ferguson.

"To the best of my knowledge and belief it was stricken out by General Marshall in person."

"Well, now, will you tell us whether or not that was a false report that you had inserted in there or was it true?"

"The report was true to the best of our knowledge and

belief and was based on intelligence that we had secured from various sources. . . . All of the items that were stricken out of this book, to the best of our knowledge and belief, were supported by documents not on file in G-2. . . . I may say this is a document that has been referred to a number of times by my chief, General Miles. He attempted to get this committee to take cognizance of this document on a number of occasions while he was testifying but nobody seemed to take an interest.'' He explained that the Far Eastern volume was supported by more than ten volumes of photostats of original documents on file in G-2.

Richardson ridiculed the entire matter. ''Here is a review made by a person two years after Pearl Harbor. It is of no more importance than a review made by the Washington *Post* or the Chicago *Tribune*.'' His equation of an official War Department report based on voluminous secret material with a newspaper review was ludicrous. Equally so was his misunderstanding of the seriousness of deleting material for the eyes of the President foreseeing war with Japan over a period of years from 1937, an action interpreted by Bratton to Yeaton as a cover-up by the Chief of Staff of the Army.

Not a single thing in the volume was fact, charged the chief counsel with some heat. ''Everything is conclusion of this witness, historically, as to what happened. I don't care how many times it has been referred to here, but I am wondering as counsel how far the committee is going to go into the hindsight of some historian as to what the situation was at Pearl Harbor when we have all this trouble here trying to get foresight.''

Murphy and Ferguson, usually antagonists, joined in pressing the issue. The former moved that Bratton be allowed to read a letter explaining the import of what had been stricken out of the volume. The colonel read a memorandum, dated August 26, 1943, for General George Strong, the Army Intelligence Chief.

The attached tab does not comply with the directive in that it contains much material other than the MA reports. The Chief of Staff desires it to be revised to contain only MA reports.

By direction of the Chief of Staff

> (signed) W. T. Sexton
> Colonel, General Staff
> Secretary, General Staff

"Do I understand everything was stricken out except MA's?" asked Ferguson. "What is an MA? That is a military attaché?"

"Yes, sir," said Bratton. "The book was all torn to pieces by the Chief of Staff and everything deleted therefrom except the raw MA and MO reports, MO meaning military observer."

Asked for an example, Bratton read parts of a confidential lecture delivered to the faculty and students of the Army War College which gave the opinion of the Far Eastern Section as to the approaching war. He then gave other examples showing partial as well as total deletions in what he claimed was Marshall's own handwriting. "There are numerous comments on the margin all through the book which I believe, and General Strong also believed, to have been made by General Marshall in person." Strong, he said, had told him this upon the return of the volume from the Chief of Staff in 1943.

There were no more questions from the committee. It was already after 10 P.M. The matter was dropped; and Bratton disappeared into obscurity.[1]

2.

Colonel Sadtler was the next witness. As bitter and disillusioned as Bratton, he also was determined to at last fight back. To the committee's surprise he reverted to the first testimony he had given the Army Board. Yes, he *had* told Gerow about the "winds" execute on December 5 and it undoubtedly meant a Japanese break with Britain

---

[1] He retired in 1952, still a colonel, and moved to Hawaii. Six years later, an embittered man, he died at Tripler Army Hospital.

and America. Then he *did* see Bedell Smith. "I said, 'The Winds message is in,' as I recall the wording."

"So you told him the Winds message was in," said Ferguson. "And did you ask him to get it to General Marshall, that word that it was in?"

"As I remember it, he asked me what I had done and I told him I had talked to General Miles and General Gerow. . . . He said he didn't care to discuss it further."

"What did that really mean, that he didn't want to discuss it further?"

"That I was through. . . . Had done as much as I could possibly do."

". . . Did he say as to whether or not he would convey this to General Marshall?"

"No, sir."

"Then, I assume, you thought your mission had been performed, when you told them that the Winds message was in?"

"I think I had gone a little too far in talking to either General Gerow or Colonel Bedell Smith."

Had Sadtler considered it was a genuine message? Yes. "So far as you were concerned, the Winds message was in and it meant war."

"Yes, sir." He also verified that, before the rebuff from both Gerow and Smith, he had prepared a warning message to Hawaii, Panama and the Philippines that read:

Reliable information indicates war with Japan in the very near future Stop Take every precaution to prevent a repetition of Port Arthur Stop Notify the Navy. Marshall.

"And you did it because of the mounting tension and flow of information which you had together with the Winds Execute at that time?" asked Ferguson.

Yes, but the message was never sent. "I did not show it to anyone. I do not know where the message is now, and I made no copy at the time."

This was the testimony that Sadtler had given to the Army Board and then, after being confronted by written denials from Gerow and Smith, had reversed to Clausen. Keefe asked for a clarification of the confusing double reverse. Did Sadtler now mean to tell the committee "positively and without question" that he was challenging the denials of Gerow and Smith?

"Absolutely," said Sadtler. "I talked to both of them." This unequivocal statement was not only an attack on the credibility of Gerow and Smith but a covert admission that Sadtler had reversed himself to Clausen out of fear of opposing the Army hierarchy.

He also declared that the "winds" intercept "was the most important message that I think I ever handled in my life." Murphy challenged its importance. After the messages that preceded it, what exactly did the "winds" message do? "It capped the climax," said Sadtler.

"In what way?"

"That everything is here. Now we have the whole thing. . . . Now, there was nothing but the Winds message, which was a message that we had been straining every nerve to get; we had everybody listening for that message."

The dramatics provided by Bratton and Sadtler were surpassed by revelations from the surprise naval witness who followed. He was Commander Lester Robert Schulz, who had taken a message to Roosevelt on the night of December 6, 1941.

In late November 1945, after a request by Ferguson to locate witnesses who had been at the White House, the Navy Pearl Harbor Liaison group, headed by Commander John Ford Baecher, had requested that Schulz, chief engineer of the U.S.S. *Indiana* docked at Puget Sound Navy Yard, Bremerton, Washington, be ordered for temporary duty in connection with the congressional investigation. Since Schulz was needed at Bremerton, it was decided to retain him on the West Coast until the committee was ready for him to testify. A week later Commander Baecher telephoned Schulz and learned that he had been on watch at the White House on Pearl Harbor eve; and that he had received the thirteen-part message delivered by Kramer at about 9:30 P.M. Schulz revealed that he had personally carried the message to the President and stood by while he read it.

Having spent the night of February 14 on board a Navy transport plane from San Francisco, Schulz had slept very little. He arrived in the capital about 9 A.M. to be met by a Navy officer who took him to the Navy Department where he talked briefly with Commander Baecher. Schulz had been reading about the hearings and disagreed completely with any innuendoes that the President could have known in advance of the Japanese attack. Not yet being aware of the significance of the Magic messages, he didn't feel that he had much to offer as a witness.

As Schulz entered the caucus room, Keefe was winding up his interrogation of Sadtler. Informed that Schulz had arrived, Ferguson hurriedly escorted him to the reception room of the Judiciary Committee for a short talk. When Ferguson returned to his seat he leaned over and whispered to Greaves, "This is it!"

After Schulz met Richardson, whom he did not then know, he was brought into the caucus room. The appearance of the mystery witness kindled interest and the explosion of flash bulbs surprised the young commander.

Richardson asked if Schulz recalled Captain Kramer coming to the White House on the evening of December 6 to deliver some papers.

"He handed them to me," said Schulz. "They were in a locked pouch. . . . I took it from the mail room, which is in the office building, over to the White House proper and obtained permission to go up on the second floor and took it to the President's study." An usher announced him and left. "The President was there seated at his desk and Mr. Hopkins was there. . . . I informed the President that I had the material which Captain Kramer had brought and I took it out of the pouch." As Schulz recalled, Mr. Roosevelt was expecting the material. There was a hush of expectation in the room. Schulz's open, bright face radiated credibility. The committee members listened in rapt silence. "The President read the papers, which took perhaps ten minutes." Then he handed them to Hopkins, who had been slowly pacing back and forth. "Mr. Hopkins then read the papers and handed them back to the President. The President then turned toward Mr. Hopkins and said in substance—I am not sure of the exact words, but in substance—'This means war.'"

There was an excited murmur, a stirring of chairs. Several photographers moved within a few feet of Schulz and began taking pictures. Startled by the flash bulbs, Schulz wondered what the excitement was about. The photographers, under orders to take no pictures once testimony began, were reprimanded and Murphy told Schulz to relax.

"Mr. Hopkins agreed," he continued, "and they discussed then, for perhaps five minutes, the situation of the Japanese forces, that is, their deployment and—"

"Can you recall what either of them said?" asked Richardson.

"In substance I can. There are only a few words that I can definitely say I am sure of, but the substance of it was that—I believe Mr. Hopkins mentioned it first—that since war was imminent, that the Japanese intended to strike when they were ready, at a moment when all was most opportune for them—"

In the excitement, Barkley could not hear. "When all was what?"

"When all was most opportune for them. That is, when their forces were most properly deployed for their advantage. Indochina in particular was mentioned, because the Japanese forces had already landed there and there were implications of where they should move next. The President mentioned a message that he had sent to the Japanese Emperor concerning the presence of Japanese troops in Indochina, in effect requesting their withdrawal. Mr. Hopkins then expressed a view that since war was undoubtedly going to come at the convenience of the Japanese, it was too bad that we could not strike the first blow and prevent any sort of surprise. The President nodded and then said, in effect, 'No, we can't do that. We are a democracy and a peaceful people.' Then he raised his voice, and this much I remember definitely. He said, 'But we have a good record.' The impression that I got was that we would have to stand on that record, we could not make the first overt move. We would have to wait until it came."

Schulz heard no mention of Pearl Harbor. "The time at

which war might begin was not discussed, but from the manner of the discussion there was no indication that tomorrow was necessarily the day. I carried that impression away because it contributed to my personal surprise when the news did come.''

Neither Roosevelt nor Hopkins mentioned sending any further warning or alert to overseas posts. ''However, having concluded this discussion about the war going to begin at the Japanese convenience, then the President said that he believed he would talk to Admiral Stark. He started to get Admiral Stark on the telephone.'' The President, so recalled the commander, was told by the telephone operator that Stark could be reached at the National Theater ''and the President went on to state, in substance, that he would reach the admiral later, that he did not want to cause public alarm by having the admiral paged or otherwise when in the theater, where I believe, the fact that he had a box reserved was mentioned and that if he had left suddenly he would surely have been seen because of the position which he held and undue alarm might be caused, and the President did not wish that to happen because he could get him within perhaps another half an hour in any case.''

''Was there anything said about telephoning anybody else except Stark?''

''No, sir, there was not.''

''How did he refer to Admiral Stark?''

''When he first mentioned calling him, he referred to him as 'Betty.'''

Schulz had made an excellent impression on all the members of the committee as well as the observers. No one doubted that he was telling the truth. As he left the room no reporters or photographers followed. They were busy with the next witness. He left alone but was soon invited by Admiral Noyes to ride with him back to the main Navy Building. Schulz was glad the ordeal was over and still couldn't understand why there had been so much excitement. It was an uneasy ride. He was somewhat in awe of the admiral and did not feel comfortable conversing with him. Schulz was also somewhat concerned about his recent testimony. Had the committee really understood

Roosevelt? After all, there was a big difference between feeling war was imminent and expecting it to begin with an attack on Pearl Harbor. So much could be inferred from the tone of voice. The President, for instance, had said, "This means war," calmly without emotion. Could he possibly have unwittingly harmed the President, whom he admired and held in high esteem?

3.

Five days later, after uneventful interrogations of eleven more witnesses, the hearings were suspended. "The committee had some differences with respect to procedure," commented peacemaker Barkley in closing, "but these differences were no doubt inherent in the situation; but they have not been too serious. . . . I might say that the committee and counsel have a vast amount of work yet to do before we get our report ready for the Congress, and I am sure we will pursue that phase of this task with the same diligence and I hope the great thoroughness with which we have concluded the hearing." Whereupon, at 5:15 P.M., February 20, the committee adjourned, subject to call of the Chair. The committee now had until June 1 to assess the evidence it had received and prepare their report.

Over a period of three months and five days there had been sixty-seven days and three nights of public hearings. The testimony of thirty-nine witnesses comprised almost 14,000 pages. Even so, many witnesses deemed important by the minority were not called. These included Bedell Smith, Forrestal, the judge advocates of the Army and Navy who had instigated the Clausen and Hewitt investigations, Marshall's orderlies and two top State Department Far East advisers, Maxwell Hamilton and Stanley Hornbeck. The latter, sent off recently to Holland as ambassador, had more to say about the Pacific Fleet than the Navy itself, according to Admiral Richardson's testimony. Hull was not recalled for Republican cross-examination on medical grounds, and Secretary of War Stimson had a heart attack the day it was announced he was to be summoned.

"The Congressional Pearl Harbor investigation, one of the longest and most extraordinary in the history of any country," commented William S. White in the New York *Times,* "closed this week, but the fog of doubt and accusation that has hung so long about that disaster has been dispelled only in part."

The day was marked by a tragedy involving an important witness. That morning, Vice Admiral Theodore Wilkinson, former head of Navy Intelligence, drove a borrowed Cadillac sedan off the ferry *West Point* at Norfolk. As the car rolled down the port side at about twenty miles an hour, a deckhand, Luke Piland, shouted, "Stop that car, man, you're driving too fast!" Piland threw a block beneath a wheel of the car but the Cadillac went over this obstruction, crashed through the forward chain and gate to plunge into the Elizabeth River. Piland saw the admiral bent over the wheel. ("I thought he would open the door and make a leap out," he later testified. "He never did straighten up any more.")

As the car hit the water, Wilkinson shouted to his wife to open her window. She did and was halfway through when the car sank. She surfaced and was rescued, but a diver found the admiral's body stuck behind the wheel. Wilkinson was still clutching the steering post. His window was wide open. "He died at the peak of his career," said Secretary of the Navy Forrestal. "There goes with him on his last journey the heartfelt 'well done' of all hands."

The freak accident sparked rumors that Wilkinson had committed suicide because he had defied the military hierarchy during his earlier testimony to the committee. He, it will be recalled, had insisted there had been messages indicating the Japanese feared the Purple code had been compromised—and then produced eleven intercepts which Marshall and others had testified did not exist.

Some supporters of Safford reasoned that, being a man of honor, Wilkinson had not been able to live with the fact that he had not come forward with the truth about the "winds" execute. Safford himself believed this. Referring to the October 1941 Mutiny on the Second Deck, he wrote, "Wilkinson was the only decent one in the lot, the only one to show any remorse." The Wilkinsons had been close friends of the Saffords and, after the tragic incident at Norfolk, the admiral's widow had come to Mrs. Safford to accuse her husband of "causing Ping's death" by his dogged persistency in the Pearl Harbor controversy.

A Naval Board of Investigation, after a thorough inquiry, concluded that his drowning was accidental "and was not the result of his own misconduct, and that his death was not caused in any manner by the intent, fault, negligence or inefficiency of any person in the naval service."

By late March Baecher reported to Forrestal that Seth Richardson had submitted a draft of a proposed report concluding that "Washington must bear a large share of the burden for what occurred on 7 December 1941." However, his assistant, Sam Kaufman,[2] would submit a draft "more in keeping with the views of the Democrats. It places the primary responsibility for the Pearl Harbor disaster on the command in Hawaii, chiefly because of failure to take reconnaissance and other action after receipt of the war warning message."

A few days later there was a surprise move. George Marshall, recently returned from China, was summoned to another session at the caucus room. He and Stark arrived on the morning of April 11. The admiral still could not remember where he was on the night of December 6 despite testimony that he had been at the National Theater attending a performance of *The Student Prince*. "It does not ring any bell with me that I was there that night, but I can assume, in view of the testimony of Commander Schulz and of others who tried to contact me, and my remembrance of having seen the revival, that I probably was there." Nor did he recall getting any telephone message later that night from the President.

---

[2]Kaufman further demonstrated his pro-Administration sympathies during the first trial of Alger Hiss.

On May 23 written answers to questions by the minority to Hull and Stimson were entered in the record. The latter responded only to those questions he felt worth answering. At twelve-fifteen the work was finished and Barkley announced that the record of the investigation was now officially closed. The inquiry, editorialized the New York *Times*, "has ended as it began on a note of Republican suspicion," and it seemed inevitable that a "majority report and a minority report—along strictly party lines—will be written."

But there was the one final dramatic surprise in this inquiry of surprises. On May 25, Captain Harold Krick and his wife had dinner with their old friends, the Starks. Krick had been the admiral's flag lieutenant and the Starks had treated the Krick children as if they were grandchildren. As the admiral was carving he casually mentioned how happy he was that the hearings were over at last. But one thing bothered him. He hadn't been able to tell the committee where he was on the night of December 6.

"Well, we know," said Krick. "We were with you at dinner; and then we went to the National Theater." The Kricks both reminded Stark that after the show the President had called. They would never forget it.

Stark did recall the dinner party and the show but, although he racked his mind far into the night, the Roosevelt telephone call remained a blank. The more he thought about his previous testimony the more convinced he became "that the committee should have this, the record should have it straight, and I got up around two or three in the morning, thinking this thing over. . . ." He wrote a letter to Barkley in longhand stating that he wanted this new evidence placed before the committee.

Five of the members of the committee were out of town but, since Stark was scheduled to leave for London on May 31 to receive a decoration, Barkley called an emergency meeting for 10 A.M. of that day in Room 312 of the Senate Office Building. Only Barkley, George and Lucas were present. Keefe promised to come later but the others were unavailable.

"Admiral," said Richardson, "if the President had told

you in his talk with you that night, assuming that you talked to him, and had told you that it was his opinion that this thirteen-part message meant war, thereby impressed you with his serious estimate of it, what would have been, in accordance with your custom, the action for you to have then taken, with that information?''

''I don't know, sir, that I would have, that we would have sent anything more. I think that I should have gotten in touch with Ingersoll and with Turner. . . . We thought, and the President knew every move we had made, that we had sent everything possible, on that premise, that war was in the immediate offing. I don't know that I would have done anything. I couldn't say.''

At last Keefe arrived. He was disturbed and unhappy at the last-minute notice. Barkley explained that the admiral was leaving for London that night and it wasn't right merely to file his letter with the committee. ''I raised the question,'' said Keefe, ''because I had understood that the hearings had, by action of the committee, been closed, and that the testimony had been closed, and I want to keep the record clear, in the absence of my colleagues, none of whom are present here this morning.''

After Krick was duly sworn by the chairman, he told about the dinner, the theater and the return to the Stark home.

''What occurred when you went into his house?'' asked Richardson.

''One of the admiral's servants advised the admiral that—''

''What did he say?''

''That there had been a White House call during the evening, sir. . . . The admiral excused himself and retired to his study on the second floor and returned.''

''How long was he there?''

''I would say approximately between five and ten minutes.'' Then he came downstairs.

''Did he say anything to you?''

''Only to the extent that the conditions in the Pacific were serious; that was the substance of it, that conditions with Japan were in a critical state, something of that sort, sir.''

"Did he say anything to you, as near as you can recall, that he had had a telephone message, on the second floor?"

"That is my inference. There is absolutely no doubt in my mind about it, sir. But I do not recall the exact statement. I do not recall that he stated, 'I have talked with the President of the United States.' But I heard, of course, the statement of the servant that there had been a White House call, and the admiral retired immediately, and he may have stated that he was going to call the White House; but I have the distinct impression that the conversation was with the White House." Did he have any impression that upon his return from upstairs Admiral Stark made any statement that his talk had been with the White House? "My impression very definitely was that; yes, sir."[3]

The interrogation was accelerated with only Lucas asking a few questions, and at 11:15 A.M. the committee adjourned, this time for good. What would have been a sensational revelation several months earlier was interred by exasperation and a desire by all parties to make an end to the matter. And so the hearings ended not with a bang but a whimper.

4.

Besides the two memoranda submitted by Richardson and Kaufman there were two others designed to assist the committee in making its report. One, by assistant counsel John Masten, concentrated on the diplomatic phase and echoed the opinions of the Democrats; the second, by another assistant counsel, Edward P. Morgan,[4] also represented the Administration's viewpoint.

These last two memoranda displeased the four Republicans. And when Barkley told reporters, after a lengthy closed session on July 6, ". . . my hope is that we can make a unanimous report," Keefe announced that he was positive there would be more than one report.

[3] In an interview with the author his wife confirmed the impression.

[4] Morgan later wrote the Tydings Committee report, described by Republicans as a whitewash of the State Department.

Within a week a majority report based on the Morgan memorandum was concluded. But there were important modifications. Morgan had stated, "Indeed, had the keen awareness of Japanese deceit and bestiality voiced by the Secretary of State characterized thinking elsewhere, the disaster of Pearl Harbor as we know it might never have occurred." This was changed to "The President, the Secretary of State, and high Government officials made every possible effort, without sacrificing our national honor and endangering our security to avert war with Japan."

Morgan's flat statement that the disaster was the failure of "the Army and Navy in Hawaii" was modified by the removal of the words "in Hawaii." Again where Morgan charged that Kimmel and Short "were fully conscious of the danger from air attack," the final report read, "Officers, both in Washington and Hawaii, were fully conscious of the danger from air attack."

On July 16 the violently anti-Administration columnist, John T. Flynn, received a startling telephone call from a Washington correspondent: Congressman Gearhart was about to join the majority in its report.

Flynn immediately wrote Gearhart that he was profoundly shocked.

I earnestly hope there is no truth in the somewhat roundabout rumor that came to me, but it was enough to surprise and grieve me. Recalling so many of the things that you said during the hearings, I simply could not credit it. . . . I would be horrified beyond expression if I could be made to believe that you had changed your mind after so much that you said appears in the record itself, to take part with these fellows in the job they were appointed to perform and which apparently they are now about to complete.

If I could believe this rumor that has come to me to be true, it would help to explain so much that has happened to this country and the Republican Party in the last dozen years. I begin to tremble for the fate of this country.

Flynn wrote Keefe about the rumor. "It confirmed what

you told me yourself and I was so greatly disturbed that I wrote Gearhart. I did not, of course, mention that you had talked to me.''

The news about Gearhart was true. Much more astounding was Keefe's signature on the majority report. He had signed after promises to alter other Morgan conclusions. Whereas Morgan had found that Hawaii had been ''adequately and properly alerted on the basis of the November 27 warnings,'' the majority agreed to conclude that ''The Intelligence and War Plans Divisions of the War and Navy Departments failed'' in this respect. The majority also consented to state as their final conclusion: ''Under all of the evidence the War and Navy Departments were not sufficiently alerted on December 6 and 7, 1941, in view of the imminence of war.''

The Washington gossip was that Gearhart had been intimidated. In 1934 he had won both the Democratic and Republican nominations and held them both until losing the Democratic primary that June. This had come about after the Administration, knowing he represented a strong anti-Japanese California district, launched an attack charging Gearhart was pro-Jap and even wore a kimono. Now to save his seat in November he had gone along with the Democrats.

The case of Frank Keefe was far different. He tried to explain to Flynn in a letter why he had signed the majority report.

I did succeed in getting many ideas incorporated through changes of language and interpretations and in the addition of conclusions. . . . However, because the whole report is slanted in the wrong direction, in my opinion, I have filed my own views in a separate report. My signature to the committee report is with reservations. Gearhart has unfortunately signed the report without any reservations, and although he thoroughly agrees with the views which I have expressed in a separate report, he could not sign the same for reasons that are best known to himself. (The fact that he may have an election coming up may have something to do with his decision.)

Keefe's 24-page "Additional Views" statement condemned not only Marshall and the Administration but also the bias of the majority report. "The committee report, I feel, does not with exactitude apply the same yardstick in measuring responsibilities at Washington as had been applied to the Hawaiian commanders. I cannot suppress the feeling that the committee report endeavors to throw as soft a light as possible on the Washington scene." Rugg and Hanify helped Keefe draft his "Additional Views," and according to the anti-Administration historian, Charles A. Beard, they "constitute an arraignment of the Roosevelt Administration's management of affairs during the months before December 7, 1941, which is, in many ways, sharper in tone than the 'propositions' filed by the two Republican Senators, Mr. Ferguson and Mr. Brewster. Indeed, in phrasing, Mr. Keefe's statement is even more like an indictment than the essentially historical Conclusions advanced by the minority. . . ."

Unfortunately for Keefe, the press sensationalized his signing of the majority report but almost completely ignored his "Additional Views," which were not released until the following day.

Unlike Beard, Flynn could find no excuse for Keefe, and wrote a blistering reply.

Why did you have to sign a report which contained so much which according to your letter you did not agree to? Why could you not have done what any reasonable man would do—refuse to sign the report and file your own, which by the way, is what you said you would do?

I know, of course, that you were angered at Senator Ferguson[5] for what you believed was the manner in which he conducted his part of the investigation

[5] Keefe was handicapped throughout the hearings, wrote Percy Greaves, "by committee rules which permitted every other member prior opportunity to question each witness. Many of the questions he had worked up were exhausted by Senator Ferguson before Keefe's turn. Time after time, Keefe saw the Senator getting credit for uncovering many important points he, himself, had been prepared to reveal. Piqued by this fact, he was determined not to sign a report sponsored by the Senator."

and that you were annoyed at Senator Brewster for not being around. But what possible excuse could this be for you to put your signature to a document containing this complete exoneration of the President and Hull and the verdict that they ''did all in their power to avert war with Japan,'' when you know that they did not and when you repeatedly said not only to me but to many others that they did not. You will see what a mess you have made of the Republican share in the investigation when you see the newspapers of the country and the use they will make of your incredible folly.

Flynn's prediction was accurate. *P.M.* wrote, ''When two Republicans joined with six Democrats in signing a majority report which absolved the late President of blame in the disaster, any claims the partisans could make that the Congressional investigation under Democratic leadership was a 'whitewash' were knocked out.''

The less partisan New York *Herald Tribune* agreed. The majority report dissipated all the wildest rumors and suspicions ''and even the minority report by Senators Ferguson and Brewster offers no clear or convincing criticism of the basic course of the Administration policy. We are left with the intricate story of what happened upon which all are now substantially agreed, and that story in turn leaves us about where we began four and a half years ago.'' Now the public had the facts on record but there was no valid guide to the future conduct of both war and diplomacy. ''The committee failed to produce that searching critique and synthesis for which some hoped. Perhaps it was a hope too high to place on any politically-appointed investigation, unavoidably involved in partisan ends.''

Despite differences expressed by the two reports, it was now obvious that the wartime debate on Pearl Harbor was over. The avid critics of Roosevelt still remained vocal but, as a partisan political question and a public issue, Pearl Harbor was dead.

The principals in the affair were still left in limbo; Short, for one, felt he had been partially vindicated. Kimmel refused to comment to reporters but privately both he and Rugg felt that they had accomplished their purpose. They had placed the bulk of the material concerning the attack on record so that some historian in future years could study it with objectivity and reach conclusions. Preservation of the material to them both meant success.

Even so, many colleagues of Kimmel's remained indignant. "The most disgraceful feature of the whole affair," said Admiral Harry Yarnell, former commandant, Pearl Harbor Naval Base, "was the evident determination on the part of Washington to fasten the blame on the Hawaiian commanders. The incomplete and one-sided Roberts report, the circumstances of the retirements of Kimmel and Short, the attempts of the War and Navy Departments to deny access to the intercepted messages by the Naval Court of Inquiry and the Army Board of Investigation, the appointment of secret one-man boards to continue investigations, and finally, the inability of the Joint Congressional Committee to secure access to pertinent files, constitute a blot on our national history."

The fate of Captain Laurance Safford was perhaps the hardest to bear. In spite of the considerable evidence to the contrary, it was believed that he was mistaken about the "winds" execute. Even friends and colleagues were convinced there had been no such message. To them it was a tragedy that a man who had done practically everything right in the years before Pearl Harbor, and had built an organization which produced a wealth of solid intelligence which later helped win the Battle of Midway, could have risked his career by the fanatic pursuit of the "winds" execute. Now his achievements were all but forgotten and he was generally regarded as a brilliant eccentric whose obsession with cryptology had affected his judgment, and who had, indeed, suffered from hallucinations. The testimony of those others who had seen the "winds" execute was so buried in the complexity and verbiage of the inquiry that the general impression was that Safford and only Safford had ever seen the message.

Less than a month after the appearance of the Joint Congressional reports, Safford visited his old friend, William Friedman, the code expert, to view a ciphering machine. After the demonstration, Friedman asked him to autograph a copy of the statement on the "winds" execute Safford had prepared for the committee. Friedman asked how Safford *now* felt about the "winds" execute.

The captain looked at him rather intently, then said, "I feel I didn't *prove* it existed." He himself had prepared a war warning to send in case higher authorities did not do so.

"But," said Friedman, "it *might* have been based on an erroneous or false 'winds' execute."

"When you're going to by-pass higher authority," retorted Safford, "be damned sure your facts are right." Not only had he prepared the warning message but he had it encoded. And the man who encoded it remembered the message.

Was this introduced into evidence at the hearings? asked Friedman. No, said Safford, the encoder had been out of the country and unavailable until the hearings were over. Safford had not wanted to bring up the matter at the time since he could produce no corroborating witness. "In case the subject is reopened," said Safford, "I know I can get him to tell his story."

Friedman later wrote on the back of the statement autographed by Safford: "It is clear that S is of firm conviction there was an authentic 'Winds Execute', that it was intercepted, decoded, passed around—and has disappeared."

And so the majority of Americans, by midsummer 1946, were convinced that the "winds" execute was either a fabrication or a delusion, that Kimmel and Short should carry the burden of blame for Pearl Harbor, that George Marshall had been maligned cruelly, and that Hull, Stimson and Roosevelt had done their best to prevent war with a nation run by bandits.

Although all these conclusions had been disproved in the course of nine investigations, the truth had become so distorted by reversion of testimony, cover-up and outright lies that the only chance for it to emerge could come if all the secret records of Pearl Harbor were declassified; and those with special knowledge, like Ralph Briggs, had immunity to talk openly. Only then could a tenth investigation, carried out in full freedom, be made.

Part 4

THE TENTH
INVESTIGATION

"The truth must be repeated again and again because error is constantly being preached around us," Goethe told a friend in 1828. "And not only by isolated individuals, but by the majority! In the newspapers and encyclopedias, in the schools and universities, everywhere error is dominant, securely and comfortably ensconced in public opinion which is on its side."

Chapter Thirteen

OPERATION Z
1932–NOVEMBER 27, 1941

1.

An American hunchback, who became a Chinese general and helped organize the revolution that crushed the Manchu dynasty, published an imaginative history in 1909 exposing Japanese plans to conquer the United States. Homer Lea's *The Valor of Ignorance* inspired a demand among certain American military and naval circles for a preventive war against Japan. Lea foresaw that the Japanese would not only make easy conquest of the Philippines but seize Hawaii and Alaska, thus gaining control of the North Pacific. This extraordinary book accomplished something not intended by the author. It inspired those Japanese who felt that Asia was being held in bondage by the West to rise against their oppressors. The Japanese publisher of the book, which bore the title *The War Between Japan and America,* managed to sell 40,000 copies. No wonder, considering its advertising appeal: "More interesting than a novel, more mysterious than philosophy, this is excellent reading material for Oriental men with red blood in their veins." It became required reading for Army and Navy officers.

In 1918 Lenin predicted that Japan and America, though presently allies, were fated to be bitter enemies. ''The economic development of these countries over the course of several decades has stored up a great mass of inflammable material which renders inevitable a desperate conflict between these two powers for mastery of the Pacific Ocean and its shores.''

Seven years later a novel came out in England; *The Great Pacific War* provided further inspiration to the Japanese and was studied at their Naval War College. Hector C. Bywater, naval correspondent for the London *Daily Telegraph,* described a Japanese surprise attack on the U. S. Fleet in Pearl Harbor, with simultaneous assaults on Guam and the Philippines, and with landings on Luzon at Lingayen Gulf and Lamon Bay. Isoroku Yamamoto was serving as naval attaché in Washington in 1925 when the novel was reviewed on the first page of the *New York Times Book Review* under the headline, IF WAR COMES IN THE PACIFIC. Undoubtedly Yamamoto, an obsessive student of naval affairs, had the book called to his attention.

American naval experts took such a surprise attack even more seriously following the Grand Joint Army and Navy Exercise held in Hawaiian waters in February 1932. Involving the major portion of the Battle Force, United States Fleet, the exercise was designed ''to train the two Services in the joint operation involved in the defense of such an area. More specifically it is to determine the effectiveness of the air, surface, sub-surface and land defenses of Hawaii to repel such an attack.''

The commander of the attack force, Admiral H. E. Yarnell, revolutionized naval strategy by leaving battleships and cruisers behind while he raced from California with two carriers, *Saratoga* and *Lexington,* and an escort of destroyers. By tradition the commander of a fleet would have his headquarters on a battleship but Yarnell, an air-minded officer, was on *Saratoga.*

The defenders were expecting the traditional naval attack but Yarnell launched 152 planes half an hour before dawn, in the dark, forty miles northeast of Kahuku Point. It was Sunday the seventh of February. Although expecting some sort of air attack, the defenders were caught by surprise when planes, hidden by rain clouds over the Koolau Range, suddenly swooped down on the Army airfields and the area near Pearl Harbor as dawn was breaking. Yarnell had gained complete air supremacy, for most of the defender's planes were on the ground in dispersed and camouflaged positions.

It should have been a cautionary lesson but the Chief Umpire concluded: "It is doubtful if air attacks can be launched against Oahu in the face of strong defensive aviation without subjecting carriers to the danger of material damage and consequent great losses to the attacking air force."

The Japanese took a different view and by 1936 their Navy War College produced *Study of Strategy and Tactics in Operations Against the United States,* which stated: "In case the enemy's main fleet is berthed at Pearl Harbor, the idea should be to open hostilities by surprise attacks from the air."

The following April another U.S. exercise was held. One hundred and eleven warships and 400 planes left San Pedro Naval Base to "attack" Hawaii by surprise. Again planes bombed Oahu's airfields into submission, enabling troops to land the next day without opposition. The attackers lost only one ship, a battleship.

Still, so little had been done to defend against a surprise attack on Pearl Harbor that H. H. (Hap) Arnold, an Army Air Corps general, sounded a public warning in 1939 after a visit to Hawaii.

On our return to Washington [he wrote] I was quoted by the newspaper commentators as having said I would have liked nothing better than to have a chance to take a crack at Pearl Harbor from the air with all those ships lying at anchor. Whether I really said it or not, the target presented was an airman's dream—a concentration difficult to find. But worse, it seemed to me—though about this I could say nothing publicly—was the lack of unity of command in Hawaii. Here the dismal idea of "responsibility of the Army and Navy being divided at the shoreline" was as sadly evident as I had ever seen it. Actually, nobody was in over-all command, and thus there was no over-all defense.

Early in 1941 Admiral Richardson, about to be relieved of his command of the Pacific Fleet because of opposition to Roosevelt's insistence that the fleet remain stationed at Pearl Harbor, complained to Stark of the inadequacy of defense against air attack. He also complained that there did not appear to be "any practicable way of placing torpedo baffles or nets within the harbor to protect the ships moored therein against torpedo plane attack without greatly limiting the activities within the harbor, particularly the movements of large ships and the landing and take-off of patrol squadrons."

This alarmed Stark, who wrote the Secretary of the Navy on January 24: "If war eventuates with Japan, it is believed easily possible that hostilities would be initiated by a surprise attack upon the Fleet or the Naval Base at Pearl Harbor." He listed the dangers envisaged in their order of importance. First came "air bombing attack" and second "air torpedo attack."

Knox replied that he completely concurred as to the importance of defending against a surprise attack on Pearl Harbor. The Army, he said, was best equipped to give full protection to the fleet; he was, therefore, passing on the information to General Short, "directing him to cooperate with the local naval authorities" in making proper defensive measures effective. From then on it became Short's turn to beg in vain for adequate material and manpower.

Despite the pleas of younger air-minded officers, the basic strategical plans of Japan's leading admirals in the thirties had been to let her enemy, America, sortie from Pearl Harbor to make the initial attack: by the time the forces met in Japanese waters, the Americans would be so weakened by harassing submarine attacks that they could be defeated in one great surface battle somewhere west of Iwo Jima and Saipan.

But once Yamamoto assumed command of the fleet he and the younger officers, influenced by the writings of Homer Lea and Bywater, began to think offensively. After observing successful fleet maneuvers in 1940, Yamamoto told his chief of staff as the paced the deck of the flagship *Nagato*, "I think an attack on Hawaii may be possible now that our air training has turned out so successfully." With one sudden blow they could cripple the American fleet at Pearl Harbor, and before it could be rebuilt Japan would have seized Southeast Asia with all its resources.

This concept of achieving decisive victory by a single surprise blow lay deep in the Japanese character. Their favorite literary form was the *haiku*, a poem in seventeen syllables expressing with discipline the sudden illumination sought in the Japanese form of Buddhism. Similarly, the outcome in *judo, sumo* and *kendo*, after long preliminaries, is settled by a single stroke. In 1904, Yamamoto's hero, Admiral Togo, had, without declaration of war, assaulted the Russian Second Pacific Squadron at Port Arthur with torpedo boats while its commander was at a party.

Preliminary discussions at naval headquarters of a surprise raid on Pearl Harbor were probably overheard. On January 27, 1941, Dr. Ricardo Rivera Schreiber, the Peruvian envoy in Tokyo, chanced to meet Max Bishop, third secretary of the American Embassy, in the lobby of a bank. Bishop was changing his money in preparation for returning to Washington. Schreiber whispered that he had just learned from his intelligence sources that the Japanese had a war plan involving a surprise attack on Pearl Harbor.

Upon return to the embassy, Bishop drafted a telegram warning the State Department of the attack, then presented it to Ambassador Grew, who was most impressed. After making a few minor changes, he ordered Bishop to have the message encoded at once and dispatched to Washington. Grew remarked that he doubted the warning would get "a hot reception" but he regarded it as serious. Later that day he wrote in his diary, "There is a lot of talk around town to the effect that the Japanese, in case of a break with the United States, are planning to go all out in a surprise mass attack on Pearl Harbor. I rather guess that the boys in Hawaii are not precisely asleep."

As Grew feared, the warning was not taken seriously in Washington. One of Stark's subordinates passed on the message to Kimmel but added, "The Division of Naval Intelligence places no credence in these rumors. Furthermore, based on known data regarding the present disposition and employment of Japanese naval and army forces, no move against Pearl Harbor appears imminent or planned for in the foreseeable future."

That same day Yamamoto wrote an official letter to the chief of staff of the Eleventh Air Fleet, outlining his surprise attack plan and requesting a secret study of its feasibility. The problem was turned over to Commander Minoru Genda, one of the Navy's most promising officers. He had already won fame for his brilliant innovations in mass long-range fighter operations. He reported ten days later that an attack on Pearl Harbor would be difficult to mount and risky, but contained "a reasonable chance of success."

Only a gambler would accept the challenge and Yamamoto was certainly that. Gambling, he told a staff officer, was half calculation, half luck. As for the Pearl Harbor attack, he said, the odds were too good not to take. "If we fail," he said fatalistically, "we had better give up the war." Whereupon he outlined his plan to Captain Kanji Ogawa of Naval Intelligence with a request that he collect as much data as possible about Hawaii. Ogawa already had a few spies in the islands—a timid German named Otto Kuhn who needed money, a Buddhist priest and two Nisei. But they were only supplying unimportant bits of information. Ogawa decided to send in a Naval Intelligence expert who had already been prepared for such a mission, Ensign Takeo Yoshikawa. He was to pose as a consular official. On March 20 Yoshikawa arrived in Honolulu.

By April the Pearl Harbor plan had a new name—Operation Z, in honor of the famed Z signal given in 1905 by Admiral Togo at Tsushima when he annihilated the Russian fleet: ON THIS ONE BATTLE RESTS THE FATE OF OUR NATION. LET EVERY MAN DO HIS UTMOST. Now it was time to turn the operation over to those who would have to put it into effect—the First Air Fleet.

*   *   *

Early that May Roosevelt asked Marshall to prepare an assessment of the defense of Hawaii against a Japanese attack. The latter wrote:

The defense of Oahu, due to its fortification, its garrison, and its physical characteristics, is believed to be the strongest fortress in the world.

Air Defense. With adequate air defense, enemy carriers, naval escorts, and transports will begin to come under air attack at a distance of approximately 750 miles. This attack will increase in intensity until when within 200 miles of the objective, the enemy forces will be subject to attack by all types of bombardment closely supported by our most modern pursuit.

Hawaiian Air Defense. Including the movement of aviation now in progress Hawaii will be defended by 35 of our most modern flying fortresses, 35 medium range bombers, 13 light bombers, 150 pursuit of which 105 are of our most modern type. In addition Hawaii is capable of reinforcement by heavy bombers from the mainland by air. With this force available a major attack against Oahu is considered impracticable.

At the bottom of the report Marshall had handwritten in reference to the 35 flying fortresses: "Due to make a mass flight to Hawaii May 20. A number of this type of planes could be dispatched immediately if the situation grew critical."

This reassuring report was never passed on to Kimmel who, later that month, complained to Stark that he found himself "in a very difficult position . . . as a rule, not informed of policy, or changes of policy . . . and . . . as a result . . . unable to evaluate the possible effect upon his own situation." He was not even sure what force would be available to him.

Although Roosevelt was reassured by the report, he still resisted the pleas of Stimson and others to put pressure on

Japan with more economic sanctions. "There will never be so good a time to stop the shipment of oil to Japan as we now have," argued Secretary of the Interior Harold Ickes, on June 23. The public, he said, would applaud the move. When Roosevelt refused to act, Ickes offered his resignation. The President argued that Japan was experiencing an internal struggle to decide whether to invade Siberia, attack Southeast Asia or make peace with America. "No one knows what the decision will be but, as you know, it is terribly important for the control of the Atlantic for us to help to keep peace in the Pacific. I simply have not got enough Navy to go round—and every little episode in the Pacific means fewer ships in the Atlantic."

Stimson was also urging the President to immediate action, this on the other side of the world where Hitler had just invaded the Soviet Union. "For the past thirty hours I have done little but reflect upon the German-Russian war and its effect upon our immediate policy," Stimson wrote Roosevelt. The Nazis, he argued, would be "thoroughly occupied in beating Russia for a minimum of one month and a possible maximum of three months." He strongly recommended that "this precious and unforeseen period of respite should be used to push with vigor our movements in the Atlantic theater of operations." On July 3 the Secretary went further, this time urging Roosevelt immediately to ask Congress for a declaration of war. But once more the President resisted any overt move.

His refusal to act in the West may have left him more vulnerable to the arguments to act in the East. The Japanese made up his mind on July 23 by forcing the Vichy government to agree to the peaceful entry of Japanese troops into French-occupied Indochina.

Stanley Hornbeck, who presided over the making of Far Eastern policy at the Department of State, regarded the Japanese as a "predatory" power run by arrogant militarists. He assured the Secretary of State that the Japanese were bluffing and so Hull, in turn, added his voice to the Stimson-Ickes demand for economic force. On the night of July 26 the President ordered all Japanese assets in America frozen, thus cutting off the main supply of oil to Japan.[1]

As a result Naval Chief of Staff Nagano, a cautious and sensible man, was caught up in the near hysteria which seized the Supreme Command.[2] He warned the Emperor that Japan's oil stock would only last for two years, and once war came, eighteen months; then concluded, "Under such circumstances, we had better take the initiative. We will win." The Emperor asked if they would win a great naval victory like the Battle of Tsushima. "I am sorry, but that will not be possible."

"Then," said the Emperor, "the war will be a desperate one."

In Washington Secretary of War Stimson was delighted. At last the Stimson Doctrine was in full effect. Japan would finally have to pay for her crimes of aggression.

The passage of five weeks without any compromising words from America increased the desperation of Japan's military leaders. "With each day we will get weaker and weaker, until finally we won't be able to stand on our

[1] Admiral Turner, then Navy Chief of War Plans, testified that the freezing order came out of a clear sky. "I had expressed the opinion previously, and I again express it, that that would very definitely bring on war with Japan. There was no possibility of composing matters after that unless Japan made a complete backdown, which it was very apparent she was not going to do."

The Economist of London later commented: "When President Roosevelt told the Americans in the 1940 election that 'I shall say it again and again and again: your boys are not going to be sent into any foreign wars' he had already committed the United States to a huge program of military aid to Britain, and had drawn up the Rainbow contingency plans for a simultaneous war with Germany and Japan, and was soon to slap on Japan the embargoes which some people still believe pushed the Japanese into their attack on Pearl Harbor."

[2] On February 13, 1915, a group of Japanese army and navy officers lunched with their American counterparts at the residence of the superintendent of the U. S. Naval Academy. The signature in the guest book of Commander Osami Nagano appears just above that of Captain Douglas MacArthur. One wonders if they ever went beyond "pass the salt" to discuss the situation in the Pacific.

feet," warned Admiral Nagano. "Although I feel sure that we have a chance to win a war right now, I'm afraid this chance will vanish with the passage of time." An initial surprise victory was essential. He was referring to Operation Z but kept this to himself. The fewer in on the secret the safer. "Thus our only recourse is to forge ahead."

The Chief of Staff of the Army agreed. "We must try to achieve our diplomatic objectives by October 10. If this fails we must dash forward." And so it was decided at an imperial conference to put a five-week deadline on diplomacy and then wage war. But the Emperor did what no other ruler of Japan had ever done. A few days after the deadline, even though there was no progress in the negotiations with America, he rescinded the decision of the imperial conference. The new Prime Minister, General Hideki Tojo, was ordered to "go back to blank paper," that is, start with a clean slate and continue sincere negotiations with America for peace. Even so the preparations for the attack on Pearl Harbor continued on schedule—just in case diplomacy proved impossible.

2.

Further warnings of a possible attack on Hawaii had already reached Washington. In June an interesting report arrived at O.N.I. from the American commercial attaché in Mexico City:

Related with my recent report on activities at Honolulu Pearl Harbor Hawaii Naval Base and the use of the word Molokai I have run across the following vital information bearing on that subject and related features.

Enclosed were two rough pencil drawings of a new type of small submarine with a maximum radius of action of four hundred miles, and fitted with remote-control electromagnetically activated diving valves and air valves. A dozen of these small submarines would be hidden under water off the island of Molokai. And when war came "the plan is to at once use this small fleet of submarines for lightning attacks on the U. S. Navy fleet anchored in Pearl Harbor.''

The American naval attaché had forwarded this report to Washington with the observation that it possibly contained "an element of truth, in spite of its apparently fantastic nature, and in spite of this officer's reluctance to report what may prove to be totally unfounded rumors."

A much more important report came to Washington from a British double agent, code-named "Tricycle." He was a Yugoslav, Dusko Popov, who had first been recruited by German intelligence. Being a patriot, he offered his services to the British. His job was to feed the Germans controlled information.

That summer he was ordered by the Nazis to set up an espionage ring in the United States. He left England two days after the invasion of Russia, stopping off at Lisbon to get orders. He was asked to study a questionnaire.[3] The second heading startled him. It was *Hawaii*. He was to locate ammunition dumps and airfields on the island of Oahu and learn complete details of Pearl Harbor, including pier installations, number of anchorages and depth of water. Recently Popov had learned of Japanese interest in the British attack at Taranto which had put half the Italian fleet out of action in a single day by aerial torpedo attacks. Obviously Pearl Harbor was to be the Japanese target of a surprise attack.

Popov was ordered by the Germans to proceed to Hawaii as soon as he had set up the spy network in America. "There was some urgency about it," recalled Popov. "The action wasn't for tomorrow but it was for soon." He communicated the news of the impending attack to the Lisbon office of British intelligence. "They got on to London and I was instructed to carry my information personally to the United States, since I was leaving in a few days. Apparently, they thought it preferable that I be the bearer of the tidings, since the Americans might want to question me at length to extract the last bit of juice."

On August 10 Tricycle left for New York on a Pan

[3] For complete questionnaire see Notes.

American Clipper carrying with him a brief case filled with the questionnaire, microdots and other material. Once aboard the plane he turned over the brief case to a British intelligence officer who promised to pass on copies to the F.B.I.

The morning after arrival in New York, Popov was escorted to the Manhattan office of the F.B.I. where, to his surprise, he was received coolly. The regional chief said he had received the material from the British and would forward it to Washington. "I refrained from asking why it hadn't gone yet. If the Americans were to counter a Japanese attack, every twenty-four hours would count."

When Popov asked if the F.B.I. wanted more details on the Pearl Harbor attack, he was told, "Well, it all looks too precise, too complete, to be believed. The questionnaire plus the other information you brought spell out in detail exactly where, when, how, and by whom we are to be attacked. If anything, it sounds like a trap."

The two main sources of his information, explained Popov, were very reliable. The first would surely warn him if the plan was a trap. The second, Baron Gronau, was an expert on Japan. "If his information is exact, there's no reason to doubt his conclusions. You can expect an attack on Pearl Harbor before the end of this year unless the negotiations with the Japanese produce a definite result." The questionnaire itself was the best source. "If that is a trap, then it means my whole mission to the United States is window dressing. And that is just not possible. The rest of my mission is too important to the Germans. They wouldn't sacrifice it and me with it. Sooner or later you'd learn you'd been had and I would be blown."

The questionnaire and corroborating material was examined by J. Edgar Hoover but he had already heard stories of Tricycle's extravagant life style. Even his code name was an affront. "It arose from his sexual athleticism," Hoover wrote. "He had a liking for bedding two girls at one time." Popov was just a Balkan playboy to Hoover, who also had no liking for double agents.

Consequently the director did not take the Pearl Harbor

plan seriously[4] and refused to allow Popov to leave for Hawaii as ordered by his German masters. The Yugoslav's insistence on petitioning Hoover in person resulted in a disaster. "I'm running the cleanest police organization in the world," stormed Hoover. "You come here from nowhere and within six weeks install yourself in a Park Avenue penthouse, chase film stars, break a serious law, and try to corrupt my officers." He pounded the desk. "I'm telling you right now I won't stand for it."

Popov sought help from William Stephenson, Churchill's secret envoy in the United States, code-named "Intrepid," but he too failed to persuade Washington to take Popov's warning seriously, as did Sir John Masterman, head of the Double-Cross System whereby German agents captured in Britain were induced to become double agents and serve the Allies. The questions concerning Pearl Harbor in Tricycle's questionnaire, wrote Masterman, were specialized and detailed. "It is therefore surely a fair deduction that the questionnaire indicated very clearly that in the event of the United States being at war, Pearl Harbour would be the first point to be attacked, and that plans for this attack had reached an advanced state by August 1941."

Early that fall another direct warning of an attack on Pearl Harbor came to Washington. Kilsoo Haan, an agent for the Sino-Korean People's League, came to the CBS office of Eric Sevareid to announce excitedly that the Japanese were going to attack Pearl Harbor before Christmas. Friends in the Korean underground in Japan and Hawaii reported they had positive proof. "One piece of evidence in the jigsaw," recalled Sevareid, "—a Korean working in the Japanese consulate in Honolulu had seen full blueprints of our above-water and underwater naval installations—spread out on the consul's desk."

Haan told Sevareid of his frustration in trying to see the higher officials at the State Department but he "always

---

[4]There are no available records in the F.B.I. concerning Popov's questionnaire. Hoover's second in command, Edward Tamm, never heard of it but if Hoover had received such information, he told the author, he would certainly have passed it on to Roosevelt.

ended up seeing very minor officials who took a very minor view of his warnings.''

Late in October Kilsoo Haan did manage to convince Senator Guy Gillette of Iowa that he had just discovered the Japanese were definitely planning an invasion for December or January. It called for not only an attack on Pearl Harbor but simultaneous assaults on the Philippines, Midway, Guam and Wake. Gillette alerted the State Department as well as Army and Navy Intelligence.

Information to the War Department also came from Major Warren J. Clear, sent in the spring of 1941 to the Far East by Army Intelligence, that the Japanese were planning to launch attacks against a chain of islands including Guam and Hawaii. He vehemently urged the garrisoning of the whole chain of islands from Oahu to Guam.[5]

[5]No record can be found of Major Clear's warnings of a Pearl Harbor attack. However, there is on file a lengthy memorandum dated November 2, 1941, which he sent to the Assistant Chief of Staff, G-2. In it he reports to the War Department on his meetings in Singapore with Air Chief Marshal Sir Robert Brooke-Popham and the G.H.Q. Military Liaison Office. This document indicates the importance of Clear's secret intelligence mission to the Far East and its high-level status. He was later promoted and awarded the Legion of Merit, the Distinguished Service Cross, the Purple Heart and the Order of the British Empire.

In 1967 Clear revealed in two letters that he was writing a book. ''. . . you can be assured that my evidence re the P.H. tragedy and the related tragedies on all the islands . . . will show that Washington D.C. had solid evidence, prior to P.H. that Japan would take *the whole chain of islands*, including attacks on Guam and Hawaii. In view of this information at hand in Washington, but *not* relayed to Hawaii and Guam, it can be established that no culpability can be rightfully placed on Admiral Kimmel or Gen. Short.'' Clear's book, *Pearl Harbor—the Price of Perfidy*, was never published.

In 1968 Clear also stated that he had heard from several high-ranking generals that he was in line to be head of Army Intelligence. ''I am referring to the matter of my promotion because it shows that the FDR cabal were blocking it all the way thru. It is not a matter of sour grapes with me. But the non-promotion shows the animus, the *fear*, that attached to anyone who might disclose facts.'' Like Ralph Briggs, Clear was ordered not to appear before the Pearl Harbor investigative committee.

He suffered a stroke and spent the last ten years of his life in a convalescent home. He died in 1980. His conservator, George Farrier, searched in vain at the author's request for a copy of his unpublished book.

3.

On the eighth of October Admiral Stark recommended to Hull that they should enter the war against Germany as soon as possible even if it meant a conflict with Japan. Eight days later, after a meeting with Roosevelt, Stimson wrote in his diary, "We face the delicate question of the diplomatic fencing to be done so as to be sure that Japan is put into the wrong and makes the first bad move—overt move." The next day Admiral Claude Bloch, commander of the Fourteenth Naval District, Hawaii, wrote Stark that the deficiencies in the defense organization of Pearl Harbor described in a letter sent almost nine months earlier still existed. Bloch urged that, in view of the tense situation, small fast craft equipped with listening devices and depth bombs as well as at least one squadron of patrol planes be rushed to Hawaii. The request was strongly endorsed by Kimmel and Short but a reply would not be received for five weeks—and this would inform Bloch that no additional ships or planes could be assigned to Hawaii at the present.

In Tokyo Prime Minister Tojo was doing his utmost to carry out the Emperor's instructions to "go back to blank paper," even after Admiral Nagano observed somberly at the October 23 liaison conference, "We were supposed to have reached a decision in October and yet here we are." The Navy was consuming four hundred tons of oil per hour. "The situation is urgent. We must have a decision at once, one way or the other." Army Chief of Staff Sugiyama agreed. "We can't waste four or five days in study. We must rush forward!"

Tojo replied that the government preferred to review the matter carefully and responsibly. At a conference nine days later it was General Tojo who supported those seeking peace, and the militarists were forced to allow Foreign Minister Togo to negotiate until midnight, November 30.

Now the problem was to agree on what sort of final proposal should be sent to America. Togo said he had drawn up two. Proposal A was a somewhat watered-down version of their previous offers. In it the Army agreed to

withdraw all troops from China, including those left as
defense against Communism, by 1966. Proposal B was to
be used as a last resort in case Hull turned down the first.
It was designed to allay Hull's suspicions about the drive
into Indochina and assure him that Japan was abandoning
any idea of a military conquest of Southeast Asia. In Proposal B Japan also promised to make no more aggressive
moves south; and, once peace was restored in China or a
general peace was established in the Pacific, Japan would
immediately move all troops in southern Indochina to the
north of that country. In return, America was to sell Japan
one million tons of gasoline.

Sugiyama violently opposed Proposal B. For hours he
and his colleagues refused to accede to any suggestion of
withdrawal from Indochina, while insisting that Hull be
asked to unfreeze Japanese assets. This was a ridiculous
proposition and Foreign Minister Togo knew he could not
possibly negotiate on such terms. In desperation he shouted,
"We can't carry on diplomacy—but we still shouldn't start
a war!"

Then proceed with Proposal A! demanded the Army and
Navy.

But Togo refused to back down and Tojo reminded everyone that the Emperor had called for "blank paper" and
they should bow to his wishes. Finally Sugiyama reluctantly acquiesced, but only if Proposal A should fail.

Next morning Togo called on Tojo and asked if the
Prime Minister would persuade "those concerned to make
further concessions" if Hull reacted favorably to either
"A" or "B." Tojo did not disappoint him. He offered to
make further compromises if the Americans also came part
way.

Now it was Foreign Minister Togo's well-nigh hopeless
task to engineer peace before the deadline. The only
chance for success in Washington, he decided, was to send
assistance to Ambassador Nomura, who had already made
several diplomatic blunders. He chose Saburo Kurusu, an
able diplomat, whose wife was an American, born of British parents on Washington Square, New York City. He set
off for America on the night of November 4.

Before he arrived Togo cabled Nomura Proposals A and

B along with secret instructions. It was in the Purple code and a translation was soon on its way to Hull. The opening sentence of the instructions gave the impression that the Japanese had given up on the negotiations.

WELL, RELATIONS BETWEEN JAPAN AND THE UNITED STATES HAVE REACHED THE EDGE, AND OUR PEOPLE ARE LOSING CONFIDENCE IN THE POSSIBILITY OF EVER ADJUSTING THEM.

Such pessimism was not in the original, for Togo had written:

STRENUOUS EFFORTS ARE BEING MADE DAY AND NIGHT TO ADJUST JAPANESE-AMERICAN RELATIONS, WHICH ARE ON THE VERGE OF RUPTURE.

The translation of the second paragraph was even more misleading:[6]

CONDITIONS BOTH WITHIN AND WITHOUT OUR EMPIRE ARE SO TENSE THAT NO LONGER IS PROCRASTINATION POSSIBLE, YET IN OUR SINCERITY TO MAINTAIN PACIFIC RELATIONSHIPS BETWEEN THE EMPIRE OF JAPAN AND THE UNITED STATES OF AMERICA, WE HAVE DECIDED AS A RESULT OF THESE DELIBERATIONS, TO GAMBLE ONCE MORE ON THE CONTINUANCE OF THE PARLEYS, BUT THIS IS OUR LAST EFFORT. . . .

The original was responsible in tone:

THE SITUATION BOTH WITHIN AND OUTSIDE THE COUNTRY IS EXTREMELY PRESSING AND WE CANNOT AFFORD ANY PROCRASTINATION. OUT OF THE SINCERE INTENTION TO MAINTAIN PEACEFUL RELATIONS WITH THE UNITED STATES, THE IMPERIAL GOVERNMENT CONTINUES THE NEGOTIATIONS AFTER THOROUGH DELIBERATIONS. THE PRESENT NEGOTIATIONS ARE OUR FINAL EFFORT. . . .

The translation then stated that, unless these proposals succeeded, relations between the two nations would be ruptured.

. . . IN FACT, WE GAMBLED THE FATE OF OUR LAND ON THE THROW OF THIS DIE.

Togo's actual words were:

. . . AND THE SECURITY OF THE EMPIRE DEPENDS ON IT.

[6]Many Japanese are convinced that this and other diplomatic messages were purposely mistranslated. No evidence could be found of this. It is far more likely that the inaccuracies came from ignorance of the stylized Japanese used by diplomats.

Where Hull read—

. . . THIS TIME WE ARE SHOWING THE LIMIT OF OUR
FRIENDSHIP: THIS TIME WE ARE MAKING OUR LAST POSSI-
BLE BARGAIN, AND I HOPE THAT WE CAN THUS SETTLE ALL
OUR TROUBLES WITH THE UNITED STATES PEACEABLY

—Togo had written:

. . . NOW THAT WE MAKE THE UTMOST CONCESSION IN
THE SPIRIT OF COMPLETE FRIENDLINESS FOR THE SAKE OF
PEACEFUL SOLUTION, WE HOPE EARNESTLY THAT THE
UNITED STATES WILL, ON ENTERING THE FINAL STAGE OF
THE NEGOTIATIONS, RECONSIDER THE MATTER AND AP-
PROACH THIS CRISIS IN A PROPER SPIRIT WITH A VIEW TO
PRESERVING JAPANESE-AMERICAN RELATIONS.

An even more inaccurate translation of Togo's specific
instructions regarding Proposal A gave Hull the false impression that the Japanese were deceitful and devious. It
had misled Hull into believing that the Japanese were trying to avoid committing themselves to a formal agreement
on any of the proposed points.

When Nomura brought Proposal A to Hull's apartment
on the evening of November 7 the Secretary of State
glanced through it hurriedly; he already knew all about
it—or thought he did—and was convinced it contained no
real concessions. His attitude was so obvious that Nomura
asked for an appointment with the President.

Unlike Hull, Roosevelt was willing to negotiate. He had
just received a joint appeal from his two military chiefs,
Marshall and Stark, urging him to do nothing to force a
crisis. They pointed out that the defeat of Germany was
the major strategic objective. "If Japan be defeated and
Germany remains undefeated, decision will still not be
reached," they said and warned the President that war
with Japan could cripple the fight against "the most dangerous enemy," Germany. They wanted no ultimatum to
Japan for three or four months, until the Philippines and
Singapore were strengthened.

Unlike Hull, Roosevelt was a practitioner of *Realpolitik*
and he responded to B with a *modus vivendi,* a temporary
arrangement pending a final settlement. He wrote it in pencil and sent it off to Hull:

6 months

1. U.S. to resume economic relations—some oil and rice—more later.
2. Japan to send no more troops to Indochina or Manchurian border or any place South—(Dutch, Brit. or Siam).
3. Japan to agree not to invoke tripartite pact even if U.S. gets into European war.
4. U.S. to introduce Japs to Chinese to talk things over but U.S. to take no part in the conversations.

Later on Pacific agreements.

This *modus vivendi* brought about the first relaxation of American rigidity, the first real hope for a peaceful settlement. Hull dutifully, if without enthusiasm, began putting it into diplomatic form. Despite personal reservations about the newly arrived special envoy Kurusu (he didn't like Kurusu's looks and "I felt from the start that he was deceitful . . .") and suspicions of his superiors back in Tokyo, Hull was still willing to negotiate.

His suspicions were "confirmed" on November 22 by an intercept from Tokyo to Nomura extending the deadline of negotiations to November 30 (November 29 Washington time).

. . . THIS TIME WE MEAN IT, THAT THE DEADLINE ABSO-LUTELY CANNOT BE CHANGED. AFTER THAT THINGS ARE AUTOMATICALLY GOING TO HAPPEN.

Even so, Hull felt it was his duty to advance his version of the President's *modus vivendi*. Upon meeting with Stimson and Knox for their usual Tuesday morning get-together on November 25, Hull explained that he was thinking of countering the Japanese demand with a proposal for a truce of three months. Stimson had opposed Roosevelt's original idea for six months but did not oppose Hull's new draft. "It adequately safeguarded all our interests, I thought as we read it, but I don't think there is a chance of the Japanese accepting it, because it was so drastic." Hull's terms were for the Japanese to evacuate their recent conquests, cease new aggressions, and in return America was to supply them with oil but only for civilian use.

The three men walked over to the White House for a noon meeting of the Cabinet. At one point Roosevelt remarked that they were likely to be attacked, perhaps as soon as Monday, December 1. The Japanese were notorious for striking without warning. "The question was," Stimson wrote in his diary, "how we should maneuver them into the position of firing the first shot without allowing too much danger to ourselves. It was a difficult proposition."

The previous day Hull had invited representatives of England, China, Australia and Holland to his office where he passed around copies of his own draft of the Roosevelt plan. The Dutch minister, Dr. Alexander Loudon, forthrightly declared that his country would support the *modus vivendi* but the other three had to wait for instructions. On the twenty-fifth the Chinese ambassador handed Hull a note from his Foreign Minister stating that Chiang Kai-shek felt that America was "inclined to appease Japan at the expense of China." Later in the day a cable for Roosevelt arrived from Churchill. He was disquieted about Chiang Kai-shek.

. . . IS HE NOT HAVING A VERY THIN DIET? OUR ANXIETY IS ABOUT CHINA. IF THEY COLLAPSE, OUR JOINT DANGERS WOULD ENORMOUSLY INCREASE.

These two reactions, coupled with Hull's own doubts and exhaustion after months of negotiating, caused him to scrap Roosevelt's *modus vivendi* that afternoon. Instead he contemplated offering the Japanese "a suggested program of collaboration along peaceful and mutually beneficial, progressive lines." His assistants began putting this new proposal into draft form.[7]

---

[7] At Sugamo Prison, after the war, Tojo told one of his most trusted advisers, General Kenryo Sato, that if he had received the original Roosevelt *modus vivendi*, the course of history would probably have been changed. "I didn't tell you at the time, but I had already prepared a proposal with new compromises in it. I wanted somehow to carry out the Emperor's wishes and avoid war." Then Tojo heaved a big sigh. "If we had only received that *modus vivendi!*"

Stimson had returned to his office to find G-2 reports that the expected Japanese invasion expedition to southeast Asia was at last under way. Some thirty to fifty ships had been sighted south of Formosa. Stimson's adrenaline flowed. He prepared a paper on this invasion for Roosevelt. The time had come at last to act, for America to act.

The next morning, November 26, Hull was telephoning Stimson that he had "about made up his mind not to give . . . the proposition [the *modus vivendi*] . . . to the Japanese but to kick the whole thing over—to tell them that he has no other proposition at all."

Stimson promptly called Roosevelt to find out if the paper he had sent the night before about the new Japanese expedition force into Indochina had been received. Roosevelt reacted so violently that Stimson wrote in his diary: "He fairly blew up—jumped up in the air, so to speak, and said he hadn't seen it and that changed the whole situation because it was an evidence of bad faith on the part of the Japanese that while they were negotiating for an entire truce—and entire withdrawal (from China)—they should be sending that expedition down there to Indochina."

Before long Hull arrived at the White House to recommend that in view of the opposition of Chiang Kai-shek they drop the President's *modus vivendi* and offer the Japanese a brand-new "comprehensive basic proposal for a general peaceful settlement." Roosevelt was still so indignant and angry at news of the Japanese attack force that he approved. That afternoon Nomura and Kurusu were summoned to the State Department. Hull presented them two documents "with the forlorn hope that even at this ultimate moment that a little common sense might filter into the military minds of Tokyo."

The two Japanese expectantly read the first paper, an Oral Statement setting forth that the United States "most earnestly" desired to work for peace in the Pacific but believed Proposal B "would not be likely to contribute to the ultimate objectives of ensuring peace under law, order and justice in the Pacific area. . . ." Instead Hull offered a new solution embodied in the second paper, marked "Strictly confidential, Tentative and Without Commitment." Kurusu read its ten conditions with dismay. It insisted that Japan "withdraw all military, naval, air and police forces from China and Indochina"; support no other government or regime in China except Chiang Kai-shek's; and in effect abrogate the Tripartite Pact among Japan, Germany and Italy.

It was even harsher than an American proposal submitted in June, and Hull had drawn it up without consulting Marshall and Stark, who happened to be in the act of drafting another memorandum to Roosevelt begging for more time to reinforce the Philippines.

Nomura was too stunned to talk. Kurusu foresaw that this American reply to Proposal B would be regarded as an insult in Tokyo. He didn't see how his government, he said, could possibly agree to the immediate and unconditional withdrawal of all troops from China and Indochina. Couldn't they informally discuss the proposal before sending it to Tokyo?

"It's as far as we can go," said the tight-lipped Hull. Public feeling was running so high that he "might almost be lynched" if he let oil go freely into Japan.

Dejected, Kurusu said that Hull's note just about meant the end, and asked if the Americans were not interested in a *modus vivendi*. This phrase had become an unpleasant one to Hull. We explored that, he said curtly.

Was it because the other powers wouldn't agree? Kurusu asked.

It was uncomfortably close to the truth. "I did my best in the way of exploration," said Hull.[8]

That same day Dr. Henry Field, an anthropologist, now serving as one of the President's bright, trusted young men, was summoned to Grace Tully's office. She acted strangely gruff and was very much to the point, in contrast to her normal friendly and relaxed manner. She told Field that the President was ordering him to produce, in the shortest time possible, the full names and addresses of each American-born and foreign-born Japanese listed by locality within each state. Field was completely bewil-

[8] Three American admirals, Ingersoll, Noyes and Schuirmann, later testified that they had not expected the Japanese to accept the Hull terms.

dered and didn't know how to begin. She explained it was to be done by using the 1930 and 1940 censuses. Field was directed to go to the office of his friend, Under Secretary of Commerce Wayne Taylor.

"You will be the fourth person called after you arrive so as not to arouse any suspicion of a high priority interview." Field was to explain the situation to Taylor, who was, in turn, to notify J. C. Capt, Director of the Census, Suitland, Maryland, to expect Field shortly. "Call me if you need further help or authorization but try to avoid this. Final tabulations and addresses are of the utmost urgency. Use your own judgment to achieve results causing the least possible chance of a breach in security." Every hour counted so a twenty-four-hour program should begin immediately. "Arrange for delivery of the documents to yourself; then bring them, addressed to me, to the guard at the main gate on Pennsylvania Avenue. He will give you a receipt for each numbered envelope. Good luck! This is a major assignment!"

Field proceeded immediately to Taylor's office. No one seemed to take any notice of him as he awaited his turn. Taylor responded to his instructions graciously and enthusiastically. "I will call Mr. Capt at once to let him know you are coming. Break this request to him gently for the Census Bureau, to my knowledge, has never received a high priority order before."

Half an hour later Field was talking to Capt, a kindly, academic type who listened attentively to his instructions. "He gasped," recalled Field, "and said that that would take months especially for California. I told him it was a No. 1 priority of the Government and he had to do it as quickly as possible. If necessary, I said, he should shut down all other work of the Bureau to compile this information. He looked surprised and said he never had an order like that and he would go to work on it at once. He pressed all the knobs on a bank of switches to call his department heads in for a conference."

When Field returned after a call to Taylor there were twenty people with Mr. Capt. "There was a hush as I entered and every eye was on me." Capt's eyes were shining. "He told them that some of them could go home with full pay and that the others were to remain on a 24-hour basis to work only on this special project." The project had begun less than ninety minutes after Grace Tully had given the assignment. Field telephoned her that all was proceeding well but he needed security from the Marine Corps. Soon each entrance of the Census Building was guarded by an armed Marine. In the meantime a bank of IBM sorting machines was set up to extract the Orientals for each state from 110,000,000 cards; then they were to be resorted for the Japanese.

The Pearl Harbor Carrier Striking Force, *Kido Butai*, was now assembled some thousand miles north of Tokyo at an island in the Kuriles, Etorofu, which possessed a large deep bay, rough in summer but strangely calm in winter. It was an ideal clandestine rallying point. One of the six carriers, *Kaga*, had just arrived from the Inland Sea where it had been loaded with modified torpedoes with wooden fins from aerial stabilizers. Only with these fins could the torpedoes run shallow enough for the Pearl Harbor waters, which U. S. Navy experts still regarded as immune from aerial torpedo attack.

Late the previous afternoon more than five hundred flying officers from all of the carriers had jammed into the aviation-crew quarters of *Akagi (Red Castle)*, a carrier converted from a battle cruiser which now displaced more than 30,000 tons. Admiral Nagumo outlined the attack. It was the first time most of the men had heard the words "Pearl Harbor." As the admiral spoke, excitement mounted and when he ended with a "Good fight and good luck!" there was a deafening cheer.

That night there was a giant *sake* party aboard *Akagi* but not attended by Nagumo. A compulsive worrier, he got out of bed long after midnight to arouse the commander, who had gone to Honolulu three weeks earlier to observe and take pictures of the Pearl Harbor entrance and the adjoining Hickam Field. He had also brought back answers to ninety-seven questions from the lone Japanese Navy spy, Yoshikawa.

Nagumo had to be reassured that Kimmel's fleet had not

transferred from Pearl Harbor. "Is there any possibility the Pacific Fleet might assemble in Lahaina?"

"None."

The next morning—the twenty-sixth in Washington—dawned bright and clear with unusually high barometric pressure for this time of year. The seas had calmed. It seemed a good omen—until one of the giant screws of *Akagi* caught in wire just as the fleet was weighing anchor, and a sailor fell into the icy waters. Thirty minutes later *Kido Butai* finally got under way except for the man overboard, who could not be found. As the armada filed past Etorofu, the heavy cruisers and battleships test-fired their guns by throwing live rounds into a hillside of the island. The sound of the guns and the splashes of snow bursting on the hill like gigantic white flowers stirred the men.

At the State Department in Washington, Hull's uncompromising answer to the Japanese was being typed out for Nomura and Kurusu.

Chapter Fourteen

THE TRACKING OF *KIDO BUTAI*
NOVEMBER 26–DECEMBER 6

1.

By the time Colonel Rufus "Togo" Bratton had arrived at his office in the Munitions Building on the morning of November 26, he was convinced that war would soon break out. For the past six months he had plotted what looked surely like a Japanese deployment for war. From the intercepted Japanese messages both in the Purple and consular codes, he was almost dead sure that the Japanese would attack the following Sunday, November 30.

The next morning, Thanksgiving, Bratton's conviction that there would be war on Sunday was strengthened. Among the intercepts on his desk he had found a message from Nomura to Tokyo bemoaning Hull's curt reply: "Our failure and humiliation is now complete." Even more indicative were intercepts from the military and naval attachés advising their chiefs in Tokyo that the negotiations had collapsed and war with America apparently could no longer be delayed.

Since Marshall was vacationing in Florida with his wife, Bratton rushed these messages to Stimson along with a G-2 report evaluating a possibility that the Japanese "might be proceeding to the Philippines or to Burma to cut off the

Burma Road, or to the Dutch East Indies,'' or to "Thailand from which they could be in a position to attack Singapore at the proper moment.''

Stimson telephoned Hull to learn what the diplomatic situation was. "I handed the note to the Japs,'' said Hull almost casually. "I have washed my hands of it and it is now in the hands of you and Knox—the Army and the Navy.''

Stimson's call had interrupted Hull's conference with his three top advisers on the Far East, Hornbeck, Maxwell Hamilton and Joseph Ballantine. The first, as usual, was urging use of arms against Japan. Hull pointed out that Marshall wanted a delay of at least three weeks and Stark wanted three months. The Navy asked for six months last February, riposted Hornbeck, and the Secretary, through his negotiations, had got them that delay. Now they wanted three more. What the President should do, said Hornbeck, is "to stop asking the Navy, and tell it.''

He assured Hull that yesterday's note would call the bluff of the Japanese. They weren't going to fight. He put his conviction on paper in a memorandum.

Were it a matter of placing bets the undersigned would give odds of 5 to 1 that the United States and Japan will not be at "war" on or before December 15 (the date by which General Gerow has affirmed that we would be "in the clear" so far as consummation of certain disposals of our forces is concerned); would wager 3 to 1 that the United States and Japan will not be at "war" on or before the 15th January (i.e., seven weeks from now); would wager even money that the United States and Japan will not be at "war" on or before March 1. . . . Stated briefly, the undersigned does not believe that this country is now on the verge of "war" in the Pacific.[1]

---

[1] In Hornbeck's draft autobiography, he attempted to explain his faulty prediction: ". . . I made the mistake of yielding to an emotional urge and committing myself on record in terms of wishful thinking and gratuitous predicting." In mid-November 1941 he had rebuked a young colleague for prophesying that Japan would go to war in desperation: "Name me one country in history which ever went to war in desperation!"

Even before Hornbeck began writing his memorandum, Stimson had made up his mind that Bratton could be right about war by Sunday. They must prepare for conflict. With Marshall out of town, Stimson himself would have to act. He asked Roosevelt for authorization to send war warnings to the commanding generals of the danger zones: the Panama Canal, Hawaii and particularly MacArthur in the Philippines.

Roosevelt must have felt somewhat like a pawn in the hands of his belligerent Cabinet. He had planned to send a reasonable reply to the Japanese yet allowed his *modus vivendi* to be drastically altered by Hull. Hull, in turn, had been influenced by Hornbeck to think the Japanese were negotiating deviously; and, almost out of pique, had discarded his own *modus vivendi* to send a reply to Japan that would not be acceptable.

Ever since Stimson had accepted the post of Secretary of War, Roosevelt had been pushed further and further toward war with both Germany and Japan. Feeling he had little choice, the President ordered Stimson to send out "the final alert." Now the Secretary of War had what he wanted. No longer a mere civilian head of the War Department, he was Commander in Chief Roosevelt's deputy. Before long Knox and Stark were in his office along with Gerow. The last two begged for more time but Stimson cut them off. "I'd also be glad to have time but I don't want it at the cost of humiliation of the United States or of backing down on any of our principles which would show weakness on our part."

Gerow presented a draft of a warning to commanders in the Pacific he had already prepared. In his own hand Stimson added "but hostile action possible at any moment" to a sentence reading "Japanese future action unpredictable." He approved the rest of the message and at 11:08 A.M. the warning went out over the absent Marshall's name. Stark's warning to Kimmel was not dispatched until late in the day.

At Pearl Harbor Kimmel was conferring with his War Plans officer. "McMorris," he asked, "what is your idea of chances of a surprise raid on Oahu?"

"I should say none, Admiral."

* * *

The first news of Hull's note did not reach Tokyo until late morning. The message was sent at once to the palace, where a liaison conference was in session. Arriving just as the meeting adjourned for lunch, Tojo read it aloud. There was dumbfounded silence until someone said, "This is an ultimatum!" Even Foreign Minister Togo, who had held forth slight hope of success, never expected this. Overpowered by despair, he said something in such a stutter that no one could understand him; the Hull note "stuck in his craw." What particularly infuriated every man in the room was the categorical demand to quit *all* of China. Manchuria had been won at the cost of considerable sweat and blood. Its loss would mean economic disaster. What nation with any honor would submit?

Hull's proposal was the result of indignation and impatience, but this offending passage had been tragically misunderstood. To Hull, the word "China" did not include Manchuria and he had no intention of demanding that the Japanese surrender that territory. The American note should have been clear on this point. The exception of Manchuria would not have made the Hull note acceptable as it stood, but it might have enabled Foreign Minister Togo to persuade the militarists that negotiations should be continued; it could very well have forced a postponement of the November 30 deadline.[2]

And so two great nations sharing a fear of a Communist-dominated Asia were set on a collision course. Who was to blame? Japan was almost solely responsible for

[2] The author asked a number of Togo's close associates what might have happened *if* Hull had clarified that point. General Kenryo Sato, learning the truth for the first time, slapped his forehead and said, "If we had only known!" Excitedly he added, "If you had said you recognized Manchuria, we'd have accepted!" General Teiichi Suzuki (director of the Cabinet Planning Board), Naoki Hoshino (Tojo's secretary-general), and Finance Minister Okinori Kaya would not go that far. Kaya, a leading politician in the postwar period, said, "If the note had excluded Manchuria, the decision to wage war on would have been re-discussed at great length. There'd have been heated arguments at liaison conferences over whether we should withdraw at once from North China in spite of the threat of Communism." At least, said Suzuki, "Pearl Harbor would have been prevented. There might have been a change of government."

bringing herself to the road of war through the seizure of Manchuria, the invasion of China, the atrocities committed against the Chinese, and the drive to the south. But the United States did not fully understand that this course of aggression had been the inevitable result of the West's attempts to eliminate Japan as an economic rival after World War I, the Great Depression, her population explosion, and the necessity to find new resources and markets to continue as a first-rate power. How could the United States, rich in resources and land, free from fear of attack, understand the position of a tiny, crowded island empire with almost no natural resources, which was constantly in danger of assault from a ruthless neighbor, the Soviet Union? America herself had, moreover, contributed to the atmosphere of hate and distrust by excluding the Japanese from immigration and, in effect, flaunting a racial and color prejudice that justifiably infuriated the proud Nipponese.

There were no heroes or villains on either side. Roosevelt, for all his shortcomings, was a man of broad vision and humanity; the Emperor was a man of honor and peace. Both were limited—one by the bulky machinery of a great democracy and the other by training, custom and the restrictions of his rule. Tojo and Togo were not villains nor were Stimson and Hull. The villain was the times. Japan and America would have never come to the brink of war except for the social and economic eruption of Europe after the Great War and the rise of two great revolutionary ideologies—Communism and Fascism.

A war that need not have been fought seemed certain to begin.

In Tucson, William R. Mathews, the editor of the *Arizona Daily Star,* a close friend of General Pershing, was writing an editorial forecasting a surprise attack on the Philippines—and Pearl Harbor.

2.

The next day, Friday the twenty-eighth, Colonel Bratton brought Stimson information about Japanese movements in Southeast Asia amounting "to such a formidable statement of dangerous possibilities" that the Secretary decided to take it to the President before he got up. It was after nine o'clock but Roosevelt, suffering from a sinus infection, was resting in bed. After reading Bratton's reports, he said there were three alternatives: "first, to do nothing; second, to make something in the nature of an ultimatum again, stating a point beyond which we would fight; third, to fight at once."

The last two were the only ones, said Stimson. Roosevelt agreed. "Of the other two, my choice is the latter one," said Stimson, and waited in vain for the President to second the motion. But Roosevelt, apparently, was still leary of taking the final step to war.

At a noon meeting of the War Cabinet, consisting of Stimson, Knox, Hull, Stark and Marshall, the President read aloud the most alarming passages of Bratton's report envisaging an imminent Japanese attack on the Philippines, or Thailand, or Singapore, or the Dutch Netherlands. Roosevelt then said there was one more possibility, an attack on the Kra Isthmus, which would effectually block the Burma Road at its beginning.

In the discussion that followed, Stimson took the offensive. Strike at the Japanese force as it went by—*without warning!* The others preferred warning the Japanese that if their expedition "reached a certain place, or a certain line, or a certain point, we should have to fight."

The President approved of this and suggested sending a personal message to the Emperor asking him to help stop the senseless drift to war. Stimson thought little of this idea. One does not warn an Emperor, he said. It would be far better to send a message to Congress reporting the danger. Then, if he wanted, Roosevelt could dispatch a secret message to the Emperor.

Roosevelt didn't feel like arguing. He agreed. He was impatient to leave Washington and take his sinus problem to Warm Springs, Georgia. He said he wanted to have a belated Thanksgiving with the children there. Stimson disapproved—this was no time to leave the capital—but he said nothing, nor did anyone else. And so the President abruptly took himself out of the crisis.

No one in Washington had warned Short that he should be on the alert for more than sabotage from local Nisei. In fact, on that November 28, General Arnold wired the commander of the Hawaiian Air Force to initiate measures immediately "to provide the following: protection of your personnel against subversive propaganda, protection of all activities against espionage, and protection against sabotage of your equipment, property and establishment. . . . Avoiding unnecessary alarm and publicity protective measures should be confined to those essential to security."

Short took this message as confirmation that he was on the right alert. Army planes were bunched together for better protection from saboteurs.

On the last day of November Tokyo ordered their ambassador in Berlin, General Hiroshi Oshima, to inform Hitler immediately that the English and Americans were planning to move military forces into East Asia and this must be countered:

. . . SAY VERY SECRETLY TO THEM THAT THERE IS EXTREME DANGER THAT WAR MAY SUDDENLY BREAK OUT BETWEEN THE ANGLO-SAXON NATIONS AND JAPAN THROUGH SOME CLASH OF ARMS AND ADD THAT THE TIME OF THE BREAKING OUT MAY COME QUICKER THAN ANYONE DREAMS.

This Purple message was intercepted and promptly translated in Washington but neither Kimmel nor Short was informed.

At the War Department Hornbeck brought Stimson a draft for the President's proposed message to the Emperor. "I read it over," recalled Stimson, "and it was a comprehensive but very long and meticulous statement of the history of the United States relations with the Far East into which had been blended the suggestions that Knox and I had made. The whole paper was thirteen or fourteen pages long and had no punch for the requirements for which we had suggested it at the conference on Friday. Poor Hornbeck looked practically worn out. He had been working very hard and was evidently very nervous and tired. He said Hull was also very much worn.''

In the evening Knox visited Stimson and they made their own draft for the finale of whatever message would be sent to the Emperor. "This was in the shape of a virtual ultimatum to Japan that we cannot permit her to take any further steps of aggression against any of the countries in the southwestern Pacific including China."

In Japan, where it was noon of December 1, the deadline had come twelve hours earlier. *Kido Butai* was well on its way to Hawaii and now, except for a last-minute diplomatic miracle, there seemed no chance that it would be called back.

The Matson liner *Lurline* was heading for the same destination but from the opposite direction. Ordinarily the ship would be crowded with tourists but on this trip there were far more defense workers aboard than passengers. She looked more like a transport than a luxury liner to Leslie E. Grogan, first assistant radio operator, who described himself as "a 260 pound blimp." The forty-seven-year-old Grogan, one of the most experienced radio operators of the Matson Line, picked up a faint signal which he could not identify. It came from northwest by west, a peculiar area for traffic at this time of year. What would anyone be doing in such northerly, rough waters? Suspicious, he strained to follow the signals. They increased, grew louder, and he could make out the call letters JCS, Yokohama. It was in some Japanese code. He stayed on after his watch ended at midnight helping Chief Operator Rudy Asplund log the signals. Grogan wrote down in his journal:

> The Japs are blasting away on the lower Marine Radio frequency—it is all in the Japanese code, and continues for several hours. Some of the signals were loud, and others weak, but in most every case, the repeat-back was acknowledged verbatum [*sic*]. It appears to me that the Jap is not using any deception of "Signal Detection" and boldly blasts away, using the Call letters JCS and JOS, and other Japanese based

stations that have their transmitting keys all tied-in together, and controlled from a common source, presumably Tokio. . . .

So much of the signals reaching us on the SS *Lurline* were good enough to get good R.D.F. [Radio Direction Finding Bearings]. We noted that signals were being repeated back, possibly for copying by crafts with small antennas. The main body of signals came from a Northwest by West area, which from our second night from Los Angeles bound for Honolulu—would be North and West of Honolulu.

Having crossed the Pacific for 30 years, never heard JCS Yokohama Japan before at 9 P.M. our time on the lower Marine Frequency, and then rebroadcast simultaneously on the lower Marine frequency from some point in the Pacific.

If anyone should ask me, I would say it's the Jap's Mobilization Battle Order. Rudy Asplund kept Captain Berndtson [the ship's master] informed and presume the Bridge Officers must have thought us "Nuts" with so much D.F. Tracking down of signals.

It is now 3 AM and am trying to cool off after that hectic session earlier.

Have jotted down all the particulars as they present themselves, and it is my desire to make a record of this because [I] sense things! Might prove worthy, who knows? GM 3.30 AM Dec. 1, 1941.

The next night, Monday, the Japanese signals were once more intercepted.

Again Rudy and I pick up without any trouble all the Japanese coded Wireless signals like last night—it goes on for two hours like before, and we are now making a concise record to turn in to the Naval Intelligence when we arrive in Honolulu, Wednesday December 3rd, 1941.

On Tuesday night the signals became even stronger as *Kido Butai* drew closer to its target.

We continue to pick up the bold Japanese General Order signals—it can't be anything else. We get good Radio Direction Finder bearings, mostly coming from a Northwesterly direction from our position. The Jap floating units continue their bold repetition of wireless signals, presumably for the smaller crafts in their vanguard of ships, etc. The Japanese shore stations JCS and JOS are keyed by remote tie-in, coming from Tokyo I presume, and if we had a recording device, it would only prove what we ourselves jot down, and we can't help but know that so much of it is a repeat back, letter for letter, because we have copied the original signals coming from Japanese land based stations, etc.

The Japs are so bold in using these low Marine frequencies too, but with all the tension we've seen up to now, it's safe to say something is going to happen, and mighty soon, but how soon? All this display means something—time will tell, and tonights Radio Detection signals have come from a NW by W from Honolulu, and from the signals, the Japs must be bunched up, biding time.

3.

The signals picked up by *Lurline* were only the shape of things to come. There was also excitement on the seventh floor of 717 Market Street in San Francisco, the main office of the Twelfth Naval District Intelligence. Lieutenant Ellsworth A. Hosner, a communications expert in civilian life, had recently been ordered to relocate the missing Japanese carrier force. For the past few days he had been feeding information to his assistant, Seaman First Class Z, a brilliant young man who had left college to volunteer in Navy Intelligence.[3] Z, an electronics expert at twenty, had

---

[3] Seaman First Class Z, an officer after Pearl Harbor, is presently internationally renowned in his field for his accomplishments. His tapes have been monitored by Carolyn Blakemore and Ken McCormick of Doubleday & Co., and will eventually be open to researchers.

already designed a device which was being used on all Navy landing craft. Z's task was to collate reports from commercial ships in the Pacific as well as the four wire services: Press Wireless, Globe Wireless, RCA, and Mackay. That morning they had received a report from one of the wire services wondering what was going on west of Hawaii. They were receiving queer signals that didn't make sense at such frequency. Hosner telephoned the other services and shipping companies. Were they getting any strange signals? Several confirmed they had. —

Using a large chart, Z managed to get cross bearings on the mysterious signals. He told Hosner it could possibly be the missing carrier force. The lieutenant alerted the Chief of Intelligence, Captain Richard T. McCollough. Hosner felt assured that not only O.N.I. but the President would be promptly informed. It was common knowledge in the office that McCollough was Roosevelt's personal friend and had access to him through Harry Hopkins' telephone at the White House.

Across the Pacific in Bandoeng, Java, the Dutch Army intercepted a Japanese message from Tokyo to their ambassador in Bangkok. It was in the consular code, which had been broken by a Dutch colonel, J. A. Verkuhl, with the help of his wife and a group of students. The message told of attacks to be launched on Hawaii, the Philippines, Malaya and Thailand. The signal to begin all operations simultaneously would come from Tokyo in the form of a weather broadcast over Radio Tokyo. It was the "winds" code setup.

General Hein Ter Poorten, the commander of the Netherlands East Indies Army, hand-carried the long message to the next building where the American military observer, Brigadier General Elliott Thorpe, a close friend, had an office. Ter Poorten asked Thorpe's secretary to leave and, after locking the door, said, "I have something here I believe of great importance to your government."

Thorpe read the intercept. "Sir, this is so important that with your permission I will go at once to Batavia and inform our senior State Department representative of this and then send it directly to Washington tonight."

By the time Thorpe arrived in Batavia the American

Consulate had closed, so he proceeded to the Hotel des Indes where Dr. Walter Foote, the consul general and the senior naval attaché, Commander Paul Sidney Slawson, lived. The former, nicknamed "Uncle Billy," ridiculed the matter and advised Thorpe to forget it. But Slawson was impressed. Since Thorpe's code book was in Bandoeng, Slawson offered to send the message in naval code to Washington. By the time it was encoded it was past midnight and the main post office, which handled overseas communications, was closed. The two pounded on the back door of the post office until a member of the night staff appeared. Thorpe explained the urgency and asked that it be sent by cable; the Japs were probably tapping the wireless. Since the message was in naval code it had to go to the War Department through the Navy Communications center. After its receipt was acknowledged Thorpe assumed that both the Army and Navy had read the message and its warning of an attack on Hawaii.[4]

On that eventful second of December Captain Johan E. M. Ranneft, since 1938 the naval attaché of the Netherlands in Washington, paid a visit to the Office of Naval Intelligence where he queried Admiral Wilkinson and other intelligence officers about the deteriorating situation in the Pacific. As usual they were most frank with Ranneft since he had done the U. S. Navy a great service. (After witnessing a demonstration of the 40-mm. Bofors gun on a Dutch ship, in the Caribbean, Captain W. P. H. Blandy, chief of Ordnance, found it so far superior to all other anti-aircraft guns that he was determined to get it for the U. S. Navy. But there were complications. The weapon had been developed jointly by the Netherlands Navy and two private companies, Hazemeyer-Signaal and the Swedish firm of Bofors. Blandy realized how difficult it would be to get Swedish approval so he asked his friend Captain Ranneft for the blueprints. Without consulting his superiors in exile in London, Ranneft procured a set of blueprints from Batavia and turned them over to Blandy. Hours later a perturbed Swedish naval attaché protested

[4] There is no record of this message ever having been received. No one has admitted seeing it; no copy has been found in any file.

this violation of patent rights. Ranneft assured him that the decision had been made by the Dutch government in London and any complaints should be lodged there.[5] A gun was made from the blueprints by a Baltimore firm, tested at Aberdeen Proving Grounds and would soon be installed on American warships.)

Ranneft was startled when one of the Americans pointed to a map on the wall and said, "This is the Japanese Task Force proceeding east." The position was halfway between Japan and Hawaii. Ranneft said nothing, only wondered how the Americans had managed to track the missing carriers. He cabled Dutch naval headquarters in London and also reported the information in person to Minister Alexander Loudon. Then he wrote in his official diary, "Conference at Navy Department, O.N.I. They show me on the map the position of two Japanese carriers. They left Japan on easterly course."

At Pearl Harbor Kimmel was asking his intelligence officer the whereabouts of the missing carriers. Lieutenant Commander Layton reported that there were a few carriers in Japanese home waters but the major force was still missing.

"What!" exclaimed Kimmel. "You don't know where Carrier Division 1 and Carrier Division 2 are?"

"No, sir, I do not. I think they are in home waters, but I don't know where they are. The rest of these units, I feel pretty confident of their location."

Then Kimmel looked at Layton as he occasionally did—with a somewhat stern countenance and yet partially with a twinkle in his eyes—and said, "Do you mean to say that they could be rounding Diamond Head and you wouldn't know it?"

"I hope they would be sighted before now."

The information given to Captain Ranneft by O.N.I. was never sent to Kimmel. That day the admiral wrote Stark that the Pacific Fleet was so deficient in auxiliaries

[5] After the war, former Secretary of Defense Dekkers told Ranneft that it was lucky he had not asked London for the blueprints. "We should have been obliged to answer 'no.'" The U. S. Government eventually paid large sums to both Bofors and Hazemeyer-Signaal.

that it could not even start any attack west from Pearl Harbor before February of 1942.

4.

Stimson was worried on that Tuesday, the second. The President had returned from Warm Springs but as yet had sent no message to the Emperor or the Congress. Harry Hopkins reassured the Secretary that Roosevelt was not weakening. Stimson convinced himself this was true from F.D.R.'s attitude at the afternoon Cabinet meeting. "The President went step by step over the situation," he wrote in his diary, "and I think has made up his mind to go ahead." He was confident Roosevelt would now not only warn the Emperor but alert the American people through a strong message to Congress. The way was at last clear. Roosevelt's words would maneuver the Japanese into firing the first shot once they crossed that certain line in Southeast Asia. In a few days the line would be crossed and the British and Dutch would have to fight. And so, at last, would America.

Yet Roosevelt showed apprehension when he was interrupted during a later meeting with Donald Nelson, head of the Supply Priorities and Allocation Board, to be told that Kurusu and Nomura were outside with Hull. "How does it look?" asked Nelson.

The President shook his head gravely. "Don, I wouldn't be a bit surprised if we were at war with Japan by Thursday."

On the third of December he seemed almost cocky. He told Secretary of the Treasury Morgenthau that he had Kurusu and Nomura "running around like a lot of wet hens" after he asked them why they were sending so many military forces into Indochina. "I think the Japanese are doing everything they can to stall until they are ready."

The Census Bureau finally had the name and address of every Japanese in the United States, a total of 126,947: the California material alone consisted of some fifty single-spaced pages. Dr. Field telephoned the commandant of the Marine Corps that the job was finally completed and thanked him for his generous assistance. After congratulating Mr. Capt and his staff, Field then drove to the White House where he turned over the last envelope containing the California material to Grace Tully.[6] Copies were distributed to the F.B.I. and the governors and military commanders in each state.

That day Washington forwarded Kimmel two dispatches advising him of Japanese instructions to embassies and consulates to burn their code books. Nothing was sent about the approaching Japanese carriers.

At 9:00 A.M. the SS *Lurline* docked at its usual pier near Honolulu's famous Aloha Tower. Grogan and Asplund hurried the few blocks up Bishop Street to the downtown intelligence office of the Fourteenth Naval District in the Hotel Alexander Young Building. After introducing themselves to Lieutenant Commander George Warren Pease, they turned over their data. "He was a good listener," recalled Grogan, "and showed little outward reflection as to what we felt was a mighty serious situation, but nevertheless, Rudy and I felt relieved in our avowed duty to pass the vital information on to the Navy for whatever value they could derive from it." Pease promised to pass on the warning but there is no record that he forwarded the information either to the Fourteenth Naval District intelligence officer, Captain Irving Mayfield, or to Washington.[7]

Within sight of the docked *Lurline*, Police Lieutenant John A. Burns, head of the Honolulu Espionage Bureau, was

---

[6] Dr. Field, who became one of the world's leading anthropologists, recently revealed that years later he requested specific information on the project. "Dr. Conrad Taueber, director of the Bureau of the Census at the time, replied that no record of this assignment could be found! Apparently, our security measures were entirely successful." In 1980, the Freedom of Information Act notwithstanding, the associate director for administration, Bureau of the Census, wrote the author: "Apparently there is some misunderstanding regarding the assistance which the Bureau actually made. Our records indicate that no request for services was made to the Census Bureau prior to the attack on Pearl Harbor by President Roosevelt or any other administrative official." A request to Miss Tully for an interview on the subject was refused. "I'm sorry to tell you that I have nothing worthwhile to contribute to your project."

[7] Pease was killed in an air crash in 1945.

entering the Dillingham Building. He proceeded up to the second floor to the office of Robert L. Shivers, the F.B.I. agent in charge. "Close the doors," said Shivers. He was a small man who prided himself on being "a deadpan F.B.I. agent," but today he was patently agitated. "I'm not telling my men but I'm telling you this." There were tears in his eyes. "We're going to be attacked before the week is out." Pearl Harbor was going to be hit. The stunned Burns asked what he could do and was told to start contacting people in town to see if anyone had any foreknowledge of the Pearl Harbor attack. No one had.[8]

In San Francisco at the Twelfth Naval District Intelligence Office, Lieutenant Hosner and Seaman First Class Z had tracked the Japanese carrier force to a position northwest of Hawaii. Were they bound for the Aleutians or Hawaii? The information was passed on to Captain McCollough who, they assumed, informed Washington through intelligence channels as well as the President through Harry Hopkins.

Late that night Barnet Nover, associate editor of the Washington *Post,* was wakened by a telephone call from a British official who begged him to come at once to his room. Once Nover arrived the official, in great agitation, explained that a Dutch officer had told him two Japanese carriers had been discovered north of the Marshalls and were bound either for the Dutch Indies or Pearl Harbor.[9] The Briton confessed he could not sleep since he was certain the carriers' destination was Pearl Harbor.

Just after midnight, in the early hours of December 4,[10]

---

[8] Burns was later three-time governor of Hawaii. Taped interviews of the John A. Burns Oral History Project were conducted in 1975 by Stuart Gerry Brown, Daniel Boylan and Paul Hooper of the University of Hawaii Department of American Studies. Burns was cross-examined by all three on this issue. Professor Hooper told this author he was convinced Burns was telling the truth; he knew he was dying.

[9] A full and more accurate account of this episode will appear in the forthcoming biography of Nover by his widow. Captain Ranneft asserts he was not the Dutch official mentioned above. It may have been Colonel F. G. L. Weijerman, the military attaché, now deceased.

[10] Safford believed it was December 4 but Briggs today thinks it may have been earlier. See Notes.

Ralph Briggs was on duty at Station M, the Navy's East Coast intercept installation. Earlier Commander Laurance Safford had driven out to Station M to inspect the new land-line telegraph for direction-finder control. He knew that the Orange intercept team had been alerted to watch out for any "winds" execute and was making a personal check of the watch assigned to that duty. He was assured that the Tokyo news and weather broadcasts were being monitored by qualified *katakana* operators.

Briggs had not met Safford on an earlier inspection but was well qualified to pick up any "winds" message. He could read Japanese and his superior, Chief Radioman DW, had instructed him to look out only for three terms: *Higashi no kaze ame, Kitano kaze kumori* or *Nishi no kaze hare.* DW privately explained to Briggs the significance of each term and that it probably would be the third, "West wind, clear," a diplomatic break with Great Britain.

Before dawn Briggs picked up on schedule the routine Japanese Navy weather broadcast from Tokyo and he began copying down in Japanese telegraphic code: *Higashi no kaze ame:* "East wind, rain." Momentarily he didn't realize its significance since he had been expecting "West wind, clear."

He quickly checked his watch supervisor's classified instructions. There was no doubt this was one of the war warning destruct messages to ministries and consulates. And it meant war with America.

He rushed to the next room and got the message on the TWX circuit to Safford's office. Then he telephoned his supervisor, who lived on the post. "DW," he exclaimed, "I think I got what we've been looking for!"

"Good. I'll be right up." Briggs was to get it on the TWX circuit downtown right away.

Briggs said he had already done that. He hung up and made an entry on his log sheet of the lead line of the message. He also included the warning characters, the date, time and frequency.

5.

During the fateful third of December an Army air corps captain had secretly brought to isolationist Senator Burton Wheeler a document as thick as a novel, wrapped in brown paper and labeled "Victory Program." The young captain, according to Wheeler's account, said he thought Congress had "a right to know what's really going on in the executive branch when it concerns human lives." As Wheeler scanned the top secret papers, his blood pressure rose. "I felt strongly that this was something the people as well as a senator should know about."

It looked to Wheeler like a blueprint for total war in Europe and Asia, contemplating total U.S. armed forces of 10,045,658 men. In righteous indignation he turned over the papers for publication to a Washington correspondent for the Chicago *Tribune*.[11]

The next morning, the fourth, it was 7:30 A.M. by the time that Major Albert C. Wedemeyer reached his office in the Munitions Building. He sensed an atmosphere of excitement. Officers were milling around amidst a buzz of conversation which ended abruptly as his secretary handed him a copy of the Washington *Times-Herald*. In consternation he read the banner headlines:

F.D.R.'S WAR PLANS

And in somewhat smaller type below:

GOAL IS 10 MILLION ARMED MEN:
HALF TO FIGHT IN AEF
Proposed Land Drive by July 1, 1943, to Smash Nazis

Wedemeyer hastily scanned the report. It was an exact reproduction of the Victory Program on which he had been

[11] According to the biographer of William Stephenson, the man called "Intrepid," the British had "planted" these documents with the help of a sympathetic American captain. "The primary aim of this deception was to use isolationist channels as a means of revealing to Hitler a 'secret plan' calculated to provoke him into a declaration of war. Even if the Japanese attacked British and American bases without warning, the British feared that the United States would not declare war on Germany."

working day and night the past few months. "I could not have been more astounded if a bomb had been dropped on Washington. . . . Here was irrefutable evidence that America was preparing to enter the war, and soon. President Roosevelt's promises to keep us out of war were interpreted as campaign oratory." Wedemeyer was the General Staff officer responsible for the preparation as well as the secrecy of the Victory Program, revelation of which might inevitably precipitate American participation in the war.

Privately he believed America should not intervene in the affairs of foreign countries unless national interest was in jeopardy. And the United States, as professional military men generally agreed, was not in imminent danger. Despite his convictions, Wedemeyer had devoted all his energies to the planning of a war for which he felt the United States was unprepared. The first to be suspected of leaking the information, he was thoroughly investigated by the F.B.I., which found him completely innocent.

Official Washington was in panic on that fourth of December. By the time Stimson returned from a three-hour session with his dentist in New York, he found his assistants depressed. "Nothing more unpatriotic or damaging to our plans for defense could very well be conceived of and for the first time in my observation of him McCloy was sunk. But the picture of this occurrence during my own day of absence rather tickled my funnybones and I cheered them up. The thing to do is to meet the matter head on and use this occurrence if possible to shake our American people out of their infernal apathy and ignorance of what this war means."

He telephoned the President. "I gave him my views on the situation and was glad to find that he agreed that we should meet the crisis head on." Stimson was relieved to find Roosevelt "full of fight" and no longer vacillating. "So the evening's discussion ended with a note of fight and optimism."

William R. Mathews, who had recently predicted an attack on Pearl Harbor in his newspaper, was interviewing Knox. Mathews asked if the Navy was ready for a surprise attack. "Hell, yes," was the answer, "but they don't dare to make a surprise attack. They know they could commit suicide.''

During the day Kilsoo Haan telephoned Maxwell Hamilton of the State Department that he had been warned by the Korean underground that the Japanese would attack Pearl Harbor the coming weekend. He was concerned enough to send Hamilton this long report:

Pursuant to our telephone conversations regarding our agents' apprehensions that Japan may suddenly move against Hawaii ''this coming weekend,'' may I call your attention to the following relevant and pertinent information.

One: The publication of U. S. Army Air Corps maneuvers throughout the Hawaiian Islands by the Japanese daily *Nippu Jiji*, Nov. 22, 1941. This timetable of air maneuvers is from November through Dec. 31, 1941, ''every day except Sundays and holidays.''

Two: The Italian magazine ''Oggi'' of Oct. 24, 1941, published an article in Rome forecasting war between Japan and America. The article forecast war between Japan and America by air and naval attack of the Hawaiian Islands and eventually attacking Alaska, California and the Panama Canal.

Haan also called attention to a Japanese book, *The Three Power Alliance and the U.S.-Japan War,* by Kinoaki Matsuo, published in October 1940. In a chapter entitled ''The Japanese Surprise Attack Fleet,'' Matsuo had written that there was no doubt that in the event of war with the United States Japan would grasp the best opportunity to strike the enemy in advance.

It is our considered observation and sincere belief, December is the month of the Japanese attack, and the SURPRISE FLEET is aimed at Hawaii, perhaps the first Sunday of December. . . .

No matter how you feel toward our work, will you please convey our apprehension and this information to the President and to the military and naval commanders in Hawaii.

In Java General Thorpe had already sent a second message to Washington warning of the attack on Hawaii and the Philippines. But he was so disquieted, he decided, on the fourth of December, to send still another, this through Consul General Foote. But Uncle Billy deleted the entire first long paragraph mentioning the location of the attacks, and only set up the "winds" code. At the end Foote added: "Thorpe and Slawson cabled the above to the War Department. I attach little or no importance to it and view it with suspicion. Such have been common since 1936."

General Ter Poorten guessed that Foote would water down the warning and sent all the details to Colonel F. G. L. Weijerman, the Dutch military attaché in Washington, with instructions to pass the information on to the highest U.S. military sources.

Thorpe sent a fourth message a little later, one directly to the Army G-2, General Miles. This message was acknowledged by Washington; Thorpe was ordered to send no more dispatches on the subject.[12] "This might have been because the War Department felt my dispatches might reach the wrong hands or for some other reason they considered adequate."

Another drama was taking place to the north, in Manila. At Asiatic Fleet Headquarters, Lieutenant Kemp Tolley was instructed to set out on a mysterious mission ordered personally by the President. He was to arm a windjammer, the *Lanikai*, a two-masted interisland schooner, with a cannon, a machine gun and provisions for a two-week cruise—and be ready to sail in twenty-four hours. Tolley was aware that his was but one of three small ships on a joint mission, and that he was to relieve the *Isabel*, commanded by Lieutenant John Walker Payne, Jr., which

---

[12] Of the four messages Thorpe sent, only two were found in War Department files: the censored one signed by Foote; and his own final message, which arrived without the paragraph warning of the Pearl Harbor attack. Somehow in transmission this vital information was deleted.

was already on her way to the Indochina coast. Three days earlier Admiral Hart had received this extraordinary order: PRESIDENT DIRECTS THAT THE FOLLOWING BE DONE AS SOON AS POSSIBLE AND WITHIN TWO DAYS IF POSSIBLE AFTER RECEIPT THIS DISPATCH X CHARTER THREE SMALL VESSELS TO FORM A QUOTE DEFENSIVE INFORMATION PATROL UNQUOTE X MINIMUM REQUIREMENTS TO ESTABLISH IDENTITY AS UNITED STATES MEN-OF-WAR ARE COMMAND BY A NAVAL OFFICER AND TO MOUNT A SMALL GUN AND ONE MACHINE GUN WOULD SUFFICE X FILIPINO CREWS MAY BE EMPLOYED WITH MINIMUM NUMBER NAVAL RATINGS TO ACCOMPLISH PURPOSE WHICH IS TO OBSERVE AND REPORT BY RADIO JAPANESE MOVEMENTS IN WEST CHINA SEA AND GULF OF SIAM. . . .

Hart had read this with consternation. "As a war measure the project was very ill-advised," he later told the Director of Naval History. "Pickets in such locations could not be useful because the Japanese were bound to have them marked down . . . which would mean no chance to let them see anything of value."

He had instructed Payne to observe the utmost secrecy. The two of them alone were to know the actual mission until the *Isabel* was at sea, and then only his executive officer, Lieutenant j.g. Marion Buaas, was to be informed of their true purpose. Their cover orders were to search for a downed Catalina. On the morning of December 5 the *Isabel* sighted a Japanese Navy plane which continued to reappear throughout the day as the ship, originally a private yacht, kept heading west. From the air the deck chairs gave the *Isabel* the appearance of a large yacht but it was obviously a warship because of four 3-inch guns mounted fore and aft as well as four Lewis machine guns on top of the pilot house.

At 7 P.M. Payne sighted the Indochina coast twenty-two miles distant. Ten minutes later he was ordered to return to Manila immediately. During the return voyage a message was received that Pearl Harbor had been attacked.[13]

---

[13] After the war Tolley, whose ship was about to set sail when bombs fell on Oahu, was convinced the mission was only a trick to incite war with Japan. Lieutenant (later Captain) Buaas shared the belief that his ship was bait for the Japanese. "The true nature of our mission was to endeavor to

In Washington it was early morning of December 5. Half of the front page of the Washington *Times-Herald* was occupied with the War Plan scandal:

WAR PLAN EXPOSÉ ROCKS CAPITAL, PERILS ARMY APPROPRIATION BILL: LONDON HAILS PROSPECT OF A.E.F.

The three subheadlines read:

Congress in Uproar; Tinkham Declares Republic Betrayed
British Press Headlines Sensational Disclosure
Administration Fears Nation's Wrath Over Secret Project

Stimson called the President; he now disagreed with Roosevelt's idea of making no comment to the newspapers regarding the matter. "Go ahead," said Roosevelt. "Tell them." At his own press conference at 10:30 A.M. he said he had nothing to say but that the Secretary of War probably did. And when Stimson got to his own press room an hour later he found it jammed as never before. He was very brief. First he asked two questions: "What would you think of an American General Staff which in the present condition of the world did not investigate and study every conceivable type of emergency which may confront this country and every possible method of meeting that emergency? What do you think of the patriotism of a man or a newspaper which would take those confidential studies and make them public to the enemies of this country?" Then

locate Japanese ships and as such it was expected that our reporting would result in an incident in which the ship would probably be sunk." Although Admiral Hart had the opportunity to tell the truth about the three small ships at the congressional hearings he did not do so. Later he admitted to Tolley that the *Lanikai* had been sent out as bait. "And I could prove it. But I won't. And don't *you* try either."

Hanson Baldwin, the noted military analyst, also believed the three vessels had been intended as "tethered goats" to lure the Japanese. "In short, Roosevelt undoubtedly believed, like millions of Americans, that the United States' vital interests required the nation's entry into war, and in order to convince a large and reluctant portion of public opinion, he wanted the Japanese to strike first."

he explained that the revelations were only unfinished studies. "They have never constituted an authorized program of the government."

During the day Roosevelt wrote Wendell Willkie, whom he had defeated at the polls the previous year, approving Willkie's proposed trip to Australia. "It would, of course, be of real value to cement our relations with New Zealand and Australia and would be useful not only now but in the future. There is always the Japanese matter to consider. The situation is definitely serious and there might be an armed clash at any moment if the Japanese continue their forward progress against the Philippines, Dutch Indies or Malaya or Burma. Perhaps the next four or five days will decide the matter." [14]

At the Cabinet meeting Roosevelt read Stimson's statement to the press. The latter was amused to find his fellow members extremely warlike. "They thought I was almost defensive in my statement. Harold Ickes grunted that it was entirely too defensive. Even Henry Wallace said that while he liked the main statement, he thought he didn't like the questions."

In his diary the Secretary of War did not mention the much more important discussion at the meeting concerning the approaching conflict. A rare detailed account of this was revealed by Secretary of Labor Frances Perkins in an oral history interview at Columbia University in 1955. She recalled that Hull was very sober and so lugubrious that the gloom fairly stood out all over him. He was disgusted with Kurusu and Nomura. "They don't mean business, Mr. President. I'm sure they don't mean to do anything. With every hour that passes, I become more convinced that they are not playing in the open, that what they say is equivocal and has two meanings to it. . . . They are the worst people I ever saw." He continued in the strongest and most blasphemous language Mrs. Perkins had ever heard him use.

As they started discussing how the Japanese would go about attacking the British, Knox suddenly interrupted.

[14] The letter was not mailed until after the attack on Pearl Harbor. The President then wrote a postscript in longhand: "This was dictated Friday morning—long before this vile attack started."

"Well, you know, Mr. President, we know where the Japanese Fleet is?"

"Yes, I know," said Roosevelt and then looked around. "I think we ought to tell everybody how ticklish the situation is. We have information, as Knox just mentioned . . . Well, you tell them what it is, Frank."

"Well," began Knox in his sputtering, excitable way, "we have very secret information that mustn't go outside this room that the Japanese Fleet is out at sea." He was extremely high strung.

Roosevelt, looking very serious and severe, kept nodding his head in affirmation. He was scowling in a puzzled manner and as Knox said, "Our information is . . ." cut him off and said, "We haven't got anything like perfect information as to their apparent destination. The question in the minds of the Navy and in my mind is whether the fleet is going south."

"Singapore?" said several.

Roosevelt nodded. "Probably. That's the presumed objective if they go south."

Knox interrupted excitedly. "Every indication is that they are going south, Mr. President. That's the obvious direction."

Roosevelt cut in. "But it's not absolutely certain that they wouldn't be going north. You haven't yet information that they're not going north. You haven't got information with regard to direction."

"That's right, we haven't, but we must conclude that they are going south. It's so unlikely that they would go north."

"Well," said the President, "there are the Aleutians. There are fishing grounds. We do know there have been very large fishing fleets in those waters in recent months, larger than usual."

Knox thought this was ridiculous. "That might be, but it's not likely."

For some reason Roosevelt persisted as if he knew something Knox did not. "They might be going north. There is no evidence that they're not going north."

Knox was equally stubborn. "No, but I must draw the conclusion that they're going south. I don't think they're out just to maneuver. We in the Navy think they must be going to do something.''

Roosevelt surveyed the group. ''Now, I want to try an experiment. They are at sea. What shall we do? If they proceed toward Singapore, what's the problem of the United States? What should the United States do? I'd like every person here one by one to answer and say what he thinks we ought to do. I want to warn you that I'm asking this for information and a kind of an opinion, not advice in the usual sense, because we're not going to take any vote and I'm not going to be bound by any advice that you give. I'm just checking to see how your minds are operating. It is a terrible problem. I hope we won't have to act on it, or settle it, but we may have to. We may have to decide to do something. What do you think?''

When Mrs. Perkins declared that they should go to the relief of the British if Singapore were attacked, Roosevelt was surprised as though expecting her to go along with the minority who opposed this course. The Secretary of Labor left the room feeling that this had been a dreadful session. ''I remember going back to my office and just sitting down kind of limp, trying to face the music myself, saying, 'Is it possible that this country will be involved in a war with Japan in the Pacific?' That had never crossed my mind, I'm free to say.'' It had been a very shattering day, yet there was still no sense of immediacy and nothing had been said that made it seem imperative to change her weekend plans. She would still go to the Cosmopolitan Club in New York City where she'd have peace enough to write a report.

In Honolulu the lone Navy spy, Yoshikawa, was informing Tokyo that three battleships had arrived in Pearl Harbor that morning, and that the carrier *Lexington* had left port with five heavy cruisers.

6.

It was about 5 A.M., December 6, Washington time, as Colonel Bonner Fellers, an American observer in Egypt, walked into the Royal Air Force Headquarters in Cairo.

The air marshal in charge of the Middle East was at his desk. His first words were: "Bonner, you will be in the war in twenty-four hours. We have a secret signal Japan will strike the U.S. in twenty-four hours."

Fellers—described by George Marshall as "a very valuable observer"—couldn't believe it. He replied that the Japanese were having a free hand in the Orient and it would not be to their advantage to attack America. But the air marshal was confident the Japanese would strike and made no secret of his elation that the United States would finally be in the war.

Fellers toyed with the idea of sending a dispatch to Washington relaying the air marshal's statement. "Finally, I decided that if the British knew of the attack, we also knew of it. Also I reasoned that if the report were false I would be in quite a pickle." [15]

About that time London was cabling Air Chief Marshal Sir Robert Brooke-Popham, commander in chief in the Far East, that they had "now received assurance of American armed support" in case of Japanese attacks on Siam, Thailand or the Netherlands East Indies.

As the morning wore on in Washington, the bad news from the Far East increased and Stimson felt that "the atmosphere indicated that something was going to happen."

At the White House Harry Hopkins was reading a cable from Averell Harriman, who had come to London after completing a mission for Roosevelt in Moscow:

THE PRESIDENT SHOULD BE INFORMED OF CHURCHILL'S BELIEF THAT IN THE EVENT OF AGGRESSION BY THE JAPANESE IT WOULD BE THE POLICY OF THE BRITISH TO POSTPONE TAKING ANY ACTION—EVEN THOUGH THIS DELAY MIGHT INVOLVE SOME MILITARY SACRIFICE—UNTIL THE PRESIDENT HAS TAKEN SUCH ACTION AS, UNDER THE CIRCUMSTANCES, HE CONSIDERS BEST. THEN CHURCHILL WILL ACT "NOT WITHIN THE HOUR, BUT WITHIN THE MINUTE." I AM SEEING HIM AGAIN TOMORROW. LET ME KNOW

[15] "Had I known what I later learned," Fellers wrote Kimmel in 1967, "I would have alerted Washington, Panama, Pearl Harbor, and the Philippines—come what may. I truly made a horrible mistake which I'll regret to the end."

IF THERE IS ANYTHING SPECIAL YOU WANT ME TO ASK.

During Knox's daily meeting with Stark, Turner, Noyes and other leading naval officers there was a long discussion on Japanese intentions. "Gentlemen," asked Knox, "are they going to hit *us?*"

"No, Mr. Secretary," said Admiral Turner, who was generally considered the spokesman for Stark. "They are going to attack the British. They are not ready for us yet."

A recently retired American diplomat, Ferdinand Mayer, walked into the Japanese Embassy on Massachusetts Avenue a little after 11 A.M. He had been given to understand that his old friend, Saburo Kurusu, would talk to him openly about the degenerating negotiations. The special envoy received Mayer warmly and talked with such amazing candor that it became increasingly evident to Mayer that he was trying to convey something of shocking import. Finally he openly declared that the situation was "one of extreme danger of war." Mayer was so impressed, he begged Kurusu to dine that evening at the home of Ferdinand Belin, former ambassador to Poland. Mayer felt he needed a witness "for this most extraordinary expression of view which, if understood by our government, must surely at least provide it with a most urgent reason to alert all possible military establishments in the Far East." Mayer wasted no time in telephoning James Dunn of the State Department of his extraordinary interview.

In the Navy Building, Mrs. Edgers was showing Chief Yeoman H. L. Bryant a partial translation of the message from Consul General Kita to Tokyo concerning the light signals from a house on Lanikai Beach. She said it read like a detective story and they both agreed it should be brought to Lieutenant Commander Kramer's attention.

Commander Laurance Safford knew nothing of this message. He was involved in composing a warning to Kimmel: "In view of imminence of war destroy all registered publications in Wake Island except this system and current editions of aircraft code and direction finder code." The message was typed out and sent to Admiral Noyes for approval but the chief of communications didn't see it until returning from the big meeting in Knox's office. Noyes had been so impressed by Turner's declaration that the Japs would not attack the United States, only the British, that Safford's proposed message made him furious. He summoned Safford. "What do you mean by a message like this," he railed, "telling the commander that war is imminent?"

"Admiral," said Safford as calmly as he could, "war is a matter of days if not hours."

"You may think there is going to be a war but I think the Japs are bluffing!"

Knowing Noyes's fear of taking responsibility, Safford said, "Wake Island has all the Pacific crypto systems that we have printed, and covering the period up to July 1942. If those systems fall in the hands of the Japanese it will go very hard with you and very hard with me, too. I want that message sent."

"Well, that makes a difference," blustered Noyes, and began to rewrite the message. Safford was appalled at the "mayhem" committed on his original dispatch, for Noyes had left out any mention of Wake Island or any warning of war.

In view of the international situation and the exposed position of the outlying Pacific islands you may authorize the destruction by them of secret and confidential documents now or under later conditions of greater urgency. . . .

To make matters even worse, the message was sent deferred precedence, which meant delivery on Monday morning.

During this discussion, Captain Ranneft, the Dutch naval attaché, arrived at the office of O.N.I. where he found Wilkinson, McCollum and Kramer. After they told of the Japanese movements toward the Kra Peninsula, Ranneft asked about the two Japanese carriers heading eastward. "Where are those fellows?"

Someone put a finger on the wall chart four hundred miles or so north of Honolulu. "What the devil are they doing there?" asked the amazed Ranneft. Someone said vaguely that the Japanese were perhaps interested in "eventual American intentions." This made little sense to

Ranneft but he said nothing. And no one mentioned anything about a possible attack on Pearl Harbor. "I myself do not think about it," Ranneft wrote in his official diary, "because I believe that everyone in Honolulu is 100% on the alert, just as everyone here at O.N.I. is."

Ranneft returned to his embassy, told Minister Loudon what he had heard, and then cabled his superiors in London.

At the Twelfth Naval District in San Francisco, Lieutenant Hosner and Seaman First Class Z had tracked *Kido Butai* to a position approximately four hundred miles north-northwest of Oahu. There was now no doubt at all. Pearl Harbor was going to be raided the next morning. After passing on their calculations to Captain McCollough the two men had a private celebration. Tomorrow the Japanese were going to get the surprise of their lives.

That morning Joseph C. Harsch of the *Christian Science Monitor* talked for half an hour with Kimmel. The admiral said that the Germans had just announced they were going into winter quarters in front of Moscow. "This means that they have given up the effort to capture Moscow this winter. This means that the Japanese will not attack us. They are too intelligent to fight a two-front war. If Moscow had fallen they could attack us without any danger of being attacked by the Russians in their rear."

Despite his reassuring words to Harsch, Kimmel was deeply disturbed. In the forenoon he summoned members of his staff to evaluate the latest reports of Japanese activity. There was still no sign of the missing carriers. He took the problem to lunch. In an attempt to slow down the killing pace Kimmel had set for himself the past months, Admiral Smith urged him to take siestas in such a tropic climate.

"Come, Smith," said Kimmel shortly, "let's get back to work."

"Well, there are times when your chief of staff would like one."

Kimmel proceeded without delay to the Planning Division office where Colonel Omar Pfeiffer, a Marine on his staff, was discussing the possible outbreak of war with Kimmel's operations officer, Captain Charles McMorris. The admiral expressed his anxiety about the Japanese intentions toward the Pacific Fleet and Pearl Harbor. He was so worried, he admitted, that it "affected his guts."

"Captain McMorris tried to allay the admiral's concern, if not premonitions," recalled Pfeiffer, "by saying that the Japanese could not possibly be able to proceed in force against Pearl Harbor when they had so much strength concentrated in the Asiatic operations. I was not a participant in the conversation but I sensed the deep feeling of concern and responsibility felt by the admiral."

Kimmel was so uneasy, he ordered Lieutenant Commander Layton to take the latest intelligence report on the concentration of Jap transport and naval transports off Indochina to Admiral Pye, commander of Combat Force, for his comments. Pye, aboard the battleship *California*, guessed that the Japanese were probably going to occupy a position in the Gulf of Siam from which to operate against the Burma Road. Layton didn't believe they would stop there. He felt their objectives were farther south, probably the oil of the East Indies since the United States had stopped its export of oil to Japan. Besides, the Japs would never leave their flanks exposed and would therefore attack the Philippines. "And we'd be at war."

"Oh, no," said Pye. "The Japanese won't attack us. We're too strong and powerful."

Layton brought these heartening words to Kimmel but he still fretted. Late in the afternoon he took his own operations officers, McMorris and DeLany, to his quarters for further discussion. Searching for solutions, Kimmel finally hit upon an idea that appealed to him: they would recall all liberty parties, put everyone on the alert, and take the entire fleet to sea after dark under silence. The other two argued that this would violate the specific orders of Admiral Stark that nothing be done to alarm the people of Honolulu. Reluctantly Kimmel agreed and it was decided what they had already done "was still good and we would stick to it."

At the Japanese Consulate in Honolulu Yoshikawa had been in touch with Tokyo all day. In one message he informed his superiors that there were still "no signs of barrage balloon equipment," that the battleships had no torpedo nets, and that there was "considerable opportunity left to take advantage for a surprise attack" against Pearl Harbor and the Army airfields. A second message was equally encouraging: "It appears that no air reconnaissance is being conducted by the fleet air arm." These messages were interrupted by the special U. S. Army monitoring station at Fort Shafter and airmailed as usual to Washington for decryption.

After his hectic day, Kimmel spent a few hours at a party but he went home early to get a good sleep. It was just another Saturday night to the citizens of Honolulu. Many were celebrating the 20-6 victory of the University of Hawaii over Willamette in the annual Shrine football classic.

7.

At the White House, dinner for thirty-four was served at eight-ten, followed by a "violin musical" by Arthur LeBlanc.

Kurusu had accepted the invitation to dine at Belin's estate in Georgetown. He repeated in substance what he had told Mayer that morning. Former Ambassador Belin was "astonished beyond measure" at the Japanese envoy's frankness. And Mayer was now more certain than ever that Kurusu was "trying in the most desperate fashion to warn us of a momentary attack somewhere."

At about 8:30 P.M. Kurusu was called to the telephone. He returned to inform the company that Roosevelt had just sent a personal appeal to the Emperor. This, remarked Kurusu, was "a clever move" since the Emperor could neither give a flat "no" or even "yes." It was sure to cause "headaches in Tokyo and more thinking."

After his dinner, Captain Ranneft was summoned to the home of Minister Loudon where he also found the military attaché, Weijerman. The minister told the two that he had just returned from the White House and that Roosevelt had told him he had sent a message to the Emperor. If there was no immediate answer, said the President, war would probably break out on Monday.

In the meantime, the first thirteen parts of the fourteen-part message to Ambassador Nomura had been decrypted. About 8:30 P.M. copies were turned over to Lieutenant Commander Kramer for delivery. He was unable to reach either Stark or Turner. The first was at the National Theater and Turner happened to be out walking one of his many Lhasa apso terriers. Kramer did manage to telephone Wilkinson and tell him "in cryptic terms" of the general sense of the thirteen parts. The Admiral instructed Kramer to take copies first to the White House, then to Knox and finally to the Wilkinson residence.

Using his wife as chauffeur, Kramer arrived at the White House shortly before nine-thirty and turned over a locked pouch to Lieutenant Lester Robert Schulz. The latter went directly to the Oval Office. The President was clipping stamps. "These are for the children at Warm Springs," he told Schulz, who had accompanied him on the recent trip to Georgia. A few minutes later Roosevelt remarked to Harry Hopkins, "This means war."

Kramer was already at the Wardman Park Hotel talking with Mrs. Knox and her guests, the O'Keiths, while the Secretary of the Navy was studying the thirteen parts. Knox was concerned enough by what he read and the ominous significance of the fourteenth part that was yet to come that he telephoned both Stimson and Hull to set up an emergency meeting of the trio at 10 A.M.

By this time Colonel Bratton had completed his deliveries. Then he drove home to Georgetown and telephoned Miles, who lived nearby. The general was not at home.

Miles was having dinner with Admiral Wilkinson and the two of them were reading the copy Kramer had recently delivered. Wilkinson thought it was just "a diplomatic paper . . . a justification of the position of Japan." Miles agreed that it had "little military significance," and there was "no reason for alerting or waking up the Chief of Staff."

Marshall was not asleep but at a dinner party a few minutes' drive from the White House. He was attending a reunion of World War veterans of the 1st Infantry Company,

R.O.T.C.[16] The gathering at the University Club on 16th Street, N.W., included Brigadier General Joseph A. Atkins, commander of the unit; Dr. A. M. Langford, dean of Peddie School; and Representative William P. Cole, Jr., of Maryland. The honored guest, General Marshall, was given a rousing "vote of confidence."

General "Hap" Arnold was on his way to Hamilton Field, California, to oversee departure of thirteen B-17s which were to take off that night for Hawaii on the first leg of a flight to the Philippines. He arrived about midnight Washington time and warned the crews of the Flying Fortresses that they would "probably run into trouble somewhere along the line." He had in mind the mandated islands in the vicinity of Truk.

Arnold also conferred with the commanding officer of Hamilton Field and his staff. "He brought word of the imminence of war with Japan and ordered the planes dispersed," read the official history of Sacramento Air Service Command. "He is reported to have expressed stern disapproval of their being huddled together." Since there were no revetments, the available pilots immediately began flying planes to other fields in the vicinity.

Army Air Corps planes on the island of Oahu were still huddled together, an approved Air Corps policy for protection from saboteurs.

In the Aleutians, PBY crews were almost exhausted from long daily reconnaissance patrols. Fortunately, recollected Captain James Bowers, a message had arrived that Saturday to "cease all activity which may be interpreted as hostile." By now all patrols had been recalled and the flight crews were involved in "a great drinking bout."

---

[16]The December 7, 1941, issue of the Washington *Times-Herald* reported on p. A-23 that Marshall had attended this reunion dinner at the University Club the previous evening. See Notes.

Chapter Fifteen

DATE OF INFAMY
"BUT THEY KNEW, THEY KNEW, THEY KNEW"
DECEMBER 7–8, 1941

1.

Early Sunday morning, Tom Nichols, sixteen, was delivering the Washington *Times-Herald*. One of his customers was the Japanese naval attaché, who lived on the top floor of the Broadmoor, a large apartment building at 3601 Connecticut Avenue. Upon rounding the hall the newsboy was startled to see two American Marines standing outside his customer's door.[1] One of the Marines took the paper and young Nichols left wondering what was wrong.

Readers of the New York *Times* were set at ease by Secretary Knox's state-of-the-Navy message on page 1: "I am proud to report that the American people may feel fully confident in the Navy. In my opinion the loyalty, morale and technical ability of the personnel are without superior.

---

[1] A review of the muster rolls of Marine units in Washington for December 1941 reveals that no such assignment had been routinely made. It must have been an emergency special detail. Why?

On any comparable basis, the United States Navy is second to none."

At breakfast, Admiral Richardson observed to his wife, "We are on the verge of war, which may break out any minute." Eight years before, while a student at the War College, he had written a thesis on Japanese policy. After breakfast he dug it up and found one of its "lessons" was: "That should it appear to her advantage to do so, she will strike viciously, effectively and unexpectedly prior to any declaration of war."

Because of the emergency meeting Knox had set up Saturday night, Stimson telephoned his military aide, Major Eugene Harrison, to say that they would have to skip riding. "Come by and pick me up. We're going to the office." They arrived at the Munitions Building about nine-thirty. In the adjoining building Stark was already in his office and would soon finish reading the entire fourteen-part Japanese intercept.

Bratton had been frantically trying to locate Marshall for half an hour. For he had received not only the fourteenth part but another message instructing Nomura to deliver the entire message to Hull at 1 P.M. He was stunned. One P.M. Washington time would be about sunrise in Hawaii! The implication was staggering. He called Marshall's quarters in Fort Myer only to learn that he was out horseback riding. He then guardedly telephoned Miles at his home. The general was impressed by Bratton's tone and started off for the Munitions Building. As soon as Miles arrived he accompanied Bratton to Gerow's office. Miles urged that the Philippines, Hawaii, Panama and the West Coast be alerted. But nothing could be done until Marshall showed up.

At 10 A.M. Captain John Beardall, Roosevelt's naval aide, delivered to the President the fourteenth part. Still in bed, Roosevelt said, "It looks like the Japanese are going to break off negotiations." He didn't seem at all "perturbed" to Beardall. Roosevelt did nothing until noon except see Admiral McIntire, the nose and throat specialist, who treated his sinus condition. For a man who had thrived on action all his career, this was a curious reaction.

It took about an hour and a half for the one o'clock

message to travel from the Munitions Building to the Navy Department, about the length of three blocks. This message alarmed Wilkinson, who wondered aloud if the Philippines and the Pacific Fleet should be alerted. "Why don't you pick up the telephone and call Kimmel?" he suggested to Stark at approximately ten forty-five. Stark lifted the receiver, then shook his head and said, in effect, "No, I think I will call the President." But the White House switchboard operator reported that the President was busy. Stark put down the phone and did nothing.

At 11:25 A.M. Marshall finally reached his office. But it took almost another hour before his warning message was filed. Stark had offered to send it by the Navy system, which was fast under pressure, but Marshall said he could get it out quickly also. He could have used a telephone with a scrambler device but he feared some eavesdropper might have a descrambler. The warning was taken to the message center with orders to send it by the fastest safe means. Since the War Department radio was temporarily out of contact with Honolulu, the vital message was sent by teletype to the Washington office of Western Union.

Just as the Hull-Stimson-Knox emergency meeting ended at noon, the Secretary of State was informed that Nomura requested an appointment with him at 1 P.M. Hull fixed the time for one forty-five. Stimson did not proceed to the Munitions Building to check with Marshall on the crisis. He had himself driven to Woodley for lunch.

At the White House, the President was telling Dr. Hu Shih, the Chinese ambassador, that he had sent a message to the Emperor the evening before. "This is my last effort for peace. I am afraid it may fail."

The S.S. *Lurline*, thirty-two hours out of Honolulu on its return trip to California, was loaded with a passenger list of 784, including the president of the University of Hawaii and the "Petty girl" model. Church services were being conducted by Commodore Berndtson in the ship's lounge.

A thousand miles northeast of Honolulu, the 2,140-ton American freighter *Cynthia Olson* was carrying lumber to Honolulu. None of the twenty-five crew members was aware that the ship was being trailed by a Japanese submarine. The *I-26* had left Yokuska on November 19 as part of the advance expeditionary force with orders to destroy American commercial and military shipping once war broke out. She had spotted *Cynthia Olson* the previous morning and her skipper, Captain Minoru Yokota, was preparing to attack.

At about 7 A.M. Honolulu time a radio operator on the *Lurline* picked up an S.S.S. signal from the *Cynthia Olson*, meaning she was being attacked by a submarine. Leslie Grogan tried to raise Pearl Harbor and San Francisco but to no avail. Finally he reached the U. S. Coast Guard Radio Station at Point Bonita, California.[2]

At 7:55 A.M. two aircraft mechanics at Hickam Field sighted a formation of planes. As they began to peel off, Ted Conway said, "We're going to have an air show." His friend noticed something fall from the first plane and guessed it was a wheel. "Wheel, hell, they're Japs!"

Dive bombers were roaring down on Ford Island. A sailor on the deck of the nearby battleship *Arizona* thought they were Army fliers on maneuvers. He shook his fist at an oncoming plane. "You're going to catch hell!"

Karl "Buzz" Boyer, radioman at NPM, the Wailupe naval radio station six miles east of Pearl Harbor, was receiving a Morse code message from the Marine Air Base twenty miles northeast: "We're being bombed and strafed; we're under attack."

"Go to bed and sober up," signaled Boyer.

"This is no drill. This is for real," came the frantic response.

Boyer took the message to his chief, who was crowded at a window with the rest of the staff, looking down on Pearl Harbor. They all thought Army planes were on milk runs, until they saw smoke puffs from anti-aircraft guns.

---

[2] It took *I-26* three or four hours to sink the lumber ship. There were no survivors. In an interview with Yokota in 1979, he maintained he had launched his attack at 8 A.M. Honolulu time. Both Commodore Berndtson and Chief Radio Operator Rudy Asplund stated it was 7 A.M., fifty-five minutes before the attack on Pearl Harbor. Grogan thought it was a little after eight but three other crew members agreed with Berndtson.

Ashen-faced, the chief read the Marine message. "Get on the line to Washington. Don't bother to code it."

At seven fifty-eight Boyer tapped out in the clear signal heard around the world:

AIR RAID ON PEARL HARBOR. THIS IS NO DRILL.[3]

Secret Agent Takeo Yoshikawa had been eating breakfast when the windows started to rattle and several pictures dropped to the floor. He ran into his back yard. Above was a plane with Japanese markings. They did it! he told himself. Perfect, with so many ships in the harbor! Clapping his hands, he rushed to the back door of Consul General Kita's official residence. "Kita-san!" he shouted. "They've done it!" Kita came out and said excitedly, "I just heard 'East wind, rain' on the short wave![4] There's no mistake." Dense black clouds were rising from Pearl Harbor. The two men, tears in their eyes, clasped hands. Finally Kita said, "They've done it at last."

Locking himself and a clerk in the code room, Yoshikawa set about burning code books in a washtub. But within ten minutes someone shouted, "Open the door!" The door caved in and Lieutenant Yoshio Hasegawa of the Honolulu police burst in with several men. They began stamping on the smoldering code books.

Admiral Halsey's task force, which included the carrier *Enterprise,* was on its way back to Pearl Harbor after ferrying a squadron of Marine fighters to Wake Island. Sixteen scout bombers from *Enterprise* were approaching Pearl Harbor. Lieutenant j.g. Earl Gallaher, pilot of the lead plane, coming in at 500 feet, saw planes at 4,000 feet with wheels down. He called over the intercom to his radioman in the rear, "What the hell is the Army doing out here on a Sunday morning? Did we miss something on the board?"

[3] At almost the same moment a similar message was being sent from NSM, the standby station at Pearl Harbor.
[4] This message was never intercepted by station MS-5 at Fort Shafter. Neither was another from Tokyo which might have been a similar execute. It had arrived at 3:20 A.M. and read: RELATIONS STRAINED BETWEEN JAPAN AND THE UNITED STATES AND BRITAIN.

There was some smoke ahead but they were always burning cane fields. Gallaher touched down at the Marine field near Barber's Point. As he taxied up a Marine sergeant jumped on the wing and shouted, "Get the hell off the ground! Can't you see what's going on?" Now Gallaher noticed grounded planes burning all over the place. He took off fast and, once airborne, broadcast to *Enterprise:* "Pearl Harbor is being attacked by the Japanese and this is no shit!" He began orbiting off Barber's Point at low level followed by his wing plane and five other *Enterprise* planes that had joined up with him. Several times Japanese fighter planes came down for a look but never fired.

Gallaher reported that the Japanese were retiring on a northwesterly course from a rendezvous point about halfway between Oahu and Kauai. They must be making a beeline for home since they were probably low on gas. He wanted to go after the enemy carriers and led the way toward Ford Island to refuel and load bombs.

Gallaher's message to *Enterprise* that the Japanese task force was to the northwest was not heeded. Other messages from Pearl Harbor gave conflicting reports. The Navy could not get a cross bearing and, when Layton reported that there was no way to tell whether the enemy was to the north or south, Kimmel was understandably irked. To make matters worse, a garbled message was received from a ship reporting two carriers south of Oahu. Orders were given to search south for what turned out to be two American cruisers.

Ironically Rear Admiral J. H. Newton's Task Force Twelve was not far from the Japanese at a point between Oahu and Midway. Signalman First Class Thomas Thalken, aboard the heavy cruiser *Astoria,* recalled that they began an immediate search for the Japanese, heading northeast by north at flank speed. This meant that they would approach *Kido Butai* in several hours. Scout planes were launched. Then came the report from Pearl Harbor that two enemy carriers were south of Oahu. But officers on the bridge of *Astoria* were convinced this was a false lead. Thalken was ordered to signal *Chicago,* Newton's flagship, "Ignore Pearl Harbor. They don't know what they're doing." But Task Force Twelve obeyed orders and turned south away from the Japanese.[5]

At Kaneohe Naval Air Station on the eastern (windward) side of Oahu, they were preparing to withstand a second strike, this one a landing to seize the entire island before the Americans could organize for defense. A group stood in the hangar area discussing what to do next when one man, turning pale, shouted, "Oh, my God—there they come!" He pointed northward toward the seaward entrance to Kaneohe Bay. "Then," recalled Lieutenant Murray Hanson, "we saw it, too: the foremast and conning tower of a Japanese battleship coming around the point heading straight for our station!"

There was frozen terror a few seconds until someone said, "Oh, hell, that's Chinaman's Hat." A prominent landmark seen every clear day had become a battlewagon. Such group hysteria was common that day.

The area around Honolulu was still smoldering by the time an RCA[6] motorcycle messenger, Tadao Fuchikami, managed to get through roadblocks and wreckage to deliver a telegram addressed to the Commanding General, Fort Shafter. And it was seven hours after the attack started before Marshall's message was decoded. The department signal officer didn't have the stomach to deliver it. He asked Colonel R. J. Fleming, a close friend of Short's, to do so. "If he jumps on you, you're used to it." Fleming brought it to Short. He read it, threw it on the desk. "This is a hell of a note!" He was angry but didn't take it out on Fleming. A copy was immediately sent to Admiral Kimmel, who told the Army courier that it wasn't of any use to him, then crumpled the paper and threw it in the wastebasket.

---

[5]It was a fortunate mistake. The Japanese had only lost twenty-nine planes and probably would have dealt such grievous damage to the two American carriers and their planes that Spruance could not have challenged the Japanese six months later at Midway.
[6]Since Western Union had no direct link with Hawaii, the message had been transmitted to San Francisco where RCA radioed it to Honolulu.

2.

At 2:26 P.M. WOR interrupted its broadcast of the Giants-Dodgers football game with the first news flash. Much of America heard the news of Pearl Harbor a moment before the 3 P.M. CBS broadcast of the New York Philharmonic concert.

Ralph Briggs was on an extended four-day pass to Cleveland as a reward from Chief Radioman DW for having intercepted the "winds" execute. DW himself had received a large bouquet of roses from Captain Safford with a note expressing his personal appreciation for the splendid job done by the Station M team in intercepting the crucial message. Briggs's first reaction was, "Good, we've done our job. Now our Navy will get the bastards!"

Laurance Safford, exhausted after two months' worry and almost sleepless nights, had slept around the clock. He was in his bathrobe eating breakfast when a friend telephoned that the Japs were bombing Pearl Harbor. He was so angry that he felt tempted to take his .38 and shoot Noyes and Stark.

His fellow cryptanalyst, William Friedman, could only pace back and forth and mutter to himself repeatedly, "But they knew, they knew, they knew."

Captain Paulus P. Powell, formerly in charge of the Japanese desk in Naval Intelligence, told his wife the radio report of the attack was a gigantic hoax. "Because knowing what he does about the situation, Admiral Kimmel would never have the fleet in port."

Tricycle, who had passed a detailed plan of the attack to the F.B.I., was triumphant upon learning the news on board a tramp steamer. "What a reception the Japanese must have had! I paced the deck, no, not paced it, I floated above it exultantly."

Another who had warned the United States, Kilsoo Haan, got a telephone call from Maxwell Hamilton of the State Department. He demanded that Haan's December 5 warning of a Pearl Harbor attack that weekend not be released to the press. "If you do," he warned, "I can put you away for the duration." Haan reluctantly promised to hold the report until the end of the war.

At their meeting that morning Stimson, Hull and Knox had all thought America must fight if the British responded to an attack on the Kra Peninsula. "But now," observed Stimson, "the Japs have solved the whole thing by attacking us directly in Hawaii." His first reaction was "relief that the indecision was over and that a crisis had come in a way which would unite all our people. This continued to be my dominant feeling in spite of the news of catastrophes which quickly developed. For I feel that this country united has practically nothing to fear while the apathy and divisions stirred up by unpatriotic men have been hitherto very discouraging." Later he told his military aide, Major Harrison, that they could "never have gotten the country to war without Pearl Harbor."

3.

That afternoon Knox noticed that the President was "white as a sheet, visibly shaken." Yet later in the day James Roosevelt found his father "sitting in a corner with no expression on his face, very calm and quiet. He had out his stamp collection he loved so much and was thumbing over some of the stamps when I came in. 'It's bad, it's pretty bad,' he said without looking up."

At about 6:40 P.M. Roosevelt telephoned Henry Morgenthau to tell him that there would be a Cabinet meeting at eight-thirty. Morgenthau reported that they were freezing all Japanese funds. "And we're putting people into all the Japanese banks and business houses tonight and we're not going to let the Japanese get in there at all."

"That's good."

The one with the keenest memory of the Cabinet meeting was Frances Perkins. She had just come down from New York in the same plane with Henry Wallace and Postmaster General Frank Walker. All three had been so involved with work that they didn't know of the Japanese attack until her chauffeur picked them up at the Washington airport. "That's impossible," all three said when told about Pearl Harbor.

The Oval Office was filled. The President, sitting at his

desk, didn't notice the three newcomers. He was studying papers, cigarette holder in mouth. Everyone sat down about 9 P.M. Mrs. Perkins was surprised that he hadn't spoken to anyone. "He was living off in another area," she recalled in a taped interview. "He wasn't noticing what went on on the other side of his desk. He was very serious. His face and lips were pulled down, looking quite gray. His complexion didn't have that pink and white look that it had when he was himself. It had a queer, grave, drawn look."

She recalled that his face was never relaxed, not for a minute. "It remained tense and screwed up around the mouth. His upper lip was pulled down and his lower lip sort of pursed in, an expression that I've seen him have many, many times. . . . It was the sort of expression that he sometimes used when people were making recommendations to him and he was saying, 'Oh, yes, oh, yes, oh, yes,' without the slightest intention of doing anything about it. . . .

"In other words, there have been times when I associated that expression with a kind of evasiveness. The fact that he wore his expression all evening means nothing. It was an observation from which I cannot rid my memory. My picture memory keeps that expression on his face throughout the evening. He never relaxed that expression once, and none of us felt like making the kind of joke or sally that would sometimes relax his face when he had that expression on. It always had remained in my deep memory as being anything but an emotional disturbance as far as I was concerned, but a deep emotional experience, which I never would rely upon, and I don't think anybody should. Nevertheless, it is the strange emotional crises of human nature that give one some of one's insight, and they are part of the imaginative function of the brain, which Aristotle described."

She recalled that his pride in the Navy "was so terrific that he was having actual physical difficulty in getting out the words that put him on record that the Navy was caught unawares. . . . It was obvious to me that Roosevelt was having a dreadful time just accepting the idea." He could have been condemning himself for the men and warships lost—because Kimmel had not been warned the attack was coming.

Mrs. Perkins was obsessed by Roosevelt's strange reactions that night. "I had a deep emotional feeling that something was wrong, that this situation was not all it appeared to be. That stuck with me all that evening and all that night. So much so that when I went home to my apartment I couldn't rid myself of it. I sat down and wrote in lead pencil on some snatches of White House paper. . . . I described this look on the President's face, and the curious emotional disturbance that I had, which carried with it the impression that something was wrong. I don't know why I wrote it down, except perhaps to remind myself in the future—not for historical purposes, but for the purpose of helping me, or somebody else, to understand the situation. The necessity of reviewing it has never risen in my experience. So when I find these notes among my papers, I not only remember them clearly, but am also still somewhat put to it to know why I did it, why I wrote them down. At the moment they seemed important to me, as though I ought to put down, while it was clear in my mind, in case I should ever need to call upon it to help me explain something upon which I might have to act, or upon which others might have to act. . . .

"I don't know what disturbs me about the whole thing, but something was wrong. Obviously he had to play a role of some sort. I don't think that I ever in my own mind cleared it to the point of saying that he played a false role that day. His surprise was not as great as the surprise of the rest of us." In her book, *The Roosevelt I Knew,* she would reveal none of these misgivings.

"I've been asked if it might not be possible that the President, recognizing that this thing had happened, felt a certain element and wave of relief that the long tension of wondering what would they do and when they would do it, and would we have to go to the defense of Singapore without an apparent attack upon ourselves, and should we go to the relief of Singapore, all these conflicts which had so harassed him for so many weeks or months, were ended. You didn't have to think about that any more. That very wave of relief might have produced in him that psychological atmosphere reflected in his facial expression of tenseness and calmness, and yet a sense that something was wrong, that there was slight evasion here.''

As the meeting was breaking up Walker, who was very close to Roosevelt, said under his breath to her, ''You know, I think the boss must have a great sense of relief that this has happened. This is a great load off his mind. I thought the load on his mind was just going to kill him, going to break him down. This must be a great sense of relief to him. At least we know what to do now.''

''Yes,'' she said, ''I think so.''

Long into the night Roosevelt worked with Hull and Under Secretary of State Sumner Welles, who were trying to persuade him to use one of their proposed war messages. ''The President was very patient with them,'' recalled Hopkins, ''and I think in order to get them out of the room perhaps led them to believe he would give serious consideration to their draft.'' After chatting with Colonel William ''Wild Bill'' Donovan and Edward R. Murrow of CBS, they all had sandwiches and beer. Finally at 12:30 A.M. the President ''cleared everybody out and said he was going to bed.''

Across from the White House the benches in bleak Lafayette Square were deserted for the first night in weeks. On the other side of the square the Veterans Administration Building remained one of the few in Washington without lights burning. And the traffic along Pennsylvania Avenue on either side of the White House was jammed. ''There is a slight deliberation in the movement of the cars,'' reported Jerry Greene of the *Time-Life-Fortune* News Bureau. ''The driver, passengers in each turn their heads, stare with unmoving lips at the White House from the time they come within range until they are beyond.'' Hundreds were walking past the tall, iron picket fence protecting the White House grounds. ''They move along quietly, talking if at all in whispers, subdued murmurs. Silence on the Avenue, despite the mob of cars, the mass of people, is apparent, deep enough to gnaw at the nerves.'' Everybody, it seemed, was "watching the White House quietly, without noise, waiting, hoping somehow to see a visible sign of retaliation."

In the White House, not far from the President's room, Mrs. Hamlin, the old friend of the Roosevelts, was trying to sleep. "I heard voices and steps far into the night."

At his home in Virginia, General George Marshall said nothing except that he was tired and was going to bed. "I sat there trying to think of something I could do or say that might help him," remembered Mrs. Marshall. "But words are futile at a time like that, so I passed his door and went into my room. I knew he would rather be alone."

The next morning Stimson told Major Harrison, "I think I'll go and see Old Knox." The two men walked across the bridge to the Navy Building and found panic. In Knox's outer office one admiral was pacing one direction while a second was pacing another as if they were on the deck of a sinking ship. Knox's naval aide told Harrison, "My God, what will the American people think of the Navy!"

At 12:29 P.M. President Roosevelt entered the House chamber in the Capitol on the arm of his son James. There was a resounding ovation as he grasped the rostrum. "Yesterday, December 7, 1941," he began in the voice that no one who heard it would ever forget, "—a date which will live in infamy—the United States of America was suddenly and deliberately attacked. . . ."

Chapter Sixteen

THE SUMMING UP

1.

It is not clear why the Navy and Army Departments deprived Kimmel and Short of vital messages from the summer of 1941 to late that November. It may have been because of Marshall's fear that the Japanese would discover that the United States had solved their Purple code; the natural tendency of intelligence officers to guard new information almost obsessively; or interservice and interdepartmental rivalries.

Although both Marshall and Stark felt it was necessary to wage war with Hitler and Mussolini, both had vigorously opposed inciting Japan to battle on the grounds that neither the Army nor the Navy was yet prepared for a two-front war. Up to the very last moment before the Hull ultimatum to the Japanese on November 27, Marshall and Stark had urged Roosevelt to respond temperately.

The President himself had been wavering until the final day despite persistent urging from Stimson, Ickes and other Japanophobes. Less than a week later Roosevelt was faced with the most momentous decision of his life when a number of reports to Washington indicated that the missing *Kido Butai* was heading eastward toward Hawaii.

These included warnings from the *Lurline;*[1] from the Twelfth Naval District (Lieutenant Hosner and Seaman First Class Z); and from General Ter Poorten and Thorpe in Java. Finally there was the meeting of Captain Ranneft at O.N.I., authenticated by excerpts from Ranneft's official diary.[2]

Ten years after the war, General Ter Poorten asked General Thorpe, "Did you really send that message I gave you?" After Thorpe gave assurance he had, Ter Poorten revealed that he had not trusted Consul General Foote to send the entire message to Washington and had sent one himself—including the mention of attacks on Hawaii and the Philippines—to Colonel Weijerman, the Netherlands military attaché in Washington. Weijerman informed him that he had personally taken this message to Marshall a

---

[1] Minutes after the *Lurline* docked in San Francisco at 3:37 A.M., December 10, Lieutenant Commander Preston Allen entered the radio room to request that the voyage log be turned over to him. Chief Operator Asplund insisted the log be taken to Commodore Berndtson, who handed it over to the naval officer with other notes on the period from November 30 to December 7. There is no record in the Navy files of these documents or the incidents that took place. The Matson Line gave the author free access to its records, which included Grogan's journal.

[2] Captain Ranneft remained as naval attaché in Washington throughout the war. In 1946 Admiral Nimitz personally presented him the Legion of Merit Degree of Commander. His citation read: ". . . Discharging his responsibilities with great skill and initiative, Rear Admiral Ranneft rendered invaluable assistance in prosecuting the war against our common enemy . . . his contributions to the development of Naval ordnance were of inestimable aid to ships of Allied Navies carrying out defensive and offensive measures against the enemy." See Notes.

About 1960 Admiral Ranneft casually mentioned to an old friend, Admiral Samuel Murray Robinson (former Chief of Procurement and Material, who had initiated the largest shipbuilding program in history), that he was amazed to keep reading that the Americans were taken by complete surprise at Pearl Harbor. How was this possible when O.N.I. officers had shown him on a chart that the Japanese task force was only some four hundred miles from Honolulu on December 6?

Robinson was stunned. He knew nothing about it and insisted Ranneft ask Admiral Stark how this was possible. Later in the afternoon Admiral Robinson called back with a terse message: it was not necessary for Ranneft to see Stark. Robinson himself had just telephoned Stark, who refused to comment on the matter.

few days before Pearl Harbor; the Chief of Staff had said, in substance, "Can you take such reports seriously?"

Confirmation of Dutch foreknowledge of the Japanese attack also came from General Albert C. Wedemeyer. In 1980 he informed the author that during a meeting in 1943 Vice Admiral Conrad E. L. Helfrich of the Royal Netherlands Navy expressed wonder that the Americans had been surprised at Pearl Harbor. The Dutch, Helfrich said, had broken the code and knew that the Japanese were going to strike Pearl Harbor. "He seemed surprised that I did not know this," recalled Wedemeyer, "and when I explained that I doubted seriously that this information was known in Washington prior to the Pearl Harbor attack, Admiral Helfrich was skeptical because it was his clear recollection that his government had notified my government."

There were other indications of imminent war that were either ignored or suppressed, including the warnings of Major Clear, Tricycle, and Army and Navy Intelligence and Communications officers such as Bratton, Sadtler and Safford.

2.

"A Fool lies here who tried to hustle the East."
Rudyard Kipling

By December 4 Roosevelt and a small group of advisers, including Stimson, Knox and Marshall, were faced with three options. They could announce to Japan and the world word of the approaching *Kido Butai;* this would indubitably have forced the Japanese to turn back. Second, they could inform Kimmel and Short that Japanese carriers were northwest of Hawaii and order them to send every available long-range patrol plane to discover this force. An attack conceived in such secrecy would necessarily depend on complete surprise for success, and once discovered out of range of its target, *Kido Butai* would have turned back.

A month before the Hull ultimatum to Japan, Ickes had written in his diary: "For a long time I have believed that our best entrance into the war would be by way of Japan."

The first bomb dropped on Oahu would have finally solved the problem of getting an America—half of whose people wanted peace—into the crusade against Hitler. And the third option would accomplish this: keep Kimmel and Short and all but a select few in ignorance so that the Japanese could continue to their launching point unaware of their discovery. This would insure that the Japanese would launch their attack. If Kimmel, Short and others had been privy to the secret, they might possibly have reacted in such a way as to reveal to the Japanese that their attack plan was known.

This course was a calculated risk but Roosevelt, like Churchill, could take a gamble. Nor did risk at that moment seem so great. Recall the memorandum the President had received from Marshall in May 1941, describing Oahu as the strongest fortress in the world, with assurances that any enemy naval task force would be destroyed before it neared Pearl Harbor. Long a Navy man, Roosevelt believed in its power. Also he had been receiving reports on the low efficiency of Japanese pilots, whose planes were second rate.[3] Consequently the Pacific Fleet would not only stem any Japanese attack with little loss to U.S. shipping but deal a crushing blow to *Kido Butai* itself. One of the keenest admirals in the Navy, "Terrible" Turner, believing this, had told the Navy Court of Inquiry, "I knew our carriers were out, and with the warnings which had been given, I felt we would give them a pretty bad beating before they got home by our shore-based aircraft and by our carriers."

Such a defeat would have been catastrophic to the Japanese militarists and perhaps eliminated Japan as a menace in the Pacific with a single blow. Moreover, Kimmel's two available carriers would be out of Pearl Harbor and those warships left were in no real danger of being sunk. Aerial

[3] Roosevelt's feeling was shared by most Americans. Famed cartoonist J. N. "Ding" Darling expressed it all in a drawing of a small, bucktoothed, scowling Japanese soldier wearing horn-rimmed glasses. He is vainly attempting to blow up a huge balloon. Across the Pacific stands a supremely confident Uncle Sam wearing a Navy cap. He is hiding a slingshot behind his back while smiling slyly.

bombs were not that much of a threat and the waters of Pearl Harbor were too shallow for a torpedo attack.

Only such reasoning could account for the events in Washington on December 6 and 7. What novelist could persuade a reader to accept the incredible activities during those two days by America's military and civilian leaders? Was it to be believed that the heads of the Army and Navy could not be located on the night before Pearl Harbor? Or that they would later testify over and over that they couldn't remember where they were? Was it plausible that the Chief of Naval Operations, after finally being reminded that he talked to Roosevelt on the telephone that night, could not recall if they had discussed the thirteen-part message? Was it possible to imagine a President who remarked, "This means war," after reading the message, not instantly summoning to the White House his Army and Navy commanders as well as his Secretaries of War and Navy? One of Knox's close friends, James G. Stahlman, wrote Admiral Kemp Tolley in 1973 that Knox told him that he, Stimson, Marshall, Stark and Harry Hopkins had spent most of the night of December 6 at the White House with the President: All were waiting for what they knew was coming: an attack on Pearl Harbor.[4]

The incredulities continued the following morning with Marshall insisting he did not reach his office until eleven twenty-five. Yet Stimson's military aide, Major Harrison, recently revealed in an interview that he saw the Chief of Staff in the War Secretary's office around 10 A.M. "I saw

---

[4] Almost the first question Knox asked Kimmel, upon arriving at Pearl Harbor on December 10, was: "Did you receive our dispatch the night before the attack?" When Kimmel replied he had not, Knox said he was sure they had sent one. This was later explained as a slip of the tongue; he was referring to the message sent by Marshall the following noon. Was it a Freudian slip when Knox wrote in his original report to Roosevelt, "The Army and Navy Commands had received a general war warning on November 27th, but a special war warning sent out by the War Department at *midnight* [author's italics] December 7th to the Army was not received until some hours after the attack on that date"? Had those meetings at the White House on the night of December 6, as reported by Stahlman, decided to send a warning to Hawaii at *midnight*—a warning which later was rescinded without Knox's knowledge?

and talked to General Marshall: and whoever said he was out riding horses lied, because I saw him and talked to him at that time." So had Commander McCollum and Lieutenant Colonel John R. Deane, one of Marshall's assistant secretaries.

And why had Stark, having seen the complete fourteen-point message by 9:15 A.M. and the 1 P.M. message an hour later, not followed the urging of subordinates to telephone an immediate warning to Kimmel? And why, after finally reading all the messages and agreeing that this meant immediate war, had Marshall composed an innocuous warning to Pearl Harbor and Manila indicating he didn't know "just what significance" the 1 P.M. delivery time meant but to "be on the alert accordingly"? And why, instead of accepting Stark's offer of the naval radio facilities or using his own scrambler phone, had the message gone by Western Union and RCA? Marshall's excuse for not using the telephone was that it might have revealed to the Japanese that the Purple code had been broken. Seven months earlier a dozen intercepted messages had revealed that the Japanese feared their top code had been broken by the United States. And immediately following the attack, the telephone connections between Washington and Hawaii were in common use.

The comedy of errors on the sixth and seventh appears incredible. It only makes sense if it was a charade, and Roosevelt and the inner circle had known about the attack.

3.

A massive cover-up followed Pearl Harbor a few days later, according to an officer close to Marshall, when the Chief of Staff ordered a lid put on the affair. "Gentlemen," he told half a dozen officers, "this goes to the grave with us." The unnamed officer, who is still alive, had lunch on May 4, 1961, with Brigadier General Bonner Fellers and Dr. Charles C. Tansill. According to the former, the officer stated that on December 7 Marshall was obviously dragging his feet regarding the warning to

Short. That was why the Chief of Staff had bound certain members of his staff not to disclose the truth; and why he himself later conveniently forgot where he was on the eve of Pearl Harbor.

The cover-up continued with Roosevelt's revision of Knox's original report of Pearl Harbor, and was carried a long step forward by the report of the Roberts Commission. One of the members, Admiral Standley, later called Justice Roberts' performance "as crooked as a snake." Standley's outspoken criticism earned him a Distinguished Service Medal and an assignment as ambassador to Moscow where he would be out of reach of indignant Republicans and suspicious reporters.

The cover-up persevered after the Army and Navy Boards reversed the conclusions of Roberts to find Marshall and Stark rather than Kimmel and Short primarily guilty of dereliction of duty. Then amendments by Stimson and Forrestal to the Army and Navy reports led much of the public to believe that Roberts had, in fact, been upheld. Too little attention has been paid to the efforts of important government, military and naval officials to reverse the findings of the Army Pearl Harbor Board and the Navy Court of Inquiry. One of the main thrusts was the attempt to prove there was no "winds" execute; and this was so successful that the majority report of the congressional hearings concluded there had been no such message since Safford alone believed in its existence. This ignored the testimony of Admiral Ingersoll and Colonels Dusenbury, Pettigrew and Sadtler that they too had seen an execute. Strong proof of its existence lies in the taped interview of Ralph Briggs by the Historian, Naval Security Group Command, on January 13, 1977. A transcript of this tape was released in 1980 at the author's request by the National Security Agency and the U. S. Navy, with a few security deletions. Briggs served forty-four years in the Navy as an enlisted man, officer and civilian specialist up to the grade of GS-13. In the postwar years he was the case officer for counterintelligence and a security review analyst in the office of the director of Naval Intelligence.

All "winds" execute messages apparently have been

lost or destroyed.[5] According to A. A. Hoehling, a former
Naval Intelligence officer and author of *The Week Before
Pearl Harbor*, panic gripped the Second Deck of the Navy
Department immediately after Pearl Harbor. "One officer
then in intelligence, now in a high post in the Navy, told
this writer that he went to his office safe one morning to
find that a number of the 'magic' dispatches were mysteri-
ously missing. He never retrieved them. ONI, in fact, had
done such a thorough housecleaning of its top-secret and
secret as well as not-so-secret files that, according to another officer on duty at that time, not even a departmental
organization chart of November and December, 1941,
could ever be found."

Although Captain Safford emerged from the hearings
branded by some as a liar and by others as a brilliant but
erratic genius who suffered hallucinations, he invented the
Super ECM shortly before leaving the service. The idea
had come to him, he said, while walking his dog; it was
the answer to a problem which "had eluded us for 15
years." In 1958 President Eisenhower signed a bill to reward Safford with $100,000 for some twenty crypto-
graphic inventions he developed. Until the day he died
Safford did his utmost to convince the world that there had
been a "winds" execute. It was to his credit that he never
told anyone about Ralph Briggs, whose career in the Navy
would have been endangered.

General V.,[6] perhaps the living person with the most

---

[5] It could be no coincidence that other vital messages and documents concerning Pearl Harbor also disappeared. These include: the material con-
fiscated by the U. S. Navy in San Francisco from the *Lurline* on
December 10; the Thorpe and Ter Poorten messages; the questionnaire
and other papers Tricycle delivered to the F.B.I.; records of the tracking
of *Kido Butai* by the Twelfth Naval District; records of Grogan's original
report to the Fourteenth Naval District on December 3, 1941; and records
of the illegal collection of names of all Japanese-American citizens by the
Census Bureau.

Perhaps further revelations of suppressed information will come from
readers of this book, for there is no cover-up today in the Army, Navy or
F.B.I.

[6] The identity of General V. will be revealed after his death. The letter,
addressed to a prominent general, is in the archives of a presidential
library.

significant inside knowledge of Pearl Harbor, commented in a recent letter that if there was anything proving Roosevelt and Marshall shared responsibility for the Pearl Harbor tragedy, it was the methods used, particularly by George Catlett Marshall.

The testimony of the Chief of Staff at the various investigations does not stand up now that the prestige and glamor of his high office have gone. It was a tragedy that a man in his high position was forced to lie. So too his two trusted subordinates, Bedell Smith and Gerow. Both had refused to pass on any warning to Hawaii on December 5. So testified Sadtler before the Army Pearl Harbor Board. He later changed his testimony to Clausen, who brought with him the rank and prestige of Marshall. But later at the congressional hearings Sadtler did reverse himself again and declared he *had* given the message to Gerow and Smith. In his letter General V. also wrote that he did not know what Roosevelt did to suppress the message and prevent action, but he *did* know that Gerow lied and *why* he lied.

Why did Gerow and Smith, perhaps the two closest subordinates of Marshall, stonewall this December 5 message? It is difficult to believe they would have acted without Marshall's orders. By this time the Chief of Staff and the Chief of Naval Operations, caught in the web, were acting as faithful servants of their Commander in Chief, the President.

It was also a tragedy that men like Stimson, Hull, Knox and Forrestal felt obliged to join in the cover-up and make scapegoats of two innocent men, Kimmel and Short.[7] Open criticism of this injustice from such prestigious naval officers as Admirals Yarnell, Richardson, King, Standley and Halsey indicated how deep were the resentment and disgust among leading Navy officers.

---

[7] Short lived quietly in retirement. The *Saturday Evening Post* offered him a large sum to co-author an anti-Roosevelt article but he refused. He died in Dallas on September 3, 1949.

Kimmel never gave up the battle to clear his record. "My principal occupation—what's kept me alive—is to expose the entire Pearl Harbor affair," the indomitable admiral told the Associated Press when he was eighty-four, two years before his death. "I don't know whether the whole

Despite shortcomings, Franklin Delano Roosevelt was a remarkable leader. Following the maxim of world leaders, he was convinced that the ends justified the means and so truth was suppressed.

The greater tragedy is that the war with Japan was one that need never have been fought. And so we must continue to mourn the victims: first the 2,403 who died on Oahu, then those whose careers were ruined—such as Kimmel, Short, Safford, Bratton and Sadtler. In a larger sense we must also mourn the millions of dead and mutilated in the unnecessary war in the Pacific: the soldiers and sailors on both sides and the innocent civilians of many countries, particularly those of Japan, who were savaged by fire bombings and atomic warfare. A final victim is the present state of the world. Imagine if there had been no war in the East. There would have been no Hiroshima and perhaps no threat of nuclear warfare. Nor would it have been necessary for America to have fought a grueling, unpopular war in Korea and a far more tragic one in Vietnam which weakened U.S. economy and brought bitter civil conflict.

The profit was the lesson learned by Japan and America through the consequences of their war. The former realized that her true allies were not the Axis, and the latter that only a strong, industrialized Nippon, working in concert with the democracies, could stabilize Asia and prevent domination by Japan's traditional enemy, Russia. But a small group of men, revered and held to be most honorable by millions, had convinced themselves it was necessary to act dishonorably for the good of their nation—and incited the war that Japan had tried to avoid. It was, to quote Nietzsche, "Human, all too human."

The mistakes and cruel acts of violence committed by both Japan and America must not be forgotten—only understood. Enemies in the past, and friends today, they must remain equal partners in the future.

story will get out. All incriminating documents have been destroyed." But he predicted history would "eventually" clear him. He received far more support from Navy colleagues than Short did from Army officers. In 1957 Kimmel was elected alumni president by his classmates at Annapolis.

Postscript

1.

After sending off the final draft of this book to my publisher, I felt sure its revelations would bring forth further disclosures. Here are several pieces of new information which should be useful to historians and researchers of the tangled Pearl Harbor case.

1. *A report from a man serving in the Aleutians regarding movements of* Kido Butai, *the Pearl Harbor carrier striking force, in the north Pacific.* Robert E. Israel, company commander of an infantry unit stationed in Dutch Harbor sent me a xerox of an original message (in his possession) from Alaska Defense Command to Headquarters 37th Infantry received at 1:05 A.M., December 6, 1941. It reads:

> RADIO REPORT:
> NAVY REPORTS
> JAP SHIPS 270 MILES
> SOUTHEAST OF DUTCH
> HARBOR.

I had previously learned from Seaman Z that there was a direction-finder station in Dutch Harbor, and that in 1944 one of its officers informed him that they too had tracked *Kido Butai* in the North Pacific. Seaman Z could not remember the man's name but was sure if I presented him with a list of those serving in Dutch Harbor he would recall it. I requested from the U.S. Navy a roster of all intelligence and communications officers in Dutch Harbor. None could be found. Since reading *Infamy*, one researcher, Gordon Heyd Evans, has been attempting in vain to locate at both the U.S. Naval Historical Center and the National Archives the logs and records of the Mid-Pacific Strategic Direction-Finder Net which, in 1941, stretched from Cavite in the Philippines, through Midway and Hawaii to Dutch Harbor. There seems to be no valid reason why these records, if they have not been destroyed, should not now be declassified.

2. *Letters from Colonel Carlton G. Ketchum, a well-known resident of Pittsburgh, revealing that J. Edgar Hoover had information the Japanese carrier force was approaching Pearl Harbor.* Ketchum had been selected by General H. H. Arnold to obtain commissioned personnel over draft age for the Air Force with specific qualifications and experience. This was a nationwide effort on a mammoth scale, ending in the fall of 1942. He related that early in 1942 he had been invited by Congressman George Bender of Ohio to attend a special meeting of a select group of congressmen and government officials at the Army-Navy Club in Washington. According to Ketchum, this was an informal group that met bi-weekly throughout congressional sessions to dine, talk freely on matters otherwise held confidential and play poker. Bender told Ketchum that Hoover, who was a member of the permanent group, was going to tell them how well known to the President and a few of his intimate advisers the Japanese plan to attack us had been. Hoover, again according to Ketchum, spoke informally and without notes to a group of men with whom (except for Ketchum) he was intimately acquainted. Before he spoke, the members were reminded of the group's usual pledge of secrecy.

"For an obvious reason I regarded all that was said there as privileged, and repeated it to no one," wrote Ketchum. But now, after reading parallel information in *Infamy*, he felt freed from that requirement of secrecy. "I of course cannot provide any verbatim quotations, but I was so impressed by what was said that I am sure I am accurate in principle in the material I am sending you herewith. Mr. Hoover said that he had had warnings from repeated sources from early fall, 1941, to within just a few days before the Pearl Harbor attack, that it was coming, and that these warnings became more specific from one time to another. He said that much more important, the President had had warnings during all of that time, in addition to those he received from Mr. Hoover, from a number of sources. He referred to a Dutch Embassy and the Dutch Secret Service in the Far East as having given such warnings. He referred to a British businessman and later to British Secret Service in Hong Kong. He said that Mr. Roosevelt had had a warning from some governmental agency in Japan, but I cannot recall who that was. He mentioned at least one other source that I am now unable to recall.

"Mr. Hoover said that in addition to President Roosevelt, these warnings were known to Harry Hopkins, the President's personal adviser, to Secretary Knox, and I think Secretary Stimson, but I am not sure about him. He was very sure, he said, that they were not passed on to General Marshall, nor to General Short, nor Admiral Kimmel, commanders in the Pacific. Hoover was told by the President not to mention to anyone any of this information, but leave it to be handled in the judgment of the President, and not to pass it on within the F.B.I., even to their men stationed in the Pacific at that time. Hoover said that the last warning or warnings came from some radio operator in Hawaii who said that they showed that a Japanese Fleet was approaching and that these came a few days before the [Pearl Harbor] attack. My recollection is that there was some discussion of the fact that this radio silence began about three days before the attack. There was discussion in that group at this point, that the Army and Navy commanders could have been warned well in advance, and could have made such arrangements as would have dispersed the fleet and scattered soldiers in camps so that the casualties would have been minimized. There were some rather bitter things said about the President's conduct which I shall not attempt at this late date to quote."

Colonel Ketchum wrote about this meeting in his auto-biography, *The Recollections of Colonel Retread, 1942-1945,* published by Hart Books, Pittsburgh in 1976. "The dinner conversation," he wrote, "was of the utmost interest principally because it dealt with the knowledge in Washington prior to the Pearl Harbor attack of the extreme likelihood of that occurrence and the parallel bombing of Clark Field in the Philippines. I suppose their rule of no quotation expired long since and that was some thirty-some years ago, but I will still observe it."

3. *Further evidence of the tracking of the Japanese Carrier Task Force during its historic voyage towards Hawaii.* It is an historical fact that Admiral Nagumo ordered strict radio silence to be observed by all ships of *Kido Butai* upon embarking from home waters in mid-November, 1941. In a two-hour Japanese TV special, "Search for the Solution of the Pearl Harbor Puzzle" (shown by Nippon TV on the forty-first anniversary of the Pearl Harbor attack), the director and producer, Tsutomu Konno, interviews Robert Haslach who is writing a history of Netherlands East Indies cryptology and intelligence during 1932-1942. Haslach, an employee of the Netherlands Embassy in Washington, D.C., displays a postwar affidavit from a Dutch naval captain named Henning who is described as a careful officer who reported no hearsay evidence, only those things he knew to be absolutely true. The Henning document, addressed to the Netherlands Royal Navy General Staff, stated that from the analysis of Japanese radio traffic it had been possible to determine that during the last week of November 1941, there was a large Japanese fleet concentration near the Kuriles. In other words, intercepted Japanese radio messages had enabled the Dutch in November 1941, to track *Kido Butai* all the way north to Hitokappu Bay in the Kuriles where the carrier force was assembling for the Pearl Harbor strike. How else could this tracking have been accomplished unless some ship or ships of the task force had *not* broken radio silence?

In his research for the Japanese TV special, Konno also

discovered in an official history compiled by the War History Office of the Japanese Defense Force (*Operation Hawaii*, published by Senshi Sosho) that one of the two submarines accompanying *Kido Butai*, the *I-23*, reported it was having engine trouble on November 30, 1941 (Tokyo time), and maximum speed was reduced to 80 percent efficiency. The submarine fell behind, soon dropping out of range of flag or light signals. There is no further record of *I-23* in *Operation Hawaii* until December 6 (Tokyo time) when it was noted that "*I-23* has finally rejoined the main body after emergency repairs." There is no record of how this submarine, which was not equipped with a direction finder, managed to relocate the carrier force.

Further research in the case of *I-23* and related matters dealing with radio silence could be fruitful. The new evidence that the Dutch tracked *Kido Butai* in late November 1941, gives credence to the tracking reported by Admiral Wilkinson to Captain Ranneft and by Seaman First Class Z. Both of these American trackings came on December 2, during the extremely rough weather which prevented *Kido Butai* from refueling for two days. Commanders of the smaller vessels, faced with emergency conditions, could have resorted to low-power transmission, Talk Between Ships, which in those days was believed to have a range of no more than fifty miles. Today it is known that under certain weather conditions such low-power transmissions can jump very long distances. During his research Konno interviewed radiomen serving on ships in *Kido Butai*. All swore they had never broken radio silence even with low-power transmissions. But several did admit they had been sorely tempted to do so because of the dense fog and heavy seas.

Konno has brought to light other important information. In Honolulu he found two subordinates of Police Lieutenant Burns. One, William Kaina, stated that the future governor of Hawaii had discussed with him F.B.I. agent Shivers' warning of a Pearl Harbor attack several days before it came. The other, Richard Miller, declared that Shivers himself had warned him of the attack. Konno also adds new information regarding the Yugoslav double agent, Popov, and raises intriguing questions on other incidents that should be further explored. All this material, according to Konno, will be made available to researchers.

4. *Confirmation from two prominent Japanese naval officers that the "winds" execute message had been received on the east coast of the United States on or about December 4, 1941, as Captain Laurance Safford had so persistently testified.* In an autobiography, *The 365 Days Before Pearl Harbor* (published by Kojin-sha, Tokyo), Captain Yuzuru Sanematsu, a leading Japanese naval historian, describes his personal knowledge of the controversial message. In 1941 he was a commander, one of two assistant naval attachés in the Washington Embassy. The attaché office was located on the second floor of the two-story Embassy administration building. On November 19, 1941, over a receiver located in the next room, their radio operator had picked up the message from Tokyo setting up the famous "winds" code. By the morning of December 4 the attaché staff was in a state of constant alert in expectation of receiving the "winds" execute. That afternoon the radio operator, Chief Petty Officer Kenichi Ogimoto, who was posing as a civilian clerk and had been "all ears" the past two weeks, rushed into the attaché office, shouting, "The wind blew!" Sanematsu ran into the radio room in time to hear the announcer repeat several times, *"Higashi no kaze ame* [East wind, rain]." No one tried to hide his emotions. What was to come had at last come! They began preparing for the destruction of the code machine, secret papers and code books, retaining only materials necessary to carry on last-minute business.

In an interview on August 18, 1982, the other assistant attaché, Lieutenant Commander Yoshimori Terai, confirmed the story, relating how he had returned on the afternoon of December 4 to find the office in commotion over reception of the "winds" execute. In another interview the previous day I informed Captain Sanematsu that Commissioned Warrant Officer Ralph Briggs had testified he had received the "winds" execute during an early morning shift, not in the afternoon. Sanematsu said it was probable that Tokyo had sent such an important message several times and that Briggs must have heard one of the early broadcasts of December 4. Why hadn't Ogimoto heard this early broadcast? Sanematsu explained that Ogimoto was the only radio operator and could not monitor broadcasts around the clock. Ogimoto, who shared living quarters with Sanematsu in a nearby apartment, was scheduled to report for duty at 9 A.M. Terai, presently a retired vice admiral, agreed that Briggs could have heard an earlier broadcast while Ogimoto slept.

Safford had first testified that he believed the "winds" execute had come on the morning of December 3. Later he changed the date to December 4. In his official taped interview Briggs testified he also believed the date was December 4. When he examined the secret files after the war for the "winds" execute, all he could find was one log, dated December 2, 1941, which appears in the picture section. He thought this might possibly be the "winds" execute. It was not and that answers the question of why it had not been destroyed.

2.

Also of interest to researchers should be comments and suggestions by readers of *Infamy* who had been connected with the Pearl Harbor controversy. Lieutenant Commander Richard E. Cragg, in charge of Research and Development at the Naval Code and Signal Laboratory in Washington during World War II, was an associate of Captain Laurance Safford and contributed more details concerning the Naval Cipher No. 3 imbroglio.

Joe F. Richardson, son of Admiral J. O. Richardson, while regarding *Infamy* as "the most comprehensive, the most judicious and the most enlightening" of books on the subject, pointed out that I had been remiss in one instance. "Today, knowing the full extent of the tragedy, a great many people find it impossible to believe that Roosevelt deliberately withheld information that could have saved so many lives, ships and planes. Hindsight makes it too monstrously evil to be credible.

"For this reason, I regret that in your summing up on

page 319 you did not place more emphasis on the failure of all hands to realize the significance of the British success at Taranto. I think this most vital link in the whole chain of disaster has never been sufficiently stressed.

"If Roosevelt believed, as did the Navy, that Pearl Harbor was immune from aerial torpedo attack and knew, of course, that bombs would be largely ineffective against the fleet, then his decision not to alert the Hawaiian command becomes more understandable. . . ."

What the Americans did not know was that the Japanese had modified their torpedoes with wooden fins so they would be more buoyant in the shallow waters of Pearl Harbor.

Henry Clausen, presently a leading Masonic executive and formerly assistant recorder for the Army Pearl Harbor Board as well as the officer selected by Secretary of War Stimson to conduct a special investigation of Pearl Harbor, wrote, "Your assiduity in developing the facts of the Pearl Harbor disaster for your *Infamy* is greatly admired. . . . Good luck in your follow-up on any leads." One lead came from a reader who wrote of a letter purportedly written to Admiral Kimmel by one of Roosevelt's sons-in-law concerning prior knowledge of Pearl Harbor. This matter was pursued by Captain Thomas Kimmel who recalled reading such a letter to his father from John Boettiger. In response to a query to one of the admiral's secretaries, Mrs. Geraldine A. Weeks, Thomas Kimmel received this letter:

"My association with your father was a brief one in 1967 from January to March for the purpose of helping him respond to mail he received on the occasion of the twenty-fifth anniversary of the attack on Pearl Harbor. He would dictate to me at his home and I would then take the letters and my dictation to my home to type.

"There was a letter from Mr. Boettiger (Anna Roosevelt's ex-husband) to your father stating that on the night of December 6, 1941, the 'family' was having dinner together at the White House. The President was called away during dinner and when he returned he stated, in effect, that war would start the next day. The letter from Mr. Boettiger simply said that he wanted to 'set the record straight' after all those years. It had always troubled him that the truth had never been aired but he had felt compelled to remain silent because of his ties, at the time, to the Roosevelt family. Your father's response was an expression of gratitude.

"At the time I had that letter in my possession, both my husband (then the commanding officer of the *SSBN Henry L. Stimson*—that caused some words from your father) and I debated about the prudence of making a copy of it. We decided, since it was not our property, we had no right. We have wished through the years our decision had been otherwise.

"There were carbons of all the responses to letters handled by me during that period in 1967 and the incoming letter was attached to the reply. They were all returned to your father to dispose of as he pleased."

Colonel Walter Dean Short, son of the general, wrote that he had once asked his father why he had not fought the case as hard as Admiral Kimmel. "His answer was substantially to the effect that he wanted to do what he could for the war effort. Therefore, he had gone to work for Ford and was acting as their traffic manager for the Jeep assembly plant in Dallas expediting the shipment of this critical vehicle to our units. He could not really do that job and marshal his own case, and the needs of the U.S. came first with him, then as always. He knew then that G. Marshall was no longer his friend but had placed his position in the FDR administration above his honor. However, Dad was sure that the Army Board would completely exonerate him. He simply could not believe that the honor of so many senior officers could have been subverted.

"After the congressional Pearl Harbor hearings he was saddened but seemed to think that history would ultimately, as you have done, exonerate him. I particularly remember him saying after the congressional hearings on Pearl Harbor, 'Poor George Marshall, he will be the only high ranking officer who will never be able to write his own memoirs.'"

Additional information on the Kilsoo Haan case has come from Thomas W. Gillette, nephew of Senator Guy

Gillette. He discussed the matter at length with his uncle in Bath, Maine, sometime in 1967. "It was then he told me about the contacts from Kilsoo Haan. He also said that Haan had contacted him in late November [1941], telling him that the Japanese Fleet had sailed, under battle orders, east, not south, to attack Pearl Harbor or the Panama Canal.

"Uncle Guy then said he had personally called on President Roosevelt and given him the information. The President's response was 'Thank you, the matter will be looked into.' The conversation was, I gather, quite brief.

"Several days later, in early December [1941], Uncle Guy called the President, telling the aide that it [the call] concerned the matter discussed with the President a few days earlier. The aide came back to the phone saying the President was busy, but the President said the matter had been taken care of.

"I asked Uncle Guy (who was in his late eighties and suffered a stroke a few months later) why he had not written memoirs to this effect. His response was that at the time he was a loyal Democrat who during the war was not about to second-guess President Roosevelt. He was certain Roosevelt used the Japanese attack to achieve a degree of national effort that would otherwise have been impossible, and felt Roosevelt had simply misjudged the damage which the Japanese would be able to inflict. When I suggested it wasn't too late to set the matter straight, he rather wearily said, 'The matter's over, nothing would be accomplished now.'"

Thomas Gillette checked the above information with his mother. "She says Uncle Guy requested [to see] and saw Roosevelt personally, due to the nature of the message. Also, [she said] Haan came to Uncle Guy because sometime earlier Uncle Guy had intervened to prevent deportation of anti-Japanese Korean students back to Korea, where they would surely have been imprisoned or killed."

Source material of the above information as well as other material, taped interviews and correspondence dealing with *Infamy* can be found after June 1983, among my papers at the Franklin D. Roosevelt Library, Hyde Park, N.Y.

Many more secrets of Pearl Harbor remain to be disclosed by those who long ago pledged silence in the name of national security and loyalty to the armed forces and President Roosevelt. There are some who believe that such volatile matters should not be raked up after forty years. But the best way to prevent present or future leaders from making similar mistakes is to bring all available information into the open. The time for secrecy has passed and it is hoped that those with privileged information will come forward like Colonel Ketchum has before it is too late. Much more can also be learned when—and if—our Allies at last open all their Pearl Harbor files to researchers.

August 21, 1982
Tokyo

Acknowledgments

I am grateful to the following archives, museums and libraries: the Alexander Library, Rutgers University (Irene Czarda); Columbia University, Oral History Research Office (Louis M. Star, Elizabeth B. Mason); the Danbury, Connecticut, Public Library; the main branch of the New York Public Library; the Library of Congress; the Yale University Library (Judith Schiff, Mary C. LaFogg); the Seeley G. Mudd Manuscript Library, Princeton University (Nancy Bressler); the Franklin D. Roosevelt Library (William Emerson, Donald Schewe, Robert Parks); the Herbert Hoover Presidential Library (Thomas Thalken, Robert Wood, Dale Meyer, George Nash, Mrs. Mildred Mather); the Dwight D. Eisenhower Library (John E. Wickman); the Harry S. Truman Library; the Archive of Contemporary History, University of Wyoming (Gene M. Gressley, Emmett D. Chisum); Chief Records Office of the Netherlands Ministry of Defense (M. J. van Druten); the Historical Department Naval Staff, the Netherlands Ministry of Defense (Commander F. C. van Oosten); the Naval Historical Center, U.S. Navy (Dean C. Allard); the Hoover Institution (Dr. Agnes Peterson, Charles G. Palm); the University of Hawaii (Stuart Gerry Brown, David Kittelson, Frances Jackson, Mona Nakayama); the George C. Marshall Research Foundation (Dr. Fred Hadsel, John Jacob, Larry Bland, Michael Shoop); and the National Archives (Dr. Robert M. Warner, William Cunlife, Timothy K. Nenninger, John E. Taylor, Geraldine Phillips, William Heimdahl, William Leary, James Trimble, Paul White and Barbara Burger).

Numerous agencies, organizations and individuals made substantial contributions to this book. Fellow historians and authors: Walter Lord, Gwenfread Allen, Walter Henry Nelson, Terence Prittie, Arthur Schlesinger, Jr., Joseph D. Harrington, B. Mitchell Simpson III, Roy Stratton, A. A. Hoehling, Richard Hanser, Ladislas Farago, Bradley Smith, Dr. Warren Ober, Dr. Martin V. Melosi, Dr. Lloyd C. Gardner, Dr. Duane Schultz, Colonel Charles D. MacDonald, Dr. Eric Roman, Dr. Roger Jeans and Associate Professor Paul Hooper.

Also Alfred Geddes; Lawrence J. Dugan; Fred Stocking; Francis A. Raven; Edward B. Hanify; the Matson Navigation Co. (Charles Regal, Fred Stindt); Walter D. Short; Mr. and Mrs. Robert Trumbull; Corney Downes; Mrs. Bonner Fellers; William Gunn; Captain Ben Ferguson; Doris Obata Kumpel; Carl E. Geiger; Ruth Harris; the Pearl Harbor Survivors Association (Ken Murray); Tom Masland, the Philadelphia *Inquirer;* Virginia Keefe Nolan; Mrs. Ralph Townsend; Mrs. Albert F. Betzel; Hugh Winston Lytle; Harry Albright; Colonel William F. Strobridge, Office of Chief of Military Service and the Center of Military History, U. S. Army; Buck Buchwach and George Chaplin, both of the Honolulu *Advertiser;* Bud Smyzer, of the Honolulu *Star Bulletin;* William A. Bernrieder; Anna C. Urband, Media Services Branch, Department of the Navy; Captain Wyman Packard, U.S.N.; Mrs. Stanley Coppel; William Cleveland; Karel Rink; Colonel Eugene Prince; Colonel William Moreland; Mrs. Elizabeth Meijer; James Moser of Doubleday & Company, Inc.; my typist, Helen Collischonn; and Mary R. Mitchell and Frances R. Furlow, who allowed me to quote from the unpublished memoirs of General Henry D. Russell.

Special mention should be made of those who contributed outstandingly to the book: Dr. Warren Kimball, Rutgers University, who loaned me a manuscript copy of his history of the Roosevelt-Churchill correspondence, recently published by the Princeton University Press; Admiral Kemp Tolley, who sent me material on Pearl Harbor which led to this book; Commander Charles C. Hiles, who spent years of his life assiduously researching Pearl Harbor and turned over all his material to me; Bruce R. Bartlett, author of *Cover-Up: The Politics of Pearl Harbor, 1941-1946,* who generously alllowed me to ransack his files; Thomas and Edward Kimmell, who gave not only their time but their material; Percy L. Greaves, Jr., an invaluable living source of the various Pearl Harbor investigations, who, besides reviewing the entire manuscript, allowed me to interview him at length and then select material from his immense collection of documents, manuscripts, notes and books; and Kacy Tebbel, my copy editor, not only for correcting mistakes but for suggesting many improvements in style and content.

Finally, I would like to thank my two editors at Doubleday, Carolyn Blakemore and Ken McCormick, who continue to make the editing process not only painless but enjoyable.

Sources

A. INTERVIEWS AND CORRESPONDENCE
(partial list)

Ambassador Max Bishop (tape)
Bennett Boskey
Karl "Buzz" Boyer
Captain John C. Burrill, U.S.N.
Robert Clack
Rear Admiral David H. Clark
Brigadier General Carter Clarke
Captain Paul Crosley, U.S.N.
Captain and Mrs. Prescott Currier, U.S.N. (tape)
Curtis B. Dall
Vice Admiral Walter DeLany
Robert Diggs (tape)
Vice Admiral George C. Dyer
Judge Charles Fahy (tape)
Brigadier General Bonner Fellers
Dr. Henry Field
Brigadier General Kendall Fielder
Major General Robert J. Fleming, Jr.
Rear Admiral W. Earl Gallaher (tape)
Judge Gerhard Gesell
Percy L. Greaves, Jr. (tape)
Edward B. Hanify (tape)
Major General Eugene L. Harrison (tape)
Colonel William F. Heimlich
Commander Charles C. Hiles
Tyler Kent (tape)
Edward R. Kimmel (tape)
Captain Thomas K. Kimmel, U.S.N. (tape)
Mrs. Harold D. Krick (tape)
Captain George W. Linn, U.S.N.

Colonel Roy F. Lynd
John J. McCloy (tape)
Vice Admiral John McCrea (tape)
Rear Admiral William C. Mott (tape)
Ken Murray
C. Roger Nelson
Thomas Nichols (tape)
Mrs. Barnet Nover
Robert Odell
Stefan T. Possony
Rear Admiral Johan E. Meijer Ranneft (tape)
T. S. N. Ranneft (tape)
Major General P. L. Ransom
Francis Raven (tape)
Major General William O. Reeder (tape)
Mrs. William O. Reeder (tape)
George W. Renchard
David W. Richmond (tape)
Frank B. Rowlett
Rear Admiral L. R. Schulz (tape)
K. M. Steiner (tape)
Judge Edward Allen Tamm
William Thompson (tape)
Brigadier General Elliott Thorpe
Lieutenant General Louis W. Truman
Martin Vitousek (tape)
General Albert C. Wedemeyer (tape)
Vice Admiral Charles W. Wellborn (tape)
Frederic Woodrough (tape)
Seaman First Class Z (tape)

B. DOCUMENTS, DIARIES, RECORDS AND REPORTS

Archival Materials
Columbia University Oral History Project
  Interviews with Frances Perkins, Admirals Thomas Hart, Kent
  Hewitt, and Royal E. Ingersoll
Hoover Institution
  Papers of Delos C. Emmons, Tracy B. Kittredge, General Walter
  Short and Robert A. Theobald
  Memoirs of Ivan Yeaton and Joseph W. Ballantine
  Collection of Stanley K. Hornbeck
Herbert C. Hoover Presidential Library
  Papers of William Castle, Herbert C. Hoover, Frank B. Keefe,
  Verne Marshall, Westbrook Pegler, Admiral John F. Shafroth,
  Charles C. Tansill, Walter Trohan and Ivan Yeaton

Library of Congress, Manuscript Division
   Papers of Cordell Hull, Felix Frankfurter, Frank R. McCoy,
   Robert A. Taft
National Archives
   Record Group 80, General Records of the Department of the Navy
   Record Group 107, Records of the Office of the Secretary of War
   Record Group 128, Records of the Joint Committees of Congress
   Record Group 335, Records of the Office of the Secretary of the
   Army
Naval History Division
   Central Security-Classified Files of the Office of the Chief of
   Naval Operations
   Papers of Harold R. Stark, Harry E. Yarnell, Thomas C. Hart,
   Arthur McCollum
Princeton University Library
   Papers of Philip G. Strong
   Diaries and papers of James V. Forrestal
Franklin D. Roosevelt Library
   Papers of Harry Hopkins, Franklin D. Roosevelt, Samuel I.
   Rosenman
   Henry Morgenthau, Jr. Collection
Rutgers University Library
   Prime Minister Winston S. Churchill Manuscripts: PREMIER 3
   Files, Prime Minister's Operational Files: PREMIER 4 Files,
   Prime Minister's Confidential Files
Harry S. Truman Presidential Library
   Papers of Harry S. Truman and Samuel I. Rosenman
University of Wyoming Library, the Archive of Contemporary
History
   Collections of Harry E. Barnes, Charles C. Hiles, Husband E.
   Kimmel, George Morgenstern, William L. Neumann, Laurance F.
   Safford
   Pearl Harbor File
George C. Marshall Research Foundation
   Papers of George C. Marshall
Yale University, Sterling Memorial Library, Manuscripts and Ar-
chives Diaries and papers of Henry L. Stimson
Government Documents
U. S. Congress. *Congressional Records, 77th-79th Congress,*
   1941-46, 87-91.
U. S. Congress. *Pearl Harbor Attack: Hearings before the Joint
   Committee on the Pearl Harbor Attack.* 79th Congress, 1st Ses-
   sion. 39 vols., 1946.
U. S. Congress. *Report of the Joint Committee on the Investigation
   of the Pearl Harbor Attack.* 79th Congress, 2nd Session, 1946.
U. S. Department of Defense. *The "Magic" Background of Pearl
   Harbor,* 8 volumes. Washington, D.C.: U. S. Government Print-
   ing Office, 1980.

U. S. Department of State. *Papers Relating to the Foreign Relations of the United States: Japan, 1931-1941*, 2 volumes. Washington, D.C.: U.S. Government Printing Office, 1943.

Unpublished Works

Hanify, Edward. "Memorandum." A report of evidence in the congressional hearings. Toland Collection.

————. Speech on Pearl Harbor at Union Club, Boston, MA, on December 7, 1979. Toland Tape Collection.

Hiles, Charles C. *Pattern of Betrayal: The Benign Conspiracy*. Hiles Collection.

Kimmel, Husband E. "Events Leading to the Congressional Investigation of Pearl Harbor." A history of Pearl Harbor. Thomas Kimmel Collection.

Lavender, Robert A. *Pearl Harbor*. His notebook and papers. Mrs. Albert F. Betzel Collection.

Russell, Henry D. Memoirs. George Morgenstern Collection, University of Wyoming Library.

Safford, Laurance. *Rhapsody in Purple*. Hiles Collection.

————. *Victims of the Kita Message*. Hiles Collection.

C. MAGAZINES

Bartlett, Bruce B. "The Pearl Harbor Coverup," *Reason*, February 1976, pp. 24-27.

Beatty, Frank E. "Background of the Secret Report," *National Review*, December 13, 1966, pp. 1261-65.

Burtness, Paul S., and Ober, Warren U. "Research Methodology: Problem of Pearl Harbor Intelligence Reports." *Military Affairs*, Fall 1961, pp. 132-46.

Butow, Robert J. C. "The Hull-Nomura Conversations: A Fundamental Misconception," *American Historical Review*, July 1960, pp. 822-36.

Chamberlain, John. "The Man Who Pushed Pearl Harbor," *Life*, April 1, 1946.

Current, Richard N. "How Stimson Meant to 'Maneuver' the Japanese," *Mississippi Valley Historical Review*, March 1957, pp. 67-76.

Esthus, Raymond A. "President Roosevelt's Commitment to Britain to Intervene in a Pacific War," *Mississippi Valley Historical Review*, June 1963, pp. 28-38.

Greaves, Percy L., Jr. "FDR's Watergate: Pearl Harbor," *Reason*, February 1976, pp. 16-23.

————. "Pearl Harbor," *National Review*, December 13, 1966, pp. 1266-72.

Harrington, Daniel F. "A Careless Hope: American Air Power and Japan, 1941," *Pacific Historical Review*, May 1979, pp. 217-38.

Hiles, Charles C. "The Kita Message: Forever a Mystery?" Chicago *Tribune*, December 7, 1966.

Kimball, Warren F. "Churchill and Roosevelt: The Personal Equation," *Prologue: The Journal of the National Archives*, Fall 1974, pp. 169-82.

Kittredge, Captain T. B. "Muddle Before Pearl Harbor," *U. S. News and World Report*, December 3, 1954, pp. 52ff.

Miles, Sherman. "Pearl Harbor in Retrospect," *Atlantic Monthly*, July 1948, pp. 65-72.

Morison, Samuel Eliot. "Did Roosevelt Start the War: History Through a Beard," *Atlantic Monthly*, August 1948, pp. 91-97.

Puleston, Captain W. D. "Blunders of World War II," *U. S. News and World Report*, February 4, 1955, pp. 109-11.

Tolley, Kemp. "The Strange Assignment of the USS Lanikai," U. S. Naval *Proceedings*, September 1962, pp. 70-83.

———. "Admiral-Ambassador Standley," *Shipmate*, September 1977, pp. 27-29.

Truman, Harry S. "Our Armed Forces Must Be Unified," *Collier's*, August 26, 1944, pp. 16, 63-64.

Whalen, Richard. "The Strange Case of Tyler Kent," *Diplomat*, November 1965, pp. 16-19, 62-64.

D. BOOKS

Allen, Gwenfread. *Hawaii's War Years*. Honolulu: University of Hawaii Press, 1950.

Anthony, J. Garner. *Hawaii Under Army Rule*. Stanford, CA: Stanford University Press, 1955.

Arnold, H. H. *Global Mission*. New York: Harper and Brothers, 1949.

Bailey, Thomas A., and Ryan, Paul B. *Hitler vs Roosevelt*. New York: Macmillan, 1979.

Barnes, Harry Elmer. *Perpetual War for Perpetual Peace*. Caldwell, ID: Caxton Printers, 1953.

Bartlett, Bruce R. *Cover-Up: The Politics of Pearl Harbor, 1941-1946*. New Rochelle, NY: Arlington House, 1978.

Beard, Charles A. *President Roosevelt and the Coming of the War, 1941*. New Haven: Yale University Press, 1948.

Berle, Adolf A. *Navigating the Rapids, 1918-1971*. New York: Harcourt Brace Jovanovich, 1973.

Biddle, Francis. *In Brief Authority*. Garden City, NY: Doubleday & Co., Inc., 1962.

Blair, Clay, Jr. *Silent Victory*. Philadelphia, New York: Lippincott, 1975.

Blum, John Morton. *Years of Urgency, 1938-1941*. Boston: Houghton Mifflin, 1965.

Borg, Dorothy, and Okamoto, Shumpei, eds. *Pearl Harbor as History*. New York: Columbia University Press, 1973.

Brownlow, Donald Grey. *The Accused*. New York: Vantage Press, 1968.

Buell, Thomas B. *The Quiet Warrior*. Boston: Little, Brown, 1974.

Bullitt, Orville H., ed. *Correspondence between Franklin D. Roosevelt and William C. Bullitt*. Boston: Houghton Mifflin, 1972.

Burtness, Paul S., and Ober, Warren U. *The Puzzle of Pearl Harbor*. Evanston, IL: Row, Peterson, 1962.

Churchill, Winston. *The Second World War*. Boston: Houghton Mifflin, 1949-60. Vol. 3, *The Grand Alliance*.

Clark, Ronald. *The Man Who Broke Purple*. Boston: Little, Brown, 1977.

Cole, Wayne S. *America First*. Madison: University of Wisconsin Press, 1953.

Current, Richard N. *Secretary Stimson: a Study in Statecraft*. New Brunswick, NJ: Rutgers University Press, 1954.

Dallek, Robert. *Franklin D. Roosevelt and American Foreign Policy, 1932-1945*. New York: Oxford University Press, 1979.

Divine, Robert A. *The Illusion of Neutrality*. Chicago: Quadrangle Books, 1962.

Eggleston, George T. *Roosevelt, Churchill and the World War II Opposition*. Old Greenwich, CT: Devin-Adair, 1979.

Emmerson, John K. *The Japanese Thread*. New York: Holt, Rinehart and Winston, 1978.

Farago, Ladislas. *The Broken Seal*. New York: Random House, 1967; Bantam, 1968.

———. *The Tenth Fleet*. New York: Obolensky, 1962.

Farley, James A. *Jim Farley's Story*. New York: McGraw-Hill, 1948.

Field, Henry. *Trail Blazers*. Miami, FL: Field Research Projects, 1980.

Flynn, John T. *The Final Secret of Pearl Harbor*. New York: Privately printed, 1950.

Forrestal, James. *The Forrestal Diaries*. New York: Viking, 1951.

Gauvreau, Emile, and Cohen, Lester. *Billy Mitchell*. New York: Dutton, 1942.

Grew, Joseph, C. *Ten Years in Japan*. New York: Simon and Schuster, 1944.

———. *Turbulent Era,* Vol. II. Boston: Houghton Mifflin, 1952.

Halsey, Fleet Admiral William F., and Bryan, J. III. *Admiral Halsey's Story*. New York: McGraw-Hill, 1947.

Harringon, Joseph P. *Yankee Samurai*. Detroit: Pettigrew Enterprises, 1979.

Hoehling, A. A. *The Week Before Pearl Harbor*. New York: Norton, 1963.

———. *December 7, 1941: The Day the Admirals Slept Late*.

(Paperback edition of above). New York: Kensington, 1978.

Holmes, W. J. *Dougle-Edged Secrets*. Annapolis: Naval Institute Press, 1979.

Hull, Cordell. *The Memoirs of Cordell Hull*. New York: Macmillan, 1948. 2 vols.

Hyde, H. Montgomery. *Room 3603*. New York: Farrar, Straus, 1963.

Ickes, Harold L. *The Secret Diary of Harold L. Ickes*. New York: Simon and Schuster, 1953-54. Vol. 3, *The Lowering Clouds, 1939-41*.

Kahn, David. *The Code Breakers*. New York: Macmillan, 1967.

Kimball, Warren F. *The Most Unsordid Act*. Baltimore: Johns Hopkins Press, 1969.

Kimball, Warren F., ed. *Franklin D. Roosevelt and the World Crisis, 1937-1945*. Lexington, MA: Heath, 1952.

Kimmel, Husband E. *Admiral Kimmel's Story*. Chicago: Regnery, 1955.

King, Ernest J., and Whitehill, Walter Muir. *Fleet Admiral King*. New York: Norton, 1952.

Kubek, Anthony. *How the Far East Was Lost*. Dallas: Teacher Publishing Company, 1962.

Langer, William L., and Gleason, S. Everett. *The Undeclared War*. New York: Harper and Brothers, 1953.

Lea, Homer. *The Valor of Ignorance*. New York: Harpers, 1909.

Lombard, Helen. *While They Fought*. New York: Scribners, 1947.

Lord, Walter. *Day of Infamy*. New York: Holt, 1957.

Manchester, William. *American Caesar*. New York: Dell, 1979.

Marshall, Katherine Tupper. *Together*. Atlanta: Tupper and Love, 1946.

Masterman, J. S. *The Double-Cross System*. New Haven: Yale University Press, 1972.

Melosi, Martin V. *The Shadow of Pearl Harbor*. College Station: Texas A. and M. University Press, 1977.

Morgenstern, George Edward. *Pearl Harbor*. New York: Devin-Adair, 1947.

Newcomb, Richard F. *Savo: The Incredible Naval Debacle off Guadalcanal*. New York: Holt, Rinehart and Winston, 1961.

O'Connor, Richard. *Pacific Destiny*. Boston: Little, Brown, 1969.

Perkins, Frances. *The Roosevelt I Knew*. New York: Viking, 1946.

Pogue, Forrest C. *George C. Marshall*. New York: Viking, 1968-73. Vol. 2, *Ordeal and Hope;* Vol. 3, *Organizer of Victory*.

Popov, Duskov. *Spy Counter-Spy*. New York: Grosset and Dunlap, 1974.

Porteus, Stanley D. *And Blow Not the Trumpet*. Palo Alto, CA: Pacific Books, 1947.

Potter, E. B. *Nimitz*. Annapolis: Naval Institute Press, 1976.

Powell, John B. *My Twenty-Five Years in Japan*. New York: Macmillan, 1945.

Richardson, Admiral J. O., as told to George C. Dyer. *On the Treadmill to Pearl Harbor*. Washington, D.C.: U. S. Government Printing Office, 1973.

Roosevelt, Eleanor. *This I Remember*. New York: Harper, 1949.

Rosenman, Samuel I. *Working with Roosevelt*. New York: Harper, 1952.

Russett, Bruce M. *No Clear and Present Danger*. New York: Harper and Row, 1972.

Sherwood, Robert E. *Roosevelt and Hopkins*. New York: Harper, 1948.

Snow, John Howland. *The Case of Tyler Kent*. New Canaan, CT: Long House, 1962.

Standley, Admiral William H., and Ageton, Arthur A. *Admiral Ambassador to Russia*. Chicago: Regnery, 1955.

Stevenson, William. *A Man Called Intrepid*. New York: Harcourt Brace Jovanovich, 1976.

Stimson, Henry L., and Bundy, McGeorge. *On Active Service in Peace and War*. New York: Harper, 1947.

Stratton, Roy. *The Army-Navy Game*. Falmouth, MA: Volta, 1977.

Sulzberger, C. L. *A Long Row of Candles*. New York: Macmillan, 1969.

Sweeny, Charles. *Pearl Harbor*. Murray, UT: Privately printed, 1946.

Tansill, Charles C. *Back Door to War*. Chicago: Regnery, 1952.

Theobald, Rear Admiral Robert A. *The Final Secret of Pearl Harbor*. Old Greenwich, CT: Devin-Adair, 1954.

Thorne, Christopher. *Allies of a Kind*. New York: Oxford University Press, 1978.

Thorpe, Brigadier General Elliott R. *East Wind Rain*. Boston: Gambit, 1969.

Toland, John. *But Not in Shame*. New York: Random House, 1961.
———. *The Rising Sun*. New York: Random House, 1970.

Tolley, Kemp. *Cruise of the Lanikai*. Annapolis: Naval Institute Press, 1973.

Tully, Grace. *F.D.R. My Boss*. New York: Scribners, 1949.

Van Der Rhoer, Edward. *Deadly Magic*. New York: Scribners, 1978.

Wayman, Dorothy G. *David I. Walsh, Citizen-Patriot*. Milwaukee: Bruce, 1952.

Wedemeyer, General Albert C. *Wedemeyer Reports*. New York: Holt, 1958.

Whalen, Richard J. *The Founding Father*. New York: New American Library, 1964.

Wheeler, Burton K., with Paul F. Healy. *Yankee from the West*.

Garden City, NY: Doubleday & Co., Inc., 1962.

Wilson, Rose Page. *George Marshall Remembered*. Prentice-Hall: Englewood Cliffs, NJ, 1968.

Winant, John Gilbert. *Letter from Grosvenor Square*. Boston: Houghton Mifflin, 1947.

Wohlstetter, Roberta. *Pearl Harbor: Warning and Decision*. Stanford, CA: Stanford University Press, 1962.

NOTES

Abbreviations

CR	Congressional Record
CUOH	Columbia University, Oral History Research Office, New York, NY
FD	Forrestal Diary, Seely G. Mudd Manuscript Library, Princeton University, Princeton, NJ
FDR	Franklin Delano Roosevelt Presidential Library, Hyde Park, NY
GCM	George C. Marshall Research Foundation, Lexington, VA
HI	Hoover Institution, Stanford, CA
LC	Library of Congress, Manuscript Division, Washington, DC
NA	The National Archives, Washington, DC
NYT	New York *Times*
PHA	*Pearl Harbor Attack: Hearings before the Joint Committee on the Investigation of the Pearl Harbor Attack,* 79th Congress, 1st Session. 39 vols., 1946.
SD	Stimson Diary, Yale University Library, New Haven, CT
TKC	Thomas Kimmel Collection
UWACH	University of Wyoming, Archive of Contemporary History, Laramie, WY

Chapter One "HOW DID THEY CATCH US . . ."

pages 3-4   Edgers story. Interview with Woodrough.
page 12   Kimmel reaction. Interviews with DeLany, Murray, Clark; Brownlow 133. *The Accused* by Donald Grey Brownlow contains much original material of high quality.

page 12   Roosevelt-Hopkins meeting. Sherwood 530-1.
page 13   Hull story. U. S. Department of State Bulletin, V: 461-64.
page 13   "Have you heard the news?" SD.
page 13   Kawakami story. K. C. Li, comp., *American Diplomacy in the Far East: 1941* (New York, 1942), 414.
page 14   "So sorry, we sank your fleet this morning." Sulzberger 176.
page 14   "The President was deeply shaken." Biddle 206.
page 14   Morgenthau story. Morgenthau diary, FDR.
page 15   "But they knew, they knew, they knew." Clark 170.
page 15   Popov story. Popov 190-91.

Chapter Two   MR. KNOX GOES WEST

page 17   "The Sun Will Soon Be Setting . . ." Melosi 3.
page 17   White House reaction. Tully 258-89.
page 18   "and slept the sleep of the saved . . ." Churchill, *Grand Alliance*, 608.
page 18   "Oh! that is the way we talked to her . . ." Arthur Bryant, *The Turn of the Tide*, 282.
page 18   Spruance story. Buell 97-98.
page 18   "If I were in charge in Washington . . ." Brownlow 139.
page 19   Knox story. Melosi 20; Knox papers, LC; Admiral Beatty article in *National Review*, Dec. 13, 1966, 1261.
page 20   Stowe story. CR 9646.
page 20   Tobey story. CR 9656-62.
page 21   "Altogether much is brewing . . ." SD
page 21   B-18 accident. Accident report, Norton Air Force Base, CA.
page 22   "He read them most carefully . . ." SD.
pages 22-23   Knox report to Roosevelt. PHA 24:1749-56.
page 23   Roosevelt meeting with Knox, Stimson, Hull, etc. Memorandum by Roosevelt, undated, President's File, FDR; Melosi 25.
page 23   "You could have heard a tiny pin drop . . ." William Bernreider letter to City Hall Press Corps, Dec. 16, 1941, Bernreider Collection.
pages 23-24   "The United States services were not on the alert . . ." NYT, Dec. 16, 1941, 1 and 7.
page 24   "as fairly extensive and unvarnished." *Nation*, Dec. 20, 1941, 626.
page 24   "it was almost possible to hear . . ." NYT, Dec. 16, 1941, 26.

pages 24-25   Stimson-McCloy meeting. SD; interview with McCloy.

page 25   Roosevelt-Mrs. Hamlin story. Hamlin diary, FDR.

page 26   "Most confidentially we are sending . . ." Stimson letter, Dec. 16, 1941, Yale University Library.

page 26   "You always wanted the Pacific Fleet." Potter 9-10.

Chapter Three   "SOME ADMIRAL OR SOME GENERAL . . ."

page 29   "How about that, Frank?" Current 170-71.

page 30   Hoover letter. Dec. 17, 1941, Herbert Hoover Presidential Library, West Branch, IA.

pages 30-31   Standley story. Standley 80 ff.; manuscript, "The Pearl Harbor Debacle," by Standley and Arthur A. Ageton, TKC.

page 32   Testimony, Dec. 23, 1941. PHA 22:31 ff.

page 33   Nimitz story. Potter 16-17.

page 33   "If the United States has been found . . ." CR, Dec. 26, 1941.

pages 33-34   "Of course, you are not here in the capacity . . ." Kimmel 151-52.

page 34   "that he desired to offer no objection . . ." Kimmel 154.

page 35   "I felt that, with all the information available . . ." Standley 84.

page 35   Kimmel's frustration. Kimmel 147.

page 35   Testimony, Jan. 2, 1942. PHA 23:1068 ff.

page 35   Murray story. Interview with Murray.

page 36   "opposed to any correction of the testimony . . ." Kimmel 157-58.

page 36   "But Mr. Roberts is only one member . . ." Kimmel 158.

page 36   "Words don't alter facts": Kimmel letter to Barnes, June 12, 1962, TKC.

pages 36-37   Standley report to Knox. Standley 88.

page 37   "We sat up until twelve o'clock . . ." SD.

page 38   "apparently persisted long after we both . . ." Standley-Ageton manuscript, "The Pearl Harbor Debacle," TKC.

page 38   "it did not present the whole, true picture." Standley 87-88.

page 38   "Is there any reason why this report . . ." Roberts to Samuel I. Rosenman in *The Public Papers and Addresses of Franklin D. Roosevelt*, Rosenman X:565.

page 38   "It is an admirable report . . ." SD.

pages 38-39   Report of the Roberts Commission, January 23, 1942. PHA 39:1-21.

page 39   "comprehensive and admirable view of the facts . . ." Beard 222.

pages 39-40   Taussig letter to Kimmel. Kimmel 177-78.

page 40   "Naturally it stirs many reflections . . ." Frankfurter to Roberts, Jan. 25, 1942, Frankfurter Papers, LC.

pages 40-41   Short story. PHA 7:3133. Original letter at GCM.

pages 41-42   "as I feared it might give the impression . . ." SD.

page 42   "It's high time we were getting rid . . ." SD.

page 42   Stimson letter to Roberts. PHA 7:3261.

page 43   "I think it is regrettable that the committee . . ." NYT, Jan. 30, 1942, 4.

page 43   "If you think it would be a good thing . . ." McCormack to Edwin M. Watson, Feb. 6, 1942. Roosevelt Papers, FDR.

page 44   "It seems to me that this committee . . ." Ernest J. King Collection, LC.

Chapter Four   "SETTLE YOURSELF IN A QUIET NOOK . . ."

page 45   Kimmel's retirement. "Facts and Correspondence," an unpublished memorandum by Kimmel, TKC.

pages 45-46   "I showed the Secretary and the President . . ." Stark to Kimmel, Jan. 27, 1942, TKC.

page 46   "I desire my request for retirement . . ." "Facts and Correspondence," TKC.

page 46   "Wait about a week and then announce . . ." SD.

page 46   "I told him the way in which . . ." "Facts and Correspondence," TKC.

page 47   "I wish for you, amid the clouds . . ." Ibid.

page 47   "Pending something definite, there is no . . ." Ibid.

page 47   "I stand ready at any time . . ." Ibid.

page 48   "I do not have to tell you . . ." Ibid.

page 49   May speech. Brownlow 148.

page 49   Mix letter. Kimmel 172.

pages 50-51   Thomas Kimmel story. Interview with T. Kimmel.

page 51   Edward Kimmel story. Interview with E. Kimmel.

pages 52-56   Kimmel story: "Events Leading to the Congressional Investigation of Pearl Harbor," an unpublished account by Admiral Kimmel, TKC; notebook and papers of Robert A. Lavender, Mrs. Albert F. Betzel Collection; interviews with Thomas and Edward Kimmel and Edward Hanify; Hanify speech on Pearl Harbor at Union Club, Boston, MA, Dec. 7, 1979, Toland Tape Collection.

Chapter Five MUTINY ON THE SECOND DECK

pages 59-65   For background on the mutiny I am indebted to A. A. Hoehling and two restricted studies in the Hiles Collection at UWACH by Captain Laurance Safford: *Rhapsody in Purple* and *Victims of the Kita Message*.

Commander Hiles's collections, which include twelve years of voluminous correspondence with Safford, have been an invaluable contribution to this book.

page 60   "I thoroughly appreciate that you would probably . . ." Kahn 25-26.

page 60   "That Noyes!" Hoehling, *Day*, 62.

page 63   "Both officers were good haters." Interview with Hiles.

page 65   "You put in the words 'war warning.'" Hoehling, *Day*, 72-74.

pages 65-68   Safford story of Cipher 3. His two unpublished studies cited above.

page 66   "You have been capsized . . ." Safford letter, May 25, 1964, to Eugene Gressley, UWACH.

page 68   "I further informed Friedman . . ." Safford letter to Hiles, Dec. 31, 1961, Hiles Private Collection.

pages 68-69   "I realized I would be one of the important . . ." PHA 36:69.

page 70   "I realize that your reply . . ." PHA, 8:3698-99.

page 71   "My dear Kramer: When the proper time comes . . ." PHA 8:3702.

page 71   Safford letter to Kramer, Jan. 22, 1944. PHA 8:3700.

page 72   Safford visit to Kimmel: Safford letter to Hiles, May 24, 1965, UWACH.

Chapter Six THE HART INQUIRY

page 73   "I feel that I am entitled to a speedy . . ." Kimmel letter to Hart, TKC.

pages 74-75   Turner testimony. PHA 26:273-75.

page 75   Knox's press release, April 14, 1944. Record Group 125, NA.

page 75   "I presume you have noted the recent . . ." Kimmel letter to Manning M. Kimmel, Apr. 27, 1944, TKC.

pages 76-77   Hanify story. Interview with Hanify.

page 77   Halsey testimony. PHA 6:325.

page 77   "I have just come from the front office . . ." PHA 29:2392.

pages 77-79   Safford testimony. PHA 26:392-95.

page 79   "I happened to remark to him . . ." Hart taped memoirs, CUOH.

Chapter Seven　THE ARMY AND NAVY CLUB

pages 80–81　　"Kimmel's waiver of its provisions . . ." Interview with Hanify; Hanify speech, Dec. 7, 1979.

page 81　　Rugg-Kimmel conversation. Interview with Hanify.

page 81　　Hanify story. Interview with Hanify.

pages 81–82　　"I have wanted it since Pearl Harbor . . ." Kimmel letter to Senator Weeks, May 25, 1944, TKC.

page 82–83　　"Mr. Chairman, why is it necessary . . ." CR 5340 ff.

page 83　　"It would be a splendid contribution . . ." CR 5402-15.

page 84　　"Nothing short of an impartial . . ." Kimmel letter to Rugg, July 13, 1944, TKC.

page 85　　"I know pretty well the general . . ." Brownlow 153; Lavender notebook; Hanify speech, Dec. 7, 1979.

page 85　　"I found the messages and many more." Lavender notebook.

page 86　　"It appeared that this assignment . . ." King 632.

page 86　　"I have never been able to understand . . ." Ernest J. King Collection, LC.

page 87　　"I'm not really very excited . . ." Interview with Richmond.

page 87　　Marshall testimony. PHA 27:11 ff.

pages 88–89　　"I have always considered Admiral Kimmel . . ." PHA 32:75.

pages 89-90　　Kimmel testimony. PHA 32:120 ff.

page 90　　Schuirmann testimony. PHA 33:731.

pages 90–92　　Rugg-Kimmel questions. PHA 33:731 ff.

pages 92–93　　Pye-Kimmel conversation. Kimmel 131-32.

page 93　　Kimmel-DeLany conversation. Interviews with DeLany and Hanify.

page 93　　"That son of a bitch . . ." Interview with E. Kimmel.

pages 93–94　　Kimmel at Army Board. PHA 28:946-47.

page 94　　"I will cooperate to the best . . ." Brownlow 159.

page 94　　"Dicky, it won't do you a Goddamn bit of good . . ." Ibid. 154.

page 95　　"Well, I never saw three officers . . ." Ibid. 157.

page 95　　"Jesus Christ, we'll adjourn!" Interview with Hanify.

page 95　　"Short, Marshall is your enemy." Brownlow 156.

page 96　　"It was an alert apprehensiveness . . ." Interview with Hanify.

page 96　　Stark testimony. PHA 32:532-33.

pages 96-97　　"Perhaps I was tired." Thomas C. Hart Papers, Naval Historical Center, Washington, DC.

page 97　　Marshall testimony. PHA 32:852 ff.

page 98　　"To give you an honest answer . . ." Interview with Hanify.

page 98   Hanify-Kramer conversation. Interview with Hanify.

pages 98-100   Kramer testimony. PHA 33:871 ff.

pages 100-01   Turner testimony. PHA 33:806 ff; Ibid. 32:619-20.

page 101   Noyes testimony. PHA 33:898.

page 101   "General Marshall came in in the last part . . ." SD.

page 102   Stimson testimony. PHA 29:2064 ff.

pages 102-03   "I was sorry to learn . . ." Stimson letter to Roosevelt, Sept. 26, 1944, Yale University Library.

page 103   Marshall testimony. PHA 29:2312.

pages 103-04   Short testimony. Ibid. 2251 ff.

page 105   "this was no longer a case of diplomatic . . ." Charles A. Willoughby and John Chamberlain, *MacArthur: 1941-1951* (New York: McGraw-Hill, 1954), 22-23.

pages 105-06   Yeaton story. Yeaton papers, HI; correspondence with Heimlich.

page 107   Safford testimony. PHA 29:2385 ff.

page 107   "It is my personal belief . . ." Russell's unpublished memoirs, Morgenstern Collection, UWACH.

pages 107-09   Marshall testimony. PHA 29:2400 ff.

pages 109-10   Bratton testimony. Ibid. 2415 ff.

page 110   "Marshall and his close associates . . ." Russell's unpublished memoirs.

page 110   Grunert story. Grunert letter to Deputy Chief of Staff, U. S. Army, Oct. 30, 1944.

pages 110-11   Sadtler testimony. PHA 29:2427 ff.

page 110   "We knew nothing of the reasons . . ." Russell's unpublished memoirs.

page 111   Navy Court of Inquiry Report. PHA 39:297 ff.

page 111   "undermine such faith as the great masses . . ." Russell's unpublished memoirs.

pages 112-13   Top Secret Army Pearl Harbor Report. PHA 39:221 ff.

pages 113-14   Rugg telegram. TKC.

Chapter Eight "YOU DO NOT HAVE TO CARRY THE TORCH . . ."

pages 115-23   Kent Case. Interviews and correspondence with Kent; British Public Records Office, FO/371/38704, File No. 2405; Snow; The Earl Jowett, *Some Are Spies* (London: Stodder and Houghton, 1940), 40 ff; transcript of Kent Trial at Central Criminal Court, Old Bailey; Whalen article in *Diplomat*, Nov. 1965; Whalen 313 ff.; Henry Taylor article in Washington *Daily News*, Sept. 5, 1944.

page 124   Kimmel letter to Truman, August 20, 1944. TKC.

page 124   "Dreyfus was on Devil's Island . . ." Broadcast transcript, Aug. 30, 1944, TKC.

pages 124-25   Remarks in Congress. CR 7573-76; 7648-51; 8110-12.

page 125   "About 72 hours before Pearl Harbor . . ." PHA 29:2252.

page 125   "There will be lots of things like that . . ." Roosevelt press conference, Sept. 22, 1944.

page 125   "The American People demand . . ." Preston Kaye letter to Roosevelt, Sept. 11, 1944, Roosevelt Papers, FDR.

pages 125-26   "fear there would be an adverse report . . ." SD.

pages 126-29   Marshall-Dewey story. "Statement for Record" by Brigadier General Carter Clarke, Record Group 457, NA.

page 129   Luce story. Eggleston 186.

page 129   Roosevelt's health. Ibid. 186.

page 130   "won't intimate in the papers . . ." *Facts on File Yearbook 1944*, 360.

pages 130-31   "We each told the other . . ." SD.

page 131   "Since trial by general court-martial . . ." PHA 39:343-45.

page 131   "by the grace of God . . ." SD.

pages 132-33   Stimson-Roosevelt conversation. Ibid.

pages 133-34   Stimson letter to Roosevelt, Nov. 22, 1944. Yale University Library.

page 134   "His wish for coordination . . ." SD.

page 135   "The exercise of hindsight . . ." FD.

page 135   "turning back to his old form . . ." SD.

page 135   "The departure of Mr. Hull . . ." Ibid.

page 135   "Now I feel as if I had a burden . . ." Ibid.

pages 136-37   Kimmel-King conversation. Kimmel memorandum, TKC.

page 138   Pettigrew affidavit. PHA 35:23.

pages 138-139   Dusenbury affidavit. Ibid. 25.

page 140   MacArthur story. Interview and correspondence with Fellers; Fellers letter to Kimmel, Feb. 1967, TKC.

page 141   "I told him that I felt . . ." FD.

pages 141-42   Safford-Sonnett meetings. PHA 18:3345.

page 142   Sonnett-Hewitt conversation with Safford. Ibid. 3346.

page 142   Kramer testimony. PHA 36:81.

pages 143-144   *"thought* that a 'Winds' message . . ." Ibid. 93.

page 144   "One of the reasons why he suggested . . ." Rugg memorandum, July 10, 1944, TKC.

page 144   "no message was intercepted . . ." PHA 36:575.

pages 145-46   "Some time during 1943 . . ." PHA 33:86.

page 146   Spalding testimony. Ibid. 90-92.

pages 146-47   Bissell testimony. Ibid. 101-2.

page 147   Richmond-Marshall story. Interview with Richmond.

page 148   "If I had received such a message . . ." PHA 35:92-93.

page 148   "an exceptionally good officer . . ." Ransom letter to author, March 27, 1980.

pages 148-49   Bratton story. Correspondence with Heimlich; Yeaton memoirs, HI; PHA 35:97-98.

page 150   "Secretary Forrestal had some very set ideas . . ." Hewitt taped interview, CUOH.

page 151   "only added to and accentuated . . ." FD.

page 151   Truman press conference, Aug. 29, 1945.

page 152   "As the stories were 'rigged' in Washington . . ." Russell unpublished memoirs.

pages 152-53   Truman press conference, Aug. 30, 1945.

page 153   "I wish Congress could forget about it . . ." Chicago *Tribune*, Sept. 6, 1945.

Chapter Nine "IF I HAD KNOWN WHAT WAS TO HAPPEN . . ."

page 158   "I simply ask the right . . ." CR 10345.

page 159   "whole legions of stories . . ." CR 10446.

page 159   "I shall never grant permission . . ." CR 10433.

page 160   "It is very distressing to me . . ." Mitchell letter to Randolph Mason, Nov. 10, 1945.

page 161   Testimony, Nov. 16, 1945. PHA 1:33 ff.

page 162   "a sneak attack upon the grave . . ." Melosi 149.

page 162   "tactic of desperation by a party . . ." NYT, Nov. 18, 1945.

page 162   "it seems almost certain that they . . ." Ibid.

pages 162-163   Richardson testimony. PHA 1:265-66.

page 163   "I have been greatly disturbed . . ." Mrs. Roosevelt to Hopkins, Nov. 20, 1945, Hopkins Papers, FDR.

page 164   "Since Senator Ferguson devoted more time . . ." Greaves unpublished manuscript.

page 166   Hull testimony. PHA 2:614-15.

pages 167-168   Kent story: Washington *Times-Herald*, Dec. 5, 1945; New York *Post*, Dec. 4, 1945; New York *World-Telegram*, Dec. 4, 1945.

page 168   "If I had more experience . . ." Interview with Kent.

page 168   "That phone call as we came in . . ." K. T. Marshall 282.

pages 169-71   Diggs on Marshall. Interview and correspondence with Diggs.

page 170   Gerow testimony. PHA 3:1036-37.

pages 170-71   Marshall testimony. Dec. 6, 1945, Ibid. 1049 ff.

page 172   Marshall testimony. Dec. 7, 1945, Ibid. 1105 ff.

page 172   Marshall testimony. Dec. 8, 1945, Ibid. 1165 ff.

page 174   Miles testimony. Ibid. 1554.

page 174   Lucas-Greaves incident. Ibid. 1372-73.

page 175   "It seems strange to me . . ." New York *Herald-Tribune*, Dec. 12, 1945; Washington *Times-Herald*, Dec. 12, 1945.

pages 175-78   Marshall testimony. PHA 3:1406 ff.

page 177   "Totally honest." Interview with Gesell.

page 177   "I felt that his performance . . ." Interview with Diggs.

page 177   Ferguson story. Interview with Greaves.

page 178   "sit and take it." J. L. Homer letter to Forrest Pogue, July 22, 1960, GCM.

page 178   Mitchell announcement to committee. PHA 4:1585-87.

pages 178-79   Barkley and George comments. Ibid. 1587-90.

page 179   Afternoon session. Ibid. 1612 ff.

pages 179-80   "What was indicated in his statement . . ." NYT, Dec. 16, 1945.

page 180   Greaves incident. PHA 4:1719-22.

pages 181-84   Wilkinson testimony. Ibid. 1793 ff.

page 180   "If you ever need a counsel . . ." Interview with Greaves.

page 184   "Now, yesterday I made the mistake . . ." PHA 4:1859-60.

page 185   Turner story: Interview with Mott.

pages 185-86   Turner testimony. PHA 4:1975 ff.

page 186   "The Committee wishes the press and all others . . ." Ibid. 2063.

Chapter Ten   THEIR DAY IN COURT

page 188   "Counsel has not yet had nor requested . . ." Barnes 453-54.

page 188   Stark-Richmond story. Interview with Richmond.

page 189   Greaves letter. Greaves Collection.

pages 189-90   Stark testimony. PHA 5:2291 ff.

page 190   "I want the truth to come out." Brownlow 164.

page 190   "It wouldn't take much for Stark . . ." Interview with Richmond.

page 191   "This was unquestionably done . . ." Kimmel memorandum, TKC.

page 191   Kimmel testimony. Jan. 16, 1946, PHA 6:2555 ff.

page 191   Kimmel testimony. Jan. 18, 1946, Ibid. 2701 ff.

page 192   "Now, Mr. Chairman, the gentleman . . ." Ibid. 2775.

page 192   "I appreciate as you do . . ." Ibid. 2825.

pages 192-93   Kimmel testimony. Ibid. 2839 ff.

page 193   "It contained the first inkling . . ." Barnes 456.

page 193   Greaves letter to Flynn, Jan. 19, 1946. Greaves Collection.

page 193   The war plan mentioned on page 185, WPL-46, dated May 26, 1941, was based upon the report of the United States-British Staff Conversations, the Joint Canada-United States Defense Plan and the Joint Army and Navy Basic War Plan. Apparently these Anglo-American plans were approved by the Secretary of the Navy on May 28, 1941. (PHA 15:1425.) The President on June 7, 1941, returned the war plan to the Navy Department after familiarizing himself with it, saying "since the report of the United States British Staff Conversations had not been approved by the British Government, he would not approve the report at this time, neither would he now give approval to Joint Army and Navy Basic War Plan. . . . However, in case of war the papers would be returned to the President for his approval." (PHA 3:995.)

On June 11, 1941, Admiral Stark instructed top Navy officials that "the highest priority in the preparation of war plans is assigned to the plans required by WPL-46. It is directed that the preparation and distribution of these plans be accomplished with the least possible delay." (PHA 5:2478.) In any case, despite the Administration's denial of a pre-war agreement with Britain, these plans based on British-American conversations were in effect prior to December 7, 1941.

They reveal that once war came Kimmel had certain offensive tasks, including raids on the Caroline and Marshall Islands. The Pacific Fleet was not ordered to deploy and patrol the Hawaiian coast. As Admiral Stark testified, "I do not think there is any place in the plan where it could tell him [Kimmel] what to do in connection with a defensive deployment." (PHA 5:2449.) The deployment was meant for the Asiatic Fleet in the Philippines. This fleet was the first addressee of the "war warning" message and the one primarily interested in the suspected Japanese expedition in Southeast Asia.

To Kimmel the war warning message meant he should ready his forces for raids on the Marshall and Caroline Islands, which meant that his fleet had to come into Pearl Harbor—to strip, fuel and make ready for possible action. That is exactly what the Pacific Fleet was doing on December 7, 1941.

pages 193-94   "when everybody above him . . ." PHA 6:2858-59.

page 194   "confident that the Navy . . ." Kimmel letter to Col. Manning Kimmel, Jan. 25, 1946, TKC.

page 194   Short testimony. PHA 6:2964.

pages 195-96   Short testimony. PHA 7:3133 ff.

pages 196-201   Roberts testimony. Ibid. 3272 ff.

Chapter Eleven SAFFORD AT BAY

page 202   ''He entered the Naval Hospital under orders . . .''
Associated Press, Nov. 13, 1945.

pages 203-06   Briggs story. U. S. Navy official taped interview,
Jan. 13, 1977, NA; Safford papers, Hiles Collection, UWACH.

pages 207-08   Hanify story. Interviews with Hanify and Mrs.
William Reeder.

pages 210-12   Safford testimony. PHA 8:3593 ff.

page 212   ''I was instructed by the Secretary of the Navy . . .''
U.S. News, Feb. 15, 1946, 22.

page 212   ''I was sitting right behind Safford . . .'' Lavender letter to Kimmel, Sept. 21, 1962, TKC.

pages 213-19   Safford testimony: PHA 8:3673 ff.

page 220   ''He was not a forensic type.'' Interview with Hanify.

page 220   ''We haven't touched the real meat . . .'' New York
Herald Tribune, Feb. 5, 1946.

pages 221-24   Safford testimony. PHA 8:3741 ff.

pages 224-26   Safford testimony. PHA 8:3839-93.

page 226   Before he left the room, Safford was stopped by
Richardson's wife. ''Captain, you were simply wonderful! You
did not let them bully you into changing your story.'' Realizing
who she was, Safford felt that this was an ''angel from heaven.''
Gordon Prange, *At Dawn We Slept* (New York: McGraw-Hill,
1981), 715.

page 226   Kramer testimony. Feb. 6, 1946, Ibid. 3893 ff.

page 227   Kramer testimony. Feb. 7, 1946, PHA 9:3929 ff.

pages 228-30   Kramer testimony. Feb. 8, 1946, Ibid. 4009 ff.

pages 230-32   Kramer testimony. Feb. 9, 1946, Ibid. 4093 ff.

pages 232-33   Kramer testimony. Feb. 11, 1946, Ibid. 4157 ff.

page 233   ''some medal of higher dignity than that which was
given to Captain Safford.'' Commander Baecher reported to Forrestal that the majority was indignant at the award to Captain Safford, particularly following his recent allegations about his
superiors. ''The suggestion had now been seriously made to me
that the Navy in order to straighten out the matter should award to
Captain Kramer some medal of higher dignity than that which was
given to Captain Safford . . . because the effect of his testimony
was to support the integrity of the higher command in the Navy
and your Findings and Conclusions.'' (Baecher memorandum to
Forrestal, Feb. 13, 1946.)

In a second memorandum to Forrestal three days later, Baecher
wrote: ''Congressman Murphy stated to me privately that while he
knew there were 'two camps in the Navy' yet he desired to know
whether it was 'a coincidence' that the award was made immediately following the attempt by majority members of the Committee to demonstrate as unfounded Captain Safford's statements

including one of his letters to Captain Kramer that 'nobody in OPNAV can be trusted.' I told him that he should consider the timing as unfortunate and as having been a mere coincidence.

"When there was delivered to Senator Lucas the opinion by the JAG [Judge Advocate General], which was to the effect that Captain Safford had seriously violated Navy Regulations in mailing the letters to Captain Kramer, Senator Lucas stated to me privately that the only comment he would be able to make when he would put the JAG's opinion in the record was that the award to Captain Safford of the Legion of Merit immediately following the publicity attending his letters to Captain Kramer showed that the 'Navy was cock-eyed.' He said he considered that the seriousness of the matter should have been apparent to anyone reading the newspapers, including those in the Navy responsible for the making and approving of awards."

- - - - - - - - - -

Chapter Twelve   "TO THROW AS SOFT A LIGHT AS POSSIBLE . . ."

pages 234-35   Clausen testimony. PHA 9:4308, 4319, 4428, 4464, 4470.

pages 235-38   Bratton testimony. Ibid. 4509 ff.

pages 238-40   Sadtler testimony. PHA 10:4635 ff.

pages 240-43   Schulz testimony. Ibid. 4659 ff; interviews with Schulz and Greaves.

page 244   "The committee had some differences . . ." Ibid. 5150-51.

page 245   "The Congressional Pearl Harbor investigation . . ." NYT, Feb. 24, 1946.

page 245   Wilkinson death. "Findings of the Naval Board of Investigation" submitted by the Chief of Naval Personnel, Rear Admiral T. L. Sprague, to the Secretary of the Navy, March 20, 1946; Washington *Evening Star*, Feb. 22, 1946.

page 246   "Wilkinson was the only decent one in the lot . . ." Safford letter to Hiles, May 24, 1965, UWACH.

page 246   Baecher report to Forrestal, Mar. 28, 1946.

page 247   Stark testimony. PHA 11:5154.

page 247   "has ended as it began on a note . . ." NYT, May 25, 1946.

page 247   "Well, we know. We were with you . . ." Interview with Mrs. Krick.

page 247   Stark-Krick testimony. PHA 11:5543 ff.

pages 252-53   Majority and minority reports, along with additional views of Keefe, *Investigations of the Pearl Harbor Attack: Report of the Joint Committee on the Investigation of the Pearl Harbor Attack*, July 20, 1946. 79th Congress, 2nd Session.

page 250   Flynn letter to Gearhart, July 15, 1946. Greaves Collection.

pages 250-51   Flynn letter to Keefe, July 16, 1946. Greaves Collection.

page 251   Keefe letter to Flynn, July 18, 1946. Greaves Collection.

page 252   "constitute an arraignment of the Roosevelt . . ." Beard 346-47.

pages 252-55   Flynn letter to Keefe, July 19, 1946. Greaves Collection.

page 252   "by committee rules which permitted . . ." Barnes 464.

page 253   "When two Republicans joined with . . . " P.M., July 22, 1946.

page 253   "and even the minority report . . ." New York *Herald Tribune,* July 22, 1946.

page 254   "The most disgraceful feature of the whole . . ." Barnes 408.

pages 254-55   Safford-Friedman conversation. This account, dated Aug. 14, 1946, was written by Friedman on the back of a Safford article, "Statement Regarding Winds Message." Friedman Collection, GCM.

page 257   "The truth must be repeated again and again . . ." Goethe, *Lexikon* (Leipzig: Alfred Kröner Verlag, 1912), 113. The translation is by Bettina Greaves.

Chapter Thirteen   OPERATION Z

page 260   "The economic development of these countries . . ." George F. Kennan, *The Decision to Intervene* (Princeton: Princeton University Press, 1958), 221-22.

page 260   "to train the two Services in the joint operation . . ." Report from the Chief Umpires, Grand Joint Army and Navy Exercise No. 4, to the Adjutant General, U. S. Army, Feb. 18, 1932. Record Group 80, NA.

page 261   "In case the enemy's main fleet is berthed . . ." Borg 237-38.

pages 261-62   "On our return to Washington I was quoted . . ." Arnold 193-94.

page 262   "any practicable way of placing torpedo . . ." Richardson letter to Stark, Jan. 4, 1941.

page 262   "If war eventuates with Japan . . ." Stark letter to Knox, Jan. 24, 1941.

page 262   Knox reply, Feb. 7, 1941.

page 263   "I think an attack on Hawaii . . ." Toland, *Rising Sun,* 150.

page 263   Bishop story. Interview with Bishop.

page 263   "There is a lot of talk around town . . ." Grew diary, Jan. 27, 1941.

page 264   "The Division of Naval Intelligence places . . ." Stark letter to Kimmel, Feb. 1, 1941.

page 264   "If we fail we had better give up . . ." Toland, *Rising Sun,* 152.

page 265   "The defense of Oahu, due to its fortification . . ." PHA 3:1093.

page 265   "in a very difficult position . . ." Kimmel memorandum to Stark, May 26, 1941.

pages 265–66   Ickes-Roosevelt conversation. President's Secretaries File, FDR.

page 267   "Under such circumstances, we had better . . ." Toland, *Rising Sun,* 86.

page 267   "I had expressed the opinion . . ." PHA 2:604.

page 267   "When President Roosevelt told the Americans . . ." NYT, July 2, 1941.

pages 267–68   "With each day we will get weaker . . ." Toland, *Rising Sun,* 118.

page 268   "Related with my recent report . . ." Intelligence Report, Office of Chief of Naval Operations, June 18, 1941. Released to the author by Defense Intelligence Agency, Sept. 22, 1980.

page 269   British Secret Service translation of the complete German questionnaire:

Hawaii. Ammunition dumps and mine depots.

1. Details about naval ammunition and mine depot on the Isle of Kushu (Pearl Harbour). If possible sketch.

2. Naval ammunition depot Lualuelei. Exact position? Is there a railway line (junction)?

3. The total ammunition reserve of the army is supposed to be in the rock of the Crater Aliamanu. Position?

4. Is the Crater Punchbowl (Honolulu) being used as ammunition dump? If not, are there other military works?

Aerodromes.

1. Aerodrome Lukefield. Details (sketch if possible) regarding the situation of the hangars (number?), workshops, bomb depots, and petrol depots. Are there underground petrol installations? Exact position of the seaplane station? Occupation?

2. Naval air arm strong point Kaneohe. Exact report regarding position, number of hangars, depots and workshops. (Sketch.) Occupation?

3. Army aerodromes Hickam Field and Wheeler Field. Exact position? Reports regarding number of hangars, depots and workshops. Underground installations? (Sketch.)

4. Rodger's Airport. In case of war, will this place be taken over by the army or the navy? What preparations have been made? Number of hangars: Are there landing possibilities for seaplanes?

5. Airport of the Panamerican Airways. Exact position? (If possible sketch.) Is this airport possibly identical with Rodger's Airport or a part thereof? (A wireless station of the Panamerican Airways is on the Peninsula Mohapuu.)

Naval Strong Point Pearl Harbour.

1. Exact details and sketch about the situation of the state wharf, of the pier installations, workshops, petrol installations, situations of dry dock No. 1 and of the new dry dock which is being built.

2. Details about the submarine station (plan of situation). What land installations are in existence?

3. Where is the station for mine search formations (minen-suchverbaende)? How far has the dredger work progressed at the entrance and in the east and southeast lock? Depths of water?

4. Number of anchorages (Liegeplaetze)?

5. Is there a floating dock in Pearl Harbour or is the transfer of such a dock to this place intended?

Special tasks.

Reports about torpedo protection nets newly introduced in the British and U.S.A. Navy. How far are they already in existence in the merchant and naval fleet?

pages 269-71   Popov story. Popov 148.
page 271   "It is therefore surely a fair deduction . . ." Masterman 80.
pages 271-72   Kilsoo Haan story. Kilsoo Haan documents, TKC; Sevareid correspondence.
page 272   Clear story. Clear letter to Kimmel, Feb. 4, 1967, TKC; Clear letter to Hiles, Nov. 3, 1967, UWACH; C. M. Horn letter to Kimmel, Dec. 9, 1966, TKC; Farrier letter to author, Feb. 29, 1980, and Apr. 4, 1980; Clear memorandum to Assistant Chief of Staff, G-2, War Department, Nov. 2, 1941.
page 273   "We face the delicate question . . ." SD.
pages 273-74   Tojo-Togo-Sugiyama story. Toland, *Rising Sun,* 123-31.
pages 275-76   Mistranslations of Japanese messages. Ibid. 132-36.
page 277   When Secretary of the Interior Ickes learned that Hull had considered offering the Japanese a three-month truce he was furious at the "appeasers" in the State Department. "If this negotiation with Japan had been consummated," he wrote in his diary on Nov. 30, "I would have promptly resigned from the cabinet with a ringing statement attacking the arrangement and raising hell

generally with the State Department and its policy of appease-
ment. I have no doubt that the country would have reacted violently. As a matter of fact some of the newspapers indicated that
they were uneasy and printed editorials deprecating any attempt at
even a partial resumption of relationship with Japan. I believe that
the President would have lost his country on this issue and that
hell would have been to pay generally.''

page 278   "I didn't tell you at the time . . ." Interview with
    General Sato.
page 279   "about made up his mind . . ." SD.
page 279   "He fairly blew up—jumped up in the air . . ." SD.
pages 280-82   Field story. Field letter to author, Mar. 24, 1980.
page 280   Ingersoll, Noyes and Schuirmann testimony. PHA
    33:751, 808; PHA 10:4757; PHA 32:551.

Chapter Fourteen   THE TRACKING OF *Kido Butai*

pages 284-85   "might be proceeding to the Philippines . . ."
    Farago, *Broken Seal*, 283.
page 285   Hull's conference. Berle 379.
page 285   "I handed the note to the Japs." SD.
page 285   Hornbeck memorandum. Emmerson 118.
page 285   ". . . I made the mistake of yielding . . ." Hornbeck
    unpublished autobiography, HI; Emmerson 116-17.
page 286   "McMorris, what is your idea . . ." PHA 6:2802.
page 287   Footnote. Interviews with Sato, Suzuki, Hoshino and
    Kaya.
page 288   Mathews story. Mathews letter to Pogue, Oct. 3, 1963,
    GCM.
page 289   Roosevelt-Stimson meeting. SD.
page 289   War Cabinet meeting. SD.
page 290   "I read it over and it was a comprehensive . . ." SD.
page 291   "This was in the shape of a virtual . . ." SD.
pages 291-93   *Lurline* story. Grogan journal, Matson Navigation
    Company Collection; *Ships in Gray,* the story of Matson in World
    War II; interviews with Charles Regal and Fred Stindt of Matson.
pages 293-94   Seaman First Class Z story. Interviews with Sea-
    man First Class Z.
pages 294-95   Thorpe story. Correspondence with Thorpe;
    Thorpe memorandum; Thorpe 51-59; memorandum of Thorpe-
    Kimmel conversation, Aug. 28, 1957, TKC.
pages 295-96   Ranneft story. Interview and correspondence with
    Ranneft; interview with T. S. N. Ranneft, his son; information
    and documents from Netherlands Department of Defense, Naval
    Historical Department, including official diary of Admiral Ran-
    neft.

page 296   Layton-Kimmel conversation. PHA 39:360.

page 297   Nelson-Roosevelt conversation. Donald M. Nelson, *Arsenal of Democracy* 182-83.

page 297   "running around like a lot of wet hens . . ." Morgenthau diary, FDR.

page 298   Grogan story. Grogan journal, Matson Collection.

pages 298-99   Burns story. John A. Burns Oral History Project, University of Hawaii, Department of American Studies. Interviews with Paul Hooper and Stuart Gerry Brown.

page 298   "Dr. Conrad Taueber, director of the . . ." Field letter to author, May 1980.

page 298   "Apparently there is some misunderstanding . . ." James D. Lincoln letter to author, May 19, 1980.

page 298   "I'm sorry to tell you . . ." Miss Tully letter to author, Feb. 19, 1980.

page 299   Nover story. Telephone interview with Mrs. Nover; PHA 29:2244.

pages 299-309   Briggs story. Briggs official interview; Safford material, Greaves Collection. In 1960 Briggs became officer in charge of the U. S. Naval Security Group Detachment at the depository for all U. S. Navy World War II Communication Intelligence and Cryptographic Archives. This gave him the opportunity to search further for any logs or messages concerning the December 1941 intercept period. He sought diligently for anything connected with the first week before Pearl Harbor, but the only thing he discovered was an operators' sign-on and sign-off log sheet. It was dated December 2, 1941, reflecting Greenwich Mean Time (GMT) as kept at intercept Station M. (See picture section.)

    This particular watch standers' log sheet was important since it confirmed the existence of the special "winds" execute intercept mission. The operator signs of the three watch standers on duty were RT (Briggs), RS and SE. The Log revealed that RS had the evening watch on December 2, 1941, and at 0402 (GMT) had started this new log sheet. He was monitoring a frequency of 12,430 kilocycles at that time. At 0500 (GMT) he was relieved by Briggs, who tuned to a new frequency of 12,275 kilocycles and began copying a scheduled broadcast. His entry read: "COPY PRESS SKDS HR ON . . . SEE OTHER LOGS." This meant: "Copying press schedule from here on, see other log sheet(s) containing entire intercept." At 1300 (GMT) an entry appeared indicating that Briggs was relieved by SE. This would have been 0800 (EST).

    Unable to find any confirming messages for this period of his watch, Briggs concluded that this log sheet may have covered the period of the "winds" execute intercept. Knowing it was unauthorized to make a copy of the log sheet itself, he wrote on the bottom:

"Below comments added on 12/5/60

I, R.T., now on duty at a NAVSECGAUDET [*sic*] as OinC [Officer-in-Charge], duly note that all transmissions intercepted by me between 0500 thru 1300 on the above date are missing from these files & that these intercepts contained the 'Winds message warning code.' My operation sign was 'RT.'"

It is possible that Briggs's earlier recollection of having intercepted the "winds" execute on December 4 is correct; and in view of no other evidence of intercepted material, the operators' log sheet of December 2 may not cover the period of this intercept. At the same time, if this log sheet does not cover the "winds" intercept, why is all the traffic intercepted from 0500 to 1300 (GMT) on 12,275 kilocycles missing from the archives today? It is interesting to note that late on the afternoon of December 2 (Tokyo Time), Admiral Yamamoto signaled the commander of the Pearl Harbor Striking Force: "Climb Mount Niitaka 1208." This meant: "Attack as planned on December 8." It thus appears very possible that a "winds" execute could have been transmitted at about the same time.

page 301   Wheeler story. Wheeler 32-33.

pages 301-02   Wedemeyer story. Interview and correspondence with Wedemeyer.

page 301   "The primary aim of this deception . . ." Stevenson 298-99.

pages 302-03   "Hell, yes, but they don't dare . . ." Mathews letter to Pogue, GCM.

page 303   Kilsoo Haan story. Kilsoo Haan material, TKC.

pages 304-05   —EMThree small vessels story. Tolley 264 ff.; Buaas letter to author, Feb. 9, 1981; Hanson Baldwin, *The Crucial Years 1939-1941*, 436.

page 306   "Go ahead. Tell them." SD.

page 306   "What would you think of an American . . ." Ibid.

page 307   Roosevelt letter to Willkie, Dec. 5, 1941.

pages 309-10   Fellers story. Interview with Fellers; Fellers letter to Kimmel, Mar. 6, 1967, TKC.

pages 310-11   "The President should be informed . . ." Sherwood 424.

page 311   Knox-Turner conversation. *National Review*, Dec. 13, 1966, 1261.

page 311   Mayer story. Hoehling, *Day*, 132-33; Mayer letters to Hoehling, June 11 and 22, 1962, Hoehling Collection.

pages 311-12   Safford story. PHA 29:2399; Safford letters to Hiles, Feb. 23, 1965, and Mar. 29, 1967, UWACH.

page 313   Ranneft story. Interview with Ranneft; documents and material from the Netherlands Department of Defense, Department of Naval History.

page 313   "This means that they have given up . . ." Brownlow 126.

page 313   Kimmel-Smith comments. Ibid. 126.

pages 313-14   Kimmel conference with Pfeiffer, etc. Ibid. 127.

page 314   Pye-Layton conversation. U. S. Navy Report, PAC, Chapter Twelve, Naval Historical Center.

page 314   "was still good and we would stick . . ." Brownlow 127; interview with DeLany.

page 315   Mayer-Belin story. Hoehling, *Day*, 179-80; Mayer letters to Hoehling, June 11 and 22, 1962, Hoehling Collection.

page 316   "These are for the children . . ." Interview with Schulz.

page 317   Bowers story. *Shipmate*, Dec. 1977; Robert Clack letters to author, Dec. 19 and 26, 1978.

page 318   Nichols story. Interview with Nichols.

page 319   Richardson story. Richardson 451-52.

page 319   Harrison story. Interview with Harrison.

page 319   "It looks like the Japanese are going to break off . . ." Hoehling, *Day*, 205.

page 320   "This is my last effort . . ." Ibid. 218-19.

pages 320-21   *Lurline* story. Grogan journal; Frances Berndtson Coppel letter to author, Oct. 25, 1979; interview with Yokota; five articles by Alf Pratte in Honolulu *Star-Bulletin*, starting Dec. 4, 1966; account by Eddie Collins, Chief Officer of the *Lurline*, Matson Collection.

page 321   Conway story. Toland, *Shame*, 29.

page 321   Boyer story. Boyer letter to author, Dec. 12, 1978.

page 322   Yoshikawa story. Interviews with Yoshikawa and Lawrence Nakatauka.

page 323   Gallaher story. Interview and correspondence with Gallaher.

page 323   Thalken story. Interview and correspondence with Thalken; record of movements of Task Force Twelve on Dec. 7, 1971, Naval Historical Center.

page 324   "Oh, my God—there they come!" *The Retired Officer*, Dec. 1979.

page 324   Fleming story. Interview with Fleming.

page 325   Friedman story. Clark 170.

page 325   Powell story. Powell letter to Kimmel, Feb. 22, 1955, TKC.

page 325   "What a reception the Japanese must have had!" Popov 190-91.

page 325   "If you do, I can put you away . . ." Kilsoo Haan material, TKC.

page 326   "But now the Japs have solved . . . ." SD.

page 326   "never have gotten the country to war . . ." Interview with Harrison.

page 326   "white as a sheet, visibly shaken." *Shipmate*, Sept. 1977, 28.

page 326   "sitting in a corner with no expression . . ." *Newsweek,* Dec. 12, 1966, 42.

page 326   "And we're putting people into all the . . ." Morgenthau diary, FDR.

pages 327-29   Mrs. Perkins story. Taped interview, CUOH.

page 329   "The President was very patient . . ." Sherwood 433-34.

page 329   "cleared everybody out and said he was going . . ." Murrow letter to Hoehling, Feb. 8, 1962, Hoehling Collection.

pages 329-30   "There is a slight deliberation . . ." Greene account, *Time-Life-Fortune* News Bureau, Dec. 7, 1941.

page 330   "I heard voices and steps . . ." Mrs. Hamlin diary, FDR.

page 330   "But words are futile at a time . . ." K. Marshall 99.

page 330   "I think I'll go and see Old Knox." Interview with Harrison.

Chapter Sixteen THE SUMMING UP

page 332   Ter Poorten story. Correspondence with Thorpe; Thorpe memorandum.

page 332   Ranneft citation. See picture section.

page 332   Robinson story. Interview and correspondence with Ranneft.

page 333   Wedemeyer story. Interview with Wedemeyer.

page 333   "For a long time I have believed . . ." Ickes diary, Oct. 18, 1941.

page 335   Stahlman letter to Tolley, Nov. 26, 1973. Tolley Collection.

pages 335-36   "I saw and talked to General Marshall . . ." Interview with Harrison; Fellers letter to Barnes, May 13, 1960, Barnes Collection, UWACH.

page 335   Knox-Kimmel meeting. PHA 24:1955.

page 336   "Gentlemen, this goes to the grave with us." Interview with Fellers.

page 338   "One officer then in intelligence . . ." Hoehling, *Day,* 244.

INDEX

WAR BOOKS FROM JOVE

07299-0	**BATAAN: THE MARCH OF DEATH** Stanley L. Falk	$2.95
07292-3	**THE BATTLE FOR MOSCOW** Col. Albert Seaton	$2.95
07510-8	**THE BATTLE OF LEYTE GULF** Edwin P. Hoyt	$3.50
07626-0	**NIGHT DROP: THE AMERICAN AIRBORNE INVASION OF NORMANDY** S.L.A. Marshall	$3.50
07294-X	**THE DEVIL'S VIRTUOSOS** David Downing	$2.95
872-16597-3	**DUNKIRK** Robert Jackson	$2.25
07297-4	**HITLER'S WEREWOLVES** Charles Whiting	$2.95
867-21223-3	**I SAW TOKYO BURNING** Robert Guillain	$2.95
07134-X	**DAS REICH** Max Hastings	$3.50
07295-8	**THE SECRET OF STALINGRAD** Walter Kerr	$2.95
07427-6	**U-BOATS OFFSHORE** Edwin P Hoyt	$2.95
07106-4	**THE BATTLE OF THE HUERTGEN FOREST** Charles B. MacDonald	$2.95
07103-X	**GUADALCANAL** Edwin P. Hoyt	$3.25
07296-6	**WAKE ISLAND** Duane Schultz	$2.95
07532-9	**BLUE SKIES AND BLOOD: THE BATTLE OF THE CORRAL SEA** Edwin P. Hoyt	$2.95
07403-9	**CLIMAX AT MIDWAY** Thaddeus V. Tuleja	$2.95
07449-7	**PATTON'S BEST** Nat Frankel and Larry Smith	$2.95
07393-8	**SIEGFRIED: THE NAZIS' LAST STAND** Charles Whiting	$3.50

Prices may be slightly higher in Canada.

TYPO bénéficie du soutien de la Société de développement des entreprises culturelles du Québec (SODEC) pour son programme d'édition.

Gouvernement du Québec – Programme de crédit d'impôt pour l'édition de livres – Gestion SODEC.

Nous reconnaissons l'aide financière du gouvernement du Canada par l'entremise du Programme d'aide au développement de l'industrie de l'édition (PADIÉ) pour nos activités d'édition.

Nous remercions le Conseil des Arts du Canada de l'aide accordée à notre programme de publication.

LE DÉSERT MAUVE

NICOLE BROSSARD

Le désert mauve

roman

TYPO
Une compagnie de Quebecor Media

Éditions TYPO
Groupe Ville-Marie Littérature
Une compagnie de Quebecor Media
1010, rue de La Gauchetière Est
Montréal, Québec H2L 2N5
Tél.: 514 523-1182
Téléc.: 514 282-7530
Courriel: vml@sogides.com

Maquette de la couverture: Martin Roux
Photo de la couverture: Joni Venett

Catalogage avant publication de Bibliothèque et Archives nationales du Québec
et Bibliothèque et Archives Canada

Brossard, Nicole, 1943-
Le désert mauve: roman
(Collection Roman)
Éd. originale: Montréal: L'Hexagone, 1987.
Publ. à l'origine dans la coll. Fictions.
ISBN 978-2-89295-249-0
I. Titre.
PS8503.R7D47 2010   C843'.54   C2009-941245-4
PS9503.R7D47 2010

DISTRIBUTEURS EXCLUSIFS:

• Pour le Québec, le Canada
et les États-Unis:
LES MESSAGERIES ADP*
2315, rue de la Province
Longueuil, Québec J4G 1G4
Tél.: 450 640-1237
Téléc.: 450 674-6237
*Filiale du Groupe Sogides inc.;
filiale du Groupe Livre Quebecor Media inc.

• Pour la Belgique et la France:
Librairie du Québec / DNM
30, rue Gay-Lussac, 75005 Paris
Tél.: 01 43 54 49 02
Téléc.: 01 43 54 39 15
Courriel: direction@librairieduquebec.fr
Site Internet: www.librairieduquebec.fr

• Pour la Suisse:
TRANSAT SA
C.P. 3625, 1211 Genève 3
Tél.: 022 342 77 40
Téléc.: 022 343 46 46
Courriel: transat@transatdiffusion.ch

Pour en savoir davantage sur nos publications,
visitez notre site: www.edtypo.com
Autres sites à visiter: www.edvlb.com • www.edhexagone.com
www.edhomme.com • www.edjour.com • www.edutilis.com

Dépôt légal: 2e trimestre 2010
Bibliothèque et Archives nationales du Québec, 2010
Bibliothèque et Archives Canada

PRÉFACE

L'érosion comme principe vital

Lorsque son roman *Le désert mauve* paraît en 1987, Nicole Brossard publie déjà depuis plus de vingt ans. Spontanément associée à la poésie, elle a pourtant aussi offert aux lecteurs un certain nombre de textes en prose depuis *Un livre* en 1970, qu'on qualifiera, selon l'extension qu'on accorde à la définition du genre, de roman ou non. Elle participe aussi à cette époque, dans les années 1970 et au début des années 1980, à de nombreux débats littéraires et culturels, où elle est parfois prise à partie. On a souvent l'impression alors que ses propres productions cristallisent certains de ces débats, qui prennent parfois des allures de conflits ouverts. Était-on favorable à ses livres (idolâtre inconditionnel, selon les critiques) ou défavorable (mesquin et bilieux, selon les défenseurs)? On pouvait avoir l'impression, un peu étouffante, qu'il fallait choisir son camp. Il reste qu'il y avait quelque chose de très stimulant à voir une œuvre littéraire provoquer autant de discussions.

Je prends la peine de rappeler très brièvement ces faits, justement parce que la publication du *Désert mauve* a paru apaiser les débats. Non pas que ce livre ait été passé sous silence, au contraire. Et on y retrouve, sans aucun doute, aussi bien le ton propre à Nicole Brossard que les principales questions qui traversaient ses livres précédents. Mais il s'agit d'une réussite incontestable, d'une œuvre *pensée*, comme il en existait encore peu au Québec. D'une facture sans doute plus classique que celle des ouvrages précédents tout en étant d'une grande originalité, il avait toutes les qualités pour rallier de nombreux lecteurs, à défaut de faire l'unanimité – mais qui imaginerait qu'une œuvre littéraire importante puisse faire l'unanimité ?

Le roman s'ouvre sur un bref récit d'une quarantaine de pages intitulé, comme le roman lui-même, *Le désert mauve*, ouvrage écrit par une certaine Laure Angstelle et publié aux éditions de l'Arroyo, aux États-Unis. Il raconte l'histoire de Mélanie, jeune adolescente vivant en Arizona, qui habite dans un motel appartenant à sa mère, près de Tucson. Elle passe le plus clair de son temps à rouler en voiture, attirée par le désert. Vivant avec une mère pour qui la réalité n'existe qu'à travers la télévision, elle affirme dès les premières lignes : « Très jeune, je fus sans avenir » (p. 31), mais un peu plus loin rappelle qu'une amie de sa mère, Lorna, l'« avait initiée à l'érosion, à tous les fantômes vivant dans la pierre et la poussière ». (p. 32) Ainsi, si elle se pense sans avenir, le passé s'ouvre à elle, un passé marqué peut-être par l'histoire événementielle, mais surtout par l'évolution des formes, par la création (et la recréation) du monde. *Le désert mauve* est bien un livre sur le passé, mais un passé qui remonte à la surface et transforme le présent.

Premier signe de cet effet du passé, le livre écrit par Laure Angstelle est acheté des années plus tard par Maude Laures à Montréal dans une librairie d'occasion. Elle en subit peu à peu la fascination, au point qu'elle décide de le traduire pour réinventer cette histoire qui la bouleverse. On pourrait dire qu'elle cherche, en s'investissant dans la traduction, à comprendre le sens précis des émotions qu'elle ressent, car «aucun livre ne peut s'écrire sans enjeu». (p. 182) Le livre de Nicole Brossard se divise en trois parties : d'abord le court récit éponyme, ensuite les différentes étapes de la réflexion menée par Maude Laures sur celui-ci et enfin, bouclant la boucle, le récit revu et réinterprété. La gageure de ce roman tient au fait que ce livre, supposément écrit en anglais, est en réalité présenté en français. Il s'agit bel et bien d'une réécriture, modifiée, du texte dans la *même* langue que Brossard propose par la voix de la traductrice. Mais ces variations, comme on le verra, ont un poids incontestable et peuvent s'interpréter de différentes façons.

Pour comprendre cet univers où les personnages ne se révèlent jamais totalement au lecteur, où les émotions affleurent chez les uns et les autres, sans véritable vecteur pour les canaliser, Maude Laures s'astreint à un véritable travail de décryptage. Elle prend une à une les différentes composantes du texte – objets et lieux, scènes, personnages, «dimensions» (désert, aube, lumière, réalité) – et en explore les virtualités avant de s'attaquer à la traduction elle-même. C'est à une lecture *juste* qu'elle veut parvenir, cherchant le rythme qui serait propre au texte. Parviendra-t-elle à en déterminer tous les enjeux en entrant « par le détail [...] dans l'univers de la narratrice » ? En cherchant « la faille, le petit endroit où le sens appelle quelques audaces » (p. 83), toutes les embûches de la traduction lui seront du moins révélées. Si « tout avait été possible dans la langue de l'auteure, [...] dans la sienne, il fallait qu'elle s'arme de patience ». (p. 83) Comme le texte original et le texte traduit apparaissent au lecteur en français, on comprend qu'il s'agit d'abord de se confronter à l'univers d'une autre, éloignée par la culture, mais aussi étrangère au sens littéral puisqu'aucune information biographique concernant Laure Angstelle n'est connue de Maude Laures (cette « Laures au pluriel », qui doit écrire une œuvre – puisque la traduction est une création – tout en assumant celle de l'autre Laure). Ainsi, vaille que vaille, dans les moments où le texte se fera le plus opaque, elle n'a d'autre choix que de s'en tenir à celui-ci et n'en déborder qu'à partir de ce que lui accorde sa lecture. Hors du texte, il n'y a – mais ce n'est pas rien – que la possibilité d'imaginer en s'investissant le plus possible dans *Le désert mauve*.

Ce brillant travail de mise en abyme, ce jeu de miroir qui est une réflexion sur le langage ne doit pas surprendre. Il s'impose depuis le milieu des années 1960 dans les publications de Nicole Brossard. Quelques années auparavant, *Picture Theory* proposait également une réflexion sur le langage où la présence de Ludwig Wittgenstein et de Gertrude Stein était manifeste, manière originale de faire vivre cette tension culturelle féconde (mais tombant trop souvent dans le cliché) que le Québec connaît, entre l'Europe et l'Amérique. Ce n'était pas la première fois non plus que l'auteure s'intéressait au livre lui-même, dans sa matérialité. En réalité, depuis sa première publication en prose, intitulée symptomatiquement *Un livre*, on peut dire qu'à divers degrés la plupart de ses romans composent avec le livre comme médiation entre le réel et la fiction. Jamais pourtant ce motif n'a été aussi riche que dans *Le désert mauve* – couleur emblématique d'ailleurs chez Nicole Brossard depuis la Plymouth mauve de Marielle dans *French Kiss*. Considéré dans sa matérialité, le livre permet d'interroger aussi bien la traduction que la lecture, l'écriture que le lien ambigu qui peut lier le lecteur et le texte. On s'identifie parfois avec passion à certains livres pour des raisons évidentes : les enjeux qui motivent nos actions, les valeurs qui orientent notre manière de penser s'y retrouvent. Mais il arrive aussi que notre inclination soit beaucoup moins claire. Qu'est-ce qui explique non pas ma reconnaissance objective des qualités d'un livre, mais une véritable obsession pour une écriture particulière qui expose des questions parfois éloignées de mes intérêts les plus immédiats, les plus conscients ? On peut adhérer facilement à un roman auquel il est possible de s'identifier s'il exprime notre milieu, notre génération, notre époque, nos problèmes, notre petit vécu. Mais les œuvres qui ont l'impact le plus grand sur nous sont souvent celles qui nous atteignent sans trop qu'on sache pourquoi dans un premier temps, parce qu'elles s'attachent à une part d'ombre de nous-mêmes. C'est bien cette sensation étrange que vit Maude Laures, la possibilité qu'une œuvre transforme notre rapport à la réalité et nous invite à voir le monde autrement. Une des qualités du roman de Nicole Brossard est bien de montrer que ce choc est *à la fois* de l'ordre de l'intellect et de l'ordre des sensations. L'idée bête selon laquelle intellection et émotion seraient séparées par une frontière étanche est un cliché éprouvant qui justifie souvent un anti-intellectualisme primaire – le penseur froid, austère, qui ne sait pas « vibrer », etc. Le minutieux travail intellectuel que Maude Laures effectue sur le roman de l'Américaine naît justement d'une émotion forte, puissante, viscérale. La passion n'est pas, contrairement à ce qu'on croit trop souvent, l'expression hyperbolique d'une sensibilité excessive, mais plutôt une attention soutenue, précise, rigoureuse, apportée au moindre détail. Rien ne décrit mieux le travail minutieux auquel s'astreint Maude Laures sur le texte de Laure Angstelle.

L'activité de traduction se présente donc dans ce roman de manière essentiellement formelle. Décryptage des mots et de leur sens, étude sémiotique de la dynamique du texte fondent l'activité de cette lectrice qu'est Maude Laures. Pourtant, ce sujet a priori austère – une femme décortique un texte écrit il y a des années par une autre femme, inconnue, en vue de le traduire – ne l'est jamais réellement, pour au moins deux raisons sur lesquelles je m'arrêterai maintenant. La première tient au fait qu'à ce travail métafictionnel sur l'écriture se superpose une importance considérable accordée à un espace singulier, celui de l'Amérique et plus particulièrement des États-Unis. La seconde repose sur le poids de l'Histoire dans le texte, apparaissant en filigrane, qui permet d'aborder des questions d'éthique concernant aussi le présent et faisant exploser les frontières spatiales. Ce travail sur l'écriture est donc traversé à la fois par un axe horizontal – l'importance de l'espace – et un axe vertical – la mémoire, l'Histoire – qui multiplient les strates de sens.

Lors de la parution du *Désert mauve*, la critique a souvent souligné la place des États-Unis dans le roman, mais on a rarement relevé le fait qu'il s'agissait d'une constante depuis plusieurs années. *French Kiss* et *Picture Theory* auparavant, aussi bien que *Le désert mauve* (ce que j'ai nommé ailleurs la « Trilogie USA » de Nicole Brossard, clin d'œil à John Dos Passos), s'ancraient également dans un territoire (nord-)américain. Publiés entre 1974 et 1987, ces trois romans sont marqués par une poétique de l'espace, indissociable d'un contexte social, territorial et culturel nord-américain. Si le premier, dans l'ordre chronologique, mettait en scène la grande cité urbaine et le second d'abord la côte Est et l'océan (tout en proposant aussi un territoire intertextuel au moins en grande partie américain), le dernier insiste sur les étendues désertiques. Mais si l'imaginaire du désert en soi est important ici, c'est bien une pensée de l'Amérique qui est d'abord convoquée.

Dès la deuxième page du roman, Mélanie raconte une anecdote qui semble (en apparence) sans importance. La première fois qu'elle rencontre Lorna, que sa mère reçoit pour le repas du soir, Mélanie « renvers[a] [s]on verre de lait et la nappe se transforma en Amérique avec une Floride qui se prolongeait sous la salière. Ma mère épongea l'Amérique. » (p. 32) Malgré la volonté de sa mère de faire disparaître une Amérique qu'elle ne tient à découvrir qu'à travers la médiation du téléviseur, l'adolescente, qui sait « distingue[r] entre le diamantin de l'Ouest et le crotale cornu, entre le troglodyte et la tourterelle triste » (p. 32) fonce, très jeune, solitaire, dans une Amérique réelle, non pas celle des grandes villes et du *melting pot*, mais celle des roches et du sable : « J'ai toujours pris la route du désert car très jeune je voulais savoir pourquoi dans les livres on oublie de mentionner le désert. » (p. 33) Autant, dès l'âge de 15 ans, elle roule à tombeau ouvert, « cherchant les reflets brûlants du soleil aveuglant » (p. 33), revisitant un des leitmotivs de la culture américaine associé à la jeunesse – sa mère ne se nomme-t-elle pas Kathy *Kerouac* ? –, autant elle est sensible à l'espèce de fausse pérennité de ce qui l'entoure. Rappelons que Lorna l'a mise en contact avec l'érosion qui fait en sorte que tout est éphémère : ce n'est qu'une question d'échelle. La lenteur des modifications du paysage ne doit pas nous rendre dupe. Tout meurt, il faut simplement parfois y mettre le temps.

C'est dans cette dialectique entre extrême vitesse de la voiture (extrême, du moins, du point de vue humain) et extrême lenteur de l'érosion que Mélanie vit son apprentissage du monde : « J'avais 15 ans et je désirais que tout soit comme en la fragilité de mon corps, cette tolérance impatiente qui rend le corps nécessaire. » (p. 34) Malgré cette volonté ontologique d'affronter le réel de plein fouet, et sans doute à cause de cette dialectique qui l'oblige à prendre en compte la complexité du réel, Mélanie n'a rien d'une adolescente suicidaire, habitée par le *No Future* de son époque : « J'avais quinze ans et de toutes mes forces j'appuyais sur mes pensées pour qu'elles penchent la réalité du côté de la lumière. » (p. 34)

Le désert mauve est une histoire d'errance, une quête désabusée mais d'une nécessité existentielle fondamentale pour Mélanie qui s'épuise à parcourir les déserts et les autoroutes. À une autre extrémité du continent, bien loin de l'Arizona et bien plus près de Boston et de New York, c'est dans une grande cité urbaine que Maude Laures découvrira ce récit, peut-être fascinée au fond de découvrir son Amérique qui est en même temps une autre Amérique tout en étant la même, l'une apparaissant en palimpseste de l'autre. Non pas celle des grandes villes modernes où les gratte-ciel n'impressionnent plus personne, mais celle des grands espaces, où le silence succède au chaos étourdissant et où les traces s'effacent autrement : « Qu'est-ce donc que le désert ? Pourrais-je m'obstiner longtemps à vouloir le décrire, à le désirer tantôt fureur de vivre, tantôt extinction uniforme de l'espoir ou belle quiétude ? » (p. 177)

La fascination de la traductrice pour ce livre tient sans doute aussi au fait qu'il s'agit d'un texte assez terrible sur le plus grand thème de la littérature, à savoir la mort. Ou plus largement sur l'extrême bord de la réalité, quand elle glisse dans la folie ou l'inconnu. Une mort tragique se produit à la fin du récit, qui ne sera pas élucidée et qui intrigue Maude Laures. Mais ce crime apparaît comme une conclusion logique pour un texte qui baigne dans une atmosphère d'attente. La route est ici une allégorie prégnante de la mort. Et si le désert se présente comme une manifestation imaginaire forte de l'errance, du vide, de la solitude, de l'immensité, il est aussi beaucoup plus prosaïquement le site des explosions nucléaires. C'est le moment d'en venir, après les sujets clés de l'écriture et de l'américanité, à celui de l'Histoire telle qu'elle s'exprime dans le texte.

J'écrivais plus tôt que le rapport à la langue dans le roman est un rapport très formel : il s'agit de comprendre la dynamique du texte pour bien le traduire, car la traductrice n'a pas d'autres éléments sous la main pour en décoder le sens, ne connaissant rien de la biographie de l'auteure, des idées qu'elle défendait, de son œuvre (Maude n'a pas retrouvé d'autres livres qu'elle aurait publiés), ni du contexte de publication. Mais la traduction ne se pense pas que dans un cadre linguistique. Si au fil des ans on propose de nouvelles traductions d'un même texte, c'est parce que le rapport social à la langue évolue. L'intelligence du *Désert mauve* tient au fait que cette réalité sociologique ne nous est jamais expliquée, mais dévoilée à même la traduction. Lisant le roman de Laure Angstelle puis la version de Maude Laures, on voit en filigrane une évolution idéologique liée à la connaissance des effets du nucléaire en tant qu'arme. Une inclinaison qui révèle une angoisse plus marquée, orientée. La crainte de l'Apocalypse n'est plus abstraite.

« Le désert est la civilisation » (p. 38) affirme Mélanie, phrase qui semble *a posteriori* ironique quand on comprend peu à peu, les signes se multipliant, que désert et explosion nucléaire se pensent ensemble. Les hommes « venaient dans le désert voir éclater leurs équations comme une humanité » (p. 33). « Comme » : la comparaison sonne à la manière d'une critique. Les équations physiques et mathématiques sont des abstractions, mais qui peuvent avoir une réalité tangible et des effets destructeurs le jour où il ne s'agit plus d'un jeu. Le Manhattan Project qui voit le jour à Los Alamos vise d'abord à préparer une arme qui pourra faire contrepoids à celle qu'on soupçonne les nazis d'être en train de mettre au point. Et pourtant, quand la première bombe explose dans le désert, près d'Alamogordo, en juillet 1945, il y a déjà plusieurs mois qu'on sait que les nazis n'ont plus les moyens, ni scientifiques, ni financiers, de préparer une arme d'envergure. De plus, ceux qui sont le moindrement informés savent que le Japon ne pourra faire autrement que se rendre, il ne s'agit que d'une question de semaines. Parmi les raisons qui expliquent pourquoi les scientifiques de Los Alamos ont mené à terme l'expérience nucléaire – ces raisons sont nombreuses et ce n'est pas le lieu ici d'en dresser la liste –, il y a le simple et très humain besoin de vérifier si la bombe allait fonctionner. Deux ans de travail ininterrompu : il ne fallait pas que ce soit inutile. Et puis, pensaient certains, cette arme était trop coûteuse et dangereuse pour être vraiment utilisée. Naïveté et vanité…

Autour de Mélanie, quelques personnages s'agitent : sa mère, Lorna Myher, une certaine Angela Parkins, géomètre qui travaille avec une équipe tout près de Death Valley Junction. Il y a aussi et surtout, alternant avec les chapitres qui laissent la parole à Mélanie, la figure de « l'homme long » qui revient comme un leitmotiv et permet de faire converger toutes les tensions qui naissent dans le récit. Liée sans qu'on ne sache de quelle façon dans un premier temps aux expériences nucléaires qui se déroulent dans le désert, son image oscille entre le pur cérébral et l'individu au bord de la folie.

On peut voir dans cet homme jamais nommé une figure de la science moderne, déchirée entre des sentiments contradictoires, au diapason des problèmes éthiques provoqués par certaines recherches, dont la mise au point de la bombe nucléaire, naissance de la *big science*, serait la plus spectaculaire manifestation. Cet anonymat est d'autant plus marqué que dans la section «Personnages», où chaque bref chapitre s'ouvre sur le nom du personnage étudié, celui sur l'homme long est composé de cinq photos abstraites qui déplacent son mystère, offrant un autre type de représentation, de la rhétorique à l'iconique. Mais ce masque anonyme est un leurre. Le portrait se précise quand on découvre, grâce à de multiples indices, que cet homme ressemble comme un frère à Robert Oppenheimer, le chercheur qui était à la tête du projet Manhattan, héros puis bouc émissaire à l'époque du maccarthysme. Oppenheimer reste sans doute l'homme le plus associé à la mise au point de la bombe et en même temps à sa critique. On ne peut imaginer personnalité plus clivée pour exprimer les déchirements du monde scientifique aujourd'hui.

L'intérêt de cette identification est double : d'une part, il ne s'agit pas d'un portrait psychologisé, mais d'une figure imaginaire *à partir* d'Oppenheimer, qui cristallise les angoisses et les questionnements autour de l'explosion de la bombe ; d'autre part, tout le court roman de Laure Angstelle, discuté, questionné, puis «traduit», est entièrement sous-tendu par une réflexion sur la mort associée au nucléaire et qui rend compte aussi, subtilement, d'une évolution historique.

« L'homme long » est enfermé dans une chambre. De nombreux signes identifient Oppenheimer : son fameux chapeau en feutre, un *pork pie hat* qu'on le voit porter sur de très nombreuses photos, les cigarettes fumées à la chaîne, la lecture du sanskrit (une des nombreuses langues qu'il pouvait lire), la récurrence des équations mathématiques qu'il écrit. Ces caractéristiques associées à sa biographie intime s'enrichissent d'informations qui rappellent l'explosion de la première bombe, utilisée à titre expérimental, nommée Trinity. Par exemple, Oppenheimer, lors de l'explosion à Alamogordo, a fait référence à un extrait du Bhagavad Gîtâ. Certains vers du poème se retrouvent textuellement (et en anglais) dans la première page où il apparaît : *I/am/become/Death* (p. 37). Extraits de leur contexte, on associe les vers au personnage qui devient, dans ce discours où la narration ne cesse de référer à une explosion meurtrière, métaphore de la mort. On pourrait multiplier les effets de résonance entre la réalité historique (et biographique). Mais il importe de bien comprendre qu'il ne s'agit pas pour autant de ce qu'on nomme communément un « roman historique ». Cela paraît assez évident en regard de ce que j'ai écrit jusqu'à maintenant ; encore faut-il voir ce que cela signifie.

Un roman historique ou un roman d'espionnage, qui raconte le déroulement des événements à Los Alamos entre 1943 et 1945 (et ils sont extrêmement nombreux), fait largement reposer ses qualités sur sa capacité à coller aux événements historiques et à intégrer une part de fiction de manière réaliste. Cette vraisemblance, ce souci de réalisme, en limite également la portée. Le propos se démarque de celui de l'historien en ce qu'il nous fait découvrir les événements de l'intérieur, du point de vue psychologique des individus. Cependant, les limites de ce genre de roman tiennent à ce que cela ne va pas tellement au-delà de ce que l'Histoire peut nous apprendre superficiellement. Le danger de la fiction est alors de se mettre à la remorque de l'Histoire (et parfois de la sociologie), sans apporter beaucoup sur le plan imaginaire.

À l'inverse de romans qui miment l'histoire en y plaquant simplement une intrigue fictionnelle, *Le désert mauve* ne cherche pas à réinscrire une figure dans l'Histoire mais à s'en servir pour penser une période historique, la réinventer. Oppenheimer est ici utilisé à cette fin, car il symbolise les espoirs et les doutes des années 1940 et 1950 à l'égard de la science. Oppenheimer est la bombe : qu'est-ce que cela signifie pour un écrivain ? Los Alamos devient parfois un lieu propice à des investigations imaginaires. De manière encore plus subtile, on pourrait avancer que Nicole Brossard se sert d'une réflexion sur la traduction pour en faire une réflexion sur l'Histoire contemporaine et exposer ce qu'on pourrait nommer un imaginaire de la fin.

L'association entre l'homme et la bombe est telle que des traces se répercutent dans son corps : « À chaque fois c'était l'explosion dans sa tête » ; « La poussière était là, raison froide qui retombait sur ses épaules » ; « Déjà la cendre, déjà le sang, déjà les cris, des bouches formidables, figées dans le silence de la nuit, luisaient comme des cristaux dans chacun de ses neurones »

(p. 51). Malgré sa fragilité, «les yeux de cet homme [étaient] fous et arrogants» (p. 51). Comme Prométhée qui subit dans son corps un châtiment pour avoir donné le feu aux hommes, Oppenheimer ressent les effets de l'énergie nucléaire qu'il a contribué à créer. Les difficultés existentielles de l'homme long se manifestent dans la gêne et l'inconfort qu'il ressent par rapport à son corps. «Il éprouvait [...] une excitation froide, mentale qui rendait intolérable chaque nerf dans son corps calme» (p. 65). Noyau d'énergie, le personnage fictionnel semble capter toutes les radiations et se trouver au bord d'une forme de désintégration. Il devient une véritable métonymie de la bombe, se transformant en une sorte de monstre.

Ce n'est souvent qu'indirectement que la destruction nucléaire se dévoile dans le roman, peu à peu, par strates ou par effet de sédimentation, mot qu'on pourrait facilement associer au roman. Ainsi, dans la deuxième partie qui concerne les réflexions de Maude Laures sur le livre, la section intitulée «Dimensions» se compose de chapitres qui rappellent différentes étapes de l'explosion: «Le désert», où elle se déroule («Le calcul exact des langages aboutis dans l'espace comme une explosion», p. 177), «L'aube», moment où aura lieu l'événement (qui «prépare le spectacle», p. 178), «La lumière» («L'aspect final de la matière», p. 181). Le roman, à travers l'homme long qui irradie (littéralement...) à chaque page, devient une réflexion sur la hantise de la mort nucléaire.

La réflexion sur le nucléaire se note à travers des modifications apportées au texte de Laure Angstelle par la traductrice. Comme si, entre le texte original publié aux États-Unis et la version montréalaise plus récente, se marquaient les effets idéologiques produits par notre connaissance de la course aux armements.

Le texte « traduit », composant les quarante dernières pages, s'ouvre avec une reproduction de sa couverture. Au fond du désert se lève un soleil éblouissant qui peut aussi bien être un champignon atomique. Le nom de l'auteure rappelle angoisse et colère provoquées par la bombe (l'allemand *angst* associé au « elle » qui qualifie le sexe de l'auteur), alors que ses initiales (L. A.) renvoient au lieu où s'ébauche la guerre froide, Los Alamos.

Les vers « *I/am/become/Death* » associés à l'homme long (maintenant appelé « l'hom'oblong ») deviennent, dans la traduction, « La mort/Je/suis/la mort ». La répétition du substantif « mort » appuie l'affirmation, qui hante le personnage. « Les yeux de l'homme étaient fous et arrogants » (p. 51) devient « Les yeux de l'homme étaient démentiellement arrogants » (p. 227). Folie et arrogance ne sont plus dissociées : l'arrogance *est* folie, celle de l'homme faustien qui voulait être un dieu. « Tout était en accéléré dans son corps soumis à ses pensées. Il était perdu » (p. 51) se développe : « Tout son corps était soumis à l'accélération. Son image s'allongeait, somme impossible, masse fantastique. Il était perdu, plus de corps en lui [...] » (p. 227). Cette dernière citation voit son corps se confondre avec la fulgurance de l'explosion nucléaire. Il était perdu ; maintenant, il *a* perdu. Les pensées disparaissent, l'accélération ne permet plus de réfléchir. Le corps s'annihile dans l'explosion, d'où le sentiment de perte.

Quant à Mélanie, si dans la version originale elle médite sur « ces hommes qui venaient dans le désert voir éclater leurs équations comme une humanité » (p. 33), dans la version traduite elle s'avère plus directe, à la fois vindicative et désabusée : « Un jour […] je serais insensible devant tout, les équations et l'humanité, sa déraison éclatée au fond du regard esseulé des hommes fous » (p. 211). La folie a eu lieu et chacun a pu en prendre la mesure. Elle est plus directe également : « J'avais quinze ans et je désirais que tout soit comme en la fragilité de mon corps » (p. 34) devient : « Je voulais que tout mon corps soit nécessaire » (p. 212 et 226). Dans un premier temps, tout est ramené à soi ; dans un deuxième temps, il s'agit plutôt d'agir sur le monde.

L'errance de Mélanie offre un contrepoids à l'enfermement de l'homme dans sa chambre. Déplacements sur l'axe horizontal en voiture et déplacements sur l'axe vertical par la mémoire se rejoignent dans une même angoisse de la destruction. L'aube revient comme un leitmotiv, ainsi que les substantifs « blancheur », « lumière » et « énergie », mots orientés vers l'explosion, mais sans offrir les repères qui les ancreraient dans l'Histoire. Il reste une ossature, une structure de l'événement, les affects qui y sont liés et plongent dans l'imaginaire contemporain.

Si les dérives de Mélanie dans l'espace affrontent les dérives intellectuelles de l'homme long, il existe un autre affrontement, qui concerne la matière. La récurrence du mot « érosion » donne une clé du roman. Le regard de Mélanie se mesure à l'érosion, fait face à la vie qui s'érode. Pour elle, s'exposer à l'érosion, c'est

« ne vouloir d'aucun mythe. Que du vrai, de la sueur, de la soif » (p. 52). S'articulent ainsi deux temporalités dans le roman, dont le désert devient l'épicentre. Lieu de silence et de méditation, il devient métaphore de la métamorphose. Maude Laures elle-même « érodera » le récit de Laure Angstelle et ce n'est qu'à ce prix qu'elle parviendra à le comprendre pleinement. Ce n'est qu'à travers les transformations subies par ce qui nous entoure, à travers cette perte, la mort qui est aussi l'impossibilité de la stagnation, que le sens surgit. Ce regard lucide – posé sur la matière dans le cas de Mélanie, sur un texte dans le cas de Maude – évacue ce que l'érosion peut porter en soi de négatif. À cette temporalité lente, s'appuyant aussi bien sur le mouvement de la pensée que sur celui de la nature qui dans les deux cas proposent des modifications du réel, s'oppose une autre temporalité, artificielle, un processus d'accélération, étroit corridor qui réduit la pensée en l'orientant vers la destruction, sorte de réification du mal à l'ère nucléaire. La transformation radicale de la matière par l'explosion d'une bombe nucléaire relève de l'insensé.

Arrêtons-nous en conclusion sur le rôle clé d'Angela Parkins, mouton noir et bouc émissaire. Cette femme qui a une formation scientifique, comme ceux qui mettent au point la bombe, est déterminée et en colère. Quand Maude Laures la décrit dans la section « Personnages », elle la voit dans sa chambre de motel, ouvrir un livre : elle « essayerait comme chaque nuit d'oublier l'image de l'enfer, refoulant dans sa mémoire la première explosion, l'immense déchirure dans l'atmosphère tremblant, les flancs de l'animal sous ses cuisses, la chute du cheval, le cheval au grand galop, l'herbe contre sa joue, un monarque qui bat des ailes sur une fleur d'acacia. Au loin, l'enfer » (p. 125). Dans cette phrase saisissante se mêlent des images qui rappellent la première explosion nucléaire à Alamogordo, mais aussi une explosion de colère, à laquelle se mêlent des images mythiques de l'Apocalypse (avec la fulgurance du cheval, on croirait voir apparaître la toile de Dürer), puis une brève image d'un éden qui disparaît avec cet enfer, au loin, mais qui donne l'impression de se rapprocher.

Cette même Angela Parkins, sorte de Cassandre des temps modernes, disparaît dans la scène finale où l'angoisse de la mort fait retour de manière moins abstraite. Elle meurt dans un bar, à l'hôtel, au milieu d'une foule, tuée d'un coup de revolver. Personne n'a rien vu. Tout le monde est coupable de n'avoir rien vu. L'homme long domine la scène, comme s'il avait tout orchestré. « Au fond de la salle, il y a le regard impassible de l'homme long » (p. 75). On ne peut rien lui reprocher en particulier. Pourtant, tandis qu'il se trouve loin du groupe, cloué dans sa chambre, son angoisse ne cesse de se manifester.

Roman sur la mort, sur l'apocalypse technologique moderne, sur l'écriture et sur la traduction, sur l'Amérique et ses paysages, *Le désert mauve* est au fond un roman sur la représentation. Quelle est la meilleure façon de poser un regard critique sur le réel à travers la littérature ? Comment rendre compte du fonctionnement même de la pensée à l'œuvre dans le travail sur un texte ? Comment exprimer l'horreur de la guerre, de la destruction, sans passer par une banale dénonciation dont la littérature n'a que faire ? De

quelle manière peut-on dire la mort sans tomber dans
les clichés du langage ? La réussite du *Désert mauve*
tient notamment à l'intrication de ses différents niveaux de sens, multiples, en sorte que le lecteur doit
lui-même dénouer les fils, construire peu à peu le sens
du texte. Nicole Brossard parvient par ailleurs, sans
« jouer à l'historienne », à mettre l'Histoire en scène,
cristallisant un épisode marquant du XXe siècle à travers certaines figures, exacerbant la réalité plutôt que
la décrivant. Bref, en travaillant vraiment sur le plan
imaginaire. Voilà quelques-unes des raisons qui font
de ce roman une parfaite réussite.

Jean-François CHASSAY

Lire, c'est aller à la rencontre d'une chose qui existe mais dont personne ne sait encore ce qu'elle sera...

Italo CALVINO

LAURE ANGSTELLE

Le Désert mauve

Éditions de l'Arroyo

Le désert est indescriptible. La réalité s'y engouffre, lumière rapide. Le regard fond. Pourtant ce matin. Très jeune, je pleurais déjà sur l'humanité. À chaque nouvel an, je la voyais se dissoudre dans l'espoir et la violence. Très jeune, je prenais la Meteor de ma mère et j'allais vers le désert. J'y passais des journées entières, des nuits, des aubes. Je roulais vite et puis au ralenti, je filais la lumière dans ses mauves et petites lignes qui comme des veines dessinaient un grand arbre de vie dans mon regard.

J'étais alerte dans le questionnement mais il y avait en moi un désir qui sans obstacle m'effrayait comme une certitude. Puis venaient le rose, le roux et le gris parmi les pierres, le mauve et la lueur de l'aube. Au loin, les ailes étincelantes d'un hélicoptère à touristes.

Très jeune, je fus sans avenir comme la baraque du coin qui fut un jour incendiée par des gars « venus de loin », disait ma mère qui leur avait servi à boire. Un seul d'entre eux était armé, m'avait-elle juré. Un seul parmi eux. Tous les autres étaient blonds. Ma mère parlait toujours des hommes comme s'ils avaient vu le jour dans un livre. Elle n'en disait pas plus et s'en retournait devant son téléviseur. Je voyais son profil et le reflet du petit peigne en argent qu'elle portait toujours dans ses cheveux et auquel j'attribuais un pouvoir magique. Son tablier était jaune avec de petites fleurs. Je ne l'ai jamais vue portant une robe.

J'avançais dans la vie, les yeux fous d'arrogance. J'avais quinze ans. C'était un délice comme un pouvoir de mourir ou de s'enfoncer dans la nuit avec des cernes autour des yeux, des espaces absolument délirants à proximité du regard.

Je connaissais bien le désert et les routes qui le traversaient. Lorna, cette amie de ma mère, m'avait initiée à l'érosion, à tous les fantômes vivant dans la pierre et la poussière. Elle m'avait décrit des paysages, certains familiers, d'autres absolument incompatibles avec la végétation et le sol aride de mon enfance. Lorna inventait. Je savais qu'elle inventait car moi je pouvais distinguer entre le diamantin de l'Ouest et le crotale cornu, entre le troglodyte et la tourterelle triste. Lorna inventait. Parfois je pensais qu'elle aboyait tant étaient rudes et impensables ses mots. Lorna n'avait pas connu d'enfance, seulement des filles après l'école à qui elle donnait rendez-vous avec ostentation à l'heure du midi. Les filles aimaient l'embrasser sur la bouche. Elle aimait les filles qui se laissaient embrasser sur la bouche.

La première fois que j'ai vu Lorna, je l'ai trouvée belle et j'ai prononcé le mot « salope ». J'avais cinq ans. Au souper, ma mère lui souriait. Elles se regardaient et quand elles parlaient leurs voix étaient pleines d'intonations. J'observais obstinément leurs bouches. Lorsqu'elles prononçaient des mots qui commençaient par *m*, leurs lèvres disparaissaient un instant puis gonflées se réanimaient avec une incroyable rapidité. Lorna dit qu'elle aimait le moly et la mousse de saumon. Je renversai mon verre de lait et la nappe se transforma en Amérique avec une Floride qui se prolongeait sous la salière. Ma mère épongea l'Amérique. Ma mère faisait toujours semblant de rien quand les choses étaient salies.

Je prenais souvent la route. Bien avant d'avoir mon permis de conduire. En plein soleil, au crépuscule, et même la nuit, je partais pendant que ma mère me criait des mots aigus qui se perdaient dans la poussière du stationnement. J'ai toujours pris la route du désert car très jeune je voulais savoir pourquoi dans les livres on oublie de mentionner le désert. Je savais que ma mère serait seule comme une femme peut l'être mais je fuyais le reflet magique du peigne dans ses cheveux, cherchant les reflets brûlants du soleil aveuglant, cherchant la nuit dans les yeux éblouis des lièvres, une lueur de vie. « À moi la confrontation de l'aridité » et j'appuyais sur l'accélérateur, folle de la maudite énergie de mes quinze ans. Un jour j'aurais l'âge et le temps nécessaire comme une date de naissance pour en finir avec la vie. Un jour, je serais *fast so fast, sharp so sharp*, un jour j'aurais devant la nécessité de l'aube tout oublié de la civilisation des hommes qui venaient dans le désert voir éclater leurs équations comme une humanité. Je roulais vite, seule comme un personnage émondé de l'histoire. Je disais « tant de fois j'ai sombré dans l'avenir ».

La nuit, il y avait le désert, les yeux luisants des lièvres antilopes, les fleurs de *senita* qui ne s'ouvrent qu'à la nuit. Il y avait sous les phares de la Meteor le corps gisant d'une humanité qui ne connaissait pas l'Arizona. L'humanité était fragile parce qu'elle ne soupçonnait pas l'existence de l'Arizona. *So fragile.* J'avais quinze ans et je désirais que tout soit comme en la fragilité de mon corps, cette tolérance impatiente qui rend le corps nécessaire. J'étais experte au volant, les yeux fous en pleine nuit, j'étais capable dans le noir d'avancer. Je savais tout cela comme un désespoir pouvant m'affranchir de tout. L'éternité était une ombre dans la musique, une fièvre du cerveau qui le faisait basculer dans le décalque des autoroutes. L'humanité était fragile, gigantesque espoir suspendu au-dessus des villes. Tout était fragile, je le savais, je l'avais toujours su. À quinze ans, je faisais semblant d'avoir oublié la médiocrité. Tout comme ma mère je prétendais que rien n'était sali.

L'ombre sur la route dévore l'espoir. Il n'y a pas d'ombre la nuit, à midi, il n'y a que certitude qui traverse la réalité. Mais la réalité est petit piège, petite tombe d'ombre qui accueille le désir. La réalité est un petit feu de passion qui prétexte. J'avais quinze ans et de toutes mes forces j'appuyais sur mes pensées pour qu'elles penchent la réalité du côté de la lumière.

Et maintenant stationner l'auto devant le Red Arrow Motel. La chaleur, le bar. Toute la surface du bar ressemble à une image télévisée : des coudes partout appuyés comme des ombres et des saletés d'humanité qui se répètent. Je bois une bière et personne ne s'aperçoit que j'existe.

Chapitre un

L'homme long dépose sa serviette sur le lit. Il a eu chaud, il défait le nœud de sa cravate. Il se dirige vers la salle de bains. Il pense à l'explosion, il y pense et ça ne suffit pas. Quelque chose. Il connaît de jolis petits sentiers, des coloris nuancés. Il hésite devant le miroir. Il se lave les mains. Il pense à l'explosion, il pense à ça et rien n'arrive dans sa tête. Il enlève son veston, le lance sur le lit. Un stylo tombe par terre. Il ne se penche pas. Il allume une cigarette. Il joue avec le rebord de son chapeau en feutre qu'il ne quitte presque jamais. Il pense à l'explosion. Il récite pour le plaisir des sons quelques phrases en sanscrit, les mêmes qui tantôt ont ravi son entourage. Il marche de long en large dans la chambre. La fumée de sa cigarette le suit comme une présence spectrale. L'homme long connaît la valeur magique des formules. Il pense à l'explosion. La moindre erreur pouvait avoir des conséquences catastrophiques. L'homme long s'allonge avec des visions blanches puis orange puis le sol sous ses pieds se transforme en jade – *I/am/become/Death* – maintenant nous sommes tous des fils de chiennes. L'homme long appuie sa tête sur l'équation.

J'avais le pouvoir sur ma mère de lui prendre son auto au moment le plus inattendu. Ma mère avait le pouvoir insoupçonné de susciter en moi une terrible solitude qui, lorsque je la voyais si rapprochée de Lorna, me ravageait car alors il y avait entre elles juste assez de silence pour que s'infiltre en moi la pensée de leur chair confondue. Un soir, je surpris dans l'obscurité de leur chambre ma mère, épaules et nuque tendues comme une existence vers la nudité de Lorna.

Je roule. J'hurle, gueul'e de rock, la bouche pleine des paroles que je chante au même rythme que la voix de femme qui fait éclater la radio. Une voix de malheur interrompt la chanson. J'hurle. J'appuie sur l'annonceur qui interrompt la musique jusqu'à ce que le tremblement de terre se dissipe au loin, raz-de-marée, se résorbe dans le bleu Pacifique. Le désert est la civilisation. Je n'aime pas quitter ma mère la nuit. J'ai peur pour elle. Les mères sont fragiles comme la civilisation. Il ne faut pas les oublier devant leur téléviseur. Les mères sont des espaces. J'aime rouler vite dans la Meteor de ma mère. J'aime la route, l'horizon en fuite, sentir le vide frais de l'aube. Je ne panique jamais dans le désert. En pleine nuit ou même en pleine tempête de sable lorsque le pare-brise se couvre peu à peu, je sais être isolée de tout, concrète et irréelle tel un personnage circonscrit au volant d'une vieille Meteor. Dans le sombre de la poussière, je sais exister.

J'écoute le bruit effrayant, le fracas du vent et du sable
sur la carrosserie. Je me soumets totalement à l'aveuglement. J'appuie légèrement deux doigts sur chaque
paupière et je regarde au-dedans de *l'espèce* intime,
tout au fond de mon cerveau s'écouler le temps. Je
vois les secondes, petites cicatrices argentées, se dépla-
cer comme des créatures. Je reconnais la trace des
créatures qui sont passées par là où les secondes forment des pyramides, des spirales, parmi les vestiges,
de beaux chevrons de grès. Une fois seulement des
mots que je n'ai pas su lire. Et leur forme s'est vite
dissipée comme s'il s'était agi d'une transcription partielle de la lumière au fond du cerveau.

   Je roulais avide. Je choisissais la nuit le désert
pour ainsi m'exposer à la violence de l'instant qui
meut la conscience. J'avais quinze ans et devant moi
l'espace, l'espace au loin qui m'amenuisait comme
une civilisation à rebours, cité perdue dans l'air tremblant. J'étais dans la Meteor de ma mère la solitude
exemplaire avec, au bout de mes pieds, un frein pour
éviter tous les désastres et pour me rappeler l'insigni-
fiance du désespoir parmi les serpents et les cactus
dans la nuit la plus bleue de tous les délires.

   Je suis le rire de ma mère quand je blêmis devant
la détresse de l'humanité. Jamais ma mère ne pleurait.
Je ne l'ai jamais vue pleurer. Ma mère ne pouvait pas
songer que la solitude fût comme une exactitude de
l'être. Elle tremblait devant les bruits de l'humanité
mais aucune solitude ne lui parvenait vraiment. Dans
les pires moments de son existence ma mère concluait :
« Ceci est un homme, il faut un lit ; ceci est une femme,
il faut une chambre. » Ma mère était obstinée comme

un homme aux prises avec le désert. Elle n'aimait pas les hommes mais elle défendait le désert comme un sentiment qui la rapprochait des hommes. C'était une femme sans expression et cela m'effrayait.

Chaque fois que je pense à ma mère, je vois des filles en maillot allongées au bord de la piscine du motel. Ce motel acheté en 1950, ma mère l'avait rénové puis passé quinze ans à le payer à coups de gestes polis, de discipline et d'énergie répétée dans la chaleur des après-midi de Tucson. Mais avant l'arrivée de Lorna, tout est vague. C'est vague et bruyant comme le va-et-vient des voyageurs, des fournisseurs, de la femme de ménage.

La présence de Lorna sera toujours liée dans ma mémoire à mes premières années d'école et tout particulièrement à mon apprentissage de l'écriture et de la lecture. J'aimais lire mais je ne me souviens pas d'avoir lu autrement qu'en la présence de Lorna. Elle m'observait, vigie statique, surveillant chaque battement de mes paupières, épiant toute trace d'émoi, le moindre signe qui pouvait trahir sur mon visage une émotion. Je suivais son manège d'un œil discret mais, lorsqu'il m'arrivait de lever les yeux vers elle, je pouvais à mon tour suivre sur ses lèvres l'étrange alphabet qui semblait constituer un rêve dans son regard. Je posais alors invariablement la question : « Qu'est-ce qu'on mange ? » comme si cela pouvait l'éloigner ou protéger la nature intime de ce que j'avais éprouvé pendant ma lecture.

Un jour alors que je cherchais des feuilles blanches pour dessiner, je vis tout au fond de la cuisine Lorna et ma mère assises sur la même chaise. Ma mère était sur les genoux de Lorna qui lui enserrait la taille de son bras droit. De sa main gauche, Lorna griffonnait. Leurs jambes étaient tout emmêlées et le tablier de ma mère était replié sur la cuisse de Lorna. Je demandai à Lorna ce qu'elle écrivait. Elle hésita puis allongea une phrase en disant qu'elle était incapable de lire ce que sa main avait tracé. J'allais m'exclamer, dire que... ça n'avait aucun sens lorsque je remarquai la souplesse de la main de Lorna dans les cheveux de ma mère.

Pourtant cette nuit. Très jeune, j'appris à aimer le feu du ciel, la foudre torrentielle ramifiée au-dessus de la ville comme un écoulement de la pensée dans le cerveau. Les nuits d'orage sec, je devenais tremblements, détonations, décharge totale. Puis je m'abandonnais à toutes les illuminations, ces fissures qui comme autant de blessures lignaient mon corps virtuel, me liaient à l'immensité. Et alors le corps fond comme une lueur dans l'abrégé des mots. Les yeux, l'existence plient devant ça qui s'avance en nous, certitude. Le désert boit tout. La fureur, la solitude.

Il y a dans le désert la poursuite des béances que font parfois les nuages. Parfois ils sont comme de petits plombs que le soleil envoie à l'horizon pour signifier l'avenir du lendemain. Je connais bien le plomb, le cuivre, les douilles et toutes les armes. Je connais les armes. Toute fille du désert apprend très jeune à tenir une arme et à conduire une auto. Toute fille jeune apprend que ce qui luit au soleil peut aussi blesser ou exciter à ce point le sentiment que l'ombre même s'empourpre.

Chapitre deux

L'homme long ne dort pas. Il pense à l'explosion. Il s'est allongé tout habillé. Ses souliers sont poussiéreux. Il songe à l'art, l'art du spectre énergétique. Il se lève et va vers la commode. Dans le deuxième tiroir, la petite revue aux couleurs chair et violacées est à sa place, au-dessous des dossiers blancs, orange et jade. Il prend la revue, s'allonge à nouveau après avoir replacé l'oreiller. Il tourne les pages, il regarde et attend que quelque chose se passe. « Maintenant nous sommes tous des fils de chienne. » L'explosion aura lieu. Dans le silence de la chambre, l'homme toise les sexes, leur coloration. Il ne voit pas les visages. Les visages, ombre de l'ombre, font des cernes blancs autour des sexes. Puis les cernes font un bruit d'explosion. Il ferme les yeux. La poussière tombe lentement comme en cet hiver à Princeton, la veille de ses vingt ans. L'homme long ne peut pas dormir. Pas plus que ses voisins de chambre d'ailleurs. À droite, il l'entend marcher, à gauche, il l'entend bouger ses feuilles de calcul. L'homme long connaît de beaux lacs bleus, la grande forêt pétrifiée aux arbres d'améthyste à tout jamais éternels. Il rêve d'un passé. Il neige dans l'éternel. Les spectres sont splendeurs. Maintenant que earth and death and tongue became thy shall not. L'homme long entend le bruit de l'explosion. Haut-le-cœur, haut-le-corps. Un dernier frisson. Il caresse son feutre mou. Il allume une cigarette.

Ici dans le désert, la peur est précise. Jamais obstacle. La peur est réelle, n'a rien d'une angoisse. Elle est nécessaire comme une journée de travail bien accomplie. Elle est localisée, familière et n'inspire aucun fantasme. Ici, il n'y a que du vent, des épines, des serpents, des lycoses, des bêtes, des squelettes : la nature même du sol.

Au motel par contre, la peur est diffuse, télévisée comme un viol, un meurtre, un accès de folie. Elle tourmente le versant crédule du cerveau, obstrue le rêve, tuméfie le tracas de l'âme.

J'avais quinze ans et je parle de la peur car la peur on n'y pense qu'après coup. La peur précise est belle. Peut-être après tout peut-on la fantasmer comme une tache aveugle qui donne envie d'éternité, comme un moment creux, imaginaire qui laisse dans le ventre une sensation forte, un effet renouvelé de l'ardeur.

Je me souviens qu'à l'arrivée de Lorna ma mère parlait souvent de la peur. Une peur blême, disait-elle, une peur lente. Lorna semblait aimer cette peur. En parlant, en riant, en marchant, en tout, Lorna attisait la peur de ma mère, une peur qui la rendait fébrile et qui transformait sa voix. Lorsque Lorna plongeait son corps musclé dans l'eau de la piscine, ma mère criait : « Lor, je t'en prie » mais Lorna ruisselait de plus belle, savourant des yeux la peur trouble de ma mère. Puis ses bras m'emportaient avec elle et ma mère encore une fois, ma mère se penchait au-dessus de l'eau, le visage inquiet. Je voyais la forme de son corps. La forme de sa tête était au-dessus de l'eau comme une comète. Ma mère était géante et alors je faisais surface.

Un jour peut-être, je raconterai ma vie. Un jour quand je n'aurai plus quinze ans et le cœur à l'esprit qui s'émerveille. C'est tout dire quand je parle de la nuit et du désert car en cela même je traverse la légende immédiate de ma vie à l'horizon. J'ai abusé des étoiles et des écrans de vie, j'ai entamé des routes de sable, j'ai assouvi ma soif et mon instinct comme autant de mots devant l'horizon magique, seule, manœuvrant d'une manière insensée pour répondre à l'énergie qui me traversait comme une nécessité, une avalanche de l'être. J'avais quinze ans et je savais désigner les personnes et les objets. Je savais qu'un brin de menace n'était que kilomètres à franchir dans la nuit. J'appuyais sur l'accélérateur et heurt, sueur, peur, ô c'est fragile le corps quand il fait si chaud, si noir, si blême, silence immense.

La nuit ! Oui, j'ai vu l'aube. Souvent. Mais la nuit, l'aube déjà rayonnait spectrale dans le spectacle du sable tourbillonnant. Je roulais. J'hurlais dans la vie, la nuit sur l'autoroute. Le jour, c'était la piscine, les filles en maillot et ma mère au bout du fil toute à son affaire du motel ou devant le téléviseur, affairée à la peur. Lorna venait près d'elle et ma mère se laissait chérir et ma mère la choisissait. C'était quotidien et vrai, sans cérémonie entre elles sinon que mon regard venait suspendre leurs gestes et obliger ainsi leurs corps à d'étranges rituels pour compenser l'équilibre perdu ou la trajectoire amorcée des bras amoureux.

Certaines nuits, la sécheresse était sombre et cela me fascinait de penser que sombre la sécheresse était un mot, tout comme moi j'étais une fille comme un mot dans la vie. Mais je pouvais exister sans comparaison. Cela était certain, aussi certain que la soif à venir quand on ne prend pas ses précautions avant de prendre la route et que les lèvres se plissent, craquent dans le vent fort et sec.

J'étais toujours certaine de tout. Des visages, de l'heure, du ciel, des distances, de l'horizon. J'étais certaine de tout sauf des mots. La peur des mots. Peur lente. Peine à prononcer. Peine à entendre. Peine dans toutes mes veines.

Une fin d'après-midi de mai, alors que j'avais quitté la route pour examiner de plus près un vieux saguaro à la silhouette mi-blessée, mi-agonique et que je chantais comme à l'accoutumée – *fever, fever, forever* m'en aller –, je sentis la peur pénible. Le saguaro vacillait, réel et irréel. Le saguaro, les mots, tous mes réflexes étaient au ralenti et bientôt il n'y eut plus de jour, plus d'aube, plus de route, plus de cactus, à peine l'instinct de penser que les mots ne sont pourtant que des mots.

Dans la boîte à gants, il y avait sous le revolver un petit carnet dont je me servais pour inscrire la date des changements d'huile et autres détails se rapportant à l'entretien de l'auto. Un crayon du garage Helljoy, trombone improvisé, retenait les pages décollées. Alors j'ai écrit sur ça, j'ai écrit *ça et encore ça et plus, ça m'excitait, ça m'a pris comme ça s'peut pas d'écrire tout ça avec des explosions dans ma tête, de petits sentiers crayeux dans les canyons. Je connais l'épiderme*

*parcheminé des grands cactus à l'agonie, tout ça,
l'animal creusant sa trace.* La peur s'en va, la peur
dévale.

L'horizon est courbe. Autour du grand saguaro,
l'atmosphère tremblant. Je rentre au motel. Je brûle le
dernier feu pleine du désir du visage de ma mère et de
Lorna. Ma mère est absente. Lorna regarde une émis-
sion. Folle lueur dans ma chambre et mes doigts là,
c'est ça, là, *yet* vacille, m'amuse, m'*envas*.

Cette même nuit, la conscience des mots fit le tour
de mon sentiment, l'enroula, le fit tourner à contre-
sens. J'eus l'impression de mille détours, de gestes graves dans la matière. La sensation de vivre, la sensation
de mourir, l'écriture comme une alternative parmi les
images. Puis la réalité devint une IMAGE. Je m'endormis à l'aube, ficelée dans mes draps, *objet* de l'image.

Je connais maintenant la peur en différé. Je passe
des heures devant le téléviseur. Je pense et passe près
de tout ça comme une enfant longe le silence et le
bruit sourd des voix qui transmettent l'inquiétude. Je
connais la réalité. Je connais l'humanité si soudainement comme une ombre dans mes yeux. Elle bouge
lentement, si lentement l'humanité dans ses désirs,
serpent lent dans le désert, elle se cache, elle mue. Elle
ne bouge plus, ce n'est que peau désertée. Mais la
peau est là, semblable, creuse, tout comme vie aux
pieds des *senitas* et des fouquières. La peur de la peau
creuse est « fortiche » comme une petite réalité fétiche
dans les beaux sentiers orange et jade. La peau fait
peur aux touristes. La peau, c'est ça.

Ce même mois, ma mère fut triste et Lorna comme
ma mère. Je harcelais ma mère pour qu'elle lise le *peu*

que j'avais écrit. Mes fautes ! Je voulais qu'elle corrige tout ça. Je laissais traîner le cahier sur le téléviseur ou sur le plancher, bien en vue. Le soir, je l'entendais raconter à Lorna quelques histoires qu'elle avait lues dans le *Time* ou le *Convention Globe*. À la fin du récit, quelqu'un mourait, s'en allait ou dévoilait un secret. J'augmentais alors le volume du téléviseur et je m'adonnais corps et âme à la toute peur puissante de la réalité.

Depuis que j'avais écrit dans le carnet d'entretien, je voyais vraiment la réalité de près. Les clients venaient du Texas, du Wisconsin, du Minnesota. Beaucoup de vieux. Quelques commis voyageurs, une fois ou deux des femmes ensemble pour qui exister semblait réellement fondé. Il m'arrivait d'écouter les conversations au bar. Les clients parlaient de sport ou d'argent. Certains appuyaient leurs dires par des chiffres, d'autres sautaient sur un mot pour en faire une phrase épicée et déclencher ainsi le rire. Les épaules s'agitaient, on offrait une cigarette au voisin, on trinquait. Puis l'ennui, les nanas et les affaires recommençaient.

Un soir, je pus enfin voir cette Angela Parkins dont ma mère parlait souvent. Elle devait avoir quarante ans. Elle était géomètre et venait ici tous les premiers mardis du mois. Elle s'assoyait au bar et discutait toujours avec deux hommes dont ma mère disait qu'ils étaient ingénieurs. Ce soir-là, je m'installai au bar, espérant surprendre une conversation qui puisse dénouer le mystère que ma mère avait créé autour d'Angela Parkins. Mais on parla en détail de structure et de perspective avec des mots dont la plupart

m'étaient inconnus. Puis Angela Parkins se tourna
vers ma mère et lui fit un brin de jasette en employant
cette fois-ci des mots simples qui résonnèrent en moi,
savoureux et colorés comme une chose intime.

La soirée se poursuivit comme à l'habitude jusqu'à ce que Angela Parkins élève la voix, hystérique,
au bord de l'ivresse. Sa voix s'emporta, culbuta dans
l'espace enfumé. Angela Parkins quitta le bar avant
onze heures et je me retirai à peu près à la même heure.
La réalité avait un sens, mais lequel ?

Le lendemain, j'avertis ma mère de mon départ
pour le Nouveau-Mexique. J'avais téléphoné à Grazie, une cousine qui habitait Albuquerque, et elle
m'avait invitée pour quelques jours.

Chapitre trois

Les yeux de l'homme étaient fous et arrogants. Il levait la tête puis la penchait et à chaque fois c'était l'explosion dans sa tête. Il y avait le plancher, le plafond, les murs et l'explosion. Tout était en accéléré dans son corps soumis à ses pensées. Il était perdu. La poussière était là, raison froide qui retombait sur ses épaules. Il ne guérirait jamais de l'hiver, lui qui aimait tant les petits sentiers et l'odeur de la rosée. Les murs de la chambre étaient, contre toute logique, pleins de son ombre. Il essaya de se concentrer sur un poème sanscrit. Trop tard. Déjà la cendre, déjà le sang, déjà les cris, des bouches formidables, figées dans le silence de la nuit, luisaient comme des cristaux dans chacun de ses neurones. Alors l'homme long se mit à tracer des chiffres sur les murs pleins de son ombre. Puis son corps épuisé glissa contre le mur. L'ombre longue s'évanouit. L'explosion était parfaite dans le jade.

Je roulais lentement. C'était plein jour, pleine lumière, chaud et sueur. Une véritable folie de rouler ainsi en plein soleil. Une épuisante solitude que je m'infligeais comme pour retrouver ce temps d'avant l'écriture, d'avant la réalité. Je roulais et le désert était maintenant vrai, dangereux, plein de dagues, de tranchants et de venin. Je m'étais juré de ne rien boire pendant les cinq premières heures de trajet. Je voulais la chaleur et la soif entières, excessives. Je voulais mon corps fiévreux, ne rien perdre de sa faconde, de son exubérance. Je le voulais tout à la fois centré et hors cadre, superposé à l'hyperréalité du bleu, obligé en chaque cellule à prendre goût le long de la réalité des routes à toutes les formes éphémères qui traversaient mon regard. Je ne voulais d'aucun mythe. Que du vrai, de la sueur, de la soif.

Je résume la réalité dans la lenteur des kilomètres. Je résume ma vie dans la lumière aveuglante. Un jour entre Phoenix et la forêt pétrifiée, *I had a dream*, flamboyant comme une ivresse, une dérive dans l'espace *la gorge a des fêlures de fêtes des horizons zones horribles de rire, des cascades qui saccagent les âges et les cages d'yeux éperdus dans la beauté impossible des écarts et des tourments qui accablent la pensée.*

J'étais maintenant entrée dans la peur de l'indicible, dans la fureur des mots, sans le vouloir j'abdiquais devant le silence. Dans le désert, on plie sans calcul avec la souplesse de l'être adonné à l'espace. L'horizon est un mirage qui oriente le corps assoiffé.

Je roulais, pensée fiévreuse, qui va vers Albuquerque et Grazie. À Grazie, je parlerais d'Angela Parkins, je lui parlerais d'une femme connue dans la nuit d'un mardi. Je frissonnerais, je balbutierais. Je parlerais d'Angela Parkins comme d'un songe dans la forêt pétrifiée. Grazie comprendrait, elle me dirait : « Parle, parle donc. Parle-moi de tout cela. Parle-moi d'Angela Parkins, de tous ses secrets gueulés dans le bar du motel. Parle-moi d'elles et d'Angela, de leurs gestes, de leurs rires dévastateurs, de leurs regards et de leurs sourires croisés, de la peur qui alarme les pensées. Parle-moi, volatile et fébrile, sois serpent et lenteur dans la beauté, sois feu et rigueur. *Light me* pour que le désert s'abîme en nous et que renaissent les ultrasons de notre enfance. *Light me because I might* un jour. »

Grazie était mon aînée de deux mois. Nous étions des « sœurs éloignées », c'est-à-dire des filles que leurs mères avaient nommées ainsi un soir alors que toutes deux enceintes s'étaient séduites et partagées comme un espoir de vingt-quatre heures. Nous étions des filles espérées dans la nuit de nos mères amantes. Je connais la réalité. Ma mère m'avait parlé d'un voyage à Dante's View, m'avait raconté promenade et point de vue, le plus saisissant à Dante's View, les plus beaux à Badwater et à Artist Drive. Puis elle avait ajouté : « Mélanie, mais la nuit. »

Je conduis lentement vers la certitude simple. Grazie m'attend à Albuquerque. À la jonction de la 🔟 et de la 🛡25, il y a des dizaines de motos, des gars qui fument en regardant le ciel. Il y a deux filles qui se parlent. L'une des filles m'envoie un *peace and love* et l'autre, à peine décalée dans l'espace, me fait un *fuck* violent du doigt, puis du coude. J'appuie sur l'accélérateur. Je connais la réalité. La peur, ça ne fait rien quand on accélère; la peur disparaît comme un point sombre dans le rétroviseur.

La route était un décalage horaire perdu dans l'air tremblant de l'horizon. J'avais quinze ans et devant moi la réalité pour m'aider à contourner l'existence. Et puis, il y avait la liberté! Là où j'ai grandi, la liberté se porte côté cœur comme une arme. Elle peut tout autant servir à surmonter la peur et la nostalgie qu'à faire du bruit dans les reins, les mâchoires et les vagins. Là où j'ai grandi, les femmes s'appliquaient de la liberté sur les joues: ça sentait l'encens, la peau lisse, la pharmacie pendant que les hommes tiraient un bon coup de liberté sur tout ce qui bougeait.

J'ai perdu le désert. J'ai perdu le désert dans la nuit de l'écriture. Il y a toujours une première fois, une première nuit qui brouille les passions, qui confond notre sens de l'orientation. Une première fois où il faut convenir que les mots peuvent réduire la réalité jusqu'en sa plus petite unité: l'évidence. Maintenant il faut que l'évidence ranime le désert et qu'à nouveau la couleur soit donnée aux troglodytes, aux serpents corail, aux lynx roux. Il faut qu'à nouveau le lièvre antilope puisse faire alterner du roux au blanc la couleur de ses flancs, il faut que les mystérieuses pierres qui marchent dans la vallée de la Mort laissent dans l'argile la trace de leur passage. Il faut que l'évidence revienne comme un désir du désert et qu'à nouveau les images m'aident à faire le vide comme si elles étaient de toutes petites ventouses installées dans mon cerveau.

Il y a des mémoires pour creuser les mots sans souiller les tombes. Je ne peux tutoyer personne. Il n'y a pas d'altérité, seulement une alternance dans l'apparence. J'ai besoin de souplesse et de tension. Il ne faut pas qu'Albuquerque explose dans ma tête.

Pourquoi je pense comme ça des mots, pourquoi en entrant dans Albuquerque le fou rire, la fatigue du fou rire, la fièvre en entrant dans le beau jeu soudain de la réalité?

Grazie se fit tendre et compagne. Elle se passionna, moqueuse et curieuse, pour mon tatouage sur l'épaule gauche, en suivit le contour avec ses doigts doux, dit qu'un jour elle se ferait dessiner une licorne sur une fesse. Puis, nous avons préparé des *sand witches* comme dans notre enfance et j'ai bu deux litres d'eau. « Tu vas bien? Oui, demain il y a une danse. Ma robe et puis regarde, tu verras, c'est magnifique. » Il y a des phrases entre nous. Qui a dit ça? « Je suis fatiguée, demain. Puis nous irons là. C'est merveilleux. C'était beau. Je me suis blessée à l'index. C'est comme tomber dans un piège ou dans un mot bleu. J'ai placé une photo près du grand miroir. Ça ressemble tellement. Dans la pénombre un bout de bois tordu m'a fait penser. Ah oui! Pour quoi faire? On est bien ici, ensemble. »

Je pense à Lorna qui ne prend pas le temps de respirer entre ses phrases. Lorna n'est intelligible qu'entre les bras de ma mère.

« Fais-moi un peu de place dans le lit. Tasse-toi. Bon, j'allume et je lis toute la nuit. Grazie, tu sais que nos mères se sont déjà aimées. Maintenant c'est l'heure de dormir. Si tu veux veiller, je te je ne je oui alors dors sinon... Quoi ! Oui, c'est doux. Tu prends tout l'oreiller. C'est mon côté. Grazie... une fois seulement, c'est tellement doux. »

La vie est comme une sensation à mille lieux. Cette nuit, je dormirai à côté du désert de Grazie et de son sommeil plein d'encens.

Chapitre quatre

Quelque part, l'homme long dans la nuit de son évanouissement retrouva ses esprits. C'était le silence de la nuit. Personne ne bougeait, ni dans la chambre de gauche, ni à droite. L'homme long se leva difficilement comme s'il avait bu toute la nuit. Il s'appuya contre le mur puis se pencha et ramassa son chapeau qui traînait par terre. Après tout, pensait-il, *demain* le ciel sera bleu. Mais l'aurore était partout explosée dans son cerveau. Sur les murs, les chiffres suintaient et venaient se confondre aux mots qui le suivaient, qui le suivaient partout dans la petite chambre. L'homme long qui avait inventé l'explosion comme un espoir de beauté savait qu'il ne pourrait pas survivre à la beauté des équations. Il ne pourrait pas survivre à son image. L'homme long se sentit fragile, plein d'une solitude amère. Il se vit brisé, miroir, fraction, incapable de chiffrer sa blessure. Alors il sombra impuissant dans la demande. Les paupières closes, les mains jointes, il pria longuement, insensible aux débris qui retombaient sur ses épaules.

Ce matin, Grazie et sa mère sont parties faire des emplettes. Je suis là, immobile dans la chambre et je regarde ce qui se passe dans la rue. Rien. Seulement la réalité. Ô m'absenter ! Un jour je sortirai de la réalité, de son scandale. La beauté est avant la réalité.

Aujourd'hui je reprendrai la route du désert et retrouverai ma mère et Lorna ainsi que le murmure des filles en maillot au bord de la piscine. La réalité sera réelle comme un cache-sexe dans l'éclairage des jukeboxes, comme un tueur à gages devant son manuel d'instructions. Le cerveau est fragile, il faut beaucoup de superstitions pour se le rallier et ne rien abîmer autour. Il n'y a plus de désert. Grazie n'aura jamais quinze ans.

Au retour, je roulai vite, *fast so fast*. Pourquoi flâner en imaginant des baisers, des enlacements, en pensant que la lumière est si belle parmi les *ocotillos* et les *mariposas* ? Ça défile les motels, les roulottes, les cabanes en tôle, les pylônes, les carcasses d'autos, les amoncellements de pneus. Le désert c'est ça. Je me suis acheté une caisse de Coke, je bois sans arrêt. J'ai soif. Ça me donne soif la réalité.

J'avais quinze ans et je regardais la réalité empiéter sur les êtres comme une distorsion tragique de la beauté. L'aura tremblante de l'humanité planait dans la lumière crue.

La réalité défilait, je plongeais dans l'humanité. C'était un regard autour des roulottes et des snack-bars. La réalité était une femme en t-shirt, immense dans ses seins, décuplée avec des enfants calqués sur ses reins, sur ses cuisses. La réalité défilait longeant le sort et les destins. C'était un corps à moitié enfoui sous le capot d'une auto, c'était un jean délavé, une paire de bottes. C'était en alternance la réalité puis le désert avec des longueurs dans la pensée. Des parenthèses à l'approche des villes. Oui, j'étais fascinée par la réalité et plus précisément par sa dimension impossible. La réalité n'est toujours que le possible accompli et c'est en quoi elle fascine comme un désastre ou offense le désir qui voudrait que tout existe en sa dimension. Je n'étais qu'une forme désirante dans le contour de l'aura qui entourait l'humanité. La réalité est un devenir espacé dans la mémoire. Il faut l'y surprendre comme une forme essentielle.

Il me fallait un corps devant l'impensable et ce corps je le produirais, omniprésente à l'aube, les nuits d'orage écartant la foudre. Ce corps, je le filtrerais de l'ignorance, du savoir et de l'impensable qui l'accablaient. Ce corps serait une équation de vie à même l'impossible réalité.

Je roulais, parfaite au bord de la solitude. Je ne désirais que l'horizon, les cactus et un peu de lumière comme naturellement le jour.

Il faisait froid dans la nuit du désert et partout où la chaleur rendait les êtres vivants, je tremblais de rendre la réalité comme un épisode en m'approchant des êtres.

Chapitre cinq

L'homme long était sous la douche. Il aimait l'eau sur sa tête. Il aimait que l'eau lui coule dessus. Il aimait que l'eau soit sans comparaison sur sa peau comme un supplice de l'esprit et alors tout son corps s'abandonnait. Il chantait et l'eau entrait dans sa bouche. L'homme long aurait voulu son corps musclé. Il aurait aimé toucher cet autre corps, caresser le torse puissant, les cuisses, les fesses dures. Il se serait senti allégé du fardeau des chiffres et son dos courbé se serait redressé prêt à tous les combats. Oui, combattre corps à corps avec d'autres hommes eût été enivrant. L'homme long imaginait l'effort des muscles, le battement du cœur, les veines gonflées, la sueur de la peur qui n'aurait pas été comme sa transpiration pendant les heures de calcul. Il aurait aimé l'action et entièrement le corps de ses ennemis. L'homme long avait oublié l'explosion. Il était entré tout vif dans l'instinct du corps et tout son être glissait silencieusement dans les muscles de celui qu'il aurait aimé être. L'homme long s'approcha du miroir, vit ses joues creuses et la barbe d'un mauvais jour. Il s'habilla avec empressement. Dehors il faisait peut-être jour mais l'homme long ne voulait pas y penser. Les rideaux étaient fermés et seule la lumière de l'explosion éclairait ses gestes.

L'homme long ne vit pas la grande enveloppe blanche
que l'on avait glissée sous la porte.

Je revoyais Angela Parkins telle que la première et unique fois que je l'avais vue, sa bouche proférant des menaces à l'endroit de l'humanité comme si elle avait eu le pouvoir de les réaliser. Que voyait-elle, Angela Parkins, quand elle regardait dans son théodolite ? Comment supportait-elle la chaleur et la soif, comment formait-elle ses lettres, ses chiffres ? Comment Angela Parkins faisait-elle l'amour quand elle n'était pas au bord de l'ivresse ?

Bientôt, je serais de retour à la maison et rien ne serait changé dans la réalité. Le soir, je regarderais la peur à la télévision. Le jour, j'observerais les filles en maillot, la nuit, j'irais écouter les conversations au bar. Le jour, ma mère serait une femme, le jour et la nuit, Lorna serait avec ma mère et je chérirais leur présence ailée. Parfois, je prendrais la Meteor. Tout ce temps, mon regard serait ailleurs tourné vers l'impensable et je serais attentive à tout. Je ne m'évanouirais pas devant la réalité. Je ne céderais en rien devant l'aura tragique. Un jour, je connaîtrais le moment parfait de l'exaltation et de l'indifférence en synchronie. Un jour, je connaîtrais le silence et le secret qui se prolonge dans les êtres afin que naissent d'autres civilisations. La beauté était avant la réalité et la réalité était dans l'écriture, un jour.

CHAPITRE SIX

L'homme long savait que le jour était là derrière les rideaux. Il ne se sentait pas encore prêt pour la lumière du jour. Il alluma une cigarette et prit le premier livre qui lui tomba sous la main. Il lisait comme avant, calmement. Ce calme semblait vouloir s'étendre partout en lui mais, au fur et à mesure qu'il le sentait s'emparer de tous ses membres, il éprouvait en contrepartie une excitation froide, mentale qui rendait intolérable chaque nerf dans son corps calme. Sa respiration était lente. Tout son être était agi dans les limites du possible. L'homme long déposa le volume au pied du lit. Il aperçut l'enveloppe. Il se leva, entrouvrit les rideaux, puis fixa la réalité du petit matin. Sur la pelouse du motel, une femme était penchée au-dessus d'un arrosoir. L'eau jaillissait pleine d'éclats. L'homme long se pencha et ramassa l'enveloppe.

J'avais roulé toute la nuit. Tucson n'était qu'à quelques kilomètres mais je n'étais pas encore prête à retrouver la peur panique.

Je m'arrêterais à ce motel tenu par une amie de ma mère. Je dirais ma fatigue et mon besoin de dormir. Elle m'offrirait une chambre. Je retournerais à la Meteor pour prendre mon sac. Dans la boîte à gants le revolver serait chaud. Je prendrais mon cahier et le stylo. Tout l'avant-midi, j'écrirais. Le climatiseur serait bruyant. Tout autour de moi, la réalité : le rideau transparent, la couleur des murs, une aquarelle superflue, un téléviseur, mon corps immobile devant le miroir. J'aurais l'impression d'une ultime compréhension de la nuit, du désert et des hasards intimes qui se succèdent en nous comme une loi de la réalité. Ma main serait lente. L'humanité ne pourrait pas se répéter. J'existerais alerte dans le questionnement.

CHAPITRE SEPT

L'homme long regarde en détail chaque photo. Maintenant, il n'y a plus de doute, l'explosion a eu lieu et elle a parfaitement réussi. Une photo est une preuve éclatante. La réalité n'est plus dans la tête de l'homme long. La réalité est sur la photo. L'homme long est libre. Il n'y a plus d'explosion dans sa tête. C'est rien ! C'est rien ! Tout est dans la photo. L'homme long épingle au mur chacune des photos. Il recule de quelques pas, se rapproche. Il observe l'explosion. Il allume. Il éteint. Il ouvre et referme les rideaux. Il cherche un bon éclairage pour l'explosion. Puis, c'est comme si soudain le noir et le blanc des photos envahissaient la chambre. L'homme long regarde par la fenêtre. Dehors, la pelouse est verte. Il y a des filles en maillot autour de la piscine. L'homme long allume une cigarette. Toute la chambre est solarisée.

Tout est si réel autour de la piscine. Je suis entrée comme un personnage dans la vie de mes quinze ans. À l'improviste, sans me douter de rien. Tout autour de la piscine, la lumière est vive. Elle contourne les bras, les seins, les cuisses, les dos, s'engouffre dans les yeux. Le regard fond.

   Il y a une jeune femme qui prend des photos de ses deux amies. Elles posent. Elles sourient mais leur sourire s'efface, blanchi par la lumière. Il y a toujours de la musique au bord de la piscine. La lumière est crue. L'éternité recommence à chaque instant. Elles conversent en riant, des paroles sans conséquence qu'elles s'échangent dans la saveur des cocktails. Pour le plaisir de la langue. Un homme vient s'asseoir près d'elles. Il entame la conversation en français. L'homme est mince. Il porte une serviette noir et blanc autour de ses hanches. Je ne comprends pas ce qu'il dit. Elles rient. Il se lève et se dirige vers le bar. La lumière est vive. Il revient avec un whisky. Il prononce des phrases courtes. Il parle avec du silence entre ses phrases. Il n'est pas de la région. Il n'est pas français. J'ai soif. Je tourne la tête en direction du bar. Quelqu'un plonge dans la piscine. L'homme ruisselant passe devant moi. Il allonge son corps sur la serviette. La lumière est crue. Le temps s'étiole. Les filles remuent leurs jambes dans l'eau. Je plonge. La réalité est un désir espacé dans la mémoire. Les motels sont tous les mêmes. Je suis dans la réalité jusqu'au cou.

Je nagerai encore un peu papillon, dauphin, ferai grenouille et chien puis j'irai prendre ma douche à l'heure où les touristes partiront pour une courte randonnée dans le désert, à cette heure où tout est si beau. Quand ils reviendront, je serai au bar et la propriétaire pour se rassurer dira que j'ai bien changé «depuis le temps», que je dois certainement avoir dix-neuf ans maintenant. Puis j'assisterai à la procession des clients qui viendront prendre place autour des tables ou s'accouder au bar, les yeux encore éblouis de mauve et d'orange.

CHAPITRE HUIT

Tout en nouant sa cravate, l'homme long récite des poèmes sanscrits. L'explosion est loin. Les photos traînent parmi les équations. Il se sent léger, enfin prêt à rencontrer les autorités. Une dernière nuit dans cet endroit puis il reprendrait sa fière allure, son charme. Il savait argumenter et convaincre, il serait impeccable. L'homme long vit son corps disgracieux dans la glace. Il mit son veston et se dirigea vers le bar.

Le bar commence à se remplir. C'est un jeudi soir. Beaucoup de touristes et d'accents. Quelques habitués qui viennent directement s'asseoir sur les tabourets en demi-cercle autour du comptoir. Je connais tout ça.

Le désert dénoue toutes les intrigues y compris celle qui derrière les yeux sollicite à l'horizon l'humanité invisible. Dans le désert, on ne survit pas sans ses quinze ans. Il faut toujours être prête à tout, imaginer des cascades, des torrents, la pluie, arrêter le soleil et inverser les probabilités dans le désir. Ici, dans le bar du Red Arrow Motel, le désert n'existe pas vraiment. Seule la soif qui disperse les désirs, petits débris dans l'âme. J'ai grandi dans le désert et je n'ai de mérite à l'aimer qu'en la solitude qui me préserve de l'immonde.

L'homme à l'accent vient d'entrer. Il fait un petit signe de la tête en direction de la table où sont assises les femmes de la piscine. Je commande une bière. La propriétaire répète comme pour elle-même que je dois sans doute avoir dix-neuf ans maintenant. Elle salue les nouveaux arrivants d'un air qui tout à la fois accueille et discipline. La musique est trop forte. Quelques couples dansent. Tauromachie des corps souples et des peaux bronzées. Au fond de la salle, l'homme mince est appuyé sur le mur et il fume.

L'aube est un principe qui exacerbe l'énergie. Je veux comprendre jusqu'à l'excès mon désir de l'aube, mon besoin de l'aube. Je demande une autre bière.

Quelqu'un me touche à l'épaule. Angela Parkins est là, alerte, vive, crue et je suis si lente à comprendre combien sa présence m'exalte. Elle dit une banalité puis circule entre les tables. La musique est trop forte. Les trois femmes ont trouvé des partenaires. L'homme de la piscine est maintenant assis à une table avec deux hommes. La musique est trop forte. Rien n'est sensuel. Les corps s'allongent et font des ombres comme des cheveux dans le visage des filles, disposent de leur sourire basané. Tout est sensuel. Angela Parkins regarde dans ma direction, dessine dans l'air un mouvement circulaire avec sa main, oui comme si elle me faisait signe, puis elle pointe du doigt en direction de la piste de danse. La musique est trop forte. La musique est trop douce. Le corps d'Angela Parkins est fanatique, rempli d'urgence. Il bondit comme un animal fougueux, capricieux, voltige et plane éperdument, éperdue Angela Parkins. Il y a des yeux posés sur chacun de nos mouvements, de nos regards. La beauté est suspendue, la beauté qui précède la réalité, Angela Parkins chante passionnément, moitié *lip-synch*, moitié *live*, la bouche arrondie par des sons éclatés. Ses mains virevoltent au-dessus de nos têtes. La paume de nos mains, parfois sa main glisse sur mes hanches, parfois, nos doigts acrobates et aériens se saisissent comme pour tourner le sens des sons au-dessus de nos têtes, tout autour de nous, parfois son regard, sa joue.

Je ne connais pas vraiment Angela Parkins et voici pourtant nos corps rapprochés un instant, puis distants, lents et longs dans la distance de l'Amérique. Nous sommes inséparables et distantes en pleine éternité. Nous sommes le désert et l'évidence au coucher des ombres. Peut-être la nuit et la couleur de l'aube. Les femmes se sont rapprochées de nous. Elles ont l'air de s'amuser. La musique est trop forte. Angela Parkins m'offre à boire. « *The same.* » Puis je cesse d'exister. Elle parle, parle, part vers je ne sais où, elle dit que ça recommence parole, sentiers, papillons et qu'elle aime ça la lenteur obligée des mots, elle dit que dans la détresse tout est envahi par le son des mots et qu'alors tout devient impossible à comprendre, elle dit que ça explose dans sa tête et que tout est à recommencer comme un revers, un lob dans l'espace du cerveau, elle répète le cerveau est fragile mais les yeux, mais les yeux, Mélanie, elle dit qu'il ne faut pas renoncer, que rien n'est impossible si la mémoire accomplit dans l'improbable la certitude qui en soi veille à l'horizon à la beauté, elle parle de l'attachement que nous avons pour certains mots et que ceux-ci sont comme de petites morts lentes dans la réalité concise.

Il est minuit trente et le bar est encore plein de clients. La musique s'empare de tout. Tout est fluide et lent dans les bras d'Angela Parkins. Le temps me manque pour comprendre. Il n'y a plus de temps. Le temps est entré en nous avec minutie comme un scalpel, le temps nous oblige à la réalité. Le temps s'est glissé entre nos jambes. Chaque muscle, chaque nerf, chaque cellule tient lieu de musique dans nos corps, absolument. Puis le corps d'Angela Parkins remue lentement. Tout son corps est attiré vers le bas. Son corps est lourd entre mes bras. Mes bras sont lourds du corps d'Angela Parkins. Il n'y a plus de musique. La sueur d'Angela Parkins contre ma tempe. La sueur sur ma main. Angela, le silence est cru. Angela ! Un tout petit dessin sur la tempe, un tout petit trou, ocelle. Angela, nous dansons, *yes*? Angela Parkins n'a plus de hanches, plus d'épaules et de nuque. Elle se dissipe. Les yeux d'Angela, vite les yeux! Il n'y a plus d'équilibre entre nous. Tout mon corps est devant le désastre. Plus un son. L'agitation tout autour comme dans un film muet. Au fond de la salle, il y a le regard impassible de l'homme long. Le désert est grand. Angela Parkins est allongée, là, exposée à tous les regards. Angela se dissipe dans le noir et le blanc de la réalité. Que s'est-il passé? C'était pourtant un homme de génie. *Of course Mélanie is* night teen.

La réalité, l'aube. La fureur dans l'aube et les galaxies. Les policiers, la craie autour du corps d'Angela Parkins. Les clients n'ont rien vu. Je n'ai rien vu. Le désert est indescriptible. Le regard fond.

Puis ce fut le mauve de l'aube, le désert et la route comme un profil sanglant. Il y a des mémoires pour creuser les mots sans souiller les tombes. Je ne peux tutoyer personne.

Un livre à traduire

Elle ne saura jamais pourquoi tout son être s'est enfoncé dans un livre, pourquoi pendant deux ans elle s'est brisée, s'est allongée dans les pages de ce livre écrit par une femme dont elle ne sait rien sinon la preuve présumée d'une existence recluse dans le temps et l'espace franchi d'un seul livre.

En somme ce livre était *innocent*. Il reposait, mince tranche de papier entre les appuis-livres. C'était un matin de décembre, d'une blancheur spectrale qui érodait les objets. Elle pensait lenteur en soustrayant du regard le livre à son équilibre. Et il basculait soulevant dans le ralenti du silence le lancinant désir qui ne la quittait pas. À l'horizontale, le livre ressemblait à une pierre tombale : un nom, un titre et l'éclat de la couverture.

L'univers était un risque. Elle était une présence minimale, un espace embué devant la fenêtre. Un jalon peut-être entre ce livre et son devenir dans une autre langue. C'était précisément à voir.

Autour d'elle, tout était bruits de l'instant, images à
conquérir. Il eût fallu dire d'un souffle. Il faudra exceptionnellement   beaucoup   d'illusions.   Comme
autant d'apparences, le recours à certaines données
sensorielles qu'elle ne peut faire siennes encore bien
qu'éblouie par la nature du risque.

   Elle aurait à nommer, à converser longuement de
l'intérieur jusqu'à ce que perplexe, jusqu'à ce que la
petite tentation de traduire l'émeuve à ce point qu'un
mot s'étire empruntant la forme d'un animal ou la
couleur au loin, mauve, et, encore dans son désir, toujours à documenter de l'horizon l'entourant.

   Il était possible que tout cela ne puisse advenir
que si, par le détail, elle entrait dans l'univers de la
narratrice dont le nom, Mélanie, lui donnait à entre-
voir un profil sur la nuit, découpé.

En ce début de décembre, alors que tombe la première neige, Maude Laures collige tout à la fois les indices de son désir et ses notes de lecture qui comme autant d'éclats de voix et de jours sans pluie entourent la piscine du motel. Elle plonge, est-ce erreur ou stratégie, écartant du revers de la main la première difficulté, celle dont elle ne parvient pas à décider si elle existe parce que prématurée ou si elle est le résultat de ses pensées disparates. « Ce n'est pas vrai » revient sans cesse, revient comme une intrusion dans ses notes, annule tous ses efforts de concentration. « Ce n'est pas vrai » revient, la refoule dans son univers, la retient de ce désir fou qui s'éternise, peur panique de se substituer à l'auteure de ce livre. Par un retour incalculable des mots, elle savait ne plus pouvoir être en mesure de se soustraire à ce qui, bien bas sous la langue, voulait.

Il lui faudrait aussi souligner ailleurs que là où le sentiment l'avait surprise, de l'étrange histoire arracher le sens et s'en tenir à l'acte ininterrompu de l'interprétation. Le pourrait-elle sans confondre l'horizon et le désert, ces espaces venus, par effraction, se greffer sur son monde urbain et sur les figures qui, en elle, ne toléraient pas de désastre ? Pourtant, elle acquiesçait avec un certain soulagement à ce livre qui sans préavis avait sapé son équilibre, l'obligeait à répartir son énergie de manière à inclure, optimale, l'alternative en chaque mot, terrée.

En ce début de décembre, son désir est grand, résulté de l'approche et de la possibilité croisées de quelques transformations.

Ce matin le ciel était bleu. Elle pouvait croire au dérèglement des sens comme à une activité mentale. Elle avait beau jeu.

Elle aurait voulu des choses luxuriantes, un dialogue peut-être afin d'illustrer cette souplesse des sens que, dans le temps fort de l'expérience, elle ressentait comme une invite au délire. Un dialogue pour que soit rectifiée sa méfiance à l'égard de tout personnage, sa fascination de l'aube et surtout pour nettoyer la peur de sa composition affective. Pour le reste, c'était énormément une idée. Une question de singularité pouvant affranchir les mots de leur saturation. Tout avait pourtant été possible dans la langue de l'auteure, mais dans la sienne, il fallait qu'elle s'arme de patience. Inépuisablement trouver la faille, le petit endroit où le sens appelle quelques audaces. La beauté était à ce prix comme une espérée lumière. Maude Laures s'était laissé séduire, *ravaler* par sa lecture. Il n'est pas toujours possible de rêver sans avoir à donner suite aux images.

S'astreindre à comprendre, ne rien négliger malgré le flot dévergondé des mots. Susciter de l'événement. Oui, un dialogue. Obliger Mélanie à la conversation. L'installer au bord de la piscine et la faire parler. Mettre de la couleur dans ses cheveux, des traits sur son visage. Oui, un dialogue somptueux, une dépense déraisonnable de mots et d'expressions, une suite qui, construite autour d'une idée, dériverait à ce point que Maude Laures aurait le temps de circuler paisiblement autour du motel, de pénétrer dans la chambre de la mère et de Lorna. Un dialogue qui lui permettrait, Mélanie emportée par les mots, de voyager à ses côtés dans la Meteor, d'ouvrir la boîte à gants, de toucher le revolver, de feuilleter le carnet d'entretien.

Tout n'est encore qu'intention de *faire passer*. Perspective répétée de l'aller-retour. Recours à l'original, néanmoins la démarche interposée, la dérive comme un choc culturel, une émotion grave semée de miroirs et de mirages.

La nuit, Maude Laures rêvait de *son livre* et le jour, avant même de s'adonner aux principes de l'audace et de la prudence, elle pensait à Laure Angstelle. Cela la rassurait de savoir qu'elle était libre de tout (imaginer) à son sujet. Certes, elle avait fait quelques recherches mais aucune n'avait donné de résultat. Laure Angstelle était l'auteure d'un seul livre publié dans une petite ville de l'Arizona. Elle pouvait l'imaginer jeune ou âgée, libre et fière, ayant peut-être connu un grand amour ou un désastre, ayant été géomètre ou physicienne, vivant encore isolée quelque part entre Globe et Gila. Ou morte, telle était l'autre perspective.

Des images qui permettent de distribuer le consentement. Une belle machine souple pouvant inverser le
rire ou le désespoir.

Dans son sommeil, Maude Laures se range du
côté de la perception, attachée cependant par quelques cordes sensibles à l'*expression* qu'elle définit
comme une substantielle proposition capable de faire
pencher la balance. Elle sait que c'est dans l'approxi-
mation que les mots d'abord. Puis au beau milieu des
images, elle voit bien que c'est *justement perçu* que le
rapport s'installe, assimile le mot promu ou l'image
survécue.

Décembre n'est qu'un aspect du risque. Un mois
dispersé dans *Le désert mauve*. Un mois fragile ex-
plosé dans la tête de Maude Laures.

Le moindre énoncé barrait les mâchoires. Alors elle cherchait l'envers des mots, avec un peu d'affolement, la doublure, lorsque la scène lui paraissait trop cruelle ou fausse. Ainsi, elle pouvait mettre en parallèle, bien que brièvement, la petite sensation qui donne lieu à l'émotion et le sens qui porte à croire. Indirectement *faire valoir le passage* dans sa langue, accélérer le sentiment, avec des effets de rutilance, le glissement.

Midi, la neige tombe encore. Redoutant ce qui la nuit longe la forme des grands saguaros veilleurs, Maude Laures traduit par « finalement la tempête vint aux yeux soustraire la réalité ». Puis, elle s'assoupit « dans la Meteor, entre deux chansons ».

Le monde de Laure Angstelle prenait place en elle et cela bien différemment de ce qu'elle avait ressenti au tout début alors que durant ses premières lectures, elle avait éprouvé le sentiment diffus d'une réciprocité. Maintenant le monde de Laure Angstelle avait en elle la portée d'une musique tout en durée qui la laissait devant sa table de travail comme un *bloc de concentration*; les yeux astreints au moindre détail pendant qu'au loin les images les plus intimes vacillaient, Maude Laures s'adaptait à toutes les intrigues pouvant, état d'alerte, disposer de sa ferveur. . . . .
. . . . et

de sa froideur. Car à l'improviste « tromper la langue » lui venait comme une réplique nécessaire afin
que soit reconstituée « la fiction », le contour tremblé
de ses effets. La froideur de Maude Laures était un
incommensurable désert blanc sillonné d'éclairs mauves. Il fallait beaucoup de rapidité dans le processus
pour que la froideur ne soit point sécheresse, pour
que Maude Laures abrite cet immense espace à découvert, recouvre chaque mot d'un autre mot sans que le
premier ne sombre dans l'oubli. Probables modula-
tions. De l'oubli, de la réplique, recouvre la raison.

Le temps qui passait était désormais un *temps de res-
tauration*, un ensemble qui, tel un arrangement floral
agencé par la pensée capable des gestes les plus men-
talement précis, s'expose à ce que soit reconstituée
son intentionnalité. Maude Laures se sentit liée par
une telle approche et, un matin de neige abondante,
elle décida de l'existence parmi les scènes et les symp-
tômes certains qui, dans la langue de Laure Angstelle,
l'avaient séduite.

Lieux et objets

LE MOTEL

Lorsqu'on arrive par la route de Phoenix, c'est le premier motel sur la gauche avec un toit métallique qui aveugle un instant et un néon MOTEL *Mauve* qui fait penser à un oiseau sur le point de s'envoler. Au moment de tourner sur la gauche, une petite élévation permet de constater que le motel est construit en forme de ⊓, avec une piscine au centre du rectangle et un stationnement qui, sous la ligne du bas, donne sur la route. Le bar se trouve entre la piscine et le stationnement. On y accède par un endroit ou l'autre. Le bar est peint en mauve et contraste avec la blancheur du bâtiment. Le néon a été installé sur son toit.

Six autos sont garées dans le stationnement, autour desquelles un garçonnet poursuit un garçon pendant qu'un autre, habillé en shérif, dégaine. Une des autos est occupée par un homme et une femme. L'homme est au volant, la femme s'apprête à refermer la portière de son côté, échange quelques paroles avec un autre homme, celui-là qui se dirige vers le bureau, une serviette à la main. Le bureau est à la droite du stationnement. À l'entrée, deux figuiers de Barbarie et un agave forment un petit espace vert. Le terrain de stationnement n'est pas goudronné. Il y a une mince couche de poussière sur les cactus.

Kathy Kerouac, propriétaire, est au téléphone, le combiné entre l'épaule et l'oreille, les mains occupées à chercher dans un fichier. Il y a une odeur de savon. Tout au fond du corridor qui mène aux chambres de l'aile droite, une femme de chambre déplace son chariot.

Kathy Kerouac raccroche, sourit et tend machinalement une fiche à remplir, reprend fiche et carte de crédit puis après quelques gestes rapides, la clé un instant en suspens au-dessus du comptoir, se penche légèrement, pointe du doigt en direction de la chambre, de la piscine en déplaçant son index en angle de soixante degrés.

Le corridor est sombre. Sur la première porte à droite, un écriteau indique PRIVÉ. Un peu plus loin à gauche, l'accès intérieur au bar, puis la piscine derrière un mur de verre. Au bout du corridor, la femme de ménage prononce un timide *buenos días*. La sortie de secours est ouverte. Au fond, dans la lumière, un homme décharge des caisses de papier hygiénique. Il porte une casquette. Ses bras sont musclés. La portière du camion est entrouverte et laisse passer un air de blues.

La chambre est grande. Les rideaux sont tirés. La fenêtre donne sur un espace en terre battue où une adolescente, appuyée sur un baril rouillé, fume un petit cigare.

LA PISCINE

Certaines chambres donnent sur la piscine. Il suffit de pousser la porte coulissante et c'est immédiatement, blanchie par la lumière, une atmosphère torride, un monde en disparition, brièvement fossile, un sentiment d'hyperréalité traversé par la sensation du sens vacillé. Ici et là quelques mouches à la surface de l'eau, au fond de l'eau, des pétales de magnolia. Tout autour de la piscine : des chaises longues, deux parasols ouverts, une distributrice de cigarettes, une autre pour la glace. La piscine est un endroit qui, occupé ou déserté, incite à la nostalgie, ce sentiment que parfois on éprouve lorsque les choses sont désolées et que la beauté gagne infailliblement le désir comme s'il était question de vivre un moment précieux.

Chaque objet reflète une lumière crue, une évidence de lumière qui épuise le regard. Aussi la plupart des personnes qui utilisent la piscine ont-elles tôt fait de se transformer en statues de sel, figées dans le temps, les yeux fermés, la tête basculée dans l'éternité, les membres lourds donnant autour du corps l'impression d'une espèce animale.

Une jeune femme se tient à mi-corps dans l'eau, sans bouger, le regard absent. Elle lève parfois la tête et ses paupières, et son regard, pourrait-on penser, implore quelque divinité. Assis à l'une des tables qui donnent sur le bar, un homme lit un journal. Ses jambes sont croisées, le poil sur sa poitrine encore lissé par le mouvement vertical du corps à la sortie de l'eau.

Quelques tuiles sont mouillées et l'éclat du rose alterne avec l'éclat métallique des distributrices, la rampe chromée de l'escalier. Un boyau d'arrosage serpente le long des chaises, disparaît sous les feuilles d'un agave en fleurs. L'homme qui lit déplace légèrement sa chaise et le son combiné du métal et de la tuile écorche l'avant-midi discret. La jeune femme fait quelques pas dans l'eau. Ses épaules, à fleur d'eau, sont comme deux récifs autour du collier couleur jade qu'elle porte.

L'atmosphère est au repos jusqu'à ce que Lorna Myher, soudain présence parmi les présences, lance sa serviette sur une chaise, s'envole au-dessus de l'eau, beau plongeon, à peine quelques gouttes d'eau qui forment un instant un prisme dans les yeux de la jeune femme. Alors, comme s'il pouvait être la cause de cet arc-en-ciel, elle tourne *légèrement* la tête du côté de l'homme qui, à ce moment précis, allonge un bras vers le sol pour y déposer les pages froissées du *Convention Globe*.

La jeune femme est sortie de l'eau. La lumière croise un instant le jade. Le corps musclé de Lorna Myher sillonne silencieusement la piscine.

L'AUTO

Éclat au loin dont on ne peut évaluer la distance, telle une ossature, un squelette poli au milieu du désert, la chose capte toute la chaleur et l'attention, attire et intrigue car dans le désert *une chose* est une présence soupçonnée de l'humain.

De près, l'auto est poussiéreuse. Sa carrosserie, ailée à l'arrière, se transforme à l'avant en une excroissance bombée comme pour une approche frontale répétée de l'horizon. Un des pneus avant est appuyé sur un gros caillou qui déforme le caoutchouc déjà gonflé par la chaleur. Le pare-chocs reflète l'image d'un cactus à coussins, surtout le rouge de la fleur dont la forme contiguë à une tache de rouille s'effiloche, rubigineuse. Le coffre de la valise est plein d'inscriptions tracées du doigt dans la poussière.

Une des portes est ouverte. Les clés sont sur le contact. Le cendrier est rempli de mégots, la boîte à gants, mal refermée. Une bande de cuir noir usée par la sueur entoure le volant. Sur la banquette, des cartes routières, une lampe de poche, un chandail, des bottes en peau de lézard déformées à l'endroit du petit orteil gauche, un livre aux pages cornées. Au pied du siège avant, un contenant en plastique est rempli d'eau aux trois quarts.

En contournant l'auto (la plaque est de l'Arizona, CHAP 1278), on peut voir au loin la présence soupçonnée de l'humain. Quelqu'un est là, debout et immobile au pied d'un vieux saguaro dont la blessure, les nervures ligneuses du squelette font une tache sombre à l'horizon. On peut penser un instant que c'est image ou mirage, une illusion comme cela peut se produire lorsque les altostratus modifient de seconde en seconde le champ de profondeur et la couleur tout autour. Mais l'adolescente se retourne et on peut la voir, d'un pas lent, d'un pas *satiné* revenir vers l'auto, insensible à la chaleur, à la lumière inexorable qui transforme les vies de chair en ossature de récit.

L'auto roule maintenant dans la direction de Tucson. Sa blancheur sur l'asphalte est absolument concrète. Jusqu'à ce que la nuit tombe et que phare parmi les phares, dragon parmi les dragons, elle rugisse au cœur de la « drague » vertigineuse qui déferle sur le boulevard Speedway.

Plus tard, à la nuit avancée, l'auto roule lentement parmi les candélabres et les « princesses de la nuit » éphémères. La nuit est douce drapée autour de l'auto, la nuit est blanche comme un silence trop longuement exposé sous les étoiles.

LE TÉLÉVISEUR

Le téléviseur est dans la pièce adjacente à la cuisine. C'est le premier meuble que l'on voit en entrant dans les trois chambres aménagées en appartement. Il fonctionne toute la journée depuis le réveil de Lorna Myher jusqu'à cette heure tardive où Kathy Kerouac, après avoir « fait sa caisse », referme la porte derrière elle et boit un dernier Coke avant de se mettre au lit.

Le téléviseur est beige, recouvert d'une étoffe de coton en dentelle sur laquelle un vase de lis artificiels repose en permanence ; à côté, un cendrier mal lavé en forme de pneu au fond duquel on peut lire G RAGE EL JOY. De chaque côté de l'étoffe, le vernis est abîmé par des cernes de verres. L'antenne en forme d'oreilles de lapin est placée vers l'arrière.

Le meuble est massif. Tel que placé dans la pièce, il faut à tout coup, par un mouvement habile des hanches, le contourner. Il arrive que par maladresse on s'y meurtrisse la chair à la hauteur de l'os iliaque.

L'écran est toujours parfaitement clair. Jamais de neige. Rarement doit-on ajuster à l'horizontale ou à la verticale la forme et les visages des assassins, des politiciens, des *comiques* qui occupent l'écran la majeure

partie du temps. Leur forme est parfaite, unidimen-
sionnelle, plate. Les parties les plus visibles sont la
cravate et la pomme d'Adam.

Où que l'on se trouve dans la pièce, le téléviseur
attire l'attention, transforme la raison d'être dans la
pièce, fût-elle une faim ou une soif pressante, dévie la
conversation ou l'interdit, donne lieu à des éclats de
voix, en particulier ceux de Lorna Myher qui com-
mente toujours avec beaucoup d'agressivité et de vulgarités l'allure et le physique des rugbymen. Durant
les intrigues policières, c'est pire ! Sa colère s'abat implacable sur toutes les figures mâles qui défigurent les
beaux paysages qu'elle imagine dans les yeux des femmes. Sa colère qui se manifeste d'abord par un va-et-
vient devant le téléviseur se transforme ensuite en de
longues phrases incompréhensibles qui alternent avec
des gémissements. Kathy Kerouac voit alors à fermer
discrètement les deux portes qui donnent l'une sur le
bureau, l'autre sur le corridor. Dans son esprit, il ne
saurait être question de scandale.

Le téléviseur reste ouvert pendant des heures et
des heures. Durant les orages, cela fait peur à Kathy
Kerouac et elle se blottit dans les bras de Lorna Myher.
Alors, elles conversent de profil, le regard inquiet devant les images qui défilent, leurs mains nouées comme
pour exorciser la peur imprécise de Kathy Kerouac, le
tremblement du corps musclé de Lorna Myher.

LE TATOUAGE

L'épaule est bronzée, la peau lisse, la chair ferme. Toutes les vingt secondes, l'éclairage du néon longe la poitrine, passe au-dessus de l'épaule, expose un instant l'imago, puis remonte vers le visage avant de se perdre dans la nuit chaude.

Les ailes du papillon sont ouvertes, et le rouge et le mauve et l'indigo se rassemblent autour du corps qui se prolonge, ovale blanc en un visage de femme au sourire lent comme dans un tableau de la Renaissance. Puis cheveux ou antennes, serpents ou spirales, la tête se termine en une série de courbes pleines d'allusions et d'images virtuelles comme si l'artiste avait voulu faire montre de son talent ou succombé, malgré le mouvement ralenti de l'aiguille dans le derme, à une exubérance soudaine. On peut d'ailleurs penser que le tatouage ait été l'œuvre de cette femme qui habite au sud près de la frontière et qui, dit-on, a tatoué tous les « esprits libres » de la région, qui, dit-on, métamorphose en oiseau, en crâne, en navire, en dragon ou en fleur les épaules, les torses, les avant-bras et les dos offerts à ses mains expertes qui savent atténuer la douleur et essuyer soigneusement l'excès de colorant et de sang à chaque étape.

C'est maintenant une nuit toute en lenteur. On entend des voix et des rires en provenance du bar.

Elles sont appuyées sur la Meteor, Angela Parkins, la tête tournée vers l'adolescente, les lèvres rapprochées du corps indélébile. Les ocelles sont comme de petites apparitions qui sur le derme pigmenté attirent le regard, un code certain pour l'espèce.

Angela Parkins relève brusquement la tête comme si elle voulait fuir une image et cela donne l'impression qu'elle est sur le point de perdre l'équilibre. L'adolescente a un mouvement vers elle. C'est à ce moment précis que la pluie s'abat, torrentielle, rideau ; et le crépitement violent de l'eau sur la carrosserie des autos, rigoles. À la faveur de la pluie répétée sur chaque surface, la nuit devient un immense son qui permet aux choses d'exister.

La pluie sur les épaules est violente. Le papillon luit de plus belle mais l'adolescente ayant croisé ses bras de manière à ce que chaque main couvre une épaule, le papillon disparaît non sans avoir laissé sur la pupille d'Angela Parkins : tête de mort, thorax, sphinx, une impression.

LE REVOLVER

Dans le premier tiroir sous le comptoir, l'objet repose sur un registre de comptabilité, le canon pointé en angle de cent vingt degrés vers un trombone qui affleure d'un mouton de poussière granulé de tabac. La crosse est appuyée sur un coin cartonné du registre.

Il y a maintenant deux ans que Kathy Kerouac n'a pas utilisé le revolver. Auparavant, elle se rendait une fois par semaine au champ de tir afin de se familiariser avec l'arme, sa pesanteur, sa portée, la résistance de la détente, le mouvement du pouce quand on abaisse le chien. Maintenant c'est à peine si elle remarque l'objet quand elle ouvre le tiroir. Seul le poids opaque de l'arme quand elle la déplace pour prendre le registre lui donne la sensation désagréable de toucher une bête sournoise.

Le revolver est toujours chargé.

Quand on ouvre la boîte à gants, le revolver scintille à tout coup. Il occupe la majeure partie de l'espace et sa forme reflétée dans un petit miroir de toilette amplifie sa dimension. Le revolver est chaud. Il arrive même qu'il faille le prendre avec un linge ou en étirant par le bas le t-shirt de manière à se faire une mitaine protectrice dans le coton.

Elle s'en sert rarement mais certains jours, quand tout semble désœuvré, on peut voir l'adolescente, le dos courbé, disposer en un demi-cercle d'un rayon de trois mètres autour de l'auto une vingtaine de cannettes vides. Le bras tendu, la tête légèrement penchée, un œil fermé, l'autre sur le cran de mire enligné sur les canettes, elle appuie sur la détente. Au printemps, quand les tarentules sortent en grand nombre, elles font de belles cibles sur le sol à découvert.

Le revolver est toujours chargé.

L'homme le transporte dans sa serviette. Il aime que les dossiers soient bien rangés, appuyés les uns sur les autres dans leurs chemises de couleurs différentes. Tout au fond de la serviette, le revolver ainsi qu'une boîte de cartouches peuvent selon l'épaisseur des dossiers servir d'appuis-livres.

Dans les chambres climatisées, le revolver est froid. L'homme en apprécie la sensation sur ses mains moites. Il lui arrive souvent de lire en tenant le revolver dans sa main libre comme si l'arme pouvait assurer une fraîcheur permanente au creux de sa paume.

Le revolver est toujours chargé. Aucune marque d'appartenance ne le distingue des centaines d'autres que l'on voit dans les magasins d'armes ou encore placés, tel que la loi l'exige, à la ceinture des commerçants.

Le bar

Lorsqu'on entre en venant directement du stationnement, la piste de danse, bien que petite et d'un beau
bois blond, donne l'impression d'un grand vide. Tout
autour, une dizaine de tables rectangulaires en méla-
mine noire, au centre desquelles on a placé un cendrier jaune en plastique, deux lorsque les tables sont
plus grandes. Au fond, la terrasse et la piscine à moitié
cachées par une tenture qui tranche entre la clarté du
jour et l'intérieur sombre. À gauche, le bar en demi-
cercle et, si on fait quelques pas vers le centre de la
salle, on peut apercevoir un juke-box ancien aux formes arrondies. Derrière le bar, un grand miroir, des
bouteilles d'alcool, un téléviseur suspendu. L'écran est
allumé. Le volume est au minimum. Lorsqu'on s'as-
soit au bar, le dos tourné à la piscine, on peut s'adonner à la rêverie en regardant les quatre affiches : un
orage au-dessus de Tucson, un parterre de lupins, des
oponces sauteurs dans les Santa Catalinas et le spectacle rare des grands saguaros sous la neige.

Derrière le bar, une femme s'affaire à vider des
caisses de bouteilles, à remplir le réfrigérateur, à noter
le plus et le moins des provisions. Le juke-box joue à
tue-tête. C'est le moment creux de l'après-midi où la
femme de ménage s'apprête à se transformer en barmaid.

Ses gestes sont lents. La fatigue commence. Dans une demi-heure, elle ira dénouer ses cheveux, mettre un peu de rouge sur ses joues, changer de blouse et de souliers. Vers neuf heures, son mari viendra la chercher et Kathy Kerouac prendra la relève. Dans l'auto, le plus jeune de ses garçons se sera endormi, les deux autres se tairont, le mari s'intéressera au montant total des pourboires.

Les gestes de la femme sont minutieux. Ses lèvres bougent continuellement quand elle compte les bouteilles et plus laborieusement quand elle inscrit le résultat.

La fille de la propriétaire vient d'entrer du côté de la piscine. Elle est en maillot de bain, nu-pieds et elle laisse des traces d'eau sur son passage. Elle salue la femme et tout naturellement son corps entre dans le mouvement rythmé de la musique. Puis elle se dirige vers le bar et regarde silencieusement la femme travailler. Elle allume un petit cigare. Se penche au-dessus du comptoir, s'étire à ce point le haut du corps qu'elle pourrait basculer de l'autre côté, retire un livre.

La fille est plongée dans sa lecture. Le juke-box est maintenant silencieux. Un cliquetis de bouteilles et de verres, des chiffres marmonnés en espagnol. Le bruit du climatiseur.

Un homme passe derrière la baie vitrée qui donne sur le corridor. Il s'arrête un instant, change sa serviette de main comme si elle était trop chargée, revient sur ses pas, entre dans le bar, commande un whisky et que l'on augmente le volume du téléviseur. La femme augmente le volume. L'homme allume une cigarette, fait pivoter son tabouret, regarde obstinément du côté de la piscine. La fille demande à la femme un crayon, souligne un passage, referme le livre, contourne le comptoir, remet le livre à sa place, baisse le volume. Kathy Kerouac entre, dit à la femme d'aller se changer, vérifie les additions. L'homme se retourne, son regard glisse sur la feuille de calcul.

Personnages

LAURE ANGSTELLE

Il est impossible de dire avec précision dans quelle ville ou à quelle croisée de chemins car on peut tout à la fois imaginer sa jeunesse au cœur du désert, à l'ombre des maisons en adobe de Myers Street, ou peut-être même penser qu'elle ait quitté à l'âge adulte une grande ville de l'Est afin d'explorer son désir, traversant le continent en quelques jours dans sa Dodge bleue, ou qu'elle se soit rapprochée du Sonora au fil des années après avoir étudié dans plusieurs universités, chacune ayant servi de point de repère au parcours inconscient qui l'avait menée vers ce grand nu à l'horizon qui tente.

Cela on peut l'imaginer ainsi que la voir marcher le long de l'enchantement qu'est le petit sentier qui monte vers les Catalinas. Elle doit avoir cinquante ans. Ses yeux bleus épient tout autour la vie qui comme à chaque crépuscule s'éternise dans le mauve. Elle tient un vieux bâton trouvé au fond d'un arroyo et qui l'accompagne dans chacune de ses marches au lever et à la tombée du jour.

On peut aussi penser que Laure Angstelle vit dans un temps qui suspend la réalité, qui parfois l'inverse dans le rêve ainsi que cela peut se produire avec des mots lorsqu'en en faisant usage on croit entrer dans l'inédit du monde et pouvoir là, la mémoire affranchie, donner au désir des formes jusqu'alors impensées, capables de nous soustraire à l'aveuglement.

On peut croire aussi que Laure Angstelle sait anticiper cet instant où l'âme *va craquer* devant la splendeur du mauve et où toute l'abstraction du monde s'engouffrera dans un mot. Femme studieuse, Laure Angstelle avait depuis longtemps familiarisé son corps et sa pensée à cet exercice qui consiste, très tôt le matin, à faire se rencontrer en quelques images rapides le cosmos, les êtres et le « bouillon gras » de la société. Mais avant que la pensée ne s'exerce à distinguer entre les paroles, les rires, le discours, le bouillon de culture, il lui fallait du silence, mettre du silence devant les êtres comme un écran car elle savait que la beauté était au prix du silence qui accordait toutes les musiques. Oui, accomplis, tourments ou passion, les désirs de Laure Angstelle s'étaient regroupés avec le temps en ce qu'il conviendrait de nommer quiétude.

Tous les jours, à la même heure, Laure Angstelle fume un petit cigare. Appuyée contre sa vieille Dodge, elle regarde le soleil découper la forme des saguaros et l'obscurité éteindre toutes les visions qui l'instant d'avant l'avaient amenée à penser que l'obscurité est un temps d'arrêt autour de l'humanité.

Elle doit avoir quarante ans. Certains soirs, on peut la voir marcher dans le vieux quartier de Tucson puis reprendre la voiture et se diriger vers le Bar Saguaro où l'attendent deux hommes qui lui parlent de poésie, auxquels elle parle d'images, d'acide et de colorant, de la texture du papier et de tous les problèmes que la lumière occasionne. C'est du blanc dont ils parlent, c'est de la lumière dont elle parle, et les voix ainsi se passionnent entrecroisées dans la fumée, l'éclairage et le bruit du climatiseur.

Peut-être a-t-elle trente ans. La sueur perle sur son visage. Elle est assise dans l'enceinte du Presidio. Elle porte une longue jupe rouge qui attire le regard ainsi que des bijoux tout autour de ses bras, de son cou, suspendus au lobe de l'oreille. Les cheveux, noirs, sont très courts. Elle écrit dans un grand cahier. Le cahier est relié et si ce n'était d'avoir surpris son geste et la blancheur des pages, on pourrait facilement le confondre avec un livre.

Peut-être vingt ans. Elle s'est fait surprendre par la pluie. Elle court vers l'auto. Le monde est une gigantesque vague qui creuse le lit des rivières, qui déborde dans les gorges assoiffées et qui fait que le corps se soumet, à bout de souffle, mouillé, sculpté dans les vêtements légers, la pointe des seins braquée sur l'horizon.

Maintenant treize ans, assise devant son pupitre recouvert de poussière, traçant de l'index des lettres et des profils sur le bois blond qui ressemble à un plancher de danse.

Tout cela on pouvait l'imaginer mais les questions demeuraient les mêmes quand il s'agissait de définir l'espace que *Le désert mauve* avait occupé dans la vie de Laure Angstelle. Était-ce un roman autobiographique ? Avait-elle été à l'origine de sa publication ou quelqu'un de son entourage, ayant lu le manuscrit, s'était-il chargé de le faire imprimer, avec ou sans son consentement ? Était-ce réellement le seul livre qu'elle ait écrit ? Car rien n'interdisait de penser que Laure

Angstelle fût un pseudonyme et que, sous son véritable nom, elle ait écrit et publié plusieurs livres. Si tel
était le cas, il fallait alors envisager la possibilité que
ce livre fût en quelque sorte un dénouement, une rupture camouflée dans l'anonymat. Peut-être avait-elle
écrit ce livre pour se libérer d'un passé, laissant au fil
des pages la peau creuse se renouveler à même le bau-
me des phrases, la part muée dans la mémoire. Peut-
être aussi l'avait-elle écrit par pure provocation, par
défi, se voulant sentir glisser, « flenchir », irrationnelle,
brisée ; peut-être avait-elle voulu écouler dans le temps,
comme un récit sans obstacle, une part d'elle-même,
la part indivise. Peut-être même n'avait-elle jamais
connu le désert et vivait-elle encore dans l'atmosphère
turbulente d'une grande ville, protégeant sa solitude
et son anonymat pour ne pas compromettre les livres
à venir ou tout simplement pour attendre le vif saisissant de la mort.

Mais tout cela qui pouvait être fantaisie n'invali-
dait pas la pensée que Laure Angstelle avait sans doute
été une femme fière, au corps agile, aux yeux pleins de
tourment, vulnérable devant la beauté et le silence,
affaissée quand la misère humaine retombait comme
un crachat sur les êtres.

Lorna Myher

Lorna Myher venait de terminer la réparation d'une courroie de transmission. Dans une demi-heure, elle aurait terminé sa journée. Il y avait maintenant deux mois qu'elle travaillait au garage Helljoy comme mécanicienne. Elle était sur le point d'allumer une cigarette lorsqu'elle vit arriver une auto, une Meteor, conduite par une femme. Le pompiste s'approcha mais la femme dit qu'il fallait regarder le moteur, peut-être la courroie du ventilateur ou l'alternateur.

Lorna Myher avait grandi dans la ville de Ajo à quelques kilomètres de la fonderie de cuivre. Elle était fille unique et vivait avec sa mère et sa grand-mère dans une maison-remorque que son père avait achetée quelque temps avant sa mort. Tous les jours, un grand nuage de fumée toxique arrêtait le temps au-dessus de la ville et Lorna Myher tournait la tête vers le sud en direction des monts Ajo. Là seulement pouvait-elle se sentir créature parmi les créatures, guettant le moindre signe de vie, suivant chaque indice susceptible de la diriger vers un terrier, une fourmilière, un nid. Elle aimait ces moments où retenant son souffle elle devenait écailles, perles, griffes, sentait son corps souple capable de tous les camouflages au milieu des épines et des baies sauvages.

Le pompiste pointa du doigt en direction de Lorna mais les deux femmes avaient déjà amorcé un mouvement pour se rapprocher. Lorna essuya ses mains sur son jean et, comme si au fond de son regard il était question de faire connaissance, elle tendit la main à Kathy Kerouac qui s'étonnant simultanément du geste et de la rugosité de la peau exerça sans le vouloir une légère pression de la paume. Les yeux de Lorna se tournèrent vers l'auto. Elle ouvrit le capot et ses mains se frayèrent un chemin parmi les pistons, les cylindres et les câbles huileux.

Lorna Myher marchait le long d'une palissade d'*ocotillos*, une fois de plus elle avait profité de la récréation pour se soustraire au regard vert de la jeune enseignante et au tohu-bohu de lettres et de chiffres qui heurtait quelque part en elle une volonté de silence, un besoin farouche des sens. Il avait plu la nuit précédente et on pouvait sentir une forte odeur de créosotiers. Elle se retourna et vit qu'une fille de sa classe courait vers elle. Lorna Myher attendit un moment puis quand la fille fut devant elle, à cette distance où les haleines peuvent se confondre, elle l'embrassa sur la bouche. La fille ferma les yeux. Le regard de Lorna glissa sur le vernis des feuilles vertes d'un créosotier, s'engouffra dans l'écarlate et le goût sucré des fleurs tout autour.

Lorna redressa son corps et dit qu'il faudrait laisser l'auto au garage pour la nuit. Devant l'hésitation de Kathy Kerouac, elle offrit de la raccompagner dans sa jeep. Durant le trajet, Kathy Kerouac parla du motel et de sa fille Mélanie qui allait bientôt avoir cinq ans.

À quinze ans, Lorna Myher en avait fini avec l'école. Elle passait maintenant la plupart de son temps au snack-bar de l'usine où travaillait sa mère. En face, il y avait un garage que des jeunes motards utilisaient pour la réparation de leurs engins. Après plusieurs mises en garde et un combat dont elle sortit victorieuse, Lorna put circuler librement parmi les outils et les moteurs. Peu à peu, la suie, la sueur, la poussière et les vulgarités refoulèrent dans sa mémoire le flanc de la montagne et le rouge orangé des *ocotillos* en fleurs.

Lorna stationna la jeep et laissa tourner le moteur. Kathy Kerouac offrit alors la perspective de prendre un verre au bord de la piscine. Deux ou trois choses à régler et elle la retrouverait aussitôt. Lorna regarda son jean et son t-shirt et demanda où elle pouvait se changer. Lorsque Kathy Kerouac vint la rejoindre à la piscine, Lorna portait un short. La blancheur de ses cuisses contrastait avec le teint foncé de son visage et de ses bras. Lorna observait une enfant qui jouait dans l'eau avec un grand dauphin, en plastique.

Lorna Myher avait vingt ans quand pour la première fois de sa vie elle vit des vagues. Ce n'était pas la mer, ce n'était pas la mer à Big Surf mais Lorna Myher éprouva une telle frénésie devant cet immense bassin aux mille tourbillons que vague après vague elle se laissa porter par le coussin jaune et noir qui, tapis magique, lui donnait l'impression de savoir nager, de tout pouvoir comme cette créature fabuleuse dont avait un jour parlé l'enseignante au regard vert. À partir de ce jour, Lorna Myher ne put se passer de l'eau. Matin et soir, elle allait à la piscine et on put bientôt la voir sillonner, papillon ou dauphin, l'eau chlorée.

Lorna accepta l'invitation de Kathy Kerouac. Pendant le repas, la fillette renversa un verre de lait. Elles parlèrent de mille merveilles, du mois de mai et de la mousse au sommet des montagnes qui donnait parfois l'impression que le désert pouvait être vaincu.

Cela, Lorna Myher se le rappelait comme si c'eût été hier. Elle regarda Kathy qui dormait profondément, un bras sous l'oreiller, l'autre allongé contre sa hanche. Lorna se leva sans faire de bruit, puis, en se rendant à la cuisine, elle ouvrit le téléviseur.

KATHY KEROUAC

La voix de Kathy Kerouac était à elle seule une présence, un enchaînement sonore de l'espace et du temps qui traversait comme un parfum les chambres, les corridors, l'appartement. Tout le motel était imprégné de sa voix grave et mélodique, une voix qui pouvait, lorsqu'on ne prêtait pas attention aux mots, faire penser à un motet. Chaque vibration des cordes vocales donnait l'impression d'un son originé de bouches multiples. Quelle que soit la situation, la voix s'adaptait et ce qui était urgent l'était, ce qui était comique le devenait et ce qui pouvait menacer prenait forme derrière le voile de la voix.

Kathy Kerouac connaissait le pouvoir de sa voix. C'était, disait-elle, sa « chose en or », une amulette qui la protégeait contre tous les désordres de l'esprit. Sa voix était un charme qui pouvait arrêter la violence et transformer la grossièreté en courtoisie, la bêtise en finesse. Aussi Kathy Kerouac avait-elle l'impression que rien n'était jamais *tout à fait* dangereux, le sentiment qu'aucune parole ne pouvait salir son univers.

Parce que sa voix avait un tel effet sur les êtres, Kathy Kerouac ne prêtait pas toujours attention à ce qu'elle disait. Car pour elle le mérite des mots était de produire cette résonance qui au fond de la gorge lui faisait accorder les plus beaux instruments, entendre les musiques les plus lointaines. Elle choisissait ses mots pour la longueur des voyelles, la mimique des lèvres qui pouvaient, si le souffle, si la langue cherchait, reproduire les plus folles complaintes et contrefaire, quand cela était, son inquiétude.

C'était à l'aide de sa voix, comme si elle pouvait lui servir d'écran, que Kathy Kerouac contemplait le langage obscur qui la liait à Lorna Myher. Contempler était le verbe car elle pouvait alors passer des heures entières, absorbée par le mouvement des voix actives et passives, leurs points de rencontre et de rupture, à essayer de comprendre ce qui dans le rythme pouvait produire un tel degré de tension, une telle alternance du désir et de l'émotion.

Quand Lorna venait tout près d'elle, Kathy Kerouac l'enveloppait de sa voix et Lorna séjournait silencieusement dans le contraste des mots, laissant aux petites apparitions qui cillaient dans son regard le soin de compléter les formes sonores qui la faisaient se languir de Kathy Kerouac. Lorsque Kathy parlait ainsi, le téléviseur sombrait au loin comme une forme de civilisation délavée.

Pour Kathy Kerouac penser en silence était une chose impensable, une forme bancale dans le rouage du corps et de l'âme aux prises avec la vie. Il lui fallait une résonance, une réponse, un écho aux sons qu'elle produisait. Aussi passait-elle une bonne partie de sa journée au téléphone. Tout était prétexte, une commande à donner, une réservation à vérifier, un contretemps qui l'obligeait à annuler sa pratique de tir. Penser dans le silence était pourtant une réalité à laquelle

elle était parfois contrainte. N'avait-elle pas à maintes reprises fui le son de sa propre voix et battu en retraite gardant un silence obtus lorsque Mélanie rentrait à l'aube ou quand il eût fallu parler plus longuement des hommes et du désert ? Elle le savait, le risque eût été trop grand d'une lamente ou d'un grand tapage dans sa voix qui l'en eût fait perdre le contrôle.

On disait de Kathy Kerouac qu'elle était une femme sérieuse, honnête et discrète, mais tout cela on le disait parce que la voix de Kathy Kerouac dissipait toute arrogance, toute colère comme un chant de sirènes. On disait que le père de l'enfant était un acteur ayant autrefois travaillé à Old Tucson. On disait qu'une femme «sans manières» habitait en permanence au Motel Mauve. On disait que Mélanie avait des manières sauvages. Tout cela on le disait mais Kathy Kerouac trouvait chaque fois manière de dire que sa propre mère avait connu la terre et que dans la chaleur elle avait œuvré, buisson, bruissement, les cris assourdis des enfants, tout au long des champs, dans la plaine, «sans manières, sans manières» parmi les ornières, les panics et la fougère folle qui ployait sous les tracteurs car le ravage était grand, ô grand ravage, disait Kathy Kerouac, les larmes aux yeux et la voix prête à toute allure à refaire le monde.

La voix de Kathy Kerouac était un espace à l'horizon. Elle pouvait crépiter, pluie torrentielle ou tempête de sable, s'allonger comme un écheveau d'acquiescements ou isoler une phrase investie dans le dédale de l'ennui.

Pourtant la voix pouvait *prendre peur*. Cela, Kathy Kerouac ne l'anticipait que trop quand les syllabes se mettaient soudain à sortir de sa bouche comme de petits fragments d'oubli qui lui donnaient l'impression de se contredire. C'était dans ces moments, quand les mots étaient tout à la fois vrais et faux, graves et légers, sur le bout de la langue et lointains dans la gorge, que l'espace refoulait dans sa bouche comme un coup porté durement.

Oui, Kathy Kerouac bien qu'elle eût l'orgueil de la voix savait repérer l'instant où sa propre voix pouvait se dissoudre dans le désordre et le chaos ou se mettre soudain à luire comme un corps nu de femme, une nuque tendue. Elle savait toujours là s'arrêter dans l'image et les mots.

Telle était l'épreuve de Kathy Kerouac qui donnait à tous l'impression d'être une femme sans expression.

Angela Parkins

Il y avait maintenant tout près de vingt ans qu'Angela Parkins exerçait son métier de géomètre. La sécheresse et le soleil avaient depuis longtemps buriné son visage. Ses yeux vifs habitués à toutes les perspectives étaient d'un noir capable d'atténuer les reflets trompeurs que la lumière blanche du désert déversait dans son œil calculateur. Son habitude de la précision en avait fait une femme déterminée, capable de représentation et ayant le sens du territoire, un grand territoire qui recouvrait plusieurs *états*.

Depuis quelques jours son équipe travaillait tout près de Death Valley Junction et elle avait décidé que ce soir elle irait à l'Opéra d'Amargosa, ce petit théâtre perdu au fond de l'aridité et des dunes imprenables qui, comme un fruit insolite découpé sur l'horizon, évoquait cet appétit de spectacle que les êtres développent quand la nostalgie accable l'esprit.

La journée s'étirait en tracés, volumes et superficies. La chaleur était insupportable. Le corps se déshydratait en quelques heures. Angela Parkins ne pensait pas à se protéger. Elle rédigeait soigneusement son rapport pendant que les hommes préparaient le retour à Death Valley Junction.

La salle est toute petite. Sur les murs, on a reproduit des loges, des balcons dorés remplis à craquer d'Espagnols en costumes du XVIe siècle. Au premier rang des femmes qui chuchotent, un mouchoir, un éventail à la main. Le rouge et le bleu des robes, poitrines toute chair, d'étranges coiffes, tout cela qui forme une civilisation quand on regarde au fond des yeux l'expression. N'était-ce pas l'expression du regard qui permettait de distinguer parmi les outils, les armes et les ornements, comment la mort pouvait être vaincue, comment les femmes, esclaves parmi les esclaves, pouvaient s'adonner dans leur forme arrondie à la vie ? N'était-ce pas dans le regard que l'on pouvait deviner l'usage de la parole et observer comme sur une carte topographique les pensées, leur profondeur, le nivellement, les petits détails qui permettent de mesurer la distance parcourue par l'esprit ?

Angela Parkins aimait le spectacle. Tous les spectacles, tout ce qui pouvait s'offrir comme un volume dans la pensée, faire tourner les dialogues en intrigues ou aboyer l'âme dans l'éternité. Elle aimait que les corps soient habités par des passions ou qu'ils puissent en exprimer les clichés, prendre des poses inégalées par aucun animal. Pour Angela Parkins, le corps était *stricto sensu* matière à sensation, chaos, atome, chair vive. Oui, elle aimait aussi les visages mais un visage est toujours si complexe et les traits peuvent en quelques secondes se transformer, si facilement induire en erreur comme de beaux masques, répandre la terreur, jeter l'âme dans le plus profond désarroi.

Elle aimait les sentiments extrêmes, les explosions de joie, de voix, les attendrissements soudains qui font léviter le corps, la parole touffue, abondante et crue car, pensait-elle, le corps doit être vorace et tout à la fois pouvoir s'envoler capricieux et ductile comme un fil de soie.

Le spectacle allait bientôt se terminer. La ballerine irait se changer, enfilerait son jean et ses bottes en peau de serpent. Les voix se croiseraient un instant à la sortie et Angela Parkins retrouverait sa chambre dans un motel perdu au fond de l'immensité.

La chambre serait banale, les murs tout beiges, la piscine déserte. Angela Parkins ouvrirait un livre récent et essayerait comme à chaque nuit d'oublier l'image de l'enfer, refoulant dans sa mémoire la première explosion, l'immense déchirure dans l'atmosphère tremblant, les flancs de l'animal sous ses cuisses, sa chute du cheval, le cheval au grand galop, l'herbe contre sa joue, un monarque qui bat des ailes sur une fleur d'acacia. Au loin, l'enfer.

Angela Parkins déposa le livre au pied du lit. Ses yeux fixèrent le mur. Qu'est-ce que la vérité ? *Alêthéia, alêthéia*. Elle était comme une butte-témoin échappée à l'érosion, spectatrice isolée, preuve. Angela Parkins s'endormit, le corps tout raide, figé comme une forme suspecte sous le drap.

Demain, il faudrait attendre le crépuscule avant de repartir vers l'Arizona. La route serait longue. Les hommes parleraient d'équipement, de nouveautés. Leurs paroles seraient vraisemblables. Il y aurait les yeux des lapins, de petites luisances sous les phares. Puis tous se tairaient et Angela prendrait le relais au volant. L'aube serait éclatante, indicible dans le mauve. Puis à nouveau, la blancheur ferait vaciller la réalité et

le sentiment cru de l'hyperréalité prendrait le dessus
sur les choses. À Tucson, le break s'arrêterait au premier motel sur la gauche.

L. Lomme long

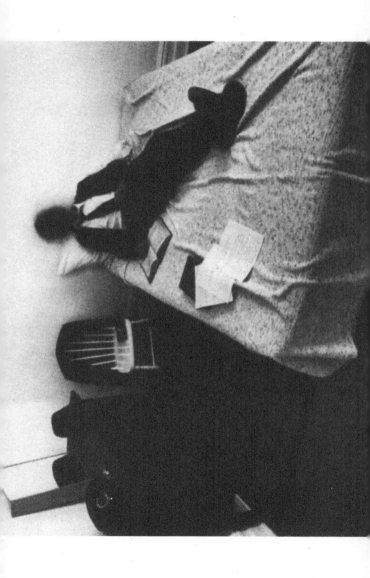

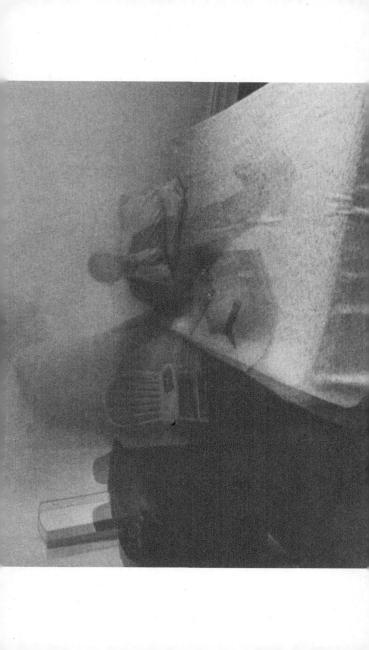

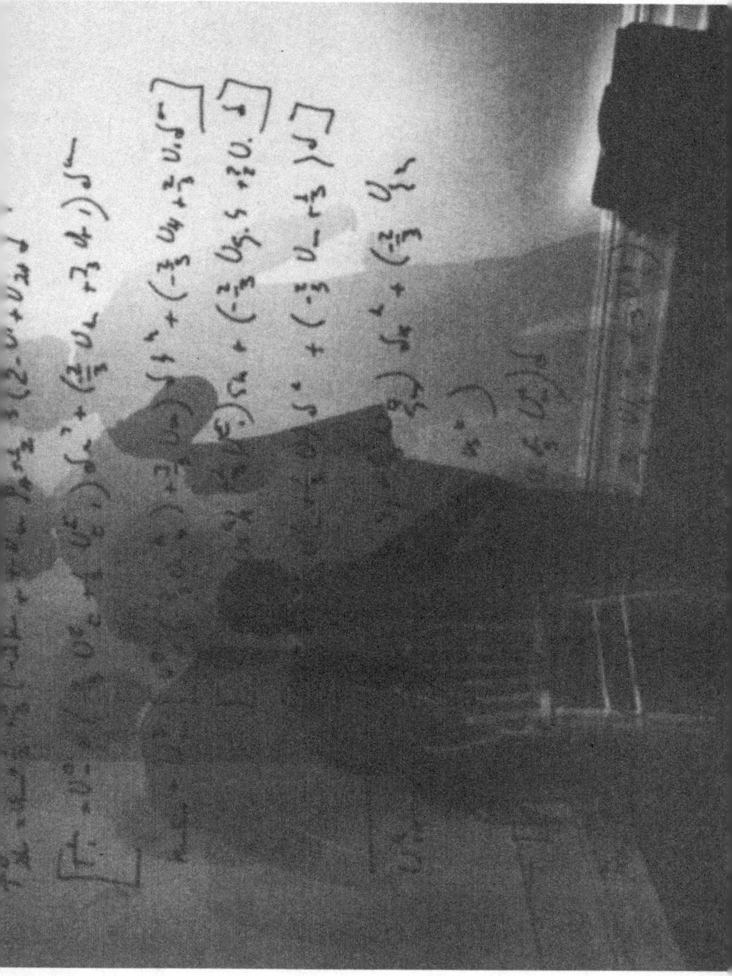

NOM L. Comme long NO

MÉLANIE

D'emblée le visage de Mélanie prend place dans l'histoire comme une figure soutenue, quelques traits indécidables de la solitude bien qu'à certains égards, quand le visage est attentif, on puisse s'interroger sur la composition même de l'air. Car vivre vite au présent assigne à certains traits leur emplacement : ride, cicatrice, au cœur du lisse, le présent s'approprie tout naturellement l'ensemble des pensées, ouvre et referme la peau, répartit le désir, l'espoir et la violence, marques circonstancielles qui arriment le visage à l'existence.

Le visage de Mélanie comme une image qui suit son cours entre la voix narratrice et le personnage, ce visage ouvre des abîmes de comparaisons. Comme tout visage, celui de Mélanie est un acte physique de la pensée. Il mime, simule, joue, tremble, effraie, charme, contraste, il retient ou rejette par chacun de ses pores le vrai, la feinte, l'image, la superstition de vivre, il acquiesce, témoigne, il nie jusqu'à ce que les muscles faciaux règlent la tension, ajustent les forces avides intérieures et la pression cumulée de la réalité. Lorsque le visage s'offre, ce sont les cheveux courts et le front dégagé, les sourcils fins, la parfaite symétrie qui donnent au désir sa configuration. Lorsqu'au contraire le visage s'obstine à vouloir plus, la bouche abrite une telle vélocité qu'on voit très distinctement les lèvres et le menton s'organiser pour l'offensive. Si les yeux interviennent, ils dessinent des ombres, des calculs, des trous comme de grandes négations, se suspendent au-dessus du vide ou encore se mettent à danser autour de quelques images hypersexuées. Mais le plus souvent les yeux, quand ils se mettent à l'écoute, enfilent l'un après l'autre les mille détails de la vitesse et de la lumière croisées.

Bien que jeune, c'est un visage habité, multiplié, non pas commun, mais portant la marque de ce qui remplit les sens abondamment et en renouvelle ainsi la théâtralité : le multiple de mourir, le multiple de passion. C'est un visage qui pourrait être qualifié de compétent, c'est-à-dire capable de compenser pour la peine l'inexpérience des traits par de subtiles mises en scène intérieures qui ont pour résultat de plisser le front, d'étirer la bouche, de soulever l'arcade sourcilière, de creuser légèrement la joue droite, tout cela afin de doser la vulnérabilité, la bonne mine et les foucades installées en Mélanie comme des contrastes.

Le visage est ressemblant, neutre et distant, capable d'assouplir la réalité. Rien de psychologique, seulement l'intensité, rush d'intensité, vitesse concentrée d'un vouloir dire sans manière. S'il fallait décrire ce visage, il faudrait cent fois recommencer les traits, la courbure du nez, les signes, les lèvres gercées qui donnent l'impression d'une grande soif et que la voix sans doute elle aussi craque dans l'air sec. Il faudrait souligner la longueur des cils, le duvet pâle sur les joues, progresser de manière à ce que le visage énonce à quelles conditions il choisit d'exister. Dans l'intervalle, la couleur panachée de l'été répété comme une seule saison sur le grain doré de la peau serait en pleine lumière, une constante. À l'ombre, le visage on n'aurait qu'à le dire absent ou consigné dans le silence avec une bouche hantée par le bruit de la civilisation.

Ainsi, bien que jeune, le visage de Mélanie ne déçoit pas. On peut le regarder en ne pensant à rien, on peut désirer discrètement qu'il s'anime le temps d'un dialogue, on peut vouloir s'en faire un masque et le porter quand le goût de vivre dépasse en nous la mesure et que le front, la mâchoire et les lèvres s'apprêtent à quelques attentats sur la réalité.

Autoportrait de Maude Laures

Tu es là, les deux bras tendus, les genoux fléchis, l'œil droit. La balle commence à monter. Tu ne la quittes pas des yeux, pourtant le bleu du ciel, le sommet des arbres, au fond du parc, le vert un instant flou, la lumière vive dans tes yeux. Tu frappes. La balle s'engouffre dans le filet, roule comme une petite tête. Ton adversaire esquisse un sourire. Tu sens la sueur sur ton cou, dans tes cheveux, le long de tes tempes. Tu passes ta langue sur tes lèvres, un goût salé. Tu voudrais être « *fast so fast* ». Tu te concentres. Tu lèves les bras. La balle est un oiseau. Tu es tendue comme un arc. Tu donnes un coup de reins. Ton corps est une oblique. Ton corps pivote. La balle traverse. Ta main glisse sur le cuir du manche. Tu penses au volant de l'auto. Tu réponds par une amortie. La balle s'écrase comme un animal foudroyé. Tu observes ton adversaire. Tu voudrais anticiper chacun de ses mouvements. Tu cherches à comprendre la raison d'être de ces courts chapitres qui donnent à l'homme long un caractère fictif. Tu t'avances vers le filet. Tu réussis ton smash. Tu penses au corps musclé de Lorna. Tu l'entends gueuler devant le téléviseur. Tu avales ta salive. Tu réponds facilement avec un lob. Tu gagnes ton service. Le soleil t'arrive dans les yeux. Tu aimerais partir au loin, te dissoudre dans la chaleur. La balle frôle ton épaule. Tu perds l'équilibre.

Tu changes le rythme. Tu l'obliges à jouer au fond du terrain. Tu la gardes à distance. Tu observes son jeu de pieds, le mouvement de son poignet, l'encolure de sa chemisette. Ses cheveux sont d'un roux flamboyant. Ses gestes gracieux. Elle doit avoir vingt-cinq ans, peut-être trente. Elle tend les bras. Sa poitrine se soulève. À chaque service, elle respire bruyamment comme si le coup allait porter, fatal. Ses gestes défensifs sont malgré tout risqués. Elle s'avance vers le filet. La partie est terminée. Vous souriez. Vous marchez le long du petit sentier vert jusqu'à la rue Joyce. Tu rentres chez toi. Tu te sers une bière. Tu étales sur ton bureau les chemises que tu as préparées pour chaque personnage. Maude Laures, dis-moi, que peut-il donc arriver en cet après-midi chaud et décousu de juillet ? Dis, que peut-il se tramer dans ton regard que tu n'as pas su comprendre quand le temps était aux premières lectures et que tu annotais ce livre insolite trouvé dans une librairie de livres usagés ? Dis-moi comment ce livre « innocent » est venu dans ta vie interrompre ta routine de fille studieuse, a dédoublé en toi le portrait car, tu le sais fort bien, Maude Laures enseignait depuis trois ans dans un collège de filles. Elle était aimée de ses élèves et la direction appréciait son enthousiasme à communiquer, son approche pédagogique. Elle ne parlait jamais de politique et les livres qu'elle mettait à l'étude ne pouvaient qu'inciter au plaisir de la lecture. On ne lui connaissait ni amant, ni mari, ni amoureuse. Elle s'entourait de beaux objets.

Lampes, tables, chaises étaient pour elle sculptures, marbre, de belles surfaces lisses et froides qui l'aidaient à penser. À Noël, elle partait vers le Sud. Après les vacances de Pâques, elle parlait de la Citadelle, des Anglais sur les Plaines, de la beauté du fleuve et toujours sa voix s'enflammait comme le feuillage en octobre. Quand septembre arrivait, ses cheveux étaient toujours très courts. Elle ne maquillait plus ses yeux depuis qu'elle portait des lentilles. Les jours de paye, elle achetait cinq ou six livres dont elle savait que la lecture allait la rassurer sur l'existence ou conforter quelque part au fond d'elle-même les aléas de ses pensées. « Aimez les livres, répétait-elle sans cesse à ses élèves, car vous ne savez par quel hasard, au tournant d'une phrase, votre vie s'en trouvera changée. »

Les soirs d'hiver, Maude Laures faisait de longues marches. Elle s'arrêtait parfois dans un petit café de la rue Bernard, parlait longuement avec la serveuse qui venait de Rivière-du-Loup. Quand la clientèle était trop nombreuse, elle s'assoyait à une table d'où elle pouvait regarder les gens passer dans le froid et observer les petits reliefs sur la devanture du cinéma Outremont.

Maude Laures aimait, bien qu'elle fût souvent entre les quatre murs de son appartement, le son cru qui accompagne la rêverie quand on s'enfonce dans la ville aux multiples outrages et dispositifs. Malgré son air distrait, rien ne lui échappait des signes et des feux qui activent l'enthousiasme ou qui, à l'opposé, refoulent toute perspective dans le grand rectangle de solitude qui sert d'écran aux poitrines urbaines.

Pour Maude Laures, la vie se résumait à trois choses : éviter toute confusion entre les hommes et la réalité, isoler les paradoxes, donner suite à ses pensées les plus impudentes. Ce n'était pourtant pas chose facile car toujours lui venait un besoin d'images et de couleurs qui la contraignait simultanément à la beauté simple de l'aube et à ce rire baroque qu'elle savait capable de tout lapider, évidence et certitude.

Et maintenant, dis-moi, Maude Laures, que peut-il donc arriver en cet après-midi chaud où tu t'apprêtes à changer de personnage, à te risquer dans le désert auprès de Laure et de Mélanie, à t'allonger, la nuit venue, sur le sol nu, les yeux aux aguets pendant que les taurides filent et que, dans la langue ancienne qui est la tienne, tu imagines encore des scènes ?

Scènes

I

Le temps recommence entre Kathy Kerouac et Méla-
nie. Les visages font un effort et on voit les lèvres et le
pli du regard obliquer à travers les mots. La chaleur
est grande, l'eau de la piscine aveuglante.

— C'est vague, il suffit d'un geste, d'une parole ou
encore que je te voie devant cette télévision.

— C'est vague ! Il y a pourtant des mots pour dire
ce que tu ressens.

— Tu regardes Lorna et tu ne vois rien autour.

— Mon regard est vaste.

— Vague. Tu ne me vois pas.

— Je vois ce que j'aime, ce qui est raison de vivre.
Tu es centrée au cœur de mon existence. Tu n'as pas
idée de ce qui m'habite. Crois-tu que ma pensée soit
libre de ton visage, de tous ces souvenirs qui s'installent
dans la mémoire au fil des années ?

– Tout pour éviter le présent, n'est-ce pas? Mais soit rassurée, je pars. Tu es à la fois trop présente et absente. Tu existes trop en moi parce que tu ne me parles jamais. Je suis obligée d'imaginer ta tendresse, d'inventer des dialogues dans lesquels tu me dis ton amour, ton estime, ton appréciation. Mais je suis lasse de toutes ces fantaisies. Je ne veux pas passer ma vie dans le désordre de l'émotion. Je veux l'horizon bien clair devant moi.

– Une fille ne va pas dans le désert se nourrir du soleil et de l'horizon. Une fille ne doit pas s'avancer jusque-là où l'œil est trompé.

– Mon regard sera vigilant. Je suis alerte dans le questionnement.

– Le soleil, la chaleur, la solitude auront raison de toi.

– La chaleur me vient de l'intérieur. Je sais être seule. Si seulement tu pouvais imaginer dans mes yeux la splendeur d'exister!

– Tu veux dire que ton ventre veut parler.

– Je dis que mes yeux parlent d'exister.

– Tes yeux sont si pleins d'arrogance et d'orgueil que forcément ils te tromperont. Tu ne sais donc pas que…

– Non, je ne sais rien. Je pars parce que tu ne m'apprends rien. Tu regardes cette télévision. Tu n'as d'attention que pour Lorna. Non, tu ne m'apprends rien.

– Tu sais, les yeux, oh! tu sauras bien assez tôt.

– Quoi, les yeux?

– Les yeux qui cherchent à devancer l'horizon. Les yeux impatients sont toujours déçus.

– Je serai vive et patiente.

– Il n'y a pas de fine manière avec eux. Il faut que les yeux pensent et quand ils pensent, il faut se soumettre. Les yeux font craquer les visages qu'ils pénètrent. Toi aussi tu te soumettras.

– Je n'ai pas peur de la mort.

– Mélanie, il ne faut pas penser à la mort. La mort est une chose quelque part inventée par les hommes pour oublier et se soustraire à la réalité.

– Ne sois pas ridicule. La mort est pour tous une rencontre.

– Je dis que les hommes ont inventé la mort parce qu'ils y pensent. Ils la cultivent tapageusement.

– Et toi, tu n'as jamais pensé à la mort ?

– Je suis devenue mortelle le jour où je t'ai donné naissance. La mort ne vient pas vers nous, c'est nous qui allons dans le temps *tout naturellement* vers la mort.

– Pourquoi me parles-tu ainsi maintenant ?

– Je t'ai toujours voulue capable et entière.

– Je le suis.

– Oui, parce que c'est ainsi que j'ai voulu que tu sois.

– Tu voudrais être tout, n'est-ce pas ? Tout pour moi, tout pour Lorna, tout pour les clients. Tu voudrais que la perfection commence avec toi. Tu voudrais passer l'éponge sur tout, faire semblant. Recommencer le monde et la loi.

– Je veux la paix, qu'il n'y ait point de massacre et d'oubli.

– *Tu n'es qu'une mère.*

– Tu crois qu'une fille peut ainsi dicter à sa mère des choses qui pourraient la rendre « facile » ! Une mère n'est jamais « facile ». Une mère fait toute la différence dans une vie.

– Une mère fait la différence si elle instruit sa fille. Une mère qui n'instruit pas sa fille mérite d'être oubliée

devant son téléviseur. Une mère ignare est une cala-
mité.

— Je t'ai instruite par mes gestes et mon courage.

— C'est avec Lorna que j'ai appris à nager, à connaître le désert. Toi, tu aurais voulu m'apprendre à pleurer. À te regarder, j'apprends la peur. On dirait que tu
as peur de tout. Mais qu'est-ce qu'une vie si on a peur
de tout ?

— Je crois que tu peux partir. Nous n'avons plus
rien à nous dire. Prends ce peigne d'argent. Il te por-
tera bonheur.

— Le bonheur ! C'est parce que tu cherches le bonheur que je t'en veux.

— Je cherche le contentement, le bien-être, le bien-
fait quotidien.

— L'aisance. Tu cherches la commodité, la facilité.

— Mélanie, tu devrais partir ou te taire car tu ne
sais plus ce que tu dis. Tu confonds violemment les
mots, tu te les appropries comme s'ils étaient des car-
rés de sucre que tu te mets sur la langue en attendant
que ça fasse effet. Pardonne-moi si je n'ai pu t'ins-
truire. J'ai pourtant cru l'avoir fait. Et cela malgré ton
mutisme, tes fugues répétées. J'ai cru que mon affec-
tion suffisait, que ma voix quelque part en toi attei-
gnait le nœud dur qui te tient lieu d'âme.

— Ce qui se noue dans le cœur se noue du silence
d'autrui. Tu sais, *ta voix*, ta belle voix ne m'a jamais
vraiment parlé. Ta voix s'est superposée à la médiocrité
qui dans ce motel écarte tout espoir. Je pars mais tu sais
que je reviendrai. Je reviendrai parce que je sais que tu
m'espéreras. Tu vois, nos yeux sont secs. C'est bon
qu'il en soit ainsi. Ne pleure jamais pour moi. Ne fais

jamais cela car alors tes larmes rejoindraient les mien-
nes et nous serions emportées, oui, je crois que nous
serions toutes deux emportées d'une seule vague.

II

Il a suffi de deux heures de route pour que le quoti-
dien devienne un petit point sombre dans la conscience.
Kathy Kerouac et Lorna Myher ont stationné la jeep.
Coupe verticale à l'horizon, leurs corps forment une
présence certaine dans le mauve.

– Presser le pas, ralentir. Il semble que nous
soyons ou trop lourdes ou légères, ou est-ce le désert
qui donne cette impression de déjouer le poids réel du
corps ?

– Auprès de toi, je garde l'équilibre. Tu es cette
eau de forte densité qui maintient le corps en surface
et qui l'empêche de sombrer bas dans le tourbillon.

– Est-ce que je mérite autant de faire-valoir et de célébration ? Je ne suis pourtant qu'une femme ordinaire.

– Et moi une grande dyke achevée de joie auprès
de toi. Tu vois, il suffit de nous éloigner de ce motel et
nous reprenons vie.

– Il suffit de laisser tranquille cette maudite télévision.

– Tu es...

– Ne me dis pas qui je suis, même si ce que je suis je ne peux le découvrir qu'avec toi.

– Parce que je te ressemble ou parce que nous sommes différentes ?

– Parce que tu es vive et que tu n'as peur de rien. Il faudrait pourtant *(malaise dans la voix)* que tu apprennes à lire.

– Tu ne peux donc te résigner à me voir telle que je suis. Je suis un corps. Un corps heureux dans l'eau. N'as-tu jamais songé que mon corps s'effriterait s'il venait à entrer dans la matière tordue des mots ? Si tu savais combien je préfère mille fois mes doigts agiles à toutes ces lignes fragiles et mille fois tordues que les hommes écrivent, que ta fille écrit.

– Mais tout le monde autour de nous sait lire et écrire.

– Tout le monde autour de nous ne fait pas, ne pense pas, ne mord pas l'oreille de son amour*e* comme nous. Personne autour de nous ne fait ce que nous faisons. Personne n'éprouve ce que nous éprouvons.

– Je suis une femme ordinaire et j'éprouve comme les autres.

– Les autres qui ? Pauvre Kathy, mon amoure. Pauvre moi, ton amoure. Qu'allons-nous devenir si tu ne m'aimes point comme je suis, si je te veux comme tu n'es point ? Combien de caresses, combien de fois les mains sur nos bouches, combien de fois l'ardeur du ventre pour que nous devenions avec exactitude ce que nous sommes ? Ou cela n'a-t-il rien à voir ?

– Mais lire est une chose nécessaire. Lire est une nourriture.

– Oui! « Qu'est-ce qu'on mange? Qu'est-ce qu'on mange? » C'est ce que répète ta fille. Et elle s'enfuit, ta fille. Moi, je dévore. Je prends. Je n'attends pas que les lignes tordues essoufflent tout mon corps et l'indisposent à ce point qu'il ne puisse tolérer les bonnes saveurs et les belles images. Ta fille, elle parle trop d'éternité.

– Ma fille est subtile. Elle comprend les choses.

– Et moi je suis grossière, je suppose! Dis alors ce que tu fais avec moi.

– Avec toi, je fais ce qui est essentiel. Je fais ma vie. J'invente ma réalité. Je cerne la certitude et tisse mon espoir.

– Tout ceci est bien abstrait. *(Silence.)* Est-ce que tu crois qu'on puisse aimer autour du corps? Qu'on puisse aimer sans odeur, sans saveur, sans que la langue n'aille chercher son sel sur la peau de l'aimée, sans le froissement des mains sur les cuisses, sans qu'il ne soit nécessaire de raffiner nos sens? Crois-tu que tu aurais pu m'aimer en faisant abstraction de mon corps, si je n'avais été qu'une image au fond de tes yeux, s'il t'avait fallu contourner mon corps pour m'élire?

– Oui, je crois que je t'aurais aimée même en n'ayant jamais trouvé ton corps. Oui, j'aurais pu t'aimer en contournant ton corps.

– Mais contournant mon corps, qui aurais-tu aimé?

– J'aurais aimé l'impossible en moi, jusqu'à en être meurtrie.

– Et tu l'aurais fait quand même?

– Quand même.

– Tu me déconcertes. Il m'est insoutenable de penser, même une seconde, que l'on puisse aimer sans que les corps ne viennent affranchir ou soutenir le désir.

– Qui parle de désir ? Je parle d'une émotion précise qui crée de la présence bien au-delà du corps réel.

– Des émotions, nous en avons plus qu'il n'en faut pour nous soustraire à la réalité. C'est le désir qui provoque toute rencontre, tout élan de vie.

– Je ne te désire pas. Je suis émue par toi. Je suis touchée à vif par tout ce qui en toi signifie. Cela est infiniment plus précieux que de te désirer. Je suis vitalement touchée par toi.

– Moi, je dis désir et vite corps à corps. Corps d'abondance, caresses, étreintes, excitation. Je veux des traces, des marques, le sang qui afflue dans nos veines. Il faut des preuves à l'amour. Des preuves charnelles sinon le corps se languit, se dissout dans la chose tordue des mots, le chaos de l'émotion.

– L'émotion est ce qui pacifie.

– Ainsi tu ne me désires pas. Mais alors que faisons-nous ensemble ? En quoi suis-je différente de ce qui te procure émotion ?

– Tu es unique.

– Non, et tu le sais bien. Personne n'est à ce point libre. Personne n'est à ce point seule au monde.

– Je présume alors qu'il n'y a pas d'explication et qu'il est futile de chercher une raison à l'amour que j'éprouve pour toi. Il est peut-être plus facile de choisir parmi la ribambelle de miroirs, de costumes et de rôles des mots plus simples, plus doux, moins crus, ordinaires.

– En amour, il ne faut pas être ordinaire. Cela m'offense de t'entendre dire que tu es une femme ordinaire.

– Tu veux dire que cela t'humilie d'aimer une femme ordinaire.

– Je ne pense pas que tu sois ordinaire. Mais oui, cela m'humilie de te l'entendre dire. J'ai passé toute mon enfance, mon adolescence à refuser de devenir une femme ordinaire. Nous étions pauvres mais cela n'était pas, à mes yeux, une excuse pour être confinée à l'ordinaire. Regarde un peu ta fille, elle non plus n'est pas ordinaire. Et tu peux être certaine que cela n'a rien à voir avec le fait de savoir lire ou non.

– Tu fais des phrases.

– Comment exister sans faire de phrases !

– Tu vois, tu es plus tordue que tu ne voudrais l'admettre.

– Je suis amoureuse. Je fais tout ce qu'il faut pour ne pas te perdre. Pour moi, cela va sans dire et sans drame.

– Pourtant la terreur est partout tout autour de nous. La glace, le *sparkle* du rire froid.

– Ce n'est pas chose que l'on peut empêcher. La terreur est. Nous n'échappons pas à ce nuage. Survoltées, révoltées ou résignées, nous sommes dans son sillage.

– Pouvons-nous contraindre le récit ?

– Le récit de nos vies, de la terreur ou de l'impossible ?

– Résumer un peu. Tout simplement. Sans violence, avec quelques points de repère.

– Nous n'avons d'autre repère que nous. Nous sommes entourées de signes qui invalident notre présence.

— Alors disons que j'aimerais que nous puissions résumer notre présence. Lorna Myher, grande dyke d'Ajo, plonge-moi dans le ravissement. Aventure-moi dans le désir. Fais tout ce qu'il faut, qu'il ne faut pas, ma confiance est absolue.

— Je ferai seulement ce qui en toi désire. C'est la seule présence que je puisse t'offrir.

III

L'épaule est bronzée, la peau lisse, la chair ferme.
L'éclairage du néon longe la poitrine, passe au-dessus
de l'épaule, expose un instant l'imago, puis remonte
vers le visage de Mélanie.

— La nuit est belle.
— La nuit est ce qui permet de soudains changements.
— La nuit est concrète.
— La nuit est oblique. D'un côté les êtres, de l'autre les bêtes. C'est pourquoi nous tremblons, la nuit venue, de ne point trouver notre lieu.
— Voici que nous nous adressons tout naturellement la parole et pourtant, Angela Parkins, je ne sais rien de vous.
— Je viens du désert.
— Que savez-vous du désert, du soleil et des hommes ? Ma mère dit que...

– Le désert est un espace. Un jour des hommes y sont venus et ils ont affirmé que cet espace était enfin conquis. Ils ont dit souffrir de leur conquête. Ils ont souffert car le désert ne permet aucune erreur. Mais les hommes ont confondu l'erreur et la souffrance. Ils ont conclu que leur souffrance pouvait corriger l'erreur de la nature, la nature même de l'erreur. Ils se sont ainsi abouchés à la mort.

– C'est une belle nuit.

– La nuit est toujours belle car elle nous oblige à ressentir avec notre peau et les yeux de l'intérieur. La nuit, on ne peut se fier qu'à soi.

– La nuit est belle en toute solitude mais votre présence me rend cette nuit encore plus vraie.

– La nuit est insolite.

– C'est parce que le corps change de rythme.

– La nuit, il faut surtout attendre que le corps change sa trajectoire dans l'univers. Qu'il se meuve de manière à ce que tous nos sens puissent transiter librement. Capter le grand vide. Quel âge avez-vous?

– J'espère ne jamais devenir comme les autres.

– Comment savez-vous que vous ne l'êtes point devenue?

– Je sais.

– J'ai soif. Il y a longtemps que vous avez fait tatouer ce papillon sur votre épaule?

– Un mois. Cela me donne de la force pour affronter la réalité. Cela me donne des ailes. Je suis Sagittaire. Cela me donne l'impression que quelqu'un a posé sa main sur mon épaule, m'a regardée, m'a instruite.

– Vous a instruite de quoi? Vous voulez vraiment qu'on vous instruise de la vie?

– Vous avez sans doute désiré cela un jour.

– J'ai fait mon chemin. Je ne dois rien à personne.

– Croyez-vous que c'est là manière de trouver la joie ?

– J'ai soif. Je passe des heures et des heures à repousser la soif. À attendre le coucher du soleil. Je passe ma vie à regarder en détail l'horizon. Je n'ai jamais songé au bonheur. Je fonce. Je brame.

– Vous connaissez cet animal ?

– Quel animal ?

– Le cerf. On dit qu'il est souvent comparé à l'arbre de vie et qu'il symbolise les renaissances. Chez les Pueblos, il représente la rénovation cyclique.

– Mélanie, qu'est-ce que vous me racontez là ?

– Ce que j'ai lu.

– Approchez-vous. Laissez-moi regarder attentivement ce papillon. Le thorax est celui d'un grand sphinx.

– Et alors ?

– *Rien.* Pourquoi avez-vous dit que la nuit le corps change de rythme ?

– Parce que c'est vrai. Croyez-vous que j'aurais osé vous suivre et vous adresser la parole au grand jour ?

– Le jour, je suis loin, au grand loin dans l'immensité. Le jour, je n'ai d'attention que pour la croûte terrestre.

– Vous ne voulez donc point que l'on vous aime ?

– Je ne suis pas aimable. Ma soif est trop grande. Mélanie, vous êtes bien jeune. Votre mère s'inquiète sans doute déjà de votre absence.

– Ma mère me connaît. Elle sait que nuit et jour j'éprouve le besoin de filer. D'aller toujours un peu plus loin devant moi pour désenclaver la réalité.

– Je crois que nous nous ressemblons.

– Sans miroir, on ne saurait le dire.

– Je crois que nos yeux savent mieux reconnaître lorsqu'il n'y a pas de reflets.

– Voilà, je suis près de vous. Me reconnaissez-vous ?

– Oui, je vous reconnais. Il est vrai que vous êtes sans âge. Vous avez toujours existé. Ne croyez surtout pas que j'invente. Je discerne parmi les signes et les indices ce qui en vous est fait pour durer. Vous n'avez pas à craindre le temps. Seule la vitesse vous abîmera.

– Ne dites pas cela. J'aime vivre vite.

– C'est bien en quoi je vous reconnais.

– La pluie.

– Restez encore un instant. La pluie ne peut qu'adoucir nos lèvres et rendre la nuit palpable.

– La pluie sur vos lèvres est fine.

– « Nous implorons de vous la pluie, le don, l'immortalité [*]. »

_____

[*] Veda, 88.

IV

On imagine la scène en écartant le rideau entre l'auteure et la traductrice. On abolit la distance en imaginant les deux femmes assises dans un café. L'une fume et l'autre aussi. Toutes deux aiment composer avec le silence mais chacune ici cherche à comprendre comment la mort transite entre la fiction et la réalité. La langue parlée est celle de l'auteure.

– J'ai craint un instant que vous ne veniez pas au rendez-vous.

– Je suis là. Soyez tranquille, je prends *la peine* d'être là.

– Je n'ai aucun droit. Vous m'êtes antérieure.

– Que voulez-vous de moi ?

– Entendre ce que je puis prendre à mon compte. Tout ce que vous me direz sera...

– Utile ?

– Nécessaire. Je vis avec ce livre depuis deux ans. Ce n'est que tout récemment que j'ai conçu le projet de le traduire.

– De quoi voulez-vous que nous parlions ?

– D'une seule chose : de la mort d'Angela Parkins. J'aimerais vous parler exactement comme j'imagine qu'Angela Parkins le ferait si elle pouvait sortir de son personnage, si elle en était la présence ultime.

– Je vous écoute.

– *Pourquoi m'as-tu mise à mort ?*

– *Tu vas vite, Angela, tu vas trop directement au cœur de l'essentiel. Ne préfères-tu pas que nous parlions d'abord de toi ou de moi, quelque part que nous retrouvions les paysages familiers de l'Arizona ?* (Silence.) *Soit, si tu le veux, nous pouvons dès maintenant parler de ta mort. Mais avant, jure-moi que tu n'as rien vu venir. Jure-le-moi.*

– *Vu venir quoi ? L'amour, la mort ? Vu venir qui ? Mélanie ou l'assassin ?*

– *Vu venir la réprobation.*

– *Quoi ! Tu m'aurais punie de ce que je suis.*

– *Je ne parle pas de toi. Je parle de tout autour de toi. L'œil. L'intolérance. La folie. La violence.*

– *Alors je n'ai rien vu venir. Certes, je me suis vue perdue, éperdue, farouche et minotaure, ivre et arrogante, joyeuse et cavalière, nostalgique et amoureuse mais je n'ai pas vu venir la folie de cet homme.*

– *Tu le connaissais pourtant.*

– *Je le connaissais de réputation. C'était un inventeur, un grand savant, mais comment aurais-je pu penser que cet homme portait en lui une telle haine ?*

– *Tu n'as rien remarqué dans son allure, dans son regard ?*

– *Il avait l'air normal. Il avait l'air d'un client normal. À vrai dire, je ne l'ai pas remarqué. Tout mon* être était dans le rythme qui me rapprochait de Mélanie.

— *Alors, je vais te dire. Je vais tenter de te dire pourquoi tu es morte aussi soudainement, absurdement. Tu es morte parce que tu as oublié de regarder autour de toi. Tu t'es trop vite affranchie et, parce que tu t'es crue libre, tu n'as plus voulu regarder autour de toi. Tu as oublié la réalité.*

— *Tu aurais pu m'aider, me faire signe.*

— *Il est vrai que je t'ai crue à l'écart du danger et des aboiements. Je t'ai imaginée passionnée et capable en cela d'éloigner le mauvais sort. Je t'ai crue plus forte que la réalité.*

— *Mais imaginant la scène, tu aurais pu en changer le cours. Tu aurais pu faire ricocher la balle ou me blesser légèrement.*

— *Non. C'était toi ou lui. Car si cet homme t'avait seulement blessée, tu te serais retournée contre lui avec une telle fureur que c'est toi qui l'aurais mis à mort. De toute manière, ta vie aurait été gâchée. Légitime défense ou non. Cet homme, ne l'oublie pas, avait bonne réputation.*

— *Tu oses me dire que pour me protéger contre cet homme, ce fou, tu as préféré m'éliminer.*

— *Je ne t'ai point tuée. Cet homme t'a tuée.*

— *Mais cet homme n'existe pas. Tu n'étais pas obligée de faire exister cet homme.*

— *Cet homme existe. On pourrait le comparer à un fil de fer invisible qui tranche entre la réalité et la fiction. En t'approchant de Mélanie, tu as voulu franchir le seuil.*

— *Je te tiens responsable de ses actes. De ma mort.*

– *Je ne suis pas responsable de la réalité.*

– La réalité est ce que nous inventons.

– *Ne sois pas cruelle envers moi. Toi qui connais la solitude, les extases et les tourments. Toi et moi n'avons jamais pensé à nous protéger. En cela, nous avons fait longue route mais la réalité nous rattrape tôt ou tard.*

– Je peux vous reprocher ce qui existe dans votre livre.

– De quel droit ?

– De vous lire me donne tous les droits.

– Mais traductrice, vous n'en avez aucun. Vous avez choisi la tâche difficile de lire à rebours dans votre langue ce qui dans la mienne coule de source.

– Mais lorsque je vous lis, je vous lis dans votre langue.

– Comment pouvez-vous me comprendre si vous me lisez dans une langue et transposez simultanément dans une autre ce qui ne peut adéquatement trouver place en elle ? Comment croire un instant que les paysages qui sont en vous n'effaceront pas les miens ?

– Parce que les paysages vrais assouplissent en nous la langue, débordent le cadre de nos pensées. Se déposent en nous.

– Je me souviens un jour d'avoir acheté un livre de géologie dans lequel j'ai trouvé une lettre. C'était une lettre d'amour écrite par une femme et adressée à une autre femme. J'utilisais la lettre comme signet. Je la lisais avant de commencer ma lecture et après l'avoir terminée. Cette lettre était pour moi un paysage, une énigme dans laquelle je m'enfonçais à chaque lecture. J'aurais aimé connaître cette femme, j'imaginais le visage de celle à qui la lettre était destinée. C'est à cette période que j'ai commencé à écrire le livre que vous voulez traduire. Oui, vous avez raison, il y a des paysages vrais qui nous détachent du bord et qui nous font entrer en scène.

— Je crois qu'il y a toujours une première fois, « une première fois où il faut convenir que les mots peuvent réduire la réalité jusqu'en sa plus petite unité : l'évidence ». Vous vous souvenez de ces mots ?

— Non, mais je crois que celui ou celle qui a dit cela avait raison. Je suis lasse. Avez-vous autre chose à me demander ?

— Je voulais surtout vous entendre parler de la mort. Mais quoi qu'il arrive nous sommes seules, n'est-ce pas ?

— Tenez-vous-en à la beauté, n'ayez peur de rien. Amortissez en vous les bruits de la civilisation. Sachez soutenir l'insoutenable : le cru de toute chose.

DIMENSIONS

LE DÉSERT

Avant tout, soutenir le regard. Vide, horizon ou lumière, c'est le mot *anatomie* qui résume ici l'apparence des choses comme une intuition prolongée de la présence de l'humain, capable parmi les formes de soutenir toutes les comparaisons. On dirait ralenti de l'énergie là même où c'est sans limite, instantanéité parfaite de la subjectivité. Affronter la durée. L'immobilité comme une saisie de la raison dans l'espace nu. L'irradiation des corps, le moment enfin venu de durer.

Depuis que je relis ce livre, je suis ancrée au point zéro, envisageant mille stratégies et points de vue qui ont tôt fait de se dissiper, abstraction, abstraction, le regard fond. Pourtant le désert comme un commentaire arraché à la réalité, une excroissance de l'espace capable de dérouter tous les silences, d'éponger la beauté, d'y engloutir la raison, le désert progresse.

Faut-il contrefaire ou résister à ce que Laure Angstelle a voulu du désert exposer comme un avertissement, une circonstance engageante ? Je suis liée par chacune de ses propositions et pourtant je dois du désert extraire tous les scolies, le moindre signe de vie, la lumière hardiment dans le regard, cela pour mon propre entendement.

Si je laisse libre cours à mes pensées, me sera-t-il possible d'imaginer le désert au loin comme une coupe transversale de la fragilité et de l'endurance, de parfaire cette coupe jusqu'à ce que des profils en sortent, évoluent dans la narration, apprivoisés comme une chaleur, une intensité ponctuée de frayeurs et d'extases ?

Non, je ne suis pas libre d'oublier *Le désert mauve* quand bien même il en irait de mon propre équilibre. Je suis au milieu d'une partition où je dois tout à la fois m'engager sans parure et répondre des images avancées par Laure Angstelle. Pourtant, au moment où j'écris ces mots, c'est la partie « grappe de fleurs » qui se déverse torrentielle dans mes pensées. Ce sont des lacs salés tout en reflet qui surgissent, surfaces givrées de la beauté.

Oui, me voici au cœur de l'émerveillement et de la déroute, parmi les minéraux et les bêtes fanatiques, entrée dans le paysage aride et solaire qui s'étend, ébauche discrète comme un rire plein d'usages. Tout est en moi disposé à la solitude qui polarise la civilisation et le réel. Car ce qui tamise ici le regard veille à restreindre le bluff, le spectacle. Ici point de vertige. Tout est séjour comme si le corps s'apprêtait à durer éternellement, scorie, sel, ossature, sans autre tragédie que la soif et l'air tremblant qui corrige la géométrie des grands saguaros, leurs petits bras comme des bornes routières au loin. Ici dans le mauve, j'oublie. J'oublie la littérature et la civilisation. J'oublie les sourires de la Renaissance et l'ambiguïté du mot *passion*, la lourdeur des membres, les têtes renversées au regard extasié, la douleur et les inclinaisons puissantes qui remembrent les émotions. J'oublie le danger. La tournure des événements. Le danger qu'il y a à vouloir tromper la réalité. Je donne entièrement du corps dans l'espace ne sachant que trop que cela ne peut durer car je ne suis pas libre d'oublier Mélanie, *ses manières de faire,* le mouvement de ses pensées, la vitesse qui la grise, qui lui ouvre un passage sur tout ce qu'il est permis d'imaginer du désespoir, de la violence, de l'anonymat et de la couleur comme un climat probable dans la végétation.

. Qu'est-ce donc que le désert ? Pourrais-je m'obstiner longtemps à vouloir le décrire, à le désirer tantôt fureur de vivre, tantôt extinction uniforme de l'espoir ou belle quiétude ?

Effacer les traces de l'humain, fasciner par ces mêmes traces, la dérision, le calcul approximatif de l'espérance de vie d'une canette, d'une carrosserie à moitié ensablée, d'un panneau de signalisation à la croisée de deux sentiers. De la disparition, traces, traces entassées. Le calcul exact des langages aboutis dans l'espace comme une explosion.

Terre, poussière, un paysage sans fenêtre, sans abri. Terre observée du silence, beauté antérieure, le désert est indescriptible.

L'AUBE

L'aube est ce qui commence, distorsion de la nuit, étrange coloration du sentiment, une version consignée de la lumière. On dit lueur, lueur d'espoir et quand cela effleure la pensée, c'est que les yeux sont fin prêts aux petites apparitions qui font renaître le quotidien. Chaque matin, l'aube blanchit le monde de tous les bruits violacés.

L'aube est discrète. Elle pourvoit tout naturellement aux profils des choses, découpe pour nous la réalité, prépare le spectacle pendant que dans nos yeux les fondus enchaînés se succèdent jusqu'au lever du soleil. L'aube expose. L'aube matière colorante qui assigne au recommencement. Aube, chaleur latente.

« Oui, j'ai vu l'aube. Souvent. » L'aube de la cérémonie de l'encens. L'aube l'été, l'aube l'hiver. L'aube des jours d'examen. L'aube des décalages horaires quand la pensée hallucine, que la mémoire se coagule comme une substance étrangère au corps et que les yeux se dessillent lentement sur des villes tout en architecture dans le matin violenté, baroque. Et aussi cette aube qui vient après que la nuit s'est embrasée d'un trop-plein d'énergie et que soudain la vie s'est mise à ressembler à des musiques lentes qui longent le corps tout entier et l'emportent.

Mais voit-on vraiment l'aube quand on laisse à la nuit le soin de s'avancer dans nos vies à ce point que la lueur du jour s'effrite dans nos yeux comme un lendemain frileux ? Peut-on dire qu'on a vu l'aube lorsque c'est déjà matin et que dans le taxi blafard qui nous ramène à la maison, l'œil capte la longue forme colorée d'un travesti, le regard fou d'un *junkie*, des mains gercées, un pantalon taché d'urine ? Voit-on l'aube quand il n'y a plus de contexte et que nos sens broient du vide appelant le sommeil, d'autres artifices pour enrober le corps ?

L'aube attire, cela est certain, l'aube fascine. Elle est au bout de la nuit, au bout de l'âme une certitude tranquille, un apaisement des yeux épris de changements et d'utopies. L'aube se mérite.

Était-ce cela, vouloir l'aube, que Mélanie avait intuitionné quand dans le Red Arrow Motel le goût de l'aube s'était violemment fait sentir en elle, goût radical comme un projet de perdition ou une volonté de disponibilité totale à tous les dérapages de l'esprit ? Besoin de l'aube, désir de défier la nuit, construisant au fil des heures des arguments, des choses émaillées tantôt lisses tantôt kaléidoscopiques donnant sur des jardins multiples ou pouvant sans avertissement conduire à l'euphorie. Vouloir l'aube, c'était se frayer un chemin parmi les intuitions furtives qui ne s'ouvrent qu'à la nuit, c'était espérer en connaître le secret dont le sens échappé à la lumière du jour ne pouvait qu'en ranimer l'attrait. Ou peut-être Mélanie avait-elle pensé qu'un peu de persévérance lui donnerait l'énergie de comprendre comment le temps peut, la nuit, se disloquer au fond des êtres et faire éclater leur histoire.

Tout ceci, je le note en me fiant à mon instinct car je ne sais vraiment comment distinguer entre « le goût de l'aube » de Mélanie et la volonté d'en finir de Laure Angstelle. N'y a-t-il pas dans ce qui affirme que « l'aube est un principe qui exacerbe l'énergie » une mise en garde, un présage de violence, un *terme* projeté ?

Je ne peux souscrire à « la fureur de l'aube ». À mes yeux, l'aube se détache comme une image sur un fond d'humilité. Un grand calme, certitude tranquille. Oui, quiétude. Un chant composé de monosyllabes parfaits et ronds qui dans la bouche font comme une horlogerie, rondeau, rose, une giration de la couleur, qui sont dans la bouche girasols, cailloux, pierres précieuses, un écoulement de la ferveur dans le temps à l'heure tranquille où la rosée se dépose toute en odeur sur le feuillage jade.

L'aube attire. On peut la qualifier d'« innocente » ou pleurer en rattrapant l'affirmation ; à l'aube, on peut facilement avoir l'intention de disparaître, de glisser son corps dans l'envers de la lumière, en douceur.

La lumière

Faut-il à nouveau soutenir le regard, orgueilleusement prétendre qu'on le peut ou imaginer la lumière comme une vague encouragée de la chaleur sur la peau, une intensité qui rend les corps translucides, capable de filtrer les poings froids et fermés que nous levons vers le ciel ? Car en pleine lumière, notre corps tout entier se dresse, aura de l'être ou animal fabuleux, doué de splendeur et d'ingéniosité.

Ainsi dans le désert la lumière travaille, dématérialisant la réalité, laissant notre regard captif de ce qui fut, hanté par « l'aspect final de la matière ». La lumière travaille sans prendre de précaution et c'est pourquoi nous cherchons quand elle dissout le corps un centre de gravité qui n'est plus. Convenir alors que même en plein désert le vertige peut, menaçant notre verticalité, nous obliger à corriger notre équilibre ou à nous soumettre sur le sol platiné de reflets à une fièvre erratique.

La lumière est traître et tout à la fois crue. On peut en observer le cheminement sur les peaux mais aussi perdre le sens de la réalité quand elle traverse la conscience, brutale, sans rémission, éloignant les points de repère et tout à la fois capable de les figer dans l'éternité. La lumière brise le regard, renvoie le regard, le remercie. Personne n'échappe au remerciement.

Dans le désert, la lumière meurtrit la réalité, déchire en tous sens le tissu fin des couleurs, supprime la forme. Nous n'avons pas de protection contre la lumière car c'est toujours en plein émerveillement que la lumière assaille et soustrait à notre regard le rapport infiniment précieux que nous avons à la réalité. Ainsi, au moment même où nous nous croyons en pleine possession du réel, voici qu'il éclate sous nos yeux, retombe sur nos épaules, joug de jade.

La lumière est crue. Comment pourrais-je déserter Mélanie ? Comment entrer dans l'angle de son regard et m'éviter la lumière ? Comment oublier l'instant ? Car c'est bien là l'histoire de ce livre. L'instant porté par un seul symbole : la lumière. La lumière écrasant toute perspective. La lumière tissant l'enjeu. Aucun livre ne peut s'écrire sans enjeu. Enjeu de vie, enjeu de mort, je ne sais encore. Mais aucun livre ne s'écrit sans enjeu, brutal et immédiat.

Tout ceci je l'écris en pensant le personnage et l'auteure songeant leur existence comme une chose attirante dans la vie, une souplesse du corps, un rythme dans la chair, un carnaval multipliant les aubes, les soies et les os dans un costume que la lumière embrouille.

C'est ainsi ! Et aussi cette image imprévue de la lumière : il·y a la fille et la mère, il y a deux chevelures, dans l'une un petit peigne argenté, son chatoiement puis à la réflexion, les angles miroités se courbent, arc-en-ciel, allant de la mère à la fille, fil de soie, lien ancien qui ravive la souplesse des cheveux, la force du cheveu. Précarité de l'image. Vitesse.

« Lumière rapide. » Là où je suis, la lumière penche la réalité du côté froid de l'hiver. La lumière est un intervalle court qui garde les démons à distance. J'apprivoise à distance. Je suis à côté. Je profite de l'incertitude, de l'ambiguïté à laquelle je sais ne pas pouvoir échapper : ma froide sensibilité contre la sensibilité excessive de Mélanie/Laure. Affrontement, validation. Question de *traitement*. Erreur probable, « transcription partielle de la lumière au fond du cerveau ». Le regard fond. La lumière persiste, aveuglante, balaie toute intimité, recommence à frôler dangereusement le temps, les tempes.

« J'appuyais sur mes pensées pour qu'elles penchent la réalité du côté de la lumière. »

La réalité

La réalité est ce que nous retrouvons par un incalculable retour des choses imagées, comme un sens familier disposé bien distinctement dans nos vies. Mais à tout cela il y a certainement, pensons-nous, un autre sens, une autre version puisque nous en rêvons comme d'une musique d'accompagnement, une voix centrée capable de nous livrer un passage, une petite ouverture. Une voix qui puisse, à égale distance de l'origine et de la mort, activer les hypothèses, adapter la parure, ajuster les plis, l'ornement, l'anecdote qui en découle comme un ouvrage, régler le mouvement alternatif de la fiction et du vrai.

La réalité *ça compte vraiment*, aussi nous adonnons-nous « petit feu de passion qui prétexte » au plus pressant de la biographie et, est-ce qu'on se trompe, on dicte à la voix des syllabes en trop qui nous font perdre le sens, qui défont l'ouvrage commencé de la voix. Mais on prend le risque, on plonge *tout naturellement* dans la réalité comme s'il s'agissait d'une catégorie valable, d'un paysage adéquat.

En pleine réalité, on la constate sans prétention toute en odeurs et nourriture ; un peu de poisson, la viande, volaille, une gousse d'ail, tout cela étalé parmi les couteaux sur la table de cuisine. Fraises, framboises dispersées, petits motifs dans le coloris du tablier. Les vendredis d'émotion, boisson fraîche, bouquet de fleurs dans un grand vase. La réalité est ponctuelle, toute en actualité, calendrier, belles photos, décembre un chien, janvier une chèvre, mai un papillon. Parfois à l'année longue, des filles nues écartées entre dimanche et la fin du mois. La réalité moule le corps, serre autour du cou, à la ceinture, taille dans le blanc, le bleu, le rose et le noir de belles formes; vieille coutume le costume. La réalité défile linéaire, longe les destins, accouple les mâles et les femelles dans de grands lits métaphoriques. La réalité file son chemin, énumère des noms de villes, des familles au complet, dénombre les morts, décline les beaux jours, la saison, les incidents. Percute. Recommence, encore faim, encore soif, encore un matin gris grégaire. Sans prétention, la réalité se promène Geiger au poing. Ça compte la réalité !

« Un jour je sortirai de la réalité », trouverai un filon, une *veine*, la petite ouverture dans laquelle il me faudra *obligatoirement ralentir*, réduire l'intensité, la vitesse de l'image. Tout refaire, corps, poids et volume, longueur de l'hiver, nature et représentation, carcasse de l'esprit.

D'ici là, je dois donner un sens à tout cela par quoi j'existe. *Le désert mauve* est un accident. Rien de tragique mais comme toute chose qui surprend, qui concourt à modifier le décor familier, l'habitude froide, ce livre m'assigne d'autres tâches. Par exemple, *isoler la réalité*, oui, l'insonoriser comme une pièce dans laquelle je pourrais m'adonner aux plus concrètes aventures de l'esprit en compagnie de Laure Angstelle et de ses personnages. Aucun bruit familier ne viendrait tromper ma perception. Certes les objets seraient les mêmes : la bibliothèque, une grande affiche du Sonora en fleurs, mes trois cactus, le lit, le téléviseur, le cendrier, la fenêtre givrée, mais rien de tout cela ne pourrait me distraire au point d'éveiller en moi quelque souvenir. La réalité serait condensée au point maximum. Je pourrais la sentir sur ma peau, suivre parfaitement la conversation entre Mélanie et sa mère, entendre tout ce que dit l'annonceur à la télévision. La réalité serait tout à fait palpable, concrète, dense. Les couleurs seraient précises, les mots utiles, univoques. J'observerais Lorna, sa démarche, ses bras musclés, un sourire, je crois. Enhardie par la présence des femmes, j'irais même jusqu'à raconter un peu de ce qui se passe dans ma vie, comment je prépare mes cours, la beauté de l'automne, les après-midi blancs de l'été, le tennis, mes partenaires, mes adversaires, les balles perdues. Ma fébrilité serait grande.

Or, nous qui aimerions isoler la réalité de la fiction, nous qui aimerions que ça compte vraiment, nous voici, par un incalculable retour des choses imagées, à nouveau parmi les bruits familiers, à égale distance du hasard et de la finalité.

LA BEAUTÉ

Un fléchissement, une chute de tonalité, un bris dans le rythme, on peut penser que la beauté s'apparente à des signes esquissés admirablement pour nous surprendre. La beauté inévitablement courbe le souffle, harmonise le vide, *soudain* les parfums qui se succèdent, la pupille, on verra, se dilate, les paupières se ferment quand même. La beauté comme s'il n'était plus question de vivre. Le moment précieux. Surface givrée. La conscience éperdue.

On peut aussi imaginer cette souplesse inconditionnelle que nous avons devant la vraisemblance, cette apparence soutenue de la volonté d'être, malgré le froid, malgré tout, la beauté, car nous le pensons parfois, la beauté voisine les sensations les plus désagréables, voisine les plus rudes façons de vivre et de parler.

La beauté, je ne sais comment dire, pourtant, dit-elle, « la beauté empiète sur les êtres ». Je ne sais comment traduire cette intention, peut-être du bonheur, peut-être de la nostalgie ou de quelque autre sentiment qui pourrait, à un moment donné d'une vie, se confondre à ce point avec la joie que telle on la dit goût d'éternité.

Dans la distance éclatée, la beauté remue, figure impossible de l'attouchement. Labelle fragrant.

« La beauté est avant la réalité », d'une antériorité polysémique, impensable, trop pacifique pour nos yeux abrégés dans la distance, incapables au loin de penser sans coupure, fragment, histoire, différence. Le corps ballotté des femmes au loin, histoire, différence. La beauté précède le désir, son fragment, l'histoire, la coupe transversale de la réalité et de la fiction. La beauté *fata* de mémoire.

« La beauté est avant la réalité. » Peut-on réellement penser que la beauté puisse être antérieure à toute réalité, *paradis perdu*, sans risquer, la coupe des phrases et l'inflexion de la voix obligées, de succomber à l'attrait certain de la nostalgie et de la ferveur croisées : une prière soutenue. L'homme, on le sait, connaît la prière, la prière est son élévation mais se pourrait-il que, par autres détours et passions de l'âme, Mélanie soit *parvenue* en toute innocence et intuition à la même résonance de l'être ? Faut-il penser que toute intuition radicale de la beauté renvoie la pensée à ce poing serré de l'imagination agenouillée, superbe d'instinct ? Faut-il penser que c'est là routine imposée à quiconque penche violemment du côté de la lumière ? Faut-il risquer que la superbe explose, beauté froide de l'hiver, « il neige dans l'éternel » ?

Beauté froide de l'éternel, la beauté intimide, je veux dire qu'elle menace suprêmement comme un langage masqué. Car cela qui prend forme dans le chaud du ventre de l'espèce se transforme, langage, bris, miroitement, séduction : la beauté, angle de réflexion, neurone sélectif, langue à la source.

Il arrive aussi qu'à l'occasion on puisse penser que la beauté n'a que faire du regard, qu'elle néantise les comparaisons, essouffle les corps souverains car la beauté ne s'aborde pas avec un instrument, fût-il notre regard à l'extrême de sa précision. La beauté saborde les motifs, la fureur de vivre, attend le moment creux où sans fin l'équation de vie surprend, nivelle au bout de l'affirmation la queue de lettre tendue.

On pourra penser tout ce que l'on voudra, la beauté achève en nous l'intime, oui, menace suprêmement comme un langage froid. Sans coupure, sans interruption du sourire, sans dénouement. La beauté procède.

La peur

La peur est une réalité qui encombre la fiction car sans elle nous jonglerions avec nos vies bien au-delà de la leçon.

La peur mobilise les espoirs et l'énergie, au nom de qui, au nom de quoi ? On dira la peur est individuelle, on dira la terreur est collective, on dira précisément l'inverse, la peur demeure une forme qui percute la fenêtre. Blessée, la peur cogne, bandée, la peur épouvante. La peur est pour toute femme un signal de repliement. Ce n'est pas sa limite, c'est dans sa tête une manière « creuse » de vigilance qui se forme entre la subjectivité et la réalité : une poche d'eau dans le regard qui rend le monde flou, pochade. La peur empêche.

On dira qu'une « trop grande sensibilité » arrime la peur au corps et qu'alors toute expertise devient impossible, ne fait que plonger la conscience dans l'affolement comme si *les images*, ô multitudes apparues, stupéfiantes installations, allaient soudain sur nous s'adonner à quelques prélèvements du moi.

La peur renvide les catastrophes, au bas du ventre, la contorsion. Il faut voir aussi le laisser-aller du visage : la grimace, la singerie absorbée par les membres sans repos. Ça épie. La bête renifle derrière l'écran du téléviseur l'odeur de bonne cuisine et de chair. La bête est insaisissable, nuit, métal, masque, «la peur luit dans la forêt pétrifiée». On dit alors qu'un vent de panique s'abat sur toute la région, au cœur et que le corps s'épuise au grand complet, s'essouffle, l'haleine et la sueur confondues. C'est rien! Peut-être n'y a-t-il rien qu'un rythme de croissance, un rire, un nerf soudain, une trop grande sensibilité. Une torsion des traits qui accélère le temps sur les visages.

«Ma mère parlait de la peur. Une peur lente, une peur blême» comme si la peur était capable de manœuvres parmi les fluides du corps, comme si de la peur pouvaient naître des sensations insolites, habiles au creux du ventre à embraser le sentiment, à nourrir l'excitation. Cette peur est inconnue de la plupart. C'est une peur dont on entend parfois parler et qui, dit-on, rend les femmes attentives aux sons surprenants que leur voix peut produire quand elles cherchent d'un même souffle à refouler la peur lente et l'attirance certaine qui, telle une inconvenance ludique et poignante, les traversent sans qu'elles n'aient de mots pour comprendre. C'est une peur incongrue qu'on voit surtout dans les îles, lorsque les îles commencent à prendre forme en nous comme un espoir qu'il faut apprendre à distinguer.

Mais autre peur, autres mots : «la peur pénible». Est-ce bris de ferveur ou ce qui contraint les sens, leur distribution sur la peau toujours prête à plus, les plis que l'on voudrait ouverts, lèvres parlantes sans que personne ne puisse s'attrister de la civilisation? La peur qu'il y a parfois à écrire comme si le réel allait s'en trouver renforcé, *ragaillardi* par des réparties, qui secrètes animent le beau souffle de vivre, qui dévoilées iraient dans la distorsion du sens achevé prendre place à côté des objets tranchants que nous utilisons pour la tâche quotidienne de vivre. La peur est étrange. Elle s'apparente aux objets que nous prenons dans nos mains, certains moins laids que d'autres, moins opaques, plus légers. Alors la peur glisse sur notre peau, rafraîchit la paume, donne momentanément l'impression que les créatures tombées dans notre regard vont pouvoir enfin se retirer sans que nos traits ne soient soumis à la torsion. Librement jusqu'à ce que : raptus.

  La peur, on la dira comme la honte, bien inutile. On dira « ça ne fait rien quand on accélère » croyant qu'il suffit de dissimuler derrière l'écran les signes déréglés du désir, de reporter la menace au bas de l'écran, *simulation*. On verra un peu de neige. On croira qu'il suffit, à la ferveur de la nuit, de rétablir *la parole*. Mais la peur, il ne faut pas se le cacher, est aussi répandue que paroles d'hommes.

LA CIVILISATION

Il est un temps de croyance où nous affinons les gestes naturels qui nous rapprochent de l'image, d'autres qui nous relancent dans le discours et la précipitation. Ce temps de croyance est un temps de civilisation, une certitude de l'être qui emplit le hasard d'architectures et d'explosions de voix. « L'inexpérience de mourir* » est pour toute civilisation une forme d'*empressement*. Une belle spontanéité capable de calculs, qui refoule, sans autre avertissement que métaphore hallucinée, la nature en nous. Or la nature on la dit partout car sous notre crâne, elle exagère, brode, bluffe, entasse mers, canyons, forêts et déserts, des aubes somptueuses, des orchidées sans nom. La nature nous remercie. Alors nous nous occupons à la réponse, cherchant dans la langue des instruments propices à nous détourner de la nostalgie qui n'en finit plus d'ouvrer parmi les décors les plus extravagants. Pourtant la civilisation est toujours bien simple : une femme, une naissance, des engins, la mort. *Le truc.* « Les mères sont fragiles comme la civilisation », dit-elle.

Il est aussi un temps de croyance qui absorbe toutes les paniques, ce temps nous l'appelons *temps de*

* Maurice Blanchot.

végétation ou, si l'on préfère, *temps d'animation*, une contrepartie sémantique de ce qui se languit, à la limite, on pourra parler d'une *cristallisation* des engins, exactement comme si on voulait signifier la transparence dure et un temps très court, *soudain*, entre l'attraction et la répulsion, une indifférence qui nous surprend.

Au repos, nous aimons penser que la civilisation est un sablier, une horloge, un quartz capable de nous donner le temps, un sous-verre qui protège contre l'habitude des cernes. Au repos, nous aimons le chien et la détente. Nous aimons bien la démographie et parfois quelques soupirs. Au repos, la civilisation nous porte à l'image, à certaines moqueries propices au dénouement, la nuit venue, de quelques fictions. Alors nous rêvons de nos gestes comme s'ils pouvaient nous dissuader de la mort.

En théorie, la civilisation est un modèle valable pour beaucoup de conquêtes et de conversions. Lettre chargée, elle accomplit des merveilles, dessine de beaux destins. C'est, dit-on, sa surface d'influence, sa *façon*.

Mais là où je suis, accouplée à la voix de Mélanie, l'humanité et la civilisation forment deux mots, une maladresse, un écart sémantique, un décalage qui blesse, une taille de l'horizon qui renvoie les versions, le versant du regard dans les choses bousculées du désir et de l'aube. Là où je suis rendue, la neige encore, côté jardin, la pluie sonore comme une transposition de l'effet, la pluie rend mon corps soumis, mes pensées braquées sur l'horizon.

Là où je suis rendue, on peut affiner l'espoir parmi les rayons drus de la lumière.

Un livre à traduire
(suite)

Il y avait maintenant plus d'un an que Maude Laures préparait *son manuscrit*. Ce matin le ciel était bleu. Deux ou trois nuages, petites béances au loin. Maude Laures ouvrit le réfrigérateur, se servit un Coke. Puis elle eut envie de partir, de prendre la route vers Québec. Le fleuve serait beau et grand sous la lumière crue de mars.

Maude Laures retourna à sa table de travail, prit le livre, enleva l'élastique qui retenait les pages décollées. Toutes les pages étaient annotées, ici le bleu *polysémie*, le vert *piste sonore*, le rouge *à vérifier*, le noir *incompréhensible*, le jaune *familier*, le rose *quel genre ?*, le mauve *quel temps ?* Dans les marges, des attentions qui pouvaient passer pour des remarques à la mine. Parfois un dessin pour faciliter la représentation.

au bas de la page **éliminer tous les** *comme* **si possible**

Maude Laures mit ses lentilles, s'apprêta devant le miroir. Elle eut soudain le sentiment qu'elle allait bientôt
n'être qu'un instrument de résonance. Elle se vit tour
à tour lyre, théorbe, viole. Le mauve se décomposa,
fut recomposé, palimpseste, dans ses yeux, un air.

Elle ouvrit le tiroir, en sortit une chemise blanche,
s'habilla, regarda un peu de réalité par la fenêtre,
confondit dans sa tête se révolter et revolver, retourna
devant le miroir, mit un peu de rouge sur ses lèvres,
puis alla s'installer devant le téléviseur silencieux. Alluma un petit cigare.

Le lit était douillet. Elle se réveilla à midi, furieuse contre elle-même comme si elle eût été une coulure noire dans la lumière. L'affiche du Sonora était en fleurs, les chemises pêle-mêle sur la table. Des coupures de journaux. Des fiches et des définitions comme autant de déflagrations dans le consentement. Maude Laures se leva, entrouvrit les rideaux. Le jour rutilant entra dans sa tête. Elle se pencha, ramassa une enveloppe, pensa que l'horizon était comme un grand nu de femme bien tentant pour les yeux. Puis elle recommença comme à tous les jours, penchée au-dessus de sa table, l'œil strict et la main tendue vers les mots qui pouvaient être rescapés du désert, à patrouiller l'espace imaginaire de Laure Angstelle. Elle pensa « cela frôle le vide », eut peur un instant puis refocalisa sa pensée sur « douille et toutes les armes ».

« Lorsque deux mots sont identiques, il ne faut pas t'en formaliser outre mesure ou te croire lésée d'un choix. La simplicité est belle patience du sens. » Maude Laures éprouvait parfois le besoin de se répéter à voix haute quelques recommandations. Il arrivait même qu'elle interrompe son travail et que, les baguettes en l'air, elle s'adonne au beau milieu de sa chambre à de longues joutes oratoires. Les mots volaient haut, volaient bas, elle les attrapait, lançait, relançait. Elle avait beau jeu, les papilles enflammées. Le dictionnaire, tant pis ! Langue de feu, laïusseuse. Lai.

Les mots étaient dans la bouche comme de petits noyaux, « la partie la plus dure et la plus brillante », une présence, un corps solide qu'il fallait après un certain temps rejeter en avançant la langue comme pour une amorce de grimace, puis d'un souffle, projeter devant soi la partie indivisible. Entre les dents, il ne restait alors que la chair et la saveur, partie comestible, une bonne denrée quotidienne. Mais un mot tout entier, on pouvait aussi le cracher.

Maude Laures aurait aimé partir pour Québec. Faire
un peu de route car elle pensait que l'image répétée de
l'autoroute pourrait servir le long des tempes à quelques comparaisons, compenser son inexpérience de la
vitesse et du délire. Car ici, pensait-elle, ici, il n'y a
rien pour enfiévrer l'imagination. L'imagination est
tout entière consacrée à nous sortir du doute et du
froid. Cependant Maude Laures persistait, elle se
voyait au volant, plissant les yeux pendant que clôtu-
res, baraques et silos surgis de la neige fondante et de
la boue luisaient enfin dans le lointain comme des
comparaisons, de petits palets qui lui rappelaient des
gestes d'enfants habiles sur la surface du fleuve à faire
ricocher des cailloux.

Aussi ce jour-là, elle travailla jusque tard dans la nuit au mot *ricocher*. Ricocher était en effet un mot qui pouvait sauver bien des situations : « Son regard et sa pensée ricochèrent, la balle ricocha et ne l'atteignit point, la balle ricocha sur une chaise, alla se perdre dans le téléviseur, la lumière ricocha sur le pare-chocs, la conversation ricocha sur un mot. »

Dans la marge, il n'y avait plus d'espace et Maude Laures se mit à cocher d'autres mots qui pourraient dans sa langue relancer le sens et lui éviter d'affronter la fin brutale d'Angela Parkins.

Encore une aube. Il fallait s'attendre au printemps. La lumière empiétait de plus en plus sur la réalité comme s'il eût été question de lui donner un sens global ou d'exposer la matière comme une nouveauté quand vient le temps de s'adapter et que les corps suggèrent des saveurs raffinées, vont d'un pas satiné, beau ralenti de l'image, à la rencontre de quelques universaux.

Trajectoire, pensait Maude Laures, trajectoire. Et elle se faisait de plus en plus à l'idée de devenir une voix autre et ressemblante dans l'univers dérivé de Laure Angstelle. Les personnages allaient bientôt se défiler les uns après les autres, devenir de petites transparences au loin, se cristalliser. Elle serait seule dans sa langue. Alors, il y aurait substitution.

Le temps était venu du corps à corps avec le livre. Un temps qui ferait place à l'étonnement devant les choses que l'on ne voit que très rarement, sises à l'arrière-plan de nos pensées. D'une langue à l'autre, il y aurait du sens, juste distribution, contour et rencontre du moi, cette substance mouvante qui, dit-on, entre dans la composition des langues et qui les rend savoureuses ou détestables. Maude Laures savait que le temps était maintenant venu de se glisser anonyme et entière entre les pages.

Plein désert, plein horizon. Au bas du ventre, là où la langue veut, une peur fine et lente commençait à sourdre, à distribuer les tâches.

C'était maintenant le printemps. La lumière était éclatante et on pouvait à nouveau prétendre que les mots iraient, du livre *innocent* au livre traduit, s'acquitter de leur fonction, emportant Maude Laures dans le flot des contraintes, des exceptions et des principes. Maintenant il faudrait, dans le non-dit, jouer serré.

Là où il y avait eu des personnages, des objets, de la peur et du désir, Maude Laures ne voyait plus que des mots. Les mots prenaient le relais, parés pour la capture des sens.

Laure Angstelle

MAUVE, L'HORIZON

Traduit par Maude Laures

Éditions de l'Angle

Le désert est indescriptible. La lumière avale tout, gouffre cru. Le regard fond. Aujourd'hui, pourtant. Très jeune, je désespérais déjà de l'humanité. À chaque jour de l'an, je la voyais se disperser dans l'espoir et la démesure. Très jeune, je filais dans l'auto de ma mère et j'allais vers le désert où je m'obstinais devant le jour, la nuit et à l'aube, à vouloir tout. Je tissais la lumière. Je roulais vite et aussi lentement ; je suivais les petits fragments de vie qui s'alignaient dans mon regard, horizon mauve.

Habile, je l'étais au jeu du discernement mais il y avait en moi un désir tel que, sans obstacle, cela m'angoissait comme un trop-plein d'énergie. Alors venaient le rose, le rouge et le bris parmi les pierres le mauve et l'aube lente. Au loin, l'éclat d'un hélicoptère à touristes.

Très jeune, il n'y eut point d'avenir et le monde ressembla à une maison incendiée comme celle qui le fut au coin de la rue par des hommes « étrangers », ma mère le disait, qui leur avait servi un verre. Ma mère pensait qu'un seul parmi eux était armé mais aucune inquiétude ne lui venait car tous les autres avaient les yeux bleus. Ma mère disait souvent que les hommes étaient libres de faire comme dans les livres. Elle terminait sa phrase puis, une fois le malaise passé, s'installait devant le téléviseur. Je regardais son profil et dans mon regard la broche à cheveux qu'elle portait

toujours se découpait comme un fil de soie. Son tablier était jaune avec de belles fleurs. Ma mère ne portait jamais de robe.

Je roulais dans la nuit, folle d'arrogance. J'avais
15 ans. C'était exquis comme un grand pouvoir, une
manière douce de se perdre dans le noir et mille scènes
délirantes aux environs des yeux.

Je connaissais bien le désert, ses petits sentiers et
les grandes routes au loin. Lorna, cette amie chérie de
ma mère, m'avait appris à donner un sens aux images
qui tremblent dans la pierre et la poussière. Elle passait de longs moments à me raconter des histoires tout
en paysages, pleines de végétations exotiques, me parlait de terres lointaines qui ne pouvaient être compa-
rées au sol de mon enfance. Lorna fabulait. Je devi-
nais que quelque part en elle une étrange passion la
poussait à inventer des noms de bêtes, à rêver de couleurs impossibles, à truquer la forme des reptiles. Je le
savais car moi je distinguais fort bien le diamantin du
corail, les aigles des piscivores. Lorna mentait. Lorna
osait dire tant de choses. Ses mots étaient si durs et
irréels que j'avais parfois l'impression d'un hurlement
quand ils franchissaient tout flamboyants le seuil de
sa bouche.

Lorna n'avait pas connu de jeunesse, seulement
des filles de sa classe avec lesquelles elle s'acoquinait à
l'heure de la récréation. Les filles l'aimaient. Elle aimait
les embrasser sur la bouche à la sortie de l'école.

La première fois que j'ai vu Lorna, je l'ai trouvée
jolie et j'ai prononcé un mot sale. J'avais 5 ans. Au
repas, ma mère souriait. Elles s'observaient et quand
elles ouvraient la bouche, il y avait une émotion. Je les

regardais attentivement, leurs lèvres surtout, comme si elles avaient été une surface prononcée du visage, un renflement qui animait jusque dans leurs yeux la conversation. Lorna s'émerveilla à propos de la mousse au sommet des montagnes, douce sur les mollets. Mon verre de lait se répandit sur la nappe qui ressembla soudain à une grande carte géographique avec un fleuve qui coula sur mes genoux. Ma mère épongea tout, fit semblant d'un jeu.

Je prenais souvent l'auto de ma mère. Bien avant que tout me soit permis. Sous le soleil, à la tombée du jour et même la nuit, je partais malgré les mots inquiets que ma mère criait et qui retombaient dans la poussière du stationnement. J'ai toujours cherché le désert, car très jeune je voulais tout connaître de la beauté, de la lumière, éloigner la peur et la mort. Je savais que ma mère éprouverait un grand vide mais je préférais aux reflets de la magie dans ses cheveux lisses le reflet brûlant du soleil, la nuit dans les yeux des lièvres, comme une saisie de la vie, m'éblouir. « À moi la violence et l'aridité » et j'accélérais, folle de cette énergie maudite qui me montait à la tête. Un jour je serais *fata de fata, edge on edge*, un jour à l'aube, je serais insensible devant tout, les équations et l'humanité, sa déraison éclatée au fond du regard esseulé des hommes fous. Je roulais vite, émondée de l'histoire, silence torride. Je répétais « tant de fois j'ai abouti dans l'utopie ».

La nuit, le désert était beauté, reflet de bêtes vives, éphémère, silence, *senitas*. Sous les phares de la Meteor, l'humanité était un gisement trompeur. L'humanité était fragile sans l'Arizona. *Si fragile*. J'avais 15 ans et

ma voix tremblait, impatiente et friable. Je voulais
que tout mon corps soit nécessaire. Je conduisais bien.
J'étais capable d'enligner en moi la nuit, de me faufiler
parmi les ombres. J'anticipais sur tout et cela me déli-
vrait temporairement de l'encombrement et des mots.
L'éternité était dans mon cerveau comme une ombre,
l'aspect foncé du désir, une musique qui me faisait
sombrer dans le décalque des autoroutes. L'humanité
était fragile, suspendue comme un univers au-dessus
des cités, explosive. Tout était fragile, je le savais, je
l'avais toujours pensé. À 15 ans, je prétendais que
tout serait fameux. Comme ma mère, je croyais que
tout était semblant de jeu.

L'ombre au passage avale l'espoir. Il n'y a pas
d'ombre la nuit, quand le soleil est au zénith. Tout est
évidence et la réalité nous transit. Mais la réalité est
enfermement, petite tombe qui trompe le désir. La
réalité est un feu de paille qui prétend. J'avais 15 ans
et de tout mon être j'appuyais sur le pan fragile de
mes pensées pour qu'elles soient penchant de l'instant, pour que ça compte vraiment la réalité.

Maintenant suivre les indications, la flèche en direction du Motel Rouge. Stationner l'auto. La sueur. Le bar. La surface polie du bar ressemble à un écran : des femmes et des hommes conversent et dans le décor se répètent comme des ombres sur le mur. On dirait des taches. J'avale ma bière et la vie continue dans le brouhaha*.

---

* Forme expressive du verbe exister, peut, selon le contexte, être péjoratif ou mélioratif.

CHAPTITRE 1

L'hom'oblong pose sa serviette sur le lit. Il fait chaud dans la chambre. Il défait le col de sa chemise. Il va vers la toilette. Il pense à l'explosion. Il l'imagine et ça ne lui suffit pas. Quoi! Il se souvient des beaux sentiers, de l'automne en couleurs. Il se regarde dans le miroir. Il s'*essuie* les mains. Il pense à l'explosion, il pense à ça et c'est le vide dans sa tête. Il dépose sa veste sur une chaise. Un crayon tombe d'une poche. Il ne le ramasse pas. Il allume une cigarette. Il tâte le rebord de son chapeau en feutre. Il pense à l'explosion. Il caresse des mots ronds qui dans sa bouche forment quelques phrases en sanskrit, des mots qui enchantent, il le sait. Il arpente la chambre. La fumée de sa cigarette forme un petit nuage au-dessus de sa tête. L'hom'oblong connaît la valeur des mots. Il pense à l'explosion. Une seule erreur de calcul pouvait changer le cours de l'histoire. L'hom'oblong s'allonge sur le lit. Des images, puis de blanche à orange la terre devient jade. – *La mort/Je/suis/la mort* – Je suis un enfant d'chienne. L'hom'oblong s'endort, une petite tombe calculée comme une forme explosive dans son corps.

Je pouvais surprendre ma mère. Elle pouvait me dérouter. Son pouvoir était grand de morceler mon regard. Lorsque je la voyais si près de Lorna et qu'entre
elles il y avait juste assez de distance pour que j'imagine en leur corps une excitation, les images défilaient
en moi, nuque, nudité, épaules heureuses.

　　J'avance. La bouche béante avalant les airs rock,
tout le rythme, hurlant paroles et vitesse. On interrompt la musique. Une voix d'homme annonce un
désastre, un tremblement de terre. J'appuie sur la voix
et elle se perd inaudible tsunami dans le lointain Pacifique. Je n'aime pas que ma mère soit seule la nuit.
Cela me hante. Les mères sont comme la civilisation,
fragiles devant leur téléviseur, oubliées comme un savoir ancien. Les mères sont de grands espaces. J'aime
rouler violemment vite dans la Meteor. J'aime l'horizon répété. Aucune peur, aucune panique ne me vient
en pleine nuit ou quand c'est nuage de sable et que je
ne vois rien devant moi. Je m'arrête, je deviens matière vive ; isolée de tout, les mains sur le volant, en-
foncée dans le sombre, j'écoute le fracas du monde
ensabler la carrosserie. Je me soumets, aveuglée. Je
regarde au-dedans du dedans mon cerveau s'avancer
dans le temps, multiplier les secondes, cristaux, créatures aériennes dans le pli des paupières. Je suis des
pistes, la trace du temps, des triangles, des spirales,
autour des ruines, des barkhanes, mobiles. Une fois

seulement, une fois seulement, j'ai vu des mots que je n'ai point su lire. Et les signes se sont aussitôt dispersés comme si au fond du cerveau le corps de la lettre ne pouvait soutenir la lumière, une telle présence.

Je roulais vorace. Je m'exposais à tous les risques pour que la conscience surgisse, violente et continue au cœur de la nuit et du désert. J'avais 15 ans, tout le temps et l'horizon devant moi. Dans l'ossature blanche de ma mère, j'étais vitesse, civilisation, au loin, cité, regard perdu, ruine à rebours. J'avançais, exemplaire de solitude, avec à mes pieds un frein pour empêcher les désastres. Il n'y a pas lieu parmi les serpents et les cactus de désespérer, car la nuit est toujours bleue comme un délire.

Je ressemble à ma mère quand l'humanité en détresse se dresse au loin et que d'un grand rire elle fait blêmir. Ma mère ne pleurait jamais. Je ne l'ai jamais vue s'adonner à un tel désordre. Sans doute ne pouvait-elle songer à la solitude avec exactitude. Pourtant ma mère tremblait quand le bruit des êtres l'assaillait mais elle restait insensible à cette chose froide et myst*érieuse* qu'est la solitude. Dans les moments les plus difficiles, elle décrétait : « Ceci est un mâle, il faut du repos, ceci est une femme, il faut du sens. » Ma mère était austère comme un homme ayant l'habitude de la nature et du danger. Elle n'aimait pas les hommes, mais elle défendait avec âpreté les sentiments aptes à endurcir la pulpe trop féconde de son imagination. C'était une femme dont la voix sans expression pouvait faire écho et soudainement inquiéter la raison, tromper le jugement.

Chaque fois que je pense à ma mère, j'imagine des filles en maillot allongées grands corps nostalgiques au bord de la piscine du motel. Ce motel, ma mère l'avait reconstruit au fil des années puis entretenu avec soin, gestes et sourires courtois malgré la chaleur des après-midi de Tucson. Mais tout est vague. Avant la venue de Lorna, il n'y a qu'un espace achalandé, rempli de clients, de vendeurs, le bruit continu de l'aspirateur.

Lorna, cette présence neuve, sera toujours dans mon souvenir comme un point de repère parmi les séances scolaires où l'écriture et la lecture se forment comme un apprentissage au savoir. Je lisais beaucoup mais, hasard étrange, toujours en la présence de Lorna. Elle m'épiait. Sur le qui-vive et silencieuse, Lorna cherchait sur mon visage à retracer les signes qui en moi faisaient images. Dès que je levais les yeux vers elle, son regard se mouillait comme si les mots qu'elle imaginait dans ma bouche pouvaient, en sa présence, se transformer ou être partagés comme une émotion. Alors, pour détourner son attention et surtout pour qu'elle ne puisse lire dans mes pensées, je parlais de manger.

Un jour alors que je voulais des feuilles blanches et qu'à toute allure je cherchais ma mère, je tombai sur la forme nouée d'une double présence. Ma mère était assise sur les genoux de Lorna et Lorna griffonnait distraitement sur son dos des lettres géantes. Je demandai des feuilles et Lorna me répondit qu'il ne servait à rien d'écrire, qu'il valait mieux jouer et crier fort. J'allais protester, dire que chaque lettre était un jeu, un oiseau, un chat, une fi... lorsque je remarquai qu'une des fleurs du tablier de ma mère était tout entière abriée par la main libre de Lorna.

Pourtant cette nuit. Très jeune, j'appris à aimer l'orage, le feu, la foudre, le tracé électrique qui éraille l'horizon comme si chaque déchirure allait ouvrir un passage aux pensées. Les nuits d'orage sec, j'explosais au loin, je serrais les mâchoires, je tremblais, tout mon corps se chargeait de larmes et de froid mental. Puis je m'abandonnais à tous les éclairs comme s'il s'agissait dans la chair d'être liée momentanément au bruit que font les neurones devant l'immensité. Alors le corps fond, abrégé comme une certitude. Le désert boit tout. La fureur et la solitude.

Dans le désert, il faut vouloir poursuivre son chemin, entrer dans la béance du monde. Quelques nuages ici et là qui frôlent l'horizon, qui dessinent de petits plombs dans l'air. Je connais l'éclat permanent du métal, les dragées, les cendrées, la grenaille. Je sais ce qu'il faut, fille du désert, je n'ai jamais cessé de croiser le fer et le sentiment.

CHAPTITRE 2

L'hom'oblong veille. Il s'est étendu encore tout vêtu. Il revoit l'explosion. Ses vêtements sont froissés, les souliers sont sales. Il songe un instant à l'art et à la beauté du spectre solaire, puis il se lève et se dirige vers la commode. La petite revue de femmes nues est à sa place, enfouie sous les chemises blanches, orange et jade. Il prend la revue, retourne vers le lit, tapote l'oreiller, s'installe confortablement. Il feuillette, il s'attarde ici, là, il attend que quelque chose arrive. « Maintenant nous sommes tous des chiens. » L'hom'oblong passe en revue les sexes. Pas de visages, surtout pas de visages ! Les sexes font des cernes autour des images labiées. Puis les cernes explosent. Il ferme les yeux. Il neige lentement comme en ce bel hiver à Princeton, la veille de ses 20 ans. C'est encore l'insomnie. La confusion entre les calculs et les résultats. L'hom'oblong connaît de grands lacs bleus, pense à la forêt, aux arbres d'améthyste à tout jamais pétrifiés. Il neige dans l'éternel. Splendeur et splendeur. « Maintenant que la mort et l'écriture sont sur la langue un interdit. » L'hom'oblong entend l'explosion. Tout son corps se raidit, forme crispée. Son feutre est tombé, mou. Il allume une cigarette.

Dans le désert, la peur est exacte, bien proportionnée, n'affiche pas de masque. Elle est utile, précise, fait du beau travail. La peur, ici, se fréquente comme une histoire naturelle. Elle est exceptionnellement sommaire, quelques illustrations : becs, crocs, dards, langue bifide.

Au motel par contre, la peur épouvante. À l'écran comme en pensée, fragmente les corps, assassine quotidiennement. La peur renifle l'ennui et fait froid dans le dos. La peur insiste, amplifie le tourment de vivre, permute dans le cerveau les certitudes et les galéjades.

J'avais 15 ans et je parle encore de la peur car elle me surprend toujours. Mais la peur exacte est belle. Chaque nuit, on peut la voir errer, relent d'éternité dans la forêt pétrifiée. Oui, la peur exacte allume le plexus et tresse d'étranges soleils dans les yeux.

Lorsque Lorna est venue vivre avec nous, ma mère hésitait à parler de la peur. Je la sentais, confuse, lente et tout à la fois prête à se déclarer. Ma mère disait : « Lorna, je suis à bout, je flaire un danger » et Lorna incarnait dans son rire, dans ses gestes, dans ses yeux, une menace imprécise qui brisait la voix de ma mère. Lorsque Lorna plongeait de tout son corps ailé dans la piscine, ma mère suppliait : « Lor, Lor, ne fais pas cela » et Lorna, amusée de la peur incongrue qui s'emparait de ma mère, me prenait dans ses bras et nous devenions dauphins, dos gris, de gros moutons sur la mer. Ma mère se penchait au-dessus de l'eau et je pouvais voir son corps comme une forme géante se découper sur le ciel. Alors la bouche pleine de bulles et balbutiante de joie, je faisais surface ; les yeux rougis par le chlore, je crachais souverainement sur le monde comme un grand dragon.

Je raconterai peut-être un jour tout cela, ma vie. Un jour quand plus rien ne me semblera vrai. C'est déjà beaucoup dire quand je parle de la nuit et du désert car en moi l'horizon immédiat affine le tranchant biographique. J'ai abusé de tout, des étoiles, de l'aube, touché la pierre, connu le métal, caressé la forme assoupie des bêtes, manœuvre tant de fois devant l'horizon magique pour que l'énergie qui me hante déferle comme une réponse, une chose audible parmi le bruit, l'instinct. J'avais 15 ans et je savais choisir entre les personnes, la doublure, le personnage. Je savais *fata de fata* qu'un soupçon de peur était dans la nuit, synonyme d'affranchissement. J'appuyais sur l'accélérateur et peur, ô nuit, bruit, c'est si fragile le corps quand le silence ne tarit point dans le noir.

La nuit ! Oui, j'ai vu l'aube. Souvent. L'aube, les spectres, le spectacle fascinant du temps tourbillon, poussière. Je filais. J'hurlais au grand jour. La nuit sur l'autoroute, je vivais fort. Puis à nouveau c'était la piscine, des filles en maillot et ma mère au téléphone tout occupée à la voix, toute vêtue de son image. Lorna s'approchait d'elle et ma mère décidait du moment, de la caresse. Dans leurs yeux, le quotidien était soudain vrai, sans écran, puis détecté par mon regard, se suspendait comme une décision.

Certaines nuits, le sombre desséchait les mots et cela me fascinait de voir la peau de délire tomber comme la fièvre à l'aube. Alors je pouvais exister sans comparaison, capable seulement d'une grande soif entre mes lèvres et le vent fort. La siccité.

J'étais toujours certaine de tout. Des gestes, du temps, de la distance, de l'horizon. De tout sauf des mots. La peur lente des mots. Une peine effrayante dans toutes mes veines.

Un jour de mai alors que la chaleur bougeait encore très fort dans l'atmosphère, je m'arrêtai au beau milieu de nulle part pour examiner un immense saguaro entre la vie et la mort. Comme à l'accoutumée, je chantais – *over and over*, partir. Puis, comme si l'horizon s'était soudainement retourné vers moi, je sentis la peur pénible s'emparer de moi. Le saguaro vacillait. Les mots. Tout était au ralenti, la vie comme une synthèse irréelle accomplie dans le corps. Mais plus de route, plus de cactus, d'aube aucune, seulement l'instinct de survie qui d'un coup fort ramène les mots à leur juste valeur.

« Du papier ! » Je retournai à l'auto, ouvris la boîte à gants, déplaçai le revolver, m'emparai du petit carnet pour écrire tout ça ou à propos de cela, j'en avais une folle envie. Ça éclatait dans ma tête, *la beauté filait douce comme une ombre, longeait de grands canyons, serpentait, arroyo, agonie, cumul, culbute, dévalait parmi les candélabres, les teddy bears, les épines et les fleurs, ça m'excitait, ça se déchaînait, brave bête, épiderme consentant*, la vie multiple. Puis la peur s'en alla blêmir au loin.

L'horizon est courbe. L'atmosphère satinée autour de l'auto. Je rentre au motel. Je roule vite, en tête, ma mère et Lorna. Ma mère est distante, Lorna, devant le téléviseur. Folle, folle déception, folle lueur dans ma chambre, vite mes doigts là, c'est ça, *wet*, vacille, m'*envas*.

Cette nuit-là, les mots tournèrent longtemps dans ma tête, s'enroulèrent autour de moi, firent tourner l'émotion. J'eus l'impression de mille boucles dans mon corps, des intuitions solennelles au sujet de la vie, à propos de la mort. Puis la réalité devint une IMAGE. Je m'endormis à l'aube, langée, sirène, objet de l'image.

Maintenant, je connais la peur en différé. Je passe mon temps devant le téléviseur. Je longe le bruit cru des voix, l'inquiétude qui se communique. Je connais la réalité. L'humanité comme une forme ombrée. Elle bouge lentement, ophidienne, peau de lenteur dans la poussière, camouflage, mue. Immobile, peau morte, petit fétiche à ras du sol, somme aux pieds des *senitas* et des *ocotillos*. La peur de la peau creuse au fond des yeux pendant que l'orange et le jade au loin forment de beaux sentiers dans le feuillage. La peau fait peur aux ignorants. La peau, c'est ça.

Ce même mois ma mère fut triste et Lorna fut douce envers moi. Je relançais ma mère pour qu'elle regarde ce que j'avais écrit. Je laissais des messages partout comme autant d'indices de mon désir. Le soir, ma mère racontait mon histoire à Lorna en omettant le récit. Lorna riait nerveusement. Alors, j'augmentais le volume et la toute peur panique prenait place dans la réalité comme un œil malpropre.

Depuis que j'avais osé écrire, la réalité s'installait en toute chose, prenait beaucoup de place. Les clients arrivaient, Texans, « oiseaux pâles » du Wisconsin et du Minnesota. Beaucoup de vieux et de vieilles. Des vendeurs. Quelquefois des femmes qui lorsqu'elles étaient ensemble faisaient du brouhaha. Encore des jeunes filles en maillot. J'écoutais les conversations au bar. Les gens appuyaient leurs dires sur des clichés, d'autres riaient grassement ; il me semblait que tous payaient cher le maigre pouvoir de vivre.

Un soir, je vis enfin cette fameuse Angela Parkins dont ma mère disait qu'elle était excessive. Elle était encore jeune. On la disait géomètre. Elle venait au bar une fois par mois. Elle discutait avec des hommes. J'écoutais leur conversation. Je ne pouvais tout comprendre et quand cela était, j'observais les physionomies. J'accumulais mes pensées puis d'un seul coup je relâchais les masques et les sourires. Seul le visage rare d'Angela Parkins continuait de m'habiter comme une chose intime.

La soirée se poursuivait lente et sans histoires lorsque la voix d'Angela Parkins détonna comme un engin d'abord insolite, ensuite menaçant. Puis la voix s'éleva hystérique et capricante, fit en moi irruption sauvage. Ma mère dit que c'était l'alcool, trop d'alcool, mais je voyais bien que dans la voix d'Angela Parkins il y avait plus qu'une simple débauche. Infiniment plus qu'une ivresse. Elle était tout entière îlot de résistance, butte-témoin au loin dans le désert. La soirée continua d'être enfumée. Angela Parkins se retira avant 11 heures. Je la suivis jusqu'au stationnement. J'avais 15 ans et je voulais que tout mon corps soit nécessaire. La réalité avait un sens. Comment ?

Le lendemain, je partis pour Albuquerque où habitait ma cousine Grazie.

CHAPTITRE 3

Les yeux de l'homme étaient démentiellement arrogants. Il bougeait sa tête de haut en bas et à chaque mouvement c'était l'explosion. Le plafond, le plancher, l'explosion. Tout son corps était soumis à l'accélération. Son image s'allongeait, somme impossible, masse fantastique. Il était perdu, plus de corps en lui, seulement la poussière qui retombait tout autour comme une raison froide. Il ne guérirait jamais de l'hiver, lui qui savait pourtant être si chaleureux quand l'odeur de la rosée lui redonnait espoir. L'hom'oblong était terrorisé. L'ombre se multipliait, aberrante et intouchable. Il rêvait de poèmes et de sanskrit mais déjà la cendre, déjà le sang entraient dans la bouche ouverte et silencieuse qui obstruait dans son cerveau la belle image aux mille cristaux qu'il avait inventée. Puis l'hom'oblong traça des chiffres sur le mur. Traça compulsivement la mort. Son corps s'épuisa contre le mur. Son ombre. L'explosion était parfaite dans le jade.

Je roulais calmement. C'était torride, lumineux. Pas de musique, pas de voix. Seulement moi. Le silence partout. J'avais choisi de m'imposer le plein soleil, d'épuiser mon corps comme si cela pouvait m'aider à retrouver le temps d'avant la réalité. Je roulais et le désert était maintenant un vrai danger sec et tranchant, plein de pièges. Je n'avais pas emporté une goutte d'eau. Je m'imposais chaleur, soif, tourments afin que les petites choses vraies que l'on voit le long des routes puissent trouver leur résolution en moi. Je voulais en mon corps civilisé que la bête résume son code, que dans l'hyperréalité du bleu les images soient réduites à quelques aperçus, que cesse le flot violent des mots. Que du vrai. Rien à penser. Du chaud, de l'asphalte.

Je résume la réalité, ma vie dans la lumière aveuglante. Un jour j'ai rêvé *full feeling* entre Phoenix et la forêt pétrifiée. Dans l'espace *tout flambait, carnaval voix l'horizon, beau bal masqué, cavalcade, la forêt fougères en furie, la beauté fougueuse, il y avait tant de mots pourtant pourvu que pensée patiente.*

J'étais maintenant entrée dans la peur de l'indicible. Sans le vouloir, j'avais franchi la limite, fractionné la frayeur et maintenant tout était décalé. Un pli énorme dans le silence. Dans le désert on plie sans calcul. Face à l'horizon, le corps s'expose, avide, à ne point trouver de sens.

Je roulais maintenant toute à la joie d'imaginer Grazie à qui je parlerais d'Angela Parkins, de cette femme connue sous la pluie dans la nuit d'un mardi. Je frissonnerais. Je fabulerais. Je raconterais feu vif, tout ce que j'avais éprouvé comme en songe dans la forêt pétrifiée. J'oserais dire tant de choses. Grazie m'encouragerait. « Encore une histoire, une autre version, ton vrai visage. Parle, dis-moi tout. Raconte aussi à propos de Lorna et de ta mère. Leur rire, leur peur, leur voix, la nuit, les paroles. Parle-moi, sois flamme, lèche, embrase pour que le mauve éveille en nous d'amples manières de songer. Allume en moi ce qui, peut-être, un jour. »

Grazie était de deux mois mon aînée. Nous étions, à ce que nos mères disaient, comme « de vraies sœurs ». Ma mère m'avait tout raconté. « C'était par une belle nuit d'avril. Nous étions toutes deux enceintes, rondes, si tu nous avais vues, rondes et veloutées, mûres, à point comme des syllabes, tout en écho au sommet de Dante's View. Si seulement, Mélanie, tu nous avais vues, mais la nuit. »

Je conduis lentement vers Albuquerque. Oh! la certitude! Grazie m'attend. À la jonction de la 🔟 et de la 🔢, il y a une bande de motards qui fument le nez en l'air. Deux filles conversent, une bouteille de bière à la main. L'une d'entre elles m'adresse un signe de victoire et l'autre, à peine décalée dans l'espace, m'« encule » violemment du majeur, puis tout le coude y passe. J'accélère. Je connais la réalité. La peur c'est rien, c'est rien quand on est *fast so fast*. La peur s'évanouit tache sombre dans le rétroviseur.

La route était comme un décalage horaire imperceptible dans l'air tremblant. J'avais 15 ans et devant moi toute la réalité pour me gâcher l'existence. Comme cette liberté qui, là où j'ai grandi, était une arme capable d'éloigner la peur et la nostalgie. Il y avait aussi une autre liberté, celle-là plus légère, qui sentait propre, l'encens et la poudre. Alors la liberté d'un seul coup PAN visait la liberté. Donne-moi une bouchée de liberté, disaient les hommes. Bouchonne-moi donc, répondaient les femmes. Ah, la liberté ce que ça fourvoyait le monde !

J'ai perdu le désert. J'ai perdu le désert dans la nuit de l'écriture. Il y a sans doute un moment où il faut savoir s'arrêter, bloquer devant la bêtise, convenir que les mots ne sont pas toujours à la hauteur ou qu'ils peuvent assombrir notre enthousiasme, déjouer nos belles manœuvres pensantes. Maintenant, il faut que l'évidence ranime en moi le désert et qu'à nouveau le serpent corail et le lynx roux bisent le sol de leurs couleurs. Il faut que le lièvre antilope retrouve sa vitesse, sa bourre blanche, que les pierres de mystère qui marchent dans la vallée de la Mort balisent de leur poids l'horizon. Il faut que l'évidence revienne, que la certitude comme un trop-plein d'images au fond du cerveau répartisse en moi le vide, m'expose totalement.

Il y a des mémoires pour creuser les mots sans souiller les tombes. Tutoyer est un enracinement. Je ne peux tutoyer personne. Point d'altérité, seulement une alternance dans l'apparence. J'ai besoin de toutes mes tensions et de légèreté. Il ne faut pas qu'Albuquerque explose dans ma tête.

En entrant dans Albuquerque, je sens la fatigue, je suis fou rire, mots tordus, tête baroque dans le beau jeu de la réalité. Soudain.

Grazie m'accueillit chaleureusement. Elle se fit tendre, attentive et joyeuse, caressa mon tatouage sur l'épaule. Très sensuelle. Puis nous avons mangé, ri, et j'ai bu sans arrêt jusqu'à ce que des phrases commencent entre nous à répartir l'enjouement, à égrener les souvenirs, à partager le temps. Grazie aimait parler et j'aimais son parfum. Elle me parla de blessure, de danse, d'une série de photos prises devant le miroir. Je ne sais pourquoi mais entre chacune de ses phrases je pensais à Lorna, à la manière qui est la sienne de se rendre intelligible entre deux phrases tordues et les bras doux de ma mère.

« Grazie, viens, il fait froid dans ce grand lit. Viens. Éloigne-toi. Allume. Éteins. Je vais lire toute la nuit. Tu ferais mieux de dormir. Tu vois bien que c'est doux, touche un peu, tu vois, attends… Une fois seulement, c'est tellement bon. »

La vie s'en va, la vie s'en va. Cette nuit, je dormirai, petite bête esseulée, dans le creux du sommeil plein d'encens de Grazie.

Chaptitre 4

L'hom'oblong émergea de la nuit et recouvra son corps. Il faisait encore sombre. Aucun bruit pour parer à l'isolement. L'hom'oblong se redressa avec peine comme si la nuit en avait été une de grande beuverie. Il s'appuya contre le mur, vit que son chapeau avait roulé au pied du lit. *Demain*, pensa-t-il, le ciel sera beau. Mais partout encore, l'aurore était en lui fragmentée. Les chiffres qu'il avait tracés sur les murs venaient à sa rencontre, le suivaient pas à pas dans la petite chambre. L'hom'oblong, qui avait consacré sa vie à espérer la beauté, comprit qu'une fois enchâssée dans la science la beauté ne pouvait que pâlir. Il ne pourrait lui non plus soutenir le rythme obligé des équations, son insatiable appétit de connaissance. Il se sentit vulnérable et amer. Il ferma les yeux et s'abandonna à la voix morcelée qui implorait en lui, *libera*, *memento*, demain le ciel serait bleu, il n'y aurait plus de déchets dans l'atmosphère.

Grazie et sa mère sont parties au centre commercial. Je suis là, derrière la fenêtre, et je regarde la réalité passer. Rien. Je ne vois rien. Seulement la réalité. Un jour, je sortirai de tout ce fatras. La beauté est avant la réalité.

Pour l'instant, reprendre la route du désert, retrouver le motel, la piscine, les filles en maillot. La réalité se montrera *topless* dans l'éclairage pendant que les tueurs à gages suivront à la lettre leurs instructions. Le cerveau est fragile. Il n'est pas facile de substituer les images, d'allier l'abîme et la plénitude en soi. Grazie n'aura jamais 15 ans.

Au retour, je roulai vite, *fata de fata*. Pourquoi rêver en imaginant des baisers, des étreintes, en pensant que la lumière est si belle parmi les fouquières et les *paloverdes* ? Ça luit les motels, les roulottes, la tôle, les pylônes, même la rouille et tous ces pneus comme des condoms séchés. Le désert, c'est ça. Je me suis acheté une caisse de Coke et je bois. J'ai soif. Ça m'assoiffe la réalité.

J'avais 15 ans et je regardais la réalité empiéter sur la beauté pour en faire parade et parodie, comme si le vice caché de la violence voulait tâter de tout. Dans la lumière crue, l'aura tremblante de l'humanité se défendait contre la réalité.

La réalité défilait. De temps à autre l'humanité se montrait autour des roulottes et des snack-bars. C'était une femme en t-shirt, grosse de mille grossesses, des enfants calqués sur le destin. La réalité défilait, longeait habilement les atavismes, le hasard, la destinée comme un courant électrique. C'était tantôt un corps à moitié enfoui sous le capot d'une auto. Tantôt un jean, un chapeau, des ombres plaquées au sol. C'était alternance de fiction, de désert et de beauté. Des étendues dans la pensée. Des épisodes à l'approche des villes. Oui, j'étais attirée par la réalité, fascinée par ses multiples facettes, sa prose écartelée entre la matière quotidienne et le chichi du désir. Mais la réalité ouvrait sans mandat dans le volume du corps pensant. Elle actualisait les routes faciles, le déjà pensé de l'instinct, humiliait le besoin passionné de splendeur. Je n'étais qu'une forme désirante dans le contour de l'aura qui entourait l'humanité. Il me faudrait la surprendre là, dans son impossible dimension.

Oui, il me fallait un corps devant l'impensable, un corps qui puisse filtrer le mensonge, la violence, la peur, la nuit comme à l'aube, un corps capable d'écarter la foudre, d'éloigner le cri tenace d'instinct.

Je roulais, parfaite au bord de la solitude. Je ne désirais que l'horizon, un peu de lumière comme naturellement le jour, l'odeur du désert.

Mais il faisait froid dans la nuit du désert et partout où la chaleur donnait vie, je tremblais qu'elle transpose tout du côté de la mort. Je tremblais de rendre la réalité comme un épisode en m'approchant des êtres.

Chaptitre 5

L'hom'oblong prend sa douche. Il aime l'eau, que l'eau caresse et assoupisse sur sa peau le tourment. Alors tout son corps s'abandonne. Il lève la tête et l'eau pénètre par la bouche, les oreilles, les narines, découpe de grandes rigoles sur le visage osseux. L'hom'oblong aurait aimé son corps musclé. Il aurait aimé toucher ce corps neuf, sentir sa poitrine, palper les fesses fermes, les bras, serrer les cuisses dures. Il se serait senti allégé du fardeau des chiffres et son dos courbé se fût redressé prêt à tous les corps à corps. L'hom'oblong aurait aimé combattre d'homme à homme. Le battement du cœur, les veines gonflées, l'effort des muscles tendus l'auraient forcément grisé et la sueur de l'épreuve n'eût pas été comme sa transpiration pendant les heures de calcul. Il aurait aimé chaque mouvement et combien le corps de ses adversaires. L'hom'oblong ne pensait plus à l'explosion. Il était action, tension, contraction et tout abandon dans les bras de celui qu'il aurait aimé être. Il sortit de la douche, se regarda dans le miroir, vit ses joues creuses. La barbe. Il s'habilla avec empressement. Dehors le jour allait se lever mais l'hom'oblong ne fit semblant de rien. Les rideaux étaient fermés. Seule la lumière de l'explosion éclairait ses gestes. L'hom'oblong ne vit pas l'enveloppe que l'on avait glissée sous la porte.

Je pensais à Angela Parkins. Je revoyais son visage tendu, sa bouche menaçante, le tir des mots, dans ses yeux, l'humanité bien ciblée. Mais que voyait-elle Angela Parkins quand son regard affrontait l'érosion ? Comment traçait-elle ses chiffres, comment ses gestes témoignaient-ils dans la chaleur et la soif de l'ivresse amoureuse ?

Bientôt je retrouverais le motel. Le soir, je m'adonnerais à la peur devant le téléviseur. Le jour, il y aurait les filles en maillot, la nuit, les conversations au bar. Le jour, ma mère serait comme une femme. La nuit, Lorna serait avec ma mère et je m'affolerais de leur présence voilée. Je reprendrais le volant. Tout ce temps, ma pensée serait attirée vers ailleurs, précise et froide. Tout ce temps, je veillerais. En réalité, je ne céderais en rien devant l'aura tragique. Un jour, je connaîtrais tout en synchronie, l'extase, les secrets qui minent par en dedans la chère civilisation. La beauté était avant la réalité et la réalité était dans l'écriture, béance.

CHAPTITRE 6

Le jour était là, derrière les rideaux, mais l'hom'oblong n'était pas encore prêt à affronter la lumière. Il alluma une cigarette, prit un livre au hasard parmi ceux qui traînaient sur la commode. Un grand calme. Un calme envahissant qui, au fur et à mesure qu'il le sentait monter en lui, était aussitôt compensé par une excitation mentale qui ravivait douloureusement chaque nerf, rendait la peau trop vivace. Il respirait lentement mais il se savait agi par une force incontrôlable. L'hom'oblong déposa le volume, aperçut l'enveloppe blanche, se leva, entrouvrit les rideaux, puis sembla s'attrister du petit matin bleu, encore bleu comme la porcelaine des dimanches midi de son enfance. Sur la pelouse du motel, une femme déplaçait un boyau d'arrosage. Le matin rutilant entra dans la tête de l'hom'oblong. Il se pencha et ramassa l'enveloppe.

J'avais roulé toute la nuit. Bientôt je retrouverais Tucson mais je n'étais pas encore prête à affronter la peur panique et le quotidien recommencé du Motel Mauve.

Je préférais m'arrêter au Motel Rouge dont la gérante était une amie de ma mère. J'inventerais une histoire, je dirais ma fatigue et mon incapacité à reprendre la route. La gérante m'offrirait une chambre. J'irais chercher mon sac dans l'auto. Dans la boîte à gants, je prendrais le cahier, le revolver serait chaud. Puis je prendrais possession de *ma* chambre. J'écrirais tout l'avant-midi. La chambre serait petite, banale, le rideau transparent, mon corps très calme en ce décor anonyme. J'aurais l'impression de tout comprendre, la nuit, Grazie, ma mère, Lorna et toutes les autres qui vivaient en moi. Je glisserais profondément dans cette chose intime qui en réalité fait loi sur tout. Ma main serait lente. L'humanité ne pourrait pas se répéter. J'inventerais. Je serais vigilante. La langue bien pendue, j'aurais de bons réflexes.

CHAPTITRE 7

L'hom'oblong examine chaque photo. Il n'y a plus de
doute, l'explosion a eu lieu avec succès. Une photo est
une preuve éclatante. La réalité qui était une épreuve
dans la tête de l'hom'oblong est maintenant forme exposée sur la photo, beau cliché. L'hom'oblong est libre. « C'est rien, c'est rien. » Tout est dans la photo.
L'hom'oblong fixe les photos sur le mur comme pour
un examen final. Il s'éloigne, se rapproche. Observe
l'explosion. Il allume, éteint, referme le rideau, cherche le parfait éclairage qui pourrait lécher la scène : la
touche finale du regard. Puis le noir et le blanc des
photos transforment toute la chambre en un immense
instantané. L'hom'oblong regarde par la fenêtre. Dehors, tout est couleur. La piscine, les maillots, les parasols, l'eau. L'hom'oblong allume une cigarette. Toute
la chambre est solarisée.

La réalité s'impose autour de la piscine. Me voici dans la vie de mes 15 ans devenue personnage, pure aventure dans le temps théâtral. La lumière est vive, glisse sur les tuiles, se décompose arc-en-ciel dans le regard. Les bras, les cuisses, les dos, les poitrines. La lumière assaille l'infiniment précieux désir de vivre.

Une jeune femme prend des photos. Deux autres posent. La musique entre dans leur sourire, quelques rires blanchis par la lumière. Les paupières clignent. La lumière est crue. Un instant, c'est l'éternité qui recommence. Le son des voix, les murmures, *ad lib*, la saveur des cocktails sous la langue. Un homme s'approche des poseuses, entame la conversation en français. L'homme est mince. Je ne comprends pas ce qu'il dit. Les femmes rient. Il se lève, va vers le bar. La lumière est vive. Il revient avec un verre de whisky. Il parle avec beaucoup de courtoisie entre ses phrases. Il n'est pas d'ici. Il n'est pas français non plus. J'ai soif. Je regarde vers le bar. Un plongeon. L'homme repasse devant moi. Il allonge son corps sur une serviette rayée de noir et de blanc. La lumière est crue. Le temps s'étiole. Les filles bavardent en ballottant leurs jambes dans l'eau. Je plonge. La réalité est un désir espacé dans la mémoire. Les motels se ressemblent, la réalité, envahissante.

Je nagerai un peu. Quelques longueurs, mammifère, cétacé, raine, puis je prendrai ma douche à l'heure où les touristes iront dans le désert voir éclater l'orange et sentir le mauve lentement les soustraire à l'angoisse. Quand ils reviendront, je serai au bar et la gérante dira comme si cela était rassurant que j'ai maintenant l'air d'une femme. Puis les yeux braqués sur le miroir derrière le bar, j'assisterai à la procession des clients qui viendront commander des alcools aux couleurs multiples et chercher dans la saveur l'effet calmant du soleil au coucher.

CHAPTITRE 8

L'hom'oblong récite des poèmes sanskrits. L'explosion est loin. Le nœud de sa cravate, bien fait. Les photos traînent parmi les équations. L'hom'oblong se sent léger, presque heureux. Il est prêt, enfin, à rencontrer les autorités. Une dernière nuit au motel, puis il reprendra sa véritable identité, son charme certain. Il sait argumenter et convaincre. Il sera impeccable. L'hom'oblong vit son corps disgracieux dans la glace. « Il neige dans l'éternel. » Il mit son veston et se dirigea vers le bar.

C'est jeudi soir. Les clients arrivent en couple ou un à un. Le bar est rempli d'accents, des touristes, quelques familiers qui font la ronde, la parade autour du bar. Je connais tout ça.

Aucune intrigue ne résiste au désert. Le désert boit tout, l'anatomie, les pensées capables en apparence d'espoir. Il faut pouvoir inventer autour de ses 15 ans. Tout pouvoir. Dramatiser, cascade audacieuse au-dessus de l'horizon, transformer l'eau vive des cascatelles en puits de lumière, immobiliser l'ombre, d'un seul élan traverser toutes les probabilités. Ici dans le bar du Motel Rouge, le désert est déplacé. Ne reste que la soif débridée comme un torrent pouvant emporter tous les ossements, le noyau sec de l'âme. J'ai grandi dans le désert. Je n'ai aucun mérite à le désirer vrai. J'ai grandi dans la solitude. Je me protège contre l'aspect craspec du monde.

L'homme à l'accent vient de faire son entrée. Il salue les femmes de la piscine. Je commande une bière. La propriétaire murmure quelques mots qui font certainement de moi une jeune femme. Elle accueille tout son monde aimablement. La musique joue à tue-tête. Des gens dansent, cherchent à accoupler leurs pas, à s'accorder en plaçant leur corps dans le rythme. Les bras se soulèvent en forme de cape comme pour capter le hâle chaud des visages. Au fond de la salle, l'homme maigre est appuyé sur le mur et il fume.

L'aube oriente l'énergie. J'ai besoin de l'aube. Je veux tout comprendre. J'ai soif. Quelqu'un me frôle. Angela Parkins remue tout autour de moi, joyeuse et cavalière. Le temps ralentit, sa présence m'exalte. La musique éclate dans ma tête. Les trois femmes de la piscine ont trouvé des partenaires. L'homme maigre converse avec deux autres hommes. La musique tape fort. Les corps s'élancent, chevaux au grand galop, crinières happées par l'éclairage, yeux bleus, visages blonds, des ombres sur le front, le sourire emporté des filles, la couleur des gestes basanés. Tout est sensuel. Je regarde Angela Parkins. Elle me fait un grand signe, vient vers moi, me prend par la taille. La musique est trop forte. La musique est encore trop douce. Le corps d'Angela Parkins cabriole, chevreuil fou aux yeux pleins de lubies. Corps de voltige, corps de vertige. On nous regarde. On nous observe. La beauté soudain, sournoisement. Ça chante entre les lèvres d'Angela, ça braille, ça brame, ça psalmodie. Nos mains se croisent, se figent, longeant le velouté de la peau, se retiennent dans le tout bas des mots. C'est comme un grand tournoi de sons. Puis sa joue enfin rapprochée.

Il y a si peu de temps que je connais Angela Parkins et pourtant nous voici dans un état de tel rapprochement. Hormis l'éternité, il n'y a plus d'espace entre nous. Nous sommes le désert et l'évidence. Dans nos yeux, plus de remous, seulement l'Amérique sonore et distante qui se confond à la couleur des peaux. Peut-être encore un peu de nuit. Les trois femmes dansent ensemble en évitant de trop se rapprocher. La musique est trop forte. Angela Parkins propose de s'asseoir.

Nous buvons la même chose. Puis dans ma tête le brouhaha cesse et Angela parle d'exister. Elle dit que tout va recommencer, paroles, sentiers, sentiments, elle dit que pleurer oblige à ralentir, que dans la détresse tous les sons envahissent les mots, qu'ils sont tout crus dans la bouche, que ça devient alors difficile de se comprendre, elle dit que ça saute dans sa tête et que s'il fallait recommencer le monde, il faudrait encore des orages, de l'électricité partout dans le cerveau, elle dit qu'il faut espérer, que la mémoire peut encore accomplir de beaux ouvrages, mais les yeux, Mélanie, elle dit qu'en réalité il suffit de quelques mots concis pour changer le cours de la mort, pour effrayer les petites douleurs, elle parle et réveille en moi l'horizon.

Il est minuit trente. La nuit continue dans la musique à se frayer un espace, creuse son nid entre nos jambes. Le temps travaille minutieusement. Muscle, nerf, cellule, peau de vertige organisent en nous les mirages, les visions. Encore un temps, une musique, nous dansons allègrement. Puis le corps d'Angela Parkins bouge si peu. Je resserre l'étreinte à la taille. Il fait chaud entre nous, sur les tempes, dans les cheveux. Angela, nous dansons? Plus d'écho, plus de musique. Nos corps ne tiennent plus ensemble. Le silence est cru. Les yeux, vite les yeux! La pupille grand œuvre du désir se fane. Des bruits de chaise, l'agitation, des voix qui portent. Le ravage est grand. L'hom'oblong regarde devant lui, complètement détaché de la scène. Angela Parkins est allongée sur le bois blond de la piste, le corps à tout jamais inflexible, exhibé, point de mire. Mélanie, fille de la nuit, que s'est-il donc passé?

La réalité, l'aube. Néant. Tout mon corps va se soumettre. Des policiers, la craie autour du corps. Personne n'a rien vu. Je n'ai rien vu venir. Le désert est indescriptible. Les yeux se fanent.

Puis ce fut le profil menaçant de toute chose. Puis l'aube, le désert et mauve, l'horizon. Il y a des mémoires pour creuser les mots sans souiller les tombes. Je ne peux tutoyer personne.

DOSSIER

- Réception critique
- Chronologie
- Bibliographie

RÉCEPTION CRITIQUE

Présentation générale

Le désert mauve de Nicole Brossard est un des rares textes québécois qui put, dès sa parution en 1987, attirer l'attention des critiques aussi bien féministes que déconstructionnistes, ceux-ci s'intéressant plutôt à ses aspects postmodernes qu'à ses perspectives idéologiques. Mais la réception positive dont jouit ce roman parmi des critiques d'approches différentes, sinon complémentaires, n'a rien d'étonnant puisque c'est au carrefour des discours féministes et postmodernes que Brossard place, en fait, son texte.

Œuvre aussi bien de synthèse que d'innovation, *Le désert mauve* reprend plusieurs des thèmes, des émotions, des situations et des stratégies textuelles déjà explorés dans d'autres œuvres brossardiennes.

Le désert mauve aborde de nouveau la problématique des genres littéraires par son mélange de genres et de discours divers – récit, journal de lecture, dialogues fictifs, éléments autobiographiques, traduction – ainsi que par l'inclusion du matériau visuel. Forçant les limites du genre romanesque, cette *interdiscursivité au féminin* et le hors-texte-devenu-texte à l'aide d'une série de photos de « l'homme long » aussi bien que des fragments extratextuels de documentation historique assurent que le quotidien, le poétique, le théorique et l'historique circulent presque sans restriction.

Le désert mauve de Nicole Brossard est l'histoire d'un ouvrage publié en Arizona par une écrivaine fictive, Laure Angstelle, et dont le titre est aussi Le désert mauve. Ce dédoublement du titre initial fait partie de toute une série de structures et de procédés narratifs marquant l'importance de l'autoreprésentation dans Le désert mauve et contribuant ainsi à son air « postmoderne ». Retrouvé dans une librairie d'occasion, le texte inconnu – et donc non canonique – de Laure Angstelle constitue la première section du roman de Brossard ; il nous fait connaître les personnages, gestes et perspectives qui seront par la suite contemplés, considérés sous d'autres *angles* de vue, et éventuellement réécrits dans le récit « traduit » de Maude Laures. L'histoire du *Désert mauve* de Laure Angstelle, c'est donc l'histoire de sa présentation matérielle, de son trajet mental et émotif dans la pensée d'une lectrice fictive, Maude Laures, et de sa transformation finale dans la traduction effectuée par Maude Laures qui compose la troisième partie du roman et qui s'intitule *Mauve, l'horizon*.

Karen GOULD
Le roman québécois depuis 1960 : méthodes et analyses

SUR LA TRADUCTION

Imaginons que ce roman, *Le désert mauve*, que cette écrivaine, Laure Angstelle, soient réels et que Maude Laures, professeure de littérature, déniche par hasard le livre à Montréal dans une librairie d'occasion. Fascinée, elle l'annote pendant un an, le traduit et le publie finalement sous le titre de *Mauve, l'horizon*. C'est là l'objet du livre de Nicole Brossard.

Hélène RIOUX
Le Journal d'Outremont

Le désert mauve: un ouvrage dans lequel elle explore, au travers la traduction que son héroïne Maude Laures fait d'un court récit et la nouvelle œuvre à laquelle celle-ci donne naissance, une approche complètement renouvelée du genre romanesque.

Corinne Durin
Spirale

Le désert mauve de Nicole Brossard: la coprésence du texte original français et de sa traduction réénonciation dans la même langue met au jour la participation créative de la traductrice – son désir, son travail de dévoilement de ce qui, dans le texte premier, se dérobe – et crée.

Pierrette Roy
La Tribune

C'est la forme même qui devient signifiante.

On assiste à une transposition constante entre deux niveaux de fiction angoissante et paradoxalement exaltante de sa traduction, puis finalement retour au premier niveau: la fiction de l'œuvre traduite. Tout au long de la lecture du livre nous transitons entre ces deux niveaux dans un mouvement de balancier. Ce rythme est donné dès le début par l'insertion de la présence de « l'homme long », intercalée entre les différentes pauses du récit et semblant n'avoir, de prime abord, aucun autre lien avec celui-ci que ceux du désert et de la folie. « L'homme long » fait converger les tensions qui émergent, qui affleurent dans le récit et qui créent une atmosphère d'attente lente et lourde. Ces tensions seront relâchées quand surviendra à la fin, d'une façon imprévue et soudaine, presque insolente, la mort.

Jean-Marie Marcotte
Mœbius

Y prime la réflexion sur le pourquoi et le comment d'un texte, sur le choix ultime entre deux signifiés, la succession des choix modelant le récit entier. Les moyens utilisés se veulent concluants : une histoire, une étape d'analyse et de questionnement, la reformulation de l'histoire. Traduction ? Si on veut, mais pas uniquement. Entre la traduction mécanique et l'investissement de celle qui devient ici une seconde narratrice, la marge est grande.

Dominique MAUREL
Nos livres

Pour ce qui concerne l'activité dans ce centre de traduction [où de jeunes traducteurs slovènes en formation se réunissaient une fois par mois à l'automne 1988 et au printemps 1989 à Ljubljana], ce roman qui joue (et déjoue à la fois) sur les passages « fictifs » voire fictionnels entre l'anglais (encore) « fictif » dans le texte et le français de la prose, et en même temps sur les passages ô combien réels entre les conceptions nord-américaines de la vie et ce fond québécois a représenté non seulement un défi tel que décrit plus haut, mais aussi et surtout un exemple extrêmement gratifiant et instructif par rapport aux « pièges » et aux « attrapes » du métier. Dans un contexte bien particulier où la langue slovène parlée par deux millions d'habitants de cette république au nord de la Yougoslavie se sent menacée de tous les côtés – « fictivement » ou « réellement », et subit depuis des siècles des pressions linguistiques des voisins – italiens et allemands et croates et les Serbes... Problème particulier aussi lorsqu'il s'agissait de réécrire ce discours particulier qu'est celui de Nicole Brossard, vue l'absence presque totale, en Slovénie, mais en Yougoslavie en général aussi, de la pensée féministe au sens nord-américain du terme, et en conséquence, de la terminologie corroborant l'idéologie, d'où les difficultés dans le choix des termes, pour ne pas

parler de la complexité symbolique brossardienne, de la polysémie des mots (par exemple la *mousse*) qui sert justement
– la complexité – à assurer la contiguïté dans la disparité –
où il s'agit, en outre, de préserver le côté phonétique ainsi
que de respecter les contraintes sémantiques, tel le *m* (de
mousse) dans les jeux de mots (encore symboliques), des
sand witches, des jeux entre Maudes et mauves et laures et
l'hor-izon… Pour ne citer que ces quelques exemples. Mais
surtout, et avant tout – cette attraction qu'opère le texte sur
le lecteur / la lectrice, par sa force, par sa cohérence, par
cette incroyable et bien sûr agréable, je dirais contagieuse
joie d'œuvrer dans le langage et par le langage – qui est
source, l'origine de cette volubilité métafictionnelle – dans
le texte et autour du texte.

Metka Zupančič
Entre le désert et l'horizon

Traduction et procédés narratifs

Tout le sens du roman tient dans le déplacement de la première version à la deuxième, dans la rencontre entre une
auteure et sa traductrice, grâce à la lecture et à la réécriture
du texte original. Mais le passage ne se fait ni sans ambi-
guïtés, ni sans perte, puisque chacune des deux versions de
l'intrigue aboutit à un événement apparemment incontour-
nable – le meurtre de la femme « intégrale » vers laquelle se
dirigeaient tout le désir et tout le sens de la possibilité du
roman de Laure Angstelle : « Le ravage est grand » (p. 248).

Un des plaisirs de la lecture de ce roman est d'assister au
tour de force par lequel Brossard nous présente, en français,
non seulement le texte original du roman, mais aussi sa traduction. Identiques jusque dans leur pagination et leur division en phrases et en paragraphes, les deux versions sont
pourtant l'expression de deux sensibilités différentes, et

c'est dans la variation de mots et d'images de la première à la deuxième qu'émerge le mouvement vers une réconciliation avec le temps et le réel. Même prise isolément, la première version (avec sa préoccupation constante de « la réalité ») représenterait un point tournant important dans l'évolution de l'écriture de Brossard. Mais c'est en faisant passer ce premier récit tout imprégné d'intensité, de vitesse et de violence à travers l'intelligence amoureuse et toute en simplicité de la traductrice Maude Laures que Brossard parvient à enraciner sa vision du désert et à l'insérer dans la durée.

L'interdépendance et l'affrontement inévitable de ces deux trajets narratifs dans la scène finale du meurtre d'Angela Parkins par l'homme long figurent l'énigme que tout le roman de Brossard explore et tente de résoudre. Meurtre aussi froid, abstrait et dévastateur que l'explosion silencieuse par laquelle la technologie pourrait annihiler la terre, et que l'homme long semble avoir accompli par le seul pouvoir de son regard haineux.

Patricia SMART
Voix et Images

Du *Désert mauve* au *Mauve, l'horizon*, du texte d'origine au texte traduit, de Laure Angstelle à Maude Laures, se produit donc un lieu de rencontre privilégiée entre deux « Laure », deux endroits en mauve et deux perspectives sur la mort d'une femme. C'est ainsi qu'une dialectique s'établit entre lecture et réécriture, car comme les théories féministes récentes de la traduction l'ont déjà révélé, cette dialectique se fait « entre deux textes et deux langues (entre le texte et la langue de départ [et] le texte et la langue d'arrivée); la traduction [ainsi conçue] devient un acte combiné de lecture et d'écriture puisque la traductrice est à la fois lectrice (et interprète du texte de départ) et auteure (du texte d'arrivée) » (Mezei, 1985 : 29).

Dans *Le désert mauve*, ce processus de différenciation et de répétition transformatrice s'effectue dans l'espoir de « faire pencher la réalité un peu plus du côté de la lumière » – sans pour autant oublier le poids de l'*évidence*. Interprète culturelle donc, qui affirme l'importance de nouvelles lectures, Maude Laures fonctionne comme médiatrice entre le mot-signe et le monde. Pour elle, ainsi que pour Brossard, lire, c'est s'engager dans une transformation du réel par le désir d'une justice de vivre qui serait autre et que Brossard ne cesse d'explorer dans son écriture.

Karen GOULD
Le roman québécois depuis 1960 : méthodes et analyses

La seconde partie, *Un livre à traduire*, commence par les réflexions de Maude Laures sur le texte de Laure Angstelle, se poursuit par la description des divers « lieux et objets » (le motel, la piscine, l'auto, le téléviseur, le bar, le revolver, etc.), des personnages (en ce qui concerne l'homme long, cette description se résume à cinq remarquables photographies classées dans une chemise) ; puis par des dialogues imaginés entre les personnages et notamment une conversation entre l'auteure et la traductrice ; finalement par les « dimensions », c'est-à-dire le désert, l'aube, la beauté, la civilisation, etc.

C'est donc à un deuxième degré que s'effectue le travail sur le texte. Et qu'opère aussi toute la magie de l'écriture. Entre les deux versions du même écrit, un décalage, mais d'une subtilité incomparable. L'anecdote, les personnages, les lieux et les objets sont pourtant identiques. La différence vient du seul fait que deux auteures le marquent de l'empreinte de leur vécu. Différence d'éclairage donc. D'ajustement du foyer. Les mots ont ce pouvoir de rendre et de trahir la réalité.

Hélène RIOUX
Le Journal d'Outremont

Les mots DÉSERT et MAUVE ne sont pas le fruit du hasard. Le désert fascine Nicole Brossard. Les couleurs aussi, surtout celles de l'aube. […] Le désert, l'aube, la lumière, la réalité, la beauté, la peur, la civilisation défient la réflexion comme le rêve.

Elle raconte, frémissante, dans une sorte de transfiguration sensuelle, la beauté du désert, l'attrait irrésistible qu'exerce sa violence, le danger vers lequel elle nous persuade d'accourir… Pour échapper peut-être à l'échec d'une civilisation.

Elle propulse des personnages d'une vitalité trépidante dans des voies sans issues. Que peut-il survenir pour ces personnages qui oscillent comme sur un fil de fer invisible qui tranche entre la réalité et la fiction, qui épuisent leur vie sans renoncer à ce que, aveuglés par une implacable lumière, ils conçoivent comme la beauté?

Roland HÉROUX
Le Nouvelliste

Le roman de Nicole Brossard, *Le désert mauve*, nous offre ce que j'appellerais une image extrême de ce présent. Un désert en Arizona, c'est-à-dire au diable vauvert, dans le bric-à-brac de la modernité; une explosion, un meurtre, quelque part, sans raison; des relations amoureuses réduites à un seul sexe; les signes d'un monde qui semble toujours sur le point de disparaître.

Cela colle à la rétine, aussi fortement que les images du désert dans *Paris, Texas* de Wim Wenders.

Gilles MARCOTTE
L'Actualité

Le désert mauve est sûrement le plus beau livre de sa carrière – un grand roman courageux et lucide, qui traverse tout le désespoir de notre civilisation et qui, grâce à la générosité de sa créatrice, nous ouvre un chemin vers l'espérance.

Quelques allusions passagères à un «Dante's View Motel» dans ce fabuleux «roman du désert» font comprendre qu'il s'agit bel et bien de *la Divine* (et humaine) *Comédie* d'une auteure qui se sait rendue au mi-temps de sa vie. Revenue des utopies (sans avoir abandonné pour autant son désir de transformer le monde), Brossard trouve dans le désert de l'Arizona une métaphore de la totalité de l'expérience humaine.

«Le désert est indescriptible» (p. 31): ainsi commence ce roman mystique et très incarné, toutes perspectives ouvertes sur l'espace «hyperréel» du désert – à la fois lieu de violence (expérience scientifique et explosion imminente), lieu postmoderne parsemé de traces humaines (canettes et carrosseries d'autos, motels anonymes où l'on vit autour de la piscine et dans les bars) et lieu de beauté indicible faite de lumière, de couleurs, d'une végétation lente et patiente qui sait résister à la mort pendant de longues périodes d'aridité.

C'est dans ses mots que réside la beauté qui transcende le désespoir de cette intrigue, mots qu'il faut goûter et garder en soi comme un vin exquis sur le palais, ou comme l'aube qu'on ne voit même pas «quand on laisse à la nuit le soin de s'avancer dans nos vies à ce point que la lueur du jour s'effrite dans nos yeux comme un lendemain frileux, [quand] dans le taxi blafard qui nous ramène à la maison… il n'y a plus de contexte et que nos sens broient du vide appelant le sommeil, d'autres artifices pour enrober le corps. Car l'aube se mérite, et, lorsqu'on a su la mériter, elle est au bout de l'âme une certitude tranquille, un apaisement des yeux épris de changements et d'utopies» (p.179).

Patricia SMART
Voix et Images

Le livre de Nicole Brossard est beau d'une beauté dure, comme celle du désert lui-même.

Lori SAINT-MARTIN
Le Devoir

VIOLENCE ET FÉMINITÉ

D'ailleurs, disons-le tout de suite, les personnages de ce livre ont quelque chose d'obsédant, qui les aveugle, scande et dérègle leurs passions.

On croirait que les intervalles de la narration consacrés à « l'homme long », personnage énigmatique, menaçant, sorte de démiurge de la destruction, vont faire basculer dans une mort prématurée une aventure et des personnages voués à la faillite.

Maude Laures (elles s'appellent bien Laure Angstelle et Maude Laures : ne pas confondre) s'invente une langue. Et quelle langue ! Elle restitue lieux et objets, donne encore plus de chair aux êtres qu'elle réinvente, recrée. Tisse une toile, règle les dialogues, les scènes, d'un roman qui renouvelle et transforme ce qui avait été une simple esquisse.

Roland HÉROUX
Le Nouvelliste

La richesse des perspectives apportées au thème de la violence dans *Le désert mauve*, ainsi que les contextes multiples de ses manifestations, reflète la variété de théories féministes sur ce sujet.

Tout comme *Les fous de Bassan* d'Anne Hébert – roman que Brossard admire beaucoup et qui a déjà suscité une reconnaissance féministe considérable –, *Le désert mauve* prépare dès son début à l'acte de violence ultime qui nous sera révélé à la fin du récit originaire et sur lequel il faudra sans cesse revenir.

Patricia Smart a déjà noté que « [l]e meurtre d'Angela Parkins par « l'homme long/oblong » [...] reproduit tous les meurtres de femmes qui parsèment les textes littéraires québécois depuis le dix-neuvième siècle, mais en plus terrifiant, parce que devenu anonyme, abstrait, portrait d'une civilisation postmoderne devenue pure technologie » (1988, p. 335). Aussi faut-il constater que, même si le texte de Brossard ne tourne plus inévitablement autour du couple hétérosexuel, la violence reste le lieu privilégié de leur rencontre.

Procédant à cet égard comme *Les fous de Bassan*, *Le désert mauve* introduit le meurtre d'une femme dans la première partie du roman, et de façon énigmatique, pour que la brutalité de l'acte puisse être interrogée, interprétée et réécrite différemment.

Cependant, la question à laquelle il faut répondre dans *Le désert mauve* n'est pas qui a tué la femme – car la responsabilité est en fin de compte collective, on l'a facilement compris – mais pourquoi l'a-t-on tuée. Comme *Les fous de Bassan*, *Le désert mauve* demande donc une réflexion sur les raisons sociale, politique et idéologique de cet acte de violence qui semble si inintelligible, si impossible à narrer au début. L'originalité du *Désert mauve*, c'est que toute la réflexion sur la violence masculine se fait entièrement entre femmes – l'assassin misogyne n'a littéralement plus de voix.

On ne devrait pas s'étonner de voir que des traces indiquant la violence de l'Histoire ont fourni une matière essentielle à la construction du *Désert mauve* ainsi qu'aux significations qui y circulent.

C'est aussi à l'aide de la présence énigmatique de cet homme inconnu, « l'homme long », que des liens se forment dans le texte avec d'autres signes de brutalité dans la culture contemporaine. De prime abord, ce personnage est un homme dépouillé de nom et d'identité fixe. Trouvé par des équations mathématiques, obsédé par des explosions qu'il imagine et qu'il essaie ensuite d'oublier ou de refouler, incapable enfin de dormir, l'homme long de Laure Angstelle n'est, à première vue, qu'une présence mal définie et brumeuse.

Angstelle, qui écrit sous la plume de Brossard, construit une thématique surdéterminée de la violence de l'ère atomique et nucléaire en relevant de nombreux éléments-fragments associés à un physicien en particulier, Robert Oppenheimer, et à un projet historique précis, « The Manhattan Project » – programme entrepris en 1942 par le gouvernement américain afin de produire une bombe atomique qui pourrait assurer une victoire militaire et mettre fin à la guerre.

Selon le peu d'indications données dans la première partie du texte (qui est le récit d'Angstelle), l'homme long, tout comme Oppenheimer, aurait voulu que cette explosion, dont il se croit responsable, soit « comme un espoir de beauté » ; il se rend compte trop tard qu'elle ne peut mener qu'à la destruction de la civilisation (p.57).

Chez l'homme long, le doute et l'incrédulité postmodernes remplacent, pour ainsi dire, l'autorité de la science atomique et nucléaire qui lui avait servi de métarécit du progrès humain. C'est pour cette raison, sans doute, que son visage, tout comme son identité masculine-virile, s'éclate dans la photo à l'intérieur du dossier tenu par Maude Laures ; c'est pour cela également que l'homme long sera renommé « l'hom'oblong » (*l'homme-au-blanc*) dans sa traduction du texte. [...]

Dans son désir de comprendre ce récit qui vit en elle depuis deux ans et auquel elle retourne sans cesse, Maude Laures mène une enquête sur la place de la violence dans la civilisation contemporaine. Elle écrira donc un chapitre intitulé « Le revolver » dans lequel elle imagine des revolvers dispersés un peu partout dans ce désert américain. Cette prolifération des revolvers ne s'effectue pas pour nous confondre sur l'identité de l'assassin, mais plutôt pour signaler la prolifération de la violence potentielle dans une société nord-américaine aux tendances agressivement « macho » ou « cow-boy ».

Karen GOULD
Le roman québécois depuis 1960 : méthodes et analyses

Il faut reconnaître pourtant que l'histoire racontée par les deux textes du *Désert mauve*, si elle est simple, est incisive, puisqu'elle mène au meurtre d'Angela Parkins, femme de carrière (géomètre) que l'alcool amène à parler peut-être trop, certains soirs, et qu'un homme (appelé « l'homme long » dans « Le désert mauve » et « hom'oblong » dans « Mauve, l'horizon ») finira par abattre, pour des raisons jusqu'à un certain point mystérieuses.

L'important à retenir est qu'Angela Parkins meurt en dansant, tombant dans les bras de Mélanie, 15 ans, l'adolescente qui occupe le centre de tout le roman.

La vie d'Angela Parkins est ainsi retirée à Mélanie, et avec elle la (nouvelle) vie qui semblait sur le point de lui venir par le biais d'Angela Parkins.

Le personnage de l'homme revient comme en force dans *Le désert mauve*, stylisé, accompagnant le personnage de la femme tant dans le contenu – on a vu le rôle important qu'il y joue – que dans le déroulement de l'écriture où le personnage masculin a droit à ses propres chapitres.

Qui plus est, l'homme long/hom'oblong est le sujet du seul déploiement iconographique du roman : cinq photos qui le représentent, toujours de biais, sans que jamais ne soit révélé son visage, dans des scènes qui reproduisent l'un ou l'autre des épisodes décrits parallèlement dans le roman et qui le concernent.

À noter, une modification amplement mise en relief, d'un texte à l'autre : le changement de nomination de cet *homme* posé comme *long* dans « Le désert mauve », le meurtrier d'Angela, et que « Mauve, l'horizon » désigne comme un *hom'oblong*,

Il y a certainement ici exhibition de quelque chose, ne serait-ce que du fait de la provocation venue du jeu de langage : la graphie atypique de *hom*, là où on attend *homme*, ne peut que faciliter l'amalgame *hom'oblong*.

Dans un ouvrage où les relations entre femmes sont si prégnantes, la tentation est forte de voir en cet homme qui se cache constamment, dont le visage est volontairement laissé invisible (selon l'angle de certaines photos, on *devrait* pourtant voir son visage), la production d'un nouveau syntagme, relativement clair au fond, et qui serait dissimulé à son tour sous l'utilisation sibylline de l'adjectif rare *oblong* : *hom'oblong / homo blond*.

La mort d'Angela Parkins, si elle abolit le personnage d'Angela, abolit aussi et surtout la possibilité d'une relation lesbienne de deuxième génération, celle d'une adolescente, fille de lesbienne, sur le point de voir se concrétiser à son tour, sur un arrière-fond de désert, sa propre naissance à la passion et au désir.

Le développement d'une passion amoureuse librement choisie ne s'avère pas être bloqué, ici, par *l'autre*, l'adversaire, cet *homme long*, justement, qui était sans doute dans le (premier) texte de Laure Angstelle un opposant, le symbole de la société mâle en général, mais par un *homo blond* qui, tout menaçant qu'il apparaisse dans cette fiction, n'en constitue pas moins pour les personnages féminins un autre elles-mêmes. Comme si le travail de traduction par Maude Laures du récit de Laure Angstelle avait abouti à un double meurtre, celui de la lesbienne libérée Angela Parkins, et celui du désir de vivre de Mélanie, mais en déplaçant le lieu de l'agression, de l'autre à soi-même, produisant quelque chose qui serait plus de l'ordre du suicide et de la renonciation que de l'agression.

Louise Milot
Lettres québécoises

Cinq pages d'illustrations prolongent la mystérieuse présence [de l'homme long], après les huit chapitres intercalés dans le récit du début et qui deviendra, en fin de roman, dans huit chapitres aussi, l'hom'oblong du texte de Laure Angstelle : *Mauve, l'horizon*, quand Maude Laures aura fini de le traduire. De quoi l'homme long, qui devient l'hom'oblong, est-il le symbole, le moteur ou la victime aveugle ? Cet homme n'est-il qu'un robot dont use une science qui peut tout détruire et qui, de fait, le détruit ? Sa tentative, une explosion, devient, grâce à la science, l'équation réussie. Au point de vue humain, cette image de beauté n'est-elle pas proposition mortelle et donc faillite ?

Roland HÉROUX
Le Nouvelliste

Mais qui est cet homme qui apparaît comme une ombre menaçante entre les chapitres ? Un savant qui s'amuse à barbouiller d'équations les murs de sa chambre. On l'imagine, plus qu'on ne le voit, étendu sur son lit de motel, sa petite revue de femmes nues à la main. Cet homme, que l'auteure va jusqu'à nous présenter en photos, toujours fait peur. Il incarne la violence et la destruction. C'est lui en même temps qui détient le pouvoir.

Aucun homme n'apprécierait, il va sans dire, d'être associé à ce fantôme. D'ailleurs, même dans l'esprit de Nicole Brossard, il ne s'agit pas d'un individu en chair et en os, mais plutôt d'un symbole, celui « d'une société qui a colonisé les femmes, bien que toutes ne soient pas exploitées », celui aussi d'une société qui a inventé la bombe.

Anne-Marie VOISARD
Le Soleil

L'originalité du récit tient avant tout à la façon dont il est construit.

Elle [Maude Laures] s'applique, tel un metteur en scène, à reconstituer le désert de l'Arizona « indescriptible », un motel avec piscine, le bar qui est peint en « mauve ». Ensuite, elle se glisse dans la peau de chacun des personnages : une mère et sa fille de 15 ans, Mélanie ; deux femmes, dont l'une est la mère, partageant à l'abri des regards indiscrets leur amour ; puis Angela Parkins, la femme libérée qui n'a pas peur de s'afficher, dans les bras de Mélanie, sur la piste de danse, celle précisément que « l'homme long » ne pourra tolérer.

Anne-Marie VOISARD
Le Soleil

Tout *Le désert mauve* s'étire en effet entre deux *livres dans le livre* : un premier texte, donné comme appartenant à une narratrice/auteure autre que celle du roman, une certaine Laure Angstelle, s'intitule « Le désert mauve » (p.29-75) ; puis la traduction de ce premier récit par Maude Laures, sous le titre de « Mauve, l'horizon », (p.207-249) *second texte dans le texte* qui clôt le roman. Entre les deux se tiendrait le travail de la transformation.

C'est tout le problème de la fabrication de la fiction qui est posé ici, par le biais de la traduction, en un certain sens la réécriture du monde.

Louise MILOT
Lettres québécoises

[Nicole Brossard] joue à fond du paradoxe du livre, à la fois objet matériel (« mince tranche de papier entre les appuis-livres »), collection de mots imprimés, et histoire (car les mots deviennent, sans qu'on sache trop comment, des personnages, des lieux, des émotions).

C'est justement de ce double passage du réel au mot et des mots au réel qu'il est question dans *Le désert mauve*. Le roman englobe trois récits. [...]

À force de manipuler les objets, d'arpenter les lieux, de faire parler les personnages muets de Laure Angstelle, Maude entre peu à peu dans le monde de l'auteur. La partie centrale du livre donne naissance à un nouveau récit, une fiction mimée, retournée, interrogée, en même temps, c'est une longue méditation sur la traduction comme acte de lecture.

La version du « Désert mauve » publiée par Maude Laures est une interprétation, dans le double sens de traduction et de commentaire.

Maude Laures se voit comme un simple « instrument de résonance », mais elle n'en donne pas moins une lecture parallèle de l'œuvre : par exemple, l'aube évoque la « fureur » pour Laure Angstelle, mais le calme et la quiétude dans l'esprit de Maude Laures. Traduire signifie alors faire coexister les paysages intérieurs de l'une et de l'autre.

Lori Saint-Martin
Le Devoir

Dans la deuxième partie du roman, qui s'avère de loin la plus longue et la plus hétérogène du point de vue de la forme, la lectrice fictive, Maude Laures, explore les raisons de son identification avec le récit de Laure Angstelle et de la résistance qu'elle y oppose. Des notes de lecture, des réflexions autobiographiques et des dialogues imaginés entre les personnages et l'auteure fictive l'aident dans cette tâche. Les méditations de Maude Laures sur le meurtre d'Angela Parkins et sur la violence grandissante de la culture nord-américaine sont au cœur même de cette entreprise d'expansion, d'interprétation et de réécriture.

En accordant une place importante à la lectrice-traductrice du *Désert mauve* au beau milieu du roman, Brossard met en relief le rôle essentiel de Maude Laures dans la construction et la circulation du sens textuel. C'est ainsi que Brossard nous fait penser non seulement à l'acte d'écrire, mais aussi aux procédés de toute lecture intime et aux émotions qu'elle peut provoquer. [...]

À travers son carnet de lecture, Maude Laures pose ainsi des questions investigatrices aux personnages d'Angstelle et y répond de son mieux à travers leurs voix telles qu'elle les imagine. Enfin, la concentration dont Maude Laures fait preuve lorsqu'elle entre en dialogues multiples avec les personnages féminins du « Désert mauve » démontre sa volonté de résister à des interprétations toutes faites sur le récit d'Angstelle et, plus généralement encore, sur la vie des femmes. La recherche sérieuse de Maude Laures est aussi sa façon de reconnaître les féminismes dans le féminisme, de faire place à une pluralité de voix féminines dans le texte.

Karen GOULD
Le roman québécois depuis 1960 : méthodes et analyses

Nicole Brossard réalise ici un singulier exploit puisque le lecteur se prend de fascination pour la nouvelle de Laure Angstelle, véritable *temps sacré*, qui ne constitue pourtant que l'objet du « roman ».

La dimension « romanesque » que désire l'auteur n'intervient qu'ensuite. Elle prend corps avec la laborieuse démarche de « traduction » que poursuit Maude Laures qui, en développant certains aspects du texte initial, ne fait que reconduire, paradoxalement, la fascination du lecteur pour ce dernier.

Complètement excentrique, le « roman » se veut pourtant, davantage qu'une illustration, une éducation où l'on verra Maude Laures, femme de peu d'envergure, « devenir une voix autre et ressemblante dans l'univers de Laure Angstelle » (p.204). Un univers résolument lesbien où les hommes ne sont associés qu'à des images de destruction et de mort.

Et pour peu que plusieurs lecteurs soient rebutés par le projet idéologique d'écriture de Nicole Brossard, il faut en reconnaître la rigueur et le fait qu'il se conjugue avec une richesse poétique et une maîtrise formelle qui jamais ne défaillent.

Patrick GONZALES
Nuit blanche

CONCLUSIONS

Un tel livre ne peut pas décevoir le public lecteur de Nicole Brossard, d'autant qu'il s'agit certainement d'un des textes de prose les plus immédiatement lisibles que cette auteure ait publié.

Nicole Brossard fait de nouveau la preuve d'une perspicacité de premier ordre, face aux courants contemporains d'écriture, et d'une très grande intelligence des faits de langage. [...]

Ce qui fait l'objet du roman, dans la centaine de pages intermédiaires dont l'utilité est de ménager le passage, du « livre à traduire » à sa « traduction » : la narratrice (fictive), vraisemblablement Maude Laures, avant de le traduire, en redispose les éléments par séries thématiques selon : les lieux et objets (p.91-107): le motel, la piscine, l'auto, le téléviseur, le tatouage, le revolver, le bar ; les personnages (p.109-147) Laure Angstelle (l'auteure), Lorna Myher (l'amante de la mère), Kathy Kerouac (la mère), Angela Parkins, Mélanie, l'homme long, et Maude Laures elle-même par le biais d'un autoportrait ; des scènes imaginaires entre ces personnages (p.149-171) ; et ce que le texte appelle les dimensions (p.173-194) : le désert, l'aube, la lumière, la réalité, la beauté, la peur, la civilisation.

À première vue, cette liberté prise par l'instance narrative de redistribuer comme à loisir le contenu de l'anecdote, apparaît comme le troisième point fort du roman, le premier étant l'idée même du livre et de sa traduction, et le second, certainement, la représentation mystifiante de l'homme long.

Quand il est question en particulier de choses aussi abstraites que la lumière ou la beauté, on est frappé de l'écart entre les deux récits plus directement fictionnalisés d'une part, et d'autre part cette réflexion intermédiaire d'auteure qui s'articule en fait autour de l'écriture, qui finit par être moins percutante, moins convaincante, et dont on serait porté à croire – injustement peut-être – qu'elle serait moins réussie que les deux textes qui l'entourent.

Disons que les deux récits du « Désert mauve » et de « Mauve, l'horizon » génèrent certainement plus de force que les réflexions centrales de la narratrice, quelque sérieux et pertinent que soit le propos de celle-ci.

Il est possible de bien saisir ce qui s'est passé, de l'histoire du « Désert mauve » à celle de « Mauve, l'horizon » en commençant par le glissement du titre, qui contient déjà tout un programme, hissant le mauve du rang d'adjectif à celui de substantif. On notera également comme ne pouvant pas ne pas être significatifs les rapports entre les noms et prénoms de la première auteure et de la narratrice : *Laure* Angstelle et Maude *Laures*. Un peu comme pour le « mauve », le prénom, sorte d'adjectif du nom se retrouve dans un deuxième temps en position de substantif, c'est-à-dire de nom véritable. [...]

Le désert mauve de Nicole Brossard : un livre important, dans le contexte d'un des cheminements d'écriture les plus sérieux de la littérature québécoise contemporaine.

Louise MILOT
Lettres québécoises

Le livre de Nicole Brossard est à la fois une brillante fiction et une réflexion sur la notion même de récit. Il pose le problème de la traduction, des mots, en d'autres mots, mais aussi du réel en caractères imprimés. La confrontation de trois textes – chacun présenté comme un livre distinct, rédigé d'une main différente – emmêle fiction et réalité, ébranle nos certitudes en matière de lecture.

Lori SAINT-MARTIN
Le Devoir

On a l'impression de suivre la recherche de l'auteure dans ses moindres ramifications, de partager en quelque sorte le travail « factuel » qu'elle a dû fournir pour parvenir à la « fabrique » de son roman.

Brossard nous a habitué(e)s au déchiffrement, à l'attention dans la lecture, à une participation active. Dans ce dernier roman, il faut suivre la fabrication du « récit » que nous sommes à lire en même temps que sa « traduction » en cours, en même temps que la « traduction du réel » que ce roman inscrit !!!

Le désert mauve : à lire absolument comme la synthèse d'une œuvre qui n'a pas encore fini de nous surprendre !

Louise COTNOIR
Arcade

CHRONOLOGIE

1943	Naissance à Montréal, le 27 novembre.
1965-1975	Cofondatrice et codirectrice de la revue littéraire *La Barre du jour*.
1967	Organisatrice des spectacles de jazz et de poésie au Pavillon de la jeunesse de l'Expo 67, à Montréal.
1968	Participation au Congrès culturel de La Havane.
1968-1972	Études en lettres à l'Université de Montréal et en pédagogie à l'Université du Québec à Montréal.
1970	Participation à la Nuit de la poésie, au Gesù. Préparation du dossier « Québec » pour la revue d'art *Opus international*.
1974	Récipiendaire du Prix du Gouverneur général du Canada pour *Mécanique jongleuse*.
1975	Membre du comité organisateur de la Rencontre québécoise internationale des écrivains sur le thème « La femme et l'écriture ». Participation au Festival international de poésie, à Toronto.
1975-1976	Réalisation du documentaire *Some American Feminists: New York 1976*, produit par l'Office national du film ; recherche et tournage en collaboration avec Luce Guilbeault ; rencontres

et entrevues avec Kate Millett, Betty Friedan, Ti-Grace Atkinson, Rita Mae Brown et Simone de Beauvoir.

1976-1979 Membre du collectif fondateur du journal féministe *Les Têtes de pioche*.

1977-1979 Cofondatrice et codirectrice de la revue *La Nouvelle Barre du jour*.

Membre du premier bureau de l'Union des écrivaines et des écrivains québécois (UNEQ).

1978 Préparation pour les éditions Coach House Press de Toronto de *The Story So Far 6 / Les stratégies du réel*, une anthologie des nouvelles écritures québécoises.

Séjour en Hongrie : lectures et rencontres d'écrivains.

1979 Organisatrice, avec Jovette Marchessault, du spectacle « Célébration », présenté au Théâtre du Nouveau Monde ainsi qu'à la salle Fred-Barry.

Participation au colloque « Production et affirmation de l'identité », à Toulouse (France).

Participation au colloque consacré aux éditions de l'Hexagone, à Toronto.

1979-1981 Codirectrice de la collection « Réelles » chez Les Quinze, éditeur.

1979-1982 Membre du jury du prix Émile-Nelligan.

1980 Participation au colloque de Cerisy-la-Salle sur la littérature québécoise.

1981 Rencontre « Writers in Dialogue » avec Adrienne Rich, à Toronto.

Conférence sur Djuna Barnes au Théâtre expérimental des femmes, à Montréal.

Tournée de lectures et conférences en Europe : Belgique, France et Italie.

Participation à la Conférence des écrivaines interaméricaines, à Mexico.

1982	Fondation de la maison d'édition L'Intégrale éditrice (essais, analyses et théories féministes).
	Participation au colloque « Émergence d'une culture au féminin » à l'Université de Montréal.
	Professeure invitée à l'Université Queen's, à Kingston (Ontario).
1983	Participation au Festival of Women's Writing, à Victoria (Colombie-Britannique).
	Participation au Congrès mondial des littératures de langue française, à Padoue (Italie).
	Participation à la conférence « Les femmes et les mots », à Vancouver.
1983-1985	Vice-présidente de l'Union des écrivaines et des écrivains québécois (UNEQ).
1984	Récipiendaire du Prix du Gouverneur général du Canada pour *Double impression*.
	Professeure invitée à l'Université Queen's, à Kingston (Ontario).
	Participation au Salon du livre de Paris.
	Participation à la première Foire internationale du livre féministe, à Londres.
1985	Participation au Forum des femmes de *La Nouvelle Barre du jour*.
	Participation à la Semaine culturelle québécoise, à Montpellier (France).
	Participation au Holland Festival, à Amsterdam.
	Participation au Festival international de poésie, à Oslo.
	Participation au Poetic Colloquium, à Vancouver.
	Participation au Festival de poésie « Borderline », à Détroit.
	Tournée universitaire à Madison, East Lansing et Minneapolis.

	Participation au premier Festival international de poésie de Trois-Rivières.
1986	Récipiendaire du BP Nichol Chapbook Award, Therafields Foundation, pour *Sous la langue/Under Tongue*.
	Tournée de lectures et de conférences en Australie : Canberra, Sydney et Adélaïde.
	Participation à la IIe Foire internationale du livre féministe, à Oslo.
	Tournée de lectures et de conférences dans le Sud-Ouest américain : Arizona, Colorado, Californie et Nouveau-Mexique.
	Tournée de lectures et de conférences aux États-Unis : Géorgie, Alabama et Caroline du Sud.
1987	Tournée de lectures et de conférences aux États-Unis : Louisiane, Kansas et Ohio.
	Professeure à la Westword School of Writing for Women, à Vancouver.
1988	Tournée de lectures et de conférences en Nouvelle-Angleterre.
	Présidente de la IIIe Foire internationale du livre féministe, à Montréal.
	Invitée au colloque « Writing and Language », à Dubrovnik (Croatie).
	Invitée au colloque « Mitominas 2 », à Buenos Aires.
	Conférence à Toronto dans le cadre de la série « Counter Talk », organisée par The Public Access Collective.
	Conférence à la New School for Social Research, à New York.
1989	Récipiendaire du Grand Prix du Festival international de poésie de Trois-Rivières pour *Installations* et *À tout regard*.

Membre du Conseil des arts de la Communauté urbaine de Montréal (CACUM); fin de mandat en décembre 1997.

Participation au colloque « Littératures francophones », à Mexico.

1990   Écrivaine en résidence à l'Université Bucknell, à Lewisburg (Pennsylvanie).

Tournée de lectures et de conférences en Italie : Milan, Bologne, Florence, Rome; et en Allemagne : Cologne, Berlin, Francfort, Munich.

Participation à la IVᵉ Foire internationale du livre féministe, à Barcelone.

Invitée au Harbourfront Festival of Authors, à Toronto.

1991   Doctorat *honoris causa* de l'Université Western Ontario.

Récipiendaire du prix Athanase-David pour l'ensemble de son œuvre.

Récipiendaire du Harbourfront Festival Prize.

Lectures de poésie au Ear Inn et à St. Marks Church, à New York.

Lecture de poésie au Festival de Trois en compagnie de l'actrice Michèle Magny et de la claviériste Danielle Boutet.

Série de lectures et de conférences à l'Université de Buffalo, à l'Université SUNY à Oswego et à l'Université Queen's de Kingston (colloque « Femmes, écritures et sociétés »).

Membre invité du Conseil des humanités du Département de langues et littératures romanes à l'Université de Princeton (New Jersey).

1992   Tournée de lectures et de conférences en Argentine et en Uruguay.

Participation au colloque international « Renvois d'ailleurs/Echoes from Elsewhere », à l'Université d'État de Louisiane, à Baton Rouge.

Rencontre internationale de poésie, à Coimbra (Portugal).

Invitée par le Bristish Art Council pour une tournée de lectures en Angleterre (avec Barbara Gowdy, Dionne Brand et Lee Maracle).

Participation à la Ve Foire du livre féministe, à Amsterdam.

Participation au symposium « Novel of the Americas », à l'Université du Colorado, à Boulder.

Conférence d'ouverture au XIIe Colloque interdisciplinaire de la Société de philosophie du Québec, « Les femmes et la société nouvelle ».

Conférence d'ouverture au colloque « La ville en rose », à Montréal.

1993   Élue à l'Académie des lettres du Québec ; présentée par Claude Lévesque.

Lectures en Alabama et en Louisiane.

Participation au colloque « After the Montreal Massacre », à l'Université Georges Mason, en Virginie.

Participation au colloque « Queer Sites », à Toronto.

Conférence d'ouverture au Congrès de l'Association des Études nordiques sur le Canada, à Turku (Finlande).

Participation au Milton Acorn Poetry Festival, à Charlottetown.

Participation au Eden Mills Writers' Festival, à Eden Mills (Ontario).

Conférence à l'Université de Toronto; lecture à l'Université York.

Lecture au Swarmworth College, à Philadelphie.

Lecture à la Lesbian Writers Series, à Los Angeles.

Conférence et lecture au Claremont College, à Los Angeles.

Conférence à l'Université de l'Arizona, à Tucson.

Lectures à l'Université de Calgary.

1994 Voyage d'écriture à Paris.

Lectures à l'Université Simon Fraser, à Burnaby, et à la Kootenay School of Writing, à Vancouver.

Tournée de lectures en Nouvelle-Écosse: Halifax, Wolfville et Church Point.

Conférence à la British Association for Canadian Studies, à York (Angleterre).

Participation au Victoria International Arts Festival.

Membre du jury pour The Women's Monument Project, à Vancouver; inauguration du monument en décembre 1997.

Conférence inaugurale Margaret Laurence et lecture à l'Université Trent, à Peterborough (Ontario).

Participation au Hemispheric Writers Symposium, à Miami.

1995 Lecture à l'Université de l'Alabama, à Tuscaloosa.

Conférence inaugurale au colloque « Corps/ corpus », à l'Université de Montréal.

Vice-présidente de la Commission du droit de prêt public, à Ottawa.

Participation à la Rencontre internationale de poésie, à Coimbra (Portugal).

Participation au symposium Site Santa Fe, au Nouveau-Mexique.

Conférence au colloque « Gay and Lesbian Writings », à l'Université Yale, au Connecticut.
Conférence à l'Université Memorial de St. John's, au Nouveau-Brunswick.

1996-1998   Présidente de la Commission du droit de prêt public, à Ottawa.
Co-conférencière avec Daphne Marlatt pour la Ravenscroft Lecture, à l'Université de Leeds, en Angleterre.
Tournée de lectures en Europe : Londres, Leeds, Durham, Dublin et Toulouse.
Conférence inaugurale au colloque de The NorthEast Modern Language Association.
Participation au Festival Slam/Text, à l'Université de la Californie, à San Diego.
Séjour à Paris : lecture à la Maison de la poésie (Théâtre Molière) avec des poètes québécois ; participation au Marché de la poésie.
Lecture et participation à la rencontre-conférence « Assembling Alternatives », à Durham (New Hampshire).
Lecture au colloque « Explorations of Post-Theory : Towards a Third Space », Université Carleton, à Ottawa.
Écrivaine en résidence au New York State Writers Institute, SUNY, à Albany.
Participation au Congrès de l'Association espagnole d'études canadiennes, à Sitges (Catalogne, Espagne). Lectures à Barcelone et à Madrid.
Tournée en Acadie : Fredericton, Saskville et Moncton.

1997   Doctorat *honoris causa* en lettres et communication de l'Université de Sherbrooke.

Conférence à l'Université de Columbia, à New York, à l'invitation de Maryse Condé.

Présentation de *El desierto malva* à Mexico : entrevues, table ronde, conférence de presse.

Lecture au Collège Saint Rose, à Albany (New York).

Séjour à Leipzig : conférence au Colloque sur le postcolonialisme et lecture à l'Institut français.

Lecture-conférence à l'Université George Mason, à Fairfax, et à l'Université Old Dominion, à Norfolk (Virginie).

Lecture à la Segue Foundation de New York.

Participation au Colloque sur le multiculturalisme de l'Université Harvard, à Cambridge (Massachusetts).

Conférence inaugurale à l'assemblée annuelle du Writer's Union, à Kingston (Ontario).

Lecture dans le cadre de la Harbourfront Reading Series, à Toronto.

Lectures à Paris, au Centre Wallonie et au Centre culturel canadien.

Participation à une table ronde (organisée par Didier Eribon) avec Pierre Bourdieu et Michael Lucey, dans le cadre du colloque « Gais et lesbiennes », au Centre Pompidou.

Lectures à Cambridge (Angleterre) à l'occasion de la parution de *Typhon dru* chez Reality Press.

Participation au colloque « Women and Text », à Leeds (Angleterre).

Conservatrice, avec Michel Marc Bouchard, de l'exposition « Mythes et réalité des gais et des lesbiennes », présentée à la maison de la culture Marie-Uguay, à Montréal.

Participation aux Études canadiennes à Milazzo (Sicile).

Séjour en France : participation au Salon du livre de Saint-Étienne ; lecture au Centre culturel canadien et à la Librairie du Québec à Paris.

Participation au International Writers Festival de Vancouver. Conférences et lectures à l'Université de Georgetown, à Washington, et à l'Université Duke, à Durham (Caroline du Nord).

Participation au Salon du livre de Guadalajara (Mexique).

1998   Écrivaine en résidence à l'Université du Québec à Montréal (UQAM).

Participation au Colloque «L'art inquiet», organisé par Louise Déry et Monique Régimbald, à l'UQAM.

Lecture dans le cadre du Québec à New York avec Michel Tremblay, Marie-Claire Blais, Denise Boucher et Michel Garneau.

Allocution inaugurale de la Rencontre québécoise internationale des écrivains sur le thème «Écriture, identités, culture».

Invitée au XXIᵉ Colloque littéraire de Zagreb (Croatie).

Invitée, avec Teresa de Lauretis, à donner un séminaire sur la théorie féministe, à Vigo (Espagne).

Participation au Festival de littérature d'Ottawa.

Participation au LiteraturWERKstatt berlin.

1999   Récipiendaire du Grand Prix du Festival international de poésie de Trois-Rivières pour *Musée de l'os et de l'eau* et *Au présent des veines*.

Conférence et lecture à l'Université de Saskatoon.

Conférence et lecture à l'Université du Massachusetts, à New Bedford.

Lecture dans le cadre du Poetry Project, à St. Marks Church, à New York.

Tournée de lectures en Autriche : Innsbruck, Graz, Vienne.

Conférence au Centre d'études canadiennes, à Bologne.

Lecture à Venise dans le cadre de la Biennale (Projet Oreste).

Lecture à Saint-Jérôme à l'invitation de la Fondation René Derouin : « Mythologie des lieux » ; table ronde : « Sommes-nous nordiques ? Mythes ou réalités » ; exposition de manuscrits.

Lecture et conférence à l'Université du Colorado, à Fort Collins.

Tournée de lectures en Espagne : Madrid, Séville, Cordoba, Barcelone.

Participation aux Journées Jacques Cartier, à Lyon (France).

2000   Allocution inaugurale au colloque « Silent Moments and Ill-Communication », à l'Université Western Ontario, à London.

Lecture de poèmes et table ronde à l'Université Georgetown (Washington) avec Joan Retallack et Carolyn Forché : « Poetry and Ethics : A Question of Language ».

Présentation de la traduction espagnole de *Vertige de l'avant-scène*, à Mexico.

Conférence sur la francophonie à l'Université de Columbia (New York) : « The Chosen Tongue ».

Participation au Salon du livre de Buenos Aires, en Argentine, et lancement en traduction de

Au présent des veines/En el presente de la pulsation.

Lecture à l'Université de San Francisco, présentée conjointement par le Département d'anglais de l'Université de San Francisco et Small Press Traffic, Literary Arts Center.

Participation, en Guadeloupe, aux Journées du Prix des Amériques insulaires et de la Guyane; participation à deux tables rondes.

Participation à la Segundo encuentro internacional de escritoras à Rosario, en Argentine; lectures et conférence à Mendoza, à Cordoba et à Buenos Aires.

Lectures et conférence à l'Université de Buffalo, dans le cadre du « Poetics Program ».

Participation à la Ve Encuentro de mujeres poetas, à Barcelone.

Participation à la IIe édition des Rencontres poétiques internationales de Dakar.

2001   Boursière du Conseil des arts et des lettres du Québec pour le studio de New York (de janvier à juin).

Invitée dans le cadre du Programme d'écrivains distingués Markin-Flanagan à l'Université de Calgary : conférence et lecture.

Lecture à l'Université Bard (New York) avec le poète John Ashbery.

Conférence à la Cité universitaire de New York (CUNY).

Invitée par l'Institut d'études des femmes de l'Université d'Ottawa à prononcer la conférence annuelle Shirley Greenberg.

Lectures à l'Université George Mason, à Fairfax (Virginie), et à l'Université Georgetown, à Washington.

Invitée par le PEN galicien et l'Unesco à participer aux Journées mondiales de la poésie à Saint-Jacques-de-Compostelle.

Lecture à l'Université Simon Fraser, à Vancouver, dans le cadre des lectures organisées par la Fondation Ruth Wynn Woodward.

Invitée à « Tongue-Tied » dans le cadre de la Saison du Québec à New York (annulé en raison de l'attaque du 11 septembre au World Trade Center).

Distinguished Visitor au Women's Studies Program de l'Université de l'Alberta, à Edmonton.

Participation au Festival international de poésie d'Aveiro (Portugal).

Conférence inaugurale aux 16th Annual Maine Women's Studies.

Conférence au College Colby, à Waterville (Maine).

Lecture à la bibliothèque de Westmount dans le cadre de la série « Tea and Oranges », à Montréal.

2002 Récipiendaire du Prix de la Société des écrivains canadiens pour le roman *Hier*.

Regents Lecturer à l'Université de Berkeley, en Californie.

Participation au Festival Metropolis Bleu, à Montréal : lecture avec John Ashbery.

Participation au colloque « À la frontière des deux genres », à Beyrouth.

Participation au Festival de poésie de Barcelone, avec George Elliott Clark.

Invitée à Ljubljana, en Slovénie, à l'occasion de la parution de la traduction d'*Installations* en slovène.

Participation à la nuit de poésie « Le premier métro », organisée par le Centre culturel canadien.

Participation au Festival Scream in High Park, à Toronto.

Participation au festival de poésie Encuentro de las poetas de America, à Morelia (Mexique).

Participation au Colloque de l'Association internationale des études québécoises à Innsbruck et lecture à Salzbourg (Autriche).

Participation au Festival de poésie de Las Palmas, aux îles Canaries.

2003   Obtention de la bourse de carrière du Conseil des arts et des lettres du Québec.

Récipiendaire du prix W. O. Mitchell pour l'ensemble de son œuvre.

Invitée d'honneur au Salon du livre de Montréal.

Participation aux Journées de poésie de Mondorf, au Luxembourg.

Tournée de lectures et de conférences au Japon : Tokyo, Nagoya et Kyoto.

Participation au Festival Stephen Leacock, à Orillia (Ontario).

Participation au Festival de Trois ; soirée « Nicole Brossard, poète », mise en lecture par Brigitte Haentjens.

Participation au Festival de poésie de Struga, en Macédoine, et de Vilenica, en Slovénie.

Participation au Festival RomaPoesia, à Rome.

Participation au WordFest de Calgary.

Participation à la Foire du livre de Guadalajara consacrée au Québec.

Lecture au Festival Voix d'Amériques, à Montréal.

2004   Lectures à Stockholm et à Oslo.

Invitée par Québec-Édition au Salon du livre de Paris.

Lecture à Tours, en France.

Participation au Quebec Festival, à Pittsburgh.
Professeure invitée au Summer Writing Program de l'Université Naropa, à Boulder (Colorado).
Lecture avec Rhizome au Centre culturel canadien dans le cadre de la Nuit de poésie, à Paris.
Séjour dans l'archipel du Svalbard, en Norvège, pour préparer le livre-exposition *Rien que l'Arctique*, édition bilingue français-norvégien.
Résidence d'écriture au Château Lavigny, en Suisse.
Participation à la rencontre « Las lenguas de América », à Mexico.
Participation à la journée « Les donneurs », à Joliette.
Lecture à l'Université de Princeton (New Jersey).
Séjour à New York; lecture et rencontre à la Maison des poètes de New York; entrevue avec Mary Ann Caws, en collaboration avec la Cité universitaire de New York (CUNY), et lecture dans le cadre de la série Belladonna.
Participation à la Foire du livre de Guadalajara; présentation de *Ayer*.

2005   Élue à la Société royale du Canada.
Directrice de la Rencontre québécoise internationale des écrivains.
Présentation de *Instal-lacions* en catalan à Barcelone et à Sabadell (Espagne).
Invitée au Cycle de conférences sur « L'extrême contemporain », au Circulo de Bellas Artes de Madrid.
Lecture et rencontre à Albi et à Carmaux, en France, dans le cadre de la XXIIIe manifestation de « Tarn en poésie ».
Lancement de *Yesterday, at the Hotel Clarendon* et célébration des 40 ans d'écriture de

Nicole Brossard au Festival Metropolis Bleu, avec des lectures de Denise Desautels, Élise Turcotte, Martine Audet, Alberto Manguel, Louise Forsyth et Susanne de Lotbinière-Harwood.

Invitée à Los Angeles dans le cadre de l'échange entre *Estuaire* et *The New Review*.

Invitée au Festival Il cammino delle comete, à Pistoia (Italie).

Lecture au Fuoricampo, groupe lesbien de Bologne (Italie).

Lecture au Literaturhus d'Innsbruck (Autriche). Rencontre à l'Université d'Innsbruck.

Participation au Festival of Words de Moose Jaw, en Saskatchewan.

Professeure au Poetry Colloquium à Sage Hill Writing Experience, dans la vallée de Qu'Appelle, en Saskatchewan.

Participation au Winnipeg International Writers Festival.

Lecture dans le cadre de la Canadian Writers in Person Series, à l'Université York, à Toronto.

Participation au Wordfest de Calgary.

Participation au Vancouver International Writers Festival.

Lecture et conférence à l'Université du Minnesota, à Minneapolis.

Lecture avec Barbara Godard au Congrès de l'Association des traducteurs, à Montréal.

Participation au premier Festival de poésie de Manzanillo (Colima) avec Rhizome, au Mexique; Foire du livre de Guadalajara; lancement de *Camino a Trieste*.

2006   Récipiendaire du prix Molson du Conseil des Arts du Canada pour l'ensemble de son œuvre.

Obtention du grade de chevalier de l'Ordre de la Pléiade, décerné par l'Assemblée parlementaire de la francophonie.

Séjour à Paris : lecture dans le cadre des Parvis poétiques et participation à une table ronde au PEN Club de France.

Lectures au Luxembourg.

Entretien avec Catherine Mavrikakis dans le cadre du Printemps de la poésie, à la maison de la culture Notre-Dame-de-Grâce, à Montréal.

Conférence et lecture à l'Université Swarthmore, en Pennsylvanie.

Participation au Festival littéraire d'Ottawa.

Invitée au Congrès des sciences humaines, à Toronto : conférence sur la ville. Participation à une table ronde sur les traductions des livres de Nicole Brossard avec, entre autres, les traducteurs Monica Mansour (Mexico), Raquet Heffe (Argentine), Pierre Joris (États-Unis), Robert Majzels (Canada) et Barbara Godard (Canada).

Professeure au Poetry Colloquium à Sage Hill Writing Experience, en Saskatchewan.

Participation au Festival Eden Mills, en Ontario.

Participation au Festival des écrivains franco-ontariens, à Toronto.

Participation au Festival littéraire de Windsor, en Ontario.

2006-2007   Écrivaine en résidence à l'Université de Montréal.

2007   Participation au Test Reading Series, avec Barbara Godard et Sharon Harris, au Center for Comparative Studies, à l'Université de Toronto.

Participation à la Nuit laurentienne : lecture à Val-Morin et hommage à Gaston Miron.

Lecture-rencontre au Département de français de l'Université du Connecticut.

Hommage à Alain Grandbois et à Nicole Brossard, avec un coup de chapeau à Benoît Jutras, organisé conjointement par l'Académie des lettres du Québec et Bibliothèque et Archives nationales du Québec (BAnQ), à l'auditorium de la Grande Bibliothèque, à Montréal.

Participation au Festival international de Coimbra (Portugal).

Professeure au Poetry Colloquium à Sage Hill Writing Experience, en Saskatchewan.

Participation au Festival international Literatura en el Bravo, à Ciudad Juárez, au Mexique.

Invitée par la revue *Dandelion* et l'Université de Calgary à des lectures-rencontres.

Participation au Colloque de la francophonie, à New Delhi, et lecture à la Bibliothèque française de Mumbai.

Participation à la rencontre Nueve siglos de poesia femenina, à Mexico.

Participation au colloque « Genre et espace », à Innsbruck (Autriche).

2008   Récipiendaire du prix du roman de la société des Écrivains francophones d'Amérique pour *La capture du sombre*.

Finaliste au Griffin Poetry Prize 2008 pour *Notebook of Roses and Civilisation* (*Cahier de roses et de civilisation*).

Lecture rencontre au Département d'études françaises de l'Université d'Ottawa.

Participation au *Cirque des mots* avec la musicienne Charmaine Leblanc.

Lecture au Salon international du livre de Québec.

Lecture à l'Université du Maine (Orono) dans le cadre du colloque *Poetry of the '70s*.

Invitée au Festival of Authors' Reading de Brno (Tchéquie).

Écrivaine en résidence à l'Université d'Ottawa.

Participation à la foire Liber de Barcelone (Espagne).

Conférence inaugurale, avec Daphne Marlatt, au colloque en hommage à Barbara Godard à Toronto.

2009   Finaliste au Rogers Writers' Prize 2009 pour *Fences in Breathing* (*La capture du sombre*).

Rencontre avec Aline Apostolska dans le cadre des Midis littéraires de la Grande Bibliothèque.

Lecture à La Coupole, à Paris, avec Madeleine Monette dans le cadre des rencontres Souffles d'elles.

Lecture avec Bruno Doucey et Abdellatif Laabi à Saint-Quentin-en-Yvelines (France).

Lecture au Centre culturel canadien à Paris et au Salon du livre de Paris.

Participation à une table ronde intitulée « Feminist Translation as Creative, Interpretive, and Community-Building Process in the Production and Reception of the Work of Nicole Brossard », organisée par la British Association for Canadian Studies à l'Université d'Oxford (Royaume-Uni), avec Louise Forsyth et Anne-Marie Wheeler.

Lecture et table ronde au Festival international Franco-Irlandais à Dublin (Irlande).

Lancement-entrevue de la traduction du roman *La Capture du sombre* sous le titre anglais *Fences in Breathing* à Toronto.

Participation au PEN World Voices Festival of International Literature à New York

Conférence inaugurale au XVIIIe colloque international de l'Association de professeurs de français de l'Université espagnole à l'Université Jaume I, Castellón (Espagne).

Conférences à Barcelone et Alicante, et enregistrement d'une entrevue à l'UNED (Universidad Nacional de Educación a Distancia) de Madrid (Espagne).

Conférence inaugurale au colloque « Queerly Changing the Narrative » à Vancouver en Colombie-Britannique.

Lecture à Paris dans le cadre de la série de lectures de poésie Résonances.

Participation au Festival international de Poésie de Medellín (Colombie).

Lecture dans le cadre du lancement de l'anthologie *Prismatic Publics. Innovative Canadian Women's Poetry and Poetics* à New York.

Table ronde et lecture à l'Université de Saskatoon en Saskatchewan.

Conférence inaugurale au colloque « La traduction à l'ère de la mondialisation » au Collège universitaire de Saint-Boniface à Winnipeg au Manitoba.

Participation au Festival Cervantino à Guanajato (Mexique).

Lecture à Berlin (Allemagne) pour lyrikline.org.

Participation au Festival Audiatur à Bergen (Norvège).

Conférence inaugurale du colloque « Mujeres Multiorgásmicas » à l'Université de Valence (Espagne).

2010   Participation au 6e Festival international de Poésie de Granada (Nicaragua).

Participation au printemps des poètes à Paris, à La Rochelle et à Saint-Quentin-en-Yvelines (France).

Participation au Festival international de poésie de Palma (Majorque).

Participation au Festival international de poésie de Namur (Belgique).

BIBLIOGRAPHIE

Poésie

Aube à la saison, dans *Trois,* Montréal, Éditions de l'AGEUM, 1965.

Mordre en sa chair, Montréal, Éditions de l'Estérel, 1966.

L'écho bouge beau, Montréal, Éditions de l'Estérel, 1968.

Suite logique, Montréal, Éditions de l'Hexagone, 1970.

Le centre blanc, avec des dessins de Marcel Saint-Pierre, Montréal, Éditions d'Orphée, 1970.

Mécanique jongleuse, Paris, Génération, 1973.

Mécanique jongleuse suivi de *Masculin grammaticale,* Montréal, Éditions de l'Hexagone, 1974.

La partie pour le tout, Montréal, Éditions de l'Aurore, 1975.

Le centre blanc, Montréal, Éditions de l'Hexagone, coll. « Rétrospectives », 1978.

D'arcs de cycle la dérive, gravure de Francine Simonin, Saint-Jacques-le-Mineur, Éditions de la Maison, 1979.

Amantes, Montréal, Les Quinze, éditeur, coll. « Réelles », 1980.

Double impression, Montréal, Éditions de l'Hexagone, coll. « Rétrospectives », 1984.

L'Aviva, Montréal, Nouvelle Barre du jour, 1985.

Domaine d'écriture, Montréal, Nouvelle Barre du jour, n° 154, 1985.

Mauve, avec Daphne Marlatt, Montréal, Nouvelle Barre du jour, coll. « Transformance », 1986.

Character / Jeu de lettres, avec Daphne Marlatt, Montréal, Nouvelle Barre du jour, coll. « Transformance », 1986.

Sous la langue / Under Tongue, édition bilingue, traduction de Susanne de Lotbinière-Harwood, Montréal et Charlottetown, L'Essentielle, éditrices et Gynergy Books, 1987.

Installations, Trois-Rivières et Paris, Écrits des Forges et Le Castor Astral, 1989.

À tout regard, Montréal, Nouvelle Barre du jour et Bibliothèque québécoise, 1989.

Typhon dru, en collaboration avec l'artiste Christine Davies, Paris, Collectif Génération, 1990.

La subjectivité des lionnes, Bruxelles, L'Arbre à paroles, 1990.

Langues obscures, Montréal, Éditions de l'Hexagone, 1992.

La nuit verte du parc labyrinthe, Laval, Éditions Trois, 1992.

Vertige de l'avant-scène, Trois-Rivières, Écrits des Forges et L'Orange bleue, 1997.

Typhon dru suivi de *La matière harmonieuse manœuvre encore*, édition bilingue, traduction de Carolyne Bergvall, Londres, Reality Press, 1997.

Amantes suivi de *Le sens apparent* et de *Sous la langue*, Montréal, Éditions de l'Hexagone, 1998 (réédition).

Musée de l'os et de l'eau, avec des gravures de Catherine Farish, Saint-Hippolyte et Sainte-Anastasie (France), Éditions du Noroît et Éditions Cadex, 1999.

Au présent des veines, Trois-Rivières et Luxembourg, Écrits des Forges et Éditions Phi, 1999.

Je m'en vais à Trieste, Trois-Rivières, Luxembourg et Limoges (France), Écrits des Forges, Éditions Phi et Le bruit des autres, 2003.

Cahier de roses & de civilisation, avec des gravures de Francine Simonin, Trois-Rivières, Éditions Art Le Sabord, 2003.

Après les mots, Trois-Rivières, Écrits des Forges, 2007.

Ardeur, avec des dessins de René Derouin, Luxembourg, Éditions Phi, 2008.

D'aube et de civilisation. Poèmes choisis 1965-2003, choix et préface de Louise Dupré, Montréal, Typo, 2007.

ROMANS

Un livre, Montréal, Éditions du Jour, 1970; Montréal, Les Quinze, éditeur, 1980.

Sold-out. Étreinte-illustration, Montréal, Éditions du Jour, 1973; Montréal, Les Quinze, éditeur, 1980.

French Kiss. Étreinte-exploration, Montréal, Éditions du Jour, 1974; Montréal, Les Quinze, éditeur, 1980.

L'amèr ou Le chapitre effrité. Théorie-fiction, Montréal, Les Quinze, éditeur, 1977; Montréal, Éditions de l'Hexagone, coll. « Typo », 1988.

Le sens apparent, Paris, Flammarion, coll. « Textes », 1980.

Picture Theory. Théorie-fiction, Montréal, Éditions Nouvelle Optique, 1982; Montréal, Éditions de l'Hexagone, coll. « Typo », 1990.

Le désert mauve, Montréal, Éditions de l'Hexagone, 1987.

Baroque d'aube, Montréal, Éditions de l'Hexagone, 1995.

Hier, Montréal, Québec Amérique, 2001.

La capture du sombre, Montréal, Leméac, 2007.

PROSE

Journal intime, Montréal, Les Herbes rouges, 1984; réédition, 1998.

Elle serait la première phrase de mon prochain roman/She Would Be the First Sentence in My Next Novel, édition bilingue, traduction de Susanne de Lotbinière-Harwood, Toronto, Mercury Press, 1998.

L'horizon du fragment, Trois-Pistoles, Éditions Trois-Pistoles, coll. « Écrire », 2004.

THÉÂTRE
L'écrivain, dans *La nef des sorcières*, collectif, Montréal, Les Quinze, éditeur, 1976 ; Montréal, Éditions de l'Hexagone, coll. « Typo », 1992.

ESSAI
La lettre aérienne, Montréal, Éditions du remue-ménage, 1985 ; nouvelle édition, 1988 ; réédition, 2009.

ANTHOLOGIES
The Story So Far 6/Les stratégies du réel, Toronto, Coach House Press, 1978.
Anthologie de la poésie des femmes au Québec (1677-1988), en collaboration avec Lisette Girouard, Montréal, Éditions du remue-ménage, 1991 ; nouvelle édition, 2003.
Poèmes à dire la francophonie. 38 poètes contemporains, Paris, Le Castor Astral et CNDP, 2002.
Baiser vertige. Prose et poésie gaies et lesbiennes au Québec, Montréal, Typo, 2006.

LIVRES EN TRADUCTION
A Book [*Un livre*], traduit en anglais par Larry Shouldice, Toronto, Coach House Press, 1976.
Turn of a Pang [*Sold-Out*], traduit en anglais par Patricia Claxton, Toronto, Coach House Press, 1976.
Daydream Mechanics [*Mécanique jongleuse*], traduit en anglais par Larry Shouldice, Toronto, Coach House Press, 1980.

These our Mothers or: The Disintegrating Chapter [*L'amèr*], traduit en anglais par Barbara Godard, Toronto, Coach House Press, 1983.

Lovhers [*Amantes*], traduit en anglais par Barbara Godard, Montréal, Guernica Press, 1986.

French Kiss [*French Kiss*], traduit en anglais par Patricia Claxton, Toronto, Coach House Press, 1986.

The Aerial Letter [*La lettre aérienne*], traduit en anglais par Marlene Wildeman, Toronto, Women's Press, 1988.

Surfaces of Sense [*Le sens apparent*], traduit en anglais par Fiona Strachan, Toronto, Coach House Press, 1989.

Die Malvenfarbene [*Le désert mauve*], traduit en allemand par Traude Buhrmann, Berlin, Frauenoffensive, 1989.

La lettera aerea [*La lettre aérienne*], traduit en italien par Luisa Muraro, Florence, Editions Estro, 1990.

Mauve Desert [*Le désert mauve*], traduit en anglais par Susanne de Lotbinière-Harwood, Toronto, Coach House Press, 1990; McClelland & Stewart, 1997; Coach House Books, 2006.

Picture Theory [*Picture Theory*], traduit en anglais par Barbara Godard, Montréal, Guernica Press, 1991; New York, Roof Press, 1991; Toronto, Guernica Press, 2006.

El desierto malva [*Le désert mauve*], traduit en espagnol par Mónica Mansour, Mexico, Editorial Joaquín Mortiz, 1996.

Baroque at Dawn [*Baroque d'aube*], traduit en anglais par Patricia Claxton, Toronto, McClelland & Stewart, 1997.

Instalationes [*Installations*], traduit en espagnol par Mónica Mansour, Mexico/Trois-Rivières, Unam/Aldus/Ecrits des Forges, 1997.

Barroco al alba [*Baroque d'aube*], traduit en espagnol par Pilar Giralt Gorina, Barcelone, Seix Barral, 1998.

Vertigo del proscenio [*Vertige de l'avant-scène*], traduit en espagnol par Mónica Mansour, Mexico, El Tucán de Virginia, 2000.

Installations [*Installations*], traduit en anglais par Erin Mouré et Robert Majzels, Winnipeg, Gordon Shillingford Publishing, 2000.

En el presente de la pulsación [*Au présent des veines*], traduit en espagnol par Sara Cohen et Alicia Genovese, Buenos Aires, Botella al Mar, 2000.

Nikki [*Journal intime*], traduit en japonais par Mitoko Hirabayashi et Bev Curran, Tokyo, Kokubunsha, 2000.

Namstitve [*Installations*], traduit en slovène par Brane Mozetič, Ljubljana, Založba Škuc, 2002.

Museum of Bone and Water [*Musée de l'os et de l'eau*], traduit en anglais par Erin Mouré et Robert Majzels, Toronto, Anansi, 2003.

The Blue Books [*Un livre*, *Sold-out* et *French Kiss*], traduit en anglais par Larry Shouldice et Patricia Claxton, Toronto, Coach House Books, 2003.

Shadow : Soft et Soif, traduit en anglais par Guy Bennett, Los Angeles, Seing Eye Books, 2003.

Diario intimo [*Journal intime*], traduit en espagnol par Raquel Heffe, Buenos Aires, Boca la luna, 2003.

Ayer [*Hier*], traduit en espagnol par Mónica Mansour, Mexico, Aldus, 2003.

An Intimate Journal [*Journal intime*], traduit en anglais par Barbara Godard, Toronto, Mercury Press, 2004.

Yesterday, at the Hotel Clarendon [*Hier*], traduit en anglais par Susanne de Lotbinière-Harwood, Toronto, Coach House Books, 2005.

Instalu [*Installations*], traduit en roumain par Magda Carneci, Pitesti, Editura Paralela 45, coll. « Germini », 2004.

Instal.lacions [*Installations*], traduit en catalan par Antoni Clapés, Barcelone, Eumo Editorial, coll. « Jardins de Samarcanda », 2005.

Fluid Arguments [inédit en français], préparé par Susan Rudy, traduit en anglais par Anne-Marie Wheeler, Toronto, Mercury Press, 2005.

Camino a Trieste [*Je m'en vais à Trieste*], traduit en espagnol par Silvia Pratt, Guadalajara, Mantis Editorial, 2005.

Notebook of Roses and Civilization [*Cahier de roses et de civilisation*], traduit en anglais par Erin Mouré et Robert Majzels, Toronto, Coach House Books, 2007.

Mobility of Light, anthologie préparée par Louise Forsyth, édition bilingue, Waterloo, Laurier Press, 2009.

Fences in Breathing [*La capture du sombre*], traduit en anglais par Susanne de Lotbinière-Harwood, Toronto, Coach House Books, 2009.

Selections: The Poetry of Nicole Brossard, anthologie, Los Angeles, University of California Press, coll. « Poets for The Millennium », 2009.

Cuaderno de rosas y civilización [*Cahier de roses et de civilisation*], traduit en espagnol par Mónica Mansour, Mexico, UNAM, 2009.

TABLE

TYPO
TITRES PARUS

(A) : anthologie ; (C) : contes ; (D) : dictionnaire ; (E) : essai ; (N) : nouvelles ;
(P) : poésie ; (R) : roman ; (T) : théâtre